THIS
LAND
IS
THEIR
LAND

THIS LAND IS THEIR LAND

THE WAMPANOAG INDIANS,
PLYMOUTH COLONY, AND THE TROUBLED
HISTORY OF THANKSGIVING

DAVID J. SILVERMAN

BLOOMSBURY PUBLISHING
NEW YORK · LONDON · OXFORD · NEW DELHI · SYDNEY

BLOOMSBURY PUBLISHING
Bloomsbury Publishing Inc.
1385 Broadway, New York, NY 10018, USA

BLOOMSBURY, BLOOMSBURY PUBLISHING, and the
Diana logo are trademarks of Bloomsbury Publishing Plc

First published in the United States 2019
This paperback edition published 2020

ISBN: HB: 978-1-63286-924-1; PB: 978-1-63286-925-8; eBook: 978-1-63286-926-5

Library of Congress Cataloging-in-Publication Data

Names: Silverman, David J., 1971- author.
Title: This land is their land : the Wampanoag Indians, Plymouth Colony,
and the troubled history of Thanksgiving / David J. Silverman.
Description: New York : Bloomsbury Publishing, 2019. |
Includes bibliographical references and index.
Identifiers: LCCN 2019022966 | ISBN 9781632869241 (hardback) |
ISBN 9781632869265 (ebook)
Subjects: LCSH: Wampanoag Indians—Massachusetts—History—17th century. |
Thanksgiving Day—History. | Indians of North America—First contact
with Europeans—Massachusetts.
Classification: LCC E99.W2 S545 2019 | DDC 974.4004/97348—dc23
LC record available at https://lccn.loc.gov/2019022966

2 4 6 8 10 9 7 5 3

Typeset by Westchester Publishing Services
Printed and bound in the U.S.A. by Berryville Graphics Inc., Berryville, Virginia

To find out more about our authors and books visit
www.bloomsbury.com and sign up for our newsletters.

Bloomsbury books may be purchased for business or promotional use.
For information on bulk purchases please contact Macmillan Corporate and
Premium Sales Department at specialmarkets@macmillan.com.

To Aquinnah and Bela Silverman,
For whom I'm thankful

CONTENTS

A Note on Spelling, Terminology,
and Dates   ix

INTRODUCTION   Mourning in America   I

CHAPTER ONE   The Wampanoags' Old World   23

CHAPTER TWO   Danger on the Horizon   61

CHAPTER THREE   Golgotha   95

CHAPTER FOUR   Reaching Out to Strangers   127

CHAPTER FIVE   Ousamequin's Power Play   175

CHAPTER SIX   A Great Man and a Little Child   205

CHAPTER SEVEN   Ungrateful   253

CHAPTER EIGHT   Ruining Thanksgiving   299

CHAPTER NINE   "Days of Mourning and Not Joy"   355

EPILOGUE   Toward a Day with Less Mourning   419

Acknowledgments   429
Glossary of Key Indian People
and Places   433

Abbreviations   439
Notes   443
Index   499

A NOTE ON SPELLING, TERMINOLOGY, AND DATES

I have modernized the spelling and punctuation of quotations from seventeenth-century sources to make it easier for readers to focus on the meaning of the words instead of on their unfamiliar forms. I have also standardized Indian proper names and place names rather than replicate the various phonetic spellings that appear in colonial documents. Despite these measures, readers will still have to confront a wide array of unfamiliar Indian personal and place-names. After all, this is a history about Indian people and places. Grappling with those names, including trying to sound them out and track them through the story, is part of the challenge of writing and reading Native American history. I have included a glossary of the Indian (and some English) names that appear in this book to help readers stay on course.

Stylistically, writing about indigenous people in a manner that is respectful and accessible poses a number of challenges. One of them has to do with whether to use the singular or plural when referring to a group, for example, "the Wampanoag" versus "the Wampanoags." Some modern Native people prefer the singular both out of convention and because it conveys a message of unity. My usual default in such stylistic matters is to defer to the descendant communities, but in this case I have decided to stick with the plural because it is consistent with how I refer to other groups of people and it captures the often-contested, fluid nature of many tribal entities during the seventeenth century.

Some mostly non-Native readers will find my use of "Indian" a bit jarring because some educators teach that it is racially insensitive. In this case, I'm deferring to the common practice of Native New Englanders and many other indigenous people in the United States, who over the generations have appropriated and come to take pride in the designation "Indian." Wherever possible, however, I refer to specific groups.

In cases where English-language terms are ideologically problematic and an equivalent from the Wôpanâak (or Wampanoag) language or a closely related Algonquian language family is known to me, I have used it after consulting with modern Wampanoag people. For instance, I sometimes use *matawaûog* instead of *warriors* because *warriors* can mistakenly connote a lack of discipline and even savagery, when in fact Wampanoag fighters were highly trained and organized.

England and its colonies used the Julian calendar until the year 1752, under which the new year started on March 25. (By this system, *Sept*ember was indeed the seventh month, *Oct*ober the eighth, and *Dec*ember the tenth.) Yet, because other European states had adopted the Gregorian calendar, which we use today, English colonists typically gave two years for dates between January 1 and March 25. I have eliminated the double dating and used the Julian year for dates. For example, a date that Plymouth colonists might have rendered as February 1, 1675/76, will appear here as February 1, 1676. By the colonial era, the Julian calendar also ran eleven days behind the Gregorian. I have not corrected that gap in my rendering of dates.

INTRODUCTION

ᘰ ᘏ

Mourning in America

Serious, critical history tends to be hard on the living. It challenges us to see distortions embedded in the heroic national origin myths we have been taught since childhood. It takes enemies demonized by previous generations and treats them as worthy of understanding in their particular contexts. Ideological absolutes—civility and savagery, liberty and tyranny, and especially us and them—begin to blur. People from our own society who are not supposed to matter, and whose historical experiences show how the injustices of the past have shaped the injustices of the present, move from the shadows into the light. Because critical history challenges assumptions and authority, it often leaves us feeling uncomfortable. Yet it also has the capacity to help us become more humble and humane.

There always have been and always will be reactionaries who accuse the tellers of such histories of iconoclasm. Today, such critics might make the charge of revisionism or political correctness. To defenders of the status quo, it does not matter if the origin myth or national history is untrue or hurtful to those it leaves out or vilifies. The point is that the story upholds the traditional social order by teaching that the rulers came by their position heroically, righteously, and even with the blessing of the divine. Such themes are favored by those guarding their privilege against the supposed barbarians at the gates.

Frank James aimed to rattle those very gates when he rose to speak at the First National Day of Mourning held in Plymouth, Massachusetts, on Thanksgiving Day in 1970. At forty-six years old, he had in some ways been preparing for this moment his entire life. He was born into the Wampanoag community of Aquinnah (or Gay Head), which, despite three centuries of white colonization, had managed to persevere on its ancestral lands on a remote peninsula on the island of Martha's Vineyard. When James was a child, Wampanoag elders could still recall bitterly how in the late 1860s and early 1870s Massachusetts had eliminated their legal status as Indians and turned their centuries-old reservations into two towns, Gay Head and Mashpee (on Cape Cod). The state's expectation was that terminating the reservations would finally make Indians as a group vanish, as nature supposedly intended, by bringing their land into the market and forcing them to scatter and assimilate among the larger American population. Not surprisingly, after that transition, Mashpee and Gay Head ranked among the poorest communities in Massachusetts. Many of the people had indeed left home in search of work, love, or escape. Most of them, however, visited home regularly and intended to return permanently someday, an option they retained because a few stalwarts steadfastly remained where they were, refusing to disappear.[1]

James's parents raised him to stand up against a society that denied who he was, misrepresented or ignored his people's past, and saddled Indian children with low expectations. He remembered them counseling him, "You must succeed—your face is a different color in this small Cape Cod community." He did just that. At fourteen years old, he adopted the Wampanoag name of Wamsutta, in honor of the Wampanoag *sachem* (or chief) who in the 1660s began organizing a multitribal resistance to colonization, contrary to the English alliance brokered by his father, Ousamequin, or Massasoit. In other words, from a young age James envisioned himself standing up and defending his people.[2]

At the same time, he figured out how to thrive in the white world. He served in the U.S. Coast Guard Auxiliary during World War II, carrying on a long tradition of Wampanoag volunteers fighting in the wars of the United States and its colonial predecessors. Then he pursued his early love for music, especially trumpet, all the way to the prestigious New England Conservatory of Music in Boston, only to discover when he graduated in 1948 that no national orchestra would hire him because of racial segregation. Undaunted, he returned to Wampanoag country to become a music teacher and then director of music in the Nauset regional schools on Cape Cod.

But those were just his day jobs. His passion was political activism to improve the lives of the Wampanoags and other indigenous people. To that end, he served as president of the Federated Eastern Indian League, a multitribal organization that sponsored youth activities and scholarships and published a monthly newsletter of happenings throughout Indian country. James also devoted his time to the study of history, knowing that a better understanding of the past was critical to reforming the present. Delving into the classic primary source accounts written by the colonists of Plymouth, what he read made his blood boil, for the true history bore little relation to the supposed tale of Thanksgiving that weighed around his people's neck like a millstone.[3]

By the time of James's childhood, the American holiday of Thanksgiving had become associated with an origin myth in which the Wampanoags played an important if supporting role. Yet that was not always the case. During the eighteenth century and the first half of the nineteenth, Thanksgiving had no link whatsoever with Pilgrims and Indians. It was a regional holiday, observed only in the New England states or those in the Midwest to which New Englanders had migrated. Individual states decided whether and when they would hold the holiday, though the traditional time was late November to mark the close of the agricultural year. The so-called First Thanksgiving, as a 1621 gathering of English colonists and Wampanoags has come to be known, was not the root of this holiday. Thanksgiving celebrations had emerged, ironically, out of the English puritan practice of declaring *fast days* of prayer to mark some special mercy or judgment from God. Running from one afternoon to the next, these fast days, or days of Thanksgiving, centered on churchgoing, solemnity, and piety, not gluttony and sport, though they usually concluded at sundown of the second day with a community feast. Gradually, during the colonial era, New Englanders began to hold days of Thanksgiving annually each spring and autumn instead of episodically, and the fasting became less strictly observed. The only continuities between the Thanksgivings of early New England and today's celebration are the gathering of family and friends to break bread and reflect on the goodness of our lives.[4]

The character of the holiday began to change only around the time of the Civil War. In 1863 President Abraham Lincoln declared that the last Thursday of November should be held as a national day of Thanksgiving, apparently in response to intense lobbying by Sarah Josepha Hale, the editor of *Godey's Lady's Book*. Hale believed that the observance would foster unity amid the horrors of the Civil War. Afterward, the tradition stuck, with some modifications to the date, and gradually it spread to the South, too. Around the same time, Americans began to think of the holiday as originating in a feast shared between the English colonists of Plymouth and the surrounding Indians. The first suggestion that such a link existed appears to date to 1841, when the Reverend Alexander Young published the only primary source account of that event, consisting of a mere paragraph of four lines. To it, Young added an influential footnote (perhaps the first and only influential footnote in history) stating that "this was the first Thanksgiving, the harvest festival of

New England." Over the next fifty years, various authors, artists, and lecturers disseminated Young's idea until Americans took it for granted.[5]

The lionization of the Pilgrims also grew out of Plymouth town's attempt to drum up civic pride and tourism. Beginning in 1769, the community's Old Colony Club began holding an annual Forefathers' Day on the December 22 anniversary of the Pilgrim landing on Plymouth Rock, as legend would have it. At this event, speeches, toasts, and promotional materials would eulogize the once obscure Pilgrims as the symbolic founders of New England and even the United States by virtue of their religious ideals, commitment to democracy, and resolve to build their colony in the face of adversity. This filiopietistic publicity campaign gradually took hold in Massachusetts, then spread nationally through Yankee writing and orations at the very same time that Americans were beginning to associate Thanksgiving with the Pilgrim saga.[6]

Yet it was one thing for the people of Massachusetts to claim the Pilgrims as forefathers and a dinner between Pilgrims and Indians as the template for a national holiday. It was quite another for the rest of the nation to go along. For that to occur, the United States first had to complete its subjugation of the tribes of the Great Plains and far West. Only then could its people stop vilifying Indians as bloodthirsty savages and give them an unthreatening role in the national founding myth. The Pilgrim saga also had utility in the nation's culture wars. It was no coincidence that authorities began trumpeting the Pilgrims as national founders amid widespread anxiety that the country was being overrun by Catholic and then Jewish immigrants unappreciative of America's Protestant, democratic origins and unfamiliar with its values. Depicting the Pilgrims as the epitome of colonial America also served to minimize the country's long-standing history of racial oppression at a time when Jim Crow was working to return blacks in the South to as close a state of slavery as possible, and racial segregation was becoming the norm nearly everywhere else. Focusing on the Pilgrims' noble religious and democratic principles, instead of on the shameful Indian wars and systems of slavery more typical of the colonies, enabled whites to think of the so-called black and Indian problems as southern and western exceptions to an otherwise inspiring national heritage. Though Americans eventually assumed that the Thanksgiving holiday and myth had marched together in an unbroken succession since 1621, those traditions were very much products of white Protestants, particularly northerners, asserting their cultural

Jennie Augusta Brownscombe, *The First Thanksgiving*, 1914. Pilgrim Hall Museum, Plymouth, Massachusetts.

Filiopietistic depictions of the "First Thanksgiving" began proliferating in the late nineteenth and early twentieth centuries as the Thanksgiving myth gained popularity. Note such historical inaccuracies as the Wampanoags appearing in Plains Indian garb (like feather headdresses and fringed buckskin), the log cabin, the tablecloth, and fine furniture. The actual feast was an earthier, more rambunctious affair than the pious, domestic scene portrayed here.

authority over European immigrants and Americans of color in the nineteenth and early twentieth centuries.[7]

Regardless of whether James was familiar with this background to the holiday, he certainly understood the ideological work of its origin story. In the standard telling, a band of pious Englishmen, referred to as Pilgrims, were so desperate for religious liberty that they were willing to brave the dangers of the angry Atlantic and the howling wilderness to build a new society in America. Dissent spread through their ranks once they realized that they had to land well north of their intended destination on the Hudson River, so they drew up an agreement, signed by all the male passengers, in which everyone pledged to abide by the rule of a democratically elected government. Generations of American schoolchildren have read the colonist William Bradford's account of how he and his fellow English did "solemnly and mutually in the presence of God and one another, covenant and combine ourselves together into a civil body politic, for our better ordering . . . to enact, constitute, and frame such just and equal laws . . . from time to time, as shall be thought most meet and convenient for the general good of the colony, unto which we promise all due submission and obedience." This Mayflower Compact (named after the colonists' ship) thus became the supposed model for the American Constitution. It was just the first of the sojourners' many trials. Sea-tossed, thin, and tattered, they finally arrived on the shores of Cape Cod hoping to make contact with the Indians and trade for food, but the Natives kept their distance. And so the English spent their first winter half starving and lost half their numbers to disease.[8]

Then a near miracle happened. For some reason, the Indians (rarely identified by tribe) overcame their caution and proved to be "friendly" (requiring no explanation), led by the translators Samoset and Squanto and Massasoit, their chief. They fed the English and taught them how to plant corn and where to fish, at which point the colony began to thrive. The two parties then sealed their newfound friendship with a feast that came to be known as the First Thanksgiving. The peace that followed permitted colonial New England and, by extension, modern America to become seats of freedom, democracy, Christianity, and plenty. As for what happened to the Indians, this myth has nothing to say. Their legacy was to present America as a gift to others or, in other words, to concede to colonialism. Like Pocahontas and Sacajawea (the other most famous Indians), they helped the colonizers and then moved offstage.[9]

Literally. Throughout James's lifetime American schools had elementary students perform annual Thanksgiving pageants in which they dressed up as Pilgrims (replete with oversized buckles on every conceivable article of clothing) and Indians (costumed as if they were from the Great Plains) to make friendship and launch the United States. Though some twenty-first-century school systems have conscientiously halted these pageants, many others (my admittedly unscientific surveys of students and primary school teachers suggests that the number is about half) continue the ritual. I myself

Enrico Causici, *Landing of the Pilgrims, 1620*, 1825. Courtesy of the Architect of the Capitol.

The myth of friendly Indians welcoming the Pilgrims is such a fundamental part of Americans' sense of themselves that it is depicted in relief in the rotunda of the United States Capitol.

remember participating in such a pageant, which closed with the song "My Country 'Tis of Thee," whose first verse reads: "My country, 'tis of thee / Sweet land of liberty / Of thee I sing. / Land where my fathers died! / Land of the Pilgrim's pride! / From every mountain-side, / Let freedom ring!" Having a diverse group of schoolchildren sing about the Pilgrims as "my fathers" was designed to teach them about who we, as Americans, are, or least who we're supposed to be. Even students from discrete ethnic backgrounds would be instilled with the principles of representative government, liberty, and Christianity while learning to identify with English colonists from four hundred years ago as fellow whites.[10]

Leaving Indians out of the category of "my fathers" also carried important lessons. It was yet another reminder about which race ran the country and whose values mattered. Lest we dismiss the impact of these messages, consider the experience of a young Wampanoag woman who in 2017 told this author that when she was in kindergarten, the lone Indian in her class, her teacher cast her as Massasoit in one of these pageants and had her sing with her classmates "this land is your land, this land is my land." Reflecting on the moment as an adult, the cruel irony was not lost on her. As a child, she only knew enough to be embarrassed about it.[11]

Like so many Indians of his time and ours, it rankled Frank James that the ideologically loaded caricature of friendly Indians inviting the Pilgrims to colonize was practically the only cameo Indians made in the school curriculum. To the extent that social studies instructors addressed Indians at all, it was in the context of the narrative of Manifest Destiny, in which they appeared as primitive savages fated to make way for a more enlightened people. There was no discussion of the civilizations they had created over thousands of years before the arrival of Europeans or how they suffered under and resisted colonization. There was especially no treatment of how they had managed to survive, adapt, and become part of modern society while maintaining their Indian identities and defending their indigenous rights. Every Thanksgiving season, Wampanoag and other Indian students throughout the United States had to listen to their teachers deny their history and even who they were. Wampanoags today commonly tell of their parents objecting to the performance of Thanksgiving pageants and associated history lessons that the New England Indians were all gone, only to have schoolteachers and principals respond to them with puzzlement and even hostility. Officials often seemed incredulous that the children and their caregivers were actual Indians. The only authentic Indians were supposed to be primitive relics, not modern, so what were they doing in school, speaking English, wearing the same kind of clothing as their classmates, living in contemporary houses, or returning home to adults who had jobs and drove cars? Year after year, generation after generation, Indian schoolchildren have had to suffer this sort of devaluation from the very authority figures who are supposed to be looking out for their interests.[12]

So when James received an invitation to deliver a speech to a Massachusetts state banquet to be held in September 1970, in celebration of the 350th anniversary of Plymouth colony's founding, he saw it as a rare opportunity to set the record straight. Yet, when he submitted a draft of the speech for review, the deputy director of the state Department of Commerce and Development rejected it as "too inflammatory" for the occasion. James, for his part, found an alternative speech drawn up by officials to be so "childish and untrue," and attempts at collaborative rewriting to be so pointless, that he pulled out of the event altogether. He was not going to be yet another Indian prop at an event celebrating the start of his people's demise. Instead, he began laying down plans for a commemoration where there would be no censors.[13]

During the late 1960s, Indians across the country drew inspiration from the black civil rights movement to launch their own

Chestnut Street School Thanksgiving, Portland, 1924.
Collections of Maine Historical Society.

Thanksgiving pageants, in which elementary school children dramatize
the mythical Pilgrim-Indian encounter, have been an American tradition
since the early twentieth century. The not-so-subtle message is that
Indians welcomed colonization, that New England colonists were the
progenitors of the United States, and that the values of Christianity,
democracy, and white authority are timeless.

campaigns for Indian sovereignty and dignity, or Red Power, as it
became known. The first, most visible sign of this campaign came
in 1969 when dozens of Indians from San Francisco and nearby
colleges occupied the old prison on Alcatraz Island, which they
claimed by virtue of a clause in the 1868 Treaty of Fort Laramie
pledging the government to return retired or abandoned federal
land to Native peoples. Ultimately, they did not get the island or the
cultural center they demanded, but during their fourteen-month
protest they did draw an unprecedented amount of attention to
Indian causes, which was the point. Meanwhile, Native activists in
Minneapolis formed the American Indian Movement (AIM) to
combat police harassment locally and the federal government's
violation of Indian treaties nationally. Within a few years, AIM

became a magnet for publicity, leading a brief takeover of the Bureau of Indian Affairs in Washington, D.C., in 1972, and then a lengthier, more violent occupation of the South Dakota village of Wounded Knee, site of the 1890 massacre of a band of Minneconjou Lakotas by the U.S. Seventh Cavalry for nothing more than holding an unauthorized dance. All across the country, Indians were declaring that they had had enough of being "at the very bottom" of American society.[14]

The next chapter belonged to Frank James. Reaching out to Wampanoag and Narragansett leaders, and even to the nascent AIM organization, he organized a "National Day of Mourning" to take place on Thanksgiving Day 1970 in Plymouth at the site of the Massasoit statue on Cole's Hill overlooking Plymouth Rock. He intended this event to serve as a counterpoint to the Pilgrim Progress march held each Thanksgiving since 1920, in which Pilgrim descendants in colonial costume made their way through Plymouth town to the cemetery of their ancestors, followed by a church service. The name, Day of Mourning, harked back not only to the recent National Days of Mourning held throughout the United States after the assassinations of President John F. Kennedy in 1963 and Martin Luther King Jr. in 1968. It also evoked the *Eulogy on King Philip* written in 1836 by William Apess, a Pequot preacher and activist who served the Wampanoag community of Mashpee. In his *Eulogy*, Apess declared the December 22, 1620, anniversary of the Pilgrims' landing and the Fourth of July to be "days of mourning and not joy" for Indians because of the evils whites had done to them. When James's moment finally came, he, like Apess incarnate, rose up before two hundred protestors from all across Indian country, media, and onlookers, and delivered the "inflammatory speech" that Massachusetts had tried to suppress.[15]

He began with the most poignant assertion of all, that he had the right to the dignity of his humanity despite society's efforts to diminish him and his people. "I speak to you as a man," he empha-sized, "a Wampanoag man. I am a proud man, proud of my ancestry, my accomplishments won by a strict parental direction," even as his family and community suffered "poverty and discrimination, two social and economic diseases." He acknowledged to his white listeners that Thanksgiving "is a time of celebration for you—celebrating the beginnings for the white man in America." For James and his the Wampanoags, the day had doleful implications. "It is with a heavy heart," he explained, "that I look back on what happened to my people."[16]

James then proceeded to tell a history of English-Wampanoag relations that turned the bedtime story of the Thanksgiving myth into a nightmare. The European mariners called "explorers" by historians were in fact slavers who raided the Wampanoag coast for years before the Pilgrims' arrival, capturing people for sale to distant places of which they had never heard. The Plymouth colonists were no better, despite their claims to piety. They introduced themselves

Frank James in front of Massasoit statue at the 1974 National Day of Mourning protest. Courtesy of the *Enterprise*. Photograph by Craig Murray.

to the Wampanoags by desecrating graves and robbing seed corn from underground storage barns. Nevertheless, Massasoit extended a peaceful hand to the newcomers, not out of innate friendliness but pity, and because his people needed allies against their Narragansett Indian rivals after the Wampanoags suffered a devastating epidemic introduced by Europeans. This horror was the dark background to the supposed First Thanksgiving.[17]

James saw little in this history to celebrate. "The action by Massasoit," he proposed, "was perhaps our biggest mistake. We the Wampanoags welcomed you, the white man, with open arms, little knowing it was the beginning of the end; that before 50 years were to pass, the Wampanoag would no longer be a free people." The dishes had barely been cleared from the First Thanksgiving before a litany of English crimes began to mount: atrocities like the New England colonists' 1637 massacre of the Pequots at Mystic Fort, which Connecticut and Massachusetts memorialized with a day of thanksgiving; cheating Indians out of their land, herding them onto reservations, and making them trespassers in their own country; exploiting Indian poverty and English control of the courts to force Indians into servitude; degrading Indians by calling them savages at every opportunity. To James, like Apess, the moral of the First Thanksgiving was that the English and their descendants betrayed the Wampanoags who had once befriended them in their time of need.[18]

The question was and still is how to move forward. The answer, according to Frank James, is to confront this history, including the fact that, as he put it, "we the Wampanoag still walk the lands of Massachusetts . . . our spirit refuses to die." James also urged the American public to consider Indians as deserving of respect as everyone else, including their colonizers. "Let us remember," counseled James, "the Indian is and was as human as the white man. The Indian feels pain, gets hurt, and becomes defensive, has dreams, bears tragedy and failure, suffers from loneliness, needs to cry as well as laugh." If Americans took the simple step of extending compassion to their Indian countrymen and countrywomen, it would make Thanksgiving Day 1970 a new beginning toward "a more humane America, a more Indian America," in which Native people could "regain the position in this country that is rightfully ours." This was a stirring message for indigenous people unaccustomed to hearing their beliefs articulated so forcefully before the general public.[19]

To James's chagrin, the event he organized turned into something other than just a time of mournful reflection and teaching. Some speakers, including the AIM provocateur Russell Means, wanted less talking and more action, declaring that "Plymouth Rock is red. Red with our blood!" and that "today you will see the Indian reclaim the *Mayflower* in a symbolic gesture to reclaim our rights in this country." He wasn't kidding. Charging down Cole's Hill to the harbor, a body of protestors buried Plymouth Rock with sand, then took over a replica of the *Mayflower* anchored at a nearby wharf. Into the water went a small cannon and a mannequin representing Captain Christopher Jones, while other activists scaled the rigging to rip down the flags of Old England. Eventually, police managed to clear the ship of protestors, only to have other Indians march drumming and singing to the Plimoth Plantation living history museum, where they disrupted a traditional Thanksgiving dinner by overturning some tables and carrying off four cooked turkeys, all the while whooping and shouting like warriors. Some of the activists even made a second assault on Plymouth Rock, painting it red. James was no shrinking violet—a bumper sticker on his car read "Custer Had It Coming"—but he felt that "national Indians" had taken things too far and left local Indians to deal with the fallout.[20]

Nevertheless, there was no question that James's National Day of Mourning had made its mark. Indigenous people and their supporters have observed it in Plymouth on every Thanksgiving since 1970 with robust national media coverage. In any given year, there are representatives from Native communities throughout the continent and even the hemisphere who recognize that their local struggles are part of an ongoing global indigenous fight against colonial assaults on their sovereignty, land, sacred sites, and cultural self-direction. Furthermore, many Indians across the United States have joined the Wampanoags in treating Thanksgiving as a time for mournful remembrance and gratitude toward the Creator.[21]

James wanted the public to understand and sympathize with why some Wampanoags and other Native Americas mourn on a day on which other Americans express thankfulness for the good in their lives. We all would be wise to take heed. It is lazy and downright wrong to dismiss the National Day of Mourning as a spectacle without substance. No doubt, some participants over the years have sought publicity and got it for such actions as placing Ku Klux Klan sheets on the statue of the Plymouth colony governor William Bradford. Yet the point of such actions has been to punctuate the deeper messages of grief and solidarity for Native Americans, and understanding, compassion, and the value of daily gratitude among Americans of all descriptions.[22]

There are so many reasons for the American public to follow James's example and attempt to reflect on the history of Plymouth and Thanksgiving with three-dimensional Wampanoags at the center. Thanksgiving eclipses Columbus Day as the one time a year when the country considers the Native American role in the nation's past. It is bad enough to have gotten the story so wrong for so long. It is inexcusable to continue the annual tradition of having a phalanx of teachers, politicians, and television producers traffic in the Thanksgiving myth, and homeowners and shopping centers sport decorations of happy Indians and Pilgrims. These practices dismiss Native peoples' real historical traumas in favor of depicting their ancestors as consenting to colonialism. To call the consequences harmless is to ignore the chorus of Native Americans, our fellow Americans after all, who say the hurt is profound, particularly to their children. This is a population that has suffered more than its fair share in the creation of the United States. Additionally, Indian men and, nowadays, women, have served in the military at exceptionally high rates in every single one of the nation's wars. In a pluralistic country, it is morally unacceptable to allow the celebration of a national holiday to damage part of the nation's people, never mind the First People.

Or, for that matter, all of the people. Whereas the identity politics of marginalized groups tends to focus on achieving justice and equality (or, in the Indian case, sovereignty), white identity politics has always—always—centered on oppressing others. Yet there has been too little public consideration about how the Thanksgiving myth teaches white proprietorship of the nation. Why should a school-age child with the last name of, say, Silverman, identify more with the Pilgrims than the Indians? After all, such a student is unlikely to descend from either group, and the descendants of both groups are Silverman's fellow Americans. If the student is taught to think of *both* Pilgrims and Indians more dispassionately as "they" instead of "we," it might be a step toward a more critical understanding of history in which all the actors can be seen as fully human, with all the virtues and shortcomings that one would expect to find in any population. At the same time, if the student is taught to think of both groups more inclusively as "we," it might contribute to a more compassionate national culture. This vision would include school curricula that treat Native American history as basic to an understanding of American history in general rather than something to be discussed only at Thanksgiving or Native American Heritage Month. Such a shift might also feature bringing Indians and their concerns into the national conversation, including having presidential candidates hold a serious discussion about their Indian policies and the state of Indian country, something this author has never seen in his lifetime.

If the public continues to insist on associating Pilgrim-Wampanoag relations with Thanksgiving, the least we can do is try to get the story right. The challenge is significant, at several different levels. Part of it has to do with the limits of historical sources, which at best make recovering the Native American past difficult, and at worst make it impossible. The Wampanoags, despite acquiring a remarkable level of alphabetic literacy during the seventeenth and eighteenth centuries, did not produce many surviving historical documents. English colonists and later white Americans—including missionaries, bureaucrats, merchants, curious travelers, and academics—created the vast majority of the written records on which historians rely. Though some of them knew the Wampanoags and their culture well, most of them did not, and though some of them believed that they had the Wampanoags' interests at heart, most of them did not. Furthermore, outsiders' accounts often ignored key aspects of Wampanoag life, such as women's roles, childhood, aging, local politics, and relations between Native communities. Other sources, including oral histories and archaeological findings, can help compensate for these biases and silences, but even then there remains so much essential information that will never be known. Until the 1970s, very few professional historians bothered to correct the record because they saw Indians as irrelevant to the story of the United States and the modern world. Better to leave indigenous people to the anthropologists across campus. Since then, however, the historical field has awakened to the dynamism and centrality of the Native American past and developed methodologies to use every possible source to recount it as best we can.[23]

This book operates under the premise that imperfect histories of Indian life are better than no histories. Acknowledging that many

Wampanoag voices and perspectives are distorted or selectively represented by the historical record is not the same thing as saying that they are absent. Indeed, they exist in greater volume than one might assume, because, from the 1620s up to the present day, the people had a remarkable knack for figuring out ways to get their points across even under trying circumstances. The fact that their history played out in a remarkably literate region, divided into several colonies and religious factions, each with their own take on Indian affairs, and blessed by a relative lack of destructive wars and severe weather incidents, has produced a rich archive with multiple vantages on Indian topics.

The customary division of American history into eras determined by the national story of the United States also obstructs our effort to understand the Native American past on its own terms. Traditionally, American history has relegated the Wampanoags to Plymouth's early years at the start of the "colonial period." To the extent that Wampanoags appear after that time, it is only in discussions of the devastating King Philip's War of 1675–76. The implication is that the people no longer mattered after their defeat, that they had all been killed or somehow disappeared. A truly Wampanoag-centered history of Plymouth and Thanksgiving requires extending the historical chronology in two directions. Rather than beginning with English contact, as if the Wampanoags were frozen in time, waiting for history to start with European colonization of the so-called New World, this book contends that centuries-long developments among the Wampanoags help explain how they behaved after the English arrival. In other words, it sees the Wampanoags as having emerged from an Indian Old World every bit as ancient and important as the past of Europe.

Additionally, this book, despite its focus on the seventeenth century, traces Wampanoag history after the Thanksgiving feast and King Philip's War up to the present day. This approach emphasizes

that, for the Wampanoags and other Indians, the colonial period did
not end in 1776 with the American Declaration of Independence.
Nor did it close following the creation or termination of their reservations. Native Americans are still experiencing colonization. They
still have to take periodic legal action to exercise sovereignty over
their land and people because too many of their fellow Americans
consider such rights to be relics of a bygone era. Many Indians
continue to fight state and federal governments to recover territory
seized from them in violation of historical treaties that are supposed
to be the basis of their government-to-government relationship with
Washington. And they still battle to revitalize their languages and
cultures in the face of generations of governmental and popular pressure to assimilate and disappear.[24]

Though this book focuses on historical Wampanoags and
strives to include their voices at every opportunity, the reader should
be fully aware that the author is not Wampanoag and this is not a
history told from a modern Wampanoag perspective. My conversations with modern Wampanoags have informed the content, but
there is material in this book that some Wampanoags will consider
dubious, outright wrong, and perhaps none of my business as an
outsider. I have done my best to take those criticisms into consideration by soliciting responses to drafts of this book from histori-
cally minded Wampanoag colleagues and discussing my ideas with
Wampanoag audiences open to hearing them. I have offered to
include dissenting opinions alongside my interpretations, all the
while acknowledging that the playing field is uneven given that I am
the author. Ultimately, the responsibility for all editorial decisions
in this book belong to me alone, and in the final analysis I have made
tough decisions based on the standards of my discipline of history.
I urge my readers to seek out the Wampanoags' own tellings of this
history, which are widely available in print, film, and online, as cited
in my endnotes. My hope is that Wampanoag and other indigenous

readers will see an informed, well-intentioned attempt to fulfill the Indian call to take Indian history seriously in the context of a greater American history. Doing so necessarily includes addressing issues that remain controversial and contested among readers of all descriptions. Again, critical history can be hard on the living. But, as one gracious Aquinnah Wampanoag elder once told me, "we do ourselves no good by hiding from the truth." I think she meant all of us. Amen.

CHAPTER ONE

꒐ꓵ

The Wampanoags' Old World

In the early seventeenth century, Europeans viewed America as a wilderness. William Bradford, Plymouth's longtime governor, repeatedly used the term in his famous account of the colony's founding, as when he described New England as "a hideous, desolate wilderness full of wild beasts and wild men." Europeans also called America a New World because it had previously been unknown to them. Yet there was little wild or new about this place, as one can see from the Plymouth colonists' own writings, even if the authors missed the point. When the *Mayflower* reached Cape Cod in November 1620, the English had only to set foot onshore to encounter evidence of a civilization created by the Cape's indigenous people, the Wampanoags, even though the Natives already had moved inland for the winter. Narrow roads wound their way from the beach through the dunes and forests to sources of drinking water and multifamily summer villages. These clearings were filled with *wetus*, the Wampanoags' houses, made of frames of bent saplings, with sleeping platforms running along the interior walls, and the people's belongings and some leftovers of past meals scattered throughout. In the summer these wetus would have been covered with mats, but when the people left the coast during the cold months, they took the mats with them, leaving the frames standing for use the next year, which is what the English found. Underground storage pits lay nearby, including one with "a fine great new basket full of very fair corn of this year . . . it held three or four bushels." Predictably, a little bit more wandering led the exploratory party to "much plain ground . . . and some signs where the Indians had formerly planted their corn." Roadways, villages, stored crops, and planting fields are hardly signs of wilderness or an undiscovered new world, whether by the standards of 1620 or 2020.[1]

Wetu.

Wampanoag *wetus* (more commonly known as *wigwams*) appeared in a variety of sizes, ranging from small domes for one or two families to longhouses capable of lodging multiple families and hosting political events. The Wampanoags covered them with reed mats in summer and with bark in winter. They left the frames standing for future use when they relocated to spring, summer, or winter sites. Remarkably, there are no surviving detailed images of New England Indian wetus from the seventeenth century, but John White's watercolor drawing of North Carolina Algonquian houses from the 1580s provides a sense of what they looked like, as does this contemporary wetu from the Plimoth Plantation museum's Wampanoag Homesite. Note, however, that there is no evidence that the Wampanoags lived in palisaded villages.

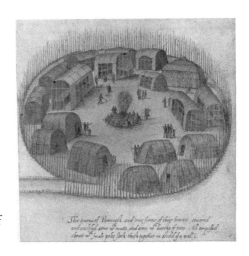

John White, "Indian Village of Pomeiooc," 1585–93. © Trustees of the British Museum.

The English liked to think of themselves as civilized and of the Indians as savages, but the sordid behavior of the *Mayflower* passengers during this probe gave the Wampanoags reason to think that they were the ones suffering a barbarian invasion. Just beyond the planting fields, the English found "a great burying place, one part whereof was encompassed with a large palisade, like a churchyard." They left the presumably elite burials within the enclosure undisturbed, but desecrated several of the nondescript ones outside it despite the obvious risk of antagonizing the people to whom this cemetery belonged. Their misconduct included ransacking the graves for funerary offerings that the Wampanoags meant for the deceased to use on the journey to the afterlife. The Wampanoags certainly did not expect their sacred gifts to become curiosities for strangers. What kind of people showed such disrespect for burials, that most sacrosanct of human rites?[2]

As the English continued their search, even the woods displayed signs that this was Wampanoag country. A spring trap made of a rope lasso attached to a bent branch managed to snag Bradford as he was walking by, providing the wary English with a needed moment of comic relief. There was "a path made to drive deer in, when the Indians hunt," in reference to the Wampanoags' communal hunts, which involved men spreading out through the woods and then gradually converging to force large numbers of game animals into a narrow space for easy slaughter. Elsewhere, the English came upon a dugout canoe left on the bank of a creek to enable travelers to cross back and forth, as if no one were worried about it being stolen. Actual Wampanoags did not care to be found, at least not yet, but this was unquestionably their *settled* place.[3]

By the end of the colony's first year, the English had gained a fuller, if still incomplete, sense of the Wampanoags' political order and lifeways. When the *sachem* (or chief) Ousamequin finally made contact with the English in March 1621 after keeping a cautious distance for months, he was clearly the people's leader. It was apparent in the train of sixty *matawaûog* (or warriors) who paid deference to him, in "a great chain of white bone [probably shell] beads around his neck," and in his dignified bearing. No mere show, Ousamequin was asserting his people's authority over the site of Plymouth colony, which the Wampanoags called Patuxet, even though he lived forty miles to the west in the sachemship of Pokanoket. He was also assuming direction of the Wampanoags' dealings with the English newcomers. It is no wonder that the English believed his proper name was Massasoit, when in actuality that was only an honorific meaning something like "the highest chief that speaks on behalf." The English also mistakenly referred to him as a king, though he represented rather than lorded over his people.[4]

An early diplomatic visit by Edward Winslow and Robert Cushman to Ousamequin's village of Sowams within Pokanoket brought Wampanoag society into even clearer view. The trip took place along a region-wide network of trails connecting dozens of communities and their fishing and gathering places. At various points along the route were holes in the ground that passersby would

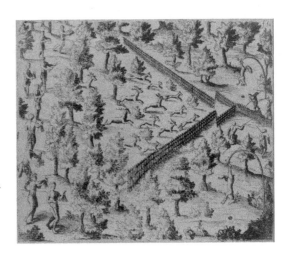

Deer drive, from Samuel
de Champlain, *Voyages et
découvertures faites en la
nouvelle France, depuis
l'année 1615* . . . (Paris: Chez
Claude Collet, au Palais, en
la galerie des Prisonniers,
1619), opp. p. 52. Courtesy
of the Library of Congress.

clear of accumulated debris or brush. Winslow understood that
these sites were mnemonic devices, or memory prompts, to initiate
the telling of a chapter of the people's history, "so that as a man
travels, if he can understand his guide, his journey will be less tedious,
by reason of the many historical discourses [that] will be related to
him." Yet only a Wampanoag would have known what story the
memorial symbolized.[5]

Not only was the route alive with history, but signs of the
people's civilization were everywhere: men using a weir to catch fish;
women ferrying baskets of shellfish they had collected; cornfields
lining the entire length of the Taunton River; forests left so free of
underbrush because of deliberately set fires that "a man may well
ride a horse amongst them." Upon their arrival at Sowams, the
English quickly had to learn and perform the protocols of Wampanoag diplomacy: the custom of visitors going straight to the sachem's
house to explain their business; sharing a pipe of tobacco before
engaging in any political talk; sleeping right next to the sachem and
his wife during an overnight stay. For a wilderness, this country had
quite a number of rules.[6]

The vastness of the Wampanoag polity was also gradually becoming perceptible. Winslow took special interest in a "great speech" by Ousamequin in which he "named at least thirty places" under his leadership, making him one of a handful of great sachems in southern New England "to whom the rest resort for protection, and pay homage unto them, neither may they war without their knowledge and approbation." In other words, Ousamequin managed the foreign relations of dozens of local communities and received "homage" (or tribute) to fund his activities, but when it came to day-to-day domestic affairs, those places were autonomous and governed by their own sachems and councils. Winslow even had to admit that "myself and others" had been wrong in saying "that the Indians about us are a people without any religion," for he had learned that the Wampanoags "conceive of many divine powers." Englishmen commonly dismissed the Natives' sovereignty and culture as no greater than that of roaming wolves because they defined difference as inferiority. Yet layers of burials containing the people's ancestors ran as deep as the tree roots. Aboveground, their civilization was evident to anyone open to seeing it.[7]

Let us discard the notion of America as a New World, never mind a savage wilderness, as there is no better way to begin a reorientation toward a Wampanoag-centered history of Plymouth and Thanksgiving. We should not be beholden to the terms and perspectives of seventeenth-century Europeans. Documentable human history in the Americas goes back at least fifteen thousand years by conservative estimates and in New England at least twelve thousand years. Whereas archaeologists trace Native American origins to Siberia and South Asia, some indigenous people contend that they sprang out of the ground into their homelands, like the corn that has sustained them for centuries. Others tell of their distant forebears migrating to the homeland from other parts of Turtle Island, as they refer to America. Despite the variety of such origin stories, they all agree on a fundamental point: Indians are not only the first people of America; they are ancient. By the time Europeans arrived on the scene, there was nothing new about this world except what indigenous people had created during their long history.[8]

If the idea of America as a New World blinds us to the antiquity of Native Americans, it also contributes to two other misconceptions about the Indian past. One is the false divide between prehistory and history. The other is that Indian authenticity depends on adherence to a supposedly unchanging culture rooted in the precolonial period. To think of America as new and of Indians as prehistorical feeds the erroneous and fundamentally racist notion that indigenous Americans had experienced little historical change before the colonial era, that they had been stuck in a rudimentary, Stone Age existence since time out of mind. Subtly, the Thanksgiving myth buttresses this fallacy by making the *Mayflower* passengers the dynamic initiators of contact with a Wampanoag population that seems to have been waiting passively to be discovered. In turn, the portrayal of Indians as static contributes to a sinister racial double bind of long standing in American culture. It posits that the Native way of life at the time of European contact was and is the only authentic Indian culture. Nobody expects the Pilgrims' modern descendants to look and act like their seventeenth-century ancestors, yet the public commonly judges that indigenous people who have changed since 1492 or 1620 have somehow relinquished their claims to be Indian. In other words, the New World concept of authentic Indians frozen in time until European contact denies Indians the right to continue to be Indians while changing with their times; it refuses to acknowledge the possibility of being a modern Indian. It is part of a colonial ideology designed to make Indians disappear.[9]

Besides being cruel, such thinking is plain bad history. No less than the English, the Wampanoags were already a people with a rich past before the arrival of the *Mayflower*, whose way of life was built on ancient precedents but continued to evolve in the face of fresh opportunities and challenges. Yes, their country was a settled place rather than a wilderness, an old world rather than new, but some core features of it, like corn cultivation and the regional authority of sachems like Ousamequin, were fairly recent developments. It takes an appreciation of those historical transformations to grasp the Wampanoags' relationship to the land, their society and culture, and the logics by which they made their decisions. Wampanoag history did not begin with the *Mayflower*. Imagine it instead as a rushing, primordial river into which the English entered as a fresh stream.

We can get a sense, but only a sense, of what the Wampanoags' old world was like before the founding of Plymouth colony by combining archaeology with historical documentation and oral histories from the early contact period. There are no chronicles about Wampanoag life before 1524, the date of the people's first recorded contact with Europeans, because the Wampanoags' ancestors did not practice alphabetic literacy. Without such accounts, it is impossible to include details of Wampanoag personas and politics in a discussion of their ancient watershed events, as such matters are not the focus of Wampanoag oral traditions. Nevertheless, archaeological evidence is unequivocal that Native America, including New England, had been developing for millennia. It is time to rediscover that old world to better understand the new world of mourning produced by the Wampanoags' encounter with the English. Taken together, they also reveal the childishness of the Thanksgiving myth.[10]

CREATING A WORLD OF PLENTY

The Wampanoags were and are so grounded in their territory that their stories of ancient times take the existence of people for granted, whereas the landscape's natural features require explanation.

Seventeenth-century Wampanoags and the neighboring Narragansetts told the English that the humanlike god Kiehtan, or
Cautantowwit, had created the original man and woman by first
forging them out of stone, but they did not love each other enough,
so he broke these models and carved new ones from wood. Other
oral histories from Wampanoags on the island of Martha's Vineyard,
though, are less interested in these first humans than in the adven-
tures of an ancient giant named Moshup, who shaped the people's
world. For instance, Wampanoags from Aquinnah say that their
ancestors came to the island to find Moshup already living there
with his wife, Squant, and their children. Moshup discovered the
place when a Thunderbird, one of the most widespread figures in
North American Indian cosmology, swooped out of the sky to seize
one of Moshup's children from the family camp. Moshup chased
the bird southward from Cape Cod across Vineyard Sound until he
reached Noepe (meaning "dry land amid waters"), now known as the
Vineyard. Finding Noepe to his liking, Moshup decided to move his
family there, and their activities left indelible marks on the terrain
that future generations of people used as prompts for their story-
telling. The peninsula of Aquinnah lacked great trees because Moshup
had used them as firewood to cook his favorite dish, broiled whale.
The multicolored clay that oozes out of Aquinnah's shoreline cliffs
originated from Moshup scooping whales out of the sea and smashing
them dead against the banks. Moshup created the treacherous shoals
off the Aquinnah peninsula by tossing rocks into the water so he
would have places to go fishing. Dense fogs were the smoke from his
pipe. And Nantucket (if an Aquinnah Wampanoag was telling the
tale) was a deposit of his pipe's ashes. In all likelihood, Nantucket
Wampanoags told a different version.[11]

Archaeologists have different ways to account for the origins of
Native New Englanders, but they concur with the Moshup stories
that indigenous people are so ancient to place as to have adapted to

Stanley Murphy, Moshup, ca. 1971. Courtesy of Chris Murphy. Photograph by Ollie Becker and Danielle Mulchay.

This mural by the late Martha's Vineyard artist Stan Murphy, which hangs in Vineyard Haven Town Hall on Martha's Vineyard, depicts the mythical Wampanoag giant, Moshup, harvesting his favorite meal, whale, against the backdrop of the multicolored clay cliffs of Aquinnah.

seismic changes to the climate and landscape. People first appear in the archaeological record of southern New England about twelve thousand years ago as small bands of hunter-gatherers tracking big game like mammoths, caribou, mastodons, and giant beaver. It was a much colder time in which so much water was trapped in ice that the sea level was ten meters below its present mark, making it possible for a giant like Moshup or even a regular-sized person to walk on land well past today's New England coastal islands.[12]

Over the next several thousand years, the warming of the earth and the melting of the last great glaciers forced a retreat of the tundra and creation of the deciduous forests we now associate with southern New England. The big game animals disappeared with the ice, probably because of a combination of human overhunting and climatic change, though the cause remains open to debate. In response, the people refocused the chase on the smaller species of the emerging woodlands, such as deer, moose, bear, rabbit, and fox. Controlled burns of the forest improved the hunt. These blazes cleared out the underbrush that impeded the hunters' pursuit and created environments in which deer, beaver, hare, porcupine, and turkey thrived. Attracted by this prey, the number of carnivorous wolves, foxes, eagles, and hawks rose in turn. This pattern leads one environmental historian to emphasize that "Indians who hunted game were not just taking the 'unplanted bounties of nature'; in an important sense, they were harvesting a foodstuff which they had consciously been instrumental in creating." Trees that survived the set fires became sources of raw material for tools, archaeologically evident in stone gouges for woodworking and axe and spear heads designed for wooden handles. The people of this era also created *mishoons*, or dugout canoes, by felling large trees and then systematically charring and scraping them out until they were capable of carrying multiple passengers and their goods miles into the open ocean.[13]

Glacial advance, then retreat, followed by rising seas, fashioned a well-watered landscape affording plenty of opportunity to use these craft. Over the thousands of years when the great Wisconsin glacier was expanding, it functioned like a bulldozer, carving out channels and basins in some places, and irregular moraines in others. Then, as it began to melt and shrink northward, it deposited massive chunks of ice and gravel until it had formed the molds for southern New England's mosaic of kettle and saltwater ponds, coastal bays, streams, slow-moving rivers, and marshes; Cape Cod alone, for instance, has 353 separate ponds. These places and the adjacent shoreline provided indigenous people with access to a seemingly unlimited amount of food. There were saltwater fish, including striped bass, sturgeon, bluefish, scup, tautog, flounder, haddock, shark, skate, and, of course, cod. In spring, alewives and shad

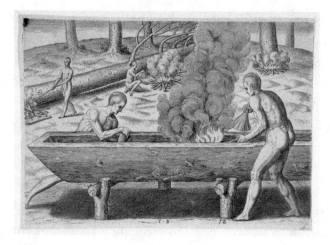

Theodore de Bry, "The Manner of Making Thear Boates," 1588, after the
John White watercolor. © President and Fellows of Harvard College.

There are no surviving images of Wampanoag watercraft during the
seventeenth century, but this painting by the Belgian artist Theodore de Bry,
after John White's paintings from coastal Carolina, provides a close
approximation. The Wampanoags created *mishoons*, or dugout canoes, by
patiently burning and scraping out the interiors of single trees. The
precolonial old-growth forests of New England enabled them to make
seaworthy mishoons as long as forty feet in length and capable of carrying
twenty people and their goods. These mishoons gave the people access to
islands such as Nantucket (thirty miles from the mainland), Martha's
Vineyard (seven miles), and Block Island (fourteen miles), to the densely
populated Indian communities of the coast, and to the rich bounty of the
sea. Today, indigenous people across New England have revived
the tradition of crafting and navigating mishoons.

appeared in astounding numbers to migrate up the rivers to spawn.
Freshwater streams and ponds also contained bass, trout, and perch,
while nearby swamps offered up turtles, frogs, and cranberries. Tidal
estuaries fed by freshwater and saltwater attracted waterfowl like
ducks, geese, and cormorants and nourished acres of edible plants
and seagrasses in which shellfish anchored. At low tide, the shellfish

were especially abundant in the form of clams, oysters, mussels, scallops, crabs, and lobsters. Between the estuaries and the wood line grew wild fruits like beach plums, raspberries, strawberries, and grapes. Herds of harbor seals lay basking in the sun on coastal rocks and remote beaches. When the people were especially lucky, drift whales became stranded on the shore, ready for the taking. Giant shell middens (or waste piles), some of them still visible today, testify to the people's increasing focus on marine resources, as do the remains of their improving technology. Take, for example, ancient fish weirs on the site of what is now Boylston Street in Boston. Native people came to this site repeatedly over fifteen hundred years, laying down some sixty-five thousand wooden stakes that they interwove with brush to trap fish at low tide for catching with spears and nets. It is one of many signs that life was good along the coast.[14]

The weir is also indicative of indigenous people shifting from nomadic tracking of animal herds to the seasonal use of the same sites year after year accompanied by an increased sense of territoriality. Beginning in the Early Archaic period, 8000–6000 B.C.E., people began following a seasonal round in which they spent the spring at riverside fish runs, summer along the shoreline, and fall and winter inland to hunt terrestrial animals. Warm weather was a time for extended family bands to gather in larger groups, which is evident in the archaeological remains of communal rituals in different parts of what later became known as Wampanoag country. For instance, sometime around the year 2340 B.C.E., several bands gathered along the Taunton River to cremate eleven bodies of their dead and bury the remains in a single large pit. The living continued to visit this sacred ground for many years. Archaeologists have found a similar site in the town of Orleans on the outer part of Cape Cod. In these places, it was as if the inhabitants were laying claim to each other and the territory itself.[15]

The people engaged in increasingly long-distance cultural and economic exchange even as they became more grounded in particular places. Sometime around the year 443 B.C.E., a new "mortuary cult" spread from the Ohio River valley throughout the eastern woodlands, reaching as far as southern New England. Called Adena by archaeologists, this culture pattern involved interring the dead in a fetal position beneath an earthen mound, sometimes surrounding the tomb with ditches and earthen rings, and placing specialized goods in the grave made of materials from as far away as Ohio, Nova Scotia, the Great Lakes, and Carolina. Precisely how this cult and its funerary objects reached southern New England must remain unknown, but clearly it disproves the popular assumption that the people of this area lived in isolation until the arrival of Europeans. It also points to the long tendrils of history, for though the Adena cultural movement does not appear to have been widespread or long-lasting, similar practices marked elite Wampanoag burials well into the 1600s.[16]

Nothing so readily disproves the fallacy that these were people without history than an appreciation of the revolutionary effects of the arrival of the bow and arrow and of maize and bean cultivation around the year 700 C.E. (known as the Middle Woodland period). The bow and arrow, which had been adopted thousands of years earlier by Arctic peoples but reached eastern North America only after 500 C.E., was a vast improvement over the spear in terms of range and portability. It instantly improved the efficiency of hunting and probably also became a weapon of war. Maize and beans came from a different direction. These crops arose in Mexico some six thousand years ago, then spread through what is now the southwestern United States and up the Mississippi and Ohio Rivers before arriving in the northeast. The expansion of maize was a stunning feat of human engineering in which cultivators—certainly women, given their responsibility for the crop—bred ever larger cobs and selected seeds that could grow in ever colder, wetter environments. There is isolated evidence of maize in New York archaeological sites from as far back as two thousand years, but there are no signs of it in New England before 1000 C.E. and not until 1300 C.E., amid a warming trend, is there proof of systematic cultivation. Beans also make their first appearance at that later date. Southern New England was the last place in America to which maize spread, as the crop cannot be cultivated successfully any farther north than lower Maine. That dividing line, between the horticulturalists of southern New England and the hunter-gatherers to the north, would have lasting implications for intertribal and Indian-European relations during the early colonial era.[17]

When and why southern New England Indians adopted maize horticulture has been subject to stringent debate. Until fairly recently, many archaeologists doubted whether southeastern New England Indians raised corn and beans at all until the 1500s and even the early 1600s. One explanation was that Indians took up farming so they could remain on the coast for longer periods of time and await the arrival of European trading vessels filled with coveted goods. Yet that theory has been swept away by the growing evidence of maize cultivation at archaeological sites dating as far back as seven hundred years, especially the discovery of a Narragansett village from 1300 to 1500 C.E. containing scores of maize kernels as well as corn hills and underground storage pits. It now appears that southern New England Indians were growing maize, beans, and squash at least two centuries before their contact with Europeans.[18]

From our vantage, this was a watershed in New England Indian history, but the people probably did not think of it as such. Tending crops did not require them to change their generations-long pattern of spending the warm months in dispersed homesteads and family hamlets along coastal estuaries and rivers. Nor did it significantly disrupt previous subsistence activities, though women, who were responsible for planting and weeding, would have had less time for gathering shellfish and wild plant foods. Indeed, horticultural produce appears to have eased some of the stress that the growing Indian population was putting on coastal resources. Of course, horticulture placed its own demands on the local environment, with maize exhausting a soil's fertility after as little as eight years of annual planting. However, coastal people discovered that they could sustain soil fertility and increase their harvest yields by using fish as fertilizer, specifically by burying a herring in each of the planting hills they made to support the cornstalks. Such adaptations enabled them to turn horticulture into yet another source of plenty alongside the teeming coastal estuaries.[19]

KIEHTAN'S GIFT

One gains a better appreciation of the choices Wampanoags made in creating their civilization through comparison with other societies in the East in which maize horticulture produced more radical transformations. The most dramatic example is the rise of the Mississippians, as anthropologists call them, between 900 and 1300 C.E. This culture centered on the confluence of Ohio and Mississippi Rivers and extended along those waterways and their tributaries north to Wisconsin, south to Louisiana, west to Oklahoma, and east to the Appalachian foothills. Leadership came from great chiefs who claimed descent from the sun, and a priesthood that claimed to control the weather so essential to the people's new crops. The Mississippians' command of waterways that reached nearly every corner of the continent enabled them to import precious materials from hundreds of miles away, which artisans then crafted into pipes, statues, ornaments, and weaponry depicting the people's religious icons. Earthen pyramids, some over a hundred feet high, contained the burials of chiefs, their wives, and their retainers, and massive amounts of grave goods. Not surprisingly, the skeletons of elites evince far better nutrition, particularly in terms of the consumption of meat, and far less physical stress (such as arthritis), than the remains of commoners. Elite graves also contain far more goods of higher quality, such as ornaments crafted from exotic materials, than those of everyday people. Atop the pyramids were chiefly houses and temples in order to locate the elites closer to the sun and symbolize the line of succession. The largest mound of a given town would sit at the head of a ceremonial plaza, around which were smaller mounds for lesser nobles. Signs of hierarchy were everywhere.

The most impressive of these towns, Cahokia, on the site of modern East St. Louis, contained 120 mounds of varying size within a five-mile-square area and boasted between ten thousand and thirty thousand residents during its heyday in the twelfth and thirteenth centuries, making it more populated than medieval London or Paris. Defensive earthworks and wooden palisades made from tens of thousands of logs protected the people from their numerous enemies. Nine smaller mound centers and dozens of villages stretching across twenty thousand square miles formed Cahokia's hinterland. Some scholars have characterized these satellite communities as suburbs. They raised the produce to feed the chiefly and priestly elite and probably contributed the labor that went into the great public works. Farther off still were remote outposts from which warriors guarded the military frontier and gathered exotic goods through intimidation and trade to funnel to the capital town. Most of these Mississippian city-states did not last into the sixteenth century—Cahokia had split apart by the fourteenth—probably because of warfare and overexploitation of the local environment, perhaps compounded by the earliest appearance of European epidemic diseases in a few cases. Yet for several hundred years they thrived, with maize horticulture as their staff of existence.[20]

Another striking example of the diverse ways Natives responded to the advent of maize comes from the Iroquoian-speaking societies of what is now upstate New York, southern Ontario, and the St. Lawrence River valley, just a few hundred miles northwest of Wampanoag country. In their case, the result was not steeply hierarchical chiefly city-states of tens of thousands of people with monumental public works but decentralized villages organized around female-descent groups. After centuries of experimentation, around 900–1000 C.E. Iroquoians took a "quantum leap" in their cultivation of maize, beans, and squash and made these crops the basis of their economy. No sooner had they completed this transition than they moved their settlements from the riversides to defensive hilltop sites surrounded by good horticultural soils. They also transformed their houses from the round or oval wetus characteristic of southern New England into multifamily longhouses as much as two hundred feet in length. Married men lived with their wives' kin, with each house consisting of a senior woman, her daughters, and their nuclear families. All these women and their children (boys and girls alike) belonged to the same totemic clan—represented by such animals as turtle, bear, and wolf—while their husbands belonged to other clans traced through their own mothers. Clan identities linked the people to members of the same clan in other villages, thereby entitling them to hospitality and support beyond their immediate kin and locality.

Anthropologists see a number of purposes to these adaptations. Female-based kin groups facilitated cooperation among women for tending crops and supervising children while able-bodied men were away hunting, fishing, trading, and warring. The custom of sending men to live with their wives' lineages reduced violence within the village because it broke up bands of biologically related men who were otherwise prone to fight males from other families for access to women. At the same time, women's dominance of house and village enabled them to project male violence outward. War parties formed when a matron called on her clansmen to bring home a scalp or captive from the enemy to serve as a symbolic or literal replacement for a dead family member. In turn, women stationed in the village oversaw the acculturation of captives from previous expeditions while warriors ventured out to capture more.

As the Iroquians consolidated this way of life, they also created a wider web of alliances to defend the home front even in the absence of the men. They began with multivillage councils of male sachems chosen by the clan matrons. These were deliberative bodies focused on collaboration and peacekeeping rather than legislative assemblies premised on majority rule. There was no single leader. The goal was to achieve consensus through discussion. In the event of stubborn disagreement, families or clans did as they wished or, in the case of serious disputes, moved to another village or formed their own. Eventually, these councils gave rise to the tribes that would constitute the Iroquois League: the Mohawks, Oneidas, Onondagas, Cayugas, and Senecas. However, before the founding of the League these tribes fought each other furiously, not for territory, but to seize captives for torture (usually in the cases of men) and slavery and adoption (usually in the cases of women and children). In response to this violence, villages of just a few hundred people consolidated into "castles" of up to two thousand or three thousand people, around which they erected palisades that sometimes ran three spiral layers thick, creating a long, narrow pathway to the entrance. Going outside to tend the surrounding fields, to fish, or to hunt was, of course, essential to the people's subsistence, but it also risked attack by enemy raiders, who could appear at any time. Iroquois archaeological sites from this era reveal numerous male skeletons riddled with arrows, separated skulls and torsos, and unburied human remains from what were probably captives. Iroquois oral histories are unequivocal that this was a terrible time to be alive, and often an even worse one in which to die.

Just as Iroquoians had earlier formed multivillage clans and tribes to reduce violence locally, in the sixteenth century they created multitribe confederacies to achieve peace regionally. Inspired by the prophet Deganawidah and his disciples Hiawatha and Tadodaho, the five nations of New York's Finger Lakes region gradually banded together into the Iroquois League or Haudenosaunee, meaning "People of the Longhouse." Like the tribal councils, League meetings of clan sachems focused not on policy-making but peacekeeping, specifically a halt to the cycles of revenge warfare. The sachems exchanged ritual words of condolence and gifts of shell beads thought to bring mourners insane with despair back into a state of society, which is to say, peace. Meanwhile, in what is now southern Ontario, five other Iroquoian-speaking horticultural nations allied to form the Wendat or Huron confederacy, probably as a defensive response to the Haudenosaunee. Though the formation of the Iroquois League suppressed revenge warfare among its member nations, it also empowered them to extend the scale of their raiding against other peoples until, by the mid- to late seventeenth century, it encompassed nearly the whole of eastern North America. Put another way, the transition to horticulture might have brought greater food security to the Iroquois, but it also spawned a militaristic culture that spread misery hither and yon.[21]

The effects of horticulture were more muted among southern New England Indians than among the Mississippians or Iroquoians. Though the Wampanoags had sachems and religious specialists, they were nothing akin to the Mississippian elite, residing high above everyone else, living off their labor, and claiming descent from the sun. New England Indians engaged in long-distance trade in exotic goods, but not on the continental scale of the Mississippians, and there was no specialized artisan class to transform those materials into status symbols for the rulers. Southern New England Indians also did not support a chiefly and priestly elite capable of marshaling great armies to reduce entire populations to tributary and even slave status. Without a mass of forced laborers, they did not build massive public monuments like the Mississippian mound pyramids, for free people would not perform such strenuous work for others. Given the Wampanoags' access to coastal estuaries full of wild foods, it would have been futile for their chiefs to try to assert control over horticultural lands as a way to starve the people into Mississippian-type submission.[22]

The differences between southern New England Indians and the Iroquois were also pronounced in several respects, though just how many is open to debate. Modern New England Indians, including Wampanoags, say their ancestors also had matrilineal, clan-based polities, but anthropologists are skeptical. Anthropologists posit instead that after New England Indians adopted horticulture, they reckoned descent from both the male and the female lines. The anthropologists' position is consistent with documentary evidence about New England Indians' patterns of chiefly succession and nuclear family residence during the seventeenth and eighteenth centuries, though these might have been colonial-era developments shaped by English pressure. More certain is that whereas the Iroquois governed themselves through counsels of clan chiefs chosen by matrons, New England Indian communities were led by individual sachems (some of them women) who inherited their office through the male line. To be sure, these sachems were no autocrats. They always consulted with councils of family heads, who, in turn, consulted with women, with the aim of achieving consensus. Additionally, the people could unseat their sachem if he or she proved to be ineffective or abusive. In these respects, the polities of southern New England Indians were akin to those of the matrilineal Iroquois. Yet Indians on the New England coast had nothing resembling the densely populated, palisaded villages of Iroquois-speaking regions. In fact, archaeologists have been unable to find any palisaded forts anywhere in New England before the 1600s, which suggests that the people did not engage in lengthy, pitched battles. Nor is there other evidence of the kind of intensive warfare and ritual cannibalism practiced by the Iroquois. Without any need to live on constant alert near fortified settlements, southern New England Indians did not rely anywhere nearly as heavily as the Iroquois on horticultural produce from nearby fields. All of which is to say, the mere two hundred miles between the Wampanoags and the Iroquoian Mohawks were sufficient to produce striking differences in their societies even though both groups cultivated corn, beans, and squash.[23]

Southern New England might not have experienced a horticultural revolution by the standards of other northeastern Indians, but this new activity did carry a host of important long-term implications. As maize horticulture grew in importance, it added to the workload of women, who took the responsibility for planting the crops with digging sticks, using clamshell hoes to form hills around each cornstalk, weeding the fields throughout the summer until harvest time, and grinding the corn into meal using mortar and pestle (an activity that contributed to many older women developing arthritis in their hands and wrists). The efflorescence of horticulture also coincided with the rise of ceramic (fired clay) vessels for cooking and storage, which women also took the responsibility for making. A Native explanation for this gender division of labor would be that edible crops had female spirits and therefore should be tended by females, unlike tobacco, which had a male spirit and was the sole plant raised by males. Many Native peoples east of the Mississippi have traditions of a woman, a Corn Mother, visiting the people in ancient times to teach them how and where to plant maize, beans, and squash, thereafter called the Three Sisters, though if such stories existed among New England Indians they went unrecorded. Women's responsibility for maize horticulture also extended from the principle, if not always the practice, that males were takers of life for the defense and sustenance of the people, whereas women were givers of life both in childbearing and plant cultivation. Anthropologists would contend that women had responsibility for this new activity because they already were in charge of raising other types of plant foods; because planting and weeding were compatible with the constant interruptions of child care duties; and because cornfields were close to homesteads where women's work took place.[24]

The rise of corn, beans, and squash also made a difference spiritually and ritually. Most of the features of Wampanoag religious life extended from their long hunter-gatherer past, which encouraged careful observation of the natural world, including the dangers it held. Thus the Wampanoags and their neighbors conceived of animals, prominent geographic features, and meteorologic forces as possessing spirits capable of bestowing and withholding favor, of doing good and ill, depending on their whim. "If they receive any good in hunting, fishing, harvest, etc.," wrote the colonist Roger Williams in the 1640s, "they acknowledge God in it." By "God," he meant their spirits, not the Christian deity. The converse was also true: "If it be but an ordinary accident, a fall, etc., they will say God was angry and did it." Wampanoags sought favorable treatment by these spirits by showing them respect through songs and dances of honor. They prayed before going on the hunt and treated the remains of the kill according to ritual proscriptions. When things went wrong—for instance, when resources failed, the weather was poor, or a sickness broke out—the people tried to figure out which spirit was unhappy with them and how to placate it.[25]

To make such a determination, Wampanoags turned to dream interpretation. Wampanoags considered dreams the product of one of a person's two souls leaving the body in the form of a luminescent blur and going out into the world to interact with powers otherwise invisible during waking hours (the other soul kept the body breathing during sleep). Dreams thus served to reveal hidden truths. Particularly important and trustworthy were messages from a person's own guardian spirit. At or around adolescence, Wampanoag males would undergo a ritual of fasting, sleep deprivation, and imbibing of emetics and hallucinogens in the hopes of making contact with a spirit protector. That force would offer the seeker a lifetime of aid and teach him a song to chant whenever he needed assistance, such as in hunting or warfare. Williams remarked on an ailing Indian man who "called much upon *Muckquachuckquànd* [the Children's God], who . . . had appeared to the dying young man, many years before, and bid him whenever he was in distress [to] call upon him."[26]

Sometimes dream signs were clear, but at other times they were inscrutable. In such cases, it was time to enlist a *pawwaw*, or shaman, someone (seemingly always male) with a deep roster of potent guardians and an uncommon ability to enter ecstatic trances in which his dream soul went forth to make discoveries. Afterward the pawwaws would exercise their variously held talents to cure, curse, enchant, prognosticate, and organize rituals dictated to them by the spirits. A Vineyard Wampanoag shaman explained to the colonist Thomas Mayhew Jr. that he had four guardian spirits who first came to him in dreams. One of them, which took the form of a man, "told him he did know all things upon the island, and what was to be done." Another, "like a Crow," lived in his head and could "discover mischiefs coming toward him." The third, a pigeon, took residence in his breast, and it "was very cunning about any business." Finally, there was a serpent spirit, which was "very subtle to do mischief, and also to do great cures." The man's faith in these beings and their powers was part of a pattern of shamanism so common across North America and hunter-gatherer societies worldwide that it must have had ancient roots.[27]

Wampanoag rituals and the forces they invoked changed as cultivation of corn, beads, and squash grew in importance. Each spring, when the running of the shad or the disappearance of the Pleiades constellation indicated that it was time to plant, the people would gather for ceremonies to secure favorable weather and a successful harvest. In August, when the first green corn appeared, and then after the fall harvest, the people would "sing, dance, feast, give thanks, and hang up garlands" in thanks and hope of future bounty. Also new was the emphasis on the deity Kiehtan, whom the Wampanoags credited not only with creating the first man and woman but with introducing the people to maize and beans. The story went that, sometime in the mists of history, Kiehtan took seeds for these plants from the fields surrounding his house, placed them in the ears of a crow, and then had the bird deliver them to the ancestors. There was more than a kernel of truth to this story, as Kiehtan resided far to the southwest, the direction of Mexico, from which these crops had actually come. Thereafter Kiehtan blessed Wampanoag farmers with "fair weather, for rain in time of drought, and for the recovery of the sick." To complete the circle of life in which Kiehtan brought the people into existence, then sent them life-sustaining crops, good weather, and health, Wampanoags believed that the souls of their dead spent the afterlife in Kiehtan's house.[28]

For that reason, shortly after the rise of corn-beans-squash horticulture, the Wampanoags and neighboring Indians in south-eastern New England began burying their dead singly in permanent graves, placing the corpse in the fetal position, covering it with red ocher, and pointing the head toward the west or southwest. The fetal position and red ocher symbolized rebirth into the afterlife, and the

westward orientation was supposed to direct the soul on its journey
to Kiehtan. In earlier times there was no standard direction for
graves, corpses might appear in either extended or flexed form, and
burial was sometimes just a first stage before exhumation and reburial
in a communal pit. The exact cause for this change is unclear, but it is
probably no coincidence that a new mortuary practice emphasizing
the journey to Kiehtan's house arose at the same time that the people
began cultivating crops thought to have originated with that very
spirit.[29]

The people were grateful to Kiehtan because the consumption
of maize, beans, and squash afforded them excellent nutrition,
particularly in conjunction with tried-and-true hunting and gathering. Eaten alone, maize is nutritionally deficient because it lacks
the amino acids lysine and tryptophan required to make proteins,
but beans contain those very compounds. At the same time, maize
provides the amino acids cysteine and methionine that beans lack.
Together, then, maize and beans provide complete nutrition, with
squashes contributing additional vitamins. These crops also comple-
ment each other in the growing cycle. Beans return nitrogen to soils
depleted by maize, maize provides beans with a stalk to climb, and
broad squash leaves at the base of the maize stalk help retain mois-
ture and protect from excessive sun and rain and the spread of weeds.
The Three Sisters thrived through their cooperation and added yet
more resources to an already rich mix of Wampanoag foods.[30]

Wampanoag communities placed different emphases on horticulture according to their particular ecological niches. For instance,
inland communities along the rivers, lakes, and ponds probably
relied more heavily on cultivated crops and, for that matter, deer
hunting than did people on Nantucket, Martha's Vineyard, or the
outer portion of Cape Cod, where marine resources were more abundant. In this respect, scholarly attempts to determine the percentage
of calories produced by horticulture—with some estimates running

as high as 65 percent—give a false sense of uniformity across a region that was actually characterized by local variability. Yet, rather than divide the people, this economic diversity helped knit them together. For instance, a Taunton River community with rich planting grounds and easy access to the game animals of the forested uplands might trade its cornmeal, venison, or bearskins to Cape and island people for seal oil, whale blubber, or deep-sea fish. Additionally, when a local economy failed because of adverse weather or enemy attack, its sister communities with different resources could offer assistance.[31]

The robust populations of southern New England Indians testify to their well-rounded nutrition. To be sure, any discussion of these figures rests on a shaky foundation. Indians did not compile censuses before the arrival of Europeans, and European counts of Indians in the early days of colonization tended to be estimates of warriors after vicious epidemics had already run their course. Nevertheless, recorded Indian testimony about their populations before the epidemics, combined with what we know about the average sizes of Indian families, has enabled scholars to produce convincing general estimates of the people's numbers. The careful work of the historian Neal Salisbury posits a range of between 126,000 and 144,000 people for southern New England as a whole (bordered on the southwest by the Quinnipiac River and on the northeast by the Saco River) and between 21,000 and 24,000 for the Wampanoags. The Wampanoag community of Patuxet on Plymouth Harbor alone was said to have held 2,000 inhabitants before the epidemics. As for neighboring peoples, the Wampanoags' northern allies, the Massachusett Indians of Massachusetts Bay, also boasted an estimated population of 21,000 to 24,000 people; the Wampanoags' Narragansett rivals to the west had the region's largest population at some 30,000 people. It would take colonists in southern New England over a century before their numbers reached the collective heights of these groups.[32]

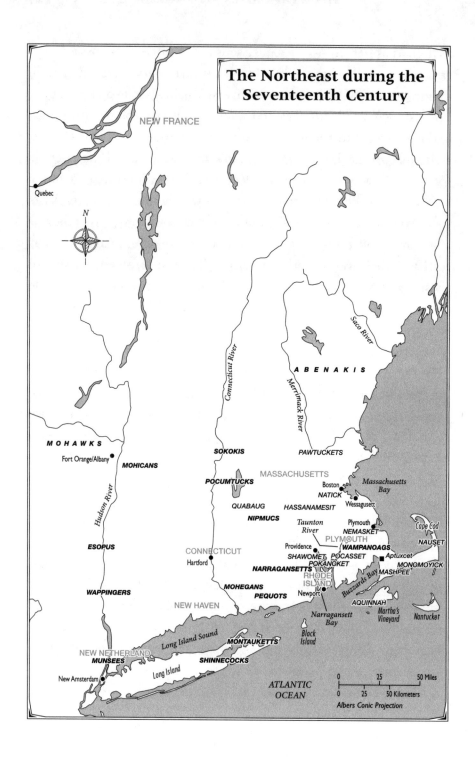

The Northeast during the Seventeenth Century

NEW FRANCE

Quebec

N

MOHAWKS
Fort Orange/Albany
MOHICANS

Hudson River

Connecticut River

SOKOKIS

POCUMTUCKS

QUABAUG
NIPMUCS

ESOPUS

WAPPINGERS

ABENAKIS

Saco River

Merrimack River

PAWTUCKETS

MASSACHUSETTS
Boston
NATICK
Wessagusett
HASSANAMESIT

Taunton
River
NEMASKET
PLYMOUTH
Providence
WAMPANOAGS
SHAWOMET POCASSET
POKANOKET
NARRAGANSETTS
RHODE
ISLAND
Newport

Massachusetts
Bay

Plymouth

Cape Cod

NAUSET

Aptuxcet
MONOMOYICK
MASHPEE

CONNECTICUT
Hartford

MOHEGANS
PEQUOTS

NEW HAVEN

Buzzards Bay

AQUINNAH
Martha's
Vineyard
Nantucket

Narragansett
Bay

Block
Island

MONTAUKETTS

NEW NETHERLAND
MUNSEES

Long Island Sound

SHINNECOCKS

New Amsterdam

Long Island

ATLANTIC
OCEAN

0   25   50 Miles

0   25   50 Kilometers

Albers Conic Projection

The needs of this growing horticultural population added to the list of duties for Native leaders. Each locality was represented by a sachem, usually a man but sometimes a woman (referred to as a *sunksquaw*) who inherited his or her position from the previous sachem, usually a father but sometimes a paternal uncle, mother, or paternal aunt. However, if the people judged the first in line of succession to be incapable of performing a sachem's responsibilities, they could bypass him or her for another candidate, just as they could remove an underperforming sachem and appoint another. The sachem handled relations with neighboring communities in consultation with a council made up of the male representatives from family lineages, a responsibility that included hosting important foreign visitors. When disputes arose between members of the same community, or when someone committed a crime, their sachem mediated the resolution or meted out the punishment. These obligations must have become more burdensome with the rising population densities afforded by horticulture. Also new was the sachem's task of allotting family planting lands in a region where fertile ground was sparse. "If any of his men desire land to set their corn," wrote Edward Winslow of the sachems, "he giveth them as much as they can use, and sets his bounds." Seventeenth-century land deeds from Indians to colonists often mention how a past sachem had granted a particular family land to cultivate, sometimes for a term limited to the life of the sachem, sometimes in perpetuity. In exchange for this and other services, the sachem received the grantee's pledges of love and loyalty and annual tribute in the form of produce, furs, choice portions of game animals, and/or labor in the sachem's fields, collected by a special military elite known as *pnieseosok*. The sachem did not hoard this wealth or immediately redistribute it, though he or she was expected to sponsor certain ritual occasions and assist the poor and needy. Rather, the main purpose of tribute was to fund the sachem's political activities. For these reasons and more, southern New England Indians called their communities *sachemships*.³³

WHO WERE THE WAMPANOAGS?

For hundreds of years, people have used "tribe" to refer to the confederacies of local sachemships known as the Wampanoags, Narragansetts, Mohegans, and Pequots. Yet this word has also been applied so indiscriminately to so many different kinds of societies throughout the world that anthropologists consider it meaningless. They prefer "paramount sachemship" to "tribe" to describe the southern New England political structure in which a prestigious and powerful (or "paramount") sachem collected tribute from a network of other local sachems to enable him to lead their foreign diplomacy, warfare, and trade and, in some cases, to spare them from his own attacks. Wampanoag oral tradition also has the paramount sachem serving as first among equals in periodic grand councils of the local sachems. These paramount sachemships or tribes were a reflection both of shared kinship and culture among the constituent peoples, and of the decision of otherwise autonomous communities to form temporary confederations under prominent, region-wide leaders.

To say that tribal divisions corresponded roughly to dialectical differences might be confusing cause and effect. All Indians in southern New England spoke one or another dialect of the broader Algonquian language family, so when people who previously spoke different dialects allied with one another, it tended to standardize their speech. Among the Wampanoags, that process was ongoing in the mid-seventeenth century, with the Wampanoags of Martha's Vineyard pronouncing some words slightly differently from mainland Wampanoags. The Wampanoags and Massachusett people to the north shared the same dialect and, perhaps not coincidentally, were close political allies. The Wampanoags also easily comprehended the Narragansetts to the west, whereas the speech of more distant Algonquian peoples such as the Eastern Abenakis of Maine or Mohicans of western Massachusetts was more of a challenge. Winslow explained that "though there be difference in a hundred miles distance of place, both in language and manner, yet [it is] not so much but that they very well understand each other."[34]

Kinship was yet another foundation for tribal identities. Members of any given Wampanoag community were likely to have relatives in other Wampanoag communities. Yet the point should not be taken too far. Wampanoags also commonly had relatives among other tribes in the region, including political rivals. A better way to think about language and kinship as elements of tribal identity is as tools that leaders used when building a confederacy of

Aquinnah cliffs. Photograph by William Waterway.

The spectacular clay cliffs of Aquinnah on Martha's Vineyard have featured prominently in Wampanoag oral tradition and economic activities since time immemorial. The cliffs still belong to the Wampanoag Tribe of Gay Head/Aquinnah. During the colonial era, the Vineyarders pronounced some words differently from mainland Wampanoags.

local sachemships. When the English arrived in southern New England, those tribes (or paramount sachemships) included the Wampanoags (meaning "Dawnland People" or "Easterners") under Ousamequin. His local sachemship was Pokanoket on the northeast of Narragansett Bay, while his paramount sachemship extended from Pokanoket, up the Taunton River to its headwaters, and due east to the tip of Cape Cod and the islands of Martha's Vineyard and Nantucket. There was also the Narragansett tribe on the west side of Narragansett Bay under the sachems Canonicus and his nephew Miantonomo, whose reach extended westward to the modern boundary of Rhode Island and Connecticut. To the northwest of the Wampanoags, in what is now central Massachusetts, was a collection of loosely affiliated peoples known as the Nipmucs, who often found themselves as pawns in the rivalries of southern sachems to reduce them to tributaries. West of the Narragansetts, in what is now eastern Connecticut, were the Pequots under the sachem Tatobem, and the Pequots' tributary, the Mohegans, under the sachem Uncas. Finally, due north of the Wampanoags was the Massachusett tribe of Massachusetts Bay under the sachem Nanapashemet, who were allied with Ousamequin and the Wampanoags against the Narragansetts. There is a long-standing tendency among scholars and the general public to think of these groups as having existed since time immemorial, hence their appearance on textbook maps labeled "Native America in 1492." Yet these were fluid political entities that formed in response to a combination of great dangers, opportunities, and charismatic leadership and might dissolve in the absence of those conditions.[35]

Marriage alliances were critical to a local sachem's ascension to paramount sachem status. Male sachems typically had several wives related to neighboring sachems or other elite families, and married off their own sons and daughters according to similar strategic considerations. For instance, though we do not have any information about the marriages of Ousamequin, we do know that after the founding of Plymouth he negotiated a marriage alliance with the sachem Corbitant of the Wampanoag sachemship of Pocasset, who had previously been chafing under his authority. This arrangement had Ousamequin's sons Wamsutta (or Alexander) and Metacom (or Philip) wed Corbitant's daughters Weetamoo (or Namumpum) and Wootonekanuske, respectively. Marriage ties of this sort, not only among elites but common people as well, were part of what made the Wampanoags a people.[36]

So did a common enemy, which appears to have been one of the bases of Ousamequin's authority. When the English arrived at Plymouth, Ousamequin lived in the village of Sowams at the head of the Mount Hope peninsula where the Taunton River empties into the east side of Narragansett Bay. This was a remarkably rich place to locate a community, as it boasted fertile fields, freshwater and saltwater resources, and many miles of broad estuaries. Yet in earlier times, at least during the lifetime of Ousamequin's father (perhaps the late 1500s), Ousamequin's people had occupied the head of Narragansett Bay, where the city of Providence is now located, as well as various nearby islands, and battled with the Narragansetts for territory and tributaries on the west bank. By the time the English arrived on the scene, the Narragansetts had driven the Wampanoags east of the Providence and Seekonk Rivers. Ousamequin's claim to paramount sachem status probably extended from his serving as a war leader of the community on the front lines of this great contest. Heading the campaign against the Narragansetts would have justified his collection of tribute from distant sachems because mobilizing matawaûog and securing allies from other tribes required material resources. At the same time, the armed might he built through his marriage diplomacy and gift exchanges enabled him to intimidate remote sachemships on the Cape and islands into paying him tribute and deferring to his will in foreign affairs.[37]

Neither the Wampanoags nor the Narragansetts left any statement on record of what their rivalry was about, but there are several possible, perhaps overlapping explanations, all related to the rise of corn-beans-squash horticulture. One is that the Wampanoags fought for control of the planting grounds of Narragansett Bay, which were among the richest in the region because they were nourished by the alluvial floodplains of nine river basins and shoreline shellfish middens, which leached the soil with the lime required to grow nitrogen-fixing beans. When the explorer Giovanni da Verrazzano visited the bay in 1524, he remarked that its "fields extend for 25 to 30 leagues; they are open and free of any obstacles or trees, and so fertile that any kind of seed would produce excellent crops." Some of the earliest archaeological evidence for horticulture among southern New England Indians comes from Narragansett Bay. Given how quickly maize exhausts the soil, it seems likely that the tens of thousands of Narragansetts and Wampanoags living along this estuary would have competed for the best tracts.[38]

Another possible factor in warfare between the Wampanoags and Narragansetts was that they were both under pressure from the fearsome Mohawks, located just to the west of the modern city of Albany, New York, to produce shell beads for them. Recall that the Iroquois League, of which the Mohawks were a part, kept peace between the member tribes through the ritual exchange of such beads. Whereas the western Iroquois League nations looked to Chesapeake Bay peoples for those manufactures, the Mohawks focused on Long Island and southern New England, sometimes through trade, but also through raid. Given that League nations began acquiring disc-shaped beads of quahog and periwinkle from southern New England at least as early as the sixteenth century, and that Narragansetts of the seventeenth century were known to send shell beads to the Mohawks regularly, it stands to reason that the Narragansetts and Wampanoags would compete for tributaries and try to reduce each other to tributary status in order to acquire the shells and labor to produce those beads in large quantities. At play in this contest were the shellfish-rich communities of Coweset, Shawomet, and Pawtuxet (distinct from the Plymouth Harbor site) on the northwest side of Narragansett Bay, with the Narragansett tribe ultimately proving triumphant. Well into the seventeenth century, the Pokanoket Wampanoags would protest that they had historical political and kinship rights to these communities despite colonists' assumption that they had always belonged to the Narragansetts. This argument hinted at a generations-old rivalry between the Wampanoags and Narragansetts for wampum-paying tributaries to meet Iroquois demand for wampum beads.[39]

A final consideration is that the Wampanoags and Narragansetts fought for control of Narragansett Bay in order to command access to European trade vessels, which began to appear intermittently at least as early as Verrazzano's voyage of 1524 and regularly by at least the early 1600s. Native people clamored after the Europeans' metal tools and implements, brightly colored cloth, mirrors, glass beads, and other jewelry. They especially prized European goods that resembled high-status indigenous productions acquired through long-distance, intertribal networks. For instance, Europeans could not help but notice that Indians had a high demand for copper even though Native leaders already possessed copper earrings and pendants from American sources. For sachems of a densely populated horticultural region trying to consolidate and extend their followings against competitors, securing a new source of exotic, luxury goods with which they could reward their supporters was a potential boon. It stands to reason, then, that when European ships began appearing in Narragansett Bay seeking trade, the Wampanoags and Narragansetts vied to dominate this traffic.[40]

All three factors—competition for planting grounds, shell-bead-paying tributaries, and long-distance trade—might have been at play in the Wampanoag-Narragansett rivalry for Narragansett Bay, which leads to a more general point about the nature of paramount sachemships on the eve of European colonization: they were fragile systems, often dependent on the political talents and resources of a single person and his or her family, rather than a set of institutions that lasted from generation to generation. A sachemship was ever a work in progress, and tribal instability was normal. At any given time, a tribute-paying community within the confederacy might break away to throw its loyalty to another paramount sachem or make a bid for independence, particularly if its local sachem lacked kinship ties to the tribute-collecting, paramount sachem. Take the Wampanoags, for example. Though the Wampanoags of Martha's Vineyard paid tribute to Ousamequin, there is no evidence that the island sachems were related to him, whereas they clearly had close connections to sachems around Massachusetts Bay. It is probably no coincidence that in the early years of Plymouth colony, Ousamequin was concerned about the islanders forming an alliance with the Bay Indians in order to buck his authority. Regional sachems also had to worry that a local sachem upstart, even a relative, might parlay military honors, a new political marriage, or a cause célèbre into a bid for power. Unhappiness with a paramount sachem's performance might prompt local sachemships to disavow his or her authority, even at the risk of war. The challenge faced by paramount sachems trying to keep multiple communities within the tribal fold was captured in the 1670s by the Massachusetts Bay missionary Daniel Gookin when he remarked that "their sachems have not their men in such subjection, but that very frequently their men will leave them upon distaste or harsh dealing, and go and live under other sachems that can protect them; so that their princes [the sachems] endeavor to carry it obligingly and lovingly unto their people, lest they should desert them, and thereby their strength, power, and tribute would be diminished." A paramount sachem like Ousamequin always had to keep one eye on his home base and another on enemies abroad. As the anthropologist Eric Johnson puts it, "The power of an individual sachem should not be assumed, but should be a topic of inquiry."[41]

When Europeans appeared in southern New England, first as explorers, traders, and slavers, and later as colonists, they entered this old world in motion. They would be met by indigenous people who had proprietorship in the land stretching back countless generations, even as they had been cultivating corn, beans, and squash on it for only a few hundred years; people who added new ceremonies dedicated to the corn-giver spirit, Kiehtan, to the dream interpretation and vision quest traditions of ancient hunter-gatherers; people who for centuries had sought exotic goods from far-off places deep in the continent even as they now also looked to the sea for vessels carrying the riches of Europe. Population growth, horticultural needs, and defensive considerations had encouraged the people of southern New England to group themselves into local and paramount sachemships or tribes. They deferred to their sachems, yet these leaders had to work constantly to maintain their followings through marriage alliances, trade, and war. None of this changed once Europeans entered the stage. Indeed, initially Native people treated colonial towns like so many new sachemships in an already crowded field. Over time Europeans tried to impose their own systems and customs on indigenous people, leaving behind a long trail of blood and mourning. But in the short term they were on Wampanoag turf, where Indian ways of doing things, old and new, dictated how things ran.

CHAPTER TWO

ᚷ ᚱ

Danger on the Horizon

When the English captain Thomas Dermer set sail for the New England coast in the spring of 1619, he knew that he was heading to a place with a growing reputation for violence between Indians and European explorers, if also for lucrative trade. Harrowing stories of the two peoples capturing and killing each other had been in circulation among sailors for years, and some accounts had been published to raise financial and political capital for colonial ventures. To get the kind of Native perspective missing in these narratives, Dermer had only to turn to one of his passengers, a Wampanoag man named Tisquantum, or Squanto for short, and ask him to recount his captivity at English hands and the subsequent nearly five-year odyssey that had at least twice carried him across the North Atlantic and was now about to bring him home, or so he thought. In surviving his ordeal and having the chance to tell his tale, Tisquantum was unique, but he was hardly alone in his suffering. He was just one among scores of other Wampanoags and Atlantic coast Indians seized by Europeans and carried across the ocean into fates lost to history. When Tisquantum shared the story of his life, in some ways he spoke for them all.[1]

He would have remembered how, in 1614, an English captain, Thomas Hunt, had anchored his ship in the harbor of Tisquantum's community of Patuxet, the very site of the future colony of

Plymouth, and invited curious Wampanoags onboard. This was no first contact episode. The Wampanoags had been dealing with shipboard European explorers intermittently since at least 1524 and nearly annually since 1602. Though these meetings tended to degenerate into bloodshed, the lure of trade was too enticing for either party to resist. Europeans sought furs, particularly beaver pelts, to sell back home and fresh food to relieve them from the heavily salted fare of their lengthy overseas journey. The Wampanoags, for their part, wanted to pick through the strangers' merchandise. First and foremost there were goods made of exotic metals like iron, brass, and tin. They included axes, knives, kettles, awls, scissors, needles, fishhooks, and combs. Certainly the Wampanoags already had their own perfectly serviceable versions of such items made out of wood, stone, and bone, but the Europeans' metal tools were sharper, more durable, and attractive by virtue of their novelty. The Europeans also carried kettles, earrings, necklaces, pendants, bracelets, and rings made of copper with a redder shine than indigenous copper, which Native people prized because they associated the color red with fire, the sun, blood, and animation. Then there were newcomers' translucent glass beads in numerous colors and patterns; brightly colored bolts of woolen cloth; shirts, pants, and stockings; mirrors that enabled the people to see themselves for the first time without looking into water; pigments of red, black, and yellow. Yes, these strangers could be dangerous, but some Native people judged that their exotic goods made dealing with them a worthwhile risk. And so Tisquantum and some of his people went aboard Hunt's vessel. They paid a terrible price.[2]

Hunt double-crossed them, seizing twenty of their men, then binding their limbs and stuffing them belowdecks. Soon seven other Wampanoags farther east at Nauset (modern Eastham) fell into the same trap and joined their tribesmen in the ship's hold for the beginning of a horrific oceanic journey toward a destiny they could barely imagine. Their greatest fear probably was that their captors intended

to torture and eat them, but it would have come as cold comfort
when they discovered Hunt's actual plan. Viewing his prisoners as
savage pagans unworthy of the dignity of civilized Christians, he
carried them all the way to Málaga, Spain, a Mediterranean port, to
sell them as slaves alongside his catch of fish. That is the last we hear
of most of these unfortunate souls, who disappeared into Iberia's
mass of bound laborers that included Islamic Moors from North
Africa, Indians from every corner of Spain's vast American dominions, and sub-Saharan Africans swept up in the burgeoning Atlantic
slave trade.[3]

Tisquantum very nearly shared this tragic end but for two
astonishing strokes of good fortune. First, a group of friars blocked
his sale, doubtlessly citing a Spanish law that had been in effect since
1542, though it was routinely ignored, that American Natives should
not be enslaved. Then, after a time lag that might have been just
months or more than a year, Tisquantum somehow made contact
with one of Málaga's many English merchants, who agreed to transport him to London so he could try to find a way home. The prospect of returning to Patuxet was not so far-fetched. A number of
Englishmen who did business in Málaga trafficked in salt cod from
the Grand Banks of Newfoundland, which put them in touch with
other sailors on exploratory probes of northeastern North America.
Such networks led Tisquantum to the doorstep of the London
merchant John Slaney, treasurer of the Newfoundland Company, a
joint-stock syndicate that underwrote fishing voyages to the North
Atlantic and aspired to found a colony on its namesake island. Slaney
was just as interested in training Tisquantum as an interpreter and
guide as Tisquantum was in him. It was still a long shot, but through
this connection Tisquantum saw the possibility of reuniting with
his people.[4]

Slaney's first assignment for Tisquantum, in the summer of 1616,
was to work for Captain John Mason at the company's settlement at

A panorama of London by Claes Van Visscher, 1616.

The era of early Indian–European contact was one of mutual discoveries, which involved Indians traveling from America to Europe and sometimes back. Usually these visits were not of the Indians' own choosing, as European explorers often seized coastal Natives for sale into slavery or training as guides and interpreters. However, occasionally the kidnapping victims managed to return, as in the cases of the Wampanoags Epenow and Tisquantum. Their visits to London and other European sites positioned them to interpret and broker diplomacy between their people and the first generation of colonists.

Cupids Cove in Conception Bay, Newfoundland, a place tantaliz-
ingly closer to Patuxet than Spain or England, but still more than
eight hundred miles distant by water. The key was to find some
captain who would agree to carry him on the next leg, which was a
reasonable possibility given that Newfoundland annually attracted
some 250 fishing vessels from England alone and had become a
rendezvous for explorers of the northern Atlantic coast. Yet Tisquantum's window of opportunity had closed by the time the autumn
chill set in. With no one to carry him south, he returned to London,
doubtlessly torn between hope and disappointment at the interruption of his quest to return to his country.[5]

There is an intriguing possibility that, during Tisquantum's
second stint in London, he met face-to-face with Pocahontas, the
other famous Native American traveler of the Atlantic. In 1616
Pocahontas was in England at the behest of the Virginia Company
of London, which wanted to use her growing celebrity status to
generate investment for the Jamestown colony. After all, over just a
few short years this daughter of Chief Powhatan (or Wahunsono-
cock) had gone from being a wartime captive of the English to the
Christian wife of the colonist John Rolfe and the key to a truce in the
long-running conflict between her and Rolfe's peoples. Pocahontas
had her own reasons for pursuing this course, but to the English she
symbolized the possibility of Native Americans consenting to colonization, and so they feted her throughout her visit to the capital. In
between meeting the king, having her portrait painted, and recon-
necting with John Smith, she lodged just a few hundred yards down
the street from the house of Slaney, where Tisquantum was staying.
Furthermore, the handlers of both Indians had mutual business interests. Given these circumstances, it seems likely that a meeting took
place. If so, Tisquantum and Pocahontas would have spoken to each
other in English rather than their Native tongues, which, though

both part of the broad Algonquian language family, were mutually unintelligible.[6]

Might Pocahontas have whispered to Tisquantum about the numbers of English who had invaded her people's country and the years of bloodletting that followed? Such a conversation would have heightened Tisquantum's anxiety to get back to Patuxet so he could help his people when the English began arriving there, too, for he would have already heard his handlers discussing such plans. One also wonders if Tisquantum learned that Pocahontas died in England in March 1617 before she had a chance to return home and tend to her people's fragile peace with Virginia. In her absence, by 1622 the Powhatans and English were furiously killing each other again.[7]

Then in 1618 it happened. During another stint in Newfoundland, Tisquantum was introduced to Captain Dermer, an associate of John Smith of Jamestown fame. In fact, back in 1614, Dermer had been part of the very exploring and fishing expedition in New England in which Thomas Hunt went rogue and kidnapped Tisquantum. By this point, Tisquantum had developed enough skill in the English language to offer his services to Dermer in exchange for passage back to Wampanoag country. As it turned out, Dermer was just the right person to whom to make such an overture.

Dermer's employer, Sir Ferdinando Gorges, was a prime mover of English exploration and colonization schemes for southern New England during the early seventeenth century and, as such, an avid collector of Indians who could serve as interpreters, guides, and cultural brokers. In 1605, for instance, Gorges had acquired five Indians taken in Maine by Captain George Waymouth, two of whom he returned in 1607 as part of an attempt to establish a colony at Sagadahoc, at the mouth of the Kennebec River. Sagadahoc failed after just one year partly because these former captives warned their countrymen to keep the English at arm's length. Yet that setback gave Gorges no pause. It took only until 1611 for him to acquire five more Indians, including two Wampanoags from Martha's Vineyard, after Captain Edward Harlow went on a captive-taking rampage stretching from Monhegan Island in Maine south to Cape Cod and the islands.[8]

Three years later, one of those prisoners, named Epenow, worked within the limits of his captivity to reclaim control of his fate. Described by Gorges as "a goodly man of brave aspect, stout and sober in his demeanor," and by Smith as a person of "wit, strength, and proportion," Epenow managed to orchestrate a homecoming by promising to lead the English to his island's fictional gold reserves. The ship carrying him home reached Vineyard waters just days after Hunt's kidnapping of Tisquantum. This time, however, the Wampanoags had the last laugh. Epenow hailed his people and, right there in front of his captors, devised a plan with them in his natal language, which the English could not understand. It would take only until the next day for the Natives to reveal what they had discussed. As designed, a flotilla of canoes surrounded the ship, whereupon Epenow jumped overboard and swam to safety while his tribesmen pinned down the ship's crew with arrows. With no one left to serve as a guide, the expedition had to return home with nothing. Yet Gorges had not yet soured on using Indians to tap into America's riches. After summoning Dermer and Tisquantum back from Newfoundland to England for a face-to-face meeting, Gorges concluded that this latest Wampanoag was worth a bet. In 1619 Gorges financed an expedition by Dermer to bring Tisquantum home and see what they could accomplish together. Tisquantum's heart must have been ready to burst with relief at the prospect of his years of exile coming to an end. Then the worry set in.[9]

Doubtless Tisquantum had already heard through the grapevine of English sailors that a terrible disease had struck the Wampanoag coast during his absence, but there was no way for him to prepare for what he saw when Dermer's ship finally reached familiar waters. Landing at Monhegan Island and then continuing south to Massachusetts Bay, the ship skirted a coastline that was usually crowded with people tending cornfields and waving furs at passing ships to signal their eagerness to trade. This time, however, there was no one to be seen or heard. Clearly something dreadful had happened. Tisquantum's anxiety must have built with every moment until the ship finally reached Plymouth Harbor, when the grim truth finally emerged. According to Nathaniel Morton, who visited the place in 1622, Patuxet and the surrounding country had turned into "sad spectacles of . . . mortality" insofar as they exhibited "many bones and skulls of the dead lying above the ground," like inverted cemeteries. The exuberant homecoming Tisquantum had been imagining for years had instead uncovered a tragedy of epic proportions.[10]

Desperate to locate any remaining family and friends, Tisquantum led Dermer inland toward the Taunton River community of Nemasket, twelve miles west of Patuxet, where he finally came upon a group of shell-shocked survivors. Those people must have been as stunned to see Tisquantum again as he was relieved to find them, for they would have assumed he was dead or captive in some far-off place after his years-long absence. Dermer failed to record the high emotions of this reunion, but, given his purpose to learn how coastal Indian society worked, he was keenly interested in Nemasket's quick decision to send news of Tisquantum and the English to Pokanoket, the tribal seat, thirty-five miles to the southwest at the river's mouth on Narragansett Bay. Two or three days later, there arrived "two kings," as Dermer characterized the Wampanoag sachems, "attended with guard of fifty armed men." Everyone must have been on edge, the English especially, given the Wampanoags' advantage in numbers. Yet Dermer was relieved to find that the sachems "gave me content in whatsoever I desired," including the release of a Frenchman "who three years since escaped a shipwreck at the northeast of Cape Cod" only to become a captive of the

Wampanoags. Dermer also managed to redeem this Frenchman's crewmate, who was being held by the Indians of Massachusetts Bay. The official narrative of these events tries to convey the sense that Dermer was in command, but the French captives were a portent that he and his crewmates might become the next ones the Wampanoags took.[11]

They very nearly were. After this meeting the men returned to their ship and continued their journey, including a stop at the Cape Cod sachemship of Satucket (modern Brewster), where Tisquantum disembarked to reconnect with friends. Unwisely, the English pushed on without him, rounding the wrist of Cape Cod and proceeding down the outer arm of the peninsula to its elbow (modern Chatham), where the Wampanoag community of Mono-moyick was located. Little did Dermer know that thirteen years earlier the men of Monomoyick had clashed with a French expedition led by Jean de Biencourt, sieur de Poutrincourt, and apparently the harsh memories ran long. In an exchange that probably began with offers of trade, armed Wampanoags suddenly took Dermer hostage and demanded a ransom for his return. However, Dermer managed to escape and turn the tables—"after a strange manner" is the extent of how he described it—capturing the sachem and two of his men, then hauling them aboard the ship. As the English began to weigh anchor, the captive chief began screaming in panic to his men onshore to return the hatchets the English had paid for Dermer's release plus an extra canoe-load of corn. Upon receipt, Dermer set the sachem free (he did not say what he did with the other two prisoners) and sailed off. The violence of this encounter could only have reinforced the Monomoyicks' distrust of Europeans. Just a year and a half later, the *Mayflower* landed thirty-five miles to the north at the edge of what had effectively become a war zone between the Wampanoags and one ship crew after another.[12]

Dermer had little time to marvel at his unlikely deliverance because even greater peril lay ahead. Anchoring at Martha's Vineyard, the crew was stunned to be greeted by a Wampanoag who spoke "indifferent good English." It was none other than Epenow, who just five years earlier had managed to hoodwink Gorges into sending him home and then orchestrated his dramatic overboard getaway from the clutches of Captain Nicholas Hobson. Dermer naively believed Epenow had overcome any resentment about his former captivity, insofar as he "laughed at his own escape and reported the story of it." Indeed, in broken English drawn from the recesses of his memory, he invited Dermer to return to the Vineyard to trade for furs after the captain completed his long voyage down the coast to Virginia. This was precisely the kind of profitable exchange that Gorges and Dermer had hoped to cultivate with the Indians when they launched the expedition. Their greed led them right into Epenow's snare.[13]

Dermer should have realized he was in danger when he returned to southern New England in June 1620, not only because it stood to reason that Epenow might be yearning for revenge, but also because the Wampanoags as a whole had turned hostile toward Europeans. Reuniting with Tisquantum at Nemasket, Dermer found that the people who had treated him so hospitably the year before now "would have killed me . . . had not [Tisquantum] entreated hard for me." The reason for their belligerency, Tisquantum explained, was that while Dermer was away in Virginia, an English vessel had anchored off Pokanoket, invited "many" of the people aboard, and then "made a great slaughter with their murderers [either daggers or small cannons], and small shot," even though the Wampanoags "offered no injury on their parts." The identity of the captain who committed this outrage went undocumented, like the traces of so many other voyages. To the Wampanoags, it hardly mattered. He was just one more in a string of vicious plunderers and slavers who left them with "an inveterate malice to the English"—all of them. Dermer and his crew had Tisquantum to thank for helping them to escape Nemasket with their lives—that is, at least until they made their way back to Martha's Vineyard.[14]

If Tisquantum warned the English that they were bound to meet more trouble on the island, Dermer paid him no heed. Eager for riches, the captain went "ashore amongst the Indians to trade, as he used to do, was betrayed and assaulted by them, and all his men slain, but one that kept the boat [the smaller trading shallop]." Dermer himself was mortally injured, suffering some fifteen wounds before escaping to the mother ship, and died after sailing back to Virginia for medical treatment. Tisquantum somehow emerged from the fray alive, but the Vineyard Wampanoags seem to have taken him captive and sent him to Ousamequin, the sachem of Pokanoket. The great leader knew this bilingual globe-trotter would be useful whenever the strangers returned.[15]

Just months later, the *Mayflower* appeared off Cape Cod, bringing to Wampanoag country a different sort of Englishmen and a whole new host of dangers and opportunities. When it did, figures like Epenow and Tisquantum, who had been to the strangers' country, who understood their language and something of their ways, would prove invaluable to shaping the Wampanoags' response. The Thanksgiving myth casts the Wampanoags in 1620 as naive primitives, awestruck by the appearance of the *Mayflower* and its strange passengers. They were nothing of the sort. Their every step was informed by the legacy of the many European ships that had visited their shores and left behind a wave of enslavement, murder, theft, and mourning.

HOGGERY AND FLOATING ISLANDS

In later years, coastal Indians who recounted their first encounters with European ships always emphasized the violence. Two colonists

Mi'kmaq petroglyph, Kejimkujik National Park. Courtesy
of the Nova Scotia Museum.

Apparently sometime during the early contact period, the Mi'kmaq of Nova
Scotia carved this petroglyph of a European sailing vessel. Contrary to
common assumptions, Indians were less awed by Europeans and their ships
than torn between, on the one hand, the desire to trade with them and, on
the other, wariness of their patterned violence.

from early New England, Phineas Pratt and William Wood, sepa-
rately recorded allegories told by the Massachusetts Indians in
which their ancestors unassumingly "took the first ship they saw for
a walking island, the mast to be a tree, the sail white clouds, and the
discharging of ordnance [cannons] for lightning and thunder, which
did much trouble them." Native men took to their mishoons to
investigate this walking island and "pick strawberries" (which might
refer metaphorically to trading for European goods, particularly
beads), whereupon the sailors opened gunfire on them. "Hoggery!"
(hoglike behavior), the Indians cried before they paddled back to
shore, or so the telling went. Of course, Indians in the early contact
period knew nothing of hogs. Yet precise details had nothing to do
with the moral of the story, which was that the people should be
wary of the treachery of Europeans, however tempting the strawberries on their walking islands.[16]

Just when the Indians of southern New England experienced their first contact with Europeans is difficult to tell, but lengthy intertribal trade networks meant that encounters taking place even hundreds of miles away sometimes brought European materials to Wampanoag country. Ever since John Cabot's 1497 exploration of Atlantic Canada, and quite possibly earlier, western European fishermen had plied Newfoundland's Grand Banks for the cod that fed royal armies in times of war and Catholics during the 165 meatless days of Rome's calendar. Shortly, these voyages extended to Nova Scotia and Maine, and the sailors began drying and salting the fish on American shores before delivering it to Europe. In turn, there arose an incipient trade with coastal Beothuks, Mi'kmaq, and other Wabanakis in which the Indians exchanged their furs for the fishermen's metal tools and utensils, glass beads, cloth, clothing, and liquor. When the summer fishing season ended and the Europeans returned home, the Indians received an additional haul of metal by ransacking the mariners' coastal drying stations, pulling apart entire buildings to salvage nails, door hinges, and hooks. This material then entered down-the-line intertribal networks from the Gulf of St. Lawrence and the Bay of Fundy all the way to Wampanoag country. At this point, intertribal trade rarely involved the exchange of intact European metal items such as kettles. Rather, Indians dismantled these objects for their raw material to use in crafting the same kinds of ornaments they customarily fashioned out of American copper, such as beads, earrings, pendants, and bracelets. Not until southern New England Indians were in sustained direct contact with Europeans beginning, apparently, in the early 1600s, would they begin to acquire and keep the foreigners' merchandise in its original forms.[17]

The first documented contact between Indians and Europeans in southern New England took place in 1524, involving the French-employed Italian captain Giovanni da Verrazzano and the Indians of Narragansett Bay, meaning either the Narragansetts or Wampanoags

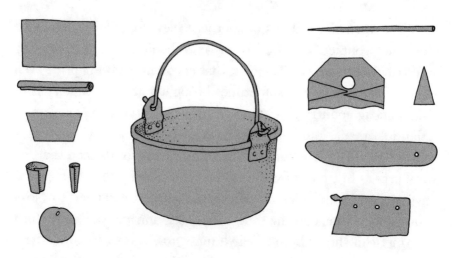

Recycling of a copper kettle. Courtesy of the New York State
Museum, Albany, NY.

Native people often dismantled European kettles so they could use the raw
metal to manufacture other tools and ornaments, as illustrated here.

or both. Verrazzano's voyage had taken him from the Carolina coast
to the island of Manhattan, and east across Long Island Sound
before he reached Narragansett Bay and Aquidneck Island, site of
the modern city of Newport. Without a history of violent encounters at such an early date, the Natives seemed intrigued if a bit wary
when the ship appeared. Twenty mishoons of men went out to greet
the vessel while keeping a safe distance. Yet the French managed to
entice them closer by tossing out bells, mirrors, and beads, "which
they took and looked at, laughing, and then confidently came on
board." It was just the beginning of much more elaborate exchanges,
initiated by the appearance of two "kings," or sachems, one judged
by Verrazzano to be forty years of age, the other about twenty-four.
The Indians were already making it clear that any foreigner wishing
to explore their country was going to have to work through official
channels and offer the people something of value in return.[18]

The Natives' preferences in trade surprised Verrazzano. When the crew "showed them some of our arms, they did not admire them, nor ask for them, but merely examined the workmanship." The captain was equally puzzled that "they do not value gold because of its color; they think it the most worthless of all, and rate blue and red above all colors." Indeed, the Indians were most interested in "little bells, blue crystals, and other trinkets to put in the ear or around the neck." Blue was an especially difficult color for Indians to produce, as their only source of blue pigment was crushed robins' eggs. Yet they prized blue as a symbol of water, sky, and the spirits of those places. With Verrazzano's appearance, now the Indians had blue goods in unprecedented amounts. By contrast, Wampanoags already possessed an abundance of ocher, copper, and plant dyes in the color red, which symbolized blood and vigor. Whether the Europeans' goods came in rare or common hues, the Wampanoags wanted them in the same ornamental forms with which they already adorned themselves, which is precisely what they got. In exchange, they supplied the crew with fresh provisions and guided the ship through local waters. Verrazzano was mightily impressed with Narragansett Bay, dubbing it "Refugio," but once he realized that it did not lead to the fabled Northwest Passage, which Europeans imagined to cut through the North American continent to the Pacific, he decided to head back to sea and continue his search elsewhere.[19]

Subsequent contacts between southern New England Indians and Europeans, including the next leg of Verrazzano's journey, are too shadowy to discern their contours and consequences. For instance, as Verrazzano headed north to Maine, he spent enough time scouting Cape Cod to sketch an accurate map of the place, but he did not mention if he had interacted with the Wampanoags there. The following year, 1525, the Portuguese captain Estevão Gomez, who was also in search of the Northwest Passage, traced southern New England from Point Judith at the southwest entrance of Narragansett Bay, past Cape Cod, where he appears to have treated the Wampanoags or Massachusett Indians to gifts of bells, combs, scissors, and cloth. If this interaction took place without incident, it was only by dint of the Indians' sheer luck, for farther up the coast Gomez seized more than fifty Natives from either Maine or Nova Scotia to sell in Spain as slaves.[20]

Given that two European vessels had visited southern New England in two consecutive years, the Wampanoags might have assumed that this was the start of a trend; but there are no surviving records of any additional contacts until 1580, and even then the details are cloudy. That year the English navigator and colonial promoter Sir Humphrey Gilbert, inspired by Verrazzano's account, sent ten men to reconnoiter Narragansett Bay in anticipation of forming a colony there. This expedition was part of a burgeoning English effort to challenge Spanish dominance in the Americas, which included English activity in Newfoundland, the lost Roanoke colony of the 1580s, and the founding of Jamestown in 1607. It is likely that Gilbert's men made contact with the Narragansetts and Wampanoags of the bay, but they left no record of it despite anecdotal evidence that they returned home with a favorable impression of the place. As to whether other Europeans had visited the area between 1525 and 1580, the possibility seems high. There were about three hundred ships a year working the Newfoundland fishery by 1550, and five hundred ships by 1580. Combined with explorations of other parts of the North American coast by the Spanish, French, English, and Dutch, it is likely that other, unrecorded encounters occurred. Yet the fact that southern New England archaeological sites dating back to the sixteenth century show a marked lack of intact metal goods, which is widely accepted as an index of sustained contact, suggests that any meetings of this sort were sporadic and brief.[21]

The Englishman Bartholomew Gosnold's expedition of 1602 was the turning point at which European visits became annual affairs,

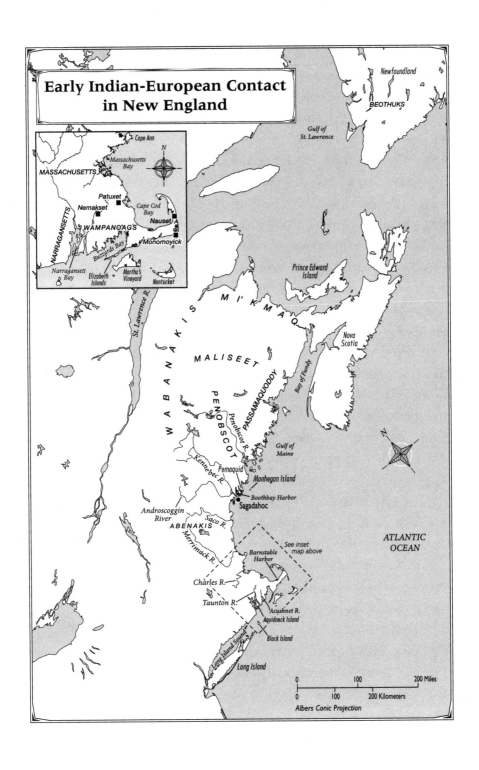

Early Indian-European Contact in New England

Cape Ann

Massachusetts
Bay

MASSACHUSETTS

N

Patuxet
Nemakset
Cape Cod
Bay
WAMPANO'AGS
Nauset

Monomoyick

NARRAGANSETTS

Narragansett
Bay
Elizabeth
Islands
Martha's
Vineyard
Buzzards Bay
Nantucket

Newfoundland

BEOTHUKS

Gulf of
St. Lawrence

St. Lawrence R.

WABANAKIS

M I ' K M A Q

MALISEET

PASSAMAQUODDY

PENOBSCOT

Prince Edward
Island

Nova
Scotia

Bay of Fundy

Penobscot R.

Gulf of
Maine

Kennebec R.

Pemaquid
Monhegan Island

Boothbay Harbor
Sagadahoc

Androscoggin
River
Saco R.
ABENAKIS

Merrimack R.

Charles R.

Taunton R.

See inset
map above

Barnstable
Harbor

N

ATLANTIC
OCEAN

Acushnet R.
Aquidneck Island

Block Island

Long Island Sound

Long Island

0		100		200 Miles

0	100	200 Kilometers

Albers Conic Projection

and usually violent ones at that. Searching for profitable commodities and a favorable place to establish a settlement, Gosnold's ship *Concord* made landfall in Maine and then turned south only to receive a startling lesson about the resourcefulness of the area's indigenous peoples and their already lengthy history with Europeans. Just off of Maine's Cape Neddick, near the modern town of York, Gosnold's ship was approached by a "Basque shallop" (a light sailboat for coastal waters) with a six-man crew. The men of the *Concord* reasonably assumed that these sailors were "Christians distressed," which was to say, Europeans. Not only were sailing vessels a European technology, but also the shallop's captain "wore a waistcoat of black work, a pair of britches, cloth stockings, shoes, hat, and band," and one of the crew sported blue britches. Yet, when the mystery boat pulled alongside the *Concord* using a grappling hook and its sailors "came boldly aboard us," the English were astonished to find that the men were Indians. Clearly this was no first contact episode for the Natives. In addition to the Indians' sailing equipment and clothing, they carried an intact copper kettle and "a few [other] things made by some Christians," and "spoke diverse Christian words, and seemed to understand much more than we, for want of language, could comprehend." They were either Mi'kmaq or other Wabanakis who had worked for and bartered with cod fisherman on Cape Breton or Newfoundland, enabling them to transform themselves into cosmopolitan, maritime middlemen in Indian-European exchange. Their encounter with Gosnold probably interrupted one of their trading expeditions along the Gulf of Maine. At a later date they also became amphibious raiders who spread terror to the northern edge of Wampanoag country.[22]

Farther south, amid the Wampanoags of Cape Cod, Martha's Vineyard, and Buzzards Bay, Gosnold's crew encountered a much different scene. The Natives possessed no sailboats, hats, britches, or any other identifiable English goods. However, copper abounded. The passenger John Brereton remarked that the Wampanoags "have chains, earrings, or collars of this metal; they headed some of their arrows herewith much." One man had "about his neck a plate of rich copper in length a foot, in breadth half a foot for a breastplate." Several others had fashioned long copper tubes and strung them on necklaces, "four hundred pieces in a collar, very fine and evenly set together." Others displayed stone pipes with copper-encased stems and mouthpieces. Wishing to know where the people acquired this material, Brereton "made signs to one of them (with whom I was very familiar) who, taking a piece of copper in his hand, made a hole with his finger in the ground, and withal pointed to the main[land] from whence they came." In other words, the Wampanoag signaled that copper came from under the earth and that his people had obtained it from the interior. However, that response missed the thrust of Brereton's question, which was whether the metal originated from some nearby mine. The answer would appear to have been no. There was so much copper among the Wampanoags at the time of the *Concord*'s visit that it could not have all come from the cold hammering of an exposed American vein, the closest of which was hundreds of miles away in another people's territory. Yet that is not to say that the Wampanoags acquired their copper directly from Europeans. The small, ornamental forms in which this copper appeared seemed to indicate that it originated with the coastal trade of Nova Scotia and Maine and arrived through Indian middlemen. One reason the Wampanoags ran excitedly along the shore "as men much admiring at us" when the *Concord* appeared was the rare opportunity to obtain such European materials firsthand.[23]

Yet the ease with which some of the Wampanoags dealt with the English suggests that there had been other, more recent contacts than surviving documents report. At Martha's Vineyard, thirteen armed men approached the *Concord* "without any fear," as if they had experience with such situations. "More rich in copper than any [Indians] before," they showed a cultivated taste for European goods, including "knives, points, and such like." Much to Gosnold's disappointment, they had no furs to trade, but they did offer up their tobacco, deerskins, and fish with "great familiarity." A history of unrecorded contacts is also suggested by the behavior of Wampanoags from the mouth of the Acushnet River near where the city of New Bedford now lies. There, the people not only seemed unsurprised by the English but also had a wide array of furs ready for barter. These Wampanoags knew what they wanted in return. One of them was drawn to a pair of knives, which he "beheld with great marveling, being very bright and sharp," contrary to the subdued Indian response to Verrazzano's metal wares decades earlier. Yet, if the Wampanoags already had some of their own metal cutting tools, Gosnold's chroniclers took no notice of it. The European strangers were not quite as strange as they had been back at the time of Verrazzano's appearance, but visits by ships like the *Concord* were still rare.[24]

Though the Wampanoags welcomed trade with the *Concord*, they knew enough through hard experience or just intuition to be circumspect of these visitors. After all, Gosnold's party was composed entirely of men, and armed ones at that, which suggested hostile intent. Their initial behavior was also unfriendly. Making camp on the thin Elizabeth Island chain extending between Martha's Vineyard and the mainland, the English quickly erected a palisade as if expecting an attack or preparing to make one. They also stole a mishoon belonging to four Wampanoags who fled on foot at the English approach. Despite these warning signs, adventurous Wampanoags reached out to the newcomers. A family on the Elizabeth Islands, including two women, visited the English and showed "much familiarity with our men, although they would not admit of any immodest touch." Likewise, when Gosnold took the shallop to visit mainland Wampanoag communities along Buzzards Bay, he received warm welcomes everywhere from "men, women, and children, who with all courteous kindness entertained him, giving him certain skins of wild beasts." If the Wampanoags had anticipated violence, they would not have exposed their women and children to the newcomers. At the same time, they probably assumed that unless their leadership got involved, eventually somebody would get hurt.[25]

After a week of these informal encounters, the English finally received a visit from the Wampanoags' "lord or chief commander" with an entourage of fifty armed men. It was unclear to everyone whether the opposite party had come to barter or battle, so Captain Gabriel Archer tried to pose the question through signs. While the ranks of Englishmen and Wampanoags stood opposite each other, staring and fingering their weapons, Archer pointed to the sachem, then "moved myself toward him seven or eight steps, and clapped my hands first on the sides of mine head, then on my breast, and after my musket with a threatening countenance." Precisely how the sachem interpreted these motions is impossible to know, but when he awkwardly mimicked them, Archer took it as a friendly gesture and thus "stepped forth and embraced him."[26]

With this, everyone let down their guard and trading commenced, followed by some good-natured, cross-cultural ribbing. The sailors found it hilarious that when the Wampanoags sat with them to share a meal of cod, mustard, and beer, "the mustard nipping them in the noses they could not endure; it was a sport to behold their faces being bitten therewith." The Wampanoags responded in kind. The English, unaware that the Natives found facial hair disgusting, fell under the false impression that "they make beards of the hair of beasts" because one of them jokingly offered a sailor a beaver pelt "for his that grew on his face." In another exchange, a Wampanoag parroted an Englishman's speech, saying to him "How now (sirrah) are you so saucy with my tobacco?" with such precision "as if he had [long] been a scholar in the language." It was all in good fun, as indicated by the Wampanoags sending up "huge cries and shouts of joy unto us" when they took to their mishoons at the end of the day, and the English responding "with our trumpet and cornet, and casting up our caps into the air."[27]

Yet even this favorable start turned violent. During the trading, the English made unmistakably angry threats after a shooting target went missing, which the Wampanoags returned with "fear and great trembling." The sailors' attempted "immodest touch" of Wampanoag women certainly did not improve relations. Even after a day of successful barter, the Wampanoags still would not go aboard the *Concord*, as if they feared being kidnapped. Recall also the English theft of a mishoon from four Wampanoags. It might not have been a coincidence that a week after the end of trading, four Wampanoags ambushed two Englishmen who had strayed from the camp to gather shellfish. An arrow struck one of the English in the side, but before the attackers could finish him off, another sailor, "a lusty and nimble fellow, leapt in and cut their bowstrings, whereupon they fled." Gosnold's initial plan had been to leave twenty of his men behind in New England as a holding party for a longer-term settlement while he returned to the mother country for reinforcements and supplies. After the Wampanoag attack, the sailors refused, perhaps having heard that a similar advance group had gone missing in 1586 at Roanoke on the North Carolina coast amid tensions with the local Indians. Instead, Gosnold loaded his ship with cedar and sassafras, the latter thought to be a cure for syphilis, raised sails, and headed for home. It would not be the last time that a Wampanoag show of force would alter colonial plans.[28]

THREE SONS

The Wampanoags understood Gosnold's visit less as a warning that Europeans would soon establish year-round colonies than as the beginning of an era in which seemingly nomadic, seafaring traders and raiders might appear at any time and then sail off, leaving behind not only a trail of coveted exotic goods but bloodshed and kidnappings as well. At once enticing and terrifying, the arrival of one of these floating islands was akin to people elsewhere in the world having horse-mounted barbarians storm through their country. These strangers had valuable gifts to offer, to be sure, but the people always had to be on guard. The Wampanoags quickly learned to shoot first and ask questions later.

Nearly every European voyage to Wampanoag country ended in violence. In 1603 the Englishman Martin Pring sailed the *Discoverer* into New England waters expecting to reman Gosnold's Elizabeth Island station. Along the way, he stopped at the tip of Cape Cod (modern Provincetown), erected a defensive barricade, and sent his crew out grubbing for sassafras. Initially, relations with the Wampanoags were as cordial as those that inaugurated Gosnold's stay. In one colorful episode, the Wampanoags plied a young sailor with "tobacco, tobacco pipes, snakeskins of six foot long . . . fawns' skins, and such like" to get him to play his cittern (a stringed instrument) while they danced around him "using many savage gestures, singing Io, Ia, Io, Ia, Ia, Io." Yet the English would not leave well enough alone. "When we would be rid of the savages company," Pring mentioned nonchalantly, "we would let loose the mastiffs," giant dogs of war, "and suddenly with outcries they [the Indians] would flee away." After weeks of such treatment, the Wampanoags began to show up for trade well armed and in large numbers, which the English interpreted as a threat. This escalation reached the breaking point when an estimated 140 Wampanoags appeared outside the palisade one afternoon, whereupon the English twice shot off their ordnance and again released the dogs. As designed, the Wampanoags withdrew, but no sooner had they departed than they set fire to the woods around the English camp. If their point was to drive the newcomers away, it worked. Pring ordered his men to set sail for home while two hundred Wampanoags gathered on the shore to prevent their return.[29]

Yet the Europeans kept coming, and soon blood started flowing. In the summer of 1605 Pierre de Gaust, sieur de Mons, lieutenant general of the French colony of Acadia, launched the first of two expeditions to explore southern New England for the site of a new colony. He arrived just weeks after Captain George Waymouth had stopped briefly on the outer forearm of Cape Cod before sailing to Maine and kidnapping five Etchemins (or Maliseet-Passamaquodies) from Pemaquid to take to England for grooming as interpreters and guides. Samuel de Champlain, who founded Québec a few years later, went along with Mons as cartographer and log keeper, producing invaluable charts and drawings of the region's harbors and the Indian settlements lining them. His sketches included Tisquantum's natal community of Patuxet, where fifteen or sixteen mishoons of Wampanoag men rowed out to the French at anchor to express "great signs of joy" and deliver "various harangues, which we could not in the least understand," though the welcome was clear. This friendly reception emboldened a handful of Frenchmen to go ashore and meet with a sachem named Honabetha, to whom they presented knives "and other trifles," much to his delight. For their part, the Wampanoags treated their weary visitors generously to fresh provisions. At this early date, before the horrors of foreign diseases had struck, Patuxet impressed the French as bountiful and busy with its "great many little houses, scattered over the fields, where they plant Indian corn . . . a great many cabins and gardens." However, full as Patuxet was with people who considered it home, the French decided to look elsewhere for a place to settle. Imagine, for a moment, how difficult it would be for the Thanksgiving myth to include the French visiting a well-populated Patuxet fifteen years before the English arrived to establish Plymouth.[30]

Danger lay ahead for the French. On July 20 they spied "a bay with wigwams bordering it all around" at Nauset on the far east side

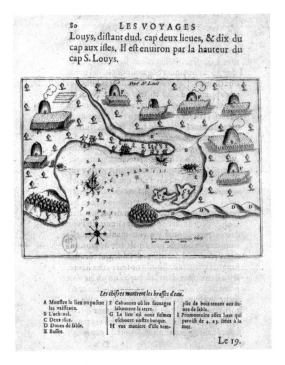

Port St. Louis (Plymouth Harbor), from Samuel de Champlain, *Les Voyages de Sieur de Champlain Xaintogeois* (Paris: Jean Berjon, 1613).

Samuel de Champlain charted a number of harbors containing Wampanoag settlements as his French expedition cruised southern New England in 1605 and 1606 looking for a place to colonize. One of those sites was Patuxet (which Champlain called Port St. Louis), the village of Tisquantum. As one can see from the houses and cornfields depicted here, Patuxet was a thriving place before the epidemic of 1616–19 wiped it out. The *Mayflower* passengers built Plymouth at this exact spot.

of Cape Cod. This majestic harbor was a hard place to overlook. A narrow break through a thin strip of barrier beach introduced a lagoon of the bluest water into which the surrounding upland seemed to melt through a confluence of streams, salt ponds, marshes, coves, and dunes. Initially, the people were welcoming, too. Once the French passed through Nauset's sandbars and made landing, "men and women visited us and ran up on all sides dancing," leading to three days of peaceful exchange and a visit to the Wampanoags' settlement by Mons and nine or ten of his men. Yet a fight broke out on the fourth day, when some Natives killed the French carpenter while robbing him of a kettle. "They are as swift afoot as horses," Champlain bristled after the attackers fled at the sound of ineffective French gunfire. The French did, however, manage to seize one Wampanoag who had been aboard their ship when the conflict began onshore. (Several other Indians had leapt overboard and swum to safety.) Under similar circumstances, other European commanders might have treated this prisoner harshly as an example. In this case, Mons showed uncommon diplomatic tact by releasing the Indian in hopes of restoring peace, and it worked. Soon, Wampanoag ambassadors approached, signaling, as far as the French could tell, that the perpetrators of this violence were not their own people. Both sides' refusal to overreact kept this incident from spiraling out of control, but it was an indication of how fragile these encounters could be. Unwilling to test his luck any further, Mons ordered his men to raise anchor for Maine two days after the murder. Perhaps it was not just for the breakers that the French named the place Mallebare ("Bad Bar").[31]

The wisdom of Mons's retreat from Nauset became readily apparent in the fall of the next year when the French resumed scouting Cape Cod under the command of Jean de Biencourt, sieur de Poutrincourt. After brief, seemingly uneventful stops at Barnstable Harbor and Wellfleet, the expedition rounded the southern tip of the Cape, barely escaping a series of ship-eating shoals, but damaging the rudder in the process. Led to safe waters by an Indian guide, the French anchored off what is now the town of Chatham, and found themselves amid an estimated five hundred to six hundred Monomoyick Wampanoags packing up their things for the move inland to winter quarters. The French, though, suspected that the Indians were sending away their noncombatants so the men could spring an attack. Keeping their eyes open and their weapons visible, the sailors spent several days exploring the area, periodically distributing bracelets and rings to Wampanoag women and hatchets and knives to the men "to keep them quiet and free from fear." Yet it was the French who were the most jittery. When a hatchet went missing, the French fired on the Monomoyicks randomly, which only sped up the Natives' preparations to leave. Now the French were doubly sure that the Wampanoags had hostile intentions.

Fight at Port Fortuné (Monomoyick), from Samuel de Champlain, *Les Voyages de Sieur de Champlain Xaintogeois* (Paris: Jean Berjon, 1613).

Samuel de Champlain's drawing depicts several violent incidents that occurred when the French visited the Monomoyick Wampanoags (of modern Chatham, Massachusetts) during the summer of 1606. Such encounters tended to turn bloody, usually when Europeans took Native people captive or overreacted to perceived Indian threats and Indian thievery. In this case, the Monomoyicks succeeded in driving off the French and convincing them to look elsewhere to found a colony.

The French also readied their own exit, but not soon enough. Early on the morning of October 15, five sailors who had spent the night near a bread oven they had constructed on the beach (they were French, after all) came under surprise attack by hundreds of Monomoyick bowmen. Shouting to their mates on the ship, "Help! They are killing us," three of the French fell dead on the spot, while another died shortly from his wounds despite musketeers rushing to his aid. Then, to add insult to injury, the Wampanoags mocked the French while they were stranded in the harbor at low tide by tearing down a cross the French had erected on the beach, unearthing the fresh grave of one of the dead sailors, and parading about in his shirt. "Besides all this," the French fumed, "[the Wampanoags] turning their backs toward the [French] barque, did cast sand with their two hands betwixt their buttocks in derision, howling like wolves, which did marvelously vex our people." When the tide rolled in and the French returned to shore to repair the damage, the Wampanoags set fire to the woods to drive them away. Suffice it to say, the French thought better of founding a settlement on Cape Cod, choosing instead to focus on the St. Lawrence River valley. If the Wampanoags had not defended their territory so stoutly, the French, not the English, might have been the first European nation to try to colonize the area, and Plymouth might never have happened. For the Wampanoags, it was a fraught proposition either way.[32]

Indians to the north also beat back would-be European colonies, of which the Wampanoags were likely informed given their connections to these people. In 1607 Gorges sent three of Waymouth's Etchemin captives back to Maine as part of an English effort to establish a fur trade colony at Sagadahoc at the mouth of the Kennebec River. The English expectation was that the redeemed Indians would convince their tribesmen to feed and trade with the colony. Instead, they advised the Etchemins to keep a guarded distance, which, combined with a brutally cold winter, forced the English to abandon the colony after less than a year. The failure of Sagadahoc was yet another example of how European violence toward Indians served less to awe the Natives than to make enemies of them and thus undermine the possibilities for trade and settlement. It probably also reinforced the impression of coastal Indians that Europeans were brutes.[33]

That lesson of Sagadahoc was not lost on Europeans, but they continued to behave more like raiders than traders, with Gorges instructing his ship captains to kidnap Indians to serve as cultural brokers, and his sailors routinely overacting to real and imagined Indian threats. In turn, a decade's worth of Wampanoag clashes with English explorers, quick on the heels of their battles with the French, proved to them that Europeans as a whole, whatever their national distinctions, were aggressive and treacherous. In 1611 Captain Edward Harlow seized three Abenakis from Monhegan Island, one of whom escaped by leaping overboard, then led his friends to cut one of the tenders (or dinghies) from the side of the ship and get it to shore. Unsatisfied with just two captives, Harlow and his men proceeded to Cape Cod, where they battled the Wampanoags and suffered three men "sorely wounded with arrows." Harlow complained, with no sense of irony, that the Cape Wampanoags were "very false and malicious, in which respect you must be more cautious in how you deal with them." The Wampanoags might have said the same of the English. Harlow attacked Wampanoags again at the "Isle of Nohono," or Nantucket. Though forced to retreat, his crew managed to capture a man named Sakaweston, who went on to live for many years in England and then serve as a soldier in central Europe among Christian forces supporting the Habsburg Empire against the Ottoman Muslims. Finally, Harlow's rampage tour reached Martha's Vineyard, where the crew seized two more Wampanoags, Cone-conam and the fateful Epenow. This was the same Epenow who years later would connive his way home and orchestrate an escape in which, according to Gorges, the Vineyard Wampanoags "wounded the master of our ship and diverse others in our company" while suffering "the slaughter of some of their people, and the hurts of others." In 1619 Epenow would exact another measure of revenge against an unwitting Thomas Dermer. He would also emerge as an enemy of Plymouth colony, providing yet another example of how the violence of this era had a long, consequential afterlife.[34]

The period between Epenow's return to Martha's Vineyard in 1614 and Dermer's voyage of 1619 were the most active and probably the bloodiest of the precolonial era. John Smith claimed that during these years at least twenty-two voyages set sail for New England from London and Devon, though records for most of these expeditions are sparse. What accounts do exist trace an escalating pattern of European-Indian clashes. In this, Smith was no exception. His lengthy experience with the Powhatans of Virginia had convinced him that if Englishmen wanted Indians' cooperation, they had to assert the upper hand immediately. He applied this principle during a 1614 voyage to New England intended to prospect for mines and hunt whales, but which spun off into a trading, fishing, and slaving expedition. At a narrow passage leading out of Little Harbor, Cohasset, in Massachusetts Bay, an unspecified "quarrel" led Indians standing on shoreline rocks to shoot arrows at the passing ship while the English onboard returned gunfire. Just thirty miles south at Patuxet, Smith and his crew were at it again, for "upon some small occasion, we fought also with forty or fifty of those [Indians]," and "though some were hurt, and some slain," he claimed that "within an hour after, they became friends." By "friends," Smith meant that after the Wampanoags had spent their arrows, the English seized six or seven of their mishoons, which the Natives ransomed for beaver pelts. It was an odd definition of friendship.[35]

The treachery of Captain Thomas Hunt, who accompanied Smith in a separate ship, produced the most lasting damage to the

English relationship with the Wampanoags. Gorges denounced Hunt as "worthless fellow" for kidnapping more than two dozen Wampanoags and selling them into Spanish slavery "for rials of eight," but he did not grasp the half of it. The victims of Hunt, dismissed by Smith as just "silly savages," of course meant a great deal more to the Wampanoags. They were cherished family members and neighbors lost to an unknown but certainly terrible fate. Surely the people back home mourned this loss, but with no sense of closure because they did not know whether their loved ones were alive or dead or would ever return. Gorges complained that, because of Hunt, "a war [was] now begun between the inhabitants of those parts and us." He was right about the effect, though his accounting for the cause overlooked that Hunt was just the worst in a string of European marauders. By the time the *Mayflower* arrived, the Wampanoags were already "incensed and provoked against the English" and still cursing Hunt's name. Poignantly, during the colonists' first year in New England, they met an elderly woman from Cummaquid (modern Barnstable) on Cape Cod who, upon seeing them, broke into a "great passion, weeping, and crying excessively" because she had lost three sons to Hunt's villainy, "by which means she was deprived of the comfort of her children in her old age." Three sons she would never see again.[36]

THEY WEPT MUCH

Though the English were the most numerous explorers of southern New England, the Wampanoags continued to encounter Europeans from other nations, sometimes with equally terrible results. Dutch activity in the region spiked after Henry Hudson's 1609 voyage up his namesake river revealed that inland Indians had rich stocks of beaver pelts to trade. By 1614 at least five Dutch ships from four different companies were trading on the Hudson and exploring and charting the nearby coast. These ventures included Adriaen Block's expedition, during which he noted that the "Wapenoks," or Wampanoags, and "Nahicans," or Narragansetts, lived on opposite sides of Narragansett Bay. Proceeding to Buzzards Bay, Block found the Wampanoags to be "somewhat shy," which he mistakenly attributed to them not being "accustomed to trade with strangers." Little did he know that their guardedness was a response to their turbulent history with Europeans.[37]

The French also remained active in southern New England despite the bloodshed that marred their voyages of 1605 and 1606. Not only did they continue to work the Newfoundland fishery, but in 1608 they also founded Québec up the St. Lawrence River, followed by fur trade posts, missionary stations, and small agricultural and fishing settlements in Nova Scotia and Maine. Occasional voyages to southern New England were an extension of these enterprises. Smith complained that when he landed north of Massachusetts Bay in 1614, French traders had already been in the area for six weeks collecting the Indians' finest beaver pelts. Yet within a couple of years two French crews met fates as dire as those suffered by the Wampanoag captives of Thomas Hunt. According to a story told in the 1620s by a Massachusetts Bay Indian named Pecksuot, in 1616 the Wampanoags enslaved some French sailors who had made it to shore after their fishing vessel wrecked off Cape Cod. (Pecksuot said the number of sailors was two, but another version says three or four.) "We made them our servants," Pecksuot boasted. "They wept much." The Wampanoag and Massachusett Indians abused the French mercilessly, stripping them of their clothes, feeding them only "such meat as our dogs ate," and transferring them from sachem to sachem "to make sport with them." One of the sailors died under such treatment. Another lasted long enough that his master permitted him to take a wife, with whom he bore a child still living after the founding of Plymouth. The others remained slaves until Dermer redeemed them in 1619.³⁸

What the Massachusett Indians remembered most about these French captives were the curses one of them uttered before he died, which to them augured the arrival of epidemic diseases and the first colonists. Pecksuot told that when the Indians asked this Frenchman about a book he read, he shot back, "It says, there will [be] a people, like Frenchmen, come into this country and drive you all away." Turning to the English colonist Phineas Pratt, to whom he related this account, Pecksuot foreboded, "We think you are they." Another version of the story, recorded by Smith and Nathaniel Morton, recalled the Indians ridiculing the Frenchman for his Christianity. Their taunts included a sachem dragging the Frenchman to the top of a hill before all his supporters below, then demanding to know whether the Christian God had the power to destroy such a great people. The Frenchman was said to have answered: "Yes, and [God] surely would [kill them], and bring in strangers to possess their land, so long as they mocked him and his God." Shortly, a terrible disease laid the people low, followed by the arrival of the *Mayflower*.³⁹

In the meantime, however, the Indians remained powerful and populous, as other Frenchmen soon discovered the hard way. Shortly after the wreck of the French fishing boat, another French vessel entered Massachusetts Bay laden with goods and eager for trade. Pecksuot remembered proposing a scheme to his sachem by which "you shall have all for nothing." According to his instructions, the sachem's men rowed out to the ship with knives hidden under piles of beaver pelts, which they offered to the French for cheap. Then, while the sailors were absorbed with these riches, the Indians drew their blades. "We killed them all," Pecksuot gloated, "then our sachem divided their goods and fired their ship and it made a very great fire." Morton's account of this event contends that the Indians spared a few of these Frenchmen to keep as slaves and that they were the ones who made the terrible hexes about the plague and colonial invasion remembered years later by the Massachusett Indians. The confusion about which French slaves made which curses speaks to the viciousness of everyone during this period of contact.[40]

The few surviving accounts of the captive French differ about particulars, but they share another broader point that Indians remained fully sovereign over southern New England even amid their victimization at the hands of Hunt and men of his ilk. The Indians not only suffered raids, captivity, and enslavement but themselves raided, captured, and enslaved Europeans in turn. The strangers did not awe them then, nor would they when the *Mayflower* appeared. Indians took the initiative to engage with shipboard explorers, knowing the risk, because they wanted trade as much as Europeans did. Despite the curses of the angry French captives, there was every reason to believe that the Natives would continue to control their own fate indefinitely—that is, until the plague came. Then the real mourning began.

CHAPTER THREE

ﾗﾆﾆ

Golgotha

Sometimes silences in the historical record can speak as loudly as words. When a significant event has occurred and there is only one surviving perspective about it, or none at all, it might mean that the powerful have suppressed or censored the voices of their opponents or the weak. A lack of evidence might also mean simply that records have been lost to the vagaries of war, natural disaster, fire, or clerical incompetence. In the case of the seventeenth-century Wampanoags, interpreting silences is infinitely more problematic. In the early seventeenth century, the Wampanoags did not yet possess the skill of writing. Therefore, most of what we know about them comes from sources produced by European men, predominantly the English, whose focus was on those aspects of Wampanoag life that affected their own security, profits, and religious interests. Curious gaps about Indians in their documents typically have to do with the colonists' indifference and hostility toward Native people's culture or simple ignorance about it.

None of these explanations, however, accounts for the paucity of Indian statements about the epidemic of 1616–19, one of the worst in Native American history. That silence speaks volumes. The English were intrigued by this disaster, partly because of its spectacle, but also because they believed it was a sign of God's omnipotence. Though the English recorded what the Indians had to say about the symptoms of the disease, and even some of their theories about its cause, that is where the conversations ended. It would appear that Native people did not want to recount how it had ripped through their communities, how the people's healers and religious specialists had struggled futilely against it, how those who could had fled in terror as the pestilence spread, and how a pall of mourning had blanketed the survivors. To dwell too deeply on these horrors would come too close to reliving them.

The historian Francis Jennings wrote poignantly that the *Mayflower* landed not in a virgin land but a widowed land. Epidemic disease had already nearly emptied a long stretch of coastline that once thronged with people. Every survivor, which is to say, practically every living person, had lost someone, and some people lost everyone. The colonist Thomas Morton used an equally powerful metaphor to describe this disaster zone in which "there hath been but one left alive to tell what became of the rest" and where unburied human remains "were left for crows, kites, and vermin to prey upon . . . It seemed to me," he reflected, to be "a newfound Golgotha." By Golgotha, he referred to the biblical hill outside Jerusalem where the Romans crucified Jesus amid the rotting remains of the empire's other victims. He meant to evoke both the macabre scene and his belief that saving grace, in the form of the English Christianity, would arise from it. He did not muse on what it meant for Wampanoags to live amid this devastation. It is hard to imagine that they saw anything redemptive in it.[1]

Morton claimed that there were no survivors to tell the tale of this disaster, but that was not true. Thousands of people had escaped the affliction, while others had convalesced, but they were not recounting it in great detail, certainly not to the English, and perhaps not even to each other. They had suffered and continued to struggle with what might be characterized as social trauma, a harsh blow to their confidence that society could protect them in the world. Unable to determine what had happened to them and why, they had diminished faith in their ceremonial leaders, healers, and the spirits they marshaled. In daylight, flashbacks of the calamity plagued them. In sleep, nightmares. Depressed, terrified, and unmoored, they clung to life trying to reconstitute some semblance of normalcy. Their psyches were too fragile for them to conjure up the misery of their ordeal through conversation. Some of them never would be ready. Nor were they willing to risk hauntings from the ghosts of the dead by speaking their names. Their silence, it would seem, was a desperate attempt to forget, to bury unspeakable memories and emotions in place of the unburied remains littering their Golgotha. The apparent goal was to create collective amnesia in order to cope, although they would probably never fully heal.[2]

Yet it was difficult to forget when no one knew for certain what had happened. The Wampanoags had no history with the disease that struck them. There was no name for it. No one knew if it would return. Most important, no one knew who or what had caused it. All of this is to say that if the initial shock of the epidemic had ebbed by the time the *Mayflower* appeared in Wampanoag country, the terror of it lingered and would continue to do so until the people determined what produced their suffering and how to prevent it from happening again. The urgency of finding those answers meant that it was impossible for the Wampanoags to exorcise their unspeakable demon. They remained constantly on alert, eyes and ears open, searching for clues, petrified about what they might find.

When the Pilgrims waded ashore, they entered the shroud of this dread mystery. Wampanoag survivors still outnumbered the hundred-odd English newcomers by a factor of sixty or more, which on the surface would suggest that the colonists did not represent much of a threat. Yet the Wampanoags' overwhelming superiority in population cannot account for the fact that they were shaken to their core and wary that the colonists might be necromancers capable of infecting the people again. Thus, to the Wampanoags, the English represented more than just potential traders, raiders, or slavers, like previous European visitors. The Natives probed to determine if these strangers had the power to revive the scourge or to protect against disease and the political threats that had arisen in its wake. The early history of the Wampanoags and Plymouth took place against this dark background of mourning, suspicion, desperation, and fear. It is the most basic element missing from the Thanksgiving myth.

The Wampanoags of the Thanksgiving myth are friendly Indians whose welcome enables the Pilgrims to establish themselves in the wilderness and plant the seeds for what would become a Christian, democratic country. There is no accounting for why the Natives extended this helping hand, no sense that their behavior was a strategic response to their historical circumstances. The story becomes much grimmer, but also much more understandable, when it acknowledges that they were reeling from their losses to an unforgiving epidemic and under relentless pressure from neighboring tribes. Only such conditions would lead them to look for help from English strangers whose nation had a lengthy track record of attacking and enslaving the people. It was not innate friendliness or a directive from God to assist Christians that drove the Wampanoags to reach out to the English. Rather, they were desperate.

"ANCIENT PLANTATIONS . . . NOW UTTERLY VOID"

Wampanoag country was an entirely different place right before the epidemic broke out, full of Native people wedded to the land by history, ceremony, spiritual relationships, and day-to-day living. In the summer of 1614, a mere two years before the people began falling ill, John Smith remarked that the southern New England coast was "so planted with gardens and corn fields, and so well inhabited with a goodly, strong, and well-proportioned people" that he judged it "an excellent place both for health and fertility. And of all the four parts of the world that I have yet seen not inhabited [by Europeans]," he extolled, "could I have but means to transport a colony, I would rather live here than anywhere." Nothing he saw presaged the disaster to come.[3]

The region was not only populated and cultivated but also commercially interconnected and politically organized into increasingly large intertribal confederacies, which would play critical roles as disease vectors. With the assistance of his Indian interpreters, Dohoday and Tatum, Smith discerned that "language and alliance" bound together the Wampanoag communities of Chawum, Paomet, and Nauset on Cape Cod, while to the north "the others are called Massachusetts, of another language, humor, and condition." The Wampanoag and Massachusett Indians had once been at odds, "but now they are all friends, so far as they have society, on each other's frontiers." Decades later, in the 1670s, Indian sources told the English missionary Daniel Gookin that before the epidemic of 1616–19 the Massachusetts Bay Indians held dominion over communities as far west as the Connecticut River and could boast three thousand warriors. They also agreed with Smith's sources that the Massachusetts "held amity, for the most part, with the Pokanokets," or Wampanoags.[4]

One reason for this friendship might have been the Massachusett Indians' need for trade partners and military allies to address opportunities and threats to their northeast. As Smith understood it, "Sometimes [they] have wars with the Bashabes [i.e., the sachem Bashaba] of Penobscot." For several years, the Mi'kmaq and Penobscots had used their newly acquired sailing vessels to cruise down to Massachusetts Bay and exchange European tools, metal, and furs for locally raised crops. This food permitted them to spend the fall and winter trapping for beaver pelts to trade to the French instead of having to devote that time to hunting deer and moose for meat. For their part, the Bay Indians acquired coveted foreign wares from still-distant sources. Initially, the alliance between the Massachusett and Wampanoag peoples might have involved the Wampanoags contributing some of their corn to this trade in return for a portion of the goods. However, the relationship became a military alliance as the Mi'kmaq and Penobscots ceased bargaining for the southern Indians' produce in favor of plundering it in murderous amphibious raids. Apparently, the Massachusett Indians looked to the Wampanoags for protection against this threat.[5]

The Wampanoags had their own need for the alliance in the form of the Narragansett threat to their west. At stake were control of Narragansett Bay's islands and tribute from the Shawomet and Coweset communities in the contested Narragansett-Wampanoag border region. Though the Wampanoags' territory was vast, Gookin's informants said that in the early 1600s they could muster only some three thousand matawaûog to answer the Narragansetts' five thousand or six thousand fighting men. Support from the Massachusett Indians more than addressed the Wampanoags' disadvantage, at least for the meantime.[6]

All of these relationships, from the Wampanoag-Massachusett alliance, to the down-the-line trade of the Gulf of Maine, to Smith's interactions with the coastal Natives, were links in a growing commercial and political chain. There had been long-distance ties between indigenous communities up and down the coast and into the interior for countless generations, but this was the first time that their networks included foreigners from across the Atlantic. The point of forging these associations was to increase the wealth and security of the people. Little could they have known that the inherent risks of dealing with strangers would include the introduction of devastating illnesses to this vibrant country.[7]

Just five years after Smith marveled at the robust condition of southern New England Indians, Thomas Dermer cruised the same

waters and encountered an entirely different scene. "I passed along
the coast," Dermer recounted, "where I found some ancient plantations, not long since populous, now utterly void, in other places, a
remnant remains, but not free of sickness." A "great mortality" that
the Indians "never heard of before" had slashed its way across the
land, after which "the twentieth person was scarce left alive," in
the estimation of the Plymouth colony historian Nathaniel Morton.
"Sad spectacles of that mortality" were evident throughout the
country in the form of the "many bones and skulls of the dead lying
above the ground." When Edward Winslow and Stephen Hopkins
traveled from Plymouth to Pokanoket in 1622, they noticed that the
entire route down the Taunton River to its mouth was lined by
formerly cleared fields being reclaimed by the woods, indicating that
once "thousands of men have lived there," but no more. Those thousands, they understood, had "died in a great plague not long since."
Once thronging, now empty, villages with undergrowth creeping
into their recesses; skeletal remains lying aboveground right where
death occurred—to the people who had survived the epidemic and
lived constantly with the memories of loved ones they had lost, the
place probably was haunted.[8]

In all likelihood, neither the Wampanoags nor most of the rest
of Native North America had ever experienced disease on this scale.
For millennia, their separation from the rest of the world had been a
boon to their health because it spared them from a host of ailments
that festered among the crowds, filth, and close human-animal
contacts of Europe, Asia, and Africa. The most lethal Eurasian
diseases developed largely because people and domestic animals
lived right on top of one another, sometimes literally. Smallpox, flu,
tuberculosis, malaria, plague, and measles all evolved from the disorders of animals. Overall, people share fifty sicknesses with cattle,
forty-six with sheep, forty-two with pigs, thirty-five with horses, thirty-
two with rodents, and twenty-six with poultry. Native Americans

had few domestic animals, only the dog in most cases, and the llama and turkey in a few limited areas of South America. Native American health also benefited from the people living usually in small, dispersed settlements. Elsewhere in the world, illnesses festered in densely populated towns and cities because of the easy communicability, open sewage, spoiled drinking water, and concentration of humans, rodents, and their disease-carrying fleas, lice, and ticks. American Indians had few urban societies outside what is now Peru, Mexico, and the Mississippi River valley. Too often, ancient Native Americans' geographic isolation and small-scale social organization are seen as having cut them off from the supposed progress enjoyed by their counterparts elsewhere in the world. Among the problems with such a view is that these conditions had spared countless generations of Indians from the very crowd diseases that made life elsewhere in the world so nasty, brutish, and short. Yet what had once been a blessing soon became a curse.[9]

The single greatest reason that Indians contracted European ailments at such high rates and died in such staggering numbers is that none of the adults had developed resistance through exposure in childhood and therefore nearly everyone became ill at the same time without anyone left to provide care. In other parts of the globe, most adults carried lifetime immunities to lethal killers such as smallpox and chicken pox after contracting them in childhood. But in America these maladies became "virgin soil epidemics," diseases to which the populations at risk had no previous contact and therefore had not developed immunological resistance. This point, above all, explains the sheer scale of the carnage. Parents, children, aunts, uncles, cousins, and grandparents all languished together. Those who otherwise might have recovered with some basic nursing died miserably without food, water, and cleaning because nobody was available to provide essential care. William Bradford's description of a smallpox outbreak among Indians in the Connecticut River valley in 1633–34 probably comes closest to capturing the wretchedness of the epidemic of 1616–19. He wrote that the Indians "fell down so generally of this disease as they were in the end not able to help one another, not to make a fire nor to fetch a little water to drink, nor any to bury the dead. But would strive as long as they could, and when they could procure no other means to make fire, they would burn the wooden trays and dishes they ate their meat in, and their very bows and arrows. And some would crawl out on all fours to get a little water, and sometimes die by the way and not to be able to get in again."[10]

The lucky few who did survive remained weak, malnourished, and psychologically frayed, thus rendering them vulnerable to additional illnesses. Consider the better-documented parallel case of the Huron or Wendat Indians of southern Ontario, who were some of New France's earliest fur trade partners and hosted Jesuit missionaries. The Hurons had not even recovered from a devastating smallpox epidemic in 1634, when they were also struck by measles in 1635, the flu in 1636–37, and smallpox again in 1639. Whether the Indians of southern New England experienced a similar disease cycle from 1616 to 1619 is unknown, but it remains a distinct possibility given their ongoing contact with European explorers and traders. Smith believed as much, contending that there had been "three plagues in three years successively near two hundred miles along the seacoast," but he stood alone in making this claim. More certain is that the survivors were stalked by famine because, during their convalescence, narrow seasonal opportunities for hunting, fishing, planting, or harvesting had come and gone without being exploited. The breakdown of society meant that there was little food.[11]

Over the next two centuries, foreign diseases would wreak such devastation among Indians throughout the continent that their introduction should be ranked among the most significant disasters in modern times. However, the New England outbreak of 1616–19 was unusual insofar as the shocking mortality appears to have been unrelated to other colonial pressures on indigenous society. In many other times and places, the rates at which Indians contracted and died from such diseases had much to do with the people being physically and psychologically stressed by forces related to European expansion. Take, for instance, intertribal wars fought to obtain indigenous slaves or animal pelts for the colonial market, and Indian-colonial wars over land and jurisdiction. Such conflicts often left Native people malnourished because of their inability to hunt and plant in safety or the enemy's destruction of their fields and food stores. Additionally, in wartime the people often clustered in unsanitary fortified settlements where viral diseases ran riot. In other words, virgin soil conditions alone rarely account for the vastness of Indian depopulation. Rarely, that is, but not never. Southern England in 1616 appears to have been one of those exceptional times and places.[12]

No one knows what disease, or diseases, struck the New England coast between 1616 and 1619. The only firsthand accounts come from the Englishmen Richard Vines and Dermer, both of whom referred to it as "the plague," a term that sometimes referred to epidemics generally and at other times specifically to bubonic plague. The Vines expedition was among the Abenakis of the Saco River, Maine, when the illness broke out in 1616, and though the Englishmen "lay in the cabins with those people that died . . . not one of them ever felt their heads to ache while they stayed there." The recollection of Vines's sponsor in England, Sir Ferdinando Gorges, was that the Maine Indians had been "sore afflicted with the plague, for that country was in a manner left void of inhabitants." Dermer arrived on the scene three years later and found that most of the people had been wiped out, though "in other places a remnant remains, but not free of sickness." He pronounced that "their disease is the plague," but added "for we might perceive the sores of some that had escaped, who described the spots of such as usually die."

Bubonic plague is not usually accompanied by sores and spots but instead swollen lymph nodes.[13]

Later accounts by colonists separated from the event by time or distance are scarcely of more help in explaining what had happened. Edward Johnson, who arrived in Massachusetts in 1630 and published an account in 1654 of the colony's first years, characterized the epidemic as "consumption, sweeping away whole families, but chiefly young men and children, the very seeds of increase." The English naturalist John Josselyn, who visited his brother in Maine in 1638–39 and again from 1663 to 1671, understood that "not long before the English came into the country, [there] happened a great mortality amongst them [the Indians], especially where the English afterwards planted, the East and Northern parts were sore smitten with the contagion; first by the plague, afterwards, when the English came by the smallpox [probably referring to the outbreak of 1622 or 1633–34]." John Eliot, a missionary who began proselytizing the Massachusetts Bay Indians in the mid-1640s, said his charges were among the lucky few who had survived "the plague and pox," while Eliot's contemporary, William Wood, wrote that the Abenakis of Maine were previously unafraid of the formidable Mohawks—that is, until they lost their male protectors to "the sweeping plague." Years later, in 1671, Gookin asked some Native elders to identify the disease, but they could only say "that their bodies all over were exceedingly yellow, describing it by a yellow garment." Gookin conceded, "What this disease was . . . I cannot well learn," though "doubtless it was some pestilential disease." The only points on which everyone agreed was that Indians died in heaps from this ailment and Europeans seemed resistant to it.[14]

There is no scholarly consensus on which disease corresponds most closely to these symptoms, the pattern of communicability, and the staggering death toll. Proposed culprits have included a combination of smallpox and measles, measles alone, yellow fever, typhoid, chicken pox, typhus, and cerebrospinal meningitis. Bubonic plague (and its outgrowth, pneumonic plague) is widely discounted as a possibility. There were no reported outbreaks of plague in English or French ports in or around 1616 from which the disease might have passed to New England, though the Netherlands was a potential vector. Even in the unlikelihood that a European or black rat carrying the plague traveled on one of the ships that visited the coast in 1616, the fleas and ticks that transmitted the disease from rats to humans and between humans were unlikely to survive New England's bitter winters. Additionally, Europeans were also susceptible to the plague, and the sources are clear that Europeans did not contract the disease of 1616–19. The epidemic was *a plague* in the general sense, but probably not *the plague* like the Black Death, which swept off a third or more of Europe's population in the mid-fourteenth century.[15]

A recent argument that the epidemic was leptospirosis is intriguing but unpersuasive. Humans contract leptospiral bacteria from water or food contaminated by rat and mice urine. As recently as 2017, there was an outbreak on the island of Puerto Rico in the wake of a devastating hurricane and an inept recovery effort by the U.S. government. There is no doubt that European sailing ships were responsible for introducing rats to southeastern New England, where they were previously unknown. However, it is unlikely that so many rats had infested southern New England by 1616 that they were capable of spoiling the people's supplies of drinking water and freshwater swimming places. To be sure, there is a documented case from the Missouri River valley in the nineteenth century in which rats infested the underground storage barns of Mandan Indians, which raises the possibility that rats did the same thing among Abenaki, Massachusett, and Wampanoag horticulturalists, poisoning them in the process. Additionally, the reported symptoms of the 1616–19 epidemic—headache, jaundice—align closely with those of leptospirosis. Yet there is one major problem with this theory. Why, if the disease was conveyed by rats, did it not affect the Narragansetts, who lived a short distance west of the Wampanoags? The fact that the disease spread among allied peoples stretching from Wabanaki to Wampanoag country but halted suddenly at the boundary between two hostile groups suggests that it passed from human to human, not from rodent to human.[16]

The strongest case is for malignant confluent smallpox. Its symptoms not only include the headache, spots, and sores (or pox) associated with the 1616–19 outbreak but also the yellowing of the skin as dense clusters of lesions break and matter together. Furthermore, this type of smallpox has been shown to kill 70 to 80 percent of its victims, never mind when those people came from a virgin soil population. Its airborne human-to-human transmission would explain why the disease corresponded to the tight-knit French-Wabanaki-Wampanoag trade network. At the same time, there are sound arguments against the smallpox theory. Gookin's informants in the 1670s did not identify the disease as smallpox, though by that time they certainly knew the disease by name and experience. An outbreak of smallpox in 1633–34 carried off large numbers of coastal Indians, including from some of the communities that had suffered the epidemic of 1616–19, which might indicate that the people had not experienced smallpox before and developed immunities to it. At the same time, it is possible (1) that most of the victims had been born in the seventeen-year interval between these epidemics, and (2) that some of the survivors of the 1616–19 outbreak might not have developed a sufficient immunological defense to smallpox during their first infection or lost it rapidly, both of which are known to occur.

If the epidemic was indeed smallpox, the victims would have suffered incredibly. The disease begins with flu-like symptoms such as splitting headaches and backaches, fever, vomiting, and intense

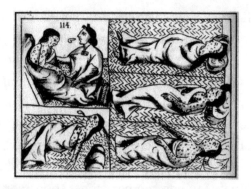

Aztecs suffering smallpox, from Bernardino de Sahagún,
Florentine Codex (ca. 1585), Book 12, Folio 54.

This depiction of the Aztecs of Mexico suffering smallpox in 1520 during the
Spanish conquest is one of the only colonial-era illustrations of its kind.
There are no such graphics of this deadly scourge among New England
Indians, though they suffered a devastating attack of smallpox in 1633. The
unidentified "plague" of 1616–19 also might have been smallpox.

anxiety. After a day or two, the fever abates briefly, then on the
fourth day returns along with the first sores in the mouth, throat,
and nose. For the next twenty-four hours, the sores spread, sometimes internally, causing bleeding from orifices like the eyes and
nose. In such cases, the pain is excruciating and eating and drinking
are difficult. More commonly, the rash spreads all over the outer
skin, particularly the hands, soles of the feet, face, neck, back, and
forearms. The sores produce agony even when they remain separated.
When they break open, ooze into each other, and congeal, the
patient's suffering becomes unbearable.[17]

At this point, the likelihood of secondary infection and death
skyrockets. The risk of mortality remains high as scabs begin to
form, sometimes coating the body in a shell that rips open with the
slightest movement. During the 1633–34 smallpox outbreak, Bradford

was horrified at the "lamentable condition" of Indians infected with the disease who "lye on their hard mats, the pox breaking and mattering and running one into another, their skin cleaving (by reasons thereof) to the matts they lye on; when they turn them a whole side will flay off at once as it were, and they will all be a gore blood, most fearful to behold. And then being very sore, what with cold and other distempers, they die like rotten sheep." After about a month, those who have survived this torment will begin to shed their scabs, remaining contagious until the last one is gone. Yet even then, the danger of spreading the infection lingers, for not only is the disease contracted by inhaling infected droplets or even dust but the pustules themselves are also potent vectors, including those shed onto clothing and bedding, where the virus can stay potent for several weeks. There it sits, hidden in ambush, ready to strike unsuspecting victims who might have assumed it had already run its course.[18]

FUTILE MEDICINE

There are no recorded eyewitness accounts of how the Wampanoags and their neighbors attempted to deal with this epidemic, but later sources about their religious, medical, burial, and mourning customs suggest what happened. Wampanoags believed that when someone grew seriously ill, and particularly when an entire community became sick, it was no accident. Someone or something caused it. Spirits punished people occasionally for their neglect of rituals, violation of taboos, or misinterpretation of directives issued through dreams. A sorcerer driven by jealousy or enmity might conjure up disease. The key was to identify the source and divine a cure. And for those purposes, the people turned to their shaman healers, known as *pawwaws*.

Normally when people fell sick, they took the mere appearance of a pawwaw as "an undoubted sign of recovery," and no wonder. Pawwaws boasted various abilities to cure and curse, uncover hidden information, influence the weather, and organize rituals. Their powers came from any one of a number of guardian spirits, but the main font was the god of the dead, known as Cheepi, Abbomocho, or Hobbamock. Cheepi was the analog of Kiehtan, whom the Wampanoags associated with the southwest, horticultural crops, pleasant weather, and the sun. Cheepi, by contrast, evoked the color black, cold, the moon, night, and the northeast wind. He shape-shifted between the forms of a serpent, a black panther, and a dead man; his very name was related to the Wampanoag word for death. His stronghold beneath the waters made Wampanoags especially leery of death by drowning and respectful of the power of swamps, where trees served as dangerous portals between Cheepi's under-world, the earthly habitations of people, and the sky. Wampanoags sought Cheepi's power because of, not despite, their fear of it. Some-times a Wampanoag couple would have their son apprentice with a pawwaw in the hope that he would "fall into a strange dream wherein Cheepian [*sic*] appears unto them as a serpent." According to the colonist Matthew Mayhew, the preparation involved "observing certain diet, debarring sleep, etc.," though it worked only for a select few. At other times, Cheepi appeared to someone unexpectedly "by imme-diate revelation." Whatever the case, a vision of Cheepi gave the seer access to secondary tutelary spirits, which thereafter inhabited the seer's body, and their stunning array of powers, such as healing, prognostication, and cursing. A young man's or woman's transforma-tion into a pawwaw (there is one recorded mention of a female pawwaw) was a momentous event, and "for two days after the rest of the Indians dance and rejoice for what they tell them about this serpent." It was to such people that the Wampanoags would have turned when they started feeling ill in the fateful year of 1616.[19]

To identify the origin of the sickness and how to combat it, the pawwaws would have fasted, danced, and thrashed themselves into ecstatic trances while "sometimes roaring like a bear, other times groaning like a dying horse, foaming at the mouth like a chased boar, smiting on his naked breast and thighs with such violence as if he were mad." These grunts and growls were the sounds of one of the pawwaw's two souls communicating with other spirits across space and time in search of answers. Meanwhile, friends and relatives of the patient gathered around, giving "attentive audience to [the pawwaw's] imprecations and invocations." Occasionally, the pawwaw would come to a stop, lead the bystanders in a chant, and then proceed as before in his "bellowing and groaning," which, Wood marveled, "thus will he continue sometimes half a day."[20]

In the worst cases, the pawwaws exited the trance to deliver the terrible news "that Kiehtan is angry, and sends them [the disease], whom none can cure." English observers were struck that, on such occasions, the patient seemed resigned to die. Maladies from other sources were treatable, as when Cheepi had sent the affliction "for some conceived anger against them," or when a necromancer had implanted a poisonous charm in the patient's body in the form of "a piece of leather like an arrowhead, tying a hair thereto; or using some bone, as of fish." If Cheepi was the cause, the pawwaw led the people in "calling upon him," whereupon "[he] can and doth help them." In the event of sorcery, the pawwaw would lay his hands on the patient and use a tube to suck out the impurity. One pawwaw explained to Plymouth's Edward Winslow that it was not he who performed the extraction "but a Skooke, that is the Snake, or Wobsocuck, that is the Eagle, [which] sat on his shoulder and licks the same. This none see but the pawwaw, who tells them he did it himself." Though the spirit was invisible to everyone else, when a pawwaw "had done some notable cure, [he] would show the imp," that is, a figurine of the spirit, "in the palm of his hand to the Indians; who with much amazement looking on it, deified them." Another possibility was that an ailing person suffered from possession by a hostile spirit, as in a case from Martha's Vineyard, when a pawwaw healed a woman by using a deerskin to capture the soul of an Englishman who had drowned in nearby waters. It required potent spiritual protectors like those wielded by the pawwaws to guard against such an array of threats.[21]

Curing ceremonies like these, held at first in individual households, then expanding into community-wide affairs, must have characterized the beginning of the epidemic of 1616–19. Yet it would have taken little time before the participants realized that their efforts were in vain. Johnson's understanding was that "their pawwaws . . . were much amazed to see their wigwams full of dead corpses and that now neither Squantum nor Abbamocho [other names for Cheepi] could help . . . and also their pawwaws themselves were oft smitten with death's stroke." At a loss for what else to do, the people could only mourn and pray that the contagion spared those who were left.[22]

There was no mistaking when southern New England Indians were in mourning. They blackened their faces with soot, mangled their hair, sometimes cut themselves, and broke out spontaneously into sobs and abject prayers. When a "strange disease" afflicted Wampanoags of Martha's Vineyard in 1643, the English saw them "run up and down till they could no longer, they made their faces as black as coal, snatched up any weapon, spoke great words, but did no hurt." Roger Williams, who had been taught to accept death as God's will, was struck during his many visits to the Wampanoags and Narragansetts that "bewailing is very solemn among them in morning, evening, and sometimes in the night they bewail their lost husbands, wives, children, brethren, or sisters." He was witnessing people who shared the agony of losing their loved ones with family and friends, giving them emotional release and human solidarity.[23]

There was to be no levity during bereavement. Southern New England Indians considered it "a profane thing either to play (as they much use to do) or to paint themselves for beauty, but [only] for mourning." No fleeting obligation, people remained in this pitiful state "sometimes a quarter, half, yea a whole year or longer, if it be for a great prince." When children died, the mood grew even more downcast. "Their affections, especially to their children, are very strong," wrote Williams, "so that I have known a father take so grievously the loss of his child, that he has cut and stabbed himself with grief and rage." Williams also "heard a poor Indian lamenting the loss of a child at break of day, call up his wife and children, and all about him to lamentation, and with abundance of tears cry out, 'O God, thou hast taken away my child! Thou art angry with me! O, turn thine anger from me, and spare the rest of my children.'" Amid the epidemic, anguished cries of this sort must have filled the air.[24]

Under normal circumstances, burial would have come next. Whether the Wampanoags, like the Narragansetts, had specialists who prepared the dead for interment is unknown. The only eyewitness account of their funeral rites, by Winslow, explained that "when they bury the dead, they sew up the corpse in a mat, and so put it in the earth. If the party be a sachem, they cover him with many curious mats, and bury all his riches with them, and enclose the grave with a pale [or fence]. If it be a child, the father will also put his own most special jewels and ornaments in the earth with it; also will cut his hair, and disfigure himself very much, in token of sorrow. If it be the man or woman of the house, they will pull down the mats and leave the frame standing, and bury them in or near the same, and either remove the dwelling or give over house-keeping." Friends and relatives remained with the deceased's family "to mourn for them . . . many days after the burial in a most doleful manner," a responsibility they considered "solemn." From this point on, no one was to mention the deceased's name, lest the ghost hear it and return to haunt the living. As Williams explained: "the dead sachem. The dead man. The dead. A dead woman. He that was here. He that was prince here. These expressions they use, because they abhor to mention the dead by name."[25]

Given these customs, imagine the scene as the epidemic of 1616–19 began to knife through person after person, house after house, community after community. Everyone still living would have been painted black and dressed in tattered clothing. The frames of empty houses with their mats or bark siding removed would have cast skeletal silhouettes against the sky, particularly at dawn or dusk. Day and night would have been filled with the sounds of pawwaws bellowing, ritual chanting and drumming, and mourners sobbing and calling on the spirits for relief. People would emerge from their dwellings to bury the dead, then return inside to continue their desperate efforts to heal the sick. Everyone would have been terrified that they were next. By and large, they were.

It is difficult to know what to make of the remains of the unburied dead so often remarked on by Europeans who arrived on the scene after the catastrophe was over. Perhaps it was as they surmised: as the epidemic grew out of control, those still standing fled the scene in horror despite the guilt and anxiety of leaving ailing loved ones to fend for themselves and die alone. Yet such a scenario is difficult to square with Winslow's observation that it was "a commendable manner of the Indians, when any (especially of note) are dangerously sick, for all that profess friendship to them, to visit them in their extremity, either in their persons, or else to send some acceptable persons to them." Williams's understanding was that the

Indians' practice was to stay with the sick and dying "unless it be an infectious disease," in which case, "all forsake them and fly . . . the living not able to bury the dead: so terrible is their apprehension of an infectious disease, that not only persons, but the houses and the whole town takes flight." It is possible, however, that what Williams interpreted as a time-worn custom was actually a new response to what the people had learned about communicability during previous epidemics.[26]

Consider, too, that the unburied dead might have been war captives without any relatives to tend to them. Indians in southern New England, as throughout North America, ranked captive taking among their primary war aims. Whereas they executed most adult male captives, the women and children would have been spared and adopted after a period of debasement and slavery. Such a population of enemy captives or their descendants might help explain Mayhew's statement in the 1690s that the Wampanoags included "many families" considered "strangers or foreigners, who were not privileged with common right," such as attending the sachem's communal hunts or having their family heads attend the sachem's council. These people were "in some measure subject to the yeomanry," or common people, which was to say, of a lesser rank than them. It is impossible to know if Mayhew accurately understood what he was seeing and if it reflected the state of Wampanoag society eighty years earlier during the epidemic of 1616–19. At the same time, it is a distinct possibility that the Wampanoag response to pestilence was not to leave all their dead unburied, but just captives without kin, for in such close-knit societies, to lack family was to lack protectors and even social identity. Whatever the reason for these remains, they became ghoulish monuments to a disaster the survivors wanted to forget and skeletal sentries warning travelers to stay away from where the unimaginable had happened.[27]

But what *had* happened? One of the worst aspects of this tragedy was that no one could say for certain. It was not as if the Wampanoags and other Indians had no previous experience with disease or premature death. Generations of them had experienced venereal syphilis, tuberculosis, hepatitis, parasites, polio, and respiratory disorders like viral influenza and pneumonia. In all likelihood, their infant and childhood mortality rates were high and average life expectancies were low by modern American standards, compounded by the risks of childbirth to women and warfare to men. But whatever had stricken them in this instance was entirely unknown. Not only did it have no name, but it also tormented survivors with the question of why it had occurred. Given the Wampanoags' understanding of how disease worked, those questions could be restated as who was responsible or what had they done to deserve this.[28]

EXPLAINING A DISEASE WITH NO NAME

As the epidemic began taking its toll despite the pawwaws' incantations, some people would have begun to wonder if one or more of the pawwaws had bewitched them. As one pawwaw explained of the powers his guardian spirit had given him, "his god, which appeared to him in the form of a snake," enabled him "to kill, wound, and lame such whom he intended mischief to." In at least one recorded case, a Wampanoag family threatened to lynch a pawwaw who had failed to cure their relative after they became convinced that he was the actual source of the trouble. Thomas Mayhew Jr.'s impression was that the Wampanoags widely feared "the pawwaws' power to kill men, and there were many stories told of the great hurt they had done by their witchcraft [in] many ways." When the Hurons experienced their sequence of deadly epidemics in the 1630s and early 1640s, they responded by executing at least half a dozen suspected witches. Whether the

Wampanoags conducted a similar purge amid the epidemic of 1616–19 is unknown, but clearly they harbored the same dread.[29]

A better-documented Indian explanation connected the epidemic to clashes with European explorers and fur traders. Some Massachusetts Bay Indians recounted that one of their French slaves threatened his abusers that his God "would be angry at them for it, and that he would in his displeasure destroy them." They did not think it was happenstance that shortly "the hand of God fell heavily upon them." Generations later, in 1792, a sixty-year-old Aquinnah Wampanoag named Thomas Cooper explained that his people formerly cured epidemics with a ritual in which a "sprightly young man" would burst out of a burning wetu and fall into a trance as if dead. When he awoke, he would tell of a vision in which he traveled "high up in the air" to meet with "a great company of white people." Only "after much persuasion," he would "obtain a promise" from them "to have the distemper laid," which, fortunately, "never failed." In other words, the people associated with Europeans the power to cause and cure epidemics, like Cheepi himself.[30]

Native people also linked the epidemic to natural wonders. "Ancient Indians" remembered that just before the outbreak, a "bright blazing comet" had streaked across the sky, first appearing, "as they say, in the Southwest," from the direction of Kiehtan, the source of incurable diseases. It remained visible for thirty days, "after which uncouth sight they expected some strange things to follow." Sure enough, the following summer, "there befell a great mortality among them, the greatest that ever the memory of father to son took notice of." They might have been referring to the comet of 1618, which with its green-blue color and uncommonly long, white triangular tail also led Christians in Europe to interpret it as an omen. Other Natives thought the sickness had something to do with an earthquake. When a tremor shook southern New England in 1638, elder

Indians told Williams that it was the fifth such event in eighty years, the first of which took place seventy years earlier, "and they always observed either plague or pox or some other epidemical disease followed 3, 4, or 5 years after the earthquake." They had come to expect that whenever ground rumbled, some horror would pour forth from the underworld.[31]

Ritual protection was the most common explanation for why the Narragansetts had been spared the disease while their neighbors to the east died in droves. Wampanoags told Winslow that they had grown "more and more cold in their worship to Kiehtan" in the years preceding the epidemic, that "in their memory he was much more called upon." By contrast, the Narragansetts "exceed in their blind

Comet over Augsburg, from the title page of Elias Ehinger, *Ludicium Astrologicum. Von dem newen Cometa welcher den 1. Decemb. 1618 am Morgen vor vnd nach 6 Uhren zu Augspurg von vilen Personen gesehen worden* (Augsburg, Ger.: Johann Schultes, ca. 1621).

Some Native New Englanders associated the epidemic of 1616–19 with a comet seen throughout the world in late 1618 and early 1619. The comet, with its bright colors and long tail, also sparked fear and inspired art throughout Europe, including this German image.

devotion" to this potent spirit. That devotion took the form of a ceremony in which the Narragansetts erected "a great spacious house" that remained off-limits to anyone but the pawwaws until an invitation went forth for everyone to convene for a spectacular destruction of wealth. Gathering up "almost all the riches they have," such as "kettles, skins, hatchets, beads, knives, etc.," the pawwaws cast these goods "into a great fire that they make in the midst of the house, and there consumed to ashes." Those who contributed the most to this sacrifice won the esteem of their people and, for that matter, drew the envy of some Wampanoags. Winslow's Wampanoag sources approved of this ritual "and wish their sachems would appoint the like" among them "because the plague hath not reigned at Narragansett as at other places about them, [which] they attribute to this custom there used."[32]

In a world full of spirits and magic, there was no way other than supernatural causes to explain the epidemic, and, in this, the Wampanoags were hardly alone. The English also widely believed that their Lord had smote the Indians to make way for Christians. Smith stood in awe that "God had laid this country open for us, and slain the most part of the inhabitants by cruel war and a mortal disease," and Johnson agreed that "by this means, Christ . . . not only made room for his people to plant; but also tamed the hard and cruel hearts of these barbarous savages." The devastation was so biblical in scale, and so obviously to the benefit of Englishmen attempting to invade the Indians' country, that John Winthrop characterized it as "a miraculous plague." God's providence seemed to be at work on behalf of his supposedly chosen people.[33]

Yet, whereas the English could use this interpretation to strengthen their faith, the epidemic left the Wampanoags spiritually adrift, uncertain of who or what had sent this terrible punishment and why, and what they should do to prevent it from happening again. The very religious leaders they counted on to handle such emergencies had failed miserably, yet it was equally unnerving that many of them and their carefully guarded knowledge had been swept away, too. As the historian James Merrell explains, "The collected wisdom of generations could vanish in a matter of days if sickness struck older members of a community who kept sacred traditions and taught special skills. When many of the elders succumbed at once, the deep pools of collective memory grew shallow, and some dried up altogether."[34]

Is it any wonder, then, that early colonists found among "those that are left . . . their courage much abated, and their countenance is dejected, and they seem as a people affrightened"? Sociologists have used case studies of disasters involving far less mortality than the epidemic of 1616–19, and stemming from better-known causes, to contend that sometimes communities as a whole experience collective trauma, meaning "a blow to the basic tissues of social life that damages the bonds attaching people together and impairs the prevailing sense of community . . . a gradual realization that the community no longer exists as an effective source of support and that an important part of the self has disappeared." In such cases, entire populations feel dazed and listless yet prone to lash out at a moment's notice. As Kai Erikson explains, "traumatized people often scan the surrounding world anxiously for signs of danger, breaking into explosive rages and reacting with a start to ordinary sights and sounds, but at the same time all that nervous activity takes place against a numbed gray background of depression, feel-ings of helplessness, and a general closing off of the spirit as the mind tries to insulate itself from further harm." Nevertheless, trauma victims cannot escape the memories of their ordeal, which return over and over again in flashbacks, daydreams, nightmares, and even hallucinations. In the most extreme cases of social trauma, of which the epidemic of 1616–19 would certainly qualify, the people suffer "not only a loss of confidence in the self but a loss of confidence in the scaffolding of family and community, in the structures of human government, in the larger logics by which humankind lives, and in the ways of nature itself." It is as if everything has fallen apart.[35]

REALIGNMENT

Societies crumble, but people pick up the pieces. All was not lost as long as some of the Wampanoags survived and had other kinfolk who could take them in and help them recover some semblance of normalcy and security. According to Johnson, during the epidemic, a number of Wampanoags deserted their country "for fear of death, fleeing more west and by south, observing the east and northern parts were most smitten by the contagion." Though the Wampanoags were at odds with the Narragansetts, certainly some of their people were related and therefore received assistance. A migration northwest into Nipmuc country also rings true because the Wampanoags and Quabaug Nipmucs maintained a close relationship throughout the seventeenth century. Some Wampanoags might have stayed away permanently, choosing to merge into their host societies despite all the associated challenges of starting anew. Yet the fact that there remained sizable, if diminished, Wampanoag communities throughout Cape Cod and eastern Narragansett Bay at the time of the *Mayflower*'s arrival, containing thousands of inhabitants altogether, indicates that most of the survivors either returned or stayed put in the first place. In this, the Wampanoags were spared the fate of so many other Native North Americans, who after suffering catastrophic losses from epidemic disease had to abandon their ancestral territories and join foreign peoples just to remain viable. The plague of 1616–19 came as close to annihilating the Wampanoags as any disaster could, but once it lifted they retained enough of a population to attempt reconstituting their lives among their own kind in their own country amid their own dead.[36]

Yet the Narragansetts, the Wampanoags' enemies living on the west side of Narragansett Bay, were not going to make this recovery easy. The Narragansetts and Wampanoags had contended with each other for years before the epidemic, from at least the time of Ousamequin's father, according to Ousamequin himself. As discussed earlier, their rivalry might have centered on any number of issues: control of Narragansett Bay's lucrative European trade; competition for tribute payers; domination of wampum production for trade with the Iroquois; expansion onto fresh planting grounds; or even just revenge for violating the taboo of mentioning a dead sachem's name. Whatever the case, the epidemic dramatically altered the balance of power. Bradford noted that whereas the epidemic had hobbled the Wampanoags, the Narragansetts "were a strong people, and many in number, living compact together, and had not been at all touched by this wasting plague." Furthermore, the Narragansetts had actually gained some population during the epidemic by taking in survivors, which makes it even more remarkable that they did not contract the disease. The Narragansetts used this newfound advantage to expand north from their base at the southwest entrance of Narragansett Bay, which was evident in "the great destitution of wood all along near the sea [bay] side" where they located their communities and planting grounds. They not only forced the Wampanoags from the head of the bay and the islands but also reduced the paramount Wampanoag sachem to their authority. As the Narragansett sachems Canonicus and Miantonomo told Williams, "Ousamequin was their subject, and had solemnly, himself in person, with ten men, subjected himself and his land to them at Narragansett." Ousamequin "acknowledged it to be true," but he qualified "that he was not subdued by war, which himself and his father maintained against the Narragansetts;

but God, he said, subdued us by a plague, which swept away my people and forced me to yield."[37]

The Wampanoags' Massachusett Indian allies were of no help in this contest because they had been hit even harder by the epidemic, which reduced them from tens of thousands of people to just a few hundred. Reports reaching Smith in England told that after the epidemic, "where I had seen 100 or 200 people" years earlier, "there is scarce ten to be found. From Pembrock's [Penobscot] Bay to Harrington's [Casco] Bay there is not 20 from thence to Cape Ann, some 30; from Taulbut's Bay [Gloucester Harbor] to the River Charles, about 40." The depopulated Charles River basin mentioned by Smith fell squarely in the Massachusett people's territory.[38]

Not only was their population thinned to the bone, but they, too, were under pressure from rival tribes. When the English established Plymouth, the Massachusett Indians said that they "were much afraid of the Tarrentines [Mi'kmaq]," who in their swift sailing vessels "used to come in harvest time and take away their corn, and many times kill their persons." In 1631, during the early days of the Massachusetts Bay Colony, the English had an opportunity to witness one of these strikes firsthand. That August, Mi'kmaq fighters stormed the Massachusett community of Agawam while it was hosting a delegation from the Pawtucket people of the Merrimac River valley just to the north. The marauders killed seven people, wounded numerous others, including three sachems, and seized one of the sachem's wives. Those who managed to escape fled to safety among the English, whom they lauded as "walls to them from their bloody enemies." Meanwhile, the Narragansetts pressed the Massachusett Indians from the south, making incursions into their hunting grounds and trading with Europeans in their territory without permission. Just years earlier, the Massachusett people had been numerous and formidable. Now they found themselves, like the Wampanoags, nearly wiped out by a strange disease and their survivors at risk of being crushed in a vise of intertribal enemies.[39]

REMEMBERING THE DEAD

If the Wampanoags are as much our fellow Americans as the descendants of the Pilgrims, and if their history can be as instructional and inspirational as that of the English, then why continue to tell a Thanksgiving myth that focuses exclusively on the colonists' struggles rather than theirs? There is no question that the colonists showed remarkable fortitude and faith in braving the dangerous Atlantic and then establishing a settlement in wintertime despite their own losses to disease and famine and the danger posed by surrounding Indians. Yet the challenges facing the Wampanoags were infinitely greater. They had suffered thousands of deaths during the epidemic of 1616–19 to the colonists' mere fifty-two in that first winter. They were subject to actual Narragansett raids compared with the colonists' speculative Indian threats. If the English viewed their tribulations as tests of faith, the Wampanoags' trials were all the more so. The English, after all, had the option of pulling up stakes and returning home to Europe, albeit to the Netherlands instead of England given the religious politics of the era. The Wampanoags already were home, fighting for the very survival of their people.

Those struggles would continue for generations to come, partly because epidemics continued to take an awful, if lesser, toll, but mostly because of Wampanoag exploitation by the colonists and their descendants. Given time and access to the natural resources that were their birthright, the Wampanoags likely would have been able to rebuild their numbers and reconstitute some semblance of life as they had once known it. But English colonization, celebrated by the Thanksgiving myth, did not permit this recovery. The colonists' engrossment of Wampanoag land, attacks on Wampanoag sovereignty, warfare against Wampanoags who resisted, and then reduction of Wampanoag survivors to servitude, near landlessness, and political impotency meant that the epidemic of 1616–19 was just the first of a relentless succession of blows that would have destroyed a less resilient people. The stunning losses of Indians to disease tell us something about why Europeans and their descendants managed to conquer not only New England but the rest of North America between the seventeenth and late nineteenth centuries. Yet disease does not come close to explaining it all. The introduction of epidemics to Native America was an accident. The bloody work of colonialism was not.[40]

There's a Wampanoag joke that goes: "Good thing for the English, or we'd all be speaking Narragansett right now." The dark humor, of course, is that, in the long term, life under English rule proved far worse for the Wampanoags than subjugation to the Narragansetts ever would have been. Furthermore, ultimately the Wampanoags and Narragansetts found themselves in the same colonial predicament, to the point that there were hardly any fluent Wampanoag- and Narragansett-language speakers left by the late nineteenth and twentieth centuries. Yet no one in 1620 could have envisioned this distant future. Their concerns were more immediate and their short-term choices, including Ousamequin's outreach to the colonists of Plymouth, made sense under those urgent pressures. Getting beyond the sanitized Thanksgiving myth to tell a more accurate history of that encounter involves reckoning with a point made by many Wampanoags today: that their storied welcome to the English was a terrible mistake, born out of the horror of a disease without a name.

CHAPTER FOUR

ん.

Reaching Out to Strangers

One of the main points of dramatic tension in the Thanksgiving myth hinges on the Wampanoags avoiding the *Mayflower* passengers for months even as the English searched desperately for them in hopes of trading for food and, the myth would have it, to make friends. Aside from one minor military confrontation shortly after the colonists' landing, the Natives appear only sporadically and always at a distance, fleeing as soon as the English become even slightly aware of their presence. No cause is given for their trepidation, but the implication is that this was a first contact episode and that they were intimidated by the mere appearance of strangers with such odd clothing and technology and fearful that they might be gods or demons. Yet even the most superficial versions of this tale contain evidence that the Wampanoags already had a history with Europeans. Midway through the story, an Indian named Samoset approaches the colonists to utter the famous words, "Welcome Englishman," in the English language. Soon he is followed by another friendly English-speaking Indian, Squanto, beginning several rounds of diplomacy that culminate in the Wampanoag-English alliance and the Thanksgiving feast. No explanation is given for how Samoset and Squanto acquired their English-language skills or why the Natives had suddenly become so hospitable. It is as if God had intervened so the colony would survive.

Moving beyond the stock characters of the Thanksgiving myth in favor of a history peopled by three-dimensional Wampanoags reveals a much more dynamic and dramatic story. The real suspense in this historical encounter had nothing to do with whether the Wampanoags were innately friendly or hostile. Rather, it resulted from an informed debate within the Wampanoag ranks about whether to wipe out the strangers before they became a threat or to seek their trade goods and possibly military support. How could the Wampanoags not have been conflicted? After all, for decades, if not longer, one group of foreigners after another had appeared on the coast to peddle their wares only to begin murdering and slaving at the slightest provocation or nothing at all. The epidemic had deepened this well of distrust because there were good reasons to believe that Europeans had caused it and might very well do so again. At the same time, the depopulated Wampanoags needed allies to fend off the Narragansetts. The *Mayflower* band, armed with guns, swords, daggers, and potentially even weaponized disease, represented one possible answer. The Wampanoags also weighed the counsel of figures like Tisquantum and Epenow, who had been to England and back and therefore better understood the potential risks and rewards of reaching out to these people. The Thanksgiving myth is true to some degree: yes, the Wampanoags did initially shrink from the appearance of the Pilgrims. However, that was not because they were overawed by the mere appearance of strangers—quite the contrary. Based on experience, they were tending to their defenses, biding their time, watching, and calculating their next move.

The Thanksgiving myth also distorts history by making the famous feast the seal of the Wampanoag-English alliance and a symbol of colonial America. Yet, to the historical actors, the event was a minor affair compared with other milestones in their relationship. English records running hundreds of pages dedicate only a handful of lines to the legendary First Thanksgiving, and then only in passing. The Wampanoags do not appear to have put much stock in it either. Though Ousamequin's son Pumetacom later shamed colonial authorities for violating the principles of friendship they had pledged to his father, he never invoked the great dinner. Coming to terms with the deficiency of the Thanksgiving myth as history means acknowledging the relative unimportance of its main act. The alliance between the Wampanoags and Plymouth took shape around other, usually less palatable episodes in which the participants were always acutely aware of how quickly it could all degenerate into bloodshed.

STRANGERS AND THEIR STRANGE BEHAVIOR

The Wampanoags of Paomet and Nauset on the eastern reaches of Cape Cod would not have been surprised at the appearance of the *Mayflower*. After all, they had more experience with Europeans than any other Indians in southern New England. Yet this latest arrival would have struck them as odd in several respects. For one, the time of year was late. Typically, European vessels came in summer, when the Wampanoags had resettled along the coast to fish and plant. The *Mayflower*, by contrast, reached the Cape in November 1620, as winter was setting in, a month or so after most of the Wampanoags had left the exposed seashore for the shelter of inland tree stands and hills. Those Wampanoags still active on the coast probably had been tracking this ship since it entered their waters and would have wondered why it dropped anchor near Paomet after failing to pass through the shoals off Monomoyick. The *Mayflower*'s passengers included not only the usual array of men in their twenties, thirties, and forties but also women and children, the first Europeans of this sort the Wampanoags would have ever seen aside from the occasional cabin boy. While the *Mayflower* was moored, these women and children occasionally made appearances on the beach to wash clothing and stretch their sea legs while the men probed inland for fresh water and somewhere to settle. Up to this point, Wampanoags other than Tisquantum and Epenow could be forgiven for wondering if Europeans had any women.

Though the *Mayflower* carried a different cross section of Europeans than the usual roughnecks, there was no way for the Wampanoags to have known the religious impulse behind its mission. Most of the 102 passengers were a type of reformed Protestant known as Separatists. Though they certainly hoped to make a living in America, and perhaps even to strike it rich, their main purpose was to create a society where they and like-minded Christians could worship as they saw fit. They would have preferred to follow this course back home in England, but they could no longer do so because, as their denominational name alluded, they had disassociated with the Church of England, the only legal form of Christianity in the country. Their issues with the state church rested on two principles. First, Separatists believed that every congregation should be a completely self-governing voluntary association. This meant that it would consist only of believers dedicated to participation in a religious community, rather than of everyone living in the parish. The congregation itself, not any outside authority, would decide who its minister would be, how its services would be run, who could join, and how it would discipline its members. Separatists entrusted their congregations with these responsibilities because they limited membership to "visible saints," people who had evinced through word and deed that they were among the few precious souls God had chosen for salvation. Godly people were to be the foundation for a godly church.

The Church of England did not work this way at all. Its power flowed down from the king, through the archbishops and bishops he appointed and the ministers they appointed. All Englishmen and Englishwomen belonged to the church regardless of their religiosity and were bound by law to attend its services. The holy ordnance of the Lord's Supper remained open to everyone except the most egregious sinners, despite the risk of profanation. To Separatists, these features meant that the Church of England was not a true church. As they saw it, its organization was a violation of the biblical model of congregational independence practiced by the apostles; state control meant religious issues would be determined by politics, not biblical truth; and its lack of discipline made it so full of wickedness that there was hardly any room left for the godly. It was, in short, an offense to God rather than a monument to him.[1]

The Separatists' other issue with the Church of England was that, though it was Protestant, it retained too many features of the Catholic Church, which distracted from what they wanted to be the focus of their services: the biblically based sermon. Like other reformed Protestants, Separatists held up the scriptures as the very word of God. They expected all lay Christians, male and female, to be literate and well read in the vernacular Bible so as to guide themselves and their families by its teachings. Yet they also contended that a true understanding of the Bible required regular preaching by a university-trained minister, lest the uneducated go astray through ignorance or the devil. To this end, Separatists made the ministerial sermon the centerpiece of their worship. Anything that diverted attention from it had to go. This meant their meetinghouses and ministerial outfits were plain, without stained glass, statues, incense, crosses (which they considered false idols), or priestly vestments. There were to be no liturgies or set prayers as in the Church of England, for Separatists thought that these rote exercises deadened the spirit. Instead, Separatists favored "prophecying" in which congregants shared extemporaneous thoughts about their faith and asked follow-up questions to the minister's preaching. They certainly did not want government interference in what their ministers and the laity could and could not say in service, yet such was always a danger in any state church.

The Separatists felt the need to separate from the Church of England because they feared that continuing to adhere to its wooden rites alongside churchgoers and church officials demonstrating no more grace than a stump was a likelier ticket to hell than heaven. The very fate of their souls hung in the balance. In favoring such a clean break, they diverged from their reformed Protestant compatriots, the puritans, or Congregationalists, who went on to found Plymouth's neighboring colonies of Massachusetts, Connecticut, and New Haven. Congregationalists subscribed in principle to the goal of continuing to try to reform (or purify) the Church of England from within, though in practice they bucked its authority in ways great and small. Otherwise, puritans and Separatists agreed about most particulars, especially once they arrived in America and escaped the shadow of the king's ecclesiastical authorities.

America was not the first place the Separatists looked to pursue their religious experiment. In 1609 the core of the *Mayflower* group had fled religious persecution in the English midlands for the safety of the Dutch Republic, stopping temporarily in Amsterdam before relocating to the textile-manufacturing town of Leiden. Like so many other religious refugees from throughout western Europe who found sanctuary in the Netherlands, for several years they enjoyed freedom of worship while toiling for little profit in the cloth trades, carpentry, and printing, among other employments. Yet within a decade they had grown weary of Leiden and skeptical about their future there. A twelve-year truce between the Protestant Netherlands and Catholic Spain was scheduled to end in 1621, and with it the likelihood of a renewal of the terrible religious wars that had previously devastated the Low Countries. Within the Netherlands, factions of the Dutch Reformed Church were taking their theological disputes into the streets and threatening to drag resident foreigners into the fray. Not least of all, James I was using his influence over the Netherlands (for England was its main source of military support) to harry the Separatists overseas, including a crackdown on their printer and church elder William Brewster. Thus the Separatist leadership began exploring opportunities to leave Europe altogether, considering sites such as Guyana, Virginia, and even a proposed Dutch colony on the Hudson River later known as New Netherland. Ultimately, they contracted with a group of investors (called Adventurers) in London led by the merchant Thomas Weston to relocate to the Hudson under the title of the Virginia Company, the same entity behind the Jamestown colony. The terms were far from ideal: for the first several years of the colony, the migrants would have to turn over most of the profits from their work to their sponsors; additionally, they were required to bring along several "strangers"—most of them other English Separatists and their sympathizers—to bulk up their meager numbers. However reluctantly, the Leiden congregation agreed to this deal because it was the best one they could get and they were impatient to begin.[2]

The drawn-out negotiations and some false starts delayed their departure well into August, thus guaranteeing that they would arrive in America with the winter chill. And that was before the debacle that began their journey. Setting sail from Southampton, England, they made it just seventy-five miles before they had to put in for repairs at the port of Dartmouth, where contrary winds kept them stranded for days even after their transports were seaworthy again. Their next attempt carried them but two hundred miles into the Celtic Sea, when one of expedition's two ships, the *Speedwell*, began leaking so badly that it had to be abandoned. The *Mayflower* accompanied it all the way back to Plymouth, England—a mere fifty miles west of Dartmouth—so it could squeeze as many of the stranded *Speedwell* passengers as possible into what was already a crowded vessel. It was early September before they could shove off again, and

Adam Willaerts, *Inscheping van een militaire eenheid aan een rivieroever*
[Embarkation of a Military Unit on a Riverbank], 1620. Courtesy of RKD—
Netherlands Institute for Art History.

This painting by the Dutch artist Adam Willaerts is thought to depict
English Separatists leaving their refuge in the Netherlands
for England in preparation for their voyage to America, where they
would found Plymouth colony.

with their numbers reduced to just 102, the remaining voyagers
knew that they had received a double blow to the chances of their
colony surviving. Packed in cheek by jowl, they tumbled for two
months across waters so violent that the ship's mast cracked and had
to be held together by a screw for the rest of the crossing. It was as if
God were testing whether the self-proclaimed saints had as much
faith as they claimed.

Still, they persevered, only to make landfall well north of the
Hudson at Cape Cod, where they had no authorization to settle.
They tried to continue south toward their chartered bounds, but
after encountering the ship-eating shoals of Pollock Rip near Monomoyick, they decided to turn back and end their exhausting journey

there, dropping anchor on November 11 in Provincetown Harbor at the northeast tip of the Cape. Bobbing up and down, with the vast ocean to one side and a sweeping expanse of sand dunes and scrub trees to the other, they huddled together to give thanks to God for their safe arrival. Yet all the while they must have been stalked by the fear that they had sent themselves on a suicide mission.

The Wampanoags probably knew they were there from the beginning. When the English sent out a small exploratory party on November 15, they immediately spied five or six Wampanoags and a dog walking along the beach at a distance. The Natives must have been there to keep an eye on this latest ship to reach their shores. Yet they had no interest in meeting these newcomers face-to-face and exposing themselves to the risk of being hauled off into overseas captivity or worse. Instead, when the English hailed them, they ran

Aerial view of Provincetown Harbor. Courtesy of the Northeast Fisheries Science Center, National Oceanic and Atmospheric Administration.

This modern aerial photograph of Provincetown Harbor, where the *Mayflower* first anchored in America, captures the stark maritime landscape even four centuries later.

in the opposite direction, prompting a chase that lasted nearly ten miles before the newcomers finally gave up. Nothing the colonists did over the next few days gave the Indians any reason to regret their decision. Trudging through the Wampanoags' summer villages and burial grounds, these strangers rummaged houses, unearthed graves, and picked through the funerary offerings, even though, as the English admitted, "we thought it would be odious unto them to ransack their sepulchers." Just what they hoped to accomplish with this desecration is unclear. Probably they were looking for evidence of the country's wealth and confirmation of their prejudices about Indian idolatry. Whatever the case, they consoled themselves that putting everything back where they found it would ease the affront.[3]

Their consciences did not prevent them from defiling yet more graves a few days later. This time the cemetery was more clearly marked, and one of the burials was "much bigger and longer than any we had yet seen. It was also covered with boards, so as we mused [wondered] what it should be . . . resolved to dig it up." The English were astonished at what they found. Under several layers of woven mats and goods was a bundle made out of "a sailor's canvass cassock, and a pair of cloth britches," or, in other words, European material. Inside was "a great quantity of fine and perfect red powder" made of ochre to symbolize rebirth into the afterlife, along with "a knife, a pack needle, and two or three old iron things." Yet the greatest surprise, which must have produced a collective gasp, was a skull with "fine yellow hair on it, and some of the flesh unconsumed." It would appear that some European, whether one of the aforementioned shipwrecked French sailors or a refugee from one of a dozen other expeditions, had received his burial rites from the Natives. And he was not alone. An accompanying package contained "the bones and head of a little child." Probably the mystery European had lived with the Cape Wampanoags and sired a son with one of their women before his death, thus earning the privilege of having his remains treated respectfully. The English, however, were uncertain how to explain what they were seeing. "Some thought it was an Indian lord and king," their account relates. "Others said the Indians have all black hair and never any was seen with brown or yellow hair. Some thought it was a Christian of some special note, which had died among them, and they thus buried him to honor him. Others thought they had killed him, and did it in triumph over him." The anxiety in this conversation is palpable even at the distance of four centuries. Given that the English had already shown their contempt for Wampanoags alive and dead, they had good reason to be nervous.[4]

Days before, this company had stumbled on another sign of previous European activity in the form of "the remains of an old fort, or palisade, which as we conceived had been made by some Christians." They would have known the difference between a European palisade made with iron-edged tools for defense by gunners and a Native one fashioned with stone instruments for bowmen. After all, their ranks included Miles Standish, who had extensive military experience in the Netherlands, and Stephen Hopkins, who had lived briefly in Jamestown in close contact with the Powhatan Indians. What they did not know was that this fort had probably been left by the 1603 Pring expedition after the Wampanoags set fire to the woods to drive the English away. It was yet another sign of the already deep and troubled history of Wampanoag-European relations of which the *Mayflower* passengers were about to become a part.[5]

If the English had been less conditioned to see the Wampanoags, as William Bradford put it, as "savage people, who are cruel, barbarous, and most treacherous," they might have taken a moment to consider what the dual symbols of the Pring fort and the European burial meant for the colony's future. There was no way to tell, of course, whether the blond-haired skull had belonged to an unwilling captive or a grateful rescue from a shipwreck. However, he clearly had become part of the community in the last phase of his life, forming a romantic relationship with one of the people's women, fathering a son with her, and becoming part of her family. In other words, playing by the Wampanoags' rules and contributing to their well-being were steps toward becoming kin with them. The rotting palisade, by contrast, was an artifact of an expedition gone wrong. Initially, Pring's men had participated in trade and even shared music making and dancing with the Wampanoags, but eventually they bullied their Wampanoag hosts as if Europeans' imaginary distinction between civilized and savage people was real. Pring's abandoned fortification was but one of many pieces of evidence from the recent past in which the Wampanoags gave lie to European claims of superiority, including the right to act as if the Natives' country were their own. The Pilgrims should have taken it as a warning.[6]

Instead, their next move was to loot the Wampanoags' stockpiles of food. Finding several heaps of sand interspersed among the Natives' planting fields and house sites, the English set to digging and discovered underground storage pits containing "diverse fair Indian baskets filled with corn, some in ears, fair and good, of diverse colors," amounting to three or four bushels. They carried away as much as they could in one of the Indians' copper kettles, which they also stole, then returned to the place two days later to thieve another seven bushels. The English credited "God's good providence" for this supposed discovery, explaining that because they had nothing to plant the next year, "they might have starved" if they had not taken this measure. Presumably, such a justification would not have satisfied the Wampanoags, who had devoted numerous hours of labor to producing this seed corn for their own people's use. Now they would have to go hungry so the English could eat. Certainly they also resented the English rifling their abandoned summer homes. The English mentioned sorting through the Wampanoags' "wooden bowls, trays and dishes, earthen pots, handbaskets made of crab shells wrought together, also an English pail or bucket." Worse still, "some of the best things we took away with us, and left the houses standing still as they were," as if restraining themselves from stealing the structures somehow mitigated the theft of what was inside. Just days into their American venture, the English had already established themselves as rotten guests.[7]

No wonder, then, that two and half weeks later, when the *Mayflower* sent out another armed expedition to look for a place to settle, a band of Wampanoags attacked. Amid "very cold and hard weather," ten Englishmen in a shallop sailed south along the inner Cape and landed somewhere near the so-called First Encounter Beach in modern Eastham. They had hoped to communicate with ten or twelve Wampanoags they had spied carving up some stranded blackfish (or pilot whales) for blubber, but the Indians were gone by the time they made it to shore. With the hour getting late, the English decided to spend the night camped on the beach behind a makeshift three-sided barricade of logs and branches, and then continue their search the next day. The Wampanoags, however, had different ideas. Sometime around midnight "a hideous and great cry" startled the newcomers awake, prompting the sentinel to shout "Arm! Arm!" and the men to fire their muskets blindly into the dark. Yet, by the time the gun smoke drifted away, there was nothing more to be heard than breaking waves. Breathing a sigh of relief, the English convinced themselves that the sound had been just "a company of wolves or such like wild beasts."[8]

They were dead wrong. At daybreak, the "dreadful" howl arose again, this time followed by a shower of arrows. "Men, Indians! Indians!" the English hollered as they rushed to fire and reload their muskets and strap on their armor. Most of the attackers dispersed when the English rushed out of the barricade, swords at the ready, but one "lusty man, and no less valiant" continued launching arrows at them from behind a tree just some twenty-five yards away. He stood his ground as three musket balls whizzed by him until a fourth shot "made the tree fly about his ears, after which he gave an extraordinary shriek and away they went, all of them." Apparently, none of the Wampanoags were hurt, nor were any of the English, though "sundry of their coats . . . were shot through and through." This terrifying incident, combined with the lack of a deepwater harbor on the Cape, was enough to convince the English to look elsewhere to establish their settlement. Once again, a Wampanoag show of force was shaping the course of colonial development, contrary to the mythology of European dominance.[9]

CONJURATIONS AND SALUTATIONS

If the Wampanoags assumed that they had repulsed another reconnaissance of their territory, they were mistaken. The English did not abandon Wampanoag country but merely shifted their attention to another part of it, the site of the village of Patuxet, from which Tisquantum hailed, just north of the Cape. The suggestion to look there came from an unidentified pilot of the *Mayflower* who had visited New England previously. He remembered Patuxet as a place of good anchorage and by the name of "Thievish Harbor . . . because that one of the wild men with whom they had some trucking [trade] stole a harping iron [harpoon] from them." The Separatists also might have made their decision after consulting Thomas Dermer's report of his 1619 journey to New England, which appeared just before the *Mayflower* began its voyage. In it, Dermer told that Patuxet's open fields, freshwater sources, defensible hills, and good anchorage were free for the taking because the recent epidemic had all but wiped out the inhabitants. "The first plantation might here be seated," he emphasized, with just "the number of fifty persons or upwards." Dermer proved correct. The Pilgrims found the harbor to be lined with "a great deal of land cleared, and hath been planted with corn three or four years ago." Sure enough, no one was there to contest this place. A coastal march of seven or eight miles turned up "not an Indian nor an Indian house." If the English wanted to settle where they would not have to fight for a beachhead, this so-called Thievish Harbor looked like the spot. They immediately gave it the new name of "Plymouth" rather than suffer a constant reminder of their own thievish behavior on the Cape.[10]

Patuxet might not have hosted a Wampanoag village any longer, but in warmer weather the people continued to resort there for fishing and shellfishing, and the surrounding country was more populated than the English appreciated. In other words, "Plymouth" remained very much a part of Wampanoag territory. Nevertheless, the Wampanoags generally steered clear of the new colonial settlement during its first couple of months, which was fortunate for the English because they were in no condition to defend themselves. Malnutrition and disease took a terrible toll on them over the winter, sweeping away half of their number and rendering a portion of the survivors too weak to perform basic labor. At times, there were just six or seven people capable of tending to all the rest under conditions that offered no comfort. Most of the colonists still had to spend nights on the drafty *Mayflower*, anchored out in the harbor, while others huddled in what few rudimentary structures they had been able to erect onshore, with nothing else to defend them in the event of an Indian raid. At the same time, Plymouth, like most infant colonies, faced the real prospect of starvation unless the Indians supplied it with food, and fast. Yet how likely were the Wampanoags to do so voluntarily? After all, this English band, never mind its predecessors, had already desecrated the Wampanoags' graves, plundered their

houses, stolen their seed corn, and fired on their men. The sick, shiv-
ering, and hungry colonists were left to wait out the seemingly
endless New England winter tormented with doubt about whether
their own ill-advised behavior toward the Natives had already
doomed their experiment and perhaps their lives.[11]

The Wampanoags were equally frightened of the colonists, if
also drawn to them by the potential for trade and alliance. Many
years after the fact, Wampanoags recalled that the appearance of
the *Mayflower* renewed a debate begun during the plague about the
meaning of a curse put on them by one of their French slaves: "that
God was angry with them for their wickedness, and would destroy
them, and give their country to another people." Some Wampanoags
already blamed the Frenchman's sorcery for the terrible sickness.
Now, with the appearance of the English, "several of the Indians
began to mind the Frenchman's words, thinking him to be more than
an ordinary man." Some Wampanoags, as they later admitted, favored
wiping out the newcomers before they turned into the conquerors of
the prophecy. Dissenters probably countered that there was no way of
knowing what horrors a rash attack might unleash, and that it was
best to proceed cautiously to discover just who these people were,
what they wanted, and what they had to offer.[12]

The moderates got the better of the argument, prompting the
Wampanoags to keep the colony under constant watch from a safe
distance, of which the English were all too aware. On December 24
and 25, Plymouth's watch sounded the alarm after hearing "a cry of
some savages" in the distance. Just a couple of days later, there were
"great smokes of fire made by the Indians about six or seven miles
from us." Then, in February, the Wampanoags grew considerably
bolder. On the ninth, an Englishman went ashore from the *Mayflower*
and discovered "a good deer killed" with its antlers removed. The
following week, a colonist stalking fowl from a camouflage of reeds

observed "twelve Indians marching towards our plantation, and in the woods he heard the noise of many more." The hunter rushed back to warn the others, but when the English sent a party to search the area, there was no one to be found, though some of the colony's tools had gone missing. The very next day, two Wampanoags appeared on a nearby hill, about a quarter of a mile off, and signaled for the English to come to them. Yet, when Standish and Hopkins took up the invitation, with Standish laying his musket on the ground as a sign of peace, the Native envoys lost heart and withdrew behind the hill, where "a noise of a great many more [Indians] was heard." Clearly, the Wampanoags were testing this odd winter settlement of foreigners.[13]

Bradford's understanding was that before the Wampanoag sachem, Ousamequin, finally reached out to the English, all the pawwaws from around the country gathered in a "dark and dismal swamp" for a three-day ceremony "to curse and execrate them [the English] with their conjurations," but his interpretation must be taken lightly. After all, Bradford considered the pawwaws to be "horrid and devilish" agents of Indian idolatry, which blinded him to the meanings of their actions. He could not have known that the Wampanoags considered swamps portals for shapeshifting spirits to pass back and forth through the three layers of the universe, underworld, earth, and sky. The pawwaws' own tutelary spirit, the horned underwater serpent, and its alter ego, the panther, would have been especially strong in such a place. True, this force gave the pawwaws' the ability to curse, but also to prognosticate and protect, services that any Wampanoag leader would have wanted to employ before undertaking a risky diplomatic mission to unpredictable strangers. There is no way to know what these shamans intended when they met in advance of Ousamequin's outreach to the English. The only certainty is that the Wampanoags saw the mission as rife with double-edged spiritual and political possibilities. The image of friendly Indians in the Thanksgiving myth ignores the angst of Wampanoag councils in the run-up to this famous moment. Rather than treat the Wampanoags as lifelike figures struggling with a historic decision, the myth reduces them to an unthreatening caricature, the better to have them hand off America to the English and then get out of the way.[14]

The Thanksgiving myth also distorts history in its depiction of the Wampanoags as naive, for when they finally made direct contact with the English on March 16, 1621, every step they took was informed by their previous encounters with dangerous, unpredictable Europeans. Take, for example, their first ambassador to the English, named Samoset. Samoset was not a resident of Wampanoag country at all but a visitor from the Abenakis around Boothbay Harbor and Monhegan Island in Maine, a people with decades of experience hosting European fishing and exploratory vessels. Apparently, Samoset had expertise as a point man in Abenaki relations with Europeans, which involved brokering trade and diplomacy and guiding visiting ships around Maine's rocky shoals. It is possible that he was one and the same with Sassacomit, one of the Abenakis taken captive to England by George Waymouth in 1605, then captured again on a return journey home, this time by the Spanish, before finally being redeemed by Sir Ferdinando Gorges and sent back to Maine. If so, such a background might help explain what Samoset was doing with Ousamequin in March 1621, insofar as the sachem might have sent for him to help deal with the strangers. Consider also the chance that Samoset was Wampanoag or Massachusett in origin, given that the English understood Sassacomit to have been a "servant"—that is, captive—of the Abenakis when Waymouth seized him. Whatever the case, during his shadowy past Samoset had developed some facility in the English language. His name might not have been of Abenaki origin at all but an Algonquian pronunciation of an English nickname, Somerset, which he used when dealing with Europeans. (At the same time, the opposite might be true, that the English called him Somerset because it approximated his indigenous name, Samoset.) Having become, in effect, a professional intercultural emissary, he showed little hesitation in dealing with the strangers at Patuxet, as he walked "boldly" into the colonists' settlement and then "saluted us in English, and bade us welcome." The English sat there, mouths agape, and "marveled at it" before they were able to gather their wits and return the greeting. It was finally time for the two peoples to talk.[15]

PEACE OR WAR?

The equipment Samoset carried, "a bow and two arrows, the one headed and the other unheaded," contained a question and a warning. It meant to ask if the English intended peace or war and to emphasize that the Wampanoags were ready for either likelihood. Yet Samoset was too skillful a diplomat to broach the issue directly. Instead, he put the newcomers at ease by asking for beer but settling for some "strong water" and a characteristically English meal of cheese, butter, pudding, and fowl. Only after a stiff drink did the conversation begin flowing. Samoset explained that he hailed "from the east, where the English fish," and could even "name various of the fishermen." For reasons he did not divulge, he had been in Wampanoag country for the past eight months—or, in other words, from around the time that Epenow sprang his assault on Dermer, raising the possibility that Samoset was there to advise Ousamequin during the fallout. Samoset claimed to know all the sachems and their followers, including Tisquantum, "who had been in England and could speak better English than himself." As to the question of where all these Indians were, Samoset "told us the place where we now live is called Patuxet, and that about four years ago all the inhabitants died of an extraordinary plague."[16]

Nevertheless, the colony was still surrounded by Wampanoags in diminished but significant numbers. Their most important sachem was Ousamequin, or Massasoit, whose people, according to Samoset, were "sixty strong." Just what he meant by that number is uncertain. It probably referred to the matawaûog of Ousamequin's local sachemship of Pokanoket, rather than the full array of bowmen the sachem could call on from other localities. The Nausets, from the outer Cape, were reportedly "a hundred strong," a point Samoset emphasized because they were "much incensed and provoked against English" after years of violent clashes with explorers. Political niceties kept Samoset from addressing the colonists' theft of the Nausets' corn and desecration of their graves as additional causes of the people's anger. However, no one missed the hint when he mentioned that the Nausets recently "slew three Englishmen" in an incident (probably the attack on Dermer) that drove two of the English survivors to Samoset's own Monhegan Island. The colonists, lest they appear intimidated, retorted that they were aggrieved, too, by the Wampanoags' theft of their tools and that if the items were not returned "we should right ourselves." They must have known, however, that in their weakness they had no chance of forcing their will on the much more numerous Wampanoags. The colony's only hope of survival rested on productive diplomatic relations.[17]

The key, of course, was for Samoset to arrange a meeting between the English and Ousamequin. To that end, the colonists reluctantly conceded to the interpreter's wish to spend the night with them, all the while keeping him under close watch. The next morning, they presented him with a knife, bracelet, and ring to deliver to the sachem. Samoset returned a day later, this time accompanied by "five other proper tall men" (who must have been stationed nearby the entire time), all dressed in deerskins, one with a wildcat fur draped over one arm. The emissaries signaled their desire for "friendship and amity" by leaving their weapons outside the settlement and greeting their counterparts with a song and dance, which were basic features of Indian protocol, however strange the English found them. Furthermore, they returned the colonists' stolen tools and presented four or five beaver skins to trade. The English were not ready to conduct business at this very moment, but they promised that soon they would buy all the furs the Wampanoags had. The Wampanoags' offer was the first sign that the colony might become economically viable.[18]

Despite the Wampanoags' overtures, their men's face paint cautioned the English about the fine line between peace and war. "Some of them had their faces painted black," the colonists observed, "from the forehead to the chin, four or five fingers broad." The color black, as the symbol of death, was a pigment for men who had ritually entered a warrior state. Like Samoset's two arrows, one sharply tipped and the other blunted, it was meant to emphasize the fragility of these negotiations.[19]

Fragile indeed. Samoset stayed with the English for the next five days, claiming to be too ill to travel, even as his Wampanoag colleagues departed to report back to the sachem. Once Samoset recovered, he left to fetch Tisquantum, with whom he returned the next day. Yet, during his absence, two Wampanoags appeared outside the English settlement and "made a semblance of daring us," in which they "whetted and rubbed their arrows and strings, and made a show of defiance," only to retreat when confronted by Standish at the head of an armed English party. Over and over again, the Wampanoags were asking: Peace or war?[20]

Handing over the reins of interpretation to Tisquantum, Samoset made his exit and apparently returned home, but it would not be the last time he entered the historical record. Three years later, the English naval officer Christopher Levett told that during his exploration of Boothbay Harbor on the Maine coast, he encountered one "Somerset, a sagamore [or sachem], one that has been very faithful to the English, and has saved the lives of many of our nation, some from starving, others from killing." True to form, Samoset took the lead in brokering Levett's relations with the coastal Abenakis. It was just a glimpse of what must have been a much larger role played by Samoset during an earlier period of Indian-European contact in Maine, but otherwise lost to the vagaries of the historical record.[21]

Back in Wampanoag country, Tisquantum picked up where Samoset left off, arriving at the colony on March 22 along with three other Wampanoags who carried beaver to trade and dried herring as a gift. They told that Ousamequin, his brother Quadaquina, and their men would arrive soon. The English were just as stunned by Tisquantum's life story as they had been with Samoset's, learning of his enslavement and escape, and his contacts with men like Dermer and John Slaney, whom some of the colonists knew personally. At this point, Tisquantum struggled with his English-language skills, but they returned in force as he exercised them over the next several months. Bradford viewed him as "a special instrument sent of God for their good beyond expectation," which is how the Thanksgiving myth portrays him. Yet eventually Tisquantum had greater ambitions than to serve as a mere translator between Wampanoag and English leaders. He wanted his own seat at the table, which would prompt both the English and Ousamequin to question whether divine blessings had anything to do with his role.[22]

If the colonists had been more attuned to Wampanoag culture, Tisquantum's very name might have tipped them off that he was even more than he appeared, which was saying something. Tisquantum was one of the names the Wampanoags used for their god of the dead, also known as Cheepi and Hobbamock, whom the English associated with the devil. Precisely what the name signified in

Tisquantum's case is uncertain, but it might have represented that he was a Wampanoag *pniese*, a special class of warrior who guarded the sachem, collected his tribute, and counseled him, particularly on matters of war. A young man became a pniese in the same manner that one became a pawwaw, by experiencing a vision of the god of the dead. Thereafter, he boasted special spiritual protection against bodily wounds and demonstrated "courage and wisdom . . . and boldness, by reason whereof one of them will chase almost a hundred men." Pnieseosok (the plural of *pniese*) were also known for being exceptionally "discreet, courteous, and humane," or, as the English might have put it, gentlemen. Tisquantum's name might also have reflected his transformative crossing of the Atlantic, the watery threshold of the god of the dead, and miraculous return home. He had become a new man, boasting linguistic and cultural skills that enabled him to pass back and forth between different human societies, like the shapeshifting horned underwater serpent and panther alternating between water, earth, and sky. Whatever the case, Tisquantum's name, like his brief career with Plymouth, suggested that he drew on special sources of power. The colony would soon find itself dependent on his talents.[23]

ENTER OUSAMEQUIN

With Ousamequin's arrival, it became clear that the colonists, regardless of their claims to sovereignty in America, were guests of the much more numerous and powerful Wampanoag people. An hour after Tisquantum's introduction to the English, Ousamequin appeared atop a nearby hill accompanied by sixty armed men. The sachem was dressed no differently from the others except that he wore "a great chain of white bone [or shell] beads about this neck" to represent light, truth, and peace. The paint on his face was not black like the members of the earlier delegation, but "a sad [or deep]

American Native American Sachem, ca. 1700. Gift of Mr. Robert Winthrop 48.246. Photography by Erik Gould, courtesy of the Museum of Art, Rhode Island School of Design, Providence.

There are no contemporary images of Ousamequin, his sons Wamsutta and Pumetacom, or any other New England sachems during the seventeenth century. However, this unidentified portrait from around the year 1700 clearly depicts someone of high status, as indicated by the subject's wampum headband, earring, and necklace, and the fact that someone judged him important enough to memorialize. English sources mentioned the Wampanoag sachems wearing similar adornments.

red," symbolizing blood, intense emotion, and the animating forces of life and war. Along similar lines, around his neck hung "a great knife on a string," ready for combat. The other men had their faces painted, too, "some red, some yellow, and some white, some with crosses, and other antic [grotesque] work." The lot of them, the English could not help but notice, were "all strong, tall, all men in appearance."[24]

For some time, the two sides just stared at each other, with Ousamequin unwilling to demean himself by approaching first, and the Plymouth governor, John Carver, likewise standing his ground. Eventually, Tisquantum broke the stalemate, bringing the English word from the Wampanoag camp that they should send someone to parlay with the sachem. Their choice was Edward Winslow, who apparently qualified for this mission by virtue of his experience as a printer who had published other Europeans' narratives about their contacts with exotic overseas people. Wisely, he began with an offer of gifts, including two knives and a copper chain with a jewel in it for Ousamequin, and a knife, a jewel, a pot of liquor, and some biscuit and butter for Quadaquina. English speeches followed, to which Ousamequin paid close attention, though it appeared that "the interpreters did not well express it."[25]

Nevertheless, these exchanges had generated enough mutual confidence to proceed with formal talks. Each side produced hostages as a guarantee of peaceful behavior, with Winslow staying under Quadaquina's watch, and six or seven Wampanoags placing themselves still under English guard. Meanwhile, Ousamequin and the rest of his men set aside their bows and arrows and entered the settlement, with Standish and an armed escort leading them to one of the houses under construction. The English did their best to create some sense of majesty under their modest circumstances, sitting the sachem down on a green rug and some cushions, then having trumpeters and drummers announce the arrival of Governor Carver. Given that the colonists were inexperienced in diplomacy and improvising each step, these displays must have come off as awkward. Carver did all he could to communicate his warm intentions, kissing the sachem's hand (which Ousamequin reciprocated), then serving him strong drink and meat. Soon, Ousamequin began trembling, which the English attributed to fear instead of realizing that this was probably the first time he had ever consumed alcohol. For his part, Ousamequin offered the colonists some of his tobacco from a bag hanging around his neck, a strain of the weed that was much more potent than any Caribbean leaf the English would have tried back in Europe. A few draws of the smoke, presumably from Ousamequin's stone council pipe, must have made them dizzy, too.[26]

Traditional accounts emphasize that this meeting produced a written treaty of seven principles, but one must be careful not to assume that Ousamequin understood the agreement as the colonists did. The English themselves worried that Samoset and Tisquantum were incapable of interpreting their words as precisely as one would want in a diplomatic setting. Another issue was that what the colonists recorded and published was intended for readers back in the home country so they would contribute money, people, and political capital to the colony. Thus one might assume that they cast these negotiations in a light most favorable to them. Finally, there was the basic matter that political terms such as "confederate," "friend," "ally," "subject," and the like are culturally specific. Therefore, the Wampanoags and English probably attributed different meanings to these words, however literally translated.

Consider, then, how the parties might have interpreted the following clauses of their "agreement." The first was "that neither he [Ousamequin] nor any of his should injure or do hurt to any of our people." It would seem obvious for Ousamequin to agree to this principle, though doubtlessly he insisted that the colonists should also refrain from injuring or hurting any of the Wampanoags, a provision that did not make its way into print. The second point was "if any of his did hurt to any of ours, he should send the offender, that we might punish him." It is inconceivable that Ousamequin assented to this condition knowingly or at least with any intention of abiding by it. The English, after all, were guests in his country, not he in theirs. Furthermore, sachems did not wield the authority to extradite their people to foreigners. Any sachem who dared to make such an attempt would at best drive away his alienated followers to another leader or lose his title. At worst, it would get him killed. Following this treaty, there was not a single case of Ousamequin ever turning over fellow Wampanoags to face English justice. Yet there are multiple examples from throughout seventeenth-century New England of sachems insisting that they alone had the right to punish the wrongdoings committed by their people—that is, unless the crime was committed in an English settlement. The first time the English demanded Indians to hand over their own kind to answer for crimes committed in Indian territory, it led to the Pequot War of 1636–37. They did not press the issue again for another forty years, but when they did by arresting, trying, and executing three Wampanoags without the consent of their sachem, Ousamequin's son Pumetacom, it became the last straw leading to the bloody King Philip's War of 1675–76. Thus there is no chance that Ousamequin ever intended to abide by the extradition clause of his treaty with the English, and it is unlikely that he ever agreed to it in the first place. It was telling of the actual balance of power that Plymouth did not dare put the matter to the test until everyone who had been present at the signing of the treaty was long since dead and gone.[27]

The remaining treaty terms are also a mix of seemingly straightforward points of agreement mixed with miscommunication. The third clause committed the Wampanoags and English alike to restore any goods stolen from the opposite party, which seems simple enough. Equally clear-cut is the fourth clause, that "if any did unjustly war against him [Ousamequin], we would aid him; if any did war against us, he should aid us." In addition to establishing trade, this mutual defense pact was the fundamental diplomatic goal for both parties, vulnerable as they were to rival tribes and European nations alike. Ousamequin said frankly that he was "willing to have peace with us" largely "because he has a potent adversary in the Narragansetts, that are at war with him, against whom he thinks we may be of some strength to him, for our pieces [guns] are terrible to them." He also wanted English weaponry for his own men, as when he gestured to Winslow to give him his sword and armor. The answer for the meantime was no, but eventually the arms trade became one of the colonists' most important services to the Wampanoags. That possibility did not mean that the English held the advantage in negotiations. Ousamequin had also demonstrated that he was "the greatest commander amongst the savages bordering upon us," as the English put it, capable of mobilizing dozens of matawaûog on short notice. Just as he wanted to employ the colonists' guns in his defense, so would the colonists benefit from the Wampanoags' protection. At the same time, if the English proved unfriendly, Ousamequin might turn his men against them, as everyone at Plymouth was fully aware. They also knew how badly the colony of Jamestown had fared during its early years because of hostility with the Powhatans. They did not want their tiny settlement to suffer the same fate or worse.[28]

The fifth clause had implications beyond what the English understood. It obligated Ousamequin to "send to his neighbor confederates, to certify them of this [agreement], that they might not wrong us, but might be likewise comprised in the conditions of peace." The English did not fully grasp that Ousamequin was not a "king" with the authority to dictate to his confederate sachems or, for that matter, his own followers. Certainly, he received their deference by virtue of his lineage, personal achievements, and special abilities, particularly when it came to foreign affairs and war, but local sachems retained the option of going their own way when they disagreed with him, just as Ousamequin had the choice of trying to force them into compliance. In other words, what Ousamequin agreed to do was try to persuade other Wampanoags to honor his policy of rapprochement with the English. The English could not conceive what a challenge that would be for him.[29]

The two final clauses were equally fraught. The sixth obligated the Wampanoags "that when their men came to us, they should leave their bows and arrows behind them, as we should do our pieces [guns] when we came to them." The Wampanoags did not need this stipulation. It was already their custom to put their weapons aside in any diplomatic setting, both as a symbol of peaceful intentions and as a safeguard against heated disagreements turning bloody. The English were the real issue, as evident in their soldiers remaining armed and at the ready during these negotiations. Afterward, Quadaquina expressed his offense at this breach of etiquette, saying "he was very fearful of our pieces, and made signs of dislike, that they should be carried away." The English complied for the time being, but this issue continued to plague their relations with the Wampanoags in the future.[30]

The final article pronounced that because of Ousamequin's consent to this treaty, "King James would esteem of him as his friend and ally." Of course, Ousamequin did not know King James personally and had no understanding of the European concept of kingship. Whatever information Ousamequin had about James would have come from Tisquantum, who probably would have likened him to a great sachem across the ocean. Given that friendship with James seemed to carry no real risk or obligation, but did seem to curry favor with the English colonists, Ousamequin might be forgiven if he assumed there was no risk in giving his assent. Little did he know that over the course of his lifetime and especially those of his sons, Wamsutta and Pumetacom, the English would try to redefine friendship with the king as subjection to his colonists. For now, however, that threat was as inconceivable as it was remote.[31]

A written treaty, which was entirely alien to the Wampanoags, would have meant less to them than demonstrations of friendship by the English. In this, the colonists did not get off to a good start. They denied not only Ousamequin's request for them to give him Winslow's sword and armor, but also Quadaquina's wish to have two of his men spend the night in Plymouth while the rest of the Wampanoags camped a half mile off. These issues, combined with the colonists' display of arms, revealed that these newcomers still had little trust for their hosts.

SLEEPOVER

Thus, much was at stake in July 1621 when the English sent a delegation consisting of Winslow and Hopkins, escorted by Tisquantum, to visit Ousamequin's village of Sowams and present the sachem "with some gratuity to bind him the faster unto them [the English]," including "a suit of clothes and a horseman's coat with some small things." At the same time, they also hoped to negotiate an end to the stream of Wampanoags who had been dropping by Plymouth ever since the March treaty. Not only did these visitors stress the colony's food supplies, but the English also feared them as a potential security threat. Different cultural expectations were also at play in this issue. Whereas the Wampanoags thought of the treaty as part of a more general friendship between entire peoples that entitled both parties to hospitality at the other's settlements, the English considered it an agreement between leaders restricted to the official terms. In an attempt to restrict the number of Wampanoags who made unan- nounced visits to Plymouth to just Ousamequin or his agents, Winslow and Hopkins intended to present the sachem with a copper chain for his ambassadors to wear whenever they came on diplomatic business. Finally, the colony wanted to ask Ousamequin to help them make satisfaction for their theft of their corn and beans the previous winter, before any trouble came of it.[32]

This was the first time any of the colonists had journeyed deeply into Wampanoag country, and, as such, it served as an education for them. The first stop was Nemasket, an inland village at the conflu- ence of the Nemasket and Taunton Rivers and one of the best shad fishing sites in the region. The English had assumed this village was located close to Plymouth because its residents visited so frequently, particularly when they were heading to and from the harbor to collect lobsters. As it turned out, Nemasket was twelve miles away. Staying at the village overnight, Winslow and Hopkins delighted their hosts by firing their gun at a crow some eighty yards off, after which the Wampanoags would not leave them alone until they did it again. The next day, following a road southwest along the Taunton,

Winslow and Hopkins confronted the haunting evidence of the 1616–19 epidemic in the form of empty fields and abandoned home-steads. Yet they also witnessed the Wampanoags carrying on with their lives, fishing at a great weir in the river, hauling baskets of shell-fish from the seashore, feasting on meals of corn, cornbread, and shad. Through such experiences, some Englishmen were beginning to see their Wampanoag neighbors as something more fully human than just savages of the wilderness. Unfortunately, there would always be too few colonists enlightened in this way.[33]

This journey also began to reveal that Tisquantum had ambi-tions beyond serving as an interpreter and go-between in Wampanoag-English relations. When the travelers arrived at Sowams, Ousamequin was out fishing and so had to be summoned back. Tisquantum advised Winslow and Hopkins to welcome the sachem home with an honorary salute from their muskets. Tisquantum had learned during his travels abroad that it was customary for Europeans to greet their leaders with gunfire and trumpets. Yet he also knew that the Wampanoags, at this juncture, were terrified of firearms. Already, at least a score of them had fallen to the shots of European explorers. The explosion, flash, and smoke of the weapons were alarming. It is also possible that the Wampanoags associated this strange technology with disease. The Narragansett word for gun, *pésckunk*, translates as "thunderstick," meaning that these tools contained the power of the Thunderbird, the analog of the underwater serpent who gave pawwaws the ability to implant poisonous objects in their enemies, like a fired musket ball. The Wampanoags would not have failed to notice that the plague struck them during those years in which they had several battles with gun-wielding Europeans. It is suggestive that during the short life of the English colony of Roanoke in the mid-1580s, the surrounding Indians attributed epidemic disease to the colonists' arms, charging "that it was the work of our God through our means, and that we by him might kill and slay whom we would without weapons, and not come near them." The Wampanoags and their neighbors harbored similar fears. In this case, all Winslow or Hopkins had to do was begin loading his musket for the women and children to scatter in terror "and could not be pacified till he laid it down again." The salute to Ousamequin would not be the last time Tisquantum exploited the Wampanoags' association of guns and disease for his own ends.[34]

For the meantime, however, Ousamequin basked in the honors the English paid to him. Taking the delegates into his house, he received their messages and promised he would send to the Cape Wampanoags to arrange for a reconciliation. He also pledged to coordinate the colonists' trade for Wampanoag corn, seed, and furs, thereby making himself the point man in potentially lucrative and prestigious relations between the two groups. In turn, the English presented him with gifts symbolizing their friendship. According to Winslow, "Having put the coat on his back and the chain about his neck, he was not a little proud to behold himself, and his men also to see their king so bravely attired."[35]

For Ousamequin, the purpose of this diplomacy was to translate his control of the English into prestige and authority among the Wampanoags and dread among his enemies. The sachem told the delegates that he wanted Plymouth to impede trade between the French and Narragansetts on Narragansett Bay, having already grasped that the French and English were distinct peoples on poor terms. Of course, this request had nothing to do with the French and everything to do with weakening the Narragansetts. He flattered Winslow and Hopkins that Narragansett Bay "was King James his country, and he also was King James his man." Certainly the sachem did not mean to resign his authority to a king he had never seen. Instead, he was trying to convince the English that they had a duty as the subjects of a king allied with him to serve, effectively, as

Wampanoag proxies. The sachem also wanted the Wampanoags to acknowledge that the colonists gave him a new source of power, and the English to know that his power was already great. He had his people gather round as he made "a great speech" with the English at his side, asserting "was not he, Massasoit, commander of the country about them? Was not such a town his, and the people of it? And should they not bring their skins unto us?" With each question, the people answered in the affirmative, a drawn-out, ritualized process that Winslow and Hopkins found "tedious."[36]

The English were about to discover just how much tedium they could stand. As the Wampanoags had communicated several times during their appearances in Plymouth, they expected political allies to treat each other as kin, which included day-to-day generosity, mutual visiting, and perhaps eventually intermarriage. In this particular instance, Ousamequin had Winslow and Hopkins spend the night at his house under conditions they found uncomfortably intimate and foreign. "He laid us on the bed with himself and his wife," the two men recounted, "they at one end and we at the other, it being only planks laid a foot on the ground, and a thin mat upon them." If this arrangement was not disquieting enough for the visitors, shortly they were joined by additional bedmates, as "two more of his [Ousamequin's] chief men, for want of room, pressed by and upon us," or, in other words, cozied up to them. Worse yet, the guests then discovered that it was the Wampanoags' custom to sing before bedtime, which, combined with "lice and fleas within doors, and mosquitoes without, we could hardly sleep all the time of our being there."[37]

The two Englishmen made a hasty exit the next day, citing their desire to keep the Sabbath at home but really because they were so tired and hungry, Ousamequin having had little food to provide them because he had not been expecting their arrival. Yet the

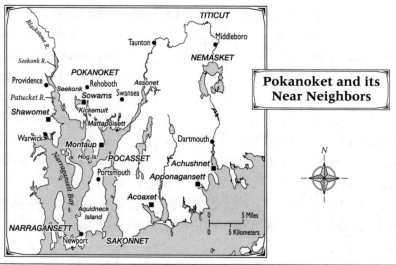

Pokanoket and its Near Neighbors

TITICUT

Middleboro

Taunton

NEMASKET

Blackstone R.

Seekonk R.

POKANOKET

Providence
Rehoboth
Assonet

Seekonk
Sowams
Swansea

Patucket R.
Kickemuit

Shawomet

Mattapoisett

Warwick

Montaup
POCASSET
Dartmouth

Hog. Is.

Portsmouth
Achushnet

Apponagansett

Acoaxet

Narragansett Bay

Aquidneck Island

NARRAGANSETT
Newport
SAKONNET

N

0   5 Miles
0   5 Kilometers

Wampanoag Country in the Seventeenth Century

Assonet River

MASSACHUSETTS

Massachusetts Bay

Charles R.

Scituate

MATTAKEESET
Marshfield
Duxbury

Monponsett Pond

Blackstone River

PATUXET
Plymouth

TITICUT

MANOMET

Taunton

Taunton R.

NEMAKSET

PAOMET

Providence

Rehoboth
ASSONET

Assawompset Pond

Cape Cod Bay

NAUSET
Eastham

Swansea

WAMPANOAGS
AGAWAM
Sandwich

NOBSCUSSET

POKANOKET
Watuppa Pond
SIPPECAN
SATUCKETT

Barnstable
Yarmouth

MONOMOYICK

MATTAKEESET

POCASSET
ACUSHNET

Narragansett Bay

Portsmouth
Dartmouth

MASHPEE

NARRAGANSETTS

Buzzards Bay

SAKONNET

Elizabeth Islands

Newport

SENGEKONTACKET

See inset map above

Naushon Is.

Martha's Vineyard
Edgartown

CHAPPAQUIDDICK

SAKEDAN
SHAWKEMO

AQUINNAH
CHRISTIANTOWN
NUNNEPOG

MADAKET
Nantucket

N

0   10   20 Miles
0   10   20 Kilometers

Albers Conic Projection

Wampanoags, and especially the sachem, must have considered this visit a success. The English had conformed to the Wampanoag expectation of mutuality as part of the alliance. For at least a day, they had lived as the Wampanoags lived. They had smoked tobacco and conversed together, exchanged gifts like friends, met the Wampanoags' wives and children, listened to their songs, and partook of their food, however meager. The English had once again demonstrated their utility, particularly on the second day when the Wampanoags prevailed on Winslow and Hopkins "to see one of us shoot at a mark." With a flash, explosion, and burst of smoke, the shooter peppered the target with hail shot, at which the audience "wondered to see the mark so full of holes." Putting such weapons to Wampanoag use was part of how Ousamequin envisioned this alliance working.[38]

TESTING THE ALLIANCE

Mutual good feeling was one thing, but translating it into action was quite another. Shortly after Winslow and Hopkins's return to Plymouth, a series of minor crises gave both parties the chance to test the other's commitment to the alliance. One such incident involved the colonist John Billington, a sixteen-year-old troublemaker from a troublemaking family, getting lost in the woods for five days before stumbling into the Wampanoag sachemship of Manomet, just southeast of Patuxet along the coast. The obvious thing for the Manomet sachem, Canacum, to do would have been to return the boy straightaway to the English. Instead, he delivered Billington to the sachem Aspinet of Nauset on Cape Cod, whose community the *Mayflower* passengers had ransacked in the weeks after their landing. Canacum appears to have had two goals in mind. For one, he was challenging Ousamequin's policy of rapprochement with the English. A sizable portion of the Wampanoags distrusted the strangers, considering them even more of a threat than the Narragansetts. Making Billington's recovery difficult was an indirect way to signal that discontent to Ousamequin and the colonists alike. Canacum and his fellow dissidents also might have been trying to take some shine off Ousamequin's luster. When they were ready to announce Billington's whereabouts, they broke the news to Ousamequin, not Plymouth, which basically forced him to go tell the English that if they wanted the boy back, they would have to go all the way to Nauset to get him. In turn, Ousamequin's reputation among the English as a powerful sachem capable of ruling over his people took a bit of a hit. For the dissidents, it was a double victory that the English would have to return to the site of their landing and confront the people whose corn they had stolen and graves they had desecrated.

The pilgrims would also have to answer for the crimes their countrymen had committed against the Wampanoags even before their arrival. Sometime in either late June or late July 1621 (the two extant accounts disagree on the date), Plymouth sent out an expedition in the *Mayflower*'s shallop to fetch Billington. It consisted of ten Englishmen, or half of the adult males in the colony, and two Wampanoag intermediaries, Tisquantum and Tokamahamon, "a special friend" appointed by Ousamequin to live with and assist the colonists and, presumably, serve as his eyes and ears. The English were justifiably nervous about how the Cape Wampanoags would receive them. On their way east across Cape Cod Bay, they put in for the night at Cummaquid, today's Barnstable Harbor, and were relieved to find the local sachem, Iyanough, "very personable, courteous, and fair conditioned . . . his cheer plentiful and various." Yet the sachem's pleasant demeanor could not shield the colonists from a "very grievous" confrontation with an elderly woman, who, at the sight of the English, began wailing because the English captain Thomas Hunt had enslaved three of her sons back in 1616. She calmed down after the colonists apologized for Hunt's behavior and gave her some "trifles" as gifts, but the episode clearly left them fearful about what lay ahead.[39]

They knew that they were sailing into potential trouble at Nauset, though they deflected responsibility for it. "We had least cause to trust them," Winslow explained, "being they had only had formerly made an assault upon us in the same place, in time of our winter discovery for habitation." Thus the English stood on their guard at anchor, even as the Natives gestured for them to row ashore. Eventually, the colonists permitted two Wampanoags to come aboard their vessel, including a man who claimed that it was his family's corn the colonists had stolen. The English promised him restitution, though they fell short of a full-throated apology by requiring him to travel to Plymouth to claim it. Nevertheless, this gesture appears to have been enough to convince the Nausets to relinquish Billington, for afterward the sachem Aspinet, at the head of a "great train" of at least a hundred people, led the boy to the beach. Wampanoag bowmen kept their distance, and everyone handling the exchange left their weapons behind. Another positive sign was that Billington was "behung with beads," doubtlessly white wampum, to represent peace. In exchange, the colonists gave knives to Aspinet and the head of Billington's host family, whereupon the two groups parted without the English visiting Aspinet's village or Aspinet inviting them. The tone of the encounter was standoffish, but it must have come as a relief to everyone that at least it was not actively hostile.[40]

The extent of Ousamequin's involvement in this affair is unclear. Perhaps after learning Billington was at Nauset, he had warned Aspinet not to do the English any harm and just return the boy, which would have demonstrated the reach of his influence to the outer limits of Cape Cod. Yet it is also possible that the exchange was a Nauset production independent of the Pokanoket sachem, which would have at once asserted Aspinet's autonomy while showing solidarity with Ousamequin's approach to the English. There is simply no way of knowing. The only thing certain is that this affair was about more than just the Nausets and the English. It was also about different Wampanoag sachems across a stretch of nearly a hundred miles negotiating the balance of power between them. That shadowy dynamic was always influencing Wampanoag-Plymouth relations, even if the colonists were often unaware of it.

The rift that Ousamequin's English alliance opened between him and other Wampanoags was far from closed, as became evident even before the Billington swap was done. While the colonists were at Nauset, an Indian runner arrived with the message "that the Narragansetts had spoiled some of Massasoit's men and taken him," which led the English to hurry their exit lest they come under attack, too. They rushed back to Plymouth to discover the news was true, "that Massasoit was put from his country by the Narragansetts." More alarming still was intelligence that Corbitant, the sachem of Pocasset, just to the east of Pokanoket, was challenging Ousamequin's authority from within the Wampanoag ranks. As the English understood it, Corbitant had grown "conversant with the Narragansetts" and was touting their support as he traveled through Wampanoag country trying "to draw the hearts of Massasoit's subjects from him, speaking also disdainfully of us, storming at the peace." Corbitant also railed against the colonists' growing roster of Wampanoag interpreters and go-betweens, which now included not only Tisquantum and Tokamahamon but also a new figure, Hobbamock. Hobbamock, like Tisquantum, carried one of the names of the Wampanoag god of the dead. He was also a fearsome pniese (or warrior-counselor) who fled to the English after a falling-out with Ousamequin, or so he claimed. It would take little time before Ousamequin and the English were glad to have him managing their affairs from inside Plymouth.[41]

The three Wampanoag go-betweens set out to investigate and attempt to negotiate an end to the crisis, only to walk into a hornet's nest. When Corbitant heard that Tisquantum and Hobbamock were at Nemasket looking for Ousamequin, he had his supporters take them prisoner, boasting that without the interpreters "the English had lost their tongue." Hobbamock managed to escape despite being held at knifepoint, true to his courageous reputation as a pniese, and then rushed back to Plymouth to announce breathlessly that Tisquantum was probably dead.[42]

As Ousamequin would have hoped, the English sprang to his defense. They quickly assembled fourteen colonists and Hobbamock under Miles Standish to march on Nemasket and, if the rebels had indeed killed Tisquantum, bring back Corbitant's head and arrest another sachem, Nepoeof, "who was of this confederacy." The mission got off to a rough start, as the plan for a nighttime raid had to be scrapped when the men got lost in the woods. Yet, as daylight broke, the troopers recovered their bearings and managed to sneak into Nemasket undetected, permitting a surprise assault on the house where Tisquantum had previously been held. Amid the fray, Hobbamock shouted that the English were there only for Corbitant, not anyone else, but that did not prevent some of the inhabitants from trying to escape or the adrenaline-filled English from injuring them in the process. To the colonists' credit, afterward they sent two of the injured Wampanoags back to Plymouth to receive medical care, though they did not mention whether these people gave their consent or had any idea what the English were going to do with them.[43]

Once order was restored, the expedition learned that Corbitant and his men had already left town, but Tisquantum was still there and very much alive. So, instead of launching a futile and hazardous manhunt, Standish pronounced that if anyone rose up against Ousamequin again or intimidated his followers, particularly Tisquantum and Hobbamock, the English "would revenge it." To punctuate the warning, Plymouth sent an armed party to the sachem Obbatinewat on the southern shore of Massachusetts Bay, who "had often threatened us (as we were informed)" even though he was supposed to be under Ousamequin. The intimidation worked, as the sachem treated the embassy "kindly."[44]

Ousamequin's backing by English defenders, who, despite their small numbers, wielded intimidating firearms, swords, and armor, was enough to quell the resistance temporarily. After the strike, in September 1621, a series of Wampanoag and Massachusett sachems put their marks to another treaty in which they pledged themselves "to be the loyal subjects of King James," which was to say, on good terms with Plymouth colony. The roster even included former dissidents such as Epenow of Martha's Vineyard and their purported ringleader, Corbitant. From this point on, Corbitant did not create any more trouble for Ousamequin that came to the attention of the English. Indeed, sometime later, Ousamequin wed his two sons, later known as Wamsutta and Pumetacom, to Corbitant's two daughters, Namumpum (or Weetamoo) and Wootonekanuske, respectively, thus creating marriage bonds that firmed up the authority of Ousamequin and his successors.[45]

The Narragansetts had no intention of permitting the English to prop up their rival unchallenged. In mid-November 1621, shortly after Plymouth received its first shipload of new colonists (thirty-seven) and fresh supplies, rumors arose that the Narragansetts "began to breathe forth many threats against us . . . insomuch as the common talk of our neighboring Indians, on all sides, was the preparation they made to come against us." An ambassador sent by the Narragansett sachem, Canonicus, to Plymouth only heightened these tensions. Speaking through the novice interpretation of Tokama-hamon, this representative asked if Tisquantum was there, appeared relieved to learn that he was not, and then delivered "a bundle of new arrows wrapped in a rattlesnake's skin." Mission accomplished, the visitor promptly turned to leave, but William Bradford, now governor of the colony, ordered him detained until the meaning of the parcel could be discerned. Tokamahamon reached the obvious conclusion that the Narragansetts were trying to say "they were enemies to us." Later, Tisquantum agreed, adding that it was a dare the English needed to answer. To that end, Bradford, probably at Tisquantum's suggestion, stuffed the snakeskin with gunpowder and shot and had the messenger return it to his sachem, unaware that Indians associated these substances with plague or at the very least powerful magic. Whether out of honor or fear, Canonicus rejected the bundle and sent it back to Plymouth unopened, leading Bradford to speculate that "it was no small terror to this savage king." The English then got to work erecting a defensive palisade around their settlement, just in case the terror wore off.[46]

GIVING THANKS

Despite the Narragansett threat looming over the colony, the English had good reason to pause for celebration in late November 1621. The colony had survived a terrible first winter and the death of half its population. The leadership had forged an alliance with Ousamequin, the most powerful sachem in the immediate area, and both parties had demonstrated their commitment to defending the other. In turn, other Wampanoag and Massachusett sachems seemed to have reconciled themselves to Ousamequin's policy, despite their distrust of the English. The colony was now capable of sustaining itself, partly through its own labor, partly through trade with the Wampanoags. Tisquantum had taught the colonists how to cultivate maize for the first time in their lives, including planting the seeds in holes made with digging sticks, forming hills around the stalks as they grew, and fertilizing each plant with herring from nearby streams, Wampanoag-style. Combined with produce from additional crops of barley and peas, fish from surrounding waters, and game from the wetlands and forest, there was finally enough to eat. Additionally, the colonists had erected seven dwelling houses and four public buildings and received their first shipload of reinforcements. Given all these developments, Plymouth had reasonable hopes for a better winter ahead—that is, if the Narragansetts did not attack.

Having passed through one crisis after another, Plymouth's leaders decided that sometime in late September or early October, after the harvest was in, the people should set aside some time to "rejoice together." It is this event that posterity has lionized as the First Thanksgiving, though the participants did not think of it as a thanksgiving. That would have meant engaging in prayerful contemplation while fasting. Rather, they planned to feast and indulge in some "recreations," including militia drill and target practice. After a session of drinking beer, "strong water," and perhaps wine, the men's uninhibited boasting probably also led to contests of (staggered) speed and strength. Modern Americans tend to imagine the Pilgrims as stern and joyless. They could be both of these things, but not on this occasion.[47]

The people's meals during these festivities bore only scant resemblance to the modern Thanksgiving spread. Before the fun began, Bradford sent out four men to go "fowling," and they brought back enough to feed the people for nearly a week. Their catch likely included wild turkey, for Bradford noted that Plymouth "took many" that autumn, despite how challenging it was for inexperienced shots to bag this surprisingly fleet creature. Yet turkey was probably not the only bird served. Accompanying it would have been "water fowl" such as ducks and geese, which "began to come in store . . . as winter approached." Venison, roasted or stewed, also would have been on the menu, given that it appears on Bradford's inventory of the colony's larders that season. Certainly there was fish aplenty, including cod and bass, "of which every family had their portion," and shellfish such as clams, mussels, oysters, lobsters, scallops, and crabs. To the surprise of many modern people, there also would have been eels, for according to Winslow "in September we can take a hogshead of eels in a night, with small labor, and can dig them out of their beds all the winter"—that was another skill Tisquantum had taught them. In other words, the legendary First Thanksgiving meal consisted largely of wild game and seafood.

Indian cornmeal in various forms also would have featured prominently at the feast. The English had spent much of the previous year trading for, raising, and harvesting maize, to the point that Plymouth finally had enough in storage to distribute "about a peck of meal a week to a person." Following the colonists' months of exposure to Indian foodways, they had likely begun preparing their own versions of the customary Wampanoag dish called *nasaump*, consisting of boiled coarse cornmeal mixed with various combinations of vegetables, fruits, and meats. Years later, John Josselyn wrote of an innovation New England colonists made to the Wampanoag recipe by cooking it with milk, something Plymouth colonists could not have done in 1621, as they did not yet have cattle or goats. Nevertheless, their preparation of nasaump would have followed the basic steps outlined by Josselyn. He explained that cornmeal "is light of digestion, and the English make a kind of loblolly [porridge] of it to eat with milk, which they call sampe; they beat it in a mortar, and sift the flower out of it; the remainder they call hominey, which they put into a pot of two or three gallons, with water, and boil it upon a gentle fire till it be like a hasty pudding;

they put of this into milk, and so eat it." Maize, cornmeal, and nasaump were just three of the many gifts for which the colonists owed the Wampanoags thanks.[48]

A number of the "traditional" foods that modern Americans associate with Thanksgiving were unavailable. For instance, there were no white or sweet potatoes. The Wampanoags did not raise these tubers, which were indigenous to South America and the Caribbean but not North America, and Europeans had not yet incorporated them into their diets. Children today will be heartened to learn that neither Winslow's nor Bradford's account mentions vegetables, though there must have been some. Yet they will be saddened that there were no pies, as the colonists did not have supplies of butter, wheat flour, or sugar. As an alternative, the English might have served fruits, for Winslow noted, "here are grapes, white and red, and very sweet and strong also. Strawberries, gooseberries, raspas [raspberries], etc. Plums of three sorts." Wild cranberries were also available, but the English do not appear to have used them. If there was dessert, it probably consisted of cornmeal fry cakes with fruit or honey, such as the Wampanoags prepared.[49]

These options reflected how far the English had come from the first winter of starvation, disease, and desperation. Though their accounts do not specify them offering prayers of thanks as part of their celebration, doubtless they did. As Winslow explained to readers back in England, conditions at Plymouth had not been "always so plentiful, as it was at this time with us, yet by the goodness of God, we are so far from want, that we often wish you [to be] partakers of our plenty." He forgot to mention that their bounty was by the goodness of the Wampanoags, too.[50]

To the colonists' surprise, they would be joined by more Wampanoag guests than the total population of Plymouth itself. While the English were enjoying some target practice and other military

drills, suddenly Ousamequin "with some ninety men" appeared at
the palisade gate unannounced. Wampanoag tradition is that this
force rushed to the scene out of concern that Plymouth was under
attack because of the sound of gunfire from the colonists' sporting.
Ironically, the English initially feared that these armed Wampanoags were the real threat. Yet the two peoples possessed just enough
trust in each other that no one overreacted. They had forged an alliance through diplomacy, trade, and mutual assistance in the face of
emergencies. Their leaders now knew each other personally and
called each other friends. In almost any other time and place, a
surprise encounter like this between so many armed colonists and
Indians would have cost lives. Instead, both sides let down their
guard. For the next three days, the two peoples "entertained and
feasted" together in what amounted to something in between a state
dinner and the kind of casual mingling that the Wampanoags
considered basic to the alliance. A few of the Wampanoags even
went out on a short hunt to make a contribution of five deer, "which
they brought to the plantation and bestowed on our governor, and
upon the captain and others." That passage closes the primary source
record of this so-called First Thanksgiving.[51]

The Thanksgiving myth promotes the idea that this event
involved Indians gifting their country bloodlessly to Europeans and
their descendants to launch the United States as a great Christian,
democratic, family-centered nation blessed by God. Yet nothing of
the sort took place in the fall of 1621. The Wampanoags' alliance
with Plymouth was not about conceding to colonialism. Their hope
was that the English would provide them with military backing,
martial supplies, and trade goods that would enable them to fend
off the Narragansetts while they tried to recover from their losses
to the epidemic of 1616–19. Once they returned to strength, they
certainly expected to continue exercising dominion in their country

over anyone living there, the English included. On a more personal level, Ousamequin wanted his control of the English and their goods to buttress his claims to authority over the far-flung, sometimes contentious network of Wampanoag sachems.

The English, for their part, had decidedly more modest plans than laying the foundations for the modern United States. They could hardly have even imagined the number of thriving English colonies that would develop in their neighborhood over the next few decades. Some of Plymouth's leaders had ambitions that, someday, someone from among their ranks would begin propagating the gospels among the Indians as a step toward Christ's Second Coming. Everyone's most pressing concern, though, was merely to create a small, stable community of fellow believers capable of earning a competent living. The alliance of peace, trade, and mutual protection with the Wampanoags was a means to that end.

Rather than the beginning of a grand American experiment, the so-called First Thanksgiving was instead a gesture to continue a friendship the two people had already established through such means as the treaty of seven articles, Winslow and Hopkins's embassy to Ousamequin, the return of Billington, the Nemasket strike, and Plymouth's exchange of threats with the Narragansetts. Yet, for the alliance to survive, such mutuality would have to become routine. The English could not expect peaceful, productive relations if they walled themselves off from the general Wampanoag population and restricted communication to the leaders. The only way the Wampanoags were going to permit them to continue living in Wampanoag country was if they continued to prove their value and show respect for the ways of their hosts. Those expectations included them shoring up Ousamequin against his rivals, internal and external. Plymouth was now an inextricable part of volatile relationships within the Wampanoag paramount sachemship and between the Wampanoags and other tribes. That position, along with continued widespread Indian hostility toward the English, meant that the future of the alliance was not between war and peace, between a pointed or blunted arrow, but who would be sacrificed for whose gain.

CHAPTER FIVE

Ꮃ Ꭷ

Ousamequin's Power Play

The English raid on Nemasket to rescue Tisquantum and intimidate Corbitant temporarily quieted but did not permanently quell Wampanoag and Massachusett Indian opposition to Ousamequin's policy of rapprochement with Plymouth. How could it be otherwise given Europeans' long track record of horrendous behavior toward coastal peoples, including the *Mayflower* passengers' grave desecrations, thievery, and even violence? Additionally, some Native people dreaded that the strangers were just as capable of spreading disease as they were of firing lead balls from iron tubes that belched fire and smoke. What sense did it make to invite this danger into the country? Ousamequin had answers to these questions. As the sachem on the front lines of the Wampanoag-Narragansett rivalry, he needed outside help, and fast, or else he and the rest of his people were going to become tributaries to their rivals. Furthermore, he could use his control of the circulation of English goods to reconstitute his authority among far-flung Wampanoag sachemships depopulated by the epidemic of 1616–19. Yet, what did the sachems whom Ousamequin claimed to lead stand to gain by his approach? Unless they were Ousamequin's relatives, it probably made little difference to them whether they paid tribute to him or the Narragansetts, except insofar as the latter carried the benefit of sparing them from

Narragansett raids. Given the Narragansetts' links to wampum-paying tributaries from Long Island, fur producers in the Connecticut River valley and Iroquoia, and a range of shipboard traders from the Netherlands, France, and England, they were even better positioned than Ousamequin to funnel European goods to their protectorates. The Narragansetts dealt with Europeans, but they did not permit them to settle near them—not yet—whereas Ousamequin had become the first sachem regionally to take such a risk. Ousamequin's title, Massasoit, proclaimed him to be a great leader, but some of the communities he claimed as followers were not quite so sure.

Ousamequin also faced trouble in the form of Tisquantum. Tisquantum was a valuable asset, certainly, for spying as well as interpretation. There were, as yet, no other Wampanoags capable of speaking the English language nearly as well as he did. However, Tisquantum had his own agenda that undercut the sachem's. Seeing that the Wampanoags and English alike depended on him, Tisquantum manipulated both sides' fears of the other, which included stirring English suspicions of Ousamequin. Apparently his ambition was to reconsolidate the surviving Patuxets, and other Wampanoags besides, under his own leadership. Without Tisquantum, Ousamequin risked losing his voice in talks with Plymouth; with him, he found himself speaking through an interpreter with a forked tongue.

The challenge facing Ousamequin was how to fend off so many threats by using the colonists while maintaining and extending his following among people who disdained them. The so-called First Thanksgiving feast had barely ended before this dilemma turned into a crisis. Ousamequin's response was a power play that confirmed his status as a great leader every bit as ruthless as those who sought to undermine him.

TISQUANTUM'S GAME

As New England's ever-so-gradual thaw began in spring, Plymouth's leaders set their sights on expanding their fur trade with local Indians. Though the colony still needed every able body for basic tasks, its sponsors in London had emphasized that unless they began seeing a return on their investments, they would stop sending supplies and reinforcements and effectively bring the project to an end. They were generally supportive of the Separatists' religious goals, but they considered the settlement to be a business venture first. Indeed, the Adventurers' demands for greater productivity from the colonists began as early as the summer of 1621 despite Plymouth having lost half of its population during the previous winter and its survivors reduced to deprivation. One sponsor, Thomas Weston, heartlessly accused the colonists of exhibiting greater "weakness of judgment than weakness of hands," and instructed them to devote less time to "discoursing, arguing, and consulting" and more to securing commodities for sale back to England. This pressure finally spurred the colony to outfit a trading expedition to Massachusetts Bay in March 1622. The Indians there might have been few in number, but their hunting territory was rich in beaver, to which they added furs they had acquired from the Wabanakis of Maine and the Pawtuckets and Pennacooks of the Merrimac River valley in exchange for their horticultural produce and European trade goods.[1]

Hobbamock, whose English-language skills appear to have been developing rapidly, warned not to trust the Massachusett Indians. His sources told him that they were still "joined in a confederacy with the Narragansetts," despite the treaty of 1621, and would cut off Miles Standish and his men at the first opportunity. None of this sounded far-fetched to the English, though they do not seem to have weighed the possibility that Hobbamock was just trying to protect Ousame-quin's domination of the trade. But then Hobbamock added a star-tling detail: Tisquantum was in on the conspiracy and would try through "many persuasions to draw us from our shallops to the [Massachusetts Bay] Indians' houses, for their [the conspirators'] better advantage" to strike. Bradford called for a council to discuss the matter, which ruled to proceed with the expedition as a show of English courage. Yet there was good reason to fear.[2]

In early April 1622, the supposed plot took another ominous, puzzling turn. Immediately after the trading mission set sail, an unidentified member of Tisquantum's family burst into Plymouth, his face bleeding profusely, to exclaim that Ousamequin, Corbitant, and the Narragansetts were meeting together at Nemasket to discuss attacking the colony while its best men were absent at Massa-chusetts Bay. As for the wound, he said one of the conspirators had struck him for speaking in defense of the English. Fortunately, the trading shallop was still within hearing range of Plymouth's guns to be called back for a council about what to do. Yet, before the English leadership made any decisions, it first tried to sort out the truth, which was a tall task. A livid Hobbamock accused Tisquantum of lying to make it appear that he and his followers were Plymouth's only true friends when actually they were false. Ousamequin remained as faithful as ever, Hobbamock stressed, and would never launch an attack on the colony without warning him first, which could not have given the English much assurance. The colonists were so dependent on just a few Wampanoags for intelligence that the best solution they could devise was to have Hobbamock's wife go on a fact-finding mission to Pokanoket, even though she and her husband might have been committed to protecting Ousamequin under any circum-stances. Days later, she returned with a message from the sachem that Tisquantum was untrustworthy and that Ousamequin would send advance warning if he heard of any threats against the colony.

The question was whether anyone was telling the truth. The English were never sure.[3]

Under Hobbamock's prodding, Plymouth's leaders concluded that the problem was indeed Tisquantum. Their investigations, the details of which they neglected to record, concluded that Tisquantum sought to drive a wedge between the colony and Ousamequin and take over as the Wampanoags' point man in English affairs. This would "make himself great in the eyes of his countrymen . . . not caring who fell, so he stood." Worse yet, he seemed to have wanted Native people to think "he could lead us to peace or war, at his pleasure. And would often threaten the Indians, sending them word in a private matter, we were intended shortly to kill them." Through these machinations, he extracted gifts from a growing number of local sachems "to work their peace," which had been the role claimed by Ousamequin.[4]

Tisquantum was at his most conniving in exploiting his countrymen's ongoing trauma from the epidemic of 1616–19. Reportedly, he spread rumors that the English "had the plague buried in our storehouse," which was to say, in the underground magazine where they protected their gunpowder from igniting accidentally. Recall that Tisquantum had earlier instructed Winslow and Hopkins to fire their guns during their visit to Pokanoket, despite the panic it caused. Remember, too, how he was probably the reason Plymouth's leaders responded to Canonicus's symbolic challenge of arrows wrapped in snakeskin by filling the skin with powder and shot and then sending it back, much to the sachem's "terror." Tisquantum used these devices to scare the people that the English had the power to unleash lethal diseases at their whim.[5]

That belief appears to have been widespread, including among the sachem class. At some point, Ousamequin himself entreated the English to direct the plague against "another sachem bordering his territories," and in the late 1630s, the Narragansett sachem, Canonicus, in a conversation with Roger Williams, "accused the English and myself of sending the plague amongst them, and threatening to kill him especially." Hobbamock asked the English point-blank whether they had the ability to afflict their enemies with disease, to which they answered that only "the God of the English had it in store, and could send it at his pleasure to the destruction of his and our enemies." This response, which the English gave honestly, would not have comforted anyone among the Wampanoags given their tradition of pawwaws using guardian spirits to attack their foes. Tisquantum wanted his people to believe that he alone was capable of controlling those who controlled the pestilence. He was playing with fire.[6]

That said, there might have been more to Tisquantum than meets the eye. It is easy to disparage Tisquantum as an underhanded opportunist, as some historians have done, because he was a loner in the world after his kidnapping and the loss of so many of his kin to the epidemic of 1616–19. Elements of that interpretation might be true, but there are other possibilities. Despite the devastation of Patuxet, Tisquantum was not the last of his kind, as evident in the fact that someone identified as his family member had been the one to sound the alarm (or false rumor) about Ousamequin and Corbitant plotting with the Narragansetts against the English. Doubtless he had other kin who had escaped the scourge. Let us assume that Tisquantum cared about them and other Wampanoag people. Why, then, would he want to undercut their sachem, Ousamequin? Perhaps Tisquantum grasped, as only he could, the long-term danger posed to the Wampanoags by Europeans, not just those in the tiny colony of Plymouth, but the multitudes who were bound to follow. He had traveled back and forth across the wide Atlantic, visited thronging European cities like Málaga and London, and colonial outposts like Newfoundland. In fact, he had seen more of the world than any of the colonists at Plymouth. Only he and Epenow among the Wampanoags had witnessed firsthand the vast populations from which the English hailed and which allowed them to keep pouring warm bodies into colonial death traps overseas. He possessed special knowledge of how their hierarchical society, quest for riches, religious arrogance, and stunning technologies not only propelled them across the oceans but also equipped them to sustain long, seemingly futile struggles far away from home against indigenous adversaries with fewer resources. Tisquantum might have thought that, given his experience, he was better prepared than Ousamequin or anyone else among the Wampanoags to lead his people in the face of this challenge, which probably few of them believed was coming no matter what he said.[7]

Clearly, though, Ousamequin did not see it this way. In late May 1622 the sachem appeared in person at Plymouth "offended and enraged against Tisquantum" and demanding his extradition. Bradford hedged, acknowledging the interpreter's crimes but calling for mercy because he "was so necessary and profitable an instrument as, at that time, we could not miss him." In other words, the governor denied the will of the very sachem on whom the colony's security and economy depended. With this, Ousamequin stormed off, but he was not about to give Bradford the last word. Shortly, one of his messengers doubled back to Plymouth to demand Tisquantum's execution, with Bradford again pleading "for our sakes . . . he [Ousamequin] would spare him." Yet the colonists' sake was not Ousamequin's concern. The next messenger from Ousamequin was accompanied by "diverse others," doubtless bowmen. They harangued Bradford that Tisquantum did not belong to the English but was "one of his [Ousamequin's] subjects, whom by our first Articles of peace, we could not retain." In other words, Ousamequin understood his treaty with the colonists to be reciprocal in nature, despite the written version obligating only the Wampanoags, not the English, to turn over those charged with cross-cultural crimes to the justice of the victim's society. The messenger delivered the

English "many beaver skins" from Ousamequin to gain their assent to Tisquantum's execution, but the gift carried a threat. It included Ousamequin's own knife and a directive that if Plymouth's leaders continued to refuse to turn over Tisquantum, they should use it themselves "to cut off his head and hands, and bring them to him [Ousamequin]." The subtext was that Ousamequin might turn his blade on them if they continued to rebuff him. This was as tense a confrontation as there had been in the history of the young Wampanoag-Plymouth relationship.[8]

At this very moment of decision, with Ousamequin's armed men staring down Bradford and his council, Plymouth's watch sounded the alarm that an unidentified ship was approaching and that it might be hostile French. Probably half-relieved, Bradford announced that he would have to postpone a decision because Tisquantum would be needed if the colony came under attack, particularly if the French had recruited Indian allies. Bradford's choice to protect Tisquantum (and, with it, his refusal to accept the gift of beaver pelts) put the sachem's men "in a great heat" and led Ousamequin himself to grow "mad with rage." In subsequent weeks, the English noticed that he "seemed to frown on us, and neither came, nor sent to us, as formerly."[9]

SOUR FACES

Ousamequin's alienation from Plymouth emboldened the colony's indigenous enemies, who suddenly appeared more numerous than even the English had imagined. According to Winslow, many of the Indians "began to cast forth many insulting speeches, glorifying in our weakness, and giving out how easy it would be before long to cut us off." The colonists still had their interpreter, but no Wampanoag leaders with whom to speak. All they could do to try to discern the state of Indian affairs was to play off Tisquantum and Hobbamock against each other, with Bradford appearing to favor the first and Standish the second. Yet it was always in question as to who was playing whom.[10]

Festering tensions between the colony and its indigenous neighbors stemmed not only from the long, foul history of English-Indian relations and Bradford's recent rebuff of Ousamequin but also from the unruliness of the passengers from the ship whose arrival had spared Tisquantum's life. The vessel, as it turned out, was not French at all but English, carrying the first of two groups of about sixty men, most of them indentured servants, intended for a new fur trade outpost on Massachusetts Bay. They were funded by none other than Thomas Weston, who had broken with Plymouth's investors and was now pursuing other colonial ventures. The Pilgrims' historical ties with Weston, never mind their moral obligations to fellow Englishmen, required them to take in and feed the newcomers, which they did dutifully throughout the summer. Yet the strains these ill-mannered men put on the colony's resources and moral standards meant that everyone breathed sighs of relief when they finally left for the Bay in early fall and settled at a site called Wessagusset (modern Weymouth). Unfortunately, these ne'er-do-wells caused trouble wherever they were. Having learned apparently nothing from previous failed colonies, Weston's men expected the surrounding Indians to feed them and resorted to theft and intimidation when trade would not suffice. By the spring of 1623, conditions had grown so dire that some Wessagusset men had abandoned the post to live with the neighboring Indians, offering the Natives their labor and tools in exchange. The Wessagusset governor, John Sanders, alerted Plymouth that he was ready to seize the Indians' produce by force to keep from starving, but Bradford urged restraint out of concern that otherwise "all of us might smart for it." Instead, Sanders abandoned the colony for Maine, claiming to be searching for food for his company.[11]

As Indian patience began running out, the Massachusett pniese, Pecksuot, cautioned the Wessagusset colonists about his people's expectations for "just dealing." He explained, "If my men wrong my neighbor sachem, or his men, he sends me word and I beat or kill my men according to the offence. If his men wrong me or my men, I send him word and he beats or kills his men according to the offence. All sachems do justice by their own men. If not, we say they are all agreed and then we fight, and now I say you all steal my corn." Wessagusset was in no condition to fight and therefore hanged one of the offenders. Yet the provocations continued unabated, creating mounting resolve among the Massachusetts Bay Indians that they would have to cut out the malignant settlement and perhaps Plymouth along with it.[12]

It did not help that the founding of Wessagusset in 1622 coincided with the outbreak of another epidemic, the timing of which the Indians did not fail to notice. The identity of the disease is unknown—once again, accounts refer to it generically as "a great plague" and "a great sickness . . . not unlike the plague, if not the same." Furthermore, the extent of its spread is unknown. Clearly, though, it had a devastating effect among the Massachusetts Bay Indians. According to Wessagusset's Phineas Pratt, "half their people died thereof," in a place where already there "were fewest of the natives of the country dwelling" because of losses from the epidemic of 1616–19. This latest pestilence also ravaged Nemasket, which Plymouth noticed only because the Wampanoags there were too sick to deliver corn the English had bought from them. The Indians' sense that they were reliving past horrors must have grown even more acute when, that same year, an English ship captain named Thomas Jones, fishing off Cape Cod for the Virginia Company, revived the well-worn English pattern of raiding coastal Wampanoag communities. Authorities in London heard that Jones "robbed the Natives there of their furs, and offered [tried] to carry some of them away prisoners," only to have his ship run aground, whereupon "the savages escaped and made great exclamation against the present planters of New England"—all of them.[13]

Plymouth wanted Indians to know that the colonists of Wessagusset were "a distinct body from us," but that was only partly true. Plymouth had not only hosted Weston's men but also partnered with them in a corn-trading mission to Cape Cod in the fall of 1622. Indian runners and boat traffic carried messages back and forth between the two colonies. Perhaps most important, Plymouth refused to do anything substantive when Native people appealed for its help against Wessagusset's abuse, despite its treaty obligation of mutual protection. To outside eyes, it certainly did not appear that Plymouth and Wessagusset were distinct.[14]

Plymouth was growing more wary of its Indian neighbors, too. Sometime in the summer of 1622, startling news arrived that the Powhatan Indians had recently launched a massive surprise attack on the colony of Virginia that killed 347 Englishmen, about a third of the total, within a matter of days. Reports of the death toll were bad enough. Worse yet were the details about how it had occurred. During eight years of peace after the marriage of Pocahontas and John Rolfe, Virginia had let down its guard and permitted the Powhatans to come and go from English settlements more or less as they pleased. The Powhatans saw a soft target and eventually took advantage of it to seize back control of territory that the English had appropriated to plant tobacco and graze livestock. On Friday, March 22, 1622, they dispersed their fighters among scattered English homesteads and villages with instructions to behave inconspicuously until they had a chance to seize the colonists' tools and turn them into weapons. The result was an English bloodbath.[15]

With this, Plymouth suddenly awakened to its own risk. After all, Ousamequin continued to keep his distance. There were "continual rumors of fears [threats] from the Indians here, especially the Narragansetts." Indians in Massachusetts Bay poured forth complaints about Wessagusset, accompanied by barely veiled threats. Even a successful English trading mission to Cape Cod in November

1622 carried ominous undertones. At Monomoyick, which had a history of violence at European hands, most of the inhabitants hid from the English and the remainder were unwilling to reveal the location of their houses. Eventually, Tisquantum was able to broker a trade for eight hogsheads of corn and beads, but then tragedy struck. As the colonists set sail, Tisquantum abruptly fell ill, blood pouring through his nose, and fell dead. Given the epidemic raging on the mainland, it is likely that he had contracted the same disease. Yet the suddenness of it all, particularly after Monomoyick's defensiveness and Ousamequin's call for Tisquantum's head, raised the distinct possibility that some agent had carried out the sachem's justice through poisoning. If so, the brilliance of the tactic was that it was impossible to tell.[16]

Captain Miles Standish had a tendency to overreact to any perceived threat even under normal circumstances, but his increased harshness toward the Wampanoags during these months provides clear evidence that Plymouth was on edge. During the final stages of the trading voyage that claimed Tisquantum's life, the colonists' shallop became so damaged that some of the men had to return home overland and leave behind their corn in a Wampanoag-style underground storage pit. But first Standish threatened the sachems Aspinet of Nauset and Iyanough of Mattakeesett that if anyone stole from these caches "they [i.e., the sachems and their communities] should certainly smart for their unjust and dishonest dealing, and further make good whatsoever had so taken."[17] He showed no embarrassment about warning the Natives against acting as his own people had previously done. Standish had a similarly disproportionate response to a minor case of theft when the English returned to the Cape in January 1623 to retrieve their corn. They "found [everything] in safety as they left it," much to their relief, but when one of the Nausets "stole certain beads, scissors, and other trifles" from the colonists' supplies, Standish grew belligerent. Despite Aspinet's record of assisting Plymouth, first in securing the return of John Billington and now in guarding the corn, Standish treated him like a subordinate, demanding either the return of the goods or surrender of the thief, "or else [Standish] would revenge it on them before his departure." The items resurfaced the next day, and the sachem claimed to have beaten the offender, which eased Standish's temper, but his earlier outburst must have reinforced Wampanoag opinion that Ousamequin's English friends were not friends at all.[18]

Amid the tensions at Wessagusset, Ousamequin's falling-out with Plymouth, and Standish's strong-arm tactics on the Cape, the English began to suspect the surrounding Indians of plotting against them. Not surprisingly, the main proponent of this view was Standish. In March 1623 he took a trading expedition to the nearby Wampanoag community of Manomet, where he received an uncharacteristically cold reception from the sachem, Canacum, one of Plymouth's putative allies. It grew even chillier with the arrival of two Natives from Massachusetts Bay, including a pniese named Wituwamat, characterized by Winslow as "a notable insulting villain, one who had formerly imbrued his hands in the blood of English and French." Wituwamat liked to taunt Englishmen that he had killed several Europeans over the years who "died crying, making sour faces, more like children than men." In this instance, he took a knife hanging from around his neck, which he had acquired from one of the colonists at Wessagusset, and used it as a prop to threaten Standish, or so Standish thought, in a speech otherwise addressed to Canacum. The problem was that Standish, who the English considered "the best linguist among us," struggled to understand what Wituwamat said. Wituwamat delivered his talk in what Standish called an "audacious manner," which probably meant in the Indians' courtly style, characterized by roundabout, mixed metaphors and theatrical use of mnemonic devices. Standish thought the point of framing it this baroque way was to frustrate him. If so, Wituwamat was largely successful, but what the captain did pick up left him distressed.[19]

Other Natives who had been in attendance confirmed to Standish that Wituwamat had been there to recruit Manomet into a general Indian uprising against the English, just as Standish thought. Apparently, Wituwamat's argument was this: the Massachusett Indians still had enough men, thirty or forty, to dispatch Wessa-gusset, but that would run the risk of Plymouth revenging it on them. But what if Wampanoags who also resented the English and disagreed with Ousamequin's policies took the opportunity to wipe out Plymouth simultaneously? Alluding to the historic Massachusett-Wampanoag alliance against the Narragansetts, Witu-wamat called for the two peoples to reunite against a common enemy. Standish's blood was boiling by the time Wituwamat finished, but he managed to retain his composure before taking his leave. He did not let down his guard the entire way home, even refusing to sleep out of fear that a Paomet Wampanoag who had volunteered to carry his luggage intended to assassinate him along the way. He attributed his safe arrival in Plymouth to his own wiles, not his burden bearer's innocence. As far as he was concerned, the colony was in imminent danger and no Indian could be trusted.[20]

English perceptions, of course, did not necessarily reflect reality, particularly given the cultural and linguistic blinders preventing them from understanding Indian politics in their full complexity. Yet, shortly after Standish returned to Plymouth, Ousamequin gave the colonists all the assurance they needed that their fears were legitimate, that there was indeed a wide-scale Indian plot against them. The lingering question today, four centuries later, was whether the sachem spoke the truth or instead exploited colo-nial anxieties and ignorance for his own ends, just as Tisquantum had so recently duped his fellow Wampanoags.

TRUE FRIENDS AND THE HOLLOW-HEARTED

The essential context was a summons from Pokanoket for the English to attend Ousamequin on what appeared to be his deathbed. *"Neen womasu Sagimus, neen womasu Sagimus!* My loving sachem, my loving sachem!" exclaimed Hobbamock. "Many have I known, but never any like thee . . . He governed his men better with few strokes than others did with many." It was Wampanoag custom for friends and relatives to come and pay their last respects when someone was fatally ill, particularly when that person was a sachem. If maintaining good relations was not enough of an incentive for Plymouth to send a representative, the accompanying news that a Dutch vessel had just run aground near the sachem's village certainly was. Plymouth's leaders had been discussing their need to open a supply line of Dutch-produced goods for the Indian trade, and now it seemed they had their opportunity. At the same time, they wanted the Dutch to know that Plymouth considered Wampanoag country its exclusive economic sphere. To these ends, the colony dispatched a team consisting of Winslow, who spoke Dutch, Hobbamock, and a temporary visitor to Plymouth named John Hamden, "a gentleman of London . . . [who] desired much to see the country."[21]

The Dutch were gone by the time Plymouth's ambassadors arrived, but with Ousamequin ailing, and Corbitant, "a hollow-hearted friend towards us," seemingly poised to succeed him, the stakes for this embassy remained high. The English visitors entered Ousamequin's house to encounter an entirely foreign, emotionally charged, potentially dangerous scene. The place was packed with Indians "in the midst of their charms for him [Ousamequin], making such a hellish noise as it distempered us that were well." That "hellish noise" probably included pulsating drums, call-and-response chants, and pawwaws dancing and inflecting, all in prayerful appeal to the spirits. Ousamequin was lying there in the midst of it, attended by a group of women who rubbed his limbs "to keep the heat in him." His condition was dire. Weak, exhausted, and probably dehydrated, he had lost his sight and seemed to be taking his last breaths. Yet he perked up a bit with the news that the English had arrived. Reaching out his hand for Winslow to take, twice he asked meekly, "'*Keen Winsnow?*' which [was] to say, 'Art thou Winslow?'" (Wampanoags struggled to pronounce the letter *L*.) When Winslow answered, "'*Ahhe*,' that is, 'Yes,'" the sachem followed with, "'*Matta neen wonckanet namen Winsnow!*' that is to say, 'O Winslow, I shall never see thee again.'"[22]

Yet he would. Whereas the Wampanoags seemed resigned to Ousamequin's fate, Winslow insisted on treating him, using his knife to force some "comfortable conserves" through his locked teeth. "Those that were about him rejoiced," Winslow recalled, "saying he had not swallowed anything in two days before." Next, Winslow applied his knife to scrape off "the abundance of corruption" that had furred the sachem's tongue and filled his mouth, preventing him from eating. It was an incredible moment: a stranger from a people the Wampanoags associated with terrible crimes, including sorcery, was using a blade to pry open their sachem's mouth and pour unfamiliar substances down his throat. Winslow must have known that he was putting the alliance to its ultimate test, with potentially severe consequences if he failed.[23]

Winslow's intervention stabilized Ousamequin enough for him to begin drinking small amounts of water and liquefied food, whereupon his sight returned, followed by his first good sleep in two nights. All the while, Winslow sat there by his bedside, monitoring his condition, including his bowel movements, which returned for the first time after an alarming absence of five days. Soon the sachem was requesting English pottage (a thick soup) with fowl, such as he had once enjoyed back in Plymouth, but Winslow advised against it until he gained more strength. Instead, the Englishman concocted

Edward Winslow. Pilgrim Hall Museum, Plymouth, Massachusetts.

This portrait of Edward Winlsow, produced by an anonymous painter in London in 1651, is the only contemporary image we have of any of the *Mayflower* passengers. Winslow figured prominently in Plymouth's early relations with Ousamequin, which included his making two critical diplomatic visits to the sachem's home village of Sowams. Winslow would go on to serve several terms as Plymouth's governor and as one of Plymouth's commissioners to the United Colonies of New England. He returned to England in 1646 during the Civil War and died in 1655 of yellow fever while serving in Oliver Cromwell's navy in the Caribbean.

his own stew of cornmeal and kernels, strawberry leaves, and sassafras, strained through a handkerchief. As everyone watched in anticipation, the sachem drank "at least a pint . . . and liked it very well." Bit by bit, Winslow's care was drawing the Wampanoag leader back from the brink of death.[24]

And so, at Ousamequin's request, Winslow became an unwitting nurse to other Wampanoags suffering from the disease. "They were good folk," Ousamequin emphasized. A reluctant Winslow obliged, going house to house to treat stranger after stranger, scraping tongues, washing out mouths, and dispensing food. Understandably, Winslow found the whole affair "offensive, not being

accustomed with such poisonous savors [smells]" as emanated from
the polluted mouths of the sick. Though no medical practitioner,
Winslow persevered. He was wise enough to his mission and increasingly sensitive enough to Wampanoag ways to perceive that there
was hardly a greater diplomatic gesture than providing this care
under such revolting conditions. This was the kind of compassion
shown not only by a friend but also by a kinsman.[25]

Winslow almost lost his budding reputation as a shamanistic
hero as suddenly as he had obtained it when Ousamequin took a
turn for the worse, apparently because of the sachem's craving for
fowl pottage. By nightfall of the second day, the sachem's pestering
had worn down Winslow's better judgment and convinced him to
prepare the dish. "Never did I see a man so low brought recover in
that measure in so short of time," Winslow explained. He spoke too
soon. Ousamequin rejected Winslow's advice to skim the goose fat
from the broth and instead made "a gross meal of it . . . as would well
have satisfied a man in health." An hour later, the sachem regurgi-
tated everything and began bleeding from the nose again. Ousamequin's violent reaction, which lasted four hours, made the Wampanoags
and Winslow fearful again that "now he would die." At a loss for what
else to do, Winslow sat there washing the sachem's face and pinching
his nose to staunch the bleeding. It must have been everything he
could do not to fixate on whether the Wampanoags would fault
him if the sachem died and what it would all mean for his fate and
Plymouth's.[26]

Yet Ousamequin did not die, and instead of receiving blame
Winslow got the credit. Scores of Indians from great distances
poured into Pokanoket just as Ousamequin began to recover for the
second time, to whom the "chief men" told of how "the English came
to see him, and how suddenly they recovered him to the strength
they saw, he being now able to sit upright of himself." When Ousamequin initially fell ill, a dissident sachem had reportedly taunted him

that "now he might see how hollow-hearted the English were," that they would not visit, that they did not wish him well. Who could say such things with a straight face any longer? Ousamequin, aglow in his recuperation and the confirmation of his political judgment, could not resist the opportunity to crow to his critics that "now I see the English are my friends and love me, and while I live I will never forget this kindness they have shown me."[27]

One might be tempted to think that such statements, as recounted by Winslow himself, were nothing more than self-serving ventriloquism, yet consider the goodwill his actions had fostered and its political implications. Back in the spring of 1621, Ousamequin took his own bold risk by reaching out to Plymouth despite widespread Wampanoag resentment of the English for at least twenty years' worth of crimes. He knew then that he would face resistance for this decision from within the Wampanoag camp and from without in the form of the Narragansetts trying to cleave off his allies and tributaries. Yet he judged the gamble to be worthwhile because, with his people laid low by the epidemic of 1616–19, the Narragansetts had already begun to treat him like a subordinate. To some degree, his bet paid off. Plymouth supplied him with gifts, trade, and political recognition that enhanced his people's material life and his authority. When Corbitant raised a minor rebellion against his policies, Plymouth helped put it down.

In other ways, though, the English merely reinforced the Wampanoags' suspicions of them. They discouraged everyday Wampanoags from visiting their settlement and kept their men on guard even when Wampanoags of high rank were around. They had partnered with the parasitic outpost of Wessagusset. They sometimes resorted to intimidation when trading with the Wampanoags for corn, rather than showing gratitude. They had harbored Tisquantum despite his treasonous double-crossing and Ousamequin's demand for his life. It was as if they did not understand that Plymouth was built atop Patuxet and remained a part of Wampa-noag country. No wonder Ousamequin withdrew from the English before he fell ill—that is, until Winslow's performance at Pokanoket. The Englishman had provided intimate, effective medical care not only for the sachem but for his people as a whole, as if he really cared about them. It was an act of tenderness and repair that transformed him and, by extension, his people into true allies.

CUTTHROATS

In return, Ousamequin slipped some startling intelligence to the English. As Winslow and his team made their way back to Plym-outh, Hobbamock shared news from Ousamequin that there was a plot brewing to wipe out Wessagusset and Plymouth. It involved an axis of sachemships stretching from Massachusetts Bay down to Cape Cod and the islands, the very places with the worst histories of English raids. Apparently the conspirators had solicited Ousame-quin's support while he was ailing, but he claimed to have rejected the offer out of hand. Now he wanted the English to know that he remained their friend. He also proffered some advice about what to do. The key was to launch a preemptive strike against "the men of the Massachusetts," whom he characterized as "the authors of this intended mischief . . . Take away the principals," he emphasized, "and then the plot would cease."[28]

If there was such a conspiracy, it seems unlikely to have involved just the outermost Wampanoag sachemships of the Cape and islands and not any of the Taunton River communities closest to Ousamequin. After all, Corbitant had led the previous drive to get rid of Plymouth, and though Ousamequin did not implicate him at this time, Corbitant certainly continued to harbor enmity toward of the English. In fact, just before Hobbamock revealed the plot, Winslow and his men had spent the night as Corbitant's guests at

Mattapoisett, a peninsula just east of Pokanoket, but it was difficult to tell if the sachem truly welcomed them. His conversation included pointed critiques of the English offset by "merry jests and squibs [sarcasm]" as if he meant nothing by it. For instance, he questioned whether the English would rush to his side if he happened to fall ill like Ousamequin. He found it puzzling that Winslow and Hamden were so bold as to pass through the country with no other protection than Hobbamock. Winslow responded that he saw no reason to fear. Well, then, Corbitant continued, "if your love be such . . . how cometh it to pass, that when we come to Patuxet, you stand upon your guard, with the mouths of your pieces [muskets] presented towards us?" Winslow dodged, as he had done in his earlier debate with Ousamequin's brother about this issue, that "it was the most honorable and respective entertainment we could give them" according to English custom. Corbitant, "shaking his head . . . answered, that he liked not such salutations." Could it have been mere coincidence that Hobbamock told what he knew so soon after they left Corbitant's company?[29]

Other Wampanoags in Ousamequin's inner circle must have shared Corbitant's loathing of the English, as the great sachem certainly was aware. Though Ousamequin never would have attempted to engage with Plymouth if he did not have popular support, there was enough opposition to make him uneasy, particularly in light of the Narragansetts threatening to cleave off Wampanoags unhappy with his rule. Ousamequin's apparent design was to direct an English strike against the Indians of Massachusetts Bay in order to intimidate Wampanoag dissidents in the Taunton River communities into rejecting Narragansett overtures and deferring to his leadership. This maneuver would also strengthen his hand when it came to collecting tribute from the outer Wampanoag sachemships of the Cape and islands. The message was that anyone who rejected his authority ran the risk of being next. This was not a policy of first resort. The ideal was for sachems "to carry it obligingly and lovingly unto their people, lest they should desert him," but that approach seemed only to embolden Ousamequin's challengers. As in Ousamequin's first entreaty to the English, it was time for him to make a power play to defend his paramount sachem status.[30]

It appears that Ousamequin truthfully told at least half the story. While Plymouth was debating what to do, it received confirmation of the plot from the Massachusett sachem, Wassapinewat, brother of a former anti-English confederate of Corbitant's named Obtakiest. Apparently, Wassapinewat wanted to distance himself from the conspiracy in the event of a colonial backlash. This development sealed Plymouth's decision to order eight men under Standish to go to Massachusetts Bay on pretense of trade and, when the people's defenses were down, assassinate the ringleaders, particularly Wituwamat. They consoled themselves that this subterfuge would be no worse than the "traps they [the Indians] lay for others."[31]

The day before this expedition set sail, additional evidence surfaced when Phineas Pratt, one of the Wessagusset colonists, stumbled into Plymouth terrified and breathless to warn that the Massachusett Indians were mobilizing. The signs were unmistakable, he pleaded. The pniese, Pecksuot (whom the English sometimes called Pexworth), had threatened Wessagusset that his knives were eager to slay Englishman, just as they had once killed the French. A Native woman whom Pratt had jokingly punched in the shoulder (why, he did not say) snapped back that soon her people would make the English pay. Most alarmingly, Native people around the Bay were stockpiling arms and ammunition, pressuring Wessagusset colonists to trade them more, and constructing a fleet of mishoons for what Pratt believed was a planned amphibious attack against Plymouth. With Indians keeping the Wessagusset fort under close watch, Pratt had been forced to sneak out under cover of night and make a harrowing twenty-five-mile trek to Plymouth while keeping off marked trails to elude pursuers. Then, as if to confirm his incredible story, a couple of days later a Massachusett Indian "pretending friendship" entered Plymouth claiming to be on his way home from Manomet when it appeared that he had actually been tracking Pratt. Leaving nothing to chance, Bradford's council decided to hold the Indian prisoner until Standish had completed his preemptive strike.[32]

As designed, the mission was a bloody affair. The expedition arrived at Wessagusset to find the colonists scattered about grubbing for wild food with no sense of danger. "They feared not the Indians," Standish reported, which he chalked up to their obliviousness. By contrast, Indians who stopped by the fort to see what the commotion was about knew that trouble was afoot. One of them baited Standish: "He saw by his eyes that he was angry." Pecksuot challenged his fellow pniese, Hobbamock, that though the Plymouth troopers intended to kill his people, he did not fear. Massachusett matawaûog whetted their blades in full view of the English, daring them to attempt the first blow, with Wituwamat once again bragging, knife in hand, that "I have killed both French and English." Nevertheless, somehow Standish was able to convince Pecksuot, Wituwamat, and two of their tribesmen to meet with him indoors the next day. Once they were seated, Standish gave the signal for his men to bar the exit and put their guests to the sword. The captain threw himself right into the fray, grabbing the razor-sharp dagger Pecksuot wore around his neck and stabbing him repeatedly with it. The English found it "incredible how much [injury] these two pnieses [Pecksuot and Wituwamat] received before they died, not making any fearful noise, but catching at their weapons and striving to the last."[33]

The supposed instigators of the plot were dead, but this was not the end of Plymouth's bloodletting. During the assassinations of Pecksuot and Wituwamat, other Englishmen stationed about the fort had also surprised and killed an additional three Indians. Later in the day, Standish's company marched out of the fort "still seeking to make spoil" and wound up in a pitched battle in which English musketeers seized open high ground while Native bowmen shot arrows at them from the cover of nearby woods. With neither party able to dislodge the other, Hobbamock threw off his coat and charged directly into the Massachusett Indian ranks, scattering them into a nearby swamp while the English lagged behind, awestruck by his bravery. At this, Standish decided to quit while he was ahead. He already grasped what future English commanders would have to learn the hard way: that colonial militiamen accustomed to open-field drills would not fare well against seasoned Indian fighters ensconced in dense, swampy terrain. Better to declare victory and head home. Some of the Wessagusset men returned with him to Plymouth, while most decided to abandon the place for Monhegan Island in hopes of catching a ride back to England from a fishing vessel. None of them were foolish enough to remain behind and take their chances with the Indians, particularly after learning that the Natives had killed three of their company in revenge for Plymouth's brutality. The troublesome fur trade post of Wessagusset was no more.[34]

The strike had done much more than just eliminate a thorn in Plymouth's side. It also sent a dire warning about the consequences of threatening Plymouth and challenging Ousamequin and his policy of English rapprochement. This was the most ferocious action by the English since the arrival of the *Mayflower*. Standish and his men had taken five Indian lives and carried home the head of Wituwamat, which Plymouth mounted atop its fort to rot alongside a flag fashioned out of a piece of linen stained with Indian blood. Fearing they were next, the Cape Wampanoags fled to defensible interior swamps instead of taking advantage of the spring fish runs and preparing their summer planting fields. "Manifold diseases" cut through their ranks under these conditions, claiming the lives of the sachems Canacum, Aspinet, and Iyanough, whom Ousamequin had implicated in the plot. From the distance of four centuries, it appears that the same pestilence that had killed Tisquantum and laid low Ousamequin had attacked the sachems amid the crowding, stress, and malnutrition of the swamp shelters. The Wampanoags did not seem to interpret it that way. Plymouth heard that as Iyanough was dying, he despaired that "the God of the English was offended with them, and would destroy them in their anger." For a time, every disaster great and small seemed only to confirm this premonition. Colonists could not help but notice that, in the wake of these events, "none of them [Indians] dare to come amongst us." The English were now known as Wotowequenage, meaning "cutthroats."[35]

THE WAMPANOAGS' NEW WORLD

From the comfortable distance of Leiden, the Separatists' spiritual leader, John Robinson, admonished them for their hasty resort to violence in the Wessagusset strike: "Oh! How happy a thing it had been if you had converted some, before you had killed any," he intoned, adding that the question for him was "not what they deserved, but what you were by necessity to inflict." Bradford agreed that shedding innocent blood was an offense to God, but he did not believe in the innocence of the Indians killed by his men. Plymouth colonists were of one opinion that a combination of Indians had been ready to slaughter them. They considered it better to keep most of the surrounding Indians in a state of intimidation while maintaining a friendship with the strongest sachem in the neighborhood than to sit passively and await a massacre like that suffered by Virginia in 1622. They also remained confident that God was still on their side.[36]

Whatever Robinson's criticisms, the colonists' approach seemed to work, at least as far as they defined it. It would be decades before there was another rumor of an Indian threat against the colony. Instead, once the shock of the Wessagusset strike wore off, most of the Wampanoag communities implicated in the plot began selling land to the English and hosting Christian missionaries. Plymouth men boasted that they felt as if they could "walk as peaceably and safely in the wood as in the highways in England." Additionally, outlying Wampanoag sachemships helped the English capture their runaway servants and, in a marked departure from previous years, assisted the survivors of English shipwrecks off the shores of Cape Cod. Robinson could rebuke Plymouth from the safety of the Netherlands that it was "a thing more glorious in men's eyes, than pleasing in God's, or convenient for Christians, to be a terror to poor barbarous people." His fellow Separatists in America preferred to live in relative security, even if it came at the expense of the people in whose country they lived and whose souls they claimed to want to save. In any case, they saw the divine at work in their enterprise. "If God had let them [the Indians] loose," reflected Winslow, "they might have easily swallowed us up."[37]

Ousamequin was the other big winner in the Wessagusset strike. He had proved his ability to harness English violence to his own ends without sacrificing any of his own people. As far as one can tell from the historical record, at no other point in his life would he face opposition from within the Wampanoag tribe to his alliance with the English, his right to represent the people in their dealings with the colonists, or his authority over communities as far away as Cape Cod, Martha's Vineyard, and Nantucket. English writers went so far as to assert that "there is now great peace amongst the Indians themselves [probably meaning the Wampanoags], which was not formerly." Ousamequin's sons would eventually succeed him without facing any noticeable palace intrigue. Hobbamock, his multiple wives, and their children set up a homestead right outside Plymouth's palisade, thereby ensuring that the colonists could do little without Ousamequin knowing about it. More European trade goods from Plymouth—including cloth, clothing, metal tools, kettles, jewelry, weapons, and more—flowed into Pokanoket than probably any other Wampanoag community. Plymouth even built a trading post right in Ousamequin's territory. This commerce enabled the sachem and his core followers to flaunt their wealth, power, and generosity and thereby enhance their prestige.[38]

Perhaps most important, the colonists' show of strength, and their continued support of Ousamequin, served to fend off the Narragansetts. It would be nearly another decade before Ousamequin faced another Narragansett attack, and when he did, the English were quick to come to his defense. In April 1632 a Narragansett force stormed into Pokanoket hoping to take Ousamequin hostage, only to have the sachem retreat to the safety of the nearby English trade house while awaiting reinforcements and provisions from Plymouth, which soon arrived under Standish. Days later, the Narragansetts withdrew for a campaign on their western boundary against the Pequots. (Indeed, the point of them trying to take Ousamequin might have been to force Wampanoag men to join this effort.) At least twice in ten years, Ousamequin's alliance with the English had deflected Narragansett aggression against him, never mind the deterrent effects of the Wampanoags' metal weaponry from Plymouth. Without such assistance, Ousamequin surely would have lost his independence and perhaps his life.[39]

Tisquantum had formerly told Ousamequin of "what wonders he had seen in England," but the sachem's secondhand knowledge gave him no reason to think that Plymouth represented a long-term threat. For all of the colonists' ferocity, they were still small in number in 1627, with just fifty-seven men over the age of sixteen, and thirty adult women, or about the size of a single small Wampanoag

community. It took until 1624 for the first head of cattle to arrive in
the colony, so how could the sachem have envisioned that such
animals would eventually overrun the country, interfering with the
Wampanoags' ability to feed themselves, and inflaming their relations with the English? What signs were there that in the 1630s
nearly twenty thousand English would pour into a new colony on
Massachusetts Bay and spill over into the buffer zone between Plymouth and Pokanoket and east to Cape Cod and the islands? American
history has a tradition of treating such developments as inevitable,
even providential, and certainly positive. From Ousamequin's
perspective in the 1620s, the very notion would have been difficult to
imagine. After all, the point of his maneuvers had been to enhance
his authority and return the Wampanoags to their former strength.[40]

After Wessagusset, colonial spokesmen turned from their
swords to their pens and recast the Wampanoags from savages into
generous hosts. They emphasized that the Natives always welcomed
strangers into their homes and fed them cheerfully with the best of
what they had even in times of scarcity. Plymouth's leaders even
went so far as to contend that Ousamequin said they could take
"what place we will, and as much land as we will, and bringing many
people as we will," in answer to critics back in England who questioned the colony's right to exist without a royal charter. Later generations of white Americans created their own versions of this trope
when they characterized the Wampanoags as inherently friendly
children of the forest who enabled Christianity, civility, and democracy to take root in America by greeting the Pilgrims with the salu-
tation "Welcome, Englishman."[41]

Self-serving, sugarcoated versions of the Pilgrim-Indian encounter
ignore that it was not the Wampanoags as a whole who reached out to
the English but Ousamequin and his core followers over the protests
and sometimes the resistance of a great many other Indians who
considered the English cutthroats. Furthermore, even Ousamequin

and those he represented had no interest in hosting a thriving colony that would displace their people. Their intention was to keep the English under their control, to draw trade goods and military assistance from them while limiting their expansion to places where the Wampanoag population was thin or the people needed assistance against the Narragansetts. Wampanoags in favor of this approach did not envision English dominance or even English-Wampanoag equality. The future they were trying to craft was about Wampanoag power under the direction of Ousamequin and his lineal successors.

Celebratory accounts of the Wampanoags' generosity have also ignored that it came with expectations. William Wood of Massachusetts was one of the few colonists to realize this point. Yes, he emphasized, Indians stood out from the English in that "they are willing to part with their mite [tiny amount] in poverty, as treasure in plenty." Yet the flip side of their munificence was that they became "disjoined by ingratitude, accounting an ungrateful person a double robber of a man." They would find many occasions in the future to become disjoined at English ingratitude.[42]

CHAPTER SIX

 λ ⌐

A Great Man and a Little Child

One reason Ousamequin's alliance with Plymouth gets such outsized attention in patriotic treatments of American history is that, on the surface, it was the peaceful exception to the violent rule of Indian-colonial relations. True enough, the Wampanoags and English did not war against each other between 1621 and 1675, which was a real accomplishment. They had even attempted to create a reciprocal friendship. This point was acknowledged by Ousamequin's very son, Pumetacom (also known as Metacom and Philip), on the eve of the war that now bears his English name. In his own history, he recalled that "when the English first came, [Ousamequin] was as a great man and the English as a little child." What Pumetacom meant by this was that though the Wampanoags were far stronger than the colonists initially, Ousamequin did not exploit this advantage. Instead, he "had been the first in doing good to the English," as if he were their protective father. For instance, he "constrained other Indians from wronging the English, and gave them corn, and showed them how to plant, and was free to do them any good, and let them have a 100 times more land than now the king [or sachem, Pumetacom] had for his own people." In exchange, Ousamequin received English military support and trade, which strengthened his authority among the Wampanoags and protected them against the

Narragansetts. It was a bargain that, by and large, paid off for both parties up until Ousamequin's death in 1660.[1]

Yet the mutual benefits of the alliance should not blind us to the very real costs for the Wampanoags. Nor should it obviate the recurrent Indian-English war scares that marked the 1620–75 era of peace and led to the brutal King Philip's War. Even before Ousamequin's passing, the "little child" of Plymouth, along with its neighboring English colonies, had begun acting ungratefully, setting the stage for Ousamequin's actual sons, Wamsutta and Pumetacom, to begin organizing a resistance movement. Predictably, from a modern vantage, the main tensions involved English encroachment on Wampanoag land by means fair and foul. However, a deeper understanding of the Wampanoag side of things requires us to do more than tally how many acres the English gained at Wampanoag expense. For the period of Ousamequin's life, it involves tracing how a mutually lucrative trade of European manufactured goods for Indian wampum and furs gradually gave way to an economic relationship centered on the English purchase of Wampanoag land. In turn, grasping why Native people sold territory when they did and to whom depends on an appreciation for the Indians' cultivation of the English as friends amid the chronic danger of war. It also invites us to consider alternative views to the Western principle that the seller of land relinquishes all rights to the buyer, and to the popular assumption that when Europeans acquired land from Indians, they also gained full jurisdiction over that territory and the people on it. Wampanoags had no such conceptions of these bargains. Wampanoag resentment over colonial encroachment stemmed partly from the English using their strength to impose their interpretation of these transactions.

Wampanoag-English tensions also fed on the internal politics of the Wampanoag paramount sachemship, particularly the efforts of outlying Wampanoag communities to loosen Ousamequin's authority over them. One of the remarkable ironies of this period is that the

Wampanoags of Cape Cod and the islands of Martha's Vineyard and Nantucket granted land to the English and hosted Christian missionaries as part of an effort to distance themselves from Pokanoket, based, in part, on earlier resentments over Ousamequin's accord with the English. By the time of Ousamequin's death, his sons and the people they represented had come to interpret English violations of Wampanoag land, sovereignty, cultural autonomy, and dignity not as peaceful coexistence, as the Thanksgiving myth would have it, but as hostility. Rejecting the old sachem's legacy, they concluded that friendship with Plymouth was a mere pretense leading to landlessness and subordination, and thus no longer worth it.

ENRICHING EACH OTHER

Trade as well as mutual defense rested at the heart of the Wampanoags' alliance with the English, which one might assume was a simple matter of both parties trying to enrich themselves. Yet these peoples had varying cultural notions of what enrichment meant. Those differences exposed the basic incompatibility of the two people's social systems and contributed mightily to the deterioration of their relationship by the end of Ousamequin's lifetime.

Among the Wampanoags, and Indian people in general, a great deal of the value of material wealth rested in the social relationships it fostered and the spiritual power it represented. One point of acquiring exotic goods was to give them away eventually. To be sure, that process could take some time. After all, Wampanoags were no different from any other people in their enjoyment of fine clothing, jewelry, and luxuries, which in the case of the European trade included shirts, coats, blankets, glass beads, rings, combs, and bracelets. They also appreciated the utility of the foreigners' durable metal tools. Yet, after a period of using those items personally, they would pass them on to others because the circulation of material wealth was the essential social lubricant in Indian country. Proposing marriage, consoling a mourner, apologizing for an insult, compensating for a crime, and an infinite variety of other social interactions all involved giving or exchanging gifts. People even buried their dead with valuable goods so their souls could carry the spirits of the objects on the journey to the afterlife. Sometimes the gods received their share, too, as in the great Narragansett ritual dedicated to Cautantowwit (Kiehtan) in which the people cast their cherished objects into a roaring central fire. To refuse to participate in these customs was to mark oneself as selfish and jealous, the qualities of witches. To conform was to promote the endless series of mutual obligations and spirit of generosity essential to the success of small, intimate face-to-face societies like Wampanoag communities. To excel at giving was to magnify one's influence.[2]

As such, sachems circulated European manufactured goods among their followers just as they did with exotic materials from the continental interior. Whether sachems did this in the course of their basic duties, like arbitrating disputes or overseeing justice, or mainly in ceremonial contexts is unknown. The only eyewitness account of sachems redistributing wealth is Roger Williams's 1644 description of a Narragansett ritual called Nickòmmo, in which elites hosted "sometimes twenty, fifty, a hundred, yea . . . near a thousand persons" for a dance, feast, and giveaway of "all sort of their goods (according to and sometimes beyond their estate) in several small parcels of goods." Each recipient would then go outside and give three shouts "for the health and prosperity of the party that gave it, the Mr. or Mistriss of the feast." Williams might have been describing the same event when he wrote to the Massachusetts governor, John Winthrop, in August 1637 that the Narragansetts "were in a strange kind of solemnity, wherein the sachems eat nothing but at night, and all the natives about the country were feasted." This ceremony appears to have been a way to symbolize that the people's bounty was a gift from their leaders.[3]

The concentration of European goods at archaeological sites within Ousamequin's sachemship of Pokanoket reflects that his core supporters enjoyed privileged access to colonial trade. Suddenly, living at Pokanoket, and probably at other Taunton River communities like Pocasset and Nemakset where Ousamequin had relatives, meant possessing wool cloth, brass and iron kettles, pewter and latten spoons, tin cups, glass bottles, iron hoes, iron axes, iron knives, iron fishhooks, iron scissors, brass arrowheads, and glass beads. Elites, such as the sachem's kin and counselors, had even greater material wealth in the forms of European clothing, swords and guns, brass rings, gold ribbon, and wooden chests with locks and keys. Within just a matter of years, these goods had become so ubiquitous that many of the people used them in the full range of their daily activities, including clearing fields, weeding, cooking, sewing, hunting, butchering, building houses, cutting firewood, and even just getting dressed. The effects were so transformative that this moment might be called a consumer revolution. Yet one should not take the point too far. There is a tendency to assume that as soon as Indian peoples had access to European trade, they became dependent on it, as if they entirely quit their former technologies and forgot how to produce them. That was not true of the Wampanoags. Along with their new imports, they continued to craft and use their own containers of clay, wood, stone, and woven grass; tools and weapons of wood, stone, bone, and shell; leather and fur clothing; rope and thread from plant fibers and deer gut; and ornaments of shell, bone, antler, and teeth. As during the early contact period, they often disassembled European goods for raw material to use in their own tools, weapons, and ornaments. Some conservatives preferred to keep doing things as they always had and probably saw the rage for foreign goods as detrimental to the people's autonomy and community values. Nevertheless, the alliance with the English, supplemented by periodic trade with the Dutch, had opened the Wampanoags to a new material world that most of them embraced to greater or lesser degree.[4]

These goods meant more than luxury or efficiency to the Wampanoags. They also represented power: diplomatic, military, and spiritual. When sachems enriched their communities, they secured a base of local political support from which to govern at home and negotiate with other Native leaders. Gift giving and trade also firmed up alliances with foreign peoples. In times of war, the sachem's arsenal of iron tomahawks and knives, steel swords, brass-tipped arrows, and, of course, firearms made all the difference. In a more general way, Wampanoag wealth symbolized spiritual potency. Northeastern Indians widely associated glass beads with crystals thought to originate from lightning bolts shot from the eyes of the mythical Thunderbird. The beads' lightness connoted positivity, life, knowledge, and well-being. Firearms, with their pyrotechnics and destructive force, also seemed to embody the power of the Thunderbird and give the bearer the shamanistic ability to implant harmful objects in an enemy. The reflective qualities of mirrors represented divination of the sort carried out by pawwaws and dream souls. In all these ways and more, European trade goods coursed with spiritual significance. Some scholars have gone so far as to contend that Indians were "trading in metaphors." A society like the Wampanoags', which associated well-being with spiritual favor, might even have interpreted the thriving trade as a sign that they were recovering from the plague of 1616–19.[5]

Whereas the Wampanoags wanted European goods but did not need them, Plymouth colony's very survival rested on the Indian trade. The colonists could hardly feed themselves, never mind satisfy their financiers' demand for furs, without the help of their

Wampanoag neighbors. It took Indian corn obtained through gifts and trade for the English to cheat starvation during their second winter and spring. Even after the colonists became agriculturally self-sufficient in 1623, they probably still relied on the Wampanoags for a portion of their meat, as it would take years before they had imported and bred enough cows, sheep, pigs, and goats to answer their needs. By the mid-1620s, the English had become productive fishermen after initially lacking the equipment and expertise, but it is likely that they continued to trade for shellfish with Native women who gathered them in Plymouth Harbor. Colonists might also have turned to Indian wage labor when it came to getting land cleared, fences built, and houses erected, though such employment is under-documented. "Frontier exchange economies" of this sort, involving Indians and Europeans bartering food and services, were basic to the survival of most early colonies. At first, Plymouth authorities discouraged their people's casual interactions with the Wampanoags, for such familiarity had enabled the Powhatans to launch their surprise strike against Virginia in 1622. Yet the trade of "small things" was so ubiquitous and probably essential that in 1640 Plymouth's General Court gave up trying to regulate it.[6]

The real problem for the English was that the market for Indian furs included European competitors with better-quality goods in larger amounts. The Dutch were their greatest rivals in this respect. The Dutch had been trading with the Indians of southern New England and Long Island since the early 1600s, and when they founded the colony of New Netherland in 1624, that traffic increased exponentially. Dutch mercantile vessels fanned out from the port of New Amsterdam on Manhattan Island to scour the northeast coast for Indian customers. This activity included regular visits to the Wampanoags of Narragansett and Buzzards Bays. The Dutch also established short-lived trade houses at such places as "Dutch Island" in Narragansett Bay, Block Island, and the Connecticut River (at

the site of modern Hartford). For Indians, Dutch trade was ideal. The Netherlands was at once the premier manufacturing and maritime trading nation of Europe during the early seventeenth century, making the Dutch the best source for cloth, clothing, armaments, metal tools, glass beads, and liquor. Better still, once the dealing was done, the Dutch typically sailed off, thereby giving New England Indians the best of both worlds: the benefit of Dutch goods without the complications of Dutch colonization. Plymouth also faced competition from English and French fishermen working the Maine coast and Massachusetts Bay. Like the Dutch, their commerce was brisk and relatively uncomplicated insofar as they dropped anchor, conducted the exchange, and then left without any expectation of further relations.[7]

Plymouth could not compete in any of these respects. The colony received no Indian trade goods between the arrival of the *Fortune* in 1621 and the summer of 1623, and those that arrived afterward were overpriced and of low quality, amounting to "only a few beads and knives, which were not there much esteemed." Furthermore, unlike New Netherland, which teemed with seasoned merchants, only a few Plymouth colonists had previous business experience. Not least of all, Plymouth's economic relations with nearby Indians, unlike those of its rivals, were inseparable from on-the-ground politics essential to the colony's future.[8]

Geography also did not work in Plymouth's favor. Neither Plymouth Harbor nor the nearby coast contained a major river providing access to the heavily forested, beaver-rich interior. (The Charles River of Massachusetts Bay hardly qualified.) In contrast, the Dutch post of Fort Orange on the upper Hudson River attracted Indians from a vast hinterland including what is now northern New England, the St. Lawrence River valley, upstate New York, and even the Great Lakes. Meanwhile, the Dutch traded from shipside at the mouths of the Connecticut and Blackstone Rivers, which ran north deep into the New England woods. Independent English traders in coastal Maine had similar advantages dealing with Wabanakis at the mouths of lengthy rivers like the Penobscot, Kennebec, Androscoggin, and Saco. To the limited extent that Plymouth managed a successful trade during its early years, it came in 1625 when Edward Winslow took the colony's surplus corn to exchange with Maine Indians, netting seven hundred pounds weight in beaver and some other furs. Yet, even then, the colony received no credit for this haul because French pirates captured the ship carrying it before it could reach the Adventurers back in England. If the Plymouth colonists had settled at their intended destination of the lower Hudson River, or at Massachusetts Bay (to which they briefly considered relocating), they would have been situated far better for the Indian trade.[9]

Despite these liabilities, Plymouth assumed a more active economic role in the region as its population and agriculture stabilized. In 1626 the colony put its finances on a surer footing by granting a group of its leading men, including Bradford, Winslow, and Standish, a monopoly on the fur trade in exchange for their assuming responsibility for the colony's mounting debt. The following year, these so-called Undertakers administered the construction of a trading post at Aptucxet at the head of Buzzards Bay, accessible from Plymouth by six hours of canoe paddling and portages along Scusset Creek and the Manomet River, nowadays enveloped by the Cape Cod Canal. The station was modest, consisting of just "a house made of hewn oak planks . . . where they keep two men, winter and summer," an attached storehouse, and a shallop to cruise local waters. Yet it finally gave Plymouth a base from which to reach the main body of Wampanoags south of the Cape and enter the lucrative trade of Narragansett Bay.[10]

Little did the English know that Apucxet would soon become a node in an extensive indigenous trade network linking coastal

Aptucxet. Photography by Vejlenser.

Plymouth's Aptucxet trading post, on the Manomet (or Monument) River at
the head of Buzzards Bay, was a node in the regional trade of indigenously
produced wampum beads and furs for European metal tools, cloth, clothing,
weapons, and ornaments. Built in 1627, the post operated into the 1650s,
when Plymouth appears to have abandoned it in response to a sharp decline
in wampum's value. The buildings shown here are a reconstruction of the
post built atop its original foundation.

manufacturers and traffickers of shell beads (or wampum) with interior producers of beaver pelts. *Wampum* (also known as *sewan* and
wampumpeag, or *peag* for short) referred to tubular white and purple
beads measuring about an inch long and an eighth of an inch in
diameter made from the inner column of the whelk and periwinkle
(in the case of white wampum) and the outer rim of the quahog (in
the case of purple). Before the Indians' acquisition of iron drills,
which bore holes through the shells more quickly and efficiently
than stone, most shell beads were discoidal in shape (imagine a coin
with a hole in the middle). The rarity of tubular beads made them a
status symbol displayed by the elite in headbands, belts, necklaces,

and earrings, and even as ornamentation for war clubs, pipes, and bowls. More generally, the circulation of discoidal and eventually tubular shell beads was part of regional politics and trade. Foreign diplomacy involved sachems exchanging fathom-long (six-foot) strings of shell beads to symbolize the depth of their domestic support (for, after all, the common people's labor and wealth went into the gift) and the sincerity of their speech. Intertribal commerce and tribute obligations carried the beads from coastal sites of production hundreds of miles into the continent. The Five Nations Iroquois, for example, required enormous amounts of processed shell for their peacekeeping rituals and possessed the military might to extort the beads from shoreline communities. In turn, the strongest coastal groups pressured neighboring peoples to pay them tribute in wampum so they could ease Iroquois pressure on themselves.[11]

Once wampum manufacturing began on a larger scale with the introduction of metal drills, and particularly when Europeans got involved in the trade, the pace of this traffic quickened dramatically. The Narragansetts and Pequots on Long Island Sound, soon joined by Dutch and English middlemen, began supplying interior peoples at unprecedented rates: archaeologists estimate that the total number of beads reaching the Iroquois in the early to mid-seventeenth century might have run into the millions. Shoreline peoples received furs in exchange, which they then traded to Europeans. The political benefits of this commerce were nearly as great as the material ones, insofar as the Narragansetts' and Pequots' value as wampum producers spared them from the Five Nations' wide-ranging raids for captives and plunder. Unfortunately, a lack of positive documentary and archaeological evidence makes it impossible to say definitively whether the Wampanoags also traded wampum, though it seems likely.[12]

It took only a few years before the Dutch discovered the profits they could reap trading with coastal Natives for wampum, then transporting the beads upriver to exchange with the Iroquois and Mohicans for beaver pelts destined for sale in Europe. Yet, rather than bet on the unlikelihood that the English would fail to make a similar discovery, in 1627 New Netherland's governor, Isaack de Rasieres, decided to share the Dutch trade secret with Plymouth in exchange for an agreement to divvy up the northeast coast into separate national commercial zones. Plymouth would direct its fur trade north to Massachusetts Bay and Maine and away from the center of Dutch enterprise on Long Island Sound. Additionally, the Dutch would supply Plymouth with wampum and trade goods and

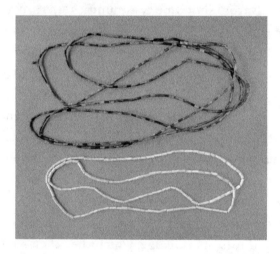

Wampum strings. Courtesy of the Peabody Museum of Archaeology and Ethnology, Harvard University, PM #99-12-10/53011 and 99-12-10/53014.

Native people of the northeast coast made *wampum* shell beads from the quahog (in the case of purple beads) and whelk and periwinkle (in the case of white wampum). The exchange of strings of wampum, like the ones pictured here, were a common part of Indian diplomacy. The strings served simultaneously as mnemonic devices (or memory aids) for speeches and as gifts that demonstrated commitment to the spoken words. European colonists often adopted this protocol, too, when dealing with indigenous people, though there is no concrete evidence that Plymouth colonists did so.

buy the colony's furs and Virginia tobacco (acquired from Virginia fishing vessels working the New England coast). It was an ambitious vision reflecting not only the multilateral state of European competition along the American coast but also the potential riches for colonies that tapped into long-distance intertribal economies, at once ancient and evolving.[13]

The plan worked only partly as designed. Consistent with Dutch hopes, Plymouth initially concentrated its trade on the Penobscot and Kennebec River valleys, finding that though the Wabanakis were uninterested in wampum at first, fashion trends and competition for social status meant that shortly "they could scarce ever get enough for them." Plymouth was the beneficiary, with its annual shipments of beaver pelts to England ranging in weight between one thousand and four thousand pounds from 1631 to 1636 to the value of ten thousand pounds. This commerce was but a fraction of New Netherland's, yet it was a vast improvement over the thin years of the previous decade. Wampum even temporarily became legal tender in Plymouth and then the other New England colonies for payment of taxes and private debts, based on the premise that the beads could be traded for beaver, which, in turn, could be sold in Europe for hard coin. Yet Plymouth's activity in Maine did not preclude it from trading south of the Cape. Though Plymouth reluctantly promised not to interfere with Dutch operations among the Wampanoags, it refused to cede its own right to trade with the tribe, "which is (as it were) at our doors," as Bradford put it. In addition to Aptucxet, Plymouth opened a trade house at the head of the Mount Hope peninsula (called Montaup by the Wampanoags) in Pokanoket. In this respect, the Dutch promotion of wampum had not diverted the English from the Wampanoag trade but drawn them to it.[14]

Though scholars widely assume that the Narragansetts and Pequots not only dominated but practically monopolized the early wampum trade in New England, mainland Wampanoags also appear to have participated in this commerce. Quahog and whelk might have been more abundant in the territories of rival tribes, but it could still be found in significant amounts throughout Wampanoag country, particularly on the shores of the Narragansett Bay sachemships of Pokanoket, Pocasset, and Sakonnet, the Buzzards Bay communities of Acushnet and Apponagansett, and throughout Cape Cod and the islands. A walk today along the beaches of these sites will amply demonstrate the point. Documentary evidence also points to Wampanoag wampum manufacturing and trade. Bradford asserted that before the Dutch-English agreement of 1627 "the Indians of these parts and the Massachusetts had none or very little of it [wampum], but [except] the sachems and some special persons that wore a little of it for ornament." Everything changed with the emergence of a European market for Indian-produced beads. "It [wampum] grew thus to become a commodity in these parts," Bradford continued, "[and] these Indians [Wampanoags and Massachusetts] fell into it also, and to learn how to make it." The Wampanoags began producing the beads with such zeal that Bradford likened the effect to that of an addictive "drug." The presence of shell blanks (unfinished attempts to craft wampum beads) and clusters of whelk columns at Pokanoket archaeological sites testifies to the Wampanoags crafting wampum, just as English and Dutch trade at Mount Hope would suggest.[15]

Much to Plymouth's frustration, it still could not control the Wampanoags' commerce with other Europeans. They dealt not only with Plymouth but with Dutch shipboard merchants, English fishermen, and, eventually, English traders working out of neighboring Rhode Island. With no oversight and few scruples, rival traders liberally supplied the Wampanoags with arms and alcohol, ignoring Plymouth's admonitions that such traffic was an affront to God and man alike. It took little time for the Natives surrounding Plymouth to grow "mad" after guns, leading Bradford to seethe that they became "ordinarily better fitted and furnished [with them] than the English themselves." In 1628 such concerns spurred Plymouth to break up a rogue trading post known as Merrymount near the former site of Wessagusset, and to banish its leader, Thomas Morton, back to England. Yet the colony could do little about other dealers who came and went faster than anyone could respond. It was all to the mainland Wampanoags' advantage.[16]

Indians found the wampum trade attractive, to be sure, but not irresistible. Strikingly, there is no archaeological or documentary evidence of wampum making on Cape Cod and the islands despite the presence of ancient coastal shell heaps filled with quahog remains. The only passing reference associating Natives from these areas with wampum comes from King Philip's War, when the Nantucket Wampanoags sent a wampum belt to Governor Edmund Andros of New York as a gesture of peace. Certainly fresh proof could surface tomorrow with the next archaeological excavation or discovery of a long-lost letter, but there is one anecdote to suggest that the outer-coast Wampanoags made a conscious refusal to produce wampum despite market pressures and enticements. In 1671 the New York governor, Francis Lovelace, instructed the English proprietor of Martha's Vineyard, Thomas Mayhew Sr., to encourage the island Wampanoags "to worke the Sewan [wampum] making." In light of the negative archaeological evidence, the meaning of his request seems to have been for them to begin this activity anew.[17]

The decision of the Cape and island Wampanoags to stay out of the wampum trade was a new way to distance themselves from Poka-noket after having failed to break free in the early 1620s. They must have known that if they began manufacturing wampum, Ousame-quin and his successors would siphon it off as tribute. Furthermore, to become wampum-paying tributaries to one paramount sachem was to invite raids from others seeking to claim these payments.

Throughout the 1630s and 1640s, the Pequots and Narragansetts, and then the Mohegans and Narragansetts, competed violently for control of wampum tributaries on Long Island, which sometimes involved direct strikes against the subject communities themselves. But if the Wampanoags of the Cape and islands did not make wampum, mainlanders could not take it, though they could try to coerce production. It is probably no coincidence that in the mid-1640s these same communities would begin hosting English missionaries and adopting Christianity, which also insulated them from Pokanoket. Yet with the unexpected arrival of thousands more Englishmen in southern New England, and an associated raising of the stakes in inter- and intratribal politics, ultimately it was impossible for any Native community to escape the destructive forces of colonialism.

SWARMING

In terms of population, Plymouth alone represented little threat to Wampanoag interests. Hardly more than two hundred English families and unattached individuals migrated to the colony between 1620 and 1633, which, along with natural births, made for at most four hundred people in the mid-1630s. Plymouth was no larger than a local sachemship. However, the so-called Great Migration following the establishment of the Massachusetts Bay Colony in 1629 increased English numbers dramatically. Massachusetts received somewhere between fifteen thousand and twenty thousand arrivals in its first eleven years, most of them seeking to escape a crackdown on puritans in England by the Anglican archbishop William Laud. The influx finally halted in the early 1640s, as the beginning of the English Civil War mobilized puritans back home against Charles I's (and Laud's) rule and briefly put them in control of the government. Yet New England was already changed irrevocably. Almost overnight,

Massachusetts had become as populated and powerful as any of the region's tribes. Furthermore, there seemed to be no end to its expansion. The young ages and relatively balanced gender ratio of its colonists, combined with the good health they experienced in America, was a recipe for natural demographic growth. The Englishwomen of the Great Migration bore on average eight children over the course of their lives. Additionally, the first two generations of New England colonists enjoyed long lives even by modern standards, with adults routinely reaching their sixties, and a striking number even their seventies and eighties. Because of these trends, the English population of southern New England climbed to over thirty-three thousand people by 1660 and was on the verge of exceeding the total number of Indians.[18]

The impact of this growth on Native people would have been significant even if it had remained concentrated in the towns ringing Massachusetts Bay, but numerous colonists promptly left for other parts of New England in search of better agricultural land and freedom from puritan religious oppression. These places included territory in and around Wampanoag country. Secondary migration from Massachusetts was the main factor in the spike of Plymouth colony's population to about two thousand people in 1643. Religious exiles from Massachusetts also relocated to the head of Narragansett Bay on the western edge of Wampanoag territory. There, under the leadership of Roger Williams, they founded the town of Providence in 1636, followed by Portsmouth and Newport on nearby Aquidneck Island, and eventually Warwick on the west side of the bay. In 1644 these towns incorporated as the colony of Rhode Island and Providence Plantations. Farther west, Massachusetts out-migrants established the towns of Windsor, Hartford, and Wethersfield on the Connecticut River, which became the colony of Connecticut, while others settled on the Quinnipiac River and founded New Haven, which became the mother town of the short-lived colony by the same name. Characterizing these developments merely as "hiving off," as many historians do, minimizes what they represented to indigenous people. The English were no longer restricted to a tiny fortified post at Patuxet, or even just a cluster of towns around Boston. They had established beachheads on every major river and harbor in the region, creating not an Indian-colonial frontier but a patchwork of European settlements interspersed among Native communities. To the First People, this was nothing short of a swarming.[19]

Meanwhile, European diseases continued to take a staggering toll on the Native population. In 1633 smallpox broke out along the coast, knifing up the length of the Connecticut River valley and then northwest all the way into Mohawk country, the St. Lawrence River valley, and possibly southern Ontario. The Narragansetts lost some seven hundred people in this outbreak. In the lower Connecticut River valley, where both the Dutch and Plymouth had opened trade houses, Bradford reported that the Indians experienced "such a mortality that of a 1000 above 900 and a half of them died, and many of them did rot above ground for want of a burial." The English established the first towns of the Connecticut colony on the sites of these disasters, just as the *Mayflower* passengers had done at Patuxet years earlier. The Massachusett Indians, survivors of the unnamed plagues of 1616–19 and 1622, also suffered mightily in 1633, which the Bay Colony governor, John Winthrop, interpreted as divine providence. He stood in awe that as "for the natives, they are near all dead of the smallpox, so the Lord hath cleared our title to what we now possess." The extent of the Wampanoags' hurt is unclear, but given that every surrounding Indian community had contracted the pox, and even twenty Plymouth colonists appear to have died from it, it is all but certain that they lost people, too, once again.[20]

The 1633 smallpox was the last large-scale epidemic on record among the Indians of southern New England, but localized eruptions continued, sometimes to devastating effect. Take, for example, the island of Martha's Vineyard. In 1643, just one year after the English founded their first settlement there, a "strange disease" attacked the island Wampanoags. According to English accounts, the Natives began "to run up and down till they could run no longer" and "made their faces black as coal, snatched up any weapon, spoke great words, but did no hurt," apparently as a ritual to ward off the contagion. In 1645 sickness returned. This time it was a "universal" "sore Distemper" that was "mortal to many of them." The Vineyard case is rare only insofar as it was documented. Contemporaneous outbreaks in other parts of Wampanoag country, however lethal, went unrecorded by the English.[21]

If the swarming of English migrants and decimation of Indians by epidemics shifted the regional balance of power, so did the English use of terroristic military might in the Pequot War of 1636–37. The direct cause of the war was Massachusetts's insistence that the Pequots extradite tribal members accused of murdering a troublemaking English merchant captain, John Stone, and his crew. Pequot sachems offered compensation for the dead in the form of gifts of land and furs, but they would not meet the English demand and probably could not without risking their own lives. For two years, tensions built, until the Manisses of Block Island murdered the sailors of another English vessel. Massachusetts, fearing that its failure to prosecute the Stone murder had emboldened Indians to take English lives whenever they pleased, sent out a rather ineffective punitive expedition against the Manisses and Pequots in August 1636. The Pequots responded forcefully with a surprise attack on the Connecticut town of Wethersfield in April 1637, in which they killed nine residents and captured two girls. Little did anyone know that this strike would be the Pequots' last victory in this war.[22]

The Pequots found themselves increasingly hemmed in and friendless as Native nations began lining up with the English to address their own long-running intertribal rivalries. The Narragansetts saw an opportunity to seize the advantage in their contest for tributaries from Long Island and hunting grounds along the Pawcatuck River on the modern Rhode Island–Connecticut border. The Mohegans were even more supportive of the English, as their sachem, Uncas, had spent years trying to escape subordinate status to the Pequots after an unsuccessful bid to get himself named the Pequots' paramount sachem. The Wampanoags sat out this conflict, as did nearly all other tribes in the region, but the English-Mohegan-Narragansett axis was more formidable than anything for which the Pequots had bargained.[23]

The next chapter of the war jolted Native people into the realization that the newly ascendant English were a dire threat. A month after the Pequot strike on Wethersfield, an army of Connecticut, Massachusetts, Narragansett, and Mohegan men made a surprise assault on a Pequot fort on the Mystic River filled with women, children, and the elderly; most of the Pequots' matawaûog were concentrated at another fort a short distance to the west, expecting the attack to come from that direction. Breaching the fort's palisade, English soldiers put the wetus inside to the torch, then placed gunmen in a cordon around the palisade outside to shoot down anyone who escaped the flames. An outer ring of mostly Mohegan bowmen (a number of Narragansetts had fled the scene in disgust at the indiscriminate killing) captured the fortunate few who made it that far. When it was all over, somewhere between four hundred and seven hundred Pequots lay dead. Captain John Mason reveled, "Then did the Lord judge among the heathen, filling the place with dead bodies." The Massachusetts Bay Colony memorialized the victory by declaring a public day of thanksgiving after its soldiers returned home safely.[24]

English mop-up operations after Mystic were nearly as destructive to the Pequots as the massacre itself, with the double effect of warning Indians far and wide of how murderous the English could be when provoked. Colonial and Mohegan forces systematically hunted down the survivors, killing most of the men and taking the women and children captive. English authorities sold a portion of their prisoners into lifetime slavery in the Caribbean and sentenced the remainder to toil in Massachusetts and Connecticut. Other Pequots became captives of the Mohegans or Narragansetts or fled to sanctuary among the Long Island Indians or tribes far to the west. (In the 1640s New Haven merchants found one Pequot band on the lower Delaware River.) In 1638's Treaty of Hartford, which effectively marked the end of the war, Massachusetts and Connecticut declared the Pequots to be extinct as a nation, but that was not true. Over the next decade, Pequot survivors would regroup, with dozens of them escaping from English, Mohegan, and Narragansett captivity to form two new communities in their ancestral territory. Nevertheless, their status as a regional power was broken, and all the Natives in the region took heed, which was just as the English had designed it.[25]

Even the Wampanoags were unnerved. On April 21, 1638, Ousamequin personally visited Boston to present Governor Winthrop with eighteen beaver pelts on behalf of his people and the "Mohegans" (probably meaning the Mohicans of the Housatonic and Hudson Rivers, a separate group from Uncas's tribe). The reason, he said, was that he heard the Massachusetts Bay Colony was mad at them and intended war. The Wampanoags might have been worried that Boston intended to punish them for offering refuge to Roger Williams and other religious exiles from Massachusetts, while the Mohicans possibly feared colonial vengeance for taking in Pequots. Winthrop reassured Ousamequin that the colony meant them no ill will, yet the sachem remained unconvinced. The following year he and his son Mooanum (later known as Wamsutta), paid a visit to Plymouth's General Court seeking a renewal of their alliance. They got it, but on the condition that they would not sell land to any Englishmen (meaning other colonies) without the court's approval, as Ousamequin had done previously with Rhode Island. The sachem readily agreed, and thus Plymouth once again pledged to defend him and his followers "against all such as shall unjustly rise up against them to wrong or oppress them unjustly." The English do not seem to have grasped that Indians now saw them as the mostly likely source of that danger.[26]

Ousamequin was hardly alone in his concern. Tellingly, the Narragansetts shared it, too, even after serving alongside the English during the Pequot War. In the attack on Mystic Fort, Narragansetts had cried out, "'*Machit, machit*'; that is, 'It is naught, it is naught because it is too furious and slays too many men.'" The Narragansetts were particularly appalled at the English slaughter of Pequot women and children, for Indian warfare usually involved taking these populations captive for eventual adoption into the victors' society. This goal would have been particularly urgent to the Narragansetts after their losses from the smallpox of 1633. The Narragansetts grew even more alienated from the English as they came to the realization that dispatching the Pequots had merely cleared the way for a new rival, the Mohegans under Uncas. Uncas used his kinship ties with the Pequots to claim spoils that the Narragansetts had expected to reap: not only did he take more than his agreed-on share of Pequot captives, but after strategically marrying three high-ranking Pequot women, he attracted other Pequot survivors who had remained on the loose. With more men at his command than ever, Uncas began intimidating the Pequots' former tribute payers on Long Island to direct their wampum payments to him despite Narragansett expectations that they would fill this power vacuum. The Mohegans also clashed with Narragansetts over claims to Pequot hunting grounds. And if all this was not enough to make the Narragansetts question their role in the war, English support of Uncas certainly was. The puritan colonies saw Uncas as a wedge against the Narragansetts and, by extension, the dissenters' colony of Rhode Island.[27]

In this context, Miantonomo came to a startling realization that Native people as a whole faced a common threat in the form of European colonists. It was an idea that, in later years, would spur Ousamequin's sons to organize a multitribal, anticolonial resistance. Yet this revelation did not come easily. In the early stages of the Pequot War, the Pequots had appealed to the Narragansetts for help, arguing that the colonists "were strangers and began to overspread the country" and would eventually turn on their Native friends. Miantonomo had not believed it at first, but now he did. Thus in the early 1640s he began touring the Indian communities on both sides of Long Island Sound as far west as the Hudson River, according to Native informants, "soliciting them to a general war against both the English and the Dutch." He urged that they needed to become "all Indians as the English are, and say brothers to one another; so must we be one as they are, otherwise we shall be all gone shortly."[28]

If Ousamequin agreed with this assessment, he did not let the English know, but he certainly had no interest in joining a resistance campaign led by a sachem from his archrivals. Instead, he used the opportunity to distance himself even further from the Narragansetts and emphasize his friendship with the English, as on July 23, 1642, when he paid a courtesy call to Boston, "attended with many men and some other sagamores [sachems]." The following year, representatives from neighboring puritan colonies encouraged Plymouth to "labor by all due means to restore Woosamequin [Ousamequin] to his full liberties in respect of any encroachments by the Narragansetts or any other nations" as per "former terms and agreements between Plymouth and him." Clearly the Wampanoags' leader had convinced the English that he was no supporter of Miantonomo's purported ambition to become "universal sagamore" of southern New England. His timing was apt, for shortly thereafter the Bay Colony jailed the Massachusetts sachem, Cutshamekin, and seized his arms on suspicion that he was conspiring with Miantonomo. The colony also hoped this measure would double "to strike some terror into the Indians."[29]

Ousamequin's effort to create daylight between his people and the Narragansetts might also have involved helping the Nipmucs of what is now central Massachusetts reach out to the English. Shortly after Ousamequin's renewal of the Wampanoags' English alliance, a group of Nipmuc sachems paid a diplomatic visit to Boston, probably at his urging. They offered their "submission" (what this term meant to the Nipmucs one can only guess), promised to "give speedy notice of any conspiracy, attempt, or evil intention," and presented a gift of twenty-six fathoms of wampum. Now the Wampanoags were no longer alone in their approach to the English. As the Massachusetts minister William Hubbard later wrote, the Nipmucs, "some have said, were a kind of tributaries to Massasoit [Ousamequin]." They would also prove to be close allies of his son Pumetacom even after his relations with the English soured.[30]

The Wampanoags and Nipmucs had extensive company in their rejection of Miantonomo's appeal for Indian unity. Not only did multiple Native sources inform the English about the plot, but it was none other than Uncas who brought it to an end. In 1643 the Mohegan sachem took Miantonomo captive in battle, after which he delivered his prisoner to the first meeting of the commissioners of the United Colonies of New England, an alliance of Massachusetts, Connecticut, Plymouth, and New Haven (heterodox Rhode Island was left out) to coordinate their Indian and military affairs. As if to affirm Miantonomo's plea that Indians needed to band together to counter English solidarity, the commissioners released Miantonomo back to Uncas for execution in Indian territory, to which the Mohegan sachem readily obliged. Once again, Native New England took notice, including the Wampanoags, who must have been at once cheered by the weakening of the Narragansetts and worried by the uncertainty of how the English would display their ruthlessness next.[31]

Ousamequin continued to rebuff Narragansett entreaties from Canonicus after Miantonomo's killing, and made sure the English knew about it. In the summer of 1644, the colonist John Brown, who had just recently built a house near Pokanoket, informed Boston that the Narragansetts had sent Ousamequin a Mohegan head and hand to solicit his support in their war against Uncas. According to Indian custom, if the sachem received these trophies, he accepted the accompanying message; but if he returned them, he spurned it. Ousamequin took the second option with a twist, delivering the body parts to Plymouth so it knew where he stood. Later that summer, Ousamequin visited William Coddington of Newport, Rhode Island, to declare "he is all one heart" with the English, evident in the fact "that Canonicus sent to him to borrow some pieces [muskets] . . . which he refused." As Ousamequin would have expected, Coddington "told him he did well so to do." The point of these gestures was to underscore the Wampanoags' abiding friendship with the colonies even as the Narragansetts and English teetered on the brink of war throughout the 1640s and 1650s. In other words, in the face of other Native people's resistance to English colonization, Ousamequin remained true to the spirit of 1621.[32]

DIRECTING COLONIAL EXPANSION
IN WAMPANOAG COUNTRY

The Wampanoags might have been unable to do anything about the Great Migration to Massachusetts Bay or the colonists' aggression against the Pequots and Narragansetts, but they had significant influence over the spread of the English into their own territory, which they used to advance their own interests. This was particularly true in the case of the religious outcasts who founded Rhode Island. When Roger Williams fled Massachusetts in the winter of 1636, he first sought refuge with Ousamequin, who placed him at a site east of the Seekonk River at the head of Narragansett Bay. Williams had been cultivating this relationship for years as a fur trader and student of the Wampanoag language. As he later recalled, in the years before his exile, he had "spared no cost . . . in gifts to Ousamequin, yea and to all his [people] . . . and therefore when I came I was welcome to Ousmequin." Yet Plymouth authorities warned Williams out of this territory, contending that Wampanoag country was part of their jurisdiction and they did not want to alienate the Bay Colony by harboring its dissidents. To avoid a confrontation, Williams relocated just a few miles west to an area at the confluence of the Moshassuck and Woonasquetucket Rivers, the intermediate zone between the Wampanoags and Narragansetts. He called the place Providence.[33]

Both Ousamequin and the Narragansett sachem, Canonicus, supported this move for similar reasons. For one, an English settlement would serve as a buffer against the other's raids. It would also provide them with readier access to English goods and services, including the use of Williams as a go-between and scribe in their relations with other tribes and colonies. As Williams told, the Wampanoags and Narragansetts used him as "their counselor and secretary . . . they had my person, my shallop and pinnace, and hired servant, etc., at command, on all occasions, transporting 50 at a time." In other words, Williams, by virtue of living in their country, had become their resource.[34]

Over the next decade, Ousamequin granted Williams and other Rhode Island colonists the right to settle and use tracts all around the northern and eastern edges of Narragansett Bay and its islands within the Wampanoag-Narragansett no-man's-land. The Narragansetts did the same, ceding land north of their core territory to which the Wampanoags also laid claim. To be sure, the English compensated the sachems for these grants—for instance, paying Ousamequin five fathoms of wampum for the right to graze livestock in what became the town of Portsmouth. However, Williams knew that these sums were merely one aspect of what the sachems expected in return. They were cultivating the English as friends to advise their people in politics, defend them in times of danger, and treat them with respect and hospitality. Williams explained that he secured the sachems' consent to build at Providence "not by monies or payment . . . monies could not do it." Rather, "what was paid was only a gratuity, though I choose, for better assurance and form, to call it a sale." Such transactions were not one-for-one exchanges of land for goods but a mutual pledge to sustain "a loving and peaceable neighborhood." Ousamequin captured this spirit in the deed for Portsmouth, stressing that he expected William Coddington and his associates to pursue a "loving and just carriage" toward the sachem, his followers, and their posterity—always.[35]

This is not to say the Ousamequin never drove a hard bargain. In 1646 Providence men met with the sachem at his house to secure grazing rights up the Blackstone River, even though they had already paid Miantonomo for his claim several years earlier. They offered Ousamequin fifteen fathoms of wampum, but he wanted European merchandise, so they settled on ten fathoms of white wampum, four coats, six of the "best" hoes, axes, and twelve knives. Insisting on immediate payment, Ousamequin sent the English in one of his mishoons with a Wampanoag guide to fetch the goods from Portsmouth. The English did as the sachem asked, only for him to reject half of the knives and a portion of the hoes as unsatisfactory. All the Rhode Islanders could do was promise "to procure the rest . . . to his liking." With the hour getting late, the colonial delegates went to bed assuming the negotiations were done, but they were not. Ousamequin woke his guests from a deep sleep and "begged two coats of us, which we promised to give him." In the morning, he also demanded musket balls, which the colonists refused, and another four coats, which they also denied because they had already gifted "a coat to his chancellor" and distributed several "small gifts" worth forty fathoms of wampum to other Wampanoags. With this, Ousamequin called off the talks, leading the colonists to return home and enter the deed into the official record without his mark of consent.[36]

Ousamequin's grants permitted the Rhode Islanders to use the land in only narrowly specified ways that did not exclude the Wampa-noags. For instance, the questionable Blackstone River cession stip-ulated that the English "could not put up houses without further agreement" and that nearby Indian planters would either fence in their fields or else depart. Likewise, though Ousamequin gave his permission for the English to settle on Aquidneck Island, he still retained the right to hunt deer there with ten of his men. Most land deeds did not record these understandings, but they were under-standings just the same. As far as the Wampanoags were concerned, the terms were whatever had been negotiated in person regardless of what the English put down in their writings. It is telling of Indian power along Narragansett Bay, and of the colonists' grasp of Indian principles of joint use of the land, that Rhode Islanders generally adhered to these agreements and satisfied Wampanoag and Narra-gansett complaints about violations, if out of self-preservation rather than moral principle. As Williams put it to the Massachusetts legis-lature in 1655, Rhode Island's "dangers (being a frontier people to the Barbarians) are greater than those of other colonies."[37]

Ousamequin also began selling colonists land within his core territory to promote a "loving and just carriage" with Plymouth at a time when war between the United Colonies and Narragansetts seemed certain. In 1640 and 1641 he ceded areas due north of Poka-noket that eventually became the Plymouth towns of Taunton and Rehoboth. A decade later, the sachem made another series of grants in quick succession: In 1649 he sold a tract along the upper Taunton

River that became the town of Bridgewater; in 1652, it was Appona-gansett on Buzzards Bay, which the English renamed Dartmouth; in 1653, he deeded Popanomscut and Chachacust Necks near Montaup and the site where his home village of Sowams had long been located. Before these cessions, a vast stretch of swampland and forest had sepa-rated the Wampanoags' Taunton River villages and Plymouth town. Now they and the colonists were living in such close proximity that one of the sachem's land deeds included his pledge "to remove all the Indians within a year from the date hereof that do live in the said tract" and to make sure "the English may not be annoyed by the hunting of the Indians in any sort of their cattle." Nevertheless, Ousamequin had good reason to think that this familiarity would breed amity rather than contempt. The point of his bargains, after all, was to show goodwill that he expected the English to return in kind.[38]

Another reason Ousamequin sold land to Plymouth was to give the Wampanoags access to particular colonists with valuable services to offer, as had been the case with Williams. Take, for instance, John Brown and Thomas Willet, who negotiated a number of these trans-actions and oversaw several town foundings, including Swansea, the closest English settlement to Pokanoket. Brown was one of the point men in Plymouth's relations with Ousamequin. When the sachem complained in 1653 that his people had "sustained great damage in their corn by the horses and other cattle" of Rehoboth, the colony sent Brown to investigate and reach a settlement. Five years later, when English authorities suspected that Ousamequin was harboring an Indian accused of murdering another Indian in the Massachu-setts Bay Colony, Brown was part of the committee to press the sachem for the suspect's extradition (to which the sachem does not appear to have obliged). Brown also seems to have helped translate several land deals and diplomatic encounters between Ousamequin and Plymouth. In other words, he interacted so frequently with the Wampanoags that he had some facility in their language.[39]

When Brown's daughter married Willet, the role of interme-
diary with the Wampanoags became something of a family enterprise. Willet was a seasoned merchant, having conducted business in
the Netherlands before arriving in Plymouth to manage the colony's
Indian trade in Maine. These experiences coalesced in the next
phase of his life, which involved trading with New Netherland
for Dutch goods that he then sold to the Wampanoags and the
merchants with whom they dealt. Considering this to be no mere
economic relationship, Ousamequin and his sons turned to Willet
repeatedly when they had disputes with their English neighbors.
Pumetacom even called him "my loving friend."[40]

Ousamequin's land sales also brought to Wampanoag country
colonists who ignored Plymouth law to sell the Natives munitions
and alcohol. The first colonists to relocate to the new towns of
Taunton, Rehoboth, and Swansea were often socially marginal characters willing to bear the uncertainty of living near the Wampanoags in exchange for escaping the oversight of puritan authorities
near Boston and Plymouth town. Not only were many of them religious dissenters, such as Quakers and Baptists, but smugglers interested in pursuing the illegal and enormously profitable Indian trade
in guns and liquor. We know about these shadowy Englishmen only
through the rare occasions that the law caught up to them. For
instance, Francis Doughty of Taunton was fined thirty shillings in
1641 for selling gunpowder to Indians, and in 1648 William Hedges
of Taunton faced the charge of failing to inform on others who had
illegally traded ammunition. Sometimes Ousamequin himself was
involved in these cases. Nicholas Hide received a stiff penalty of
twenty-five pounds in 1652 for outfitting Ousamequin with a gun,
while William Cheesebrough of Seekonk spent two weeks in jail
and forked over six pounds for "mending two locks for pieces
[muskets]" belonging to the sachem. The reason Cheesebrough's
offenses came to light was that Ousamequin had complained about

The mark of Ousamequin, 1649 land deed to Bridgewater. From the Collection of the Old Bridgewater Historical Society.

Written land deeds were the colonists', not the Indians', mechanism for recording land transfers. Indians relied on oral agreements and the memory thereof. Nevertheless, Ousamequin and the Wampanoags often managed to get their understandings of land deals recorded in these documents. Wampanoags not only assumed but often insisted that the colonists' purchase of discreet "use rights" to the land (such as the right to plant crops, graze animals, and build houses) did not extinguish Indian use rights to hunt, gather, fish, and sometimes even plant and reside in the same territory. Recorded joint-use agreements reflect Wampanoag power during Ousamequin's lifetime. The decline of these agreements as the English population grew introduced irreconcilable tension into Wampanoag-English relations and contributed mightily to the descent into war.

him causing some unspecified "affray." The English in the Taunton
River towns were even more brazen in their sale of liquor to Indians,
as reflected in Plymouth's repeated and apparently futile prohibi-
tions against the traffic. It would appear that one of the Wampanoags' purposes for selling land was to gain access to such contraband.
This black market is about as contrary to the Thanksgiving myth as
one can imagine.[41]

Of course, a final benefit of these sales was that they provided
Ousamequin with a windfall in goods for the enrichment of his
people and consolidation of his following. For instance, in the 1649
sale of forty-nine square miles that became Bridgewater, Ousamequin received seven coats, nine hatchets, eight hoes, twenty knives,
four moose skins, and sixteen and a half yards of cotton. Three years
later, the Apponagansett cession netted him an additional thirty
yards of cloth, eight moose skins, fifteen axes, fifteen hoes, fifteen
pairs of britches, eight pairs of stockings, eight pairs of shoes, one
pot, and ten shillings' worth of other goods. Ousamequin certainly
did not intend to use all these items himself. The point was to
distribute them among his supporters. The seeming inequity to
modern eyes between the high long-term value of the land and low
worth of the goods does not take into account how Wampanoags
would have seen things. They did not know that soon after the tools
had broken and the cloth had frayed, the English would use their
superior numbers and military might to assert exclusive rights to the
ceded territory. Nor could they predict that Miantonomo's prescient
warning would come true: "You know our fathers had plenty of deer
and skins, our plains were full of deer, as also our woods, and of
turkeys, and our coves full of fish and fowl. But these English having
gotten our land, they with scythes cut down the grass, and with
axes felled the trees; their cows and horses eat the grass, and their
hogs spoil our clam banks, and we shall all be starved."[42] More
inconceivable still would have been the idea of future generations of

Wampanoags relegated to tiny reservations on which it was impossible to make a living by the people's traditional methods. There was no certainty about these outcomes in the 1640s and 1650s, even though farsighted leaders like Miantonomo predicted them.[43]

BREAKING AWAY

Whereas Ousamequin used land sales to enhance his authority in various ways, similar transactions by the Wampanoags of Cape Cod and the islands appear to have served partly as attempts to distance themselves from his demands. There is scant evidence of eastern Wampanoag sachems consulting with Ousamequin about these deals, never mind giving him a cut, in contrast to Ousamequin's leading role in cessions throughout the greater Taunton River valley and adjacent coast. That the eastern Wampanoags meant to signal their independence is evident in the fact that their communities also began hosting Christian missionaries around the same time. Everyone understood that this decision involved closer relations with the English not only religiously and culturally but politically, to the detriment of Pokanoket.

English offers to buy eastern Wampanoag land began coming in fast and furious in the 1630s, followed by a spate of sales by local sachems. Plymouth colony approved the founding of the town of Sandwich (at the shoulder of the Cape) in 1638, followed quickly by Barnstable and Yarmouth on the middle Cape in 1639, and then Eastham on the outer Cape in the late 1640s and early 1650s, though sometimes the authorization to create these towns took place before the English had actually purchased the land for them. Meanwhile, island Wampanoags permitted the Watertown, Massachusetts merchant Thomas Mayhew Sr. and a small group of his compatriots to settle on the Vineyard in 1642, and then a band of religious dissidents and aspiring fishermen to plant themselves on Nantucket, twenty-eight miles offshore, in the 1660s. Though the islands fell within Wampanoag country, they remained outside any colony's jurisdiction until the crown annexed them to New York in 1671 and then Massachusetts in 1691. They were never a part of Plymouth colony. To the Wampanoags, the difference was negligible. On the Cape and islands alike, these colonists clustered near harbors, bays, inlets, coastal ponds, and river mouths, where there was good anchorage, easy access to fishing, and plenty of salt grass to feed livestock. These also happened to be the areas used most intensively by the Wampanoags.[44]

Like Ousamequin, the Cape sachems had their understandings about shared use of the land and multiple Wampanoag claimants written into the colonists' land deeds. For instance, when the English tried to purchase Billingsgate in the sachemship of Nauset, they first cut a deal with the sachem Mattaquason, only to discover that they also had to pay another sachem named George (the successor of Aspinet) and then an additional claimant called Lieutenant. Yet, even after these three transactions, they still did not enjoy exclusive access to the land. The Nauset Wampanoags, "as natural inhabitants of the place," reserved the rights to collect shellfish, carve up drift whales, and plant on Pochet Island. Initially, George's followers also asserted their liberty to plant on another neck within the ceded area, which the English were responsible for fencing to keep out livestock. However, eventually the English, "finding it inconvenient for us to have Indians at both ends of the town," paid a "valuable sum" to convince the Wampanoags to relocate and assume responsibility for their own enclosures. Clearly, the Natives had no intention of leaving the area just because the English had arrived. They planned for the two peoples to live side by side. Colonists grudgingly respected these terms for the meantime so as to "not cause or breed any disturbance amongst the Indians," who, as yet, represented a legitimate military threat.[45]

Contrary to the assumption that land sales plunged Indians into colonial subjugation, some deeds required the English to pay tribute to the local sachem, as if they were joining Wampanoag society rather than buying the land from out of it, which is doubtlessly how the Wampanoags conceived of these arrangements. In Barnstable, the English were obligated to build sixty rods of fence "near unto a certain parcel of ground which the [sachem] Nepoyetum possesseth," plow Nepoyetum's land, and build him a house with floorboards, a chimney, and an oven. Nepoyetum reserved the right to gather wood and spend the winter wherever he pleased. Likewise, the sachem Seeknout of Chappaquiddick on the Vineyard permitted the English to graze cattle on his land between late fall and early spring, but in exchange he expected a piece of beef from every head of cattle they slaughtered, an agreement that colonists honored "all the sachem's days." The point of such terms was to make land sales to the English a means of long-term Wampanoag benefit.[46]

The Cape and island Wampanoags also profited from the English market for Indian labor and products, which gave them access to European manufactured goods independent of Ousamequin. One can see such arrangements in a 1646 complaint by the Mattakeesett (or Yarmouth) Wampanoags that a Mr. Offrey owed them six coats of trading cloth and a pair of small britches as compensation for their having gone sturgeon fishing for him, "and now not to pay them for their labor, they take it very ill." During the same period, the Nauset Wampanoags reportedly maintained a fishing fleet of seven or eight boats, by which they had "taken abundance of sturgeon and cod and bass this spring," apparently for sale to the English. This newfound opportunity to trade labor, fish, shellfish, venison, fowl, and feathers for European merchandise enabled the eastern Wampanoags to live richer material lives than ever before despite colonists encroaching on their territory. They even began acquiring horses in noticeable numbers, with ten different

Nausets purchasing mounts from colonists in Eastham between 1670 and 1672. These Natives could not have conceived that within a generation they would have little land left on which to use the horses to ride or plow.[47]

THE EBB AND FLOW OF FAITH

If any of these developments gave Ousamequin pause, he did not mention it, but he certainly took issue with English missionary outreach to the eastern Wampanoags. The Reverend John Eliot, who evangelized Natives near Boston in places like Natick and Punkapoag, is often held up as the consummate puritan missionary, partly by virtue of the lengthy paper trail he left behind. Yet a host of lesser-known figures also pursued the work on the Cape and islands to equally remarkable effect. The Mayhews of the Vineyard were the first and most recognized of the lot, starting with Thomas Mayhew Jr. in the mid-1640s, then expanding in the late 1650s and 1660s to include Thomas Mayhew Sr. (Junior having disappeared at sea in 1657) and his grandsons, John and Matthew. William Leveridge, Richard Bourne, and Thomas Tupper (and Bourne's and Tupper's descendants) preached throughout the Cape, while Peter Folger (Benjamin Franklin's grandfather) tended to the Nantucket Wampanoags after a brief stint on the Vineyard. John Cotton Jr. also began his missionary career on the Vineyard before relocating to Plymouth, from which he evangelized the nearby Wampanoag communities of Assawompset, Titicut, Herring Pond, and Manomet. All the while, Eliot was active among the Wampanoags' kin around Massachusetts Bay, which meant that the geography of the missionary campaign formed a broad C shape from the tip of the Cape north through the eastern breadth of Wampanoag country, culminating just west of Boston. This was the same network of peoples Ousamequin had implicated in the plot against Wessagusset and Plymouth.[48]

New England did not host Spanish-style missions run out of Christian compounds by full-time priests backed by soldiers. All English missionaries had to balance family duties (as Protestant officiants were allowed to marry) and full-time jobs ministering to colonial congregations. Having little time to spare, the missionaries focused their attention on the Wampanoags living closest to their towns, with instruction taking place in Wampanoag communities in the Wampanoag language, with the assistance of Wampanoags themselves. Indeed, the spread of Christianity depended on an increasingly long roster of Wampanoag missionaries, which included Wuttananmatuk, Meeshawin, and Sakantuket (or Peter) on Cape Cod; Assassamough (or John Gibbs), Joseph, Samuel, and Caleb on Nantucket; and Hiacoomes, John Tackanash, John Nohnoso, and Joshua Mummeecheeg on the Vineyard. Such figures were indispensable at translating and transmitting the Christian message in ways that resonated with their own people, which was considerable work. It included not only preaching but slow, painstaking question-and-answer sessions that probed innumerable similarities and differences between Christianity and Wampanoag religious belief and practice. Through such exercises, the Wampanoags not only gained a thorough education in Christian doctrine but shaped it to fit their own traditions. Not least among those traditions was the centrality of local, face-to-face relationships given the key roles Wampanoags played as missionaries to their own people. In other words, though the missions certainly reflected English influence, they were not yet a sign of colonial dominance. For the meantime, even Christian Wampanoags remained in charge of their own destiny.[49]

It was no coincidence that the missionaries got their start in the 1640s when southern New England Indians were reeling from fresh bouts of disease, the shock of the bloody Pequot War, and the likelihood of a clash between the Narragansetts and the English. Christianity helped address all these emergencies and more. Some Native people gave Christianity a hearing because they suspected that the colonists' good health and military success was a reflection of their spiritual power. As one Native Christian told the English, previously he had "low apprehensions of our God" as a "mosquito god," but after the Pequot War he "was convinced and persuaded that our God was a most dreadful god" insofar as a single English gunner was able "to slay and put to flight a hundred Indians." Indians routinely asked their missionaries to help heal the sick and inquired about Christianity's power to ward off and cure disease. A Mashpee Wampanoag named Wuttananmatuk recounted in 1665 that after three of his children died in just one year, "I thought God was angry at me," which led him to the church community. Another Mashpee named Waopam also recalled how "I thought of my father that his gods could not deliver him from death, but this God could." Such ideas in the midst of a decades-long Wampanoag health crisis, combined with the widespread Native opinion that Christianity offered protection against the curses of pawwaws, provided ample motivation to explore the colonists' religion.[50]

Christian Wampanoags were unequivocal that they considered the faith not as something brand-new but as a fresh source to rediscover ancient spiritual power and protection lost to them because of deaths of so many elders during the epidemics. One Cape Wampanoag asserted that "their forefathers did know God, but after this, they fell into a great sleep, and when they did awaken they quite forgot him," an idea that was widespread among Native people. Others said that well before the colonial era they had experienced visions of the same teachings that the missionaries propagated, including one in which a man appareled like the English, carrying a thing like the Bible, told them "that God was moosquantum or angry with them, and that he would kill them for their sins." As for why they had forgotten or misinterpreted these lessons, the Vineyard

Wampanoag Tawanquatuck told Thomas Mayhew Jr. that "a long time ago, they had wise men, which in a grave manner taught the people knowledge, but they are dead and their wisdom is buried with them." Native people turned the missionaries' religion into a new way to express indigenous truths by melding Wampanoag religious concepts and spirits with their rough Christian equivalents. To no small degree, this process was a natural result of using Wampanoag-language terms to communicate analogous Christian principles. For instance, the Wampanoags referred to God as "Manitou," making him the wellspring for the spiritual force, *manit*. Hell became the underwater lair of Cheepi, whom the Wampanoags conflated with the devil. In these ways and more, some Wampanoags found Christianity to be a means of reinvigorating old religious ideas to meet the stresses of a new era.[51]

The Wampanoags also hosted missionaries to defuse the colonists' aggression when war loomed constantly. One of Eliot's charges told him directly that he first came to Christianity because "sometimes I thought if we did not pray, the English might kill us." Likewise, in 1654 the Narragansetts asked Roger Williams to petition "the high sachems of England that they might not be forced from their religion, and for not changing their religion be invaded by war. For they said they were daily visited by threatenings from Indians that came from about the Massachusetts, that if they would not pray they should be destroyed by war." The English did not make such threats directly because there was no need. No one could mistake that colonists were more peaceful toward Christian Indians and hostile toward others. Indeed, funds for missionary work raised by the London-based charity, the New England Company, were disbursed by the United Colonies, a military alliance aimed at Indians.[52]

The missions came with numerous practical benefits for Indians that reinforced their political calculations. Initially, English missionaries were sources of manufactured goods among Cape and island Wampanoags less involved in the fur and wampum trades than Pokanoket and the other Taunton River communities. Eliot, and probably his counterparts on the Cape and islands, made it a point "never [to] go unto them empty, but carry somewhat to distribute among them," which included "mattocks, shovels, and crows of iron, etc." He also paid Indians for performing "civilized" work in their own towns such as building fences and square-framed houses and having men perform agricultural tasks. Wampanoags who served in the offices of preacher, church elder, or schoolteacher drew coveted salaries from the New England Company. Christian schools run initially by English missionaries but eventually by Native instructors taught literacy in the Wampanoag language to a wide range of children and adults. Boys who distinguished themselves in these lessons, particularly if they came from politically powerful Wampanoag families, might enroll in boarding school near Boston and perhaps even enter Harvard College, as did Joel Hiacoomes and Caleb Cheeshahteaumuck from the Vineyard during the 1660s. Attending these schools did more than expose the boys to eccentric English knowledge and manners, though it certainly did that. It also put them in a position to form interpersonal connections with elite colonists that they could apply to the benefit of their people.[53]

Eventually, literate Wampanoags, and those to whom they read aloud, had a collection of published works targeted toward them. Beginning in the 1650s, Eliot and his Indian partners, Cagenhew and James Printer (or Wawaus), began putting the Wampanoag language into print, culminating in the publication of an entire Wampanoag-language Bible in 1663, the first Bible ever published in North America. A string of other Wampanoag-language religious tracts and educational guides followed until such writings could be found in a sizable percentage of Christian Wampanoag homes. By

Stephen Coit, portrait of Caleb Cheeshahteaumuck, 2010. Image used with permission of the artist.

In 1665, Caleb Cheeshahteaumuck, son of the sachem of Nobnocket on Martha's Vineyard, became the first indigenous person to graduate from Harvard College. He died of consumption shortly after finishing his degree. Harvard College's charter committed it to "provisions that may conduce to the education of English & Indian youth of this Country in knowledge and godliness." A handful of other young Wampanoag and Nipmuc men also attended Harvard during this period. They represented the intense religious, political, linguistic, and cultural exchange that characterized Christian missions and Christian schools in Wampanoag country and beyond.

1674, roughly a third of Wampanoag Christians, mostly from Cape Cod and the islands, could read in their natal language, and some 16 percent could write in it. A slim minority were literate in English. These were remarkable accomplishments in light of the fact that alphabetic literacy was completely foreign to the Wampanoags when this educational campaign began. Though the primary point was to give the people direct access to the Bible, the worldly benefits were obvious given the centrality of written land deeds, court documents, account books, petitions, and letters to colonial society. The

Wampanoags' achievements in literacy were historic and critical to the future of their relations with the English, and all the participants knew it.[54]

Christianity also offered the Wampanoags the protection of some of their territory from the English, though missionaries who used their positions to speculate in Indian land were as much a part of the problem as the solution. Everyone could plainly see that the missions would fail if the English totally displaced Indians interested in Christianity. Unfortunately, Indians facing the threat of English encroachment made up a disproportionate number of the Christians. One answer was to create "praying towns," communities in which colonial governments guaranteed the land to Christian Indians forever in order to promote the Natives' churchgoing and other English-style reforms. In general, these praying towns were not new creations; instead, they usually involved an existing community declaring itself to be Christian, submitting itself to colonial authority, and, not least of all, agreeing to a land cession somewhere else. The best known of these praying towns were in Massachusetts near Boston and associated with the evangelical work of Eliot. They included Natick (founded in 1651), Punkapoag (1653, now Canton and Stoughton), Wamesit (1653, now Lowell), Hassanamesit (1654, now Grafton), Okommakamesit (1654, now Marlboro), and Nashobah (1654, now Littleton). Oft overlooked is that there were also two praying towns in Wampanoag country. The first was Mashpee on Cape Cod, created in 1665 when the sachems Wepquish and Tookenchosin granted the area around Mashpee Pond, the Santuit River, and Waquoit Bay to the local Indians "forever: and not to be sold or given away from them by anyone without all their consents." The following year, the sachem Quatchatisset of Manomet confirmed this decision. The missionary Richard Bourne often receives credit for the creation of Mashpee praying town

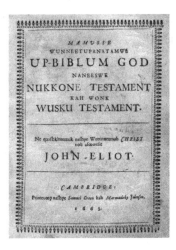

Title page of the Wampanoag Bible.

In 1663, the press at Harvard College began printing the first Bible ever produced in the Americas—in the Wampanoag language. It was the first of a long series of religious publications in Wampanoag designed to reach the growing Christian Indian population among the eastern Wampanoags, Massachusett Indians, and Nipmucs, who had been learning to read in their own languages in mission schools. The translation of the Bible into the Wampanoag tongue was a collaborative process involving not only the English missionary John Eliot (to whom most of the credit is typically given) but his Native colleagues Cagenhew, Wawaus (or James Printer), and doubtless a number of other Indian figures. Modern Wampanoags have drawn on these colonial-era texts as part of their revival of the Wampanoag language.

because he drew up the paperwork that gave it legal standing with Plymouth, but it should not be overlooked that his own land speculation had contributed to the emergency that made a reservation necessary in the first place.[55]

Another Wampanoag praying town formed on Martha's Vineyard, where the land purchases of the missionary and proprietor

Thomas Mayhew Sr. were driving Christian Wampanoags to distraction. The Vineyard Wampanoags asked their other missionary, John Cotton Jr., in 1666 "whether it be a righteous thing for Mr. M [Mayhew] to buy away so much of the Indians' lands?" Finally, in 1669 they prevailed upon Mayhew and the Takemmy sachem, Keteanummin, to agree to the formation of the praying community of Christiantown (or Mannitootan) in modern Tisbury, consisting of a square mile of reserved land. Elsewhere on the island, in sachemships like Aquinnah, Sengekontacket, and Chappaquiddick, Christian Indians had to fend off English land encroachment without such safeguards.[56]

The praying towns' obstruction of sachem land sales was but one of many ways that Christianity factored into politics between Native people. A number of *local* sachems supported the mission, because, regardless of their religious commitment, they could harness Christianity to their political ends by having themselves or their family members fill church and school offices. Furthermore, embracing Christianity would earn them English protection against outside aggressors, including the paramount sachems to whom they wished to cease paying tribute. By contrast, paramount sachems saw Christianity as a Trojan horse for the colonies to cleave off their tributaries despite the disclaimers of English missionaries that "if any of the praying Indians should be disobedient (in lawful things) and refuse to pay tribute unto their sachems, it is not their religion and praying to God that teaches them so to do, but their corruption." Tribute-collecting sachems were not buying it. Eventually, Eliot was forced to admit that the paramount sachems, to a person, opposed Christianity because "they plainly see that religion will make a great change among them [their followers], and cut them [the sachems] off from their former tyranny . . . and as for tribute, some they are willing to pay, but not as formerly." It should come as no surprise, then, that whereas local sachems like Papmunnuck of Mashpee, Mittark of Aquinnah, and Tawanquatuck of Nunnepog became stalwarts of their community churches, not a single paramount sachem in southern New England was willing to host a mission. Uncas of the Mohegans and Ninigret of the Narragansetts, for instance, drew Eliot's denunciations as "open & professed enemies against praying to God," to which he added that "whenever the Lord removes them, there will be a door open for the preaching of the Gospel in those parts."[57]

Ousamequin, despite his engagement with the English, always rejected the mission and reportedly admonished Plymouth just before he died not to evangelize his people. Earlier in life, he had pressured the sachem Nohtouassuet (or Notooksact) of the Vineyard sachemship of Aquinnah to hold firm against the Mayhew mission even as Nohtouassuet's son, Mittark, was in favor of Christianity. Eventually, Ousamequin took his intervention a step further, issuing death threats that required Mittark to spend three years in exile on the east end of the island. Ousamequin also appears to have taken his complaints directly to the Vineyard proprietor, Thomas Mayhew Sr. Thomas's grandson, Matthew Mayhew, recalled that on some unspecified date around midcentury, an Indian "prince who ruled a large part of the mainland," undoubtedly Ousamequin, came to the island with an entourage of eighty men, "well armed," to meet with Thomas about "something wherein the English were concerned." This conference, which ended with "Mr. Mayhew promising [the sachem] to effect what he desired," was probably the impetus for Mayhew's half-hearted insistence that Christian Indians were obligated to follow their sachems in civil matters. Additionally, it put the English on notice that Ousamequin was "a great enemy to our Reformation on the island," and elsewhere, too.[58]

DARKENING SKIES

In his last years, and perhaps earlier, Ousamequin could tell that the experiment he had helped launch was not going to last. It had been premised on the English population remaining small and concentrated at depopulated Patuxet and the contested Wampanoag-Narragansett borderlands while providing the Wampanoags with military protection on demand and trade goods in abundance. For most of Ousamequin's life, the English had served these purposes. But with every passing year the tensions inherent in this arrangement were rising to the surface. The English began swarming Indian country following the Great Migration, and, given the rate of the colonists' natural growth, there was no end in sight. Nascent English settlements had a great deal to offer their Indian neighbors in terms of trade, services, and a market for wage work, and living alongside one another seemed possible as long as everyone abided by their joint-use agreements. However, as the English population and especially their livestock herds grew, invariably they trespassed on Wampanoag resources and colonists began claiming shared places as their sole possessions. The English also became increasingly assertive about the primacy of their jurisdiction despite the Wampanoags' assumption that colonists had been buying their way into Native society to live as friends and allies. Mutually beneficial trade helped dampen these tensions, but that binding force was coming to an end during the 1650s and 1660s. The value of wampum plummeted during these years as a result of a decline of furs in the New England hinterland, a glut of furs in Europe, a glut of wampum in New Netherland, and a rise in other forms of currency as the colonies became more involved in Atlantic trade. In turn, New England governments gradually stopped accepting wampum for payment of taxes and then for private debts. This situation left land as the coastal tribes' only vendable resource of significance. The missions also threatened, for they demonstrated that the colonists were not content merely to engross Indian resources but wanted the Natives to adopt their entire way of life. It did not give the English pause that the communities most interested in Christianity intended to use the missions to loosen the authority of Ousamequin, the very sachem who had welcomed the first colonists to Wampanoag country.[59]

Conditions were building toward the very kind of military conflict that Ousamequin had spent his entire career trying to avoid. Already the English had led a massacre of the Pequots, killing hundreds, enslaving and selling off dozens more, and shattering them as a regional power. War scares between the United Colonies and Narragansetts were nearly constant, with Uncas egging on the English against his intertribal enemy, the English eager to take the bait, and the Narragansetts raising their fears by seeking allies among the Mohawks, Pocumtucks, and Dutch. Indians throughout the region were building up arsenals of European weaponry, both to defend themselves against one another and to prepare for the eventuality of war with the English. The long list of English provocations prompted Canonicus to ask of his close ally, Roger Williams, "Did ever friends deal so with friends?" Of course, his were Narragansett sentiments, not Wampanoag, but the two rivals were developing like minds as colonial expansion increasingly placed them in the same predicament.[60]

Ousamequin must have been pained at the idea of the coming storm. Nevertheless, at the end of his life he handed over his office to his eldest son, Mooanum, despite the likelihood of him taking a more confrontational stance toward the English. Mooanum's decision at this time to change his name to Wamsutta might have been designed to signal such a change in policy. It was common for Indian leaders to adopt new names when faced with a new challenge in life. Though becoming sachem would have been sufficient reason alone for Wamsutta, he seems to have been indicating something more, involving pushback against English expansion and even outreach to the Narragansetts. If so, he had the support of his brother, Pumetacom, and a critical mass of Wampanoag people, which probably factored into Ousamequin's decision to step aside before his death. However, the old sachem was careful to instruct his sons that, whatever course they took, they should never harm the family of his old friend John Brown, who had come to symbolize the reciprocal Wampanoag-English world the old sachem had built. He also made one last demonstration of the value of his approach to colonial affairs, helping the Quabaug Nipmucs frame an appeal to Massachusetts for assistance in fending off attacks by Uncas and the Mohegans, who were trying to reduce them to tributary status. As in Ousamequin's own diplomacy with Plymouth earlier in his career, the move paid off, with Massachusetts stationing an armed guard at Quabaug, issuing a warning to Uncas, and requiring the Mohegans to release Nipmuc captives they had taken in earlier raids. Yet this was a minor success in an otherwise sorrowful last stage of Ousamequin's life as he witnessed his sons organizing a resistance movement around the rallying cry that the English had betrayed their father's generous spirit.[61]

CHAPTER SEVEN

ㅈㆍ

Ungrateful

Wamsutta and Pumetacom insisted that they were friends of Plymouth just like their father. Yet their world was not his. By the time Ousamequin died in 1660, leaving his office to them, English missions, land encroachment, double standards of justice, and colonial interference in Native people's affairs had strained the historic alliance almost to its breaking point. Wamsutta and Pumetacom represented a younger generation of Wampanoags who came of age well after the dark days of the epidemic of 1616–19 and no longer viewed Plymouth as a source of the people's strength but as their greatest threat. The Wampanoags were particularly bitter toward Plymouth because it failed to reciprocate Ousamequin's protection and provision of the colony during its uncertain early years. Instead, it proved to be greedy and power hungry, willing to use any means to reduce its supposed Wampanoag friends to landlessness, subordination, and even slavery. Ingratitude was an especially repugnant quality in the tightly knit, kin-based Indian world in which people were expected to give without restraint and show appreciation to those who did. In the context of English aggression, the charge of colonial thanklessness easily morphed into the accusation of betrayal.

Such widely shared anticolonial sentiments fed a growing sense of common cause among the southern New England tribes. Calls for

Indian unity emanating from the Pequots and then Miantonomo in the 1630s and 1640s had failed because intertribal rivalries seemed more pressing than the theoretical long-term danger of the colonies. Yet by the 1660s Indians all across the region could plainly see that the English rose at their expense by using underhanded dealing and military threats to engross Indian land, and divide-and-conquer tactics against Indian polities. Such concerns did not eclipse political fights between or within tribes, which continued apace, or necessarily lead to violent resistance. Some groups decided the best course was to throw in their lot with the English. Yet there was a growing urgency that unless the people pushed back collectively against the burgeoning colonial threat, it would grow too powerful for them to do anything about it. The irony was that Wamsutta and Pumetacom, the very sons of the colonists' friend Ousamequin, were the ones who picked up this mantle. Their fifteen years of leadership before the outbreak of King Philip's War in 1675 does not comport with the long peace trumpeted by the Thanksgiving myth. Rather, it was marked by repeated war scares with the English partly as an outgrowth of their attempts to mobilize an anticolonial league.

The brothers might have been subtly indicating this change on June 13, 1660, when they visited Plymouth and Wasmutta explained "that in regard his father is lately deceased . . . he being desirous, according to the custom of the natives to change his name, that the Court would confer an English name upon him." The magistrates obliged by evoking names of two prominent figures from Greek antiquity, dubbing Wamsutta "Alexander Pokanoket" and Pumetacom "Philip." Just what the English meant by these choices is uncertain. The only explanation comes from the Massachusetts minister William Hubbard, who claimed many years later that the point was to mock Pumetacom's "ambitious and haughty spirit." Yet this statement, coming as it did after Pumetacom had taken up arms against the English, is suspect. A more interesting question is why the brothers asked the English to rename them in the first place. It was probably no coincidence that they made this request right after airing grievances against the English. They complained that roving hogs from the English town of Rehoboth had damaged the Wampanoags' corn at Annawamscutt (modern Barrington, Rhode Island) and Kickamuit (just east of Montaup). Wampanoags found colonists hypocritical and hostile for refusing to keep their livestock enclosed on their own land even as they zealously prosecuted Wampanoags who injured the trespassing animals. Wamsutta also objected that the English had bargained with a Narragansett sachem to purchase Wampanoag territory, which was part of a growing pattern of the colonists setting up straw sellers as a step toward browbeating the Indians with legitimate rights into releasing their claims. The brothers' final order of business before soliciting new names was to seek the colony's permission to buy gunpowder, despite its ban on sales of munitions to Indians. Plymouth authorities, reluctant to set a dangerous precedent but also wary of insulting the sachems, decided instead to gift the powder to them. None of the English seem to have connected the brothers' complaints to their request for ammunition and then their assumption of new names, but perhaps, with the benefit of hindsight, we should. The sequence might have been a subtle diplomatic threat of a sort common in Indian country, a way for Ousamequin's sons to hint that they were about to become different leaders from their father. They were prepared to seize on the colonists' own technologies, resources, and even names to turn back colonial expansion. Ingratitude had its costs.[1]

WAMSUTTA THE SACHEM, WAMSUTTA THE CAUSE

Wamsutta rose to power as the pressures driving English demand for Wampanoag territory were cresting. The children and even grandchildren of the Great Migration generation were coming of age and producing their own offspring, raising the colonial population of southern New England in 1670 to somewhere between sixty thousand and seventy thousand people, about double the total number of Natives. Like their forebears, their ambition was to establish their own farms, which could only mean expanding at the Indians' expense. Furthermore, New England agriculture was increasingly focused on exporting beef and pork to feed the slaves of the burgeoning sugar plantations of the Caribbean. Animal husbandry required extensive tracts of cleared pasturage, the best sort of which was located along the banks of creeks, rivers, and salt marshes that marked Wampanoag and Narragansett country. Add to these factors the vast profits that could be earned from land speculation, and it is easy to grasp why the English badgered Wampanoag sachems to part with their territory.[2]

Yet that does not fully explain why sachems like Wamsutta and Pumetacom decided to sell, particularly in light of their manifest resentment of colonial expansion. Neither of these sachems nor any of the other local Wampanoag sachems who alienated their people's land during the 1660s and 1670s gave their reasons, but several overlapping possibilities exist. Obviously, like Ousamequin, they coveted the pay that colonists offered, which included not only manufactured goods but, increasingly, wampum. Colonial sources showed no curiosity for why the Wampanoags traded for beads they were perfectly capable of manufacturing themselves, but, once again, we should. In all likelihood, Wamsutta's and Pumetacom's followers and tribute payers could not keep up with the brothers' demand for wampum to sponsor their far-flung intertribal diplomacy about checking colonial expansion. The sachems probably also used wampum from land sales to buy munitions from Rhode Islanders and the Dutch with the expectation that if a pan-Indian resistance movement came to fruition, they would use the arms to seize back land that had purchased the guns in the first place. Not least of all, Pumetacom repeatedly deeded land to to the English to defuse their suspicions that he was plotting against them. He made these concessions to English extortion to buy time and gather strength.

Wamsutta might have sold land to fund a campaign for Indian unity, but the most immediate effect was to alienate Wampanoags and Englishmen alike, including his own wife. Ousamequin had trained his eldest son to handle the responsibility of negotiating with the English by including him in several land transactions during the early to mid-1650s. When Wamsutta took over the public responsibilities of the sachemship from his father in 1657, he tried to establish right away that he was no English lackey. However, it was telling of the extent to which English land encroachment would dominate his short-lived rule that when he pronounced, "I Wamsutta am not willing at present to sell all they do desire," it appeared in a deed of sale for part of what is now the city of Fall River. The fact of the matter was that ceding land to the English and trying to keep his people quiet about it became a signature of Wamsutta's time in office. In 1659 his wife, Namumpum (later Weetamoo), the sunk-squaw of Pocasset, received a third of the goods he had been paid for the 1657 Fall River grant, with her portion consisting of twenty yards of blue trading cloth, two yards of red cloth, two pairs of shoes, two pairs of stockings, two broad hoes, and an axe. In other deals, he reserved tracts for the Native inhabitants "to plant and sojourn upon." Despite these measures, his deals sometimes pushed his people too far. On March 8, 1662, Wamsutta released his claims to the west end of Martha's Vineyard to William Brinton of Newport, Rhode Island, which so spooked the people of Aquinnah that they dropped their previous opposition to the Mayhew mission, apparently in an effort to secure English allies against the sachem's overreach. They had good reason for worry. Two months earlier, Wamsutta had sold Peter Talman of Newport a massive area bounded in the north by the Seven Mile River in modern Attleborough, extending east to Cockesit in modern West Bridgewater, then south to the shoreline and west to Narragansett Bay, thereby encompassing most of the sachemship of Sakonnet and part of Pocasset.[3]

Namumpum was not having it. Her marriage to Wamsutta was supposed to be a mutually beneficial alliance between Pokanoket and Pocasset, not an invitation for her husband to market her people's territory. Thus, on June 3, 1662, she appeared before the Plymouth General Court to complain, accompanied by Tatacoman-caah, son of the sunksquaw Awashonks of Sakonnet and probably one of Namumpum's relatives. It must have been the second time they had raised the matter, for, back in March, Plymouth had depu-tized the trader Thomas Willet "in case the sunksquaw should be put off her ground by Talman, to see that she be not wronged in that behalf." This was no act of benevolence, for the colony also charged Willet to use this emergency to urge the Sakonnets to sell their land to Plymouth before Wamsutta did.[4]

Willet had another mission as well: to inform Wamsutta that Plymouth did not take kindly to him selling land to Rhode Island. Yet Wamsutta continued to do as he pleased, including a bargain conducted just days after Willet's visit in which he ceded Providence a tract of land between the Seekonk and Pawtucket Rivers in exchange for one hundred fathoms of wampum and other goods. Six weeks later, he provoked Plymouth again by confirming a sale to a group of men from Hingham, Massachusetts, to a fifteen-mile-square tract along the Bay colony's border with Plymouth. Under the circumstances, Namumpum and Awashonks must have submitted their protests against Wamsutta to Plymouth knowing that the colony would leap at the chance to assert its authority along the contested boundary with Rhode Island. Little did any of the polities grasp how far this dispute ultimately would go.[5]

What happened next was and is shrouded in mystery and controversy. The agreed-on details are as follows: In the summer of 1662, Plymouth summoned Wamsutta to appear in court, but the sachem ignored it. In response, Plymouth sent out ten dragoons under Major Josiah Winslow to arrest him. This squad tracked down Wamsutta and a group of his men at a hunting camp at Monponsett Pond near the head of the Taunton River, took him into custody, and brought him in for questioning. Suddenly, the sachem fell ill and the English released him, only for him to die shortly after. Beyond this broad outline of events, surviving accounts disagree on nearly all the specifics. First, there is the cause of the English summons. Plymouth's official records mention only the issue of Wamsutta selling land to Rhode Islanders, but three other accounts written by colonists right after King Philip's War also cite rumors of the sachem conspiring with the Narragansetts. The most dependable one is a private letter written in early 1677 by the Plymouth minister and missionary John Cotton Jr. to provide information for Increase Mather's history of Indian-colonial relations in New England published later that year. Though Cotton did not move to Plymouth until 1667, five years after the events in question, he personally knew the officials who carried out the mission to retrieve Wamsutta, spoke Wampanoag himself, and had regular contact with Wampanoag people, who would have had their own perspectives on these matters. He had no discernible reason to invent reasons for Wamsutta's arrest, and he was unequivocal that Plymouth's cause was a "report being here that Alexander was plotting or privy to plots against the English." Precisely what that report said, Cotton did not relate. However, it likely charged that the sachem had been in secret talks with the Narragansetts and storing up arms, for in future years the English would make similar accusations against Wamsutta's brother, Pumetacom, and widow, Namumpum.[6]

English sources also differ on the sequence of events leading to Wamsutta's arrest. Mather and William Hubbard painted a dramatic scene in which Winslow and the dragoons surprised the Wampanoags, seized their muskets, then demanded Wamsutta's surrender, with

Winslow pressing a pistol against the sachem's breast and declaring "that if he stirred or refused to go, he was a dead man." Cotton related a much calmer exchange, which Mather apparently rejected for his published history because it was insufficiently theatrical. In Cotton's telling, the Wampanoags saw the English coming and were so unalarmed that they did not even bother to interrupt their breakfast. Instead of Wamsutta fulminating at Winslow, Cotton had him calmly explaining that he had delayed appearing at court because first he wanted to consult with his friend Captain Thomas Willet, who was away in New Netherland. There was no gunpoint arrest. Rather, "Alexander freely and readily without the least hesitancy consented to go." Cotton's version has the greatest ring of truth to it, even as he might have sanitized it. Winslow had an aggressive streak, but he would have understood that drawing a weapon on a sachem as powerful as Wamsutta and then dragging him before English authorities was a sure-fire way to start a war. It would have been unprecedented. That said, on the eve of King Philip's War, Pumetacom recalled bitterly about how the English had "forced" his brother "into court," though he might have been referring to the presence of the armed soldiers rather than Winslow drawing his pistol. The actual events must remain unknown.[7]

Pumetacom believed that the English used foul play to kill Wamsutta while he was in their company. After the encounter at Monponsett Pond, Wamsutta, his followers, and the English troops proceeded to the house of Magistrate William Collier in Duxbury. They then agreed to split up and reconvene later at Winslow's estate in Marshfield so Governor Thomas Prince (or Prence), who had to be summoned from his home on the outer Cape, could attend. Wamsutta voluntarily reappeared after two or three days, as promised, but unexpectedly fell ill as talks began. The English seemed genuinely concerned about him, as they rushed him to a certain "Mr. Fuller" so he could administer the sachem "a potion of working physic [medicine]." Yet Wamsutta only grew worse after this treatment. His

A view from the Island looking over East Monponsett

"East Monponsett Lake, Halifax, Massachusetts," SAILS Digital
History Collections, accessed February 8, 2019,
https://sailsinc.omeka.net/items/show/1413.

In 1662, an English force led by Josiah Winslow intercepted the Wampanoag
sachem, Wamsutta (or Alexander), at a hunting camp on Monponsett Pond
and took him into custody to answer a Plymouth court summons.
Contemporary accounts disagree whether Winslow used threat and force.
Regardless, Wamsutta fell fatally ill while in English custody. Some
Wampanoags suspected that Wamsutta died from English poison.
Pumetacom (or Philip) succeeded Wamsutta as sachem and later led his
people to war against the English.

men tried to rush him back home to their own doctors, but it was
too late. He died shortly after his arrival at Montaup, "as they judged,
poisoned," as Pumetacom later put it. With this, Wamsutta went
from being the Wampanoags' sachem to their martyr.[8]

POISONED RELATIONS

If there had been any question about whether Pumetacom supported a multitribal resistance against the colonies, the suspicious circumstances of Wamsutta's death appear to have answered it. Not only was Pumetacom enraged, but so were his people, thereby giving him a popular mandate to undertake such a bold and perilous initiative. If English sources are correct, he got to work right away. It took only until August 1662, just weeks after he took office, before the colony heard rumors "of danger of the rising of the Indians against the English." Pumetacom denied it all in "a large and deliberate debate of particulars," and even volunteered to surrender another brother, perhaps Sonkanuhoo, as a hostage until the magistrates could investigate, which they declined. So instead the new sachem offered up something greater, emphasizing that he did "earnestly desire the continuance of that amity and friendship that had formerly been between this government and his deceased father and brother." As proof, he pledged to keep the peace and sell land only to Plymouth.[9]

Despite the sachem's avowal of the alliance, the English were onto something with their concerns about the strange new pattern of Wampanoag-Narragansett relations. Back in 1660 Wamsutta had led his men in war against Uncas and the Mohegans, the Narragansetts' longtime archenemy. Wamsutta's main goal was to assert his tributary claims to the Quabaug Nipmucs, which Uncas challenged, but he was certainly aware that the Narragansetts would welcome Wampanoag-Mohegan hostilities. Rumors of Wamsutta plotting with other Indians surfaced two years later, leading to the events surrounding his death. Perhaps not coincidentally, in October 1663 Pumetacom complained to Plymouth that Namumpum, Wamsutta's widow, along with her new husband, "Quiquequanchett," had been hosting Narragansetts without his permission. Namumpum's actions seem like a continuation of Wamsutta's intertribal diplomacy; indeed, she and Wamsutta might have charted this course together from the beginning. Her quick remarriage appears to have been part of that outreach, given that her new spouse was probably Quequegunent, son of the Narragansett sunksquaw Quaiapen and nephew of Nini-gret, the Niantic-Narragansett sachem. Ninigret had a history of trying to foment a multitribal resistance movement against the English, largely because of their protection of the Mohegans, while Quaiapen would emerge as one of the Narragansetts' most militant leaders during King Philip's War. Namumpum's efforts to forge an anticolonial Wampanoag-Narragansett alliance harked back to her father Corbitant's campaign in the 1620s to break with Ousamequin and rally the two tribes against Plymouth. Pumetacom did not explain this context to Plymouth because he was only opposed to Namumpum overstepping him rather than to the coalition building itself. For once, English authorities should have been more alarmed than they were. Their only response was to affirm Pumetacom's primacy in foreign affairs while urging him to return some mishoons he had seized from the Narragansetts when they were visiting Pocasset.[10]

The rapid pace of Pumetacom's land sales to Plymouth during these years probably had something to do with his outreach to the Narragansetts insofar as the payments in trade goods and wampum enabled him to bestow impressive gifts as part of this diplomacy, while keeping the English happy decreased the chances of them probing too deeply into his business. In 1664 the sachem sold William Benton of Rhode Island the area of Mattapoisett Neck (or Gardiner's Neck) near Montaup, thereby violating his earlier pledge to deal only with Plymouth. Just four years later he ceded his English neighbors an eight-mile-square tract northwest of Swansea, followed by another sale of all the meadowland just north of Montaup. This was not a case of the sachem going rogue against the will of his people. A number of these deals recorded the explicit consent of a roster of his counselors and other leading men. Nevertheless, each transaction drew English settlements closer to Montaup and, with them, a rise in the sort of disputes over territory, resources, and jurisdiction that fueled Pumetacom's effort to organize Indians against the colonies in the first place.[11]

To say that Pumetacom had popular support for his sales does not mean that there was no opposition. A number of Wampanoag people voiced their concern that he had lost control over the process. In 1668 Tom Pawpawino, Tom Aththowannomit, and Tom Mothohtom of Mattapoisett Neck begged Plymouth not to accept any offers for their

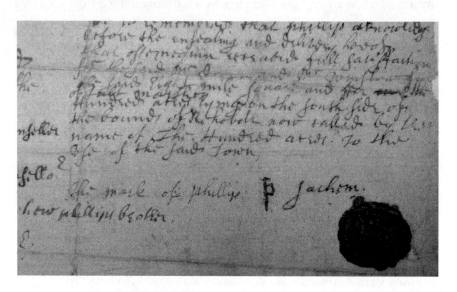

Pumetacom's mark, March 16, 1668. Courtesy John Carter
Brown Library, Providence, Rhode Island.

Pumetacom (or Metacom, Metacomet, Philip, King Philip) put his mark to a number of land deeds between 1662 and 1675, which, combined with the sales of Ousamequin, Wamsutta, and other sachem contemporaries, effectively surrounded his base of Montaup with English claims and towns. It appears that Pumetacom used a number of these sales to acquire wampum for intertribal diplomacy and munitions for his warriors, all in anticipation of a war with the English that he hoped would return this land to his people.

territory, "for we are afraid that our sachem will dispose of our land without our consent, which is a very unjust thing." This petition might have been the impetus for Pumetacom's own undated request for Plymouth not to pressure him for any new cessions for seven years. Yet that was asking too much. Even Roger Williams wondered aloud whether land lust was becoming the puritans' false idol, writing, "God Land will be (as now is) as great with us English as God Gold was with the Spaniards." Accordingly, it took only until 1669 for Pumetacom to alienate another five hundred acres just above Mattapoisett Neck to the town of Swansea. Then in 1672 he transferred a four-mile-square tract south of Taunton, and another three-by-four-mile parcel southwest of the Three Mile River. In barely a decade, he had literally surrounded his home base of Montaup with English land claims.[12]

Pumetacom was hardly the only sachem involved in runaway land deals with the English, which would have come as cold comfort to the Wampanoag people. Up the Taunton River, the sachems Josias Wampatuck, Pamantaquash, and his son, Tispaquin, were also alienating the timbered, well-watered lands in and around Titicut and Nemasket, bringing the English ever closer to the Wampanoags of Assawompset Pond. The colonists were so relentless that Pamantaquash, in an effort to protect his successors, petitioned "that neither Tispaquin nor his son be pressed to sell lands by any English or others whatsoever." Once again, it was wishful thinking. During the 1660s and 1670s, colonists also prevailed on the local sachems of Buzzards Bay to make nine different sales of lands along the very estuaries that the Wampanoags needed for their subsistence. Meanwhile, similar patterns were playing out among the Nipmucs to the north and the Narragansetts to the west. Increasingly, nowhere was safe from English swarming.[13]

Indian resentment over these developments naturally extended from the colonists' growing unwillingness to abide by the letter or spirit of joint-use agreements. Imagine the Natives' frustration when they returned to spring fish runs to find the streams dammed up or fenced off, or cattle grazing on their planting fields, or woods they depended on for fuel and building materials cut down, or their dogs killed for threatening the colonists' sheep. Such incidents mounted with every passing year without resolution. For instance, on March 3, 1663, a group of Englishmen in Taunton acknowledged that some of their townsmen had violated the "long practiced" custom of tolerating the Indians planting their corn in the "remote parts of the community . . . to their [the Indians'] great impoverishing." The following year, Pumetacom accused the English of Rehoboth with felling his timber. Yet the greatest strain on joint use was English livestock or, more specifically, the unwillingness of colonists to fence in their animals. Practically every year complaints poured into Plymouth from every corner of Wampanoag country about English cattle, horses, and pigs devouring the people's crops. Sometimes the animals even swam around fences the Wampanoags had built across peninsular necks of land to keep them out. When the Wampanoags killed the trespassing animals, or when their dogs attacked them, or when livestock wandered into Indian deer traps, colonists sued for damages. It made Wampanoags wonder why the English valued Indian property so little yet expected their own wandering four-legged private property claims to carry such weight.[14]

Indians found it even more astonishing that when they experimented with raising livestock, especially pigs, the English refused to share pastureland and obstructed Indian competitors from selling pork on colonial markets, contrary to their admonitions that Indians should live in a "civilized" manner. In 1669 the Rhode Island town of Portsmouth even demanded Pumetacom to remove pigs he had put to feed on the aptly named Hog Island, a literal stone's throw from the sachem's village, arguing that he had already sold that exclusive right to the Englishman Richard Smith. The plague of English beasts was so bad that John Eliot considered it to be one of the greatest obstacles to propagating Christianity because it left Indians infuriated toward colonists and unwilling to live near their towns. Yet for some English that was precisely the point: the more difficult it became for Wampanoags to share space with colonial neighbors, the more likely they were to withdraw and sell the contested territory.[15]

When English herds failed to drive Indians off the land, some colonists turned to outright fraud, occasionally with an assist from rogue Wampanoags who wanted to line their own pockets and grab power. Pocasset was a prime target for these schemes by virtue of its rich meadowlands and location within the contested jurisdictional claims of Rhode Island and Plymouth. After Namumpum's 1662 protest of Wamsutta's sale of part of her territory, Captain John Sanford and John Archer of Portsmouth convinced her to sign over the land to them, purportedly so they could guard it until the emergency had passed and then return the title to her. Obviously, she had faith in these men. Yet they were unworthy of her trust. Sometime before October 1667, Archer tried to use Namumpum's temporary grant to erect a homestead at Pocasset, which the Wampanoags could only see as a first step toward an influx of English claimants. Before matters went too far, "several Indians" confronted Archer, "abusing of him by dispossessing him of his house and otherwise at Pocasset." A subsequent investigation uncovered that Archer was the culprit rather than the victim. Portsmouth residents Richard and Mary Sisson testified that Archer had confessed to them that his deed "was a cheat . . . to deceive Namumpum of her land." He and Sanford had even admitted that their swindle left them "troubled in conscience," though not enough to abandon it.[16]

This kind of treachery cut the Wampanoags deep. Namumpum's daughter, Weetama (whose name Namumpum would later adopt, probably after her daughter's death), and her husband, Josias Wampatuck, complained that Namumpum had followed Sanford's advice because she trusted that he was her "great and good friend." She did not mean to sell her land, quite the contrary. She only wanted "to preserve her interest from Alexander's [Wamsutta's] intrusion [or sale of her land]." Making this betrayal worse was that Namumpum's followers had already "spared so much lands" to the English "upon reasonable terms," to the point of having "straightened ourselves to the great discontentment of our people . . . and now to be defrauded and defeated of the small portion we have reserved for us and our people to subsist on, will lose something more than we shall be able to bear." Citing their ignorance of English law, Weetama and Wampatuck asked Plymouth to appoint an attorney for them and hand over all documents relating to their lands. They no longer had any confidence in their own English contacts because those who claimed "to be most faithful . . . prove most treacherous and deceitful." Statements of this sort were becoming so frequent as to constitute a running Wampanoag critique of English colonialism.[17]

The Wampanoags' recognition that their sachems' sale of land was as much a part of the problem as the English purchase of it led growing numbers of them to demand individual title or communal reservations. One of the first instances of this sort arose in 1666 when a man named Watuchpoo complained that his local sachem, Quatchatisset, had sold territory along Buzzards Bay belonging to generations of Watuchpoo's family. Pumetacom got involved as paramount sachem and proposed that colonists should treat Quatchatisset's sale as just a preliminary step toward bargaining with common Indians still living on the tract, whom he considered still possessed of the right to decide whether to stay or go. On the Vineyard, this kind of two-tiered system of land claims became standardized because everyday Wampanoags simply refused to vacate the areas their sachems had alienated. English land speculators and Wampanoag sachems alike had to concede that the "sachem rights" of Indian leaders and the "planting rights" of regular people were two different things that colonists would have to purchase in separate transactions in order to secure clear title. Wampanoags elsewhere applied this principle selectively, but widely enough for cases to be found in a variety of locales. At Titicut, opposition to the land sales of Josiah Chickataubut was so great that he granted his followers three miles on the east side of the upper Taunton River to enjoy "peaceably . . . without interruption from me," which his son, Josias Wampatuck (Weetama's husband), confirmed with the promise that this tract would belong to the "Titicut Indians and their Indian heirs forever." Titicut thus became the only Indian reservation in the region that was not a praying town. The people living there, like a growing number of Natives across southern New England, would need it.[18]

MURDEROUS

Jurisdictional fights went hand in hand with English expansion as colonial courts tried to establish their authority over a growing range of Indian-colonial and even Indian-Indian affairs. During most of Ousamequin's lifetime, the colonies tended to address such issues through the sachems in diplomatic settings rather than courtrooms. Yet, during Wamsutta's and Pumetacom's tenures as sachem, all the New England colonies began empowering their magistrates to seize Indians with overdue debts to English creditors. In 1659 Rhode Island went so far as to authorize the sale of Indians into overseas slavery when they were convicted of theft or property damage and failed to pay restitution, fines, and court costs, particularly when they had demonstrated "insolency" to English officers. No colonial magistrates ever dared attempt to wield this power, but courts in Providence and Newport did try sixteen cases involving fourteen Indians over the next decade. Plymouth also became more assertive in extending its jurisdiction over Indians. In 1665 it established "select courts" in every town with the power to adjudicate minor civil suits and issues of Indian-English property damage. Its colony-level courts also began aggressively prosecuting Indians accused of thievery and assault and meting out harsh punishments, including whipping, branding, and forced servitude. Such measures would have been unthinkable in Ousamequin's day.[19]

As one would expect, murder cases were particularly charged, given the high stakes and wide cultural gulf between Wampanoag and English ways of handling this crime. Colonists insisted on carrying out capital execution against the guilty individual, consistent with English legal tradition. By contrast, Indian custom was for the leaders of the perpetrator and victim to negotiate compensation or punishment or else leave it to the victim's kin to exact revenge against the murderer's kin, thereby putting pressure on families to keep their members in line. Generally, sachems appear to have been ambivalent about the English insistence on punishing Indians who committed murder against colonists within colonial towns. Perhaps it seemed pointless to contend over this issue, given how easy Indians found it to break out of jail and escape to safety, which seems to have been common. The greater question was whether the English were so bold as to try to assert their jurisdiction over murders between Indians, particularly those committed in colonial settlements.[20]

Two such cases arose in 1674. The first, in Plymouth, involved two obscure figures and ended without incident after an English jury returned a verdict of minor manslaughter and set the accused free. The second case was potentially more combustible because it concerned intertribal as well as Indian-colonial affairs. In it, a Wampanoag known as Quaoganit/Poagonit or Old Man stood accused of killing his Narragansett wife and her Narragansett lover in or around Providence. The Narragansetts demanded the execution of both Quaoganit and an additional Wampanoag chosen at random, asserting that it was their custom to have "two to put to death for the said two killed, and out of Philip's men, for that the murdered were related to the Narragansetts, and the murderer to Philip." English authorities would consent only to the punishment of the murderer himself. Ultimately, something of a compromise was reached. A Rhode Island jury, which remarkably included three Indians, found Quaoganit guilty and ordered him executed by hanging. After carrying out the sentence, the colony delivered the body to the Narragansetts as a self-preserving courtesy. Yet it was not enough to satisfy the Narragansetts, who "showed great indignation" that "before the English came, they could do what they wished with Philip's [Pumetacom's] party." We are left to imagine Pumetacom's reaction. The colonies' assertion of the right to try and execute his followers did not bode well for the sanctity of any sachem's jurisdiction or any Indian's life in the face of ongoing English expansion.[21]

There were other festering intercultural tensions that rose to the surface during Quaoganit's trial. The case prompted Rhode Island's General Assembly to debate whether juries should consider an Indian's testimony as legitimate as an Englishman's. Ultimately, it ruled that Indian witnesses were permissible in this instance, but only because it concerned Indians alone, not colonists. Indians were privy to such discussions and easily grasped the bigotry behind them, as evident in Native people's complaints that "the English slighted their witnessing" just because they were Indians. The distrust cut both ways. Colonial authorities found it difficult to prosecute Quaoganit because "Indians have been reluctant to come in and give testimony in legal proceedings for fear of being arrested themselves." Indian indebtedness to English creditors had become so widespread, and the colonies' prosecution of it had grown so aggressive, that Indians feared the English would exploit every opportunity to seize them and force them into servitude. Clearly, Ousamequin's alliance with the English was in shambles.[22]

A TIME OF CRISIS, NOT PEACE

Pumetacom faced a herculean task to transform Indian fears of the English menace into a broad resistance movement. First there was the challenge of convincing rival sachems that their shared grievances against the English were more important than their many differences. Beyond that, he had to forge a consensus on what to do about it and foster trust that everyone would stay true to the end. The grinding diplomacy involved him sponsoring conferences at which he would present gifts to visiting sachems and their counselors to open their ears to his message. Everyone would feast, smoke, and dance together in the name of peace and solidarity. Then they would speak their minds about his proposals. Afterward, the delegates would disband to consult with their home communities before returning for additional rounds of talks. Yet, before they did, Pumetacom, even as he advocated for the common cause, would warn that any sachem who did not go along with his plans risked losing their supporters and tributaries to him.

This threat applied particularly to the Narragansetts, given their shared border and history with the Wampanoags. Pumetacom signaled as much in 1666 by making a "promise" to support Pomham, sachem of the Narragansetts' tribute-paying community of Shawomet, if the Narragansetts tried to force him off his lands. Shawomet fell within the once contested Narragansett-Wampanoag border region from which Canonicus had driven Ousamequin after the epidemic of 1616–19. In subsequent years, the Narragansett sachems Canonicus and Miantonomo had given the English permission to form the town of Warwick in Shawomet territory despite Pomham's vocal opposition. Subsequent fights between the Shawomets and neighboring colonists over joint use and jurisdiction grew so disruptive by the 1660s that the Narragansett sachems Pessacus and Ninigret demanded Pomham and his followers to hand over all of Warwick

Neck to the English. Enter Pumetacom, who had a rival claimant to the Shawomet sachemship, named Nawwushawsuck, living under his protection. Pumetacom contended that a united Pokanoket and Shawomet "will be too great a party against those two [Narragansett] sachems." In this, Pumetacom was doing more than just asserting his ancestral rights to the area. He was setting himself up as a protector of aggrieved Narragansett tributaries and, ultimately, recruiting them against the English.[23]

That same year, Pumetacom also lent his support to the Montauketts and Shinnecocks of Long Island in their long-running campaign to free themselves from the Narragansetts' tributary demands. The offer came, fascinatingly enough, in an English-language letter written by Pumetacom's Harvard-educated Wampanoag scribe, John Sassamon, and addressed to the chief officer of the colonial town of Southampton. The sachem wanted the English of that community to warn "your neighbors, the Indians" that Ninigret was about to launch another raid against them. "Tell them from me," he implored, "that they shall not pay any more tribute to Ninigret." He counseled the Long Island Indians to fortify themselves against the assault and, when it finally came, to call for his aid through the Manisses of Block Island. The Manisses, he explained, would not "anyway align with Ninigret, for they are as I am." In other words, they were already a part of his growing coalition of disaffected Narragansett tributaries. Pumetacom wanted the English to think that he was only trying to buy time for Native Long Islanders so they could present their case to royal officials. The real point, though, was to bring the Montauketts and Shinnecocks into his fold. Pointedly, Pumetacom emphasized that the Long Island Indians would not just be substituting one oppressor for another by aligning with him. What made his leadership appealing was his promise that "as for myself, I will not lay my hands upon you."[24]

Pumetacom finally provoked a Narragansett response when he convinced the Nipmucs of Quantisset to cut off their tribute payments to Quaiapen, Ninigret's sister. Quaiapen had just succeeded her deceased husband, Mixano, as leader of a series of Narragansett villages near what is now Exeter, Rhode Island. Unwilling to brook Pumetacom challenging her authority so soon after it began, she responded furiously with a September 1667 raid

Pumetacom's letter to the Indians of Long Island, May 7, 1666. *Colonial State Papers*, 1/20, No. 68, National Archives of the United Kingdom, Kew.

As an English-language letter dictated by an Indian leader to an Indian scribe, then sent from one Indian community to another, this document is one of a kind. Pumetacom had his fateful interpreter, John Sassamon, address it to the English of Long Island to deliver to the Long Island Indians to encourage them to reject the tributary demands of Ninigret of the Narragansetts. It appears to have been part of his effort to raise a coalition of indigenous allies for an anticolonial resistance.

against Quantisset in which her men destroyed houses and plundered wealth. It was telling of the shadowy, multilateral politics of
this contest that Quantisset appealed to Pumetacom for help, only
to have Ninigret divert him by stoking a crisis between him and the
English. Pumetacom, Ninigret charged, had been conspiring with
the French and Dutch to go to war against the New England colonies, "and so not only to recover their lands sold to the English, but
to enrich themselves with [the colonists'] goods." This rumor was
especially alarming because England was in the midst of a naval
conflict with the Dutch during which it had conquered New Netherland. Additionally, a land war was brewing in Europe pitting
England against France and the Dutch Provinces over the fate of the
Spanish Netherlands. Though it might seem inconceivable today
that Pumetacom was engaged in diplomacy with the French, whose
colony on the St. Lawrence River was hundreds of miles away, the
notion was not far-fetched given the vastness of the Wampanoags'
networks, which included Abenaki allies of New France. The Dutch
threat also rang true, for Dutch colonists remained the majority in
the English colony of New York that had replaced New Netherland.
Dutch naval forces would even briefly retake the colony in 1673
before finally handing it back to the English. If Ninigret contrived
this story, he had done his research first.[25]

English sources on the ground also perceived that the Wampanoags were up to something. Thomas Wilmot of Seekonk informed
Rhode Island's assembly that "the deportments of the Indians, especially of Philip . . . giveth great occasion of suspicion of them, and
their treacherous design." When Plymouth sent Josiah Winslow to
Pokanoket to investigate, he found "the first reporter" of the
rumor "to be one of Philip the said sachem's men, who freely and
boldly did avouch it to his [Pumetacom's] face." It was enough to
make colonial New Englanders fear that they were "like to be
hazarded by the invasion of the common enemy, or by treachery

from amongst the Indians." Rhode Island went so far as to order any Indians in English settlements to be disarmed, arrested, and interrogated. Clearly, many colonists believed the threat was real.[26]

Pumetacom, of course, claimed total surprise and innocence and even volunteered to surrender his weapons until the matter could be resolved. He pledged to have always upheld his father's "faithfulness to the English, by whom he and his progenitors had been preserved from being ruined by the Narragansetts." If such spurious rumors destroyed his people's historic relationship with Plymouth, it would be "little less than death to him, gladding his enemies, grieving and weakening his friends." Why, he asked, would he ever ally with England's imperial rivals? He claimed that they were his foes, too, citing an incident from a year earlier in which a French or Dutch ship seized eighteen of "his people" from the Vineyard. (A French man-of-war had, in fact, been spotted off the island in July 1666.) The entire war scare, he charged, was nothing more than a scheme by Ninigret, who had hired a Wampanoag agent to make the false accusation before Winslow's party. Roger Williams himself testified that the accuser was known to have been "a very vile fellow formerly." Pumetacom even produced a letter from an unnamed Narragansett sachem backing his version of events, though under direct questioning that source "utterly disclaimed that he had or could say any such thing concerning Ninigret." Plymouth finally concluded that the crisis was a mere result of Pumetacom's "tongue . . . running out" rather than an actual plot. Despite issuing the sachem a fine of forty pounds to pay for the expedition to Pokanoket and resolving to "keep a watchful eye over him," the colony decided "to continue terms of love and amity."[27]

That love and amity was sorely tested yet again in 1669 as rumors flew back and forth that the Pequot sachem, Robin Cassacinamon, had hosted a great dance attended by long-standing archrivals Ninigret and Uncas. Their joint presence startled the

English because, as the interpreter Thomas Stanton put it, they had "durst not look at each upon [the] other this 20 years but at the muzzle of a gun or the pile of an arrow." By this, he meant that they had always been enemies in a fight for tributaries and revenge over Uncas's execution of Miantonomo. Even Cassacinamon had often been at odds with Ninigret and Uncas in his quest to secure the Pequots' independence from Narragansett and Mohegan dominance. Now, for some reason unknown to the English, these three rivals were meeting face-to-face. More alarming still, the dance reportedly included "northern Indians" associated with the French. Other rumors had Ninigret, once the scourge of the Long Island Indians, suddenly presenting those people with gifts of guns and wampum to recruit them into an alliance with "as many of the Indians as he could in all parts" to "kill all the English . . . that they might get their lands from the English." Ninigret's daughter, Weunquesh, was said to be traveling throughout the country, inviting Indian delegates to attend another great meeting, "the greatest dance . . . that ever was in the Narragansett." Rhode Island heard that seven of Pumetacom's "ancient men," including counselors, had been with Ninigret for nine or ten days contriving "a plot or combination among the Indians to cut off the English." With so many former enemies gathering presumably to discuss their common interests and common threats, Stanton proclaimed, "It's not far from as great a hazard as ever New England yet saw."[28]

For weeks, war seemed imminent until Ninigret went before a Rhode Island investigatory committee and convinced it that the colonies had overreacted. The sachem claimed that his dances had been merely ceremonial. Most of his "Wampanoag" visitors were not Wampanoag at all but his own men who had just been living temporarily at Pocasset (which, for some reason, the English did not think to question). The rest were simply craftsmen teaching the Narragansetts how to "make bark houses." He attributed the damaging rumors to a Long Island Indian who wanted to scuttle Ninigret's real purpose, which, he stressed, was to promote peace between former enemies. The panic was just a misinterpretation of innocuous activities. Rhode Island agreed, finding "no just ground of jealousy as to [Ninigret's] intentions," a conclusion that was probably motivated by a desire to keep the United Colonies from sending an army through Providence and Warwick into Narragansett country, but also convincing enough to defuse the crisis.[29]

Ninigret might have been so persuasive because he had given up hope for a successful multitribal resistance after being rebuffed by the Mohawks, who were indispensable. Not only did the Mohawks boast the most formidable warriors in the region, but they controlled access to Albany, easily the most important market in the region for guns and ammunition. Additionally, if coastal peoples rose against the English, they would need the Mohawks to open their territory west of the Hudson River to serve as a refuge for their noncombatants. During this war scare, Pequot leaders had even intimated "that they must go to the Mohawks' country to live for they had so much trouble here that they was wearied out with it." For years, Ninigret had cultivated the Mohawks as the Narragansetts' counterweight to Uncas's alliance with the English. He knew better than anyone that, without the Mohawks, even the united tribes of southern New England had little chance of rolling back colonial expansion.[30]

Yet 1669 was a bad time for such entreaties to the Mohawks. English New York had recently replaced Dutch New Netherland as the Mohawks' main supplier of European goods, including arms. The Mohawks could not risk alienating its new trade partner by warring against its countrymen in New England, particularly at a time when the tribe was already overstretched, battling with New France and Indian enemies. Thus, when Connecticut's John Mason, a thirty-year veteran of Indian-colonial affairs, wrote the Mohawks urging them to keep out of the anticolonial plot, they responded favorably that they would not "meddle with these [matters], they say, for fear [of] displeasing the English." Rather, they pledged, "they will prove our real friends." This answer, which the coastal sachems certainly received as well, was a devastating blow to the prospects of New England Indian unity. With it, Ninigret abandoned the cause, and over the next several years his and Pumetacom's men engaged in several clashes, even amid Wampanoag rapprochement with the rest of the Narragansetts. No one explained the source of this trouble, but there is a likely explanation: Ninigret, who had always seen the Mohawks as the key to a large-scale Indian resistance to the colonies, had rejected Pumetacom's league in the absence of Mohawk support.[31]

Nevertheless, events in 1671 suggest that Pumetacom was far from abandoning his vision. In a vague incident that February or March, a group of Wampanoags nearly came to blows with neighboring English over the colonists' trespassing animals. When Pumetacom ignored a summons from Plymouth to explain, the colony dispatched Hugh Cole to investigate, only for him to stumble on a community seemingly preparing for war. Twenty or thirty Wampanoag men brandishing clubs intercepted Cole at the entrance of Mount Hope Neck, declaring that they would resist any English attempt to arrest their people for trial. Cole did not doubt their resolve, particularly after entering Pumetacom's village to find the people busy making bows, arrows, and spears and putting their firearms in working order. There were also foreign Indians present who struck Cole as "better armed than I have usually seen them." Suffice it to say, Cole beat a hasty retreat back to English territory without fulfilling his mission. A few days later, Pumetacom and an estimated sixty gunmen marched to the outskirts of Swansea, then turned back without doing any damage. Their unmistakable point was that they were ready to fight if the English continued to engross what little land they had left, torment them with wandering livestock, and then threaten them with invasion, fines, and even capital execution when they defended themselves. The sachem and his people had reached the limits of their patience.[32]

THE NEAR WAR OF 1671

Over the next month, English authorities received a string of star-tling reports that the Wampanoags and Narragansetts were preparing jointly for war against the colonies. The Massachusetts governor, Richard Bellingham, heard that "multitudes" of armed Natives were marshaling, "instigated by the devil and evil-minded English and French." The word from Rhode Island was that both tribes were in "warlike preparations" and threatening their colonial neighbors by asking "why they came from their own country and wished them to be gone [or else] they would flay them as they do cattle." Pumetacom and "the squaw sachem," probably Weetamoo (who had just changed her name from Namumpum), were said to have delivered five baskets of wampum to the Narragansetts to secure an alliance. Amid these "continuous rumors of invasions from the Indians," the town of Newport once again declared a round-the-clock state of defense. Newporters lived in such close proximity to the Wampanoags and Narragansetts that they could literally witness the back-and-forth mishoon traffic and even shoreline assem-blies that informed these startling reports.[33]

Plymouth called for a treaty conference to be held in Taunton on April 10, 1671, claiming that it hoped to avert violence, though doubtless it was also motivated by the prospect of fining Pumetacom to wrest another land cession from him. The meeting was nearly sabotaged, however, by an explosive rumor that two hundred Indians planned to capture Governor Prince and his men en route and hold them for ransom. Josiah Winslow's understanding—and he did not name his source—was that Indian forces had already assembled for this mission, when "one wiser than the rest" convinced the others to call it off because the English "were now awakened." The Wampanoags reportedly decided that it was better to let the colonies "grow secure again" before reviving such ambitious plans. Another informant claimed that nothing but "foul weather" had prevented the Indians from striking, which would have been followed by "the cutting off of Taunton, Swansea, and Seekonk."[34]

Under such circumstances, the summit barely took place as scheduled, and though no minutes survive, there are enough surviving anecdotes to glean that the English dictated the terms rather than negotiated them, which probably means that they were accompanied by a formidable guard. How else could they have induced Pumetacom and his counselors to concede "that they had been in preparation for war against us . . . not grounded upon any injury sustained from us, nor provocation given by us, but from their own naughty hearts." There is no other conceivable scenario under which the sachem would have "agreed" to the humiliating provision to turn over all his people's firearms, including those he and his men had carried to Taunton. He made clear that he considered the treaty illegitimate by ignoring the terms once he was back within the safe confines of Montaup. By early May, he had relinquished only an additional sixteen or seventeen muskets, some of them unserviceable, even though, according to Governor Prince, "it is well known that he had at least six score [120]" back in March. Prince believed not only that the Wampanoags withheld their guns but that they continued to stockpile them, "not to defend themselves against Mohawks but probably against us if we should attempt to take in their arms."[35]

Pumetacom tried to deflect the demands of colonial authorities by assisting them in the arrest of a Nipmuc named Ascook, charged with the killing of an Englishman on the road outside Dedham, Massachusetts. Springfield's John Pynchon praised Pumetacom for how "industriously active" he was "to discover the murderer," though he was not blind to the fact that the sachem cooperated "so [the colonists'] jealousy may be removed from him." As for Ascook, a Massachusetts court ordered him hanged and decapitated, his head left to rot publicly in Boston. Ironically, this execution, carried out with Pumetacom's assistance, would earn the English more Native enemies and Pumetacom more allies. When the time for war finally came, Ascook's father, Matoonas, constable of the Nipmuc praying town of Pakachoog, would lead his community in arms against the people who had executed his son, not the sachem who aided them under duress.[36]

Pumetacom cooperated in the Ascook case because he feared that his dispute with the English was building toward a catastrophic showdown in which Plymouth would attempt to seize his people's guns by force. Indeed, the colonists' fear of Indian conspiracy, encouraged by their desire to engross what was left of the mainland Wampanoags' rich territory, led them to demand the other Taunton River sachemships to disarm, too, based on the charge that they had been "in compliance with Philip in his late plot." In June, Winslow and his troops successfully forced the issue at Nemasket and Assawompset. Then, for good measure, Plymouth issued William, son of the Assawompset sachem, Tispaquin, a harsh fine for stealing and branding a mare belonging to a colonist of Duxbury, knowing that Tispaquin would have to sell yet more land to pay it. Still, Sakonnet and Pokanoket withheld their guns, which Governor Prince took as a sign that "there is scarce any of them, but would imbrue their hands in the English blood." He was not going to wait to see if he was correct.[37]

Soon Awashonks capitulated, faced as she was with the prospect of an impending attack from an expedition of 102 Englishmen and 40 Natives (probably Cape Wampanoags) raised by Plymouth. On

July 24, she signed articles of agreement in which she submitted herself and, conspicuously, her Sakonnet lands to Plymouth's authority. These concessions might have rested in the misplaced hope that the colony would fulfill its reciprocal pledge to protect her office and territory from "such as will not be governed by her." Yet Plymouth's decision to levy her a fifty-pound fine for its trouble and expense, which she could only pay through a land cession, revealed that its promises were empty. So did Plymouth's warning that it retained the option to confiscate Sakonnet territory to pay for the subdual of "incendiaries" who refused the order to disarm. Given that this mission would be led by such figures as Josiah Winslow and Constant Southworth, who were among the colony's most aggressive land speculators, Awashonks had no cause to doubt that the colony meant what it said on that point.[38]

While Awashonks folded, Pumetacom raised the stakes, "making unkind carriages toward us," as Plymouth put it, and hosting "many strange Indians," especially "diverse Sakonnet Indians, professed enemies to this colony." In late August, Plymouth issued another summons for the sachem to appear before the General Court, threatening his "reducement by force," but tried to ease the affront by including his old friend James Brown (son of John) on the team that delivered the message. It did not work. The party arrived at Montaup just as the people were concluding a dance at which alcohol had been flowing freely, including into Pumetacom's cup. With tempers high and inhibitions low, Brown and Pumetacom exchanged heated words, during which the sachem knocked the hat from Brown's head as if to demand the same respect due to an English elite. (Brown, as a Quaker, did not doff his hat for any man.) Talks resumed the next day once everyone had cooled off and sobered up, but Pumetacom still rejected Plymouth's order. Instead, he had decided to accept a last-minute invitation from the praying town of Natick and John Eliot to present his quarrel with Plymouth to the judgment of the Massachusetts Bay Colony. In fact, the sachem planned to head north immediately to state his case. Meanwhile, Plymouth entered a discussion with Rhode Island about mutually coordinating their defenses, citing "more than ordinary causes to suspect and believe the Indians are treacherously inclined against the English in general." Plymouth viewed Pumetacom's appeal to Massachusetts as part of that treachery.[39]

Pumetacom arrived in Boston dressed to impress and hopeful that he had seized the upper hand. Accompanied by a large, well-armed entourage, he marched through town awing colonial onlookers with his "coat . . . and buckskins set thick with these [wampum] beads in pleasant wild works [designs] and a broad belt of the same . . . valued at twenty pounds." His speech also commanded English respect. After hearing his version of events, Massachusetts admonished Plymouth for its presumption in demanding an independent sachem to answer its summons. Pumetacom was not Plymouth's subject, the Bay colony lectured, but rather the leader of a separate polity under a shared king. True, he had formerly made pledges of fidelity, but those were no more than "a neighborly and friendly correspondency," not an acquiescence to Plymouth's rule over him. Furthermore, Boston warned that "the sword once drawn & dipped in blood may make him as independent upon you as you are upon him."[40]

Buoyed by his success in Boston, Pumetacom accepted Plymouth's suggestion to submit their dispute to a panel of arbitrators from Massachusetts and Connecticut and even to hold the proceedings in Plymouth. He had no idea that Plymouth had already fixed the outcome by convincing Massachusetts authorities that their earlier ruling in Pumetacom's favor had been wrong on its merits and shortsighted when it came to the colonies' shared interest to reduce Indian power. Expecting a fair hearing, the sachem showed up on September 29, took his seat, and only then realized that he had walked into a diplomatic ambush. There, on the site of the former Wampanoag village of Patuxet, where Ousamequin had first welcomed the English, the purportedly neutral judges ganged up on their "common enemy," as Plymouth referred to him, and forced him to yield in nearly every particular. The subsequent "agreement" declared that Pumetacom had indeed been plotting with the colonies' "professed enemies" and stockpiling arms. Furthermore, he had treated Plymouth's ambassadors with "great incivility" and tried to alienate fellow English colonies from one another. If he did not "humble himself" and "amend his ways," the English as a whole would make him "smart for it," which he did not doubt, given the presence of colonial soldiers. With no good options, Pumetacom did the only thing he could and formally submitted his people not only to the king of England but Plymouth, too. He must have known that this concession gave Plymouth a basis to justify even more aggressive assertions of its jurisdiction and land claims in the future. He probably reasoned that it hardly mattered because Plymouth was going to do whatever it wanted regardless of principle. This affair, like colonization as a whole, was little more than crass exercise of power, not a morality play.[41]

The other clauses of this settlement proved as much. The sachem pledged to pay an unprecedentedly large fine of one hundred pounds, requiring still more land cessions of the sort that had produced the war scare in the first place. To represent his submission, he would deliver five wolves' heads to Plymouth each year, if it was possible to get them. The Wampanoags would have found this condition especially offensive, inasmuch as their very name for "wolf" was closely related to their term for "cousin." The English also stipulated that Pumetacom would refer all future grievances with Plymouth to Plymouth's own judgment and never go to war or sell land without Plymouth's approval. Strictly enforced, these provisions would reduce Pumetacom from a paramount sachem to a minor official in the colonial bureaucracy with nominal rule over a nearly landless people. Yet, with a proverbial gun to his head, he and six counselors gritted their teeth and applied their marks to a supposed treaty of peace that might as well have been a declaration of war.[42]

The spate of Wampanoag land sales following this submission was as much a sign of the people's determination to resist as it was of Plymouth's heightened sense of dominance. On the one hand, these transfers were a direct result of Wampanoags' need to pay fines Plymouth had levied against them for the war scare. On the other hand, it is likely that Pumetacom and his allies used the extra proceeds to replace guns confiscated by the English and to acquire wampum for use in intertribal diplomacy, all with an aim toward building a coalition to fight the colonies and take back the ceded acreage. Long gone were the days of Ousamequin, when Wampanoags could imagine such transactions as part and parcel of an alliance of friendship between equals, and an integration of the English into Wampanoag society.

The cessions came fast and furious, often under dubious circumstances. In 1672 Pumetacom mortgaged twelve square miles of land to Taunton to pay off a debt of 83 pounds, followed quickly by the sale of a four-mile-square tract nearby for the sum of 143 pounds. From Sakonnet, Awashonks nearly kept pace, including a 1674 transaction in which she, her husband, Wawweeyowitt, and their son, Samponock, alienated "all their land" to Newport's James Barker Jr. and Caleb Carr Jr. Yet, whereas Pumetacom's conveyances were to Plymouth's advantage, Awashonks's deals with Rhode Islanders once again threatened the old colony's claims. In response, Plymouth threw its support to a bid by Awashonks's son, Mamaneway, to replace his mother as sachem, contrary to its earlier vow to support her rule. Not coincidentally, Mamaneway promptly led a group of relatives in selling Sakonnet Neck to Plymouth's Constant Southworth. He also began attending the missionary John Cotton Jr.'s sermons at Acushnet, as if to give his and the colony's crooked dealing the color of Christian righteousness.[43]

This case was but one of several examples that, if the English had their way, sachems like Mamaneway would become mere colonial placemen to sell all the land from under feet of their followers. Awashonks, though, refused to surrender without a fight and led her people in physically preventing Mamaneway from conducting a ceremonial transfer of the land to Plymouth. Lacking his mother's following, but enjoying the support of the English, Mameneway could only answer with a lawsuit filed in Plymouth. The fact that the court accepted his motion and awarded him five pounds, legal costs, and confirmation of his title was a direct blow against the Wampanoags' rights to choose their own leaders and protect their lands. Awashonks's appeal of the ruling was still in progress when King Philip's War made the issue moot. In the interim, however, the Englishman Benjamin Church had moved onto Sakonnet Neck in the expectation that soon other colonists would join him. The threat of English encroachment was growing so intense that, in May 1675, Awashonks's neighbor, Weetamoo, said that she was willing to make do with less land as long as it was bounded by rivers (she probably had the Acoaxet, Assonet, and Taunton Rivers in mind), "by which they have great dependence of fish." Yet she did not know how to secure even this meager claim because she and her people had "great fear of oppression from the English" and no faith that any of them would respect her title.[44]

When the English were not propping up sachem pretenders in order to secure land cessions, they turned to lawsuits. In Assawompset, the sachem Tispaquin's generous grants to the English were not enough to protect his son, William, from charges filed in

1672 by Josiah Winslow for nonpayment of a horse and other goods in the amount of twenty-four pounds. William, having no means to pay, mortgaged a triangular piece of land measuring three miles on the east and four miles on the west. It was probably carved out of the tract that Tispaquin's predecessor, Pamantaquash, had tried to cordon off from sale to the English. There was only one problem with Winslow's extortionist scheme: Plymouth law did not permit mortgages to pay off debts. Yet Winslow dispensed with this inconvenience the next year by ascending to the governorship of the colony and having the General Court alter the law in his favor. It was insulting enough to the Wampanoags when everyday colonists behaved like land sharks. Now the very occupant of the seat once held by Ousamequin's allies John Carver and William Bradford was displaying such aggression, despite being the scion of Ousamequin's other primary English friend, Edward Winslow. It would only have deepened the Wampanoags' bitterness that Josiah Winslow had also been at the center of Wamsutta's controversial arrest and death. An enemy of the Wampanoags was now at Plymouth's helm. For the sons of men Ousamequin had once trusted to stoop so low symbolized that the Wampanoag-English alliance had truly become meaningless.[45]

Pumetacom was the greatest target of Plymouth's relentless efforts to degrade the Wampanoags under the color of law. In 1673 John Allen and Hugh Cole of Swansea slapped Pumetacom with a two-hundred-pound lawsuit for failing to come into court and testify to the legitimacy of a land deed. The very next year, Peter Talman also sued the sachem for a whopping eight hundred pounds, claiming that he had forfeited a 1661 bond for land in what is now the town of Tiverton, Rhode Island. Clearly the English viewed Pumetacom's formal subjection to Plymouth in 1671 as a fresh opportunity to harass him and his people through the courts, with the apparent goal of

Josiah Winslow, 1651. Pilgrim Hall Museum, Plymouth, Massachusetts.
Josiah Winslow (1628–1680) served as Plymouth's major-commander of
military forces in 1656, commissioner to the United Colonies of New
England from 1658 to 1672, and governor from 1673 until 1680. With the
English population and power growing, he turned away from his father,
Edward's, approach of sensitive Indian diplomacy in favor of strong-arm and
underhanded tactics to engross Wampanoag land and subject the
Wampanoags to English authority. His aggression contributed mightily to
the outbreak of King Philip's War.

reducing them to utter landlessness. None of this legal bullying had
anything to do with justice and certainly not gratitude.[46]

SHIFTING LOYALTIES

The war scares not only inflamed relations between the mainland
Wampanoags and the English but widened already deep fault lines
between Christian Wampanoags of the Cape and islands and the
Taunton River sachemships under Pumetacom. During the mid-
1660s, Christian Wampanoags used the occasion of Ousamequin's

death and his sons' supposed plotting to lobby their English missionaries for help in establishing a Christian magistracy. Their intention,
it would appear, was to distance themselves from the impending
conflagration on the mainland. The process began in 1665 when
the Mashpee Wampanoags appointed six men—Papmunnuck,
Keencomsett, Watanamatucke, Nanquidnumacke, Kanoonus, and
Mocrust—to serve alongside Richard Bourne as justices and consta-
bles. Plymouth approved but was at pains to emphasize "that what
homage accustomed legally due to any superior sachem be not hereby
infringed." Time would prove these words to be hollow. A similar
reform took place on the Vineyard six years later, in 1671, amid the
most serious war scare to date. The Christian Wampanoags and
Thomas Mayhew Sr. arranged to have each Native community elect
three Christian magistrates to hold formal courts presided over
by the local sachem, who would exercise a veto over all decisions.
Wampanoags would run the system, but for the meantime they agreed
to consult with Mayhew on their choice of officers. Nantucket
Wampanoags would adopt parallel measures over the next couple of
years. It was precisely as Ousamequin had once feared.[47]

These steps took the Christian Wampanoags out of Pokanoket's orbit and halfway into the English fold. On the Vineyard and
Nantucket, Wampanoags who appealed the decisions of their own
courts had their cases heard by English magistrates, who could rule
according to their own definitions of justice. The greater concern
for Pumetacom was that if the Christian Indians appealed their
disagreements to English courts, they would no longer need him to
arbitrate stubborn local cases, thus reducing his authority and
tribute. Pumetacom was still fulfilling this role as late as 1665. That
year, English authorities charged a group of Nantucket Wampanoags
with murdering the passengers of a shipwreck, the victims of which
included the Vineyard Wampanoag Joel Hiacommes, who had been
on his way back home to pay a visit before his graduation ceremony

from Harvard. Faced with the impossible question of whether to turn over the accused to colonial justice, the Nantucket sachem, Nicka-noose, headed for the mainland to seek the advice of his "head sachem," Pumetacom. Afterward, Pumetacom himself appeared on Nantucket, probably to lend his assent to the hanging of the killers while ensuring that the judicial executions stopped there. This is the only case of its kind on record because the trend was toward Christian Wampanoags phasing Pumetacom out of their business entirely. In July 1674, for instance, two Wampanoags from Potonumecut on the outer Cape brought a local disagreement to Plymouth's courts instead of Pokanoket. No wonder Indian opponents of Christianity charged that "English men have invented these stories to amaze us and fear us out of our old customs, and bring us to stand in awe of them, that they might wipe us off our lands, and drive us into corners, to see new ways and living and new places, too." From this perspective, the missions were inseparable from the colonists' appropriation of Wampanoag land, jurisdictions, and livelihoods, which is to say, the English subjugation of Native people.[48]

Christian Wampanoags did not see it that way. They called themselves "praying Indians" in reference to their distinctive way of petitioning God and Jesus, but the "praying" part of that label appears to have meant more to them than "Indians." After all, Indian was every bit as novel an identity as Christian. Eventually, Indian identity would become more salient through colonists' treatment of indigenous people as a single group and the rallying cries of Native militants. In the meantime, however, kinship networks and the face-to-face community carried far more weight in the decisions of praying Indians than any nascent sense of race or even of tribe. Finding Christianity to be a source of spiritual inspiration, comfort, practical skills, English alliance, and especially local solidarity, that is where they turned. Furthermore, they used the faith to reinvigo-rate old regional ties through back-and-forth visiting for ordinations, baptisms, celebrations of the Lord's Supper, public confessions, and a host of other religious events. One such "church gathering" at Mashpee in 1670 brought together Indian and English Christians from throughout the Cape, Martha's Vineyard, Nantucket, and the Massachusetts praying towns for a day of fasting and prayer, the installation of church officers, and public agreement to a church covenant of rules and responsibilities. The participants, Indians and English alike, referred to each other as brothers and sisters. They thought they had a rich future together.[49]

For Pokanoket, that was part of the problem, and it was only growing worse as missionaries targeted even more mainland Wampanoag and Nipmuc communities. By the 1660s the vigorous evangelical work of Cape and island Wampanoags had reached Pokanoket's threshold. This campaign was given additional impetus by the relocation of the Wampanoag-speaking missionary John Cotton Jr. from Martha's Vineyard to Plymouth, from which he preached itinerantly as far west as Tispaquin's and Awashonks's territory. Joining him in the field was the Harvard-educated Indian John Sassamon, who set up ministry in Nemakset in the early 1670s after years of working as an interpreter and scribe for Pumetacom. The great question was whether the mission would also make inroads among the heavily populated Wampanoag communities of Pokanoket and Pocasset at the Taunton River's mouth.[50]

Under Wamsutta, the answer was clearly no. Early on, John Eliot could see that "young Ousamequin [referring to Wamsutta] is an enemy of praying to God, and the old man [Ousamequin himself] too wise [discerning] to look after it." Yet Eliot was hopeful, probably naively, that Pumetacom might prove more receptive. In the winter of 1663–64, Pumetacom, probably at Sassamon's urging, solicited Eliot for Wampanoag-language books so he could begin learning to read. Eliot's son, John Jr., himself an aspiring missionary, used this entreaty as a wedge for him and the praying Indians to evangelize the sachem. John Eliot appears to have drawn on their conversations for a series of semifictional dialogues that he published to raise support for the mission and help train missionaries. In them, Pumetacom explains that his main reservations about Christianity are that "you praying Indians do reject your sachems and refuse to pay them tribute," that non-Christians would abandon him for other sachems if he took up the faith, and that church discipline obviated his authority. As late as 1674, the Massachusetts missionary Daniel Gookin wrote that "some of [Pumetacom's] chief men, as I hear, stand well inclined to hear the gospel," but they and the sachem himself were held back by Pumetacom's "sensual and carnal lusts."[51]

It is no easier to read Pumetacom's ambivalent weighing of Christianity from this historical distance than it was for his English contemporaries. Perhaps it was a half-hearted gesture to maintain his weakening hold over the Cape and island Wampanoags. It is possible, too, that he was genuinely curious about a religious movement that had galvanized a sizable number of his people. Probably it was camouflage for his anticolonial diplomacy. Whatever the source of his interest, it came to an abrupt end following the 1671 war scare in which the Natick praying Indians' offer of arbitration led him into Plymouth's clutches and the Christian Wampanoags showed their determination to continue their experiment in coexistence with the English.

The 1671 crisis exposed the long-developing rift between Cape Cod and island Wampanoags who had allied with the English through Christianity and Taunton River Wampanoags who still followed Pumetacom. In early June, representatives from the Cape Wampanoag communities of Paomet, Nauset, Satucket, Nobscusset, Monomoyick, Wequaquet, and Mattakeesett appeared in Plymouth to express their fidelity to the colony and promise to reveal anything they heard about conspiracies against the English. Clearly, they wanted to reduce the possibility of the English implicating them in the plot. They and the English were of one Christian blood, they contended, and should settle their differences like men, not wolves. Over the next two months, other communities followed, with forty-five men from Mashpee and other inner Cape sachemships signing articles of friendship in early July, and the Vineyard sachems pledging to Thomas Mayhew "to subject themselves to his majesty, and to fight against his enemies and the enemies of his subjects if called thereto." Despite their own grievances about English encroachment, the people of the Cape and islands had no desire to end their Christian alliance with the colonies, certainly not based on the politics of mainland communities from whom they had been drifting away for decades. If Pumetacom was going to recruit support for his resistance against the English, he would have to look elsewhere.[52]

INTERPRETING THE MARCH TO WAR

The interpreter and preacher John Sassamon, like his counterparts on the Cape and islands, was determined to protect himself and his family from the mounting threats of English expansion and war. On March 1, 1674, amid yet another scheme by Plymouth to wrest land from Tispaquin, Sassamon prevailed on the sachem to grant him, his daughter Assaweta (or Betty), and her husband, Felix, a tract at Assawompset Pond. Part of that area is known today as Betty's Neck. On the surface there was nothing exceptional about this grant. Over the years it had grown increasingly common for sachems to distribute private parcels of land to their followers to get them to concede to other cessions to the English. Yet that does not appear to have been the case in this instance, and Sassamon was no mere follower. Harvard educated and thus trained for the ministry, he probably had a greater command of the English language and literacy than any other mainland Wampanoag. During the 1660s, his talents had earned him the influential job as interpreter and scribe for Wamsutta and then Pumetacom, a position that involved him in numerous land transactions. He had also played a role in Pumetacom's short-lived interest in Christianity. Ultimately, however, Sassamon and Pumetacom had a falling-out. Sassamon's evangelizing might have had something to do with it, particularly after the failed intervention of the Natick praying Indians during the crisis of 1671. More certain is that Pumetacom came to view Sassamon as a spy for the English. While tensions in 1671 were at their height, Pumetacom and his new interpreter, Tom, had railed against Sassamon "for reporting that any Narragansett sachems were there" in Wampanoag country. Around this same time, Sassamon was also involved in a vaguely understood incident in which Pumetacom instructed him to draw up a writing to protect the sachem's remaining land, only to have Sassamon falsely set off some of it for himself. When "it came to be known" to Pumetacom, Sassamon "then . . . run away from him." No wonder Pumetacom considered Christian Indians to be lying double-crossers.[53]

Perhaps Sassamon deserved this characterization. Perhaps he was duplicitous, traitorous, and a fellow worshipper with the English at the altar of God Land. Maybe he manufactured crises between the Wampanoags and the English, attempting, like Tisquantum in the 1620s, to carve out an influential role for himself. Yet there is another possibility. Consider that Sassamon, from his close-up vantage of Pumetacom's diplomacy, believed war was coming and therefore did what he could to avert it and to protect himself and his kin in the event that his efforts failed. This scenario appears to have been the case in 1674. Less than a year after his receipt of the Assawompset deed, Sassamon made a winter's visit to the Plymouth governor, Josiah Winslow, to warn that "Philip . . . was endeavoring to engage all the sachems round about in a war," a concern shared by colonists living near Montaup. It was the last time the English saw Sassamon alive. His next appearance was as a corpse, discovered by

Indians beneath the ice of Assawompset Pond. (His hat, musket, and a brace of ducks were left sitting nearby.) Soon the colony had Indian testimony that some of Pumetacom's men had strangled Sassamon and staged the crime scene to make it appear that he drowned by accident. Instead of letting the matter go as a purely Indian concern, Plymouth decided to test the limits of its authority in Wampanoag country. It pushed the issue to the breaking point.[54]

Plymouth's response in the late spring and summer of 1675, involving the arrest, trial, and execution of three Wampanoags for the murder of Sassamon in Wampanoag territory, and the colony's seeming resolve to implicate Pumetacom, was the final insult that drove the mainland Wampanoags to war. Certainly we should not have it bear anywhere near the full weight for hostilities, because, as the pattern of the 1660s and 1670s illustrates, the English would have contrived another way to incite the Wampanoags eventually. The power of the Sassamon affair was that it crystallized the long deterioration of the Wampanoag-Plymouth alliance from one of mutual protection to systematic English exploitation of their supposed Indian friends. For decades, the English had by hook and by crook grasped at the Wampanoags' lands, tributary networks, cultural autonomy, and jurisdiction. English disrespect for Wampanoag sovereignty had grown so brazen that Plymouth now felt entitled to judge and capitally execute Wampanoags for purported incidents that involved only Wampanoags on Wampanoag land. The apparent next step was to arrest Pumetacom himself, or at least to fine him once again, in order to cajole him into ceding what little land and authority he had left, as the English had done to him four years earlier. Unless the Wampanoags were willing to accept this debasement, there was nothing left for them to do but fight.[55]

The story told here is an interpretation, not a simple relation of facts. It could be and has been told differently. Some historians have concluded that the war scares, and perhaps even the Sassamon "murder," were figments of the English imagination. From this perspective, the colonists' view of themselves as civilized Christians and Indians as savage pagans, combined with their ambitions to seize Indian territory and reduce the Indians to subservience, made them quick to see threats in innocuous Indian behaviors and eager to stamp out the supposed danger and collect the spoils.[56]

This line of argument is unconvincing on several counts. For one, it portrays southern New England Indians as passive victims who were remarkably willing to suffer colonial aggression without defending themselves. Expanding our view continentally shows that multitribal leagues in defense of Indian sovereignty occurred practically everywhere that Indians faced pressures similar to those in New England, producing such conflicts as Kieft's War (1640–45), the Pueblo Revolt (1680), the Tuscarora War (1711–15), the Yamasee War (1715–16), and Pontiac's War (1763–64), among others. Dismissing the Wampanoag war scares as self-interested English overreactions also discounts the pattern of Natives making verbal and military threats in the face of English provocations. It paints English colonial society with too broad a brush, assuming that the tangled interests of men who simultaneously speculated in Indian land and held war-making governmental offices drove their entire society. It is certainly true that colonists generally lusted after Indian land, but those living cheek by jowl with the Wampanoags and Narragansetts, such as the residents of Rehoboth, Swansea, Taunton, Portsmouth, Providence, and Newport, also understood the grave danger to their lives and estates of goading their Indian neighbors to violence. Most of them were not eager for war. Yes, the English commonly viewed Indians as deceitful savages, but some of the same figures who sounded the alarms of Indian plotting also knew the Wampanoags as fellow traders and diplomats and possessed a basic familiarity with the Wampanoag language and Wampanoag customs. They could tell when their indigenous neighbors were acting out of the ordinary. Some of them lived so close to Indian communities, or interacted with Indians so regularly, that they could see it with their own eyes, and in Wampanoag eyes.

The thrust of the narration here rests on the premises that Native people collectively grasped the danger that colonial society posed to them and began the slow process of making common cause to address those common threats. This interpretation is a likely case, not a foolproof one. Given the fraught nature of surviving historical sources, it cannot be otherwise. Yet, from this historian's perspective, Pumetacom was trying to put together a multitribal resistance to colonization during the 1660s and 1670s, building on the diplomacy of his brother Wamsutta and sister-in-law, Namumpum/ Weetamoo. Viewed through this lens, colonial accusations that Pumetacom was plotting were less self-interested excuses for an armed land grab, though they certainly doubled as that, than reflections of Indian political and military pushback against clear and present dangers. As Pumetacom himself would explain on the eve of the war bearing his English name, he and his kind had reached the limits of their patience with ungrateful colonists who had betrayed their trust and generosity.

CHAPTER EIGHT

Ruining Thanksgiving

The span of the water between Mount Hope Neck, where Pumetacom's village stood, and Aquidneck Island, where the English towns of Portsmouth and Newport were located, is barely one mile. To someone on the ground gazing across this channel, it seems even closer. The distance is so short that, by the 1670s, the Wampanoags and English of these places would have been accustomed to seeing the light and smoke from each other's fires and hearing the sounds of each other's lives—percussive drumming and hammering, the barking and bellowing of domestic animals, the singing of people taking part in shamanistic rituals and church services. They could also easily track each other's mishoons and shallops as they crossed back and forth between the two peoples' settlements carrying traders, diplomats, wage workers, and even friends on social calls. Natives and newcomers were more than just rivals for control of southern New England. They were a constant and sometimes intimate part of each other's lives.

Yet when John Easton, Rhode Island's lieutenant governor, and four other colonial delegates ferried across the narrows in June 1675 to meet with Pumetacom at Montaup, tensions between the Wampanoags and English were at an all-time pitch. Plymouth had just arrested, tried, and executed three of the sachem's followers for the murder of John Sassamon, which in and of itself was an unprecedented colonial

Bristol Neck, Rhode Island, 1765. Courtesy of the Library of
Congress Prints and Photographs Division.

This mid-eighteenth century painting depicts Montaup (or Mount Hope
Neck), the seat of Pumetacom, almost a century after the English seized it
from the Wampanoags in King Philip's War. It was the site where
Pumetacom and John Easton discussed Wampanoag-English tensions on the
eve of the war. During the seventeenth century, it probably was more
forested than it appears here.

breach of internal Wampanoag affairs and disregard of Wampanoag
life. The Wampanoags feared, however, that English "justice" would
not end there. They knew that Sassamon, just before his death, had
informed the Plymouth governor, Josiah Winslow, that Pumetacom
was in the final stages of plotting a multitribal anticolonial war.
History taught that, at best, the English would use this charge to
saddle Pumetacom with enormous fines to extort land cessions from
him. Most of them believed the worst: that next "the English would
hang Philip . . . that they might kill him to have his land."[1]

However, that was not going to happen without a fight, which
Pumetacom showcased by calling in matawaûog from surrounding
Wampanoag communities and parading them in arms right up to
the very edge of the border of Swansea, the nearest English town. To

the colonists of Swansea and other nearby communities, such as Taunton, Rehoboth, and Portsmouth, whose encroachment on Wampanoag land had helped precipitate this crisis in the first place, it no longer seemed to be a question of whether Pumetacom would strike, but where and when. Still, Easton remained confident as he was crossing Mount Hope Bay that good-faith diplomacy could snuff out this fire before it spread out of control. As he explained, "For forty years time, reports and jealousies of war had been so frequent that we did not think that now a war was breaking forth."[2]

It took little time before Easton realized that war was indeed happening. Pumetacom signaled his resolve (and mimicked the colonies' past mistreatment of him) by greeting the Rhode Islanders at the head of forty armed men. The English, though unnerved, maintained enough composure for the two sides to sit "friendly together," only to discover that Pumetacom intended this meeting as an airing of grievances instead of a negotiation. The conversation began with Easton emphasizing that the purpose of his embassy "was to endeavor that they [the Wampanoags] might receive or do no wrong." Pumetacom retorted "that was well—they had done no wrong, the English wronged them." Easton pleaded that he had no interest in rehearsing the old, tired act in which "the English said the Indians wronged them and the Indians said the English wronged them." He wanted only to settle the Wampanoags' feud with Plymouth "in the best way, and not as dogs decided their quarrels." Pumetacom granted that "fighting was the worst way" but went on to explain why it seemed to be the only option left for his people. After all, their lifetime of abuse at English hands spoke louder than Easton's promises.[3]

As the sachem told it, the colonies' forced subjugation of the Wampanoags in 1671 had destroyed what little faith the Natives had in negotiated settlements with the English. He recalled bitterly that when he submitted his grievances with Plymouth to the judgment of Massachusetts and Connecticut, "all English agreed against them [the Wampanoags], and so by arbitration they had had much wrong, many miles square of land so taken from them; for English would have English arbitrators." Additionally, when the Wampanoags surrendered a portion of their arms "that thereby jealousy might be removed," the English refused to return them until Pumetacom coughed up one hundred pounds, even though he had already signed their treaty. The need for the Wampanoags to sell off territory in order to meet such fines meant "now they had not so much land or money," so little in fact "that they were as good to be killed as to leave all their livelihood." In other words, they had nothing left to lose.[4]

Trying to be constructive, Easton proposed setting up another arbitration without New England judges, presided over by a mutually acceptable Indian sachem and the royal governor of New York, Edmund Andros. Andros had some credibility in Native circles because his patron, James Stuart, the Duke of York, directed him to check the imperiousness of New England puritans, including their abuse of Indians. The Wampanoags admitted that "they had not heard of that way, and said we honestly spoke," which provided Easton with a glimmer of hope. Nevertheless, Pumetacom snuffed out that flickering light as he returned to a deeper historical account of why fighting, "the worst way," was necessary. Historians have characterized the sachem's talk as the lament of someone pushed by Plymouth from one side, and by his own angry men from the other, into a war he did not want. That interpretation makes sense only if one denies that Pumetacom had been trying to organize a multitribal resistance against the English for more than a decade. But if one subscribes to the view espoused here, that he had a long track record of trying to rally the region's Indians against the colonies, his words read far differently. They look like a principled declaration of war.[5]

Pumetacom's history of English wrongs against his people comes through the fog of translation so clearly that, just as Easton alluded, he must have delivered it before in other diplomatic settings. This time, however, with the threat of violence looming, he succeeded at having an Englishman take his words seriously enough to put them down in writing. The sachem's take was that fifty-five years of Wampanoag-English relations boiled down to colonists' failure to live up to the principles of their alliance with Ousamequin. He recalled that when the *Mayflower* passengers arrived in Wampanoag country in 1620, his father, Ousamequin, "was as a great man and the English as a little child." Ousamequin could have wiped out the tiny Plymouth colony if he had wished. Instead, he held back its enemies, sustained it with provisions, and granted it ample tracts of land. And how did the English show their gratitude now that they had become the great man? In 1662 Plymouth had taken Ousamequin's own son, Wamsutta, into custody and, Pumetacom alleged, assassinated him by poisoning because they suspected him of plotting with other tribes. More recently, they had concocted the Sassamon murder trial as a pretense to kill Pumetacom, too. The little child could not have been more ungrateful than to kill the very sons of the great man who had protected it from the world.[6]

The colonists' attacks on Ousamequin's family members were just a few of the many ways they disrespected the Wampanoags as a people. After bilking the Wampanoags of their land through such means as setting up straw sellers, the English released livestock to trespass on what little territory the Indians had left, even when the Natives had moved "30 miles from where the English had anything to do." When Wampanoags harmed the beasts out of self-preservation, colonists prosecuted them and issued fines to engross more acreage. Wampanoag leaders, starting with Ousamequin, had always thought that "when the English bought land of them, they would have kept their cattle upon their own land." Additionally, colonists were "eager to sell the Indians liquors," because they knew that drunk Indians "spent all" on more spirits and trade goods and signed land deeds without regard to the contents. The English did not seem to care about the terrible fallout. Natives in their cups "ravaged upon the sober Indians." Whenever intoxicated Wampanoags harmed the colonists' livestock or other personal property, English magistrates went after them instead of the grog dealers, issuing fines and requiring payment in land, even though it was illegal in the colonies to sell alcohol to Indians. Was this how friends treated friends?[7]

There was also the matter of colonists using Christianity as a stalking horse. It was bad enough that about half of the Wampanoag people had adopted Christianity and sworn off Pokanoket's authority, without fear of reprisal because the English offered them protection. Now colonists had used the testimony of two false, self-serving praying Indians in the Sassamon murder case to execute three of Pumetacom's men and implicate the sachem himself in the crime. Pumetacom considered these witnesses and Christian Indians in general to be "in everything more mischievous, only dissemblers," and "by their lying to wrong their kings [or sachems]." The English gave the praying Indians plenty of assistance in this regard, because in colonial courts "if twenty . . . honest Indians testified that an Englishman had done them wrong, it was as nothing, and if but one of their worst Indians [meaning praying Indians] testified against any Indian" in disfavor with the English, "that was sufficient." How did any of these developments represent gratitude toward Ousamequin and his people?[8]

Clearly, the little child of Plymouth had grown into a thankless, covetous, unprincipled adult. If the Wampanoags who once served as benefactors to the colony allowed this English exploitation to continue, they would be left with nothing, maybe not even their own lives. Why, then, Pumetacom asked rhetorically, would he put any faith in any negotiated settlement? History taught that it would just become a vehicle for the English to use some technical violation as an excuse to kill him.[9]

Easton's answer was that Pumetacom was about to start a fight he could not win. Though the colonies were divided over religion, land, trade, and dozens of petty matters, they would unite in a common defense if Indians took up arms against any one of them. Collectively, "the English were too strong for them [the Wampanoags]." Pumetacom had a cutting rejoinder ready for that argument. In that case, he advised, "then the English should do to them [the Indians] as they did when they were too strong for the English." That was to say, he challenged the colonies to show the same level of generosity and sufferance toward his people as Ousamequin had once displayed toward them. The sachem's overarching point was that Indians and English alike knew this wish would never come true and, thus, there was nothing left to say. The time for war had come.[10]

From the perspective of Pumetacom and other Indian militants, war could hardly make things worse. Yet, if doing nothing was resignation to a future of impoverishment, exploitation, and degradation at English hands, warring against the English and their Indian allies put precious lives immediately at risk. Even in the event of a victory—whatever that would mean—Native communities would have to endure killing, disease, famine, captivity, enslavement, and immeasurable stress. People who cared about each other would wind up on opposite sides of the conflict. As in practically all Indian-colonial wars, the colonial side would include thousands of Indians, which in this instance meant the Mohegans, Pequots, Ninigret's Niantics, Massachusetts praying Indians, and even the Christian Wampanoags of the Cape and islands. It is safe to assume that none of these groups wished for English dominance and that all of them more or less sympathized with Pumetacom's cause. Yet they saw no prospect of success in battling an English population that could draw on the resources of several colonies and even of an Atlantic empire. Prioritizing the interests of their closest kin and local communities, they sided with the colonies. This kind of choice is what made the colonial regime so sinister. It forced indigenous people either to participate in the destruction of their cousins and friends and, ultimately, a cherished way of life, or else face the deaths of their immediate family members. To Pumetacom and his followers, such concessions had become too much to bear, and so they went to war, despite knowing the terrible possibilities. There were no good alternatives for Native New Englanders in the bloody summer of 1675.

TRYING TIMES

A major source of Pumetacom's frustration was that Plymouth used its investigation of Sassamon's death and prosecution of his accused killers to turn the Wampanoags' formal submission to the colony back in 1671 into a reality. English authorities summoned the sachem to court in late February 1675, shortly after the discovery of Sassamon's body. However, with Pumetacom denying responsibility and a lack of any firm evidence to the contrary, the magistrates "dismissed him friendly" despite their doubts. Then the following month there was a break in the case. A Christian Indian named Patuckson came forward claiming to have witnessed three of Pumetacom's men—Mattashunannamo, Tobias, and Tobias's son Wampapaquan—strangle Sassamon and place him beneath the ice of Assawompset Pond, then carefully arrange his belongings on the surface to make it appear as if he had fallen in and drowned by accident. Another Christian Indian, William Nahauton of the praying town of Punkapoag, soon reported hearsay to the same effect. That was enough for English authorities to renew their inquiry. Unearthing Sassamon's corpse, Plymouth held a coroner's inquest and found bruises and other signs that suggested Sassamon's neck had been broken by the "twisting of his head around; which is the way that the Indians sometimes use when they practice murders." Furthermore, the Indians who discovered Sassamon's body said that his lungs did not expel any water as they removed his corpse from the pond, meaning that probably he had not drowned. The clincher came when English magistrates ordered Tobias to approach Sassamon's corpse whereupon it began "bleeding afresh, as if it had newly been slain," which the English considered a supernatural way to identify murderers. It was sufficient proof for Plymouth's magistrates to authorize the arrest and trial of the three suspects, apparently without consulting Pumetacom.[11]

Nothing in the colonists' prosecution of this case followed what the Wampanoags, or even some English, would have considered justice. We do not know how the colony took the defendants into custody. It is difficult to imagine the men surrendering voluntarily without Plymouth making some threat against their home communities. A more likely scenario is that the English seized them forcefully. Plymouth held Mattashunannamo and Wampapaquan in jail—which Indians widely considered a form of torture—until trial, but permitted Tobias to go free on bail, which was less an act of mercy than manipulation. Authorities released him only after his local sachem, Tispaquin, and Tispaquin's son, William, put up bond in the form of a one-hundred-pound mortgage for land, which included none other than Assawompset Pond, where Sassamon's body had been found. Finally, on June 1, Governor Josiah Winslow and his seven assistants heard the case following English, not Wampanoag, standards of jurisprudence. The court did, however, make the diplomatic gesture of adding six Indians, certainly Christians, as consultants to the colonial jury of twelve men. None of the accused had a court-appointed lawyer to advocate for them, as legal representation in colonial New England courts was still rare in

practice if not in principle. When the jury came back with the unanimous verdict of guilty, the magistrates sentenced the three men to
death, thereby violating another basic judicial standard of requiring
two eyewitnesses to a capital crime (Patuckson was the only one in
this case).[12]

Mattashunannamo and Tobias met their ends by hanging on
June 8, but Wampapaquan received a brief reprieve. His rope either
slipped or broke and upon his surprise landing he began pleading
frantically for his life. Easton, from the distance of Rhode Island,
heard that Wampapaquan "confessed [that] they three had done the
fact." The two rival puritan historians of King Philip's War, the
Reverend Increase Mather of Boston and the Reverend William
Hubbard of Ipswich, disagreed with Easton that Wampapaquan
admitted his guilt. Their understanding was that he said only "that his
father and the other Indian killed Sassamon, but that himself had no
hand in it, only stood by and saw them do it." Some historians have
wondered if the English had staged the broken rope "accident" precisely
to extract such a confession. Either way, once Plymouth had its testimony, it ordered Wampapaquan "shot to death within said month."[13]

Pumetacom and his people viewed Plymouth's arrest, trial, and
execution of his men as a hostile violation of Wampanoag sovereignty. Even if Sassamon had been murdered, it was a purely Wampanoag matter within Wampanoag territory. Pumetacom fumed that
"whatever was only between . . . Indians . . . they would not have us
prosecute." The same was true even if he had ordered Sassamon's
death, which he did not admit. After all, "it was their [the Wampanoags'] law to execute whomever their kings [sachems] judged
deserved it, and that he had no cause to hide it." In other words,
only Wampanoag law governed Wampanoags in Wampanoag territory. Ousamequin's alliance with Plymouth had always rested on
this principle.[14]

Even if one sets aside the central question of jurisdiction, Pumetacom considered the entire trial a sham. He accused Patuckson of bearing false witness against the executed men to avoid paying back a debt he owed to one of them and because he thought it "would please the English so, to think him a better Christian." Pumetacom also charged the other witness, William Nahuaton, with having a vendetta against him for rejecting his Christian entreaties. Nahuaton had been one of two praying Indian ministers who approached the sachem in August 1671 proffering Christian counsel as the solution to his standoff with Plymouth. Pumetacom had followed this advice, only to have colonial arbitrators rule against him in Plymouth's favor. This bait and switch, as Pumetacom saw it, left him more embittered than ever against the praying Indians, including Nahuaton. Nahuaton returned the sentiment in the Sassamon trial by lying on the stand, or so Pumetacom alleged. The whole Sassamon murder trial was rigged as far as Pumetacom was concerned, aimed less at the executed men than at him. If ever there was any lingering doubt that the Thanksgiving alliance's principles of mutual respect and friendship were as good as dead, this was it.[15]

When the trial started in early June, the Wampanoags of Montaup began to "gather strangers" around Pumetacom for his protection "and to march about in arms towards the upper end of the neck . . . near to the English houses." Their obvious message was that if Plymouth tried to arrest their sachem, they would resist violently. The question was whether they were going to fight anyway. Several English authorities who had negotiated their way through previous war scares believed that this "cloud might blow over" if Plymouth avoided any direct moves against Pumetacom. Yet the Wampanoags interpreted the trial as an English test of whether they would tolerate colonial authorities flouting their sovereignty to take their people's lives. If they did not fight back now, there would be no limits to the colonists' subjugation of them.[16]

By all accounts, the Wampanoags' young men were especially incensed, with Pumetacom claiming that their rage exceeded his control. Yet, to outside eyes, he remained very much in charge. Shortly after the executions, a letter from John Brown of Swansea dated June 15 notified Plymouth that Pumetacom was hosting a dance of gun-toting matawaûog from "Narragansett, Coweset, Pocasset, Shaowmet, [and] Assawompset." Women were packing up their children and household things to take refuge among the Narragansetts, though the Wampanoags had once looked to the English for protection against that tribe. "The truth is," Brown concluded, "they are in a posture of war."[17]

Indeed they were. Shortly after Brown's visit to Pokanoket, Awashonks summoned the colonist Benjamin Church to attend a dance she was holding, which, as Church noted, "is the custom of that nation when they advise about momentous affairs." Church was one of the first Englishmen to settle in Sakonnet, and clearly Awashonks had come to value his counsel. She wanted to speak with him because she recognized that this crisis threatened to destroy a decades-long experiment between the Wampanoags and English in which familiarity had bred not only contempt but sometimes comity and cooperation. Awashonks sent her invitation to Church through Roland Sassamon, who, like his deceased brother, John, could speak and write in English as well as Wampanoag, certainly by virtue of a formal education in missionary schools. The shared history of the Wampanoags and English was also embodied in Charles Hazelton, the son of one of Church's tenants, who accompanied Church on his mission to Sakonnet. Young Hazelton could speak Wampanoag, which he must have picked up from Wampanoag playmates and neighbors. One of the pressing questions at Awashonks's dance was whether the future would have any room for cross-cultural friendships like the one between the sunksquaw and Church, and and for cross-cultural figures like Roland Sassamon and Hazelton.[18]

Church arrived at Sakonnet to find hundreds of Indians drumming, chanting, and circling around a great central fire, and Awashonks herself "in a foaming sweat." It was one of their ways of deciding whether to accept Pumetacom's entreaty "to draw her into a confederacy with him in a war with the English." Seeing Church had arrived, Awashonks and her counselors stepped aside to speak with him. They began by pointing out the presence of six matawaûog from Pokanoket who "made a formidable appearance, with their faces painted, and their hair trimmed up in combed-fashion, with their powder horns and shot bags at their backs, which among that nation is the posture and figure of preparedness for war." These men brought Awashonks warning that the English were gathering an army to invade Wampanoag country and that, when they did, Pumetacom's retaliatory strikes "would provoke the English to fall upon her." In other words, Sakonnet's fate was sealed whatever Awashonks decided, so it would be best for her people to throw their full support to the cause. Church, of course, advised her to take another path, which was "to knock those six Mount Hopes on the head, and shelter herself under the protection of the English." For now, Awashonks hedged her bets by permitting Church to approach Governor Winslow on her behalf for instructions about how to keep her community safe and neutral. Yet she would never get the chance to weigh Winslow's response because the war reached Sakonnet first.[19]

At Pocasett, the decision appeared already to have been made. Church went straight there from Sakonnet only to find that most of Weetamoo's men were at Pokanoket mobilizing with other Wampanoag fighters. Reportedly, Pumetacom had just given them the go-ahead that, the next Sabbath day, "when the English were gone to meeting, they [the Indians] should rifle their [the colonists'] houses and from that time forward kill their cattle." Church reported

Weetamoo, like Pumetacom, saying that her men acted "against her will," but these words also ring hollow, however accurately conveyed. After all, Weetamoo probably shared Pumetacom's belief that the English had poisoned her former husband. She certainly blamed them for repeatedly trying to swindle her out of land. She had been at the forefront of the Wampanoags' rapprochement with the Narragansetts, which was part of what made the Wampanoags believe that an anticolonial uprising might be possible in the first place. Not least of all, her sister remained married to Pumetacom. Nevertheless, Church urged her, too, to seek the protection of her "friend" Governor Winslow, a puzzling characterization given Winslow's history of high-handedness with Indians and stated belief that Weetamoo was "undoubted a secret friend to Philip." No, if the people went to war, she would be among the sachems to lead it.[20]

After the failed meeting between Easton and Pumetacom, the people's matawaûog spent several days goading their English neighbors to draw first blood, because, as Easton understood it, "their priests [pawwaws] informed them if they began [the violence] they should be beaten and otherwise not so." On Saturday, June 19, a group of matawaûog ransacked Job Winslow's wisely abandoned house at the north end of Mount Hope Neck. The next day, the Sabbath, the men stepped up their aggression, just as Church had been told they would. A group of them reportedly mocked the local English blacksmith by asking him to sharpen the very hatchets they threatened to use against his people. When he refused, citing "God's day" as a time of rest, they retorted "they knew not who his God was, and that they would do it." They then proceeded to loot some abandoned homes, setting two of them ablaze. On the way back to Montaup, they detained a wayward colonist, "giving him this caution, that he should not work on his God's day, and that he should tell no lies," which they clearly meant as a jab at the hypocrisy of Christians. News of these alarming developments prompted Governor

Winslow to order militia and unidentified "Friend Indians" to rendezvous at Taunton under the command of Major William Bradford, son and namesake of the governor who had helped forge Plymouth's historic compact with Pumetacom's father, Ousamequin. Winslow also alerted Massachusetts that it was probably only a matter of time before the Narragansetts and Nipmucs joined the Wampanoags in arms.[21]

The English could not marshal their troops quickly enough. Wampanoag matawaûog continued to sack homes and kill livestock

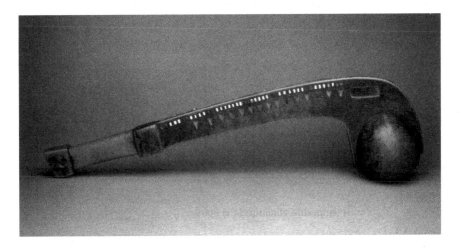

Ball club (also known as King Philip's war club). Image courtesy of the Trustees of Reservations, Fruitlands Museum.

This exquisite club is reputed to have belonged to Pumetacom. It certainly belonged to an elite warrior. The solid head is from the ball root of a maple tree, while the handle is decorated with arrowhead-shaped carvings and inlaid with wampum. Its provenance is unknown, but legend has it that a white clergyman, the Reverend John Checkley, bought it from Wampanoag people in the 1840s before it passed through several hands and came into the possession of the Fruitlands Museum in the 1930s. Someone stole it from the museum in 1970, and then it showed up again at a yard sale in 1995, whereupon the museum recovered it.

throughout Swansea until finally, on June 23, part of the pawwaws' premonition came true: an English boy gunned down a Wampanoag plundering his family's farmstead on Mattapoisett, or Gardiner's Neck. According to Easton, afterward a group of Wampanoags shouted to colonists hunkered inside the nearby Bourne garrison, demanding to know "why they shot the Indian." The English replied by asking whether the man was dead, and when the Natives answered yes, the boy who pulled the trigger dismissed it as "no matter." This exchange just confirmed why the Wampanoags were in a state of war in the first place and provided further incentive for them to abandon their restraint. The next day, Wampanoags began ambushing colonists throughout Swansea whom they caught tending their corn or returning from the meetinghouse after a day of fasting to seek God's protection of their community. The nine dead and two mortally wounded included the boy who had fired the first shot and his father who authorized it, which Easton read as God's providence and which the Wampanoags probably saw as just desserts.[22]

SWAMPED

Winslow believed that he could end this conflict "in a few days" if only his troops could execute a north-to-south sweep of the Mount Hope peninsula while Rhode Island boatmen patrolled the surrounding waters. He failed to appreciate the enormity of this task, particularly given how unprepared colonial troops were to ferret out Indians hidden among the woods, swamps, and thick fields of seagrass and reeds that characterized the Wampanoag coast. When the English began their campaign on June 28, they plodded along in line formation as if expecting the Wampanoags to meet them in open battle or somehow to stumble on an unsuspecting village. Instead, they made themselves easy targets for ambush.[23]

Over and over again, Englishmen fell to the shots of an enemy they could barely see and who disappeared back into the bush ahead of any counterstrike. Each night the troops returned to their camp fewer in number but with greater wells of frustration, only to try again the next day amid the mounting ruin of charred colonial homesteads and mangled English bodies. Wampanoag fighters had dismembered some of the dead and arranged their parts in grisly displays to warn English soldiers that they should abandon their mission before they were next. Finally, on June 30, the English slogged their way to the southern tip of the peninsula, from which they could easily see the shores of Pocasset and Sakonnet to the east and Aquidneck Island to the west. Yet there were no Wampanoags to be found. Somehow, Montaup's large civilian population had managed to escape by mishoon across Mount Hope Bay to the territories of Weetamoo and Awashonks, even as the English were guarding against this contingency.[24]

In what would be a signature of this war, the colonists' hasty next step drove Montaup's Wampanoag neighbors firmly into Pumetacom's camp. Though the people of Pocasset and Sakonnet had taken in their Montaup cousins, that did not mean they were fully committed to fighting the English. Reportedly, Awashonks and her son, Peter, had initially wanted to accept Church's offer of refuge, but they held back, probably because of the danger of being shot at by colonial troops or lynched even if they managed to reach the English lines. Already, colonial society was in a "fury against all Indians." Still, those risks did not stop a Pocasset known as Alderman from crossing over to Aquidneck with his family and offering his services to the English—including informing them that Pumetacom and his followers had escaped from Montaup. Even Weetamoo's own latest husband, Petonowowet (or Peter Nunnuit), defected to the colonists. Yet, if other Pocassets and Sakonnets were still torn about what to do, the English pursuit of the Montaups into their territory made the decision for them. The invaders numbered just three dozen men—other troops had been assigned to build a fort on Mount Hope Neck or march on Narragansett country as a warning to that uncertain tribe—but their treatment of everyone as hostile compelled a defense. A Sakonnet named George later explained that when fighting began at Montaup, "diverse of them [Sakonnets] sat still and minded their work at home." However, once the English carried the fight to Pocasset and Sakonnet, including torching abandoned homes and killing elderly people unable to escape to the swamps, "some of the [Sakonnet] Indians did then go to Philip, and fight with him against the English." The Wampanoags made their newfound enemies pay for this rashness, unleashing a ferocious guerrilla attack on them after two days of lying quietly in wait. The English, musket balls whizzing about their ears and piercing their clothing, just barely escaped with their lives by retreating to the shore and hailing a boat from Aquidneck to come rescue them. The Wampanoags knew, however, that it was only a matter of days before another, larger squad returned to finish the job. At that point, their only remaining options would be flight or surrender, both of which meant that many and perhaps most of them would lose their lives and liberty.[25]

When all seemed to be lost for the people of Montaup, Pocasset, and Sakonnet, their mainland Wampanoag and Nipmuc allies sprang into action, attacking colonial towns throughout the Taunton River valley and even deep into Massachusetts to divert English troops from their search-and-destroy mission. On July 9 Tispaquin struck Middleboro with such overwhelming force that the local militia was forced to retreat to the garrison and watch helplessly as the enemy put the entire town to the torch. It must have given the sachem some measure of satisfaction to have revenged the lives of Mattashunannamo, Wampapaquan, and Tobias on the very lands Plymouth had swindled from his people. Later in the week, Totoson of Mattapoisett led his men on a three-town blitz that killed "many people" and burned thirty houses at Dartmouth (modern New Bedford) and left parts of Swansea and Taunton "greatly destroyed." If all this was not enough to redirect English attention, then a July 14 assault by the Nipmuc sachem, Matoonas, against the town of Mendon, forty miles west of Boston, certainly was. Not only was this the first concrete evidence that the Wampanoags had the support of other Native people, but some of Matoonas's matawaûog consisted of praying Indians. English authorities had always expected the praying towns to serve as their first line of defense in the event of an Indian-colonial war. Yet now they seemed at risk of becoming a vanguard of Indian attack.[26]

Finding it impossible to defend everywhere at once, on July 19 the English called in their units for a renewed push into Pocasset, believing that a defeat of Pumetacom and Weetamoo would quell the resistance before it spread any farther. They knew that the Wampanoags were hunkered down in one of the area's cedar swamps. The problem was flushing them out from the boggy, dense terrain while defending against unpredictable Native ambushes. "We shall never be able to obtain our end this way," exclaimed the Plymouth captain James Cudworth shortly after the mission began, "for they [the Wampanoags] fly before us, from one swamp to another" and "pick off our men." Facing mounting losses in lives and treasure with little to show for it, it took only a few days before the English command called a halt to the drive and reassigned the troops once again. It put some of them to work building a new fort to control Weetamoo's territory, transferred others to a new "flying army" tasked with responding quickly to the multiplying Indian attacks on colonial towns, and decommissioned others to reduce the already spiraling costs of the war. This easement of English pressure was just the chance Pumetacom and Weetamoo needed to make their escape. Leading at least several hundred people on foot, they exited their swampy hideouts, headed north off the main paths, crossed west of the Taunton River at Assonet, and made a beeline for the Narragansett/Nipmuc borderlands. The fact that they went undetected until July 30 was testimony to their superior knowledge of the land, organization, and stealthy travel. It also was a reflection of their desperation, as they were literally running for their lives.[27]

Their fate at this critical moment hinged on the successes and failures of years of intertribal diplomacy conducted by Pumetacom and Weetamoo. Stressed and exhausted after days of marching double time, they made temporary camp at Nipsachuck, an area of hills and swamps near the headwaters of the Woonasquatucket River, twelve miles northwest of Providence. Not coincidentally, this was the territory of the Narragansett sunksquaw, Quaiapen, to whose son Weetamoo had once been married. The Wampanoags knew they could count on her protection while they recouped their energy and determined what to do next. If they continued north, they could find refuge among the Quabaug Nipmucs, whom the Pokanoket sachems had claimed as their protectorates since at least the days of Ousamequin. As Matoonas's raid on Mendon signaled, his people were equally committed to the Wampanoags' defense as the Wampanoags had once been to theirs. To the south, some of the Narragansett sachems supported the cause, but others, particularly Ninigret, were doubtful. Nevertheless, the Wampanoags knew that if they were to have any chance of dislodging the English troops who now occupied their territory, they would need the Narragansetts on their side.[28]

The time of decision was shorter than they anticipated, because not only were the English in pursuit, so was a bevy of the colonists' Indian allies. No sooner had news of the war reached the Mohegans than Uncas declared his support of the English, volunteered fifty men to assist in the campaign, and delivered two of his sons to Boston as hostages. At least fifty praying Indians from Massachusetts also stepped forward to assist colonial troops. Despite constant English suspicions that their Indian allies were playing a double game, Native guides led colonial forces to the very edge of the Wampanoag camp on August 1 and then served with distinction in a bloody four-hour battle conducted in disorienting predawn light. Wampanoag losses that day were reportedly severe, including four "captains" (or *múckquomp*), but their valiant resistance allowed the rest of the people to escape. Pumetacom, Tispaquin, and their followers continued northwest toward the Nipmuc country, while Weetamoo, Awashonks, and their followers broke south toward the Narragansetts. These were the friends and relatives who would provide the Wampanoags with succor so they could mourn the lives they had already lost and recover their strength. After all, they would need every ounce of fortitude they could muster for what was already turning into a regional war.[29]

"A KIND OF MAZE, NOT KNOWING WELL WHAT TO DO"

The descendants of colonial New Englanders dubbed this conflict King Philip's War, as if Pumetacom bore responsibility for its start and spread. Yet it was the English treatment of Indian neutrals and even allies as a fifth column that drove growing numbers of them into the resistance. Connecticut's Wait Winthrop inadvertently expressed the point with his observation that "the Bay and Plymouth seem to be resolved to make their work with all the Indians either to make them sit [in submission] or else to destroy them." The attack on Sakonnet and Pocasset was bad enough in this respect. Many times worse was the English enslavement of scores of Wampanoags who sought English protection at the start of the war, which signaled that there was no depending on the colonists' word or honor. Some eighty Wampanoags, mostly women and children, had remained behind at Pocasset during Pumetacom and Weetamoo's

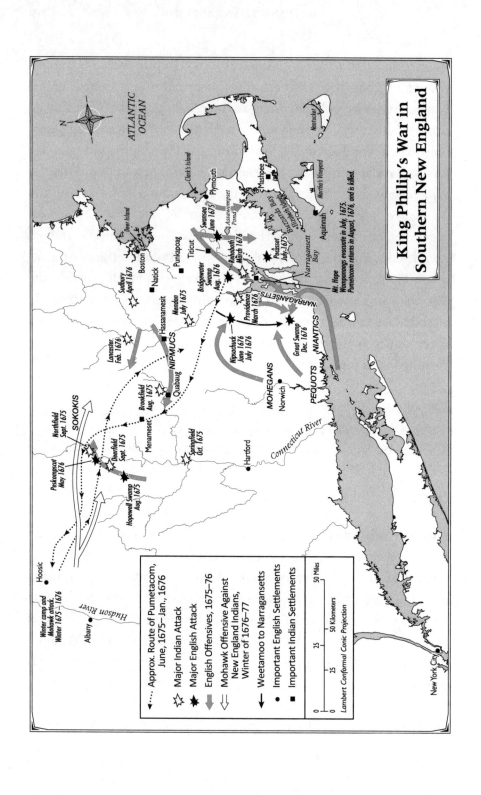

King Philip's War in Southern New England

ATLANTIC OCEAN

Nantucket

Martha's Vineyard

Aquinnah

Mashpee

Wampanoags evacuate in July, 1675, Pumetacom returns in August, 1676, and is killed.

Clark's Island

Plymouth

Swansea June 1675

Assawompset Pond

Rehoboth March 1676

Pocasset July 1675

Narragansett Bay

Buzzards Bay

Elizabeth Islands

Mt. Hope

Deer Island

Punkapoag

Titicut

Boston

Natick

Sudbury April 1676

Hassanamesit

Mendon July 1675

Bridgewater Swamp Aug. 1676

Providence March 1676

NARRAGANSETTS

NIANTICS

Great Swamp Dec. 1676

Lancaster Feb. 1676

NIPMUCS

Quabaug

Brookfield Aug. 1675

Nipsachuck June 1676 July 1676

MOHEGANS

Norwich

PEQUOTS

SOKOKIS

Northfield Sept. 1675

Peskompscut May 1676

Deerfield Sept. 1675

Menameset

Springfield Oct. 1675

Hartford

Connecticut River

Hopewell Swamp Aug. 1675

Winter camp and Mohawk attack, Winter 1675-1676

Hoosic

Hudson River

Albany

New York City

Legend

- ···· Approx. Route of Pumetacom, June, 1675– Jan., 1676
- ☆ Major Indian Attack
- ★ Major English Attack
- ⬅ English Offensives, 1675–76
- ⬅ Mohawk Offensive Against New England Indians, Winter of 1676–77
- ← Weetamoo to Narragansetts
- ● Important English Settlements
- ■ Important Indian Settlements

0   25   50 Miles
0   25   50 Kilometers

Lambert Conformal Conic Projection

escape, assuming that the English would show mercy to surrendering noncombatants. They were dead wrong. They had the unfortunate fate of being discovered by the Massachusetts rogue Samuel Mosely, who captained an independent company made up of some of the most desperate elements of colonial society. His force included Dutch privateers released from jail in Boston in exchange for military service, indentured servants fighting to free themselves from their contracts, and adventure-seeking teenagers too young for regular units. Massachusetts had authorized this crew to operate outside the normal chain of command on the condition that its compensation would come in the form of plunder and captives and not regular pay. It was a topsy-turvy operation in which English bound servants would themselves become enslavers and former sea raiders would become land pirates, except now their booty took the form of human beings. These men had little concern with whether the Indians they took were noncombatants or even allies of the English. All Natives who crossed their path were fair game. Indeed, Mosely's dragnet in Wampanoag country apparently snared a number of "Eliot's Indians," which is to say, Christians. Hauling the terrified prisoners to Boston, Mosely sold them in two installments of fifty-five pounds and twenty-six pounds. It was the beginning of a year-long reign of terror by Mosely's band against the colonies' Indian friends as well as foes.[30]

Mosely was an especially vile character, but he was hardly alone in his use of the war as an opportunity to profit from the sale of Indian people. In August, Plymouth ordered the enslavement of 112 Wampanoags in its custody, some of whom had turned themselves in at Apponogansett (or Dartmouth) on promises of quarter from Captain Samuel Eells. Plymouth's justification for violating Eells's pledge was that a number of the men had participated in recent hostilities. As for the rest—women, children, and the elderly—the magistrates ruled that they were accomplices for having failed to reveal Pumetacom's "poisonous plot." The next month, Plymouth's General Court sentenced another fifty-seven Wampanoags to "perpetual servitude" even though they had turned themselves in to the town of Sandwich "in a submissive way." Somehow the magistrates viewed them as being "in the same state of rebellion as those previously condemned." Plymouth kept its Native captives in a holding pen until the end of September, then loaded 178 of them onto a ship bound for Cádiz, Spain, for sale into slavery. Proceeds went toward helping the colony meet the mountainous financial burden of the war. It was the beginning of a trend. By the next year, the colonies had enslaved upward of two thousand Native people and distributed them throughout the vast range of England's dominions and its foreign markets, from Plymouth to the Portuguese Wine Islands and Taunton to even Tangier.[31]

Whatever short-term profits the English gained from these sales, it cost them dearly in lives and estates in the long run because Indians otherwise inclined to sit out the war or even side with the colonies realized that doing so would render them vulnerable to enslavement. Church saw that the colonists' betrayal of Indians who turned themselves in expecting leniency was not only a moral travesty but a tactical one. "Had their [the colonies'] promises to the Indians been kept, and the Indians fairly treated," he bemoaned, "'tis probable that most if not all the Indians in those parts had soon . . . surrendered themselves; which would have been a good step towards finishing the war." John Eliot agreed, protesting that if the English extended one hand in peace while holding shackles in the other, it is "like to be an effectual prolongation of the war and such an exasperation of it, as may produce we know not what evil consequences." How right they both were.[32]

Among the evil consequences was the decision of the "Friend Indians" or "River Indians," as the English called the Pocumtucks, Norwottucks, and Sokokis of the upper Connecticut River valley, to join the resistance. Though some men from these communities served alongside the English in the early days of the war, colonial troops distrusted them, charging that they purposefully shot high and celebrated the enemy's victories. Rumor had it that they were merely waiting for the chance to waylay English forces from behind. Even the Mohegans said that the River Indians could not be trusted, though that probably had something to do with hostilities between the two groups dating back to at least the 1640s. The English of Connecticut River towns such as Springfield, Deerfield, Hadley, and Northampton had so little confidence in the loyalty of their Indian neighbors that they demanded them to turn over their arms, only to have the sachems bluntly refuse. Native leaders cited the danger of Mohawk attack, which was quite real, but the more pressing reason must have been their fear that colonists would use the opportunity to put them in chains. After all, "innocent Indians" everywhere were now exposed to "the rash cruelty of our English," as Plymouth's own Thomas Walley put it. Boxed into a corner by colonists who insisted that Indians were enemies no matter what they did, the River Indians ambushed the expedition sent to confiscate their weapons, then spent September and October striking English towns up and down the valley. By the time they were done, several communities lay in ashes and dozens of colonial troops lay dead. Hubbard, like many of his English contemporaries, believed these attacks revealed the Natives' true identity as "children of the devil." He would not acknowledge how his own people's persecution of their Friend Indians was creating a self-fulfilling prophecy of a regional uprising.[33]

In this respect, nobody was in a tighter bind than the praying Indians, who neither the English nor the warring Indians trusted. It made little difference to the English that the praying towns of Massachusetts contributed dozens of men to the campaign against the Wampanoags in the summer of 1675. Colonial troops suspected them, like the River Indians, of conspiring with the enemy under the color of loyalty. By August, a string of Indian attacks against English settlements in Nipmuc country had turned these doubts into outright accusations, Mosely's company seized on the opportunity to raid the Nipmuc praying town of Hassanamesit, take fourteen of the residents prisoner, then march them "pinioned and fastened with lines from neck to neck" fifty miles back to Boston. These captives included none other than James Printer, who had played a central role in the publication of the Wampanoag-language Bible. Meanwhile, English authorities were struggling to contain popular fears of praying Indian duplicity before they burst into bloody vigilantism. The same day Mosely's band entered Boston with its coffle of prisoners, August 30, Massachusetts officials ordered the rest of the Christian Indians confined to just five of their fourteen praying town. If they went more than a mile outside their respective village centers, colonists had license to treat them as enemy combatants.[34]

Yet even that measure failed to pacify the colonial public, whose anxieties were building into a frenzy. They charged that praying Indians slipped intelligence to enemy Indians and even committed several acts of arson in outlying English towns, though without any firm evidence. Leaders who preached moderation and due process, never mind that the praying Indians were the colonists' fellow Christians and royal subjects, faced public ridicule and even death threats. The likelihood of mob violence, plus the concern that enemies lay hidden within the ranks, prompted the Massachusetts General Court in October to order all the praying Indians removed to a concentration camp on barren, frigid Deer Island in the middle of Boston Harbor. They would have to leave most of their property behind, including the "civilized" farming implements and household goods that had formerly symbolized their alliance with the English. Instead, those items became plunder for the English, the praying

Indians' co-religionists, who took advantage of the Natives' absence to loot their towns.[35]

Now it was time for Indian fears to run amok. The removal order, particularly in light of Plymouth's enslavement of unthreatening Wampanoags, put the Natick Indians "in fear that they should never return more to their habitations, but be transported out of the country." Narragansetts heard a rumor that the English had seized "all the praying Indians" so they could be "killed by Boston men." That was not true in the strictest sense, but it took only a month before the five hundred Christian Indians on Deer Island began suffering starvation, exposure, and disease. Some colonists in Boston were indeed calling for their heads.[36]

Residents of the Nipmuc praying town of Hassanamesit, other than the fourteen men of theirs taken captive by Mosely, were fortunate to have delayed their removal for several weeks longer than Natick and Punkapoag, only to face another dreaded choice. As the deadline to turn themselves in grew near, Nipmuc militants marched into the community to seize its corn and issue their own ultimatum: the people could either come with them, join the resistance, and be treated as kin, or take their chances with the English. Faced with no good options, the Hassanamesits took the offer "somewhat willingly, others of them unwillingly," as the praying Indian James Quannapaquait related. He reflected back on that day that "before they went away [with the warring Nipmucs] they were in a great strait, for if they came to the English they knew they should be sent to Deer Island, as others were . . . and others feared they should be sent away to Barbados, or other places." Even the Hassanamesits' English missionary, Daniel Gookin, could sympathize that, when faced with these "two evils," they decided "to choose the least, at least as it to them appeared."[37]

A devil's bargain also confronted Wampanoag praying Indians on the Cape and islands. The mainland Wampanoags were their relatives with whom they shared a number of grievances against the English, so they could fully sympathize with the decision to go to war. Yet in other ways their colonial experience was so different from the mainlanders in degree as to be different in kind. The fact that Wampanoags still vastly outnumbered the English on the Cape and especially the islands made the colonists of those places tread with a lighter foot. Jurisdictional disputes were still rare, and the English made no attempts to fine their Indian neighbors into ceding land. English encroachment was a growing problem, but there are no cases on record of Cape and island colonists using straw sellers or bogus deeds in the process. In most locales, the English continued to respect joint-use agreements and the "planting rights" of common Indians. Most important, Christianity bound the people together and fostered trust, above all among the leadership class of both societies. That trust would make all the difference during these perilous times.

The Cape and island Wampanoags were certainly aware of mainland colonists' antagonism toward Indian neutrals and even allies. Shortly after the war broke out, Vineyard Wampanoags working as field hands for colonists near Boston dropped their tools and headed for home because "the English were so jealous and filled with animosity against all Indians without exception." Doubtlessly, offshore Wampanoags had family and friends sold into slavery by Plymouth or interned by Massachusetts on Deer Island. And, of course, they knew all the details about the English army rampaging through mainland Wampanoag communities during the first weeks of the war. The stakes could not have been clearer.[38]

Christian Wampanoags did everything they could to express their fidelity to the English short of volunteering their men for military service until it was absolutely necessary. In August 1675, right after the mainland Wampanoags escaped into Nipmuc country, several leading Nantucket Indians appeared before the island's colonial court to "disown Philip," resubmit to the authority of King

Charles II, and surrender a handful of weapons as a symbolic gesture. They also sent a wampum belt representing peace to the governor of New York, whose colony had jurisdiction over Nantucket during the war. Over a dozen Cape sachems and their counselors followed suit in an October visit to the Plymouth General Court. Collectively, they pledged to deliver up all "strange Indians which are enemies to the English" and support the colonial war effort, which they would have to fulfill sooner than they liked. As if to test their loyalty, just days later the Cape Cod town of Barnstable prevailed on the sachem Keencomsett to cede it land along the community's border with Yarmouth, and then the following month secured another seven acres from him. There was no break from colonial land sharking, even in wartime.[39]

Despite these measures, "too many of our English" remained "unreasonably exasperated against all Indians," according to the missionary Matthew Mayhew. The infection even spread to Martha's Vineyard, despite its history of peace brokered through a shared Christianity. There, fearful colonists rallied around the island Wampanoags' longtime nemesis, Simon Athearn, to demand the Natives' disarmament. However, the island's colonial governor and missionary Thomas Mayhew Sr. knew that force was not an option, not with the local Wampanoags boasting at least ten times the population of the English. All he would permit was for an English embassy to pose the issue to Mittark, the sachem of Aquinnah on the west side of the island, whose people "were mostly to be doubted." Adding to the inherent danger of this mission was that Mittark was fresh off thwarting a challenge to unseat him by his brother, Ompohhunnut. If Mittark caved in to the English, Ompohhunnut could use it as a basis to rally support for a revival of his claim. At the same time, Mittark knew that an outright rejection of the request to disarm threatened to light a powder train that could explode the peace, as had occurred in the Connecticut River valley. What, then, to do?[40]

Mittark's answer was an inventive counterproposal in which there would be no clear winners or losers and everyone would have to show a degree of mutual trust. No, his people would not turn over their weapons because, as he argued, it "would expose them to the will of the Indians engaged in the present war, who were not less theirs than the enemies of the English." This explanation was stretching the truth more than a little because the island and mainland Wampanoags remained kin despite their differences over Christianity and tribute. He stood on firmer ground with the contention that his people "had never given occasion of the distrust intimated." Yet, whereas in the Connecticut River valley the Indians had left the matter there, prompting the English to try to seize their guns forcibly, this negotiation ended far differently. The Aquinnah Wampanoags, drawing on the literacy skills they had learned through the mission schools, produced a writing in the Wampanoag language that declared that, as loyal subjects of the crown, they would assist the English in this war. In exchange they expected colonial authorities not to disarm them but to furnish them with munitions and employ them as an island guard.[41]

It was an audacious plan, yet it won the day over vocal opposition from some English quarters. Japheth Hannit, a leader in the Native church, served as captain of the Wampanoag militia throughout the conflict, "being firmly set, if possible," according to the Mayhews, "to maintain and preserve peace betwixt the English and Indians." He kept the English so well informed about goings on among the Vineyard Wampanoags, lest they imagine the worst, that Experience Mayhew credited him for "the preservation of the peace of our island . . . when the people on the main were all in war and blood." The English returned the trust, outfitting their Wampanoag neighbors with guns despite concerns that the Natives would turn these weapons against them. "The temporal sword is good," explained Thomas Mayhew Sr. to the Connecticut governor, John Winthrop Jr., in October 1675, but "the spiritual sword is longer and more sharp." Spiritual bonds between the Wampanoags and English of the Vineyard left him confident that the two peoples could and would work together "to the utter overthrow of those heathen that despise him [God]."[42]

Yet that peace was always at risk because everyone worried, with good cause, that those on the other side wanted to kill or capture them. Throughout the war, Plymouth maintained a guard at the shoulder of the Cape to prevent Indians from passing between the peninsula and the mainland. The English warned that they would treat as hostiles any Cape Wampanoags discovered west of the town of Sandwich without a pass. That restriction must have heightened the Cape and island Wampanoags' sense of being held hostage. In February 1676 Plymouth risked provoking the eastern Wampanoags further when it ordered the removal of their cousins from Nemakset to Clark's Island in Plymouth Harbor "and not to depart from thence without license from authority upon pain of death." The colony did not explain how these Nemaskets wound up in English custody or why it decided to confine them. Perhaps colonial forces captured them in the field, but a likelier explanation is that they were Christians from the congregation of the murdered interpreter and preacher, John Sassamon, who merely wanted to sit out the conflict. Whatever the case, Plymouth's callous treatment of them, in imitation of Massachusetts's Deer Island policy, combined with its earlier enslavement of Wampanoags who surrendered, infuriated even Wampanoags still allied with the English. In April 1676 the Reverend Thomas Walley of Barnstable lamented, "We had some hope the Indians with us might have proved faithful, and been a help to us; but they see our weakness and confusion, and take great notice of the severity shown towards the squaws [women] that are sent away, some of them much grieved, others, I fear, provoked. They say we cannot so easily raise armies as send away poor squaws." There was no mistaking the strains in this partnership.[43]

Fundamentally, what held the alliance together was everyone's awareness of the terrible consequences if it broke. Numbering some three thousand people, the easternmost Wampanoags could have easily dispatched the English of Nantucket, the Vineyard, and the Cape if they joined the resistance. Plymouth town itself would have been at risk of being sacked. Yet the Cape and island Wampanoags faced grave dangers, too. They knew Massachusetts would eventually make them pay if they took up arms against Plymouth. Given their locations on islands and a peninsula, they would be easy targets for naval or amphibious attack. Additionally, many of these Wampanoags had become Christians who believed that God imposed harsh judgment on those who violated his law. Fear of his wrath during the fallout of the Pequot War and the epidemics of the 1640s had drawn many of them to Christianity in the first place. In all likelihood, they saw the war, or rather the keeping of the peace, as a test of their faith.

FORMER ENEMIES UNITED

The stakes for the resistance were doubly high in the Narragansetts' choice of sides. Though the Narragansetts' population had declined significantly since the days of Canonicus and Miantonomo, they still boasted some two thousand men of fighting age and between eight and ten thousand people overall. If they took up arms against the English, Rhode Island and even Connecticut were in peril, and the colonies' Mohegan and Pequot allies would have to devote more resources to guarding their home fronts and less to pursuing the enemy. Perhaps most important, the Narragansetts represented the best chance of recruiting the Mohawks into the war, as those two tribes had been close allies since at least the early seventeenth century.[44]

The colonies had good reason to believe that a sizable portion of the Narragansetts not only sympathized with the warring Wampanoags but intended to join their campaign soon. The Narragansetts shared practically every grievance of the mainland Wampanoags against the English, to which they added the United Colonies' decades-long obstruction of their campaign to kill Uncas as revenge for his murder of Miantonomo. Every war scare since the 1660s had cited evidence of Wampanoag-Narragansett rapprochement such as joint dances and conferences. Furthermore, when King Philip's War broke, a number of Narragansetts were living among the Wampanoags because, as they explained, they had been "removed by the English, having got their land." Through such developments, a growing cross section of Wampanoags and Narragansetts considered each other "kindred" with an obligation to come to one another's defense.[45]

In the first days of the war the collected Narragansett sachems promised the English that they would reject any Wampanoag requests for aid and turn over any Wampanoags who sought refuge with them, but Ninigret of the Niantic band was the only one of them serious about these terms. The rest were either firmly behind the resistance and just waiting for the right time to show their colors or cautiously leaving their options open. By appearances, Quaiapen, Ninigret's sister, was the strongest advocate for war. During the fight for Montaup and Pocasset, she accepted three English heads from Wampanoag messengers, thereby signaling her support for their cause. She must have had a strong popular mandate for this decision. Indeed, at the very moment the Narragansett sachems were pledging their neutrality to the English, bands of Narragansett matawaûog rampaged through nearby English settlements, killing the livestock, driving laborers from their fields, robbing and burning abandoned houses, and making "threatening speeches." The very next day, a body of armed, painted Narragansett men marched into Warwick, then suddenly turned back, sending a clear warning of their readiness if the English insisted on war. These incitements, combined with reports of Narragansett mishoons crossing the bay to reach the Wampanoags, led Roger Williams, who knew them better than any other Englishman, to contend that their promises were "but words of policy, falsehood, and treachery."[46]

Ninigret and neutral-minded leaders such as Pessacus and Canonchet did what they could to maintain the peace without actively supporting the English. Ninigret proposed a grand plan to end the war that would have involved him visiting sachems throughout the region to persuade them to deny aid to Pumetacom, then convincing the Wampanoags to give up the fight in exchange for everyone but the war leaders receiving quarter. Presumably he imagined many of the surrendered Wampanoags being forced to live under Narragansett governance like so many Pequots after the Pequot War. Some Narragansett sachems turned over severed Wampanoag heads to the English, with Ninigret emphasizing that he hoped "the English will take notice of his fidelity." Rhode Island's William Harris, however, suspected that these trophies came from the bodies of Wampanoags the English had already killed or from Wampanoags against whom the Narragansetts had a particular grudge. Either way, they represented the genuine desire of at least a portion of Narragansett society to stay out of this war.[47]

The Narragansetts' offer of refuge to Weetamoo and her followers made that impossible, even if they did not intend it as a sign of hostility toward the English. After all, the point might have been merely to shelter and defend vulnerable friends and relatives. Yet the United Colonies did not see things that way. For decades, that puritan confederation had been itching for a war with the

Narragansetts in order to seize their rich lands and subjugate Rhode
Island. Now, with this clear breach of treaty, it had not only an excuse
to attack the Narragansetts but convincing evidence that they
intended to join the Wampanoags in arms. Any lingering doubts
evaporated with the news that Weetamoo had married the Narragansett sachem, Quinapin, who would soon emerge as one of his
people's most respected military leaders. Meanwhile, unbeknownst
to the English, Quaiapen was constructing a great stone fort in the
hills of what is now Exeter, Rhode Island, replete with bastions for
gunmen and underground chambers for the shelter of noncombatants. Indian informants revealed that the Narragansetts' strategy
was to maintain their tacit neutrality through the winter and then
strike the English in spring, when sprouting greenery would provide
camouflage for their fighters. True or not, the English believed it.[48]

Unwilling to wait and see what the Narragansetts would do
next, the United Colonies decided to act preemptively in December
1675 with a thousand-man invasion of the tribe's heartland. The
campaign centered on a massive fort the Narragansetts had constructed
on four or five acres in the middle of a swamp in what is now South
Kingstown, Rhode Island. Crowded with dozens of wetus, untold
amounts of stored food, and hundreds of people of all ages, it was
literally the winter headquarters for Narragansett society. Normally
the site's bogs and thickets would have made it inaccessible to the
heavily laden colonial troops, but severe cold froze the muddy
water solid enough to permit them to march over the terrain. The
subsequent attack turned into a replay of the massacre at Mystic
Fort decades earlier. Once the English and their 150 Mohegan and
Pequot allies breached the palisade, they put the place to the torch
and shot down those who tried to escape the flames, killing hundreds
of people and destroying essential food and war materials. Suffice
it to say, this carnage sealed the issue of whether the Narragansetts would join the war against the English. Back in the 1620s,

Wampanoag-Narragansett hostilities had provided the wedge for the English to found a colony at Patuxet and form an alliance with Ousamequin. Now, fifty years later, English guns were driving the Wampanoags and Narragansetts together into an alliance sealed with blood.[49]

TURNS OF FORTUNE

Despite the Narragansetts' devastating losses at the Great Swamp, Indian resistance forces got the best of this war during its opening phases. Throughout the fall of 1675 and spring of 1676, they raided English towns up and down the Connecticut River valley, throughout Nipmuc country, and on both sides of Narragansett Bay. Twice they targeted sites within the heart of English population and power, as in March 1676, when they struck Clark's garrison in Plymouth, only three miles or so from the town center, and in April, when they attacked Sudbury, Massachusetts, just twelve miles from Boston. The Natives achieved these victories by avoiding pitched battles, favoring instead ambushes on marching troops and supply trains. Their assaults on colonial settlements usually involved matawaûog taking up positions under cover of darkness, firing on the sleepy residents when they awoke at dawn, driving the survivors into fortified blockhouses, and then burning and plundering at will before retreating. Outside of the immediate vicinity of Boston, all of colonial New England was vulnerable.[50]

By the war's end, Native forces had struck fifty-two English communities, completely razed seventeen of them, caused an estimated £150,000 in property losses, and placed acute stress on the colonies' finances. Of Plymouth's fourteen towns, only those on the Cape escaped attack, and six were either destroyed or sustained major damage. Dozens of English suffered Indian captivity after the trauma of witnessing the deaths of family and friends. Colonial society seemed so incapable of defending itself that Massachusetts held a serious discussion about whether to wall off its inner ring of towns, leaving everything and everyone else outside exposed to the enemy.[51]

Conditions were no better for the English in "down east" Maine, where colonists had goaded the surrounding Wabanakis into war by attempting to confiscate their arms and take hostages despite a complete lack of evidence that these people were confederates of the Wampanoags. The Wabanakis responded by wiping out nearly all the colonists' riverside farmsteads and coastal fishing stations, a campaign that lasted well after the final shots had been fired in southern New England. Generations of Wabanakis, with a strong assist from New France, would carry on the fight for their homeland well into the mid-eighteenth century. They had plenty of strategic reasons to do so, but part of what drove them was the memory of English treachery during King Philip's War. Any Indian descended from survivors of that war learned the terrible history of how the English had preferred the certainty of treating all Indians like enemies rather than gambling on the trustworthiness of their Native friends.[52]

The war spread so quickly and unexpectedly that many English concluded that the Indians were an instrument of God's judgment. The question was for what. Staunch puritans in Massachusetts blamed lax morals and passed sumptuary laws banning men from wearing long hair, women from "following strange fashions in their apparel," and unmarried couples from riding from "town to town" unchaperoned "upon pretense of going to lecture." Plymouth leaders wondered if God smote them because of their lax treatment of Quakers, at least compared with Massachusetts. Dissenters countered that God chastised all of puritan society for its harsh persecution of them. All the English could agree about was that the war had little to do with genuine Indian grievances, which speaks volumes as to why the Natives felt compelled to fight in the first place.[53]

DIVIDE AND CONQUER

The warring Indians also linked their fortunes to the spirits, but other Native people were the greatest determinants of their fate. This was especially true of the Mohawks, as Pumetacom and his confederates learned the hard way while they spent the winter of 1675–76 camped at the confluence of the Hoosic and Hudson Rivers at the eastern edge of Mohawk territory. Two factors had lured them this far west. The first was that it gave them access to multiple sources of arms and ammunition. Albany's Dutch merchants remained the most active traders of weaponry in the region. Though New York prohibited direct sales to Native combatants, arms dealers and their customers navigated around this impediment by using the local Wappingers, Housatonics, and Mohicans as middlemen. New England militants also received guns, powder, and shot from Québec, delivered to them by French fur traders and their Abenaki allies via the Richelieu River and Lake Champlain. These supplies gave the resistance the means to keep up the fight despite the loss of the English market.[54]

Yet the most important purpose of spending winter quarters at Hoosic was to recruit the Mohawks to join the cause. The English had done Pumetacom a great favor in this regard both by enlisting the help of the Mohegans, whom the Mohawks reviled, and by attacking the Narragansetts, who were the Mohawks' long-standing allies. If the warring Indians secured Mohawk help, never mind that of the Mohawks' fellow Iroquois League nations, they had a realistic prospect of seizing back most of their territory and confining New England colonists to Boston and its inner ring of towns. According to Hudson valley Indians, Pumetacom presented the Mohawks with three hundred fathoms of wampum "to engage them against the English or to sit still at New York." The Mohawks' response, as James Quannapaquait understood it, was that they would assist the warring Indians by furnishing them with ammunition from Albany and attacking the Mohegans, but would not fight the English. The Mohawks possibly sealed these commitments by presenting Pumetacom with gifts of their own. According to Church, at the war's end, the sachem's most cherished objects of state included three elaborately decorated wampum belts edged with red hair that he "got in the Mohawks' country." If this account is true, it points to Pumetacom's recognition of how much at stake the resistance had in the Mohawks.[55]

Little did Pumetacom expect that the Mohawks' decisive role would include a February attack on his Hoosic camp in which they killed about fifty militants and drove the rest away from their arms depots. Over the next several months, the Mohawks kept up the pressure by sending small bands of their warriors against the warring Indians as they fled east. Not only did they kill and capture untold numbers of people, but they forced the survivors to retreat all the way back to their homelands, where English troops and their Indian allies were waiting for them. In all these respects, the Mohawks' turn against the resistance was a pivotal moment in the war.[56]

The Mohawks' decision came as a surprise to Pumetacom, but there were obvious reasons for it. First and foremost, New York's governor, Edmund Andros, encouraged them with gifts of trade goods and munitions. The implicit threat was that he would close the Albany arms market to them if they failed to comply. Given that the Mohawks needed weapons from New York to pursue their ongoing conflicts with several other Indian nations, the tribe was in a weak position to say no. In any case, Pumetacom's ranks now included Pocumtucks and other River Indians against whom the Mohawks had warred for years. The strike against Hoosic was a way to deal them another blow. Another factor might have come into play as well. The Boston minister Increase Mather contended that the Mohawks turned on Pumetacom only after he had some of their people murdered and tried to pin it on the English. The scheme backfired when the Mohawks discovered this bloody deceit. Fact or fiction, we will never be able to tell unless additional evidence materializes someday. Yet the underlying premise of the story, that Pumetacom was desperate for the Mohawks' support only to have them become his foes, was utterly true.[57]

The variety of forces pushing and pulling the warring Indians back to their home territories in the spring of 1676 signaled that the resistance was on the verge of collapse. Their main concern was to escape the terror of the Mohawks, even as they knew that returning to the coast exposed them to the risk of English attack. They were also stalked by hunger, having sometimes been reduced to consuming foods of last resort or going without while being pursued by the Mohawks, the English, and the colonists' New England Indian allies. Back on familiar ground, they could take advantage of seasonal fish runs and hidden stores of seed corn, but only if they could avoid detection by the enemy. Their ammunition was short, but not exhausted, and neither were they. Despite the warring Indians' ordeals, they continued to rack up successful raids against English towns, some of which they had already lashed the previous fall. A March 28 assault against Rehoboth by Indians identifying them-selves as "Wepunuggs [Wampanoags], Cowesett[s], [and] Sakonnet[s]" killed forty-three English and destroyed twenty-eight houses and barns. Just days later, a band of Narragansett, Wampanoag, Nipmuc, and River Indian matawaûog wiped out another sixty-three English soldiers and twenty allied Cape Wampanoags in an ambush along the Blackstone River, then turned their attention to Providence, which they burned to the ground.[58]

Sauvage Iroquois (Iroquois Indian), from Jacques Grasset de Saint-Sauveur, *Encyclopédie des Voyages* (Paris: Se trouve chez l'auteur, chez Deroy, libraire, et chez les principaux libraires de la Republique, 1796).

The decision of the Mohawks of the Iroquois League (or Haudenosaunee) to ally with the English in King Philip's War, which involved driving the anticolonial Indians away from their arms markets on the Hudson River and then pursuing them east, was arguably the most significant turning point in the war.

As the smoke billowed up, the attackers called on the veteran interpreters and diplomats Valentine Whitman and Roger Williams to parlay with them, but when Williams began pleading for mercy and accusing the warring Indians of behaving like wolves, the Natives turned the tables to lecture him about why the English were at fault. Echoing Pumetacom's conversation with Easton the previous year, a Narragansett fighter called Nawhaw (known as Stonewall John to the English) retorted to Williams that "we [the English] had forced them to it . . . we [the English] broke articles [of peace] and not they (as I alleged)." Nawhaw emphasized that colonial forces had "driven us out of our own country and then pursued us to our great misery, and your own." After all, only Pokanoket and Pocasset had taken up arms against the English at first. It took the English attacking and otherwise intimidating Indian neutrals and friends for other communities to join the fight. Part of the English strategy was to starve the warring Indians into submission by driving them away from the planting fields and fishing places of their home communities. To some extent it had worked, insofar as anticolonial forces certainly were hungry, but still they would not submit. Instead, Nawhaw observed sardonically, "we are forced to live upon you," which was to say, by pillaging the English.[59]

Williams warned that the Indians' victories would not last. The English would pursue this war however long it took, forcing their enemies to remain on the run, unable to plant, until finally they surrendered. Even if the war dragged on for years and sapped the colonies' will, King Charles II "would spend ten thousands before he would lose this country." For all the damage Indians could inflict in the short term on vulnerable places like Providence, the fact was that English society had vaster resources that enabled it to fight a losing war longer than Natives could fight a winning one.

The matawaûog had heard these threats before, and they remained as unimpressed with them as ever. Their answer was that "they cared not for planting these ten years. They would live upon us, and deer," just as the English had grown accustomed to living off plundered Indian land and labor. As far as Native fighters were concerned, they were in this campaign for the long haul.

Yet their bravado began to wane as growing numbers of Indian people threw their support to the English side. By the spring of 1676, it had finally dawned on Plymouth and Massachusetts that recruiting rather than alienating Indians was their best chance of ending this war as quickly and inexpensively as possible. It was unmistakable that Connecticut's enlistment and even arming of the Mohegans and Pequots had spared the colony a great deal of hurt while enabling its forces to track the enemy with uncommon success. The Mohawks' critical strike against Pumetacom's Hoosic camp and ongoing pursuit of the warring Indians as they fled east also awakened colonial leaders to the value of Indian allies. Without any shame, the colonies asked for assistance from the same Christian Indians they had persecuted during the first nine months of the war and received a positive response. The praying Indians, whatever their trepidation, saw this as an invaluable opportunity for their men to prove their worth to the English and secure compensation to ease the suffering of kin still held on Deer and Clark's Islands. They joined Massachusetts and Plymouth forces in the field in ever greater numbers throughout the spring and summer campaigns of 1676, drawing widespread praise for their performance, including teaching plodding English soldiers how to operate in the woods and swamps. A unit of Cape Wampanoags, who were "forward to serve" under their own "Captain Amos," was particularly noteworthy for the bravery of its men, including George Wompey, Old Thomas, John Thomas, Peter Pompano, Abraham Jonas, and Tom Sipson. Yet perhaps the praying Indians' most important influence on the outcome of the war was to show warring Wampanoags what life would be like if they surrendered. It would require them to adopt the colonists' religion, contribute matawaûog to colonial military campaigns, and accept colonial governance. In other words, they would have to submit.[60]

That dreadful choice grew ever more sufferable when the other option was death. By the late spring and early summer of 1676, the resistance began to crumble under pressure from seemingly every direction. Militarily, Indians in resistance faced attack by the Mohawks from the northwest—who they called their greatest "terror"—Connecticut-Mohegan-Pequot forces from the southwest, and mixed Massachusetts–Plymouth–praying Indian units from the

east. Martial stores were in critically short supply. In a series of
defeats for the resistance between April and June, the English and
their Indian allies killed or captured dozens of the enemy while
suffering hardly any casualties themselves. By appearances, the
warring Indians were unable to shoot back because of a lack of
gunpowder and serviceable muskets. The people were also going
hungry because enemy forces had driven them away from spring
fishing camps along the rivers of the interior while harrying any
Indians they found at key planting, shellfish gathering, and food
storage places near the coast. Not to be overlooked, the people's
malnutrition, stress, and close living quarters for defense exposed
them to lethal camp diseases "such as at other times they used not to
be acquainted withal." These afflictions, according to the warring
Indians' own testimony, carried off far greater numbers "than by the
sword of the English." In hopes of cutting their losses, growing
numbers of anticolonial Wampanoags swallowed hard and accepted
an English offer of clemency in exchange for military service against
the remaining Indians in arms.[61]

The most detailed account of this process comes from a narrative attributed to Church but in fact written by his son from Church's
notes many years after the fact. Given that this telling makes Church
the hero of practically every major turning point of the war and a
voice of reason when everyone else was blind with fury and prejudice, it must be used with caution. Yet, on the issue of Wampanoags
switching sides late in the war, many of the details ring true and are
confirmed by other sources.[62]

The shift began, according to Church, in late May or early
June 1676, when he happened to spy some Wampanoags fishing off
Sakonnet Point while he was passing by on a boat bound for Rhode
Island. As the Natives later explained, they were there "to eat clams
(other provisions being very scarce with them)." Discovering that
these people were Sakonnets, and that his old friend Awashonks was

Massachusetts Bay Colony Peace Medal. Courtesy of National Museum
of the American Indian.

This medal issued by the Massachusetts Bay Colony in the summer of 1676
was supposed to help colonists identify Indians who had allied with the
English. Recipients probably included praying Indians the colony had
previously forced into concentration camps on barren Deer Island, and
Wampanoags like the Sakonnets who switched sides late in the war in
exchange for quarter. The Native figure with a bow and arrow comes from
the Massachusetts Bay Colony seal but, strikingly, without the normal
accompanying blurb "Come over and help us."

nearby, Church proposed sitting down to talk, despite everyone
fearing that the other party might spring a trap. Church was startled
when his Sakonnet escorts led him "to a convenient place to sit
down" only for "a great body of Indians . . . being all armed with
guns, spears, [and] hatchets" to emerge out of a nearby field of long

grass and surround him. One of the men threatened Church with his tomahawk, accusing the Englishman of having killed his brother at the start of the war. The other Sakonnets intervened, but their angry glares made Church fear for his life. Awashonks was on edge, too. When Church offered her a salutary drink of rum from a shell, she made him take several swigs before she would taste it out of concern that it was poisoned. It was a reflection of both sides' desperation to end this war that they were willing to hear each other out despite their deep mutual distrust.[63]

Though Church had no authorization from Plymouth to conduct such negotiations, he renewed the offer he made during the opening phase of the war to help lead the Sakonnets out of the anti-colonial ranks and into English protection. If the Sakonnets surrendered, he pledged, the English would spare their lives and not sell any of them out of the country. However, the price for quarter was high. In exchange, the Sakonnets would have to subject themselves again to colonial authority and provide matawaûog to the English for the remainder of the war. After much discussion, the Sakonnets accepted the terms, but no sooner had they agreed than it appeared that Church had betrayed them. While the Sakonnets were distracted with their deliberations, a "great army" under Major William Bradford had entered Pocasset and now was just hours away from cutting them off. Fortunately for everyone, uncommonly cool heads prevailed. Informed by Church of his agreement with the Sakonnets, Bradford held back the troops and allowed the peace plan to continue. Awashonks's son, Peter, would go to Plymouth to finalize the new alliance with Governor Winslow. Meanwhile, Awashonks would lead her people toward Sandwich under a white flag to await the results of this diplomacy. In the meantime everyone would have to exercise restraint. After all, there was ample yearning for revenge and fear of perfidy on both sides. The Sakonnets, in particular, must have been plagued with worry that the English would kill or enslave them at any moment. Yet somehow Awashonks, Church, and Bradford maintained discipline among their ranks as they set off together into the unknown.[64]

While Awashonks marched her people east, Peter, accompanied by George and David Chowahunna, were in Plymouth hashing out the Sakonnets' future. "If our women and children can be secured," they emphasized, "we will do any service we can by fighting against the enemy." Plymouth agreed on the condition that the Sakonnets also pledge to surrender anyone in their custody who had committed hostilities against the English. Additionally, Peter was to serve as a hostage for the Sakonnets' fidelity. The question was whether this fragile agreement could withstand the vengefulness and distrust generated by a year of brutal warfare. The Reverend Joshua Moody of Portsmouth, New Hampshire, counseled Plymouth to be wary of these new allies, stressing that "their words are good and fair. [Yet the] Lord only knows what is in their hearts . . . there is no trusting of them. They often mean worst when they speak best." Wampanoags must have harbored similar opinions about the colonists, who, after all, had betrayed them too many times to count. This experiment was a dangerous gamble for everyone.[65]

The Sakonnets symbolized this shift with a ceremony performed at the mouth of the Sippican River near the head of Buzzards Bay. According to Church, who claimed to have been an eyewitness, it involved everyone sitting in concentric circles around a great fire while the war captains sequentially struck at it with their weapons, "making mention of all the several nations and companies of Indians in the country that were enemies to the English." Then, one by one, they returned to their seats among the people. As they explained to Church, "they were making soldiers for him, and what they had been doing was all one swearing of them." Such rituals marking the transition from peace to war or from one side of a conflict to another are well documented among Native people of this era. Fire, as Indians knew, created as well as destroyed, enabling fresh growth to emerge from the ashes of a burned forest or field and, analogously, new relationships to form from the horrors of war. The lingering question was what kind of fire this one would prove to be after the dancing was over.[66]

The Sakonnets, followed by increasing numbers of other Wampanoags, switched to the English side not because they had a change of heart or because their loyalities were thin. The decision was wrenching for them. Yet they had children and other loved ones to protect and were unwilling to see them killed, enslaved, or forced to seek refuge far away from their cherished homelands. Seeing no prospects for victory or even an acceptable loss with honor, they made the hard choice for the sake of their most vulnerable members and future generations. It was the right move insofar as the English kept their promise to spare the Sakonnets' lives and permit them to return to at least a portion of their lands. Yet the guilt must have haunted the survivors for all their remaining days.

By May 1676 Plymouth and Massachusetts had added the manpower of three companies of Wampanoags and other praying Indians to the colonies' armed forces. Some eighty praying Indians recruited from the Deer Island internment camp performed "so faithfully" and effectively, according to Daniel Gookin, that they killed an estimated four hundred of the enemy and even managed to ease some colonists' "former hatred of them," though the problem of Englishmen attacking them at random remained. Another fifty Cape Wampanoags marched with Bradford's Plymouth troops, drawing the praise of Hubbard for having "all along continued faithful and joined with them [the English]." Then there was Church's company, which began with twenty or thirty Sakonnet men and twice as many English and grew steadily as it cornered Wampanoag fighters and gave them a choice between the sword or submission. There were, of course, still numerous Wampanoag stalwarts, including Pumetacom, who preferred death to putting their fate in the hands of the English. Yet the others, hungry and exhausted as they were, accepted the uncertain offer of mercy, partly because it was extended by military units that included their own kind.[67]

The effect was dramatic. According to Hubbard, between June and October there were "seven hundred Indians subdued either by killing or taking captive, by the means of Captain Church and his company . . . besides three hundred that have come in voluntarily to submit themselves." Thomas Walley agreed, adding that Plymouth's "greatest success if not the only success" came "when Indians are employed." He considered this pattern to be "a humbling providence of God that we have so much need of them and cannot do our work without them. It should teach us to be wise in our carriage towards them." It was for these reasons that the Sakonnets' defection "broke Philip's heart," as reported by the colonists' Indian captives.[68]

Anticolonial Wampanoags eked out a few more successful strikes even in the populated recesses of Plymouth colony, as when Tispaquin's men burned a series of houses and barns in Bridgewater, Halifax, Plymouth, and Scituate. Yet these were the last gasps of a collapsing war effort. In late May or early June, Mohawk raiders cut off Canonicus and a body of Narragansetts as they fled toward the Piscataqua River of Maine. By July 2 English and Indian forces had killed Quaiapen and her band. Pomham was dead by the end of the month. Matoonas surrendered himself on July 27 and went straight to the gallows on Boston Common. (Bostonians executed some fifty Indians that season, a black mark that public memorials have yet to acknowledge.) Days later English-Sakonnet forces captured Pumetacom's sister and another 173 Indians along the Taunton River near Bridgewater and killed his uncle Uncompoen. Then, on August 6, the English took twenty-six mostly Pocasset Wampanoags and discovered Weetamoo's body drowned in the Taunton River. She had been part of the spirit of resistance from its start.[69]

All the while, Pumetacom had managed several narrow escapes from Church's forces as they pursued him through the swamps of Wampanoag country, each time killing and capturing some of his men and confiscating his supplies. On August 12 his luck finally ran out. As if to symbolize the very reason the sachem had taken up arms in the first place, it was a Christian Wampanoag, the Pocasset named Alderman, who shot him dead. Mopping-up operations continued for several weeks more, and intermittent fighting continued in the upper Connecticut River valley and Maine for years to come, but in southern New England, the conflict was essentially over. The English, with invaluable assistance from their Indian allies, had conquered the country of the mainland Wampanoags, Narragansetts, Nipmucs, and Pocumtucks, and either killed, captured, or dispersed nearly all their people.

The best estimate, that the Indians had lost three thousand people during the war to disease or wounds, only begins to capture the extent of their hurt. For months after the fighting had slowed to a trickle, starving, terrified Native people straggled into English settlements pleading for mercy, some of them mere children on their own. Men who surrendered joined other Indian prisoners in jail or holding pens until authorities could determine whether they had committed hostilities during the war. Basic standards of evidence had no bearing on these rulings. The slightest suspicion was enough for English judges to sentence Indians to die on the gallows before hostile crowds. The same macabre scene played out over and over again in the public squares of Plymouth, Boston, and Newport throughout the summer and fall of 1676.

Perhaps two thousand Indian women, children, and even men who somehow convinced the English that they had done no harm received sentences of slavery. Then they confronted the terrifying questions of where, for whom, and with whom they would toil. Their fates rested in the hands of the town meetings and special committees that managed their sales, and the Atlantic merchants and local householders who purchased them at auction. In Providence, one of the officers who distributed Indian slaves was the elderly Roger Williams, to whom Ousamequin had provided refuge when he fled the religious persecution of Massachusetts puritans in the winter of 1635–36. Generally, the colonies shipped off all Indian males over the age of fourteen, mostly to the brutal sugar plantations of the West Indies, and even to Gibraltar, where they rowed the king's galleys and built his stone fortress. Most of the rest worked in New England households to answer daily to their conquerors. Though such bondage was supposed to be temporary, in practice the English forced most of these prisoners and their offspring to serve for life. As late as the American Revolution, descendants of Indians taken by the English during King Philip's War could still be found as slaves in every corner of New England and many other British dominions. The colonists' exploitation of them was testimony to the multiple ways the destructiveness of this war radiated through generations to come, even as the Indians' persistence spoke to their will to survive under the most dehumanizing conditions.[70]

Perhaps the most obvious fact of the colonial era belied by the Thanksgiving myth is that Indian losses were the colonies' gain, a point that is clearest in the settlement of King Philip's War. The English enslavement of Indian captives, and pocketing of the proceeds from their sale, is just one revolting example. The colonies' annexation of Indian land by conquest is yet another. Though Massachusetts permitted the praying Indians to return to some of their towns, and Plymouth allowed Wampanoags who served in the English forces to resettle on small reservations at Sakonnet, Assawompset, and Titicut, the colonies seized nearly all the territory of the Indians they had defeated as the spoils of war. Plymouth, having no means to pay its veterans, allotted them confiscated Wampanoag lands at Assonet, Assawompset, Agawam, and Sippican, most of which the recipients then sold off to speculators. Church returned to Sakonnet and engrossed the best land that once belonged to his "friend" Awashonks. It was just the beginning of a frenzy of speculation in Wampanoag country by Church to lay the foundation for the towns of Dartmouth, Little Compton, Tiverton, and Freetown, among other municipalities. As for Montaup, Plymouth successfully asserted its claims to the area against Rhode Island (Rhode Island would get it back in 1747), then sold it to a group of Massachusetts investors who incorporated it into the town of Bristol. Among its early leaders was William Bradford's grandson. One wonders if he had learned of the days "when the English first came," when that very land was the seat of the Wampanoag sachem, Ousamequin, who treated the colonists "as a great man" would "a little child."[71]

MOURNING

In the short term, the most overwhelming effect of the war on Wampanoag survivors was mourning, which was so powerful that it cuts through the victorious colonists' own records. By June 1676 Indian prisoners were telling their English captors that Pumetacom was "ready to die . . . for you have now killed or taken all his relations." Those relations included his wife, Wootonekanuske, and nine-year-old son, whose name the English did not record. Church's forces had captured them on August 2 somewhere between the Taunton River and Assawompset Pond, right in the heart of Wampanoag country where the war began. The Boston minister Increase Mather gloated at the agony this must have caused Pumetacom, for he knew that "the Indians are marvelous fond and affectionate towards their children besides other relations." Yet, whereas the English could afford to dispose of other Indian captives with little thought, Pumetacom's family members had a public profile that risked drawing the attention of authorities in London. Thus Plymouth delayed ruling on their status until the ministry could discuss whether there was a biblical sanction for holding the son responsible for offenses committed by his father. After all, Deuteronomy 24:16 states clearly that "the fathers shall not be put to death for the children, neither shall the children be put to death for the fathers: every man shall be put to death for his own sin." In the end, Plymouth decided not to execute the boy. Instead, it sold him into West Indian slavery.[72]

Another day of mourning occurred after the English discovered Weetamoo's drowned body in the Taunton River. Reveling in their victory, colonial troops decapitated her and placed their trophy on a pike within sight of a holding pen full of injured, terrified Wampanoag prisoners of war. The English purpose was to torment their defeated enemy, and it had the desired effect. At the brutal sight, the captives "made a most horrid and diabolical lamentation, crying out that it was their Queen's head."[73]

The Sakonnets and Cape and island Wampanoags must have mourned, too, even as their service with the English had spared their communities certain destruction. The Sakonnets lived under the supervision of Church, who thereafter had cheap access to their labor to run his several plantations in their confiscated territory and the command of their fighting men in the New England colonies' running wars against the Wabanakis of Maine. The Cape and island Wampanoags also retained all their lands and a strong degree of the sovereignty with which they had entered the war. However, all of them were acutely aware that the regional balance of power had shifted, thereby requiring them to remain constantly on guard against colonial efforts to appropriate their land and labor and to respond cautiously whenever disputes arose. Like the Sakonnets, they also had to live with the guilt of having turned on distant kith and kin to preserve their inner circles of friends and family. Their service included capturing refugees who fled to them or the nearby Elizabeth Islands during the summer and fall of 1676 and handing them over to the English for likely sale into slavery. Their trauma from this experience might account for why oral traditions make no mention about this impossible choice. The people appear to have agreed to suffer in silence in order to produce a collective amnesia about a moment too painful to revisit.[74]

No one's mourning could have been greater than that of Wootonekanuske, Weetamoo's sister and Pumetacom's wife. Wootonekanuske would have been filled with anxiety and sorrow, too. Not only did she fear for the fate of her child and herself, but she would have known about the death and decapitation of her sister on August 6. She was spared the ordeal of having to gaze upon Weetamoo's severed head, but she could not escape the colonists' grisly display of her own husband's remains. She and her son had been captives of the English for ten days when Church's forces finally caught and killed the great Wampanoag sachem. According to Church's posthumous account, he ordered that none of Pumetacom's remains should be buried, "forasmuch as he had caused many an Englishman's body to lie unburied and rot above ground." Instead, Church had him beheaded and quartered. Pumetacom's severed hands went to Alderman, who sold one of them for a quick profit, but held on to the other one to show as a trophy to those willing to pay for the thrill.[75]

Pumetacom's head went to Plymouth, the very site where his father, Ousamequin, had once feasted with the English. Colonial authorities placed it on a pike outside the walls of the town and left it there to rot for twenty years. English records do not say what happened to Wootonekanuske afterward, whether she managed to avoid execution and survive her months as a prisoner, only for Plymouth to sell her into overseas slavery, like her son. However, if that was her ill fortune (which seems probable), her husband's decaying head might have been one of the last things she saw of her country. The next place she arrived, like so many hundreds of other Native people, would have been one Caribbean island or another to toil the rest of her days under the whip of an overseer. What room does the Thanksgiving myth make for her story?[76]

Days after shooting Ousamequin's son dead and cutting him into pieces, Plymouth and Massachusetts announced that they would observe August 17 as a day of thanksgiving in praise of God for saving them from their enemies.[77]

CHAPTER NINE

ン ㇒

"Days of Mourning and Not Joy"

New England colonists and their successors had every reason to believe that they would have the last word on King Philip's War, because, as the saying goes, the victors get to write the history. The English, after all, had not only killed and dismembered Pumetacom, who symbolized the resistance to them. They had slaughtered, enslaved, and dispersed any Indians in arms who refused to surrender, and then seized their lands. Those Wampanoags, Narragansetts, and Nipmucs who remained in southern New England would never again be able to threaten the colonies. With the completion of this bloody business, the conquerors got to telling their version of what had happened. Their triumphant histories portrayed the sachem as having almost single-handedly led his people into a misguided rebellion by virtue of his supposedly savage pride and susceptibility to the devil, only to be crushed by a superior, civilized people favored by God. They even named the war after him. Later accounts in this vein in the nineteenth and early twentieth centuries served as more than just chronicles of New England's greatest contest. They also glorified the rise of white "Anglo-Saxons" and the demise of Indians all across America.[1]

Yet King Philip's War was not the last chapter of the Wampanoag people. A number of Wampanoag communities persevered through the horrors of that disaster and then the next three centuries of

355

subjugation to colonial rule, which was even more nightmarish than Pumetacom had predicted. The English used their dominance in the postwar era to engross most of what little land the Wampanoags had left, reduce the Wampanoags to debt peonage, and force them into the most dangerous, degrading jobs in the colonial economy. So merciless was their exploitation that they used the color of law to seize and reacculturate Wampanoag children to the point that the survival of the Wampanoag language was in doubt. All the while, Wampanoag people adapted to their straitened circumstances to keep their communities together, protect whatever land and autonomy they could, and pass down their values to succeeding generations. Rather than credit the Wampanoags for their resilience, white society in the nineteenth and twentieth centuries used their reforms under duress and marriages with non-Indians to deny that they were Indians at all and call for an end to what few official protections they still could claim. Pumetacom and his people had taken up arms against the English despite knowing the steep odds because they could not imagine colonists lording over them. The Wampanoags who survived King Philip's War engaged in another kind of battle, which involved determining when to concede to colonial pressure, and then just how much, and when and how to push back. Surviving as a people in the face of a society that wanted to dispossess them and deny who they were was their great contest. It is a struggle—a fundamentally colonial one—that has lasted to this very day.[2]

Not only did the Wampanoags survive despite colonial efforts to make them disappear, but periodically they also told their own historical accounts that disputed American society's narrative of a manifestly destined colonial ascendancy and inevitable Indian demise. In petitions, testimony, and public speeches, they echoed Pumetacom's accusation that New England society was an ungrateful child to a generous Wampanoag father. They felt betrayed because they asserted Ousamequin's aid to Plymouth to be their legacy, to which they added

Wampanoag Country, 1700–Present

■ Wampanoag Communities
● Nearby city/town

Mattakeesit

Plymouth Center

Cape Cod Bay

Taunton R.

Titicut
Assawompset Pond

Monument Pond

Nauset

Betty's Neck

Great Herring Pond

Herring Pond

Potonumecut

Troy-Watuppa

Watuppa Pond

Indian Town

Nobscusset

Dartmouth

Narragansett Bay

Monomoyick

Mashpee

N

Elizabeth Islands

Sakonnet

Christiantown

Edgartown

Chappaquiddick

Gay Head/Aquinnah

Martha's Vineyard

Sakedan

Nantucket

New Guinea

0   10   20 Miles
0   10   20 Kilometers
Albers Conic Projection

their own long track record of cooperating with the English and their successors. They have charged their oppressors with unfaithfulness repeatedly over the course of more than three hundred years.

Whereas Pumetacom's sense of betrayal left him angry and militant, Wampanoag statements on colonialism ever since King Philip's War have tended to express a deep sense of mourning. And no wonder. The people have mourned white society's rejection of Ousamequin's vision of Wampanoag-colonial coexistence. They have mourned the victors' desecration of the indigenous natural world in which the ancestors limited their population and consumption to ensure plenty for generations to come. They have mourned how capitalism and Christianity have promoted individualism, acquisitiveness, and selfishness at the expense of traditional values such as community, giving, and modesty. They have mourned the scourges of depression and substance abuse among members of their community who felt no control over their lives. They have also mourned because so few outsiders have seemed to care. It is well past time to take heed of what they have endured and what they have said about it as a way to learn and cultivate empathy toward our countrymen and countrywomen, the First People.

COPING

Just how the Wampanoag survivors coped with the aftermath of King Philip's War is largely lost to history. No one recorded their reflections on what the war had meant, and literate Indians were not writing about it. Perhaps it was something they refused to discuss in order to forget. Perhaps they judged it too perilous to share such thoughts, given the English propensity to seize on the slightest evidence of hostility as an excuse to send Indians into slavery or to the executioner. Perhaps the English simply were uninterested in what Indians had to say. Yet we can be sure that Wampanoag survivors on the Cape and the islands, despite their grudging support of the English during the war, would have quietly mourned the losses of their people on the opposing side. After all, Pumetacom's followers had been the colonists' enemies, not theirs. It is also likely that they provided refuge to some of their close kin from the mainland who escaped the English dragnet but who also went unnoticed by colonial authorities, which was how the Natives would have wanted it.

These silences reflected how dramatically the war had shifted the balance of power in the English favor. To be sure, as late as 1690, Indian and English populations within Plymouth colony remained roughly equal at 4,300 people each, largely because of the Wampanoag majority on Cape Cod. Factor in the Vineyard and Nantucket, where in 1680 there were about 2,500 Wampanoags to fewer than 700 English, and it might appear that Native people remained in charge. Yet regionally that was no longer the case. Despite English deaths from the war, the colonial population grew from 52,000 in 1670 to 68,000 in 1680, largely through natural increase. Southern New England's collective indigenous population stood, at most, at only 15 percent of that number. Equally to the point, the New England colonies had demonstrated that they would brutally suppress any Indian resistance to their dominance. This did not mean that Native people no longer posed a danger. Abenakis operating from distant bases continued to raid outlying English settlements in western Massachusetts, New Hampshire, and southern Maine well into the eighteenth century. However, it was no longer possible for groups like the Wampanoags, living squarely among the English, to conceive of a successful armed uprising. Vulnerable as they were, they had to invent other ways to defend their families, communities, and values.[3]

One answer was to take up Christianity in as public a manner as possible. Even Wampanoags who were cynical about the faith could plainly see that Christianity had been critical to the Cape and island communities' safe if uneasy passage through the war. They also understood that the church was the best way to cultivate English advocates to help them navigate colonial officialdom, protect their lands, and acquire the literacy needed to grasp colonial documents. Some of them, probably constituting a minority, interpreted the outcome of the war as a sign that the Christian god rewarded his followers and chastised nonbelievers, despite the horrors of Deer Island. For most of the rest, the protection Christianity offered from the English was the only impetus they needed. There were other options for Native people in southern New England, as evident in the fact that it would be decades before appreciable numbers of Mohegans, Pequots, and Narragansetts adopted Christianity. For mainland Wampanoags, though, the most dependable path seemed to be the one followed by their Cape and island kin.[4]

The Vineyard Wampanoags played a major role in helping their tribesmen take this critical step. John Hiacoomes, son of the first Wampanoag Christian, Hiacoomes, left the Vineyard in 1687 to preach to the eighty-person village of Assawompset, soon to be joined by his fellow islander Thomas Sissetom. Other Vineyard Wampanoags evangelized the Sakonnets, who had reestablished themselves at various sites in their ancestral territory now claimed by the towns of Little Compton and Dartmouth. These missionaries included "worthy" John Momonaquem and his "merciful" wife, Hannah Ahhunnut, the "pious and godly" couple Jonathan and Rachel Amos, and "faithful" Japheth Hannit. All of them came from leading Wampanoag families that for decades had used church offices to buttress their status. Now they were sharing the lessons of how to incorporate Christianity into Wampanoag life with their mainland cousins. It took only until 1689 before Increase Mather was praising Sakonnet as a "great congregation."[5]

The Vineyard Indians were the most active missionaries in Wampanoag country, but they were hardly alone. Joining them were a score of Wampanoag and English evangelicals from across

Plymouth colony. Plymouth town's own minister, John Cotton Jr., continued his prewar preaching circuit throughout the north shore of Buzzards Bay (including Waweantick, Sippican, and Mattapoisett), the Taunton River (including Titicut, Assawompset, and Queehequassit), and greater Sakonnet (including Acushnet, Apponagansett, and Acoaxet). On the inner Cape, the Englishman Thomas Tupper and the Natives Ralph Jones and Jacob Hedge ministered to Indians in and around Sandwich, while the Wampanoag Simon Papmunnuck (son of the sachem Papmunnuck) headed a Mashpee congregation of more than two hundred people. On the outer Cape, the Indians Tom Coshaug (grandson of the sachem Mattaquason) and John Cosens and the Reverend Samuel Treat of Eastham tended to Wampanoag meetings at Potonumecut, Nobscusset, and Monomoyick. By the 1690s, according to Mather, there were thirty-seven Indian preachers and seven or eight English preachers active in Wampanoag country, never mind Native deacons and teachers. These churchmen tended to between twenty and thirty meetings of "some thousands of souls" on the mainland, plus ten congregations on the Vineyard and Elizabeth Islands and three on Nantucket. King Philip's War might have diminished enthusiasm for missionary work among colonists in Massachusetts, but in Wampanoag country, the postwar era was the height of that campaign, largely because of Native initiative.[6]

These efforts contributed to making church life one of the binding elements between Wampanoag communities, thereby enabling them to continue holding tribal gatherings without alarming the English. Certainly kinship, language, and shared values bound the people together just as they had since time immemorial. Yet now Christian ceremonies became the most visible of their public events. In 1710 the English minister Josiah Cotton reported that church services at Herring Pond, near the shoulder of Cape Cod, regularly attracted Wampanoags from "the further end of Plymouth," by

South-west view of the Indian Church in Marshpee.

"South-west View of the Indian Church in Marshpee," from Jonathan Warner
Barber, *Historical Collections: Being a General Collection of Interesting Facts . . .
Relating to the History and Antiquities of Every Town in Massachusetts* (Worcester,
MA: Warren Lazell, 1844), 48. Courtesy of Old Sturbridge Village.

Christianity became even more fundamental to Wampanoag life after King
Philip's War as Indians sought new means to organize their people without
alarming the English. Meetinghouses, like this one at Mashpee, became
centers not only for worship but for regional tribal gatherings and political
organizing. In other words, the Wampanoags turned the church from a
colonial imposition into an institution for the expression of their
peoplehood and sovereignty.

which he meant Mattakeesett (Pembroke), Nemasket, and Assawompset. The same went for Mashpee, where Native people sometimes traveled on foot from as far as ten miles away to attend Sunday
services. By the mid-eighteenth century, if not before, it had become
an annual tradition for "the Indians of Martha's Vineyard and the
neighboring Indians of the continent" to gather in Mashpee to "celebrate holy communion together," just as they had traditionally
marked the harvest at this time of year. When it came to the social
importance of these affairs, what the participants believed and felt
in their hearts about Christianity was rather beside the point. Some
of them might have been genuine converts who believed they were
saved, knew puritan doctrine thoroughly, and upheld Christian standards of piety. Commitment to Christianity ebbed and flowed among

some other people, just as it did among the English. Still others probably went along merely for the sake of appearances while continuing
to follow ancient Wampanoag rites in private. Regardless, they all
came together on this public Christian occasion, some to worship,
others to "frolic."[7]

Even normally skeptical colonial observers were mightily
impressed with the level of Christian learning and civilized reforms in
these communities. After soliciting letters from Englishmen
throughout the missionary field, the Boston minister Cotton Mather
discovered to his surprise that the Natives were "so far Christianized,
as they believe there is a God, and but one God, and that Jesus Christ
is the savior of the world," providing "just foundation to hope, that
they are traveling the right way [to] Heaven." Schools run by a combination of Wampanoag and English instructors were producing
equally dramatic results. A 1698 examination of all the Indian
towns in Massachusetts (which, after 1691, included Plymouth
colony and the islands) by the ministers Grindal Rawson and Samuel
Danforth found Native people, particularly children, making
impressive progress at reading and writing in the Wampanoag
language at almost every stop. Twelve years later, Josiah Cotton, son
of John, reported that over a third of the Monument (or Manomet)
Pond Wampanoags near Plymouth could read, with the skill widely
shared among men and women.[8]

Marks of civility, as the English defined it, were on the rise, too.
Rawson and Danforth generally praised the Wampanoags as "well
clothed," "diligent laborers," and "sober." The Natives had adopted
several features of English farming, such as animal husbandry and
plowing, though the English failed to notice that the Indians invariably grazed their livestock in common and that oftentimes the
community sachem owned the plows and oxen and received tribute
in exchange for lending them out. These features were yet more
examples of how the Wampanoags were adapting their customs

to the demands of colonialism. Strikingly, Indian congregations continued to require public conversion narratives for full church membership (including access to the Lord's Supper), a high standard that many English had abandoned since the height of the puritan movement in the mid-seventeenth century. No colonial observer bothered to dwell on the irony of Indians rather than colonists upholding what was once the signature of colonial New England religious life.[9]

Despite such praise from English elites, Christian Indians tended to attract racial resentment and even hostility from colonists of lesser status. The Vineyard missionary Matthew Mayhew, writing

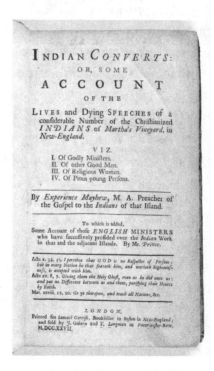

Title page of Experience Mayhew, *Indian Converts: Or, Some Account of the Lives and Dying Speeches of a Considerable Number of the Christianized Indians of Martha's Vineyard* (London: printed for S. Gerrish, and sold by J. Osborn and T. Longman, 1727). Courtesy of the American Antiquarian Society.

in 1690, chastened Englishmen whose impiety disqualified them for church membership, but took offense "that Indians should be accounted worthy." Decades later, little had changed. Experience Mayhew complained in the 1720s that too many colonists rejected the possibility of there being "sincere religion or godliness among this poor [Indian] people." He conceded that there were some "vicious" Indians just as there were some vicious English, but that was no reason "to judge and condemn *all*, for the miscarriages of *some* among them . . . They are no worse by nature than others, or we ourselves," he emphasized. In fact, they boasted "a considerable number of godly people among them." To emphasize the point, Mayhew published a book, *Indian Converts*, in 1727 that contained 128 short biographies drawn from four generations of model Christian Wampanoags. Yet Mayhew was spitting into the wind. His English neighbors did not want to respect Indians as fellow Christians because they knew what came next: they would feel pressure to treat Native people with dignity.[10]

FALLING OFF THEIR FEET

The principle that Christianity gave Wampanoags rights the English were bound to respect was far from the practice. With every passing year, colonists increased their pressure on Indians to abandon their claims to previously shared resources and even to their independently owned lands. As the English felled the woods, they extended their fences ever deeper into the landscape, which not only physically obstructed the Wampanoags' movement but warned them that English law considered the enclosed ground to be exclusive private property. In the absence of physical barriers to the land, legal ones met English ends. In 1680 the town of Eastham on the outer Cape prohibited the Nauset Wampanoags from gathering pine knots and tar and cutting wood on the town commons, even though they had done so customarily for decades. Thirty years later, Eastham also denied the Wampanoags access to "some particular swamps for peeling of bark," leaving the Natives fearful "that we should be cut off and deprived of all the benefits of the land and hindered from living by the water." The Nausets liked to think of themselves as the friends and co-religionists of their English neighbors, but such ordeals led them to conclude that "we are distressed, despised people."[11]

Disputes between the Wampanoags and the colonists of Nantucket and the island of Chappaquiddick off Martha's Vineyard centered on the Natives' right to graze livestock on their own land. Earlier in the seventeenth century, island sachems had sold the English grazing rights without considering that their people might someday want to exercise that privilege or even that they had ceded it at all. Yet when the Wampanoags began acquiring horses and sheep decades later and putting them out to graze with the colonists' animals, the English responded by impounding the beasts and fining the owners. The Nantucket Wampanoags warned that they "could not forbear, but must fight if these law were prosecuted on them." They were astounded by the gall of colonists "forcing us to pay for using our own lands" and then corruptly serving as "judges of their own cause." Though "poor in estate [and] not versed in English law," the Wampanoags knew they had morality on their side because they were "taught wrong by the light of nature."[12]

Unfortunately, the struggle for the land was about might, not right. By the early eighteenth century, the English on the Vineyard had grown so brazen as to flood tiny Chappaquiddick with more than one thousand head of livestock and then bury the sachem, Jacob Seeknout, in litigation to obstruct his opposition. They knew the only way he could afford to pay his lawyers was by selling the very land he was trying to protect. The Chappaquiddick Wampanoags were hardly alone in their concern that such schemes would force them "to flee into some remote wilderness."

Complaints about the English commandeering Native woodland, pasture, herring runs, and every other kind of resource
echoed from all corners of Wampanoag country. This was how
the English dismantled the legacy of joint use and demonstrated
the limits of their Christian fellowship and gratitude in the post–
King Philip's War era.[13]

Wampanoags who lived on reservations guaranteed to them by
the colonial government had the best chance of weathering these
storms because the law was supposed to prevent them from selling
their land. At the same time, Wampanoags quickly came to realize
that when colonial outsiders, however well intentioned, claimed to
know better than the people themselves what was best for them, it
was a Trojan horse for the erosion of their sovereignty and, ultimately, the engrossment of their resources. It took little time for
evidence to mount that when the English pressured the Wampanoags to retreat to reservations and cede the rest of their territory in
hopes of cutting their losses, it was only a matter of time before the
grifters came calling for more.

Nevertheless, reservations were the best of several bad options
for Wampanoags faced with the threat of colonial encroachment.
The prewar sanctuaries of Mashpee, Christiantown, and Titicut
remained intact in the late seventeenth century, soon to be joined by
several other protected territories. They included a 190-acre plot on
Watuppa Pond, in what is now the city of Fall River, set aside by
Massachusetts in 1701 for Sakonnets who "have been very serviceable to the crown in the late wars with the Indians." More than just a
reward, the reservation served the dual purpose of encouraging
Sakonnets to relocate quietly as colonists displaced them from other
land Plymouth had promised them in exchange for switching sides
in King Philip's War.[14]

By comparison, English authorities turned Aquinnah (or Gay
Head) into a reservation of sorts out of embarrassment that one of

Signatures from the Petition of the Gay Head Indians to the Massachusetts General Court, September 5, 1749. SC1/series 45X. Massachusetts Archives Collection. Vol. 31, p. 645, dated September 5, 1749.

These signatures from a 1749 Wampanoag-language petition from the Aquinnah (or Gay Head) Wampanoags to the Massachusetts General Court seeking protection of their land reflect the central role of the church in Wampanoag efforts to combat the plague of English encroachment. The author of the petition, Zachariah Hossueit (or Howwoswee), was minister of the Aquinnah congregational church. Most of the signatures are also in his hand. The division of the signatures by sex mirrors the sex-segregated seating of Indian church services, suggesting that the community drew up and affirmed the petition after Sunday meeting.

the region's model Christian Indian communities faced total dispossession. In 1687 the sachem, Joseph Mittark, sold all of Aquinnah to Thomas Dongan, the royal governor of New York, for thirty pounds. Just what Mittark was thinking when he made this deal is uncertain. Perhaps he imagined that he had enlisted Dongan to act like a paramount sachem and protect the land against Aquinnah's covetous English neighbors. It is also possible, given the outrageous terms, that Mittark did not understand what the agreement meant when he signed it. Whatever the case might have been, the people of Aquinnah were unwilling to accept their sachem's poor judgment as a fait accompli. When Dongan's agent, Matthew Mayhew, began trying to settle tenants on the land, the Aquinnah community responded with a document written in the Wampanoag language and dated 1681 that threatened to make the governor's purchase null and void. The people claimed it recorded a ruling by the deceased sachem Mittark (Joseph's father) and his counselors "that no one shall sell land. But if anyone larcenously sells land, you shall take back your land, because it is forever your possession." Any future sachem who violated this principle would lose his seat, or "fall forever," as this manuscript put it. In other words, the Aquinnahs' position was that Joseph Mittark never had the authority to alienate their homes in the first place.[15]

This paper put colonial authorities in a serious bind. English purchases of Indian land often depended on recorded Indian oral testimony to verify which Native people had the right to sell and on what terms. Now the Aquinnah Wampanoags were applying the same method to *block* an enormous grant to one of the most powerful figures in the colonies. This was not a case of one or two Indians agreeing about what had been said or done at some past date. The entire Aquinnah community agreed that the proceedings of Mittark and his counselors had been written on the spot in 1681. Their presentation of the document some twenty years after the fact was entirely consistent with the colonists' own example of registering deeds for Indian land years and even decades after they had supposedly been signed. Yet, if the English accepted this testimony, it would not only draw Dongan's wrath but also open the door for Indians to contest other colonial titles. Indeed, no sooner had the Aquinnahs presented their case than other Wampanoags suddenly discovered their own archived papers challenging English claims to other sites on the Vineyard, Nantucket, the Elizabeth Islands, and Assawompset. Clearly, Wampanoags across the region had coordinated a strategy to take back their land by employing the colonists' own technologies of writing and land deeds and by weaponizing oral testimony.[16]

Predictably, English authorities threw water on this fire before it grew too hot, ruling that all these papers "were not true but forged and false." Yet before Dongan could return to the task of parceling out Aquinnah to English renters, in stepped the New England Company, the London-based sponsor of the region's missions to Indians. With its showpiece community of Christian Indians "threatened to be ousted" and "scattered up and down the continent," and, the Company feared, "returning to the barbarous customs of their ancestors," the organization prevailed on Dongan to sell it his title. Practically out of nowhere, the threat of the Aquinnah Wampanoags' dispossession had ended almost as soon as it began.[17]

However, there was a substantial cost. The New England Company, framing itself as a "Kind Father," decided, over the Aquinnahs' opposition, that henceforth it would fence off and lease six hundred acres of their territory to raise funds for the Natives' schools and church officers. Furthermore, when the lease came up for renewal in 1723, the Wampanoags' complaints that "the Land was theirs and their [Ancestors'] and that they never sold it" did not hinder the company from renting out the tract for another fourteen years and expanding it by four hundred acres within a rod of the people's burial ground. The Aquinnah Wampanoags were glad to be rid of Dongan, but they believed correctly that the New England Company had taken advantage of their misfortune to assert a paternal governance they did not want and an ownership claim to their land that they did not recognize. They saw the organization for what it was: a colonial overlord. Under these conditions, they made the life of the company's tenant miserable, killing and impounding his cattle and tearing down his fences while emphasizing their birthright at every turn.[18]

The Aquinnah people had a few critical advantages in mounting their defense. For one, they lived on a peninsula, so there was only one entry point and no question when the English had breached the line, particularly once they put up a bar gate. Additionally, their nemesis was a single distant company formally dedicated to their welfare rather than a disorderly array of land speculators, poachers, trespassing livestock, and expansionist towns. Wampanoags living on smaller reserves surrounded by rapacious English neighbors were less able to resist than the Aquinnahs. Take, for example, the Matta-keesett Wampanoags of east-central Cape Cod, who lived on a 160-acre reservation known as "Indian Town" between the Bass River on the east and Long Pond on the west. In 1713 they consented to this arrangement with the town of Yarmouth only because runaway English growth threatened to dispossess them entirely. Elsewhere on the eastern Cape, colonists had already appropriated most of the land of the Wampanoags of Paomet (or Billingsgate) and Mono-moyick (or Monomoy), leaving just the hundred-acre Potonumecut Reservation on Pleasant Bay and a handful of scattered, individually owned parcels. Yarmouth proclaimed that Indian Town was for the Natives' "use forever to live upon and for planting and firewood." Yet the limits it placed on the Wampanoags' activity all but guaranteed that the reserve would remain underpopulated and impoverished. Yarmouth prohibited the Mattakeesetts from taking in other Indians, thus handicapping their ability to address the mounting loss of their people to whaling, military service, and disease. Nor would it allow the people to lease out their land to the English, even when they were away pursuing other opportunities. Such restrictions, combined with the colonists' increasingly exclusive claims to resources surrounding the reservation, meant that Indian Town, like Watuppa, was less a place to live and work full-time than a base from which the people fanned out to find other ways to make a living.[19]

A harsher example still was the Titicut Reservation on the upper Taunton River, which in its conception in 1664 was supposed to be three miles long and guaranteed to the Natives "forever." Forever turned out to be sixty years. By 1724 the Titicut people had grown so frustrated by the English of Bridgewater and Middleboro poaching their firewood and enclosing their planting and fishing grounds that they gave up any pretense of retaining the original grant. Instead, they settled for just one hundred acres with clearly marked bounds and a renewed pledge from Boston to defend the lines. Eventually they would discover how hollow that promise was, too. It took only until 1741 before Titicut's English advocates sounded the alarm that neighboring colonists and creditors were on the verge of gobbling up what little was left of the reserve.[20]

One by one, Native communities tried to stem these losses by deposing sachems who sold land without the people's consent and transferring oversight of their territory to counsels of family representatives and church officials. After Aquinnah's removal of Joseph Mittark, it raised no one to take his place. Likewise the Takemmy Wampanoags of the Vineyard swore off the sachem Zachariah Pooskin after he and his predecessors had reduced the Christiantown reserve to a mere 160 acres and the Takemmy sachemship as a whole to hardly more than that. Henceforth they governed themselves by what they cleverly called a "legal town meeting." The Sakedan Wampanoags of Nantucket followed suit in 1741, agreeing as "town people and church people" to unseat the sachem Ben Abel for "selling our land from us to the English." They emphasized that Abel had "no other power but only what he had from us." (Their use of the past tense was not accidental.) Communities that failed to take such measures soon found themselves practically landless, as was the case throughout most of Nantucket Island, in the Vineyard sachemships of Nunnepog, Chappaquiddick, Sengekontacket, and Nashuakemuck, and in Paomet, Nauset, Momonoyick, and Satucket on the outer Cape.[21]

Yet the removal of the sachems could not stem the hemorrhaging of land because the sheer poverty of the common people often forced them to sell, too. It was hard enough to resist the temptation under the stress of relentless day-to-day expenses. When costly life crises occurred, as they invariably did, there was sometimes little other choice. At any given time, a household might face crippling injuries to breadwinners, steep medical expenses, the need to pay for a family member's burial, or the threat of loved ones being forced into jail or servitude for overdue fines or store debts. Everyone knew that selling the land would make it even harder for future generations of Wampanoags to make ends meet, but sometimes urgent demands did not permit long-term decision-making.[22]

Too often this process is mischaracterized as Indians "losing" their land, as if their own errors were mainly responsible. No doubt, some of their own misjudgments contributed to the crisis, but the English were the primary culprits by far. They were the ones who used trespass, poaching, control of Wampanoag debt, and command of the courts to force the Wampanoags' hand. Even territory the English were supposed to share with Indians according to joint-use agreements or that English law technically protected for the Natives' sole use was vulnerable. Wampanoags did not lose their land any more than Indians elsewhere on the continent. No, colonists and their successors took it through every means at their disposal.

The hurt was profound. Colonial expansion, after all, denied the Wampanoags access to the sites where they had buried their loved ones, where their history had unfolded, where they had hunted, fished, gathered, and danced since time immemorial. The Wampanoags knew the names and characteristics of every plant, animal, run of water, and hill in these places. They believed the Creator had birthed their kind into their homeland to live in perpetuity. Even today, Wampanoag people diagnosed with depression commonly struggle with a feeling of helplessness as white society cuts them off from their territory only to ruin it through overdevelopment and pollution. Consider, too, the strident terms the Mashpee Wampanoags used in a 1752 Native-language petition protesting English trespass. They declared:

This Indian land, this was conveyed to us by these former sachems of ours. We shall not give it away, nor shall it be sold, nor shall it be lent, but we shall use it as long as we live, we together with all our children, and our children's children, and our descendants, and together with all their descendants. They shall always use it as long as Christian Indians live. We shall use it forever and ever . . . Against our will these Englishmen take away from us what was our land. They parcel it out to each other, and the marsh along with it, against our will. And as for our streams, they do not allow us peacefully to be when we peacefully go fishing. They beat us greatly, and they have houses on our land against our will. Truly we think it is this: We poor Indians soon shall not have any place to reside, together with our poor children, because these Englishmen trouble us very much in this place of ours.

This English-language version of the Mashpee people's letter can only hint at the extent of their agony. As the Wampanoag language keeper Jessie Little Doe Baird explains, a literal Wampanoag translation of "take away from us what was our land" is something closer to "fall off of our feet," as if colonists were pulling up the people by their roots from the soil in which the Creator had planted them.[23]

Colony- and, later, state-appointed guardians were supposed to protect the Indians against English encroachment. Though sometimes they slowed the process, too often they used their positions to give themselves, their friends, and family members the inside track on acquiring Indian resources at a discount. The system began in 1694 when Massachusetts, which had just annexed Plymouth and the islands, authorized its governor to appoint an English guardian for each Indian reservation with the power to expel and prosecute trespassers, sell communal resources like wood, distribute the proceeds, and adjudicate minor crimes and cases of debt. The law's intent was honorable, but its provisions were a recipe for corruption. After all, the Indians had no say in the choice of their guardians or formal influence over their decisions. Additionally, the guardians were certain to have conflicts of interest because, as elites who lived near Indian communities, their personal or family fortunes invariably included profits from Native land and labor. The abuses of the Chappaquiddick guardian Benjamin Hawes were so flagrant, including trying to get himself named as next in line to the office of sachem, that the Wampanoags charged he "had made a league with the devil" against a Christian people. Their objections grew even more furious after 1746 when Massachusetts gave the guardians discretion to assign their Indian charges to specific parcels of land and lease out the "excess" to colonists. Aquinnah protested that "before this new law came, the English had not power to do as they pleased, as to this our land," while Mashpee added sarcastically, "We thought we had as good a right to our lands as Englishmen have to theirs." Both peoples agreed that the guardians left them "poorer" and "do us more hurt than good" because they "hearken too much to the English who are not our friends and don't care how much we are."[24]

In 1760 Mashpee took the fight to remove the guardians all the way to London, sending Reuben Cogenhew with a list of complaints that reached the ears of the king, his Privy Council, and the Board of Trade, which oversaw the colonies. Imperial scrutiny suddenly inspired Massachusetts to respond to Mashpee, including a meeting between Governor Francis Bernard and Cogenhew—whom Bernard disparaged as "a very self-important fellow"—after the Indian's return home. The result was legislation in 1763 to redefine Mashpee—but no other Indian community—as a self-governing district managed by five overseers chosen by the Wampanoags, two of whom (the clerk and treasurer) had to be white. Mashpee would maintain this status for the next twenty-five years. Not coincidentally, during this period, Mashpee petitions to the legislature halted. It was a sign that Indian community self-governance and territorial sanctity was compatible with colonial society, if only colonial society would permit it.[25]

FIGHTING FOR THEIR LIVES

The main problem for the Wampanoags was that, try as they might to exercise self-determination, they were subject to a political and legal system in which they had no representation but which did answer to a white populace generally hostile to their interests. Before King Philip's War, Wampanoags had governed themselves with little interference from colonial officials. When disputes arose between the Wampanoags and English, they were typically handled through negotiation, not colonial dictate, unless an Indian happened to commit a crime in an English town. As the Chappaquiddick sachem, Seeknout, put it, Indians expected the English to abide by the principle that "your order should come to us, rather than your officer," meaning that the English would address problems through the sachems, rather than trying to enforce their will directly on the Wampanoag people.[26]

Yet no sooner had King Philip's War ended than colonial courts began persecuting Wampanoags under the guise of justice. As early as 1678, Plymouth courts sentenced three Wampanoags named Cartoonas, Simon, and Joel to lifetime slavery outside New England for stealing twenty-five pounds from Zachariah Allen of Sandwich. This ruling was no mere excess while adrenaline from the war continued to run high. Throughout the 1680s, Plymouth ordered Wampanoags "out of the country" for crimes like theft, assault, and rape to which colonists would normally receive corporal punishment and fines. Mashpee was so desperate to prevent the English from selling its own Tom Wampetuck into overseas slavery for his inability to pay court fines that in 1685 it confirmed a disputed land deed alienating some of their reserved territory. The regional balance of power had shifted so dramatically that even the islands' English courts became more aggressive despite the Wampanoags' vast local population majority. In 1688 Vineyard magistrates threatened three Wampanoags with seven years of slavery each if they failed to pay damages for killing English-owned oxen and sheep. A year later, the island's court executed a Wampanoag named Pommatook, who confessed to having killed his pregnant girlfriend back in 1664. This was a projection of English power that would have been unthinkable without sachem consent at the actual time of the murder.[27]

The courts became even more intrusive once Massachusetts absorbed Plymouth and the islands and instituted its Indian guardian system. Though the guardians handled petty crimes committed on the reservations and debts under forty shillings, all serious Indian crimes, major debts, and off-reservation offences were the jurisdiction of regular justices of the peace and upper-level English courts, as was the case with colonists. Native people understood this change for what it was—a major blow to their self-rule, which had previously included their own Indian-run courts with the right of appeal to the English. Robbed of that autonomy under the new system, Native people stopped referring their disputes with other Indians to the courts in favor of trying to handle them informally or not at all. The leading men of several Outer Cape communities complained in 1703 that under the new order, "the young men of said Indians have imbibed an opinion that their former laws are vacated, and so will yield no obedience thereto, but everyone acts according to his own will." Experience Mayhew reported the same results on the Vineyard, writing that the Indians "are disgusted that they have not the same authority allowed as formerly they had . . . and will seldom inform the English authority of such breaches of law as are among them." Wampanoags remained willing to participate in the English system as coequals with the power to govern their own people, but not as subordinates.[28]

Yet they *were* subordinates, as demonstrated by the courts' exploitation of its power to force Indian men, women, and even children into servitude. By the 1690s English judges had tempered the sentencing of Natives to overseas slavery, but instead they began ordering Indian lawbreakers to toil as servants locally to compensate the people they had wronged or to cover the costs of their prosecution. There were at least twenty such cases in Plymouth county courts between 1698 and 1735, with sentences ranging between one and twelve years, for an average of 4.3 years. Similar patterns could be found in the rest of the courts of Cape Cod and the islands. In 1716 the Nantucket court sentenced the Indians Jo Skinny and John Moab to eight years of labor each, on top of thirty stripes from the whip, for stealing eighty pounds from Stephen Coffin Jr. Seven years later, Vineyard magistrates went so far as to punish the Native Abraham Jonathan with a full eighteen years of bondage for stealing a storage chest containing one hundred pounds' worth of silver and paper money. Most criminal cases produced shorter terms but with such frequency that almost any Indian who entered the courts during the eighteenth and early nineteenth centuries faced the likelihood of exiting in servitude. The English called this system "justice." Natives must have had another name for it.[29]

Unsatisfied with the supply of cheap, bound labor produced by criminal convictions, English lenders and courts turned to the exploitation of Indian debtors and their family members. Throughout the post–King Philip's War era, it became the norm for Wampanoag and other New England Indian families to purchase food and clothing on credit from colonial merchants because they no longer had enough territory to provide for themselves. It was also normal for colonists to carry debt because of New England's chronic shortage of circulating currency. Englishmen, like Indians, charged what they needed at the store throughout the year, made occasional payments through barter or cash deposit, then, if they could, accounted for the rest each December. The difference was that Indians were so pinched by white encroachment and the disruption of their families by judicial servitude that they disproportionately fell into the ranks of "desperate debtors," which meant they were unlikely ever to pay. When their creditors filed lawsuits against them the problem grew worse because court costs, jail charges, and penalties sometimes doubled or tripled the original debt. It was nearly impossible for Indians to win these cases, "both Judges and Jurors, being all parties in the cause," as Nantucket Wampanoags put it. Unless the Native debtor had land to sell—which excluded those from protected reservations—the courts sentenced him or her to servitude until all the bills were paid. Despite contracts stipulating the length of service, in fact there was no telling when it would end because authorities added time to these sentences whenever servants fell into trouble or became pregnant. Obviously such penalties encouraged some masters to invent charges of misbehavior and sexually exploit their subordinates. In every which way, this system was a trap.[30]

It even targeted Indian children. Sometimes young people wound up as servants by simple virtue of accompanying their bound mothers. Such was the case with Tobias Potter of Christiantown, who spent his early childhood in a mainland English home where his mother, Elizabeth Uhquat, toiled, until Uhquat sent him at age nine to work for another colonial family because she could not afford to keep him even after her own release. Oftentimes the courts bound out orphaned Indian children, or even children who had lost just one parent, based on the prejudice that they were inherently better off in white households than in supposedly disorderly and vice-ridden

Indian ones. In most cases, however, it was the parents themselves who sold the children into servitude in what can hardly be called a choice. To be sure, they crossed their fingers that their children would emerge from the experience fluent in English and literate, though colonial masters routinely shirked their contractual responsibility to teach reading and writing. Yet foreign language and literacy lessons were not enough to convince Indian parents to turn over their own children to English families who, at best, felt nothing for them. They did so because they could see no other way. Sometimes sacrificing one child to creditors was the only way to keep the parents free and earning money so the rest of the children did not wind up as servants, too. Still another factor was that so many Indian families were in disarray because of debt peonage that family and friends could not help care for one's children in times of desperation. It was a nightmare.[31]

Take, for instance, Joseph Quasson of Monomoyick, who was born in 1698 and lived with his parents for his first six years. "Then," he recalled, "my father died five pounds in debt to Mr. Samuel Sturges of Yarmouth. I was bound out to him by my mother on that account." Quasson remained a servant of one Englishman or another until well after he had become a man. Likewise, in 1728 Gershom Barnabus of Mashpee not only agreed to perform three years of whaling for John Otis but indentured "his two children namely Moses Barnabus, a boy of about five years old last August & a girl named Jerusha of about three years old. Moses to serve until age 21. Jerusha until 18," in exchange for fifteen pounds a year. This money probably kept him and his wife out of bound service and kept open the slim possibility of them earning enough to buy back their tiny children's freedom. The following decade, the Wampanoag Robin Meserick and his wife committed their young sons, John and David, to serve Gideon Holloway until the boys reached the age of twenty-one unless the parents somehow figured out a way to pay back Holloway the enormous sum of fifty-six pounds within three years. To have done otherwise would have put the parents, and by extension the boys, in servitude anyway. Imagine the heartbreak, anxiety, self-loathing, and wrath tearing at the Meserick family and so many other Wampanoag households during these ordeals.[32]

Though Wampanoags protested this exploitation in the most moving terms, English authorities were more concerned with protecting the interests of white creditors. As early as 1700, Simon Popmonet, George Wapock, and John Terkins pleaded to Boston that their fellow Mashpees were "a people that do own the Great Jehovah and his son our Lord Jesus Christ" and who had "demeaned ourselves peaceably at all times . . . and assisted our English neighbors both in former and late wars with their and our Indian enemies." Nevertheless, creditors and the courts seized on their debts to make "ourselves and our poor children . . . servants for an unreasonable time." They wanted the legislature to prohibit the English from extending Indians credit and collecting it if they did. Yet Boston would not go that far and never bothered to say why. The most it would do was require a guardian's consent for any indenture contact, paying little regard to how simple it was to procure those signatures.

A half century later, little had changed. The missionary Gideon Hawley recalled that when he first arrived at his missionary post in Mashpee in 1757, he was shocked to discover that

> every Indian had his master . . . Their children were sold or bound as security for the payment of their fathers' debts as soon as they were seven or eight years old, which two Justices of the Peace with the consent of the parents was easily obtained, were authorized to do at the desire of their

creditors. These Indians and their children were transferred from one to another master like slaves.

The problem was so pervasive, and the English political will to do anything about it was so weak, that in 1760 the worn-down Mash-pees conceded, "We can't at present think of any other method to prevent it." No wonder. As late as 1794, Hawley could still report "many" Mashpee children serving as bound laborers, and thirteen years later still James Freeman counted 100 of 242 Aquinnah Wampanoags living away from home, "being children put out to service in English families, and other whale men." As Pumetacom had once feared, the English had reduced the Wampanoags to servitude in their very own homeland.[33]

Earnings from whaling and fishing and, to a lesser extent, soldiering provided the best opportunities for Native men to keep their families out of indentured service. The whaling and fishing industries grew steadily from seventeenth-century origins as modest enterprises operating close to shore until, by the mid-eighteenth century, whalers were hunting the breadth of the Atlantic basin for months at a time. Nantucket Island alone hosted more than eighty ships employing more than one thousand men by the eve of the American Revolution, while New England as a whole required another four thousand shiphands, many of whom were Indian. "Go where you will from Nova Scotia to the Mississippi," wrote Hector St. John de Crèvecour of Nantucket and the Vineyard in 1782, "and you will find almost everywhere some Natives of these two islands employed in seafaring occupations." No sooner had he finished writing these words than the industry expanded to the Arctic, Pacific, and even Indian Oceans. The length of voyages increased from months to years, and the ships grew so large in order to accommodate onboard tryworks (or blubber boiling stations) that the epicenter of the fleet moved from shallow Nantucket harbor to deepwater New Bedford, Massachusetts. Located in the heart of historic Wampanoag territory, a mere twenty miles' sail from Aquinnah, New Bedford's bustling port soon hosted what one observer characterized as "a greater variety of human species than is elsewhere to be found under the bright sun of Christian civilization. Europeans there are of every flag and language; Native Yankees . . . Gay Headers and negroes; aboriginals and Africans; Island Portuguese as plenty as whales'-teeth; with an occasional sprinkling of Chinese, Luscars, Australians, and Polynesians, cannibals and vegetarians." It is no coincidence that one of the characters in Herman Melville's 1851 whaling adventure, *Moby-Dick*, is Tashtego, a Wampanoag harpooner from Gay Head (or Aquinnah).[34]

Demand for Native soldiers grew in lockstep with whaling. England was at war with France in North America on and off from 1688 through 1763, with the Lake Champlain–Lake George region, northern New England, and the Canadian Maritimes among the most active theaters for Indians serving with colonial armies. Overlapping with and sometimes outlasting these conflicts were wars between Massachusetts and the Maine Wabanakis in which the Bay Colony often employed semi-independent Indian ranger companies composed largely of Wampanoags. Then came the Revolution and War of 1812, which mobilized all of American society, including Indians. The cumulative effect of these wars on Wampanoag life was dramatic. By one count, New England Indians, particularly Wampanoags, served at twice the rate of their English neighbors during the imperial wars. The Sakonnet community, for instance, built on its tradition of service for the English in King Philip's War to fill units led by Benjamin Church or his descendants in King William's War (1689–97), Queen Anne's War (1702–13), Governor Drummer's War (1722–25), King George's War (1744–48), and then the Seven Years' War (1756–63). Mashpee contributed a higher percentage of its men to provincial and continental forces during the Revolution than any other town in Massachusetts. Such patterns suggest that nearly every able-bodied Indian man from southern New England served in the military at least once during his life.[35]

Decent pay partly accounts for the high rate of Indian participation in maritime work and soldiering, but only partly. The whaling and fishing industries offered employees set shares of whatever profits their voyages earned. The more skilled the laborer, the greater his share, regardless of his race, though merchants usually reserved

Captain Amos Haskins, c. 1850. Courtesy of the New Bedford Whaling Museum.

Captain Amos Haskins (1816–1861), an Aquinnah Wampanoag, was a rare example of a Native whaler who rose to the highest ranks of the industry. At the age of thirty-five, he captained his first voyage, on a ship coincidentally named *Massasoit*. His accomplishments allowed him to build a comfortable life for himself and his family in the port city of New Bedford. The vast majority of Native whalers were less fortunate. White creditors and the courts exploited their debt to force many of them into this dangerous service for most of their adult lives. It was part of a larger pattern of debt peonage that drove Indian men into the military and Indian women and children into household labor for whites.

the highest-paying positions for whites. Typically a whaler's or fisherman's pay took the form of credit added to his individual account at the employer's company store. If he had managed to keep his debts in check, a lucrative voyage could earn him enough to build a house and purchase some extras. Military service could also be profitable, despite its association with the most desperate elements of society. The combination of enlistment bonuses, wages, plunder, and scalp bonuses could earn a Native soldier as much as a good whaling venture, with the added incentive that recruiters sometimes also promised to tend to his family's welfare while he was away. Not least of all, both at-sea work and military service carried manly prestige because of the danger and wide geographic range of these activities, which made them something like substitutes for the decline of intertribal warfare and hunting. Some special Indian units in the colonial military permitted Wampanoags to serve alongside friends and relatives under elite men from their communities. To no small degree, then, Wampanoags valued these activities.[36]

Yet most Native men did not perform this work on their own terms. Rather, white people who controlled their debts or indentures compelled them to do it. By one count, roughly three-quarters of Indians who served on Nantucket whaling crews during the 1720s and 1730s were servants whose earnings went directly to English masters. Even technically free Indian mariners were usually caught in a vicious cycle of debt peonage. More often than not, their meager shares were insufficient to pay for the work clothes and equipment they had bought on credit to perform their labor in the first place, never mind to clear the debts they had incurred to care for their families. An unsuccessful voyage meant having to sign on to another one, and sometimes a series, just to keep creditors at bay. The Nantucket Wampanoags tried to call attention to their plight by complaining that their merchant overlords forced them to chase whales even on Sunday. "How can we any ways be like Christians," they questioned, "when we should be praying to God on the Sabbath day morning then we must be rowing after whale or killing whale or cutting up whale on Sabbath day . . . [O]ur masters lead us in darkness and not in light."[37]

It grew darker still when merchants and authorities conspired to swindle hopelessly indebted mariners into using their children's freedom as collateral on the gamble of a whaling share. As Hawley explained it, "First the father is forced to go whaling. The boys are put up in sureties. When whaling fails to pay the debt, the boys are given up." And, he might have added, the father commits to go to sea again. As late as 1804 the Christiantown Wampanoags were still protesting that "our men are sent [on] long voyages to sea by those who practice in a more soft manner that of kidnapping, and when they return with ever so great success they are still in debt and have nothing to receive." From the late seventeenth through the early nineteenth centuries, nearly every Wampanoag whaleman pursuing the leviathan was just as assuredly being chased by creditors.[38]

Military service was no different. The best study of this issue finds that half or more Indians in military service were indentured servants, which was seven times the rate of colonial soldiers. Most of the rest of Indian soldiers were technically free but had accumulated such unmanageable debts that they were also beholden to their creditors. Too often, these lenders or their relatives were the very Englishmen who led the Indians' military companies and served as their guardians. For instance, Richard Bourne, a descendant of the missionary to the Mashpee Wampanoags by the same name, raised more than a quarter of his hundred-man Indian force in 1724 just by calling in his or his family members' accounts. Another two Indians in his unit were indebted to his second-in-command, Lieutenant Jeremiah Hawes. Still other Wampanoags "enlisted" because their creditors or masters had been drafted (Indians were not subject to the draft) and demanded that they serve as substitutes. Experience Mayhew recalled the case of Samuel James of Sengekontaket, who "being pressed to go as a soldier into the war . . . was most grievously distressed on that account, and came weeping to me, praying me, if it were possible to get him released; telling me, that his leaving of his wife would be a greater grief to her than she was able to endure." In all these scenarios, the Indian soldier never saw his pay, which leads one scholar to conclude that "debt was clearly the primary mechanism for the recruitment of Indian men for the army, much as it was in the whaling industry." Indeed, Native men often shuffled between the military and whaling in alternate seasons throughout most of their adult lives. In other words, they were performing the most dangerous, brute work for the benefit of the very society that oppressed them, as they themselves realized. After serving in Massachusetts forces five times between 1725 and 1750, losing a leg, and then sinking into poverty without financial relief from the colonial government, the Christian Wampanoag preacher William Simon of Titicut rued that all his suffering extended from him having "ventured my life in defense of the English people." Likewise, the people of Mashpee questioned why Massachusetts allowed their guardians to tyrannize them when "we have never been against the English, but united with them against their enemies."[39]

Wampanoags knew the answer was that whites typically stereotyped them as lazy drunkards incapable of civilized living and even of caring properly for their children. This characterization remained constant even amid otherwise important changes in white New Englanders' racial depictions of Indians. During the century after King Philip's War, when Indian-colonial warfare remained a constant feature of colonial life, it was common for whites to dehumanize Indians and call for their destruction, even as white elites promoted missionary work to prepare Indians for eventual incorporation into white society. Consider a New London publisher's decision in 1721 to reprint Wait Winthrop's 1678 ode to the English veterans of the Great Swamp Massacre. Winthrop, scion of New England's most prestigious family, compared the Natives who defended their homes on that bloody day to "a swarm of flies, they may arise . . . yea Rats and Mice or Swarms of Lice." It was but a small step from calling Natives vermin to advocating their extermination. During the Seven Years' War of the 1750s, there were multiple incidents of white New Englanders, in taverns and even in church, declaring that the only way to convert Indians was by "powder and ball," or, in other words, by deadly force. No wonder that later in the century an anonymously authored broadside published in Boston under the title "The Indian's Pedigree" half joked that the race of Indians descended from the mating of the devil and a hog.[40]

When not likening Indians to demons and beasts, white racial rhetoric tended to cast them as pathetic, attributing their poverty and subordination to their supposedly inherent shortcomings rather than to exploitation by a more powerful colonial society. As the Massachusetts lieutenant governor, Thomas Hutchinson, admitted in 1764, "We are too apt to consider the Indians as a race [as] being by nature inferior to us, and born to servitude." Thirty years later, Samuel Badger, minister to a white congregation in what had once been the thriving praying town of Natick, told the Massachusetts Historical Society that Indians "are generally considered by white people, and placed, as if by common consent, in an inferior and degraded condition, and treated accordingly." He added that whites felt free to take "every advantage of [Indians] that they could, under color of legal authority, and without incurring its censure, to dishearten and depress them." The same white people trafficking in these racial aphorisms had Christian Indians as neighbors and sometimes as fellow parishioners during Sunday worship, though they always consigned them to seats at the back of the meetinghouse. Clearly they did not see Indians, Christian or not, as either equal in the flesh or before God.[41]

By the nineteenth century, what little sense of responsibility eastern whites had once accepted for Native people's troubles was gone. The ugly business of Indian-white warfare had shifted west, and the rhetoric of violent extermination along with it. Now it became possible to muse that Indians' supposedly innate savagery fated them to recede and disappear in the face of white expansion. Supposedly, Indians absorbed only the worst qualities of white people, like drinking and debt, and none of the best ones, like thrift and hard work. Thus they deteriorated through contact with whites and then eventually disappeared. Over the next few decades, whites developed these ideas to convince themselves that God destined Indians for extinction to make way for a superior, Christian, enlightened, democratic, white civilization. This thinking, which eventually morphed into a white conquest ideology known as Manifest Destiny, and, for that matter, the Thanksgiving myth, conveniently allowed whites to abdicate responsibility for their murderous conquest and oppression of Native people. They attributed it to just the natural, divine order of things.[42]

Americans today so closely associate Manifest Destiny with the Mexican-American War of the 1840s and the Plains Wars of the mid- to late nineteenth century that it is easy to overlook how eastern whites had propagated some of its tenets, too, in the context of dealing with local Indians like the Wampanoags. Take, for example, the Boston writer William Tudor, who in 1820 cited the Wampanoag example to contend that it was "hopeless" to civilize Indians and that the "unfortunate race" faced "inevitable destruction." The *Atlantic Monthly* made the same point in an 1859 account of Aquinnah, which concluded that "the Indian" was simply incapable "of exchanging his own purely physical ambitions and pursuits for the intellectual and cultivated life belonging to the better class of his conquerors . . . Civilization to the savage destroys his own existence and gives him no better one—destroys it irredeemably and forever."[43]

Native people rarely told whites about how such treatment made them feel, but when they did, their statements were filled with pain and sorrow. The Pequot William Apess, who ministered to Mashpee in the 1830s, reflected that though he descended from a family of sachems, "this availed nothing with me; the land of my fathers was gone; and their characters were not known as human beings but as beasts of prey. We were represented as having no souls to save, or to lose, but as partridges upon the mountains. All these degrading titles were heaped upon us. Thus, you see, we had to bear all this tide of degradation, while prejudice stung every white man, from the oldest to the youngest, to the very center of the heart." "Why should I try?" a Christiantown Wampanoag put it differently to state authorities in 1849. "The prejudice against our color keeps us down."[44]

One reason whites were able to treat Native people so cruelly was that their population continued to grow by leaps and bounds, while Indian numbers plummeted. Massachusetts had expanded to more than 235,000 people by the eve of the American Revolution, with local Indians representing barely 1 percent of that figure. Even on just the Cape and islands, the non-Indian (and overwhelmingly white) population of 22,470 in 1776 dwarfed that of local Wampanoags by a factor of at least ten. Following King Philip's War and well into the 1800s, Wampanoag men tended to live short lives because of their perilous work as whalers, fishermen, and soldiers. For instance, between 1750 and 1779, Nantucket lost 38 ships and 494 sailors, which, given that an estimated 5 of 13 whalemen were Native, would put the number of Indian dead from that port alone at about 190. The wide-ranging travel of Wampanoag mariners and soldiers, and labor of other Wampanoags in port towns with international traffic, exposed their people to an endless succession of deadly diseases that ground down their already thinned populations. In 1730 smallpox decimated the Wampanoags of Monomoyick on the outer Cape, "so that there is scarce any grown person of the Indians left in this Town." Six years later, another smallpox epidemic killed up to half of the Yarmouth Wampanoags, while in 1738 an unnamed sickness carried off large numbers of people at Mashpee. The worst case on record from this period was an outbreak of yellow fever in 1763–64, which slayed more than two hundred Wampanoags on Nantucket, including nearly all the adults, plus some thirty-nine Vineyard Wampanoags, mostly at Chappaquiddick, and an unknown number at Mashpee. In the American Revolution, twenty-five of the twenty-six Mashpee men who served in one Barnstable regiment died before returning home and the one who did survive brought back with him a camp disease that took the lives of seventy people from a total population of less than three hundred. This was a demographic crisis by any measure, made infinitely worse, let it be remembered, by white society taking advantage of its overwhelming strength to degrade Native people in ways great and small.[45]

INSIDERS AND OUTSIDERS

The premature loss of their people to disease and work-related deaths on top of whites' appropriation of Indian land and labor made it nearly impossible for families in the smallest Wampanoag communities to make ends meet. By 1815 there were only six Native households at Indian Town in Yarmouth, eight at Potonumecut in Eastham, eight at the head of Buzzards Bay, and six at Sengekontacket on the Vineyard, all of which had nearly twice as many women as men. Even more depopulated were the Wampanoag hamlets of Mattakeesett (Pembroke), Sippican (Rochester), Betty's Neck (Assawompset), Wareham, Acoaxet, Apponagansett, and Acushnet (near Dartmouth).

Some of the people had relocated to larger Wampanoag communities, where it was sometimes possible to make a reasonable living and find marriage partners. Such places included Mashpee (about 400 people in 1800), Aquinnah (some 250), Herring Pond (about 100 people), and, to a lesser extent, Chappaquiddick (some 90) and Watuppa (50 to 75). Others had gone to live with the Narragansetts of Rhode Island or the Mohegans or Pequots of Connecticut. Otherwise, most young people who managed to escape bound servitude sought opportunity and companionship in the "colored" wards of New England seaports and cities. Whites considered the "mixed" population of these neighborhoods to be black, but the people had a more nuanced sense of themselves. As the supposedly black representatives of Nantucket's "New Guinea" neighborhood wrote in 1822, "there are among the colored people of this place, remains of the Nantucket Indians, and that nearly every family in our village are partly descended from the original inhabitants of this and neighboring places."[46]

The challenge of maintaining the larger communities included integrating male outsiders whom Native women had married because of the shortage of Wampanoag men. These newcomers came from a variety of backgrounds, as captured by Mashpee's white missionary, Hawley, who detested the trend as "miscegenation." In 1787 he complained that Mashpee "has been an asylum for the poor Natives and their connections . . . for we have had an East Indian, a native of Bombay, married to one of our females, and another from Mexico, besides several Dutchmen from [the British] General [John] Burgoyne's army . . . From Mohegan and other places in Connecticut, from Narragansett and other places in Rhode Island, as well as from various towns in the Massachusetts." The "Dutchmen" were Hessians (German mercenaries) who had fought for Britain during the Revolution. Hawley also counted a number of black men at Mashpee. As the New England states phased out slavery after the

Dorcas Honorable. Collections of the Nantucket Historical Association.

Dorcas Honorable (née, Esop; ca. 1770–1855) came from a prestigious line of Nantucket Wampanoags and lived out her long life on the island. White Nantucketers seized on her passing in 1855 to proclaim her the last of the Nantucket Wampanoags, part of a broader trend of white New Englanders insisting that Indians were disappearing as if by nature. Such talk was an extension of the national ideology of Manifest Destiny and of a colonial racial logic in which Indian identity diminished through mixture (the better to make Indians vanish and open their land to whites), whereas blackness spread (the better to expand the servile workforce).

Revolution, the free black population often found work in the same places as Wampanoags because white society consigned both groups to low-status jobs. Romantic relationships between black men and Wampanoag women developed in turn, with the couples sometimes moving to the reservations to settle down. At Mashpee, such men included Sepney Pollards, "a negro from near Boston"; "Negro Cuff"; "Drover a Negro"; a "Portugal Negro" (or Cape Verdean); "Fornnis a Negro from N[ew] York"; and "Newport Mye Negro." There were twenty-six black men on the reservation in 1800. More than just love matches, Wampanoag women who wanted to get married often had no choice but to bring in partners from the outside. As for the newcomers, they could hardly believe their stroke of luck in successfully courting women with access to land. Yet these relationships introduced profound tensions into how Wampanoag communities operated internally and dealt with white society.[47]

It was difficult to ease newcomers into the communal practices of large reservations like Mashpee and Aquinnah, where people could enclose as much open land as they needed for as long as they wanted, so long as they did not sell any of it to outsiders. This custom left white observers stunned that "while one proprietor has but half an acre, and another has over a hundred acres, there is no heartburning, no feeling that the latter has more than his share." Local "stinting committees" fenced off certain tracts of land for the people to graze their livestock in common, and Aquinnah even operated a common planting field that it plowed at public expense. Otherwise, woodland, cranberry bogs, hunting grounds, fishing spots, clay deposits, berry bushes, and medicinal plants were available to everyone. The people sometimes gathered as a community to harvest and sell these resources in bulk to fund public services like poor relief. One Massachusetts official, assuming that jealousy and selfishness were naturally the dominant features of all human societies, marveled that these places were "almost realizing the wildest dreams of the communists."[48]

Yet communalism was not the wild dream of most of the males who married into Native communities. They associated manhood with independent decision-making, including capitalizing on the value of their labor and property on the market. These were particularly sensitive issues for black men recently emancipated from slavery, who defined freedom, in part, as the right to enjoy the same liberties as white men. Yet Indians did not consider the issue open for discussion. As early as 1784, some Aquinnah Wampanoags began to denounce "the new comers the strangers," while at Mashpee the people worried that the "Negroes and English who have happily planted themselves here . . . unless they are removed will get away our lands & all our privileges in a short time." To guard against such a risk, these communities started to keep censuses that distinguished between "proprietors" with economic and political rights and "non-proprietors" who lived there as guests of their wives, and not always welcome ones.[49]

A common problem involved male outsiders dropping off their destitute Wampanoag wives and children for the community to support and then going to sea, even when the woman's only link to the community was through her parents or even grandparents. Aquinnah judged such behavior to be "not right," emphasizing that "we are willing to do all we can for Gay Head poor; but we are not willing to maintain people that do not rightly belong on Gay Head, for we have no means of supporting them." Tensions between insiders and outsiders reached a pitch when absentee Indians from mixed marriages tried to claim land rights in the community and even to sell these parcels to fund lives elsewhere. In 1823 Christiantown found itself embroiled in two lawsuits over such issues. With less than three hundred acres fully divided among forty or fifty people, the community argued that if it lost these contests, "we are undone." Yet, given the large number of descendants who lived off-reservation in desperate conditions, married to outsiders who viewed land as a commodity, troubles of this sort were constant. In the 1840s Christiantown suffered through two more legal cases, "which arose in consequence of negro men marrying women amongst them." Similar "difficulties" and "unhappy contention" led Chappaquiddick to call for a renewed ban on the sale of its land to any outsiders and the state legislation requiring "that when a foreigner shall marry and settle among us, he shall be subjected to the same law to which we are." Without such vigilance, the reservations were in real danger of dissolution.[50]

One way Wampanoag communities responded to the threat of newcomers and indigent returning absentees was by elevating

Wampanoag women to the political fore, a position that they have held ever since. Sometime around the turn of the eighteenth century, Mashpee and then Aquinnah decided that only the Indian wives of mixed marriages, not the husbands, could represent their families in the town meeting and lay claim to land. As the Aquinnah minister Zacheus Howwoswee explained in 1860, "We the proprietors on Gay Head wish to conduct our own business separate from the foreigners & strangers. We never have allowed them any poll [voting] right on Gay Head, therefore they have not any in our land but work on their wife's portion of land." Not coincidentally, in the nineteenth century white observers began remarking for the first time about Wampanoag women "taking the same liberty of speech" as their men in public settings. This change corresponded to a dramatic rise in the number of Wampanoag women signing petitions to white authorities between 1750 and 1850 at a rate even higher than their proportion of the total adult population. Of course, the Wampanoags had a tradition of elite women sometimes serving as sachems. Additionally, oral traditions contend that women's councils had always influenced community decision-making, and women had always governed their households. Yet it took the challenge of integrating newcomers in the late eighteenth and early nineteenth centuries before everyday Wampanoag women played such an assertive public political role.[51]

A more subtly detected but no less profound effect of these mixed marriages was the further weakening of the people's use of the Wampanoag language. The century-long pattern of whites forcing Native children into indentured servitude, and then young adults into whaling, soldiery, or household service, had removed countless individuals from Wampanoag communities for most of their formative years, thus robbing them of the experience of acquiring the language through face-to-face exchanges. When they returned to their communities as adults, often they had little or no command of their ancestral tongue. Another, more minor destructive influence was the New England Company's cessation of Wampanoag-language publications in the 1720s, with the express purpose of encouraging Native people to learn English. Yet the real hammer blow to the language came after the Revolution in the form of mixed marriages. Doubtless some outsiders and their children learned to speak Wampanoag, but with English already on the rise, most mixed households probably spoke it as their first language. If and when the children of these relationships left the reservation to work for whites, it all but ensured that they would be English-only speakers.

Creeping damage to the Wampanoag tongue accumulated throughout the eighteenth century before turning dire in the early nineteenth. Consider the following sequence: in the 1720s Experience Mayhew judged that Vineyard Wampanoags understood their own language "much better" than English. This was also the case at Mashpee, where in 1724 the Reverend Joseph Bourne could not get the people to assemble "unless he will preach to them in their own language." As late as 1753, the Mashpees complained in a letter written in Wampanoag that they "had no need" for the schoolmaster provided for them by the New England Company because he spoke only English and "we cannot understand him, only a few can." Yet just four years later the Mashpees asked Hawley to preach in English alongside the Native minister Solomon Briant because "some of us did not understand the Indian dialect fully." Likewise, a 1767 celebration of the Lord's Supper involving the Natives of Cape Cod and Martha's Vineyard included a morning service in Wampanoag and afternoon worship in English because though "the Indians are fond of retaining their own Language . . . they generally however understand English, especially the younger ones among them."[52]

A generation later, English had clearly spread at the expense of the Wampanoag tongue. In 1802 Hawley estimated that at Mashpee "the English language is now more copious perhaps than any of the old language, and is enough for an Indian to know." The Vineyard missionary Frederick Baylies, who was as familiar with the island Wampanoags as any outsider, judged in 1823 that there were only "six Indians who can talk Indian" and "not one who can read Indian." By the same token, when Samuel Davis went to Mashpee in 1838 to compile a Wampanoag vocabulary, he was told by an unnamed "half blood" informant, aged forty, that "in his infancy he learned the English tongue. These specimens there, of the aboriginal, he has acquired, from the old Natives of whom scarcely any more remain that speak it."[53]

Certainly these overconfident pronouncements by white outsiders were shaped by the racial ideology of Indian disappearance and failed to capture the full complexity of Wampanoag-language use in these communities. There must have been Wampanoags who knew more of their ancestral language than they would reveal in public, even to other Indians, as part of the tradition of keeping sacred knowledge guarded until the appropriate time. Mashpee Wampanoags tell that their last fluent speaker, before the recent revitalization of the language, was still alive in the early 1950s. A greater body of people continued to drop whatever Wampanoag words and phrases they did know into predominantly English-language conversations, thereby signaling their solidarity with other Wampanoags past and present. Nevertheless, fluency in the language was so rare by the 1830s that it could no longer function as the people's public speech.

To many Wampanoags, the growing dominance of English at the expense of their natal tongue felt like loss, not just change. Over the generations, Wampanoag people had made a host of cultural adjustments to the demands of colonization without compromising their sense of who they were. After all, they had adopted Christianity by infusing it with their own beliefs and values and running their churches with their own officers. They had taken up animal husbandry to compensate for the colonists' encroachment on their hunting grounds and the decline of wild game. They had opened schools and taught their children literacy in Wampanoag and English both to access the Bible and to exercise control over the written documents that were part and parcel of colonial life. They had incorporated manufactured clothing into their wardrobes and certain foreign foods into their cuisine for reasons of taste and declining access to wild resources. Yet all along they had continued to identify themselves as "Gay Head Indians," "Mashpee Indians," "Herring Pond Indians," and the like, because they continued to live on their ancestral lands, with their own people, telling their own special stories, passing down time-tested values, and, not least of all, speaking their own language.

The Wampanoag language had been like a barrier of beach-front dunes holding back the raging colonial sea. Its erosion seemed as permanent as the loss of shoreline, leaving the people feeling empty and vulnerable. In the late nineteenth century, the botanist Edward Burgess visited the Wampanoag community of Aquinnah, where elders told him stories about Zachariah Howwoswee, who was the last Indian minister to preach in Wampanoag until his death in 1821 at age eighty-three. The elders remembered that whenever Howwoswee switched the language of his sermons from English to Wampanoag, "there were but few of them could know what he meant . . . and they would cry and he would cry." Howwoswee knew his listeners could not understand his words, but hearing their people's speech fostered a sense of their collective history, suffering, and anxiety about the future. As Howwoswee put it, speaking Wampanoag was a way "to keep up my nation." Hope could be found in a prophecy—which turned out to be true—that the language would awaken after seven generations, but as it slept the people felt its absence deep in their hearts.[54]

WHITE INSISTENCE ON INDIAN DISAPPEARANCE

Local whites twisted the knife by seizing on the Wampanoags' marriages with outsiders, particularly blacks, and the weakening of the Wampanoag language to contend that the Indians were on the verge of disappearance. This was New England's own regional twist on the national racial idiom of Manifest Destiny. It held that Indian "blood" was weaker than that of other races, meaning that the child of an Indian and a non-Indian became a "half-blood," the child of that "half-blood" and another non-Indian became a "quarter-blood," and then, eventually, all trace of the Indian vanished, which is precisely what whites who coveted Indian land wanted to happen. By contrast, white Americans thought of black blood as polluting, so that any degree of African descent made one black. It was not coincidental that such a formulation expanded the servile black labor pool to the benefit of white people. In other words, whites' inconsistencies in reckoning Indian and black racial identities were not illogical at all. They were entirely in line with white colonial desires.[55]

The Wampanoags constantly endured the weight of these white racial judgments. For instance, in 1818, when the white Vineyard missionaries Joseph Thaxter and Frederick Baylies reported to Boston on the problem of Indian whalers and debt, they included an editorial that there were few "pure" Natives left: "they are a mixture of everything." Baylies tried to prove his point in 1823 by compiling a "blood quantum" census of every Vineyard Native he could identify, which involved breaking down their ratio of Indian, black, and white "blood" into halves, quarters, eighths, and sixteenths. Just how he came up with these figures, he did not say, but he used them to confirm his predetermined conclusion that "it is not probable there ever will be another Indian child born on the island." Baylies certainly was a white man of his times. A committee appointed in 1827 to survey all the Indians in Massachusetts concluded that "those of the full blood do not probably exceed one hundred" and "exhibit little of the characteristics of their race, except the power of patient and silent sufferance." Another committee twenty years later took this idea a step further by concluding that "the admixture of African blood" was "the only one common to all the different tribes." Some of the Wampanoags' less sophisticated white neighbors had cruder ways to express the same sentiment. According to the *Atlantic Monthly*, white Vineyarders often used "nigger" to refer to "these half-breeds." By the twentieth century, and perhaps earlier, country whites in southern New England derided local Indians as "monigs," meaning "more nigger than Indian."[56]

The Wampanoags did not take these slurs lying down. Proudly self-identifying as "Indians and people of color" of particular Native communities, they spent the first decades of the nineteenth century pressing for the removal of their guardians and state recognition of their right to self-rule. They emphasized that the land had belonged to their people since ancient times, giving them an inherent right to be free from the guardians' power to lease out and even sell tribal territory. Hannah Perry of the Watuppa reservation added that her people's guardians did not treat them with the "kindness and humanity to which they think they are entitled" but "with contempt." By 1833 the Mashpees had reached the limits of their patience not only with their guardians but with their white minister, Phineas Fish, who preached to a congregation made up almost entirely of whites from neighboring towns despite collecting his salary from a charitable fund for evangelizing Indians. Most of the Indians attended Baptist services led by one of their own, Blind Jo Amos. Yet Fish prohibited them from using the Mashpee meetinghouse. Daniel Amos lambasted Fish: "We do not believe in you trying to make us believe that we have not as good a right to the table of the Lord as others, that we are kept back merely because our skin is of a different complexion, and we find nothing in so doing to justify you in the scripture." Declaring "that all men were born free and equal; that as a tribe they were determined to rule themselves," the Mashpees took back possession of their meetinghouse and obstructed a party of whites from hauling away firewood cut on the reservation. Barnstable County officials responded by declaring the Mashpees to be in a state of "riot," then arrested their new preacher, the Pequot William Apess, and another of their leading men on charges of trespass and assault.[57]

Apess made them pay, rhetorically at least. Following in the footsteps of the Mohegan Indian minister Samson Occom, who in the 1760s and 1770s became the first published Native American autobiographer, hymnist, and poet, Apess already had several publications under his belt by the time he arrived in Mashpee. Yet the so-called riot gave him fresh material with which to work and a receptive Yankee audience. For years, New England had been the epicenter of white opposition to President Andrew Jackson's inhumane removal of the Cherokees and other southern Indian tribes from their ancestral lands to territory west of the Mississippi. Now the Mashpee protest awakened those same critics to the fact that there were Indians in their own backyard to whom New England state governments denied basic rights. Apess seized on the moment. With the support of the abolitionist William Garrison and other members of Boston's progressive literati, Apess delivered a series of public lectures (subsequently published) highlighting the troubles of Mashpee and Indians everywhere at the hands of self-righteous, hypocritical white Christians. He also provided a pointed lesson on New England's colonial history that continues to influence debate over the stories Americans tell about Thanksgiving.[58]

Apess's *Eulogy on King Philip* reversed the emerging myth of the pious Pilgrim Fathers to transform the Wampanoags into heroes and the English into villains. In Apess's hands, "Massasoit" (Ousamequin) was a model of kindness "that would do justice to any

Christian nation or being in the world" because he patiently suffered "the most daring robberies and barbarous deeds of death that were ever committed by the American Pilgrims." Apess meticulously laid out all the foul details of English misbehavior in the founding of Plymouth, including the kidnappings, grave robbing, theft of Wampanoag corn, and unprovoked massacre of Indians at Wessagusett. The same men who committed these crimes had the impudence to turn to Massasoit for help, and the chief, to his moral credit, obliged. "No people could be used better than they were," Apess intoned about the Pilgrims. The Wampanoags "gave them venison and sold them many hogsheads of corn to fill their stores . . . Had it not been for this humane act of the Indians, every white man would have been swept from the New England colonies." Apess even considered Massasoit to be a better Christian than the Pilgrims who called him a savage. After all, the self-styled saints returned Massasoit's generosity by attempting to reduce the Wampanoags through every foul means they could contrive.[59]

Apess also declared Massasoit's son, Philip (or Pumetacom), to be "the greatest man that ever lived upon the American shores" for leading his people in resistance against this exploitation. Apess went so far as to rank Philip above George Washington, white Americans' Father of the Country, because he fought against a darker tyranny and for greater freedom with far fewer means at his disposal. Additionally, Philip always treated his enemies with honor, quite unlike white people's barbarity toward Indians during King Philip's War and in every war against them since. Yet Apess's most important political point was that Philip was a sage for taking up arms rather than submitting to white people's indignities. Apess invited his listeners to imagine Philip coming back from the dead to discover that Indian life under colonial rule was just as unbearable as he had feared it would be. "How true the prophecy," lamented Apess, "that the white people would not only cut down their groves but would

"Mr. William Apes [*sic*], a native missionary of the Pequot tribe of Indians," frontispiece to William Apess, *A Son of the Forest: The Experience of William Apess, A Native of the Forest, Comprising a Notice of the Pequot Tribe of Indians, Written by Himself* (New York: published by the author; printed by G. F. Bunce, 1831). From the Collections of the New York Public Library.

While serving as preacher to the Mashpee Wampanoags in the 1830s, the Pequot William Apess helped lead a movement by his people to take back control of their local meetinghouse from an indifferent white minister, and control of their land from ineffective state guardians. His campaign included speeches and publications in which he introduced the idea that the Fourth of July and anniversary of the Pilgrims' landing were "Days of Mourning" for Native people because of the evils of colonization.

enslave them . . . Our groves and hunting grounds are gone, are dead are dug up, our council fires are put out." Whites like President Jackson were intent either on "driving the Indians out of the states" or, like New Englanders, "dooming them to become chained under desperate laws." Either way, there was no justice for Indians in white America, which was the outgrowth of "a fire, a canker, created by the Pilgrims from across the Atlantic, to burn and destroy my poor unfortunate brethren."[60]

For that reason, Apess declared, "let every man of color wrap himself in mourning" on the twenty-second of December, which was the anniversary of the Pilgrims' landing in Plymouth, and on the Fourth of July celebrating the founding of the United States. In Apess's view, Indians should treat those dates as "days of mourning and not joy . . . Let them rather fast and pray to the great Spirit, the Indian's god, who deals out mercy to his red children, and not destruction." Apess's message would continue to resonate among the Wampanoags long after he was gone.[61]

Unfortunately for Wampanoags everywhere, the Mashpee revolt also convinced a number of white authorities that it was not only strange but wrong to have Indians subject to state law without the status of citizenship. In the short term, their empathy helped Mashpee get much of what it wanted, insofar as Massachusetts turned Mashpee into a self-governing district with most of the powers of other towns except the right to send representatives to the state's General Court. There would be no more guardians, just popularly elected town officers. Furthermore, Fish was fired and Mashpee received half the amount of his annual salary to use at its own discretion. These were real victories. Yet, in the longer term, Apess's campaign had the unintended effect of prompting the state to explore whether it should revoke indigenous people's special status, including the legal protection of their lands, and put them on a purportedly equal legal footing with whites.[62]

To most Wampanoags, citizenship tied to the elimination of their legal status as Indians did not represent a gift, but a culmination of two centuries of colonial exploitation. When Indians, including the Wampanoags, demanded their rights, they did not mean the same thing as African Americans who wanted the same freedoms, protections, and responsibilities as whites. To Indians, "equality" of that sort was subjugation, because it would require them to pay taxes to a government that did not heed their voice. Furthermore, it would subject them to courts officiated by whites and expose their lands to confiscation when their taxes, fines, or debts went unpaid. This was not what they meant when they called for justice. They meant sovereignty, the sanctity of their lands, and recognition as the First People. In the case of the Wampanoags, that respect also meant honor for their historic role as welcoming hosts and allies of the English.

That opinion rang through loud and clear when Massachusetts authorized commissioners in 1849 and 1861 to evaluate all the Indian communities in the state for citizenship. Expecting to find squalor, drunkenness, and dysfunction, the investigators were surprised to discover that most Wampanoags led dignified lives. They were economically self-sufficient through a combination of wage work, animal husbandry, farming, fishing, and the sale of common resources like berries, wood, shellfish, clay, and pasture. All but a few lived in comfortable framed houses, sometimes with multiple rooms, decorated "with pictures and curiosities collected in the eastern and southern seas." They were churchgoing people, mannerly, and, contrary to stereotype, "temperate and chaste." Their values included an emphasis on formal education. "Many of the parents are very desirous that their children and youths should become as well educated as the white people among them," the commissioners boasted. Consequently, "about every native can read and write." Most remarkable of all was the effectiveness of the Indians' town meeting government, the infrequency of litigation between them, and the people's generous support of the poor. In nearly every respect they seemed perfectly qualified to exercise the rights and responsibilities of citizenship.[63]

Yet most Wampanoags did not want it. Though white authorities hoped to find Indians complaining their special legal status and receipt of state aid made them no more than vassals, the majority felt nothing of the sort. At Chappaquiddick, elders lectured the commissioners that, since whites had swindled them out of nearly "the whole island . . . they feel that they have the right to expect protection in the enjoyment of the few acres left to them." Citizenship would rob them of that security because "most of them would soon become the prey of shrewder and sharper men outside, that the little property they possess would soon be wrested from them and that they would

Jane Wamsley, from *Harper's New Weekly*, September 1860, 451.

Aquinnah's Jane Wamsley and Deacon Simon Johnson were leading voices in the mid-nineteenth century against the efforts of Massachusetts to force citizenship on the Wampanoags and divide their common lands into taxable, sellable private-property tracts. Despite the majority of the Wampanoags sharing her opinion, the commonwealth forced these measures on the Wampanoags in the late 1860s and early 1870s as something of a northern iteration of southern Reconstruction.

Deacon Simon Johnson, 1861.
Courtesy of the Martha's
Vineyard Museum.

be turned out, destitute, upon the cold charities of the world. The community would be consequently broken up, and scattered among those who would have no particular sympathy with them." The same opinion echoed through community after community, as did a belief about the people's entitlement to outside funds for the support of education, religion, and poor relief. The commissioners found it puzzling that Native people "have a vague idea that the state has large funds drawn from the sale of lands which would have been theirs . . . so that whatever they receive is but a just due." After all, the Wampanoags had once been the "great father" to the "little child" of Plymouth.[64]

One reason whites found this thinking so odd was that they did not see the Wampanoags as bona fide Indians in the first place. Whereas the Wampanoags defined their Indianness in terms of belonging to families and communities of Indian heritage, whites used the racial notion of "purity" and adherence to a timeless "traditional" culture as the standards. This was a double bind if ever there was one, because Indians could either disappear by keeping their Indian identity but refusing to meet the challenges of their times, or they could adapt and thereby sacrifice their status as Indians. Given that the Wampanoags had survived the vagaries of colonialism for more than two centuries, they clearly fell into the latter category, as whites would have it.

The Reconstruction period following the Civil War provided the impetus and political cover for state authorities to impose this supposedly natural demise on viable Wampanoag communities. The Fourteenth and Fifteenth Amendments, granting citizenship to all natural-born Americans and the right to vote to all citizens, did not affect the Wampanoags technically because they exempted "Indians not taxed," which in the New England context meant Indians living on reservations. Nevertheless, in practice the new constitutional order signaled the end to the people's separate legal status, including their protected reservations. One factor was that white authorities denied that the Wampanoags were really Indians. As Governor William Claflin put it, the Natives' protective status "should exist no longer" because "these persons are not Indians in any sense of the word. It is doubtful that there is a pure-blooded Indian in the State . . . A majority have more or less of the marked characteristics of the aboriginal race, but there are many without a drop of Indian blood in their veins . . . the characteristics of the white and negro races have already nearly obliterated all traces of the Indian." Another influence was that a vocal minority within Wampanoag communities believed that they had the ability and should have the right to compete in American society on the same footing as everyone else. Composed mostly of "foreigners" and those Indians who had succeeded in the outside world, including within the colored ranks of the Union Army, members of this faction wanted the chance to profit from their own land, vote for the officials who governed them, and escape the degradation of being state supervised like lunatics and wards. Most Wampanoag people opposed such a change, fearing that "by being incorporated as a town we shall soon lose our identity as Indians." Yet the national tide was too strong to hold back.[65]

Massachusetts was determined to force citizenship on the Wampanoags even though the majority of them did not want it. Legislation passed by the state General Court in 1869 and 1870 declared all Indians within the commonwealth to have the same rights and duties as everyone else. In turn, it ordered the division of the people's common lands into private property tracts. Mashpee and Aquinnah (then called Gay Head) were incorporated as independent towns. Smaller Wampanoag communities, such as Christiantown and Chappaquiddick on the Vineyard and Herring Pond on the mainland, became part of their surrounding white-majority municipalities, which posed a dire threat to them as distinct Indian places. Thereafter, the pressures of taxation and debt forced some families off the land, the search for employment lured others away, and the desire to live among an Indian majority brought others to Gay Head and Mashpee. A few resolute families remained in the smaller hamlets, conscious that they symbolized their people's historic connections to the place and anchored the community's dispersed social network, but sometimes even they had to give way. In 1907 for instance the city of Fall River forced the last Wampanoag family living on what was left of the Watuppa reservation to vacate in order to make way for a reservoir. Even amid such displacement and diaspora, the people generally stayed in touch, held periodic community and tribal reunions, and visited their ancestral territory, but their fears that citizenship would lead to their dispossession had materialized.[66]

"INDIANS HAVE ALWAYS LIVED HERE"

Mashpee and Aquinnah nearly fell into the same trap. By the early twentieth century, whites had obtained title to most of the land in these communities, and the year-round Indian populations had declined significantly. State census returns (admittedly an imperfect measure of a people who tended to evade white officials) show Aquinnah's Wampanoag population dropping from 204 in 1861 to 162 in 1900, to 98 in 1940, and Mashpee's population following a similar regression. Yet these were still Indian places. Most white landowners used their properties only for summer vacation homes or bases for seasonal hunting and fishing, typically with Indian guides. The remoteness of Mashpee and Aquinnah and their reputation as "colored" towns discouraged all but a small handful of whites from living there full time. Indians remained in charge of local government, which they used to turn their towns into de facto tribal organizations. They held town meetings in winter, when they knew their people would be the only ones around to vote. They elected and appointed their own people to town offices, thereby enabling them to monopolize otherwise rare salaried positions. They underrated the assessable real estate of their relatives and friends and permitted taxes to go uncollected when their people were unable to pay (a practice that occasionally drew state scrutiny). They protected town common lands like the Gay Head cranberry bogs and clay cliffs so they could continue to hold tribal ceremonies there. In so many respects, the Wampanoags had figured out how to make town and tribe indistinguishable while keeping white authorities out of their business.[67]

The people's local dominance enabled them to infuse their community life with Wampanoag values. Wampanoags treated practically all the land in Gay Head and Mashpee, whether individually owned or not, as a tribal commons that everyone could cross to hunt, fish, and gather. There were few fences and no NO TRESPASSING signs. The widespread practices of allowing any relative or friend in need to settle on one's land, and of leaving the land to several heirs and then neglecting to record these arrangements, meant that the individual private property tracts created by the Enfranchisement Act became a jumble of overlapping claims that obstructed outsiders from acquiring clear title. As had been the case for centuries, these places remained bastions of Wampanoag communalism and safe havens for relatives returning from their ventures abroad among outsiders. "Indians have always lived here" was how the people explained these practices.[68]

The people also periodically expressed a broader Wampanoag and even pan-Indian identity and political solidarity. Local celebrations in 1920 of the three-hundredth anniversary of the Pilgrims' landing in America inspired a number of Wampanoags to participate in order to highlight their ancestors' role in this historic event. Eight years later, Mashpee's Eben Queppish, a veteran of traveling Wild West shows, and Nelson Drew Simons, an alumnus of the Carlisle Indian School, drew on their experiences in these diverse Indian settings to call for a revival of the Wampanoag tribe. Their organizing included a 1928 powwow held at the Old Indian Church at Herring Pond, which united Wampanoags from throughout the

Amelia Watson, *The Road to Gay Head*, 1888. Courtesy of the
Martha's Vineyard Museum.

This painting of the road to Gay Head captures the remoteness that helped the Aquinnah Wampanoags retain control of their territory long after the Commonwealth of Massachusetts divided it into private-property tracts and incorporated it as a town.

region. The event's insignia was of an Indian in a Great Plains–style headdress and the saying "I Still Live." It was a pointed response to the pathos of white tercentenary orations lamenting the extinction of the New England Indians even as those same occasions frequently had Wampanoags serving as honorary "chiefs" and "princesses." The revived Wampanoag Nation chose as its supreme sachem the Reverend Leroy C. Perry of Pocasset, who took the name "Ousamequin."[69]

The Wampanoags' insistence that they remained a people with a birthright to their homelands and a moral right to respectful treatment by American society took on added urgency after World War II, particularly during the 1960s and 1970s, as the economic vibrancy and suburbanization of the Cold War United States produced a flood of whites to Mashpee and Gay Head. Many of the outsiders wanted seasonal vacation homes by the ocean, but a critical mass were retirees, self-employed, or long-distance commuters who planned to live there year-round. Almost overnight, the newcomers seized control of town government and began erecting physical and legal barriers to lands the Wampanoags had enjoyed for countless generations, most glaringly in the form of the New Seabury condominium complex on the coast of Mashpee. At the same time, the federal government, at the urging of the Massachusetts senator, Ted Kennedy, was considering designating a vast stretch of Cape and island territory, including a portion of Gay Head, as a protected wildlife preserve, which would have obstructed the Wampanoags' access to their cranberry bogs, clay cliffs, and fishing and gathering places. For a century, the people had been fending off privatization and the atomization of family that accompanied it, contrary to long-standing white predications that their extinction was inevitable. Now they confronted the very real possibility of their total dispossession.[70]

Like Ousamequin, who saw the English alliance as a means to help his people assert their independence from the Narragansetts, like the generations of local Wampanoag leaders who drew on the

Mashpee Indians, 1929. Courtesy of the Boston Public Library,
Leslie Jones Collection.

The Wampanoags continued to hold tribal social and political events,
including powwows, long after the Commonwealth of Massachusetts
declared their Indian legal status to be over. Sometimes these events drew
Wampanoags and other Indians from throughout the region. This kind of
organizing often coincided with other local and state commemorations of
historical events in which the Wampanoags feared they would be ignored or
misrepresented, such as the 1920 three-hundredth anniversary of the
founding of Plymouth colony. As media, especially Hollywood, increasingly
trafficked in stereotyped images of Plains Indians, the Wampanoags adopted
this dress, such as elaborate feather headdresses, as part of their ceremonial
regalia. Some of it appears in this picture.

resources of missionary organizations to steel their people against
hostile colonial forces, Mashpee and Gay Head responded by seeking
the intervention of the federal government. In this, their model was
the Passamoquoddies of Maine, who in 1975 had sued their state in
federal court for the recovery of tribal territory ceded since the
passage of the Trade and Intercourse Acts of the 1790s. The Passamoquoddies' contention was that the Trade and Intercourse Acts
had given the federal government the sole power, exclusive of the

states, of negotiating with Native people for their land. Thus any cession to which Washington, D.C., had not been a party (which was to say, all of them) was null and void. The politically charged proceedings resulted in a settlement awarding the Passamoquoddies, Penobscots, and Houlton Maliseets $81.5 million, including a buyback of hundreds of thousands of acres that became federally recognized tribal reservations. Since the Commonwealth of Massachusetts had similarly dispossessed the Wampanoags of Mashpee and Aquinnah in the nineteenth century without federal approval, these communities saw an opportunity to restore their historic rights and protect their threatened lands.[71]

They were also inspired to take this course by the Red Power movement of the late 1960s and 1970s, which called for a recovery of Indian sovereignty and dignity and for the United States to honor its historic treaties with Native people. Though some conservative Wampanoags found the Red Power AIM organization (or American Indian Movement) too confrontational and showy, a great many others, particularly young people, considered it a model for Indians to stand up for themselves.[72] Organizing locally as tribal communities, regionally (through the Federated Eastern Indian League), and nationally (through the Coalition of Eastern Native Americans and American Indian Congress), they worked as never before "to build Indian pride and unity."[73]

The path was not easy or, at first, clear. A federal judge quashed the Mashpee Wampanoags' initial attempt to recover their lands based on a ruling that they had not maintained their status as a tribe throughout their history and therefore did not have proper legal standing to bring suit. This judgment drew on the very assumptions of Indian racial purity and unchanging Indian culture that whites had used for nearly two centuries to try to make Indians disappear. However painful and insulting this decision was for the Mashpees, it carried the benefit of demonstrating that a successful legal strategy first required Wampanoag communities to obtain federal recognition as tribes through procedures newly defined by the Bureau of Indian Affairs in 1978. The application process was numbingly bureaucratic and more than a little degrading, for, as many Wampanoags commented, they did not need outsiders to tell them who they were in an existential sense. Furthermore, debates over the ends of obtaining such recognition led to sometimes divisive politics between family members, friends, and neighbors. Yet those arguments were an outgrowth of newfound opportunity. When the Gay Head/Aquinnah Wampanoags finally received federal recognition in 1987, followed by Mashpee in 2007, it represented a bold new era in Wampanoag life.[74]

The Wampanoag people are currently experiencing a revival by any definition. One might characterize this period as one of decolonization in the sense that the people are reasserting their sovereignty and cultural and economic self-determination. Federal recognition has permitted the tribes to recover portions of their ancestral territory and put them in federal trust to create what are currently a 481-acre reservation at Aquinnah, a 170-acre reservation at Mashpee, and another 151 acres for the Mashpees at Taunton. The status of the Mashpee Wampanoags' reservation, however, has recently been thrown into peril by a decision from the Department of Interior that the federal government did not have the authority to take land into trust for the tribe in the first place according to the Indian Reorganization Act of 1934. The issue currently lies with the federal congress. One hopes that it will rule in the Mashpee Wampanoags' favor, because reservations serve as sites of tribal government, social activities, and, in the case of Aquinnah, an affordable housing complex built on indigenous architectural principles. Federal grants have provided opportunities for educational, medical, cultural, and entrepreneurial initiatives, which, among other results, have allowed greater numbers of Wampanoag students to follow the path of Caleb

Cheeshahteaumuck and Joel Hiacoomes to college. At the time of this writing, the Aquinnah Wampanoags are moving forward with a plan to offer high-stakes bingo on their reservation, while Mashpee is seeking congressional approval for a full-fledged casino in Taunton, Massachusetts. The decision to take up gaming has produced contention within tribal communities and between the tribes and surrounding towns. Indeed, it spurred the lawsuit that led to the Department of the Interior's adverse ruling against Mashpee in the first place. However, these ventures, if successful, have the potential to raise the fortunes of communities that have long ranked among the poorest in Massachusetts and that once had generations of their children seized from them on the basis of their financial indebtedness.[75]

Most poignantly, modern Wampanoags are increasingly able to speak back to colonial power and, more important, to each other, in the Wampanoag language. The story of how this came to be will someday be considered as fundamental to Wampanoag history as Ousamequin's outreach to the Pilgrims or Pumetacom's resistance movement. In the early 1990s Mashpee's Jessie Little Doe Baird had a series of dreams in which Wampanoag ancestors spoke to her in a language she could not understand. Her interpretation of this vision with the assistance of elders led her on a historic mission. Despite shouldering the responsibilities of a family with four young children and a job as a social worker, she entered the elite graduate program in linguistics at the Massachusetts Institute of Technology for years of painstaking work driven by a sense of sacred duty. Combing through Wampanoag-language materials from the colonial period, including the Bible, sermons, instructional tracts, letters, petitions, and court records, she compiled vocabulary lists of thousands of words and identified grammatical patterns. She then compared her findings with Algonquian languages closely related to Wampanoag, such as Passamaquoddy and Delaware. Once she had a firm command of the language, she went on to teach it to others, holding nighttime language classes, summer language camps, and eventually an immersion school for Wampanoag children. Such efforts won her a 2010 MacArthur Foundation "Genius Grant," in addition to numerous other accolades, which have further contributed to the pathbreaking grassroots work of the Wôpanâak Language Revitalization Project. Wampanoags are now teaching the language in Mashpee High School to permit the tribe's young people to continue this education. In awakening the Wampanoag language from a sleep that so many outsiders characterized as death, this movement has captured the historic resilience of the Wampanoag people and their determination to chart their own future as a sovereign people in their own homeland.[76]

A number of the Wampanoags known by this author continue to mourn the suffering wrought on their people by colonists and their successors who arrived calling themselves friends only to become conquerors and exploiters. Yet for the People of the Dawnland, the sun is rising again. As it does, it will cast light on the resting place of Ousamequin, whose remains and funerary offerings the Wampanoags reclaimed in 2017 from museum archaeological collections after a dogged twenty-year search. They then gathered in a special ceremony on a bluff overlooking Narragansett Bay to restore those materials to their original burial site. There, in the heart of Wampanoag country, a people who other Americans insisted had vanished honored their history and prayed in their language.[77]

ʾ ʾ

Toward a Day with Less Mourning

Most of us who are not Wampanoag or American Indian will never fully grasp the raw emotions indigenous people associate with Thanksgiving. Yet the nation can and should move toward such an understanding. Doing so will be a small step toward creating a more welcoming environment for Indians in the national culture of the United States after generations of hostility and indifference. Taking Indian people's perspectives into account will also shed light on how fundamentally the nation's character has been shaped by white people's conquest and ongoing subjugation of Native America. Failing to come to terms with the hubris and destructiveness of that process—or, worse, seeing it as a glorious part of America's supposed greatness—conditions the people of the United States to perpetuate those evils in new forms. If how we tell history is one of the ways we shape our present and future, we can do no better than to rethink the myth of the First Thanksgiving and its role in the Thanksgiving holiday.

Wampanoags themselves are conflicted about their people's cameo in this tradition. Roland Mooanum James, who has succeeded his late father, Frank, in leading the National Day of Mourning protest, has no use for the Thanksgiving celebration. As he declared at the 2017 rally, "Today we say, 'no thanks, no giving.'" His position has a great deal of support among contemporary Wampanoags, though the number of tribal members who attend the National Day of Mourning has declined over the years as it has addressed a greater range of ills sometimes only tangentially involving Native people. Some Wampanoags now acknowledge their collective mourning in other family and community gatherings. Darius Coombs of Mashpee says that some of his tribespeople set aside Thanksgiving to recognize those they've lost. Others also address *what* they've lost, because, as Aquinnah's Jonathan Perry explains, so much of the prosperity for which other Americans are thankful came at Native people's expense. This feeling of victimhood is especially poignant given that Wampanoag communities still suffer high levels of poverty, with all its associated ills, while living in the shadow of sometimes garish wealth. Wampanoag people in southeastern New England are faced daily with the sight of outsiders' extravagant coastal estates, occupied for only six or eight weeks in summer, built atop places where the ancestors are buried and where some of them fished, hunted, and gathered within memory. The image sickens and depresses. And yet there is no escaping it or the sense that other Americans revel in it. Around the time of Thanksgiving, one cannot drive past neighbors' lawns or go to the store without confronting happy Pilgrim and Indian decorations, or turn on the television, radio, or computer without being bombarded with Pilgrim and Indian themes. The symbols of inequity, ingratitude, and injustice that time of year are relentless, even if the National Football League's Washington Redskins club isn't playing in one of the televised holiday games.[1]

At the same time, some Wampanoag people take pride in the attention their people receive during the Thanksgiving season and see it as an opportunity to educate the general public. As Mashpee's Bethia Washington puts it, "We always get called in the month of November . . . The positive thing about this time of year is that we are thought of. That opens the door to greater learning and understanding." She is disappointed, though, that "then we're not here the rest of the year." Some of the Wampanoag staff at the Plimoth Plantation living history museum paint their faces black in mourning the week of Thanksgiving to open conversations with museum patrons who expect patriotic themes. Having observed these interactions firsthand, I'm struck by the patience, thoughtfulness, and sense of responsibility of the Wampanoag interpreters, who say that change comes one mind at a time.[2]

The Mashpee Wampanoag tribal chairman Cedric Cromwell captured these ambiguities effectively in a 2012 address. He remarked, "The Thanksgiving holiday is a complicated day for our people. We are forever intertwined with the American Thanksgiving myth, however inaccurate it may be. Some of our people choose to observe this day as a Day of Mourning. Some choose to celebrate in a thoroughly American way. Many choose a different path, spending the day with family and friends but acknowledging our unique history and connection to this day." The response of Aquinnah's Linda Coombs to the question of how Wampanoags observe Thanksgiving is "you could talk to ten people and get ten different answers." Yet nearly all of them, she emphasizes, believe "that the whole concept of Thanksgiving as it's generally seen or practiced in this country is kind of like a superficial layer over what's really on the ground." In other words, it is a sugarcoating of the past and present abuses of Native people by European colonists and their successors.[3]

A growing, critical mass of progressive educators have begun doing away with Pilgrim pageants and depictions of indigenous people as relics of the past. Instead, their students reflect on the history of colonialism and the modern issues confronting Native America, particularly the Wampanoags. The Southern Poverty Law Center, one of the nation's leading institutions for advancing tolerance and justice for the most vulnerable members of American society, has rightly criticized traditional grade-school celebrations of Thanksgiving as damaging to Native and non-Native students alike. It contends that festive Pilgrim and Indian imagery, and Thanksgiving pageant depictions of friendly Indians consenting to colonialism, "contributes to the indoctrination of American youth into a false narrative that relegates indigenous peoples to the past and thus turns real human beings into costumes for a few days a year. It's not just bad pedagogy; it's socially irresponsible ... Teaching about Thanksgiving in a socially responsible way means that educators accept the ethical obligation to provide students with accurate information and to reject traditions that sustain harmful stereotypes about indigenous people." In recent years, educators have developed numerous resources to heed this call, including lesson plans that treat the evolution of American Thanksgiving celebration as an object of study itself, and that link the events of the 1620s to the ongoing struggles of the Wampanoags and other Native peoples to defend and regain their land, sovereignty, and cultural self-determination.[4]

Nevertheless, there is still a very long way to go. In my college courses, half or more of the students (largely ages eighteen to twenty-two) still report having performed in Thanksgiving pageants as children. I've come across one reason why during the fifteen years that I've been contributing to workshops to help primary and secondary school social studies teachers enhance their content. Those instructors have widely complained that they feel woefully underprepared to address Native American history even as they recognize its glaring absence in their curricula. At the same time, the statewide standardized tests that largely dictate their lessons require little knowledge of the Native American past. So instead of incorporating indigenous people into American history writ large and using their experiences to challenge the dominant narratives, social studies teachers commonly set aside a week or two in November to stumble through the Pilgrim-Wampanoag story and then drop Indians from consideration.

These educators come from every corner of the United States: red states and blue states; urban, rural, and suburban. It's the same set of issues practically everywhere.

Fixing this problem in the schools, never mind society as a whole, requires political action at several different levels. Parents need to withhold their children from Thanksgiving pageants if the teachers insist on putting on these performances despite all the evidence of the damage it causes. Teachers have to pressure their book-purchasing committees for texts that incorporate Native actors more robustly and accurately. They must insist on maps that not only depict Native people but place them in the right place at the right time, as opposed to textbook illustrations that portray America as an empty continent claimed by two or three imperial powers, waiting for the United States to absorb it as if by divine will. Educators of every level must call on state-level test-making agencies to design questions reflecting what we know to have been true: that Native people had a dynamic history of thousands of years before the arrival of Europeans; that they remained numerous and powerful well into the mid- to late nineteenth century; and that their experiences from then until now provide a powerful corrective lens to the self-congratulatory theme of progress that has so often driven American history telling.

Wampanoag people have offered up many thoughtful ideas about what such reforms might look like in American accounts of the First Thanksgiving. There is nearly unanimous opinion that the pageants must go. "As Native Americans," writes Mashpee's Paula Peters, "we endure regular acts of cultural degradation from children dressed up for Halloween in outfits that are a reflection of our traditional regalia, to team mascots of sports fans wearing feathers and face paint mocking ancient spiritual rites and traditions." It's bad enough when such insults take place out in public. It's downright intolerable in an educational setting like school. Mashpee's

Ramona Peters counsels that teachers of young children should dispense with the Thanksgiving myth and focus more on the sentiment of being thankful. "Gratitude is the most powerful Thanksgiving story, from my perspective as a Wampanoag," she emphasizes. "When young children grasp gratitude in a real way, beyond ritual, our country will be greater." Her recommendation is to spare young students not only the mythmaking but also the disturbing history of epidemics, betrayal, and war. That is best left until the upper grades, when students are more mature. She does not advocate getting rid of the holiday—not at all. She contends that "we can all be proud that our country has a national holiday centered upon simply being thankful." She just does not want it attached to damaging misrepresentations of her people and inaccurate, sanitized history.[5]

Among the most common Wampanoag hopes is for the general public to acknowledge their existence today, outside the November "National Native American Heritage Month" observed since 1990, instead of assuming that they somehow disappeared shortly after the First Thanksgiving. "We don't count in the everyday life of America," asserts Linda Coombs, "and I think that perception has to change." When Mashpee held its own "thanks giving" in December 2016, tribal citizens and friends paid gratitude to the Creator that "we are still here," with Chairman Cromwell reminding everyone that "our people have remained on this land for generations and will continue to thrive and prosper for many more."[6] What if, instead of propagating a linear history that associates American progress with Indian extinction, our Thanksgiving lessons taught a circular history in which the ancient indigenous past fed into the age of encounter and colonialism and in turn led to the modern decolonization efforts of the Wampanoags and other Native people? Changes of this sort would go a long way to creating a more inclusive, truthful, and healing holiday. "I can actually envision a day when a 'National Day of Mourning' will no longer be necessary," muses Paula Peters, "as acknowledgement of our history from a balanced perspective will bring closure to old wounds." She delivered these thoughts in 2009 to a surprisingly receptive audience of Massachusetts *Mayflower* descendants that tends to be guarded about the reputation of its ancestors. If that group can receive her words constructively, the rest of us can, too.[7]

Even the town of Plymouth, whose tourist industry depends on tying an uplifting Pilgrim story to the greatness of the United States, has begun to come around, albeit grudgingly and incrementally. Native people have given it little choice. In 1997 Plymouth police pepper-sprayed a crowd of National Day of Mourning protestors and roughly arrested twenty-five of them for marching without a permit (something the town had never required of them) and unlawful gathering. The police department's explanation was that it was trying to avoid trouble of the sort that occurred the previous year when Indian marchers disrupted the town's Pilgrim Progress procession by colonial descendants in period costume. Instead, the officers' overreaction drew a lawsuit by the United American Indians of New England, which organizes the National Day of Mourning, charging police brutality, and threats of an economic boycott of the town. Facing a potentially expensive public relations disaster, Plymouth agreed to a settlement, which included paying for and displaying two new plaques demanded by the protestors. One, mounted on Cole's Hill near the Massasoit statue, commemorates the National Day of Mourning. It acknowledges that for many Indians "Thanksgiving Day is a reminder of the genocide of millions of their people, the theft of their lands, and the relentless assault on their cultures. Participants in the National Day of Mourning honor Native ancestors and the struggle of Native peoples to survive today." A second plaque, in Post Office Square, is dedicated to Metacomet (King Philip), son of Ousamequin. It addresses how he "called on Native people to unite to defend their homelands against encroachment," only to go down to defeat to the English, who killed him, mutilated his body, displayed his severed body parts, and sold his wife and son into slavery. Without question, Plymouth's celebratory attractions like the Pilgrim Hall Museum, the *Mayflower II* replica, and Plymouth Rock dwarf these testimonials to the darkness of colonialism. Yet the plaques are an unprecedented step toward balancing the historical ledger. The extent to which Plymouth and the state of Massachusetts includes Native voices and perspectives in the 2020 quadricentennial events marking Plymouth colony's founding will be telling of whether this episode was part of a revisionist trend or a sidebar to the same old story. As the indigenous elder Tall

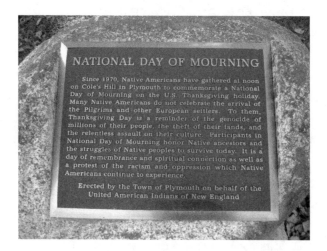

National Day of Mourning Plaque. Photograph by Melissa Doroquez.

A year after the 1997 National Day of Mourning descended into a melee in which Plymouth police arrested twenty-five protestors only to face accusations of brutality from the United American Indians of New England, the two sides reached a settlement. The town of Plymouth dropped all charges, paid the UAINE's legal charges, donated money to Indian education programs, and installed the above and opposite plaques. In exchange, the UAINE withdrew the threat to sue for damages. The content of the plaques says it all.

Metacomet (King Philip) Plaque. Photograph by Bill Coughlin.

Oak counsels, Thanksgiving and the anniversary of the Pilgrims' landing should be times for introspection and reflection rather than celebration.[8]

The current American struggle with white nationalism is not just a moment in time. It is the product of centuries of political, social, cultural, and economic developments that have convinced a critical mass of white Christians that the country has always belonged to them and always should. The myth of Thanksgiving is one of the many buttresses of that ideology. That myth is not about who we were but how past generations wanted us to be. It is not true. The truth exposes the traditional tale of the First Thanksgiving as a myth rather than history, and so let us declare it dead except as a subject for the study of nineteenth- and twentieth-century American culture. What we replace it with will tell future Americans about how we envision ourselves and the path of our society. We should think wisely and compassionately about our choice, together.

ACKNOWLEDGMENTS

My greatest debt is to Wampanoag people who have shared their stories, expertise, and criticism to make this a better book. I floated my early ideas for this project by a generous Wampanoag audience at the Aquinnah Cultural Center run by Linda Coombs. Afterward, old friend Tobias Vanderhoop offered sage advice on how to go about community outreach on this charged topic. Later, Darius Coombs granted me permission to shadow the Native staff members at the Wampanoag Homesite at Plimoth Plantation as they interacted with visitors during the week of Thanksgiving. I've also profited from conversations and critiques of this manuscript by Ramona Peters and Jonathan Perry. Thank you all. I realize that this is not the book you would have written, or that future Wampanoag historians will write, but I hope that you'll see a good-faith effort to rethink some of the colonialist assumptions and language that slipped into earlier drafts.

Two semesters' worth of students in my Pilgrims and Indians seminar at George Washington University have served as captive audiences for the ideas of this book, and one class suffered through an early draft. They deserve to be acknowledged individually for contributing to this work in ways great and small. My gratitude to Hail Alhashem, Sarah Breault, Brett Cassidy, Andrew Cohen, Sarah Coleman, Geoffrey Commons, Ronni Farid, Lauren Forrer, Sam Indelicato, Vijay Ishwar, Elise Keim, Aidan Kolenik, Adam Liberman, Keegan Mullen, Ben Raffel, Deanna Reyes-Guerra, Jack

SaFranko, Sam Santini, Caitlin Shaffer, Matthew Shine, Libby Silber, Miles Stepleton, Nathaniel Weaver, and Matthew West.

In turning this project from an idea to a proposal and then finding a publisher, I've been most fortunate to have Lisa Adams of the Garamond Agency representing me. Since then, the team at Bloomsbury has been more patient with me than one could hope and every bit as professional as one would wish. Special thanks to my editor, Anton Mueller, for talking through my ideas at each critical stage, and to Morgan Jones and Barbara Darko for polishing my prose, drafting and redrafting maps, and even helping to come up with a title.

Several scholarly institutions provided resources and forums to develop this book. My home academic institution, George Washington University, offered research grants that funded visits to archives, historical sites, museums, and tribal knowledge keepers. Michael Zuckerman's salon once again served as a sounding board for my initial ideas and a critical source of new directions. Audiences at Davidson College and the Newberry Library graciously heard lecture versions of this book and responded with the right mix of encouragement and pointed feedback.

Friends and family came through once again. Inestimable colleagues Linford Fisher, Michael Oberg, and Daniel Richter read full drafts and suggested more helpful revisions than I had any right to expect. Oberg even transcribed my text photos of his hand-written marginalia. William Carter's wisdom and moral clarity guided this project through one trouble spot after another. Holly Herbster and Charlotte Taylor, both archaeologists, kept me informed of findings from the trenches. My good chum and fellow historian Drew Lipman, and the linguists Ives Goddard and the late, great Roy Wright, helped me work through some issues of fact and interpretation. I remain responsible for all errors and shortcomings in the pages that follow.

My parents, Richard and Julia Silverman, were, as always, unflaggingly supportive during the writing of this book, as they have been throughout my career. They even took on the duty of preparing Thanksgiving dinner in 2017 so I could spend the day in Plymouth on research.

My wife and fellow historian, Julie Fisher, has lovingly listened, read, critiqued, and then repeated the process again, all the while enriching this work with her own research and outreach to descendant communities. I'm a lucky man to have her in my life, and this book is better because of her.

My daughters, Aquinnah and Bela Silverman, have been largely patient as I've dragged them to historical sites and drowned them with historical anecdotes. They've grown into wonderful young women while I've been writing this book. Throughout that time, I've teased them that they would get the dedication only if they committed to reading the whole thing, and even then that it might go to our dog, Jake, depending on their behavior and his. The dog has been a good boy, but this time, at least, he will have to wait.

GLOSSARY OF KEY INDIAN PEOPLE AND PLACES

Abenakis: Algonquian-speaking peoples of southern Maine and northern New England. Part of the wider Wabanaki people.

Acushnet: Wampanoag community in the neighborhood of modern New Bedford, MA.

Aquinnah: Also known as Gay Head. A Wampanoag community on a peninsula on the southwest of Martha's Vineyard. Became the official name of the town of Gay Head in 1997. Home of the federally recognized Wampanoag Tribe of Gay Head/ Aquinnah.

Aspinet: Sachem of Nauset on eastern Cape Cod in the 1620s.

Assawompset Pond: Body of water near the head of the Taunton River, to which it is connected by the Nemasket River. Within the Nemasket sachemship (modern Middleboro and Lakeville). Site of the death of the linguist/scribe John Sassamon.

Awashonks: Sunksquaw of Sakonnet in 1670s and 1680s. Wife of Wawweeyowitt. Mother of Samponock and Mamaneway.

Canacum: Sachem of Manomet, just south of Plymouth, in the 1620s.

Canonicus: Sachem of the Narragansetts until his death as an old man in 1647. Uncle of Miantonomo. Father of Mixano.

Cassacinamon, Robin: Sachem of the Western Pequots of Nameag, Noank, and Mashantucket from the 1640s until his death in 1692.

Chappaquiddick: A Wampanoag sachemship on easternmost Martha's Vineyard.

Cheepi: The Wampanoag god of the dead. Associated with the color black, underwater places, the moon, night, cold, the horned winged serpent, and panthers. Source of the power for pawwaws (shamans) and pnieseosok (counselor-warriors).

Christiantown: A praying town and then reservation in the sachemship of Takemmy (now West Tisbury) on Martha's Vineyard.

Corbitant: Sachem of Pocasset (modern Tiverton, RI) during the 1620s. Father of Weetamoo and Wootonekanuske.

Coweset: Tribute-paying community of the Narragansetts on the west side of Narragansett Bay.

Cummaquid: A Wampanoag community of Cape Cod, on the site of modern Barnstable Harbor, under the sachem Iyanough.

Epenow: Wampanoag from Martha's Vineyard, taken captive by Edward Harlow in 1611. Returns home in 1614. Leads attack on Thomas Dermer and crew in 1619. One of several Wampanoags to sign a treaty with Plymouth in 1621.

Gay Head: Also known as Aquinnah. A Wampanoag community on a peninsula on the southwest of Martha's Vineyard. Becomes the official name of that community when Massachusetts incorporated it as a town in 1870, until switching back to Aquinnah in 1997.

Haudenosaunees: People of the Longhouse. Also known as the Iroquois League. A five-nation confederacy including the Mohawks, Oneidas, Onondagas, Cayugas, and Senecas. Featured prominently in southern New England as a military force and market for wampum beads produced on the coast.

Hobbamock: Another name for Cheepi. Also the name for a Wampanoag pniese who assisted Plymouth as an interpreter and counselor.

Iroquois League: See Haudenosaunees.

Iyanough: Sachem of Cummaquid and Mattakeesett (Barnstable and Hyannis) on Cape Cod during the 1620s.

Kiehtan: Also known as Cautantowwit. Wampanoag, humanlike spirit associated with the sun, corn, and the land of the afterlife in the Southwest.

Mamaneway: Son of Awashonks.

Manisses: The Indians of Block Island. Tribute payers to the Narragansetts. Implicated in the murder of John Oldham in 1636. Courted by Pumetacom in the late 1660s.

Manomet: A Wampanoag sachemship just south of Plymouth.

Mashpee: A Wampanoag community on Cape Cod. Designated a praying town in 1665. Incorporated by Massachusetts as a town in 1870. Home of the federally recognized Mashpee Wampanoag Tribe.

Massachusett Indians: A people centered on Massachusetts Bay with close cultural and political connections to the Wampanoags. Decimated by the epidemics of 1616–19, 1622, and 1633. Residents of several of the praying towns associated the with missionary John Eliot.

Massasoit: The chiefly title of Ousamequin.

Matawauôg: The word for warriors in the Narragansett language, a close relative of the Wôpanâak (or Wampanoag) language.

Mattapoisett: A peninsula just east of Montaup. Sometime residence of Corbitant, sachem of Pocasset.

Metacom: The short name of Pumetacom, son of Ousamequin and paramount sachem of the Wampanoags.

Mi'kmaq: Native people of Nova Scotia. Part of the broader Wabanaki people.

Mishoon: Dugout canoe.

Mittark: Sachem of Aquinnah during the mid- to late seventeenth century.

Mohawks: One of the five nations of the Huadenosaunees (or Iroquois League). Located on the Mohawk River, just west of the Hudson River and modern-day

Albany. Figured prominently in southern New England as a military force and market for wampum beads produced on the coast.

Mohegans: A tribe or paramount sachemship in what is now southeastern Connecticut. Led in the seventeenth century by the sachem Uncas. Allies of the English in the Pequot War and King Philip's War. Rivals of the Narragansetts. Federally recognized today with a reservation in Uncasville, CT.

Monomoyick: Wampanoag sachemship on southeast Cape Cod on the site of modern Chatham.

Montaup: Pumetacom's village after which the Mount Hope peninsula is named. On the site of the modern town of Bristol, RI.

Mooanum: Wamsutta's earlier name.

Moshup: An ancient giant featured in the lore of the Vineyard Wampanoags.

Namumpum: See Weetamoo.

Narragansetts: A tribe or paramount sachemship centered on the west side of Narragansett Bay. Led in the early seventeenth century by the sachems Canonicus and Miantonomo. Collected tribute from communities stretching from Long Island in the south to Nipmuc country in the north. Contended with the Wampanoags during the early to mid-seventeenth century. Allies of the Wampanoags during King Philip's War. Federally recognized today with a reservation in Charlestown, RI.

Nauset: Wampanoag sachemship on eastern Cape Cod on the site of the modern town of Eastham.

Nemasket: Wampanoag community twelve miles west of Plymouth.

Nipmucs: Native people of what is now known as central Massachusetts. Particular communities paid tribute to the Mohegans, Narragansetts, or Wampanoags.

Ousamequin: Wampanoag name meaning "yellow feather." Born probably in 1590s. Sachem of Pokanoket and paramount sachem of the Wampanoags. Father of Wamsutta (or Alexander) and Pumetacom (or Philip). Ally of Plymouth colony. Dies in 1661.

Pamantaquash: Sachem of Assawompset. Predecessor of Tispaquin.

Patuxet: A Wampanoag community on the site where the English later built Plymouth town. Home of Tisquantum. Decimated by the epidemic of 1616–19.

Pawtuxet: Native community on the west side of Narragansett Bay that paid tribute to the Narragansett tribe. Courted by Pumetacom in late 1660s. Located between the English towns on Warwick and Providence. Led by the sachem Socononoco.

Pequots: A tribe or paramount sachemship from what is now southeastern Connecticut. Shattered by the English and their Native allies in the Pequot War of 1636–37. Reconsolidated in the mid-seventeenth century under the sachem Robin Cassacinamon. Allies of the English in King Philip's War. Western Pequots are federally recognized today with a reservation in Mashantucket, CT.

Pocasset: Wampanoag sachemship on east side of Narragansett Bay (modern Tiverton, RI) under sachem Corbitant and then sunksquaw Weetamoo.

Pokanoket: Name of the sachemship led by Ousamequin and then his sons, Wamsutta and Pumetacom. Sometimes used as the name for the entire Wampanoag tribe. Included territory now within the modern towns of Bristol, Warren, and Barrington, RI, and Seekonk, Swansea, and Rehoboth, MA.

Pomham: Sachem of Shawomet (modern-day Warwick, RI) and a tributary of the Narragansetts.

Pumetacom: Also known as Metacom, Metacomet, Philip, and King Philip. Son of Ousamequin, brother of Wamsutta, and husband of Wootonekanuske. Sachem of Pokanoket and paramount sachem of the Wampanoags. Led his people to war in 1675–76.

Quadaquina: Brother of Ousamequin.

Quaiapen: Narragansett sunksquaw. Also known as Matantuck, Magnus, and the "Old Queen." Sister of Ninigret. Wife of Mixano. Mother of Scuttup. Killed by English-Indian forces on July 2, 1676.

Quantisset: A Nipmuc community of the Quinebaug River valley.

Quinabaag: A Nipmuc community of the Quinebaug River valley.

Socononoco: Sachem of Pawtuxet and a tributary to the Narragansetts.

Sakonnet: Sachemship at the southeast tip of Narragansett Bay. Led by the sunksquaw Awashonks in the 1670s and 1680s.

Samoset: A Maine Wabanaki from around Boothbay Harbor and Monhegan Island. Spoke some English by virtue of his interactions with fisherman and possibly captivity in Europe. Brokered the first diplomacy between the Wampanoags and the English of Plymouth.

Samponock: Son of Awashonks and Wawweeyowitt.

Sassamon, John: Harvard-trained interpreter, scribe, and preacher. Father of Assaweta (Betty). Worked for Wamsutta and Pumetacom in the 1660s, then preached at Nemasket and Assawompset. The trial over his supposed murder sparked King Philip's War.

Satucket: Wampanoag sachemship on Cape Cod on the site of modern Brewster.

Seeknout: Sachem of Chappaquiddick in the mid-seventeenth century.

Sengekontacket: A Wampanoag sachemship in what is now the town of Oak Bluffs on Martha's Vineyard.

Shawomet: Native community of what is now Warwick, RI. Tributary to the Narragansetts. Courted by Pumetacom in the late 1660s.

Sowams: Ousamequin's home village within the sachemship of Pokanoket. Located on the site of modern Barrington, RI.

Squanto: See Tisquantum.

Takemmy: A Wampanoag sachemship in what is now the town of Tisbury on Martha's Vineyard.

Tatacomancaah: Son of Awashonks of Sakonnet.

Taunton River: Or Titicut River. The main inland waterway of the Wampanoag people, running from just west of Plymouth to Pokanoket on Narragansett Bay.

Tispaquin: Also known as the "Black Sachem." Sachem of Assawompset. Father of William Tispaquin.

Tisquantum: Patuxet Wampanoag taken captive in 1614 by Thomas Hunt. Traveled to Spain, England, and Newfoundland. Returned to Wampanoag country in 1619. Served as interpreter and political go-between for Wampanoags and Plymouth until his death in 1622.

Titicut: A mixed Wampanoag-Massachusett Indian community on the upper Taunton River under the sachems Chickataubut and Josias Wampatuck.

Tokamahamon: A Wampanoag appointed by Ousamequin in 1621 to be a "special friend" to Plymouth.

Wabanakis: Like the term *Wampanoag*, means "People of the Dawnland" or "Easterners." Refers to various Native people of what is now Maine and the southern Canadian Maritimes, including Abenakis, Maliseets, Mi'kmaq, Penobscots, and Passamaquoddies.

Wamsutta: Also known as Mooanum and Alexander. Son of Ousamequin. Brother of Pumetacom. Husband of Namumpum. Succeeded father as Wampanoag paramount sachem in 1661. Dies in 1662 from what some Wampanoags suspected was English poisoning.

Wawweeyowitt: Husband of Awashonks.

Weetamoo: Also known as Namumpum. Daughter of Corbitant. Sunksquaw of Pocasset. Wife of Wamsutta, Quiquequanchett, Petonowowet, and Quinapin. Prominent Wampanoag leader during King Philip's War. Found dead on August 6, 1676.

Wootonekanuske: Daughter of Corbitant. Sister of Weetamoo. Wife of Pumetacom. Captured and probably sold into slavery by the English in King Philip's War.

ABBREVIATIONS

AAS
American Antiquarian Society, Worcester, MA.

CONQUESTS AND TRIUMPHS
Matthew Mayhew, *The Conquests and Triumphs of Grace: Being a Brief Narrative of the Success which the Gospel hath had among the Indians of Martha's Vineyard (and the Places adjacent) in New-England.* London, 1695.

CPGNE
Corporation for the Propagation of the Gospel in New England, Records, New England Historic Genealogical Society, Boston, MA.

DCCR
Dukes County Court Records, Office of the Clerk of Courts, Dukes County Courthouse, Edgartown, MA.

DCD
Dukes County Deeds, Dukes County Registry of Deeds, Dukes County Courthouse, Edgartown, MA.

DCGSP
Dukes County General Sessions of the Peace, Records, Office of the Clerk of Courts, Dukes County Courthouse, Edgartown, MA.

EARLE REPORT
John Milton Earle, *Report to the Governor and Council, Concerning the Indians of the Commonwealth, Under the Act of April 6, 1859.* Senate Document No. 96. Boston, MA, 1861.

ELIOT TRACTS
Michael P. Clark, ed., *The Eliot Tracts: With Letters from John Eliot to Thomas Thorowgood and Richard Baxter.* Westport, CT, 2003.

GAY HEAD REPORT
Richard L. Pease, *Report of the Commissioner Appointed to Complete the Examination and Determination of All Questions of Title to Land, and of all Boundary Lines between the Individual Owners, at Gay Head, on the Island of Martha's Vineyard.* Boston, MA, 1871.

GIP
Guardians of Indian Plantations, Records, Massachusetts State Archives, Boston, MA.

INDIAN CONVERTS
Laura Arnold Leibman, ed., *Experience Mayhew's Indian Converts: A Cultural Edition.* Amherst, MA, 2008.

MA ARCHIVES
Massachusetts Archives Series, Massachusetts State Archives, Boston, MA.

MHS
Massachusetts Historical Society, Boston, MA.

MHSC
Massachusetts Historical Society, *Collections.*

NCD
Nantucket County, Deeds, Registry of Deeds, Town and County Building, Nantucket, MA.

NCR
Nantucket County, Records, Registry of Deeds, Town and County Building, Nantucket, MA.

NE CO. MSS.
New England Company, Records, Guildhall Library, Corporation of London.

NEHGR
New England Historic Genealogical Register.

NEHGS
New England Historic Genealogical Society, Boston, MA.

NEQ
New England Quarterly.

PLP
Passed Legislation Packets, Massachusetts State Archives, Boston, MA.

PLYMOUTH RECORDS
Nathaniel B. Shurtleff and David Pulsifer, eds., *Records of the Colony of New Plymouth*, 12 vols. Boston, MA, 1855.

REPORT OF THE COMMISSIONERS
F. W. Bird, Whiting Griswold, and Cyrus Weekes, *Report of the Commissioners Relating to the Condition of the Indians*. Massachusetts House Document No. 46. Boston, MA, 1849.

RHODE ISLAND RECORDS
John R. Bartlett, ed., *Records of the Colony of Rhode Island and Providence Plantations in New England*, 10 vols. Providence, RI, 1856–65.

ULRIA
Unpassed Legislation Relating to Indian Affairs, Massachusetts State Archives, Boston, MA.

UNITED COLONIES RECORDS
Acts of the Commissioners of the United Colonies of New England. Vols. 9 and 10 of *Plymouth Records*.

WILLIAMS CORRESPONDENCE
Glenn La Fantasie, ed., *The Correspondence of Roger Williams*, 2 vols. Hanover, NH, 1988.

WINSLOW, *GOOD NEWS*
Kelly Wisecup, ed., *"Good News from New England" by Edward Winslow: A Scholarly Edition*. Amherst, MA, 2014.

WMQ
William and Mary Quarterly, 3rd series.

YALE INDIAN PAPERS
https://yipp.yale.edu/

NOTES

INTRODUCTION: MOURNING IN AMERICA

1   Gloria Levitas, "No Boundary Is a Boundary: Conflict and Change in a New England Indian Community" (PhD diss., Rutgers University, 1980); David J. Silverman, *Faith and Boundaries: Colonists, Christianity, and Community among the Wampanoag Indians of Martha's Vineyard, 1600–1871* (New York: Cambridge Univ. Press, 2005); Kevin A. McBride and Suzanne G. Cherau, "Gay Head (Aquinnah) Wampanoag Community Structure and Land Use Patterns," *Northeast Anthropology* 51 (1996): 13–39; William A. Starna, "'We'll All be Together Again': The Federal Acknowledgement of the Wampanoag Tribe of Gay Head," *Northeast Anthropology* 51 (1996): 3–12; Christine Tracey Gabrowski, "Coiled Intentions: Federal Acknowledgement Policy and the Gay Head Wampanoags" (PhD diss., City University of New York, 1994); Ann Marie Plane and Gregory Button, "The Massachusetts Indian Enfranchisement Act: Ethnic Contest in Historical Context, 1849–1869," *Ethnohistory* 40, no. 4 (1993): 587–618.

2   Frank James, "National Day of Mourning," in Siobhan Senier, ed., *Dawnland Voices: An Anthology of Indigenous Writing from New England* (Lincoln: Univ. of Nebraska, 2014), 455.

3   A profile of James can be found in "Wamsutta Frank James Obituary," *Boston Globe*, February 23, 2001. On the Federated Eastern Indian League, see Earl H. Mills, *Talking with the Elders of Mashpee: Memories of Earl H. Mills, Sr.* (Mashpee, MA: self-pub., 2012), 91–93.

4   James W. Baker, *Thanksgiving: The Biography of an American Holiday* (Lebanon: Univ. of New Hampshire Press, 2009), 14–30.

5   Baker, 13 ("the first Thanksgiving").

6   Baker, 62–77; Anne Blue Wills, "Pilgrims and Progress: How Magazines Made Thanksgiving," *Church History* 72, no. 1 (2003): 138–58.

7   Baker, *Thanksgiving*, 98–114; Nina Baym, "Early Histories of American Literature: A Chapter in the Institution of New England," *American Literary History* 1, no. 3 (1989): 459–88; Christine Arnold-Lourie, "Baby Pilgrims, Sturdy Forefathers, and One Hundred Percent Americanism: The Mayflower Tercentenary of 1920," *Massachusetts Historical Review* 17 (December 2015): 35–66; Matthew Frye Jacobson,

Barbarian Virtues: The United States Encounters Foreign Peoples at Home and Abroad, 1876–1917 (New York: Hill and Wang, 2000).

8   William Bradford, *Of Plymouth Plantation*, ed. Chauncey Ford, 2 vols. (Boston: Massachusetts Historical Society, 1912), 1:191.

9   James Deetz and Patricia Scott Deetz, *The Times of Their Lives: Life, Love, and Death in Plymouth Colony* (New York: W. H. Freeman, 2000), 1–29; Jean M. O'Brien, *Firsting and Lasting: Writing Indians Out of Existence in New England* (Minneapolis: Univ. of Minnesota Press, 2010), 20.

10   Baker, *Thanksgiving*, 115–28.

11   Plimoth Plantation Wampanoag Homesite staff member, in-person conversation with author, November 22, 2017, Plymouth, MA.

12   Experiences of this sort are treated in Dawn Dove, "Alienation of Indigenous Children in the Public School System," in Senier, *Dawnland Voices*, 523–25; Dennis Zotigh, "Do Indians Americans Celebrate Thanksgiving?" Natural Museum of the American Indian (blog), http://blog.nmai.si.edu/main/2013/11/do-indians-celebrate-thanksgiving.html (accessed 01/31/2019); "Wampanoag Divided over Whether to Join Plymouth Thanksgiving Festivities," Aljazeera America, http://america.aljazeera.com/articles/2014/11/27/wampanoag-dividedoverwhethertojoinplymoutthanksgivingfestivitie.html (accessed 01/31/2019); Tony Chamberlain, "Vanishing Indians," *Boston Globe*, October 5, 1975. See also the Southern Poverty Law Center's "Teaching Tolerance" guidelines on Thanksgiving in the classroom: https://www.tolerance.org/magazine/teaching-thanksgiving-in-a-socially-responsible-way (accessed 01/31/2019).

13   "Indian Charges Censorship, Spurns Orator's Role," *Boston Globe*, September 24, 1970.

14   Daniel M. Cobb, *Native Activism in Cold War America: The Struggle for Sovereignty* (Lawrence: Univ. of Kansas, 2008); Troy R. Johnson, *The Occupation of Alcatraz Island: Indian Self-Determination and the Rise of Indian Activism* (Champaign: Univ. of Illinois Press, 1996); Paul Chaat Smith and Robert Allen Warrior, *Like a Hurricane: The Indian Movement from Alcatraz to Wounded Knee* (New York: The New Press, 1996), esp. 171–268; Peter Matthiessen, *In the Spirit of Crazy Horse*, new ed. (New York: Viking, 1991); Stephen Cornell, *The Return of the Native: American Indian Political Resurgence* (New York: Oxford Univ. Press, 1988); and Joane Nagel, *American Indian Ethnic Renewal: Red Power and the Resurgence of Identity and Culture* (New York: Oxford Univ. Press, 1996).

15   O'Brien, *Firsting and Lasting*, 183.

16   James, "National Day of Mourning," 455.

17   James, 456.

18   James, 456.

19   James, 457–58.

20   "Mourning Indians Dump Sand on Plymouth Rock," *New York Times*, November 27, 1970 ("red"; "reclaim").

21 "Indians Take Over *Mayflower II*: Stage Plymouth Protest," *Boston Globe*, November 27, 1970; "Mourning Indians Dump Sand on Plymouth Rock," *New York Times*, November 27, 1970; Russell Means and Marvin Wolf, *Where White Men Fear to Tread: The Autobiography of Russell Means* (New York: St. Martin's Griffin, 1995), 175–78.

22 See the discussion of the National Day of Mourning on the website of James's organization, United American Indians of New England: www.uaine.org.

23 Philip J. Deloria, "Historiography," in Deloria and Neal Salisbury, eds., *A Companion to American Indian History* (Malden, MA: Wiley-Blackwell, 2002), 6–24; Ned Blackhawk, "American Indians and the Study of U.S. History," in Eric Foner and Lisa McGirr, eds., *American History Now* (Philadelphia: Temple Univ. Press, 2011), 378–401; Susan Sleeper-Smith et al., eds., *Why You Can't Teach United States History without American Indians* (Chapel Hill: Univ. of North Carolina Press, 2015); James H. Merrell, "Second Thoughts on Colonial Historians and American Indians," *WMQ* 69, no. 3 (2012): 451–512; Patricia Galloway, "How Deep Is (Ethno-)History? Archives, Written History, Oral Tradition," in *Practicing Ethnohistory: Mining Archives, Hearing Testimony, Constructing Narrative* (Lincoln: Univ. of Nebraska Press, 2006), 1–33.

24 Kevin Bruyneel, *The Third Space of Sovereignty: The Postcolonial Politics of U.S.-Indigenous Relations* (Minneapolis: Univ. of Minnesota Press, 2007).

CHAPTER 1: THE WAMPANOAGS' OLD WORLD

1 Bradford, *Of Plymouth Plantation*, 1:156 ("hideous"); *Mourt's Relation: A Journal of the Pilgrims at Plymouth*, ed. Dwight B. Heath (Bedford, MA: Applewood Books, 1963), 21 ("plain ground"), 22 ("basket").

2 *Mourt's Relation*, 34 ("burying place").

3 *Mourt's Relation*, 23 (trap), 27 ("path"), and generally 18–40; Bradford, *Of Plymouth Plantation*, 1:162–71.

4 *Mourt's Relation*, 55–57 ("chain" on 57); Bradford, *Of Plymouth Plantation*, 1:200–203. On the meaning of "Massasoit," I am drawing on the insights of Jessie Little Doe Baird, a Wampanoag linguist.

5 Winslow, *Good News*, 107 ("travels"); Katherine Grandjean, *American Passage: The Communications Frontier in Early New England* (Cambridge, MA: Harvard Univ. Press, 2015), 3–4. On the storied landscape, see Russell G. Handsman, "Landscapes of Memory in Wampanoag Country—and the Monuments upon Them," in Patricia E. Rubertone, ed., *Archaeologies of Placemaking: Monuments, Memories, and Engagement in Native North America* (Walnut Creek, CA: Left Coast Press, 2008), 161–94; Eva L. Butler, "The Brush or Stone Memorial Heaps of Southern New England," *Bulletin of the Archeological Society of Connecticut* 19 (April 1946): 2–12; Stephen Jett, "Cairn and Brush Travel Shrines in the United States Northeast and Southeast," *Northeast Anthropology* 48 (Fall 1994): 61–67; Christine M. DeLucia, *The Memory Lands: King Philip's War and the Place of Violence in the Northeast* (New Haven, CT: Yale Univ. Press, 2018), 16.

446   **NOTES TO PAGES 27–32**

6*Mourt's Relation*, 60–65 ("horse" on 64). On pipe smoking, see Isaack de Rasieres to Samuel Blommaert, ca. 1628, in Sydney V. James, ed., *Three Visitors to Early Plymouth* (Bedford, MA: Applewood Books, 1997), 73.

7*Mourt's Relation*, 65–68 ("great speech" on 66); Winslow, *Good News*, 102–3 ("religion"), 107 ("resort"). On English views of Indian leaders, see Karen Ordahl Kupperman, *Indians and English: Facing Off in Early America* (Ithaca, NY: Cornell Univ. Press, 2000), 90–103. On the "cant of conquest," see Francis Jennings, *The Invasion of America: Indians, Colonialism, and the Cant of Conquest* (Chapel Hill: Univ. of North Carolina Press, 1975).

8Among many works, see Brian Fagan, *The Great Journey: The Peopling of Ancient America* (New York: Thames and Hudson, 1987); Richard Shutler, ed., *Early Man in the New World* (Beverly Hills: Sage Publications, 1983); Colin G. Calloway, *One Vast Winter Count: The Native American West before Lewis and Clark* (Lincoln: Univ. of Nebraska, 2003); Peter Nabokov, *A Forest of Time: American Indian Ways of History* (New York: Cambridge Univ. Press, 2002).

9O'Brien, *Firsting and Lasting*; Brian W. Dippie, *The Vanishing Indian: White Attitudes and U.S. Indian Policy* (Lawrence: Univ. Press of Kansas, 1982); Philip J. Deloria, *Indians in Unexpected Places* (Lawrence: Univ. Press of Kansas, 2004).

10For models of how to connect pre- and postcontact history, see Neal Salisbury, "The Indians' Old World: Native Americans and the Coming of Europeans," *WMQ* 53, no. 3 (1996): 435–58; Daniel K. Richter, *Before the Revolution: America's Ancient Pasts* (Cambridge, MA: Belknap Press of Harvard Univ. Press, 2011); James F. Brooks, "Women, Men, and Cycles of Evangelism in the Southwest Borderlands, A.D. 750 to 1750," *American Historical Review* 118, no. 3 (2013): 738–64; Stephen Warren, *The Worlds the Shawnees Made: Migration and Violence in Early America* (Chapel Hill: Univ. of North Carolina Press, 2014); Juliana Barr, "There's No Such Thing as 'Prehistory': What the Longue Durée of Caddo and Pueblo History Tells Us about Colonial America," *WMQ* 74, no. 2 (2017): 203–40. Generally, see Pekka Hämäläinen, ed., "The Changing Histories of North America before Europeans," *OAH Magazine of History* 27, no. 4 (2013): 5–7; Peter R. Schmidt and Stephen A. Mrozowski, eds., *The Death of Prehistory* (New York: Oxford Univ. Press, 2013).

11Winslow, *Good News*, 103; Roger Williams, *A Key into the Language of America* (1643), ed. John J. Teunissen and Evelyn J. Hinz (Detroit: Wayne State Univ. Press, 1973), 197; William S. Simmons, *Spirit of the New England Tribes: Indian History and Folklore* (Lebanon, NH: Univ. Press of New England, 1986), 172–216.

12Dean R. Snow, *The Archaeology of New England* (New York: Academic Press, 1980), 102–3; Elizabeth S. Chilton, "New England Algonquians: Navigating 'Backwaters' and Typological Boundaries," in Timothy Pauketat, ed., *Oxford Handbook of North American Archaeology* (New York: Oxford Univ. Press, 2012), 264; Barbara Blau

Chamberlain, *These Fragile Outposts: A Geological Look at Cape Cod, Martha's Vineyard, and Nantucket* (New York: Natural History Press, 1964), 156–57.

13 William Cronon, *Changes in the Land: Indians, Colonists, and the Ecology of New England* (New York: Hill and Wang, 1983), 51 ("instrumental"); Snow, *Archaeology of New England*, 183–84; Chilton, "New England Algonquians," 264–65.

14 *Historic and Archaeological Resources of Cape Cod and the Islands: A Framework for Preservation Decisions* (Boston: Massachusetts Historical Commission, Office of the Massachusetts Secretary of State, 1986), 9–10, 13; John T. Cumbler, *Cape Cod: An Environmental History of a Fragile Ecosystem* (Amherst: Univ. of Massachusetts Press, 2014), 16–22; Elena B. Décima and Dena F. Dincauze, "The Boston Back Bay Fish Weirs," in Kathryn Bernick, ed., *Hidden Dimensions: The Cultural Significance of Wetland Archaeology* (Vancouver: Univ. of British Columbia Press, 1998), 57–72; Kathleen J. Bragdon, *Native People of Southern New England, 1500–1650* (Norman: Univ. of Oklahoma Press, 1996), 122; Chamberlain, *These Fragile Outposts*, 98; Jonathan K. Patton, "Considering the Wet Homelands of Indigenous Massachusetts," *Journal of Social Archaeology* 14, no. 1 (2014): 87–111.

15 Snow, *Archaeology of New England*, 155–56, 171–72; Chilton, "New England Algonquians," 265–66; Handsman, "Landscape of Memory," 170–72; Frank Kemp, "The Coburn Site: A Burial Complex on Cape Cod," *Bulletin of the Massachusetts Archaeological Society* 22, nos. 3–4 (1961): 33–41.

16 Snow, *Archaeology of New England*, 279–80; James W. Bradley, "Native Exchange and European Trade: Cross-Cultural Dynamics in the Sixteenth Century," *Man in the Northeast* 33 (1987): 41.

17 Chilton, "New England Algonquians," 267–70; Christopher Jazwa, "Temporal Changes in a Precontact and Contact Cultural Landscape along the Southern Rhode Island Coast," in Ben Ford, ed., *The Archaeology of Maritime Landscapes* (New York: Springer, 2012), 134; Elizabeth A. Little, "Kautantouwit's Legacy: Calibrated Dates on Prehistoric Maize in New England," *American Antiquity* 67, no. 1 (2002): 109–18; John P. Hart and C. Margaret Scarry, "The Age of Common Beans (*Phaseolus vulgaris*) in the Northeastern United States," *American Antiquity* 64, no. 4 (1999): 653–58; Kevin A. McBride, "Native American Cultures in Transition: The Eastern Long Island Sound Culture Area in the Prehistoric and Contact Period," *Connecticut History* 55, no. 1 (1994): 5–21; James W. Bradley, *Archaeological Investigations at the Carns Site, Coast Guard Beach, Cape Cod National Seashore, Massachusetts* (Lowell, MA: Northeast Region Archaeology Program, National Park Service, 2005), 1, 47; Robert J. Hasenstab, "Fishing, Farming, and Finding the Village Sites: Centering Late Woodland New England Algonquians," in Mary Ann Levine, Kenneth E. Sassaman, and Michael S. Nassaney, eds., *The Archaeological Northeast* (Westport, CT: Praeger, 2000), 139–53.

18 Jazwa, "Temporal Changes," 134.

19 Lynn Ceci, "Fish Fertilizer: A Native North American Practice?" *Science*, April 4, 1975, 26–30, doubted that the use of fish fertilizer was a long-standing

Wampanoag practice. Rather, she posited that the Wampanoag interpreter, Tisquantum, learned the use of fish fertilizer from European colonists on Newfoundland, which he then taught to the colonists of Plymouth. That theory has since been disproven by archaeological evidence of Wampanoag use of fish fertilizer before the seventeenth century. See Fiske Center for Archaeological Research, "Sandy's Point, Yarmouth, MA," http://www.fiskecenter.umb.edu/Proj ects/Sandys_point.html (accessed 01/31/2019); Nanapashemet, "It Smells Fishy to Me: An Argument Supporting the Use of Fish Fertilizer by the Native People of Southern New England," in Peter Benes, ed., *Algonkians of New England: Past and Present* (Boston: Boston Univ. Press, 1993), 42-50; Stephen A. Mrozowski, "The Discovery of a Native American Cornfield on Cape Cod," *Archaeology of Eastern North America* 22 (Fall 1994): 47-62. On horticultural development as a "non-event," see Bragdon, *Native People, 1500-1650*, 58, 71, 83, 86, 89; John P. Hart and William A. Lovis, "Reevaluating What We Know About the Histories of Maize in Northeastern North America: A Review of Current Evidence," *Journal of Archaeological Research* 21 (2013): 175-216; Mary Beth Williams and Jeffrey Bendremer, "The Archaeology of Maize, Pots, and Seashells: Gender Dynamics in Late Woodland and Contact-Period New England," in Cheryl Claassen and Rosemary A. Joyce, eds., *Women in Prehistory: North America and Mesoamerica* (Philadelphia: Univ. of Pennsylvania Press, 1994), 147; McBride, "Native American Cultures in Transition," 10-12; Alan Leveille, Joseph Waller Jr., and Donna Inghamet, "Dispersed Villages in Late Woodland Period Coastal Rhode Island," *Archaeology of Eastern North America* 34 (2006): 71-89; Chilton, "New England Algonquians," 268-69; James W. Bradley, et al., *Historic and Archaeological Resources of Cape Cod and the Islands: A Framework for Preservation Decisions* (Boston: Massachusetts Historical Commission, 1986), 44-45; Jazwa, "Temporal Changes."

20 Salisbury, "Indians' Old World," 439-40; Thomas E. Emerson and Timothy R. Pauketat, *Cahokia: Domination and Ideology in the Mississippian World* (Lincoln: Univ. of Nebraska Press, 1997); Pauketat, *Cahokia: Ancient America's Great City on the Mississippi* (New York: Viking Press, 2009); Alice Beck Kehoe, "Cahokia, the Great City," *OAH Magazine of History* 27, no. 4 (2013): 17-21.

21 Snow, *Archaeology of New England*, 313-19 ("quantum leap" on 314); Snow, *The Iroquois* (Malden, MA: Blackwell Publishing, 1994), 21-75; Snow, "Evolution of the Mohawk Iroquois," in David S. Brose, C. Wesley Cowan, and Robert C. Mainfort Jr., eds., *Societies in Eclipse: Archaeology of the Eastern Woodland Indians, A.D. 1400-1700* (Tuscaloosa: Univ. of Alabama Press, 2001), 19-26; Daniel K. Richter, *The Ordeal of the Longhouse: The Peoples of the Iroquois League in the Era of European Colonization* (Chapel Hill: Univ. of North Carolina Press, 1992), 19-29; Dena F. Dincauze and Robert J. Hasenstab, "Explaining the Iroquois: Tribalization on a Prehistoric Periphery," in Tim Champion, ed., *Centre and Periphery: Comparative Studies in Archaeology* (New York: Routledge, 1995), 67-87.

22   On control of crop production as the key to political centralization, see James C. Scott, *Against the Grain: A Deep History of the Earliest States* (New Haven, CT: Yale Univ. Press, 2017).

23   Bragdon, *Native People, 1500–1650*, 140–55, 160–61; Gaynell Stone, ed., *Native Forts of the Long Island Sound Area*, vol. 8 of Readings in Long Island Archaeology and Ethnohistory (Stony Brook, NY: Suffolk County Archaeological Association, 2006).

24   Carolyn Merchant, *Ecological Revolutions: Nature, Gender, and Science in New England* (Chapel Hill, NC: Univ. of North Carolina Press, 1989), 72–73; Theda Perdue, *Cherokee Women* (Lincoln: Univ. of Nebraska Press, 1998); Chilton, "New England Algonquians," 267–70; Elizabeth S. Chilton, "Ceramic Research in New England: Breaking the Typological Mold," in Levine, Sassaman, and Nassaney, *Archaeological Northeast*, 97–114; Bragdon, *Native People, 1500–1650*, 92–95, 115; Marc A. Kelley, T. Gail Barrett, and Sandra D. Saunders, "Diet, Dental Disease, and Transition in Northeastern Native Americans," *Man in the Northeast* 33 (1987): 113–25; Marc A. Kelley, Paul S. Sledzik, and Sean P. Murphy, "Health, Demographics, and Physical Constitution in Seventeenth-Century Rhode Island Indians," *Man in the Northeast* 34 (1987): 1–25.

25   Williams, *Key into the Language*, 189 ("any good").

26   Williams, 190.

27   Henry Whitfield, *Strength out of Weaknesse; Or a Glorious Manifestation of the Further Progresse of the Gospel among the Indians in New England* (London: printed by M. Simmons for John Blague and Samuel Howes, 1652), in *Eliot Tracts*, 239 (four spirits); William S. Simmons, "Southern New England Shamanism: An Ethnographic Reconstruction," in William Cowan, ed., *Papers of the Seventh Algonquian Conference, 1975* (Ottawa: Carleton Univ. Press, 1976), 217–56; *Conquests and Triumphs*, 11–12; William Wood, *New England's Prospect* (1634), ed. Alden T. Vaughan (Amherst: Univ. of Massachusetts Press, 1977), 101; Åke Hultkrantz, *The Religions of the American Indians* (Berkeley: Univ. of California Press, 1981).

28   Winslow, *Good News*, 103; Williams, *Key into the Language*, 190, 194, 197; Wood, *New England's Prospect*, 100 ("fair weather"), 111; William Scranton Simmons, *Cautantowwit's House: An Indian Burial Ground on the Island of Conanicut in Narragansett Bay* (Providence, RI: Brown Univ. Press, 1970), 50–58; Simmons, *Spirit of the New England Tribes*, 45–47 ("garlands"); Simmons, *The Narragansett* (New York: Chelsea House Publishers, 1989), 26.

29   Merchant, *Ecological Revolutions*, 75–77; Lynn Ceci, "Watchers of the Pleiades: Ethnoastronomy among Native Cultivators in Northeastern North America," *Ethnohistory* 25, no. 4 (1978): 301–13; Susan G. Gibson, ed., *Burr's Hill: A Seventeenth-Century Wampanoag Burial Ground in Warren, Rhode Island* (Providence, RI: Haffenreffer Museum of Anthropology, 1980); Francis P. McManamon, James W. Bradley, and Ann L. Maggenis, eds., *The Indian Neck Ossuary*, vol. 5 of *Chapters in*

the Archeology of Cape Cod (Boston: Brown Univ., 1987), 23; William Turnbaugh, *The Material Culture of RI-1000: A Mid-Seventeenth Century Narragansett Indian Burial Site in North Kingston, Rhode Island* (Kingston, RI: Division of Cultural Resources, North Atlantic Regional Office, National Park Service, U.S. Department of the Interior, 1984); Bragdon, *Native People, 1500–1650,* 232; Paul Robinson, Marc Kelley, and Patricia E. Rubertone, "Preliminary Biocultural Interpretations from a Seventeenth-Century Narragansett Indian Cemetery in Rhode Island," in William Fitzhugh, ed., *Cultures in Contact: The European Impact on Native Cultural Institutions in Eastern North America,* A.D. *1000–1800* (Washington, D.C.: Smithsonian Institution Press, 1985), 107–30.

30 Neal Salisbury, *Manitou and Providence: Indians, Europeans, and the Making of New England, 1500–1643* (New York: Oxford Univ. Press, 1982), 31; Charles C. Mann, *1491: New Revelations of the Americas before Columbus* (New York: Alfred A. Knopf, 2005), 212–24; Cronon, *Changes in the Land,* 43–46; Merchant, *Ecological Revolutions,* 74–83.

31 Bragdon, *Native People, 1500–1650,* 83; Elizabeth A. Little and Margaret J. Schoeninger, "The Late Woodland Diet on Nantucket Island and the Problem of Maize in Coastal New England," *American Antiquity* 60, no. 2 (1995): 351–68; Scott Nixon, "Marine Resources and the Human Carrying Capacity of Coastal Ecosystems in Southern New England before European Contact," *Northeast Anthropology* 68 (2004): 1–23; Lucianne Lavin, "Coastal Adaptations in Southern New England and Southern New York," *Archaeology of Eastern North America* 16 (1988): 101–20; David J. Bernstein, *Prehistoric Subsistence on the Southern New England Coast: The Record from Narragansett Bay* (San Diego: Academic Press, 1993); Kevin A. McBride and Robert E. Dewar, "Agriculture and Cultural Evolution: Causes and Effects in the Lower Connecticut River Valley," in William F. Keegan, ed., *Emergent Horticultural Economies of the Eastern Woodlands* (Carbondale: Center for Archaeological Investigations, Southern Illinois University at Carbondale, 1987), 305–28; Elizabeth S. Chilton, "Archaeology and Ethnohistory of the Contact Period in the Northeastern United States," *Reviews in Anthropology* 29 (2001): 343; Hasenstab, "Fishing, Farming, and Finding the Village Sites," 139.

32 Salisbury, *Manitou and Providence,* 22–30. See also Daniel Gookin, "Historical Collections of the Indians in New England," *MHSC,* 1st ser., vol. 1 (1792): 147–49.

33 Winslow, *Good News,* 108 ("sets his bounds"); Elizabeth A. Little, "Three Kinds of Indian Land Deeds at Nantucket, Massachusetts," in William Cowan, ed., *Papers of the Eleventh Algonquian Conference* (Ottawa: Carleton Univ. Press, 1980), 61–70; Bragdon, *Native People, 1500–1650,* 100, 137, 143–48. On *pnieseosok,* see Winslow, *Good News,* 106–7, 108; Bragdon, *Native People, 1500–1650,* 189–90, 214–15; R. Todd Romero, *Making War and Minting Christians: Masculinity, Religion, and Colonialism in Early New England* (Amherst: Univ. of Massachusetts Press, 2011), 26–27, 63–64.

34 Winslow, *Good News*, 111; Ives Goddard, "Eastern Algonquian Languages," in Bruce G. Trigger, vol. ed., *Northeast*, vol. 15 of *Handbook of North American Indians*, gen. ed. William C. Sturtevant (Washington, D.C.: Smithsonian Institution, 1978), 70–77.

35 Generally, see Marshall Sahlins, *Tribesmen* (Englewood Cliffs, NJ: Prentice-Hall, 1968), 20–27.

36 Kathleen J. Bragdon, "Island Queens: Women Sachems on Martha's Vineyard and Nantucket in the Colonial Period," in Elizabeth S. Chilton and Mary Lynne Rainey, eds., *Nantucket and Other Native Places: The Legacy of Elizabeth Alden Little* (Binghamton: State Univ. of New York Press, 2010), 89; Bragdon, *Native People of Southern New England, 1650–1775* (Norman: Univ. of Oklahoma Press, 2009), 112–13; Peter A. Thomas, "In the Maelstrom of Change: The Indian Trade and Cultural Process in the Middle Connecticut River Valley, 1635–1665" (PhD diss., University of Massachusetts at Amherst, 1979), 29–39; Chilton, "Archaeology and Ethnohistory," 345–56.

37 Christopher L. Pastore, *Between Land and Sea: The Atlantic Coast and the Transformation of New England* (Cambridge, MA: Harvard Univ. Press, 2014), 22.

38 Elizabeth A. Little, "Kautantouwit's Legacy: Calibrated Dates on Prehistoric Maize in New England," *American Antiquity* 67, no. 1 (2002): 115; Lawrence C. Wroth, ed., *The Voyages of Giovanni da Verrazzano, 1524–1528* (New Haven, CT: Yale Univ. Press, 1970), 139 ("fields extend").

39 Paul Otto, "Henry Hudson, the Munsees, and the Wampum Revolution," and Jon Parmenter, "Separate Vessels: Hudson, the Dutch, and the Iroquois," in Jaap Jacobs and Louis Roper, eds., *The Worlds of the Seventeenth-Century Hudson Valley* (Albany: State Univ. of New York Press, 2014), 91–92, 109; Bragdon, *Native People, 1600–1750*, 47, 97.

40 Mary Ann Levine, "Determining the Provenance of Native Copper Artifacts from Northeastern North America: Evidence from Instrumental Neutron Activation Analysis," *Journal of Archaeological Science* 34 (2007): 572–87; McBride, "Native American Culture," 12; Bradley, "Native Exchange and European Trade," 41; George R. Hamell, "Wampum: White, Bright, and Light Things Are Good to Think," in Alexandra van Donegan et al., eds., *One Man's Trash Is Another Man's Treasure* (Rotterdam: Museum Boymans-van Beuningen, 1996), 45; Parmenter, "Separate Vessels," 109; Stuart A. Reeve and Katerine Forgacs, "Connecticut Radiocarbon Dates: A Study of Prehistoric Cultural Chronologies and Population Trends," *Bulletin of the Archaeological Society of Connecticut* 62 (1999): 19–66; William A. Ritchie, *The Archaeology of New York State* (New York: American Museum of Natural History, 1965), 179; Bragdon, *Native People, 1500–1650*, 35, 47, 97.

41 Gookin, "Historical Collections," 154 ("such subjection"); Eric S. Johnson, "Community and Confederation: A Political Geography of Contact-Period Southern New England," in Levine, Sassaman, and Nassaney, *Archaeological*

Northeast, 155–68 ("topic of inquiry" on 158); Johnson, "The Politics of Pottery: Material Culture and Political Process among Algonquians of Seventeenth-Century Southern New England," in M. S. Nassaney and E. S. Johnson, eds., *Interpretations of Native North American Life: Material Contributions to Ethnohistory* (Gainesville: Univ. Press of Florida, 2003), 119–20; Bragdon, *Native People, 1650–1775*, 205; Sahlins, *Tribesmen*, 16.

    The sachem Mittark of Aquinnah on the Vineyard descended from Nohtoakset, a "Sachim that came from the Massachusetts Bay" but lived on the Vineyard. See *Indian Converts*, 161. Likewise, sometime during the 1600s a high-ranking figure named Wannamanut came from Massachusetts Bay to the island sachemship of Takemmy, where he married two "noblewomen." See DCD, 3:133; Suffolk Files no. 12248, pp. 31–32, Mass. State Archives, Boston.

CHAPTER 2: DANGER ON THE HORIZON

1   On travel accounts, see Peter C. Mancall, *Hakluyt's Promise: An Elizabethan's Obsession for an English America* (New Haven, CT: Yale Univ. Press, 2007). On Tisquantum, see Neal Salisbury, "Squanto: Last of the Patuxet," in Ian K. Steele and Nancy L. Rhoden, eds., *The Human Tradition in Colonial America* (Wilmington, DE: Scholarly Resources, 1999), 21–36. Andrew Lipman's forthcoming biography of Tisquantum uses "odyssey" as its framework. On Indians traversing the Atlantic, whether forcibly or voluntarily, see Carolyn Thomas, *Indians Abroad, 1493–1938* (Norman: Univ. of Oklahoma Press, 1943); Olive P. Dickason, *The Myth of the Savage and the Beginnings of French Colonialism in the Americas* (Edmonton: Univ. of Alberta Press, 1991), 203–29; Harold L. Prins, "To the Land of the Mistigoches: American Indians Traveling to Europe in the Age of Exploration," *American Indian Culture and Research Journal* 17, no. 1 (1993): 175–95; Alden T. Vaughan, *Transatlantic Encounters: American Indians in Britain, 1500–1776* (New York: Cambridge Univ. Press, 2006); Jace Weaver, *The Red Atlantic: American Indigenes and the Making of the Modern World, 1000–1927* (Chapel Hill: Univ. of North Carolina, 2014); Coll Thrush, *Indigenous London: Native Travelers at the Heart of Empire* (New Haven, CT: Yale Univ. Press, 2016).

2   Amelia M. Trevelyan, *Miskwabik, Metal of Ritual: Metallurgy in Precontact Eastern North America* (Lexington: Univ. Press of Kentucky, 2004), 117–19; Christopher L. Miller and George R. Hamell, "A New Perspective on Indian-White Contact: Cultural Symbols and Colonial Trade," *Journal of American History* 73, no. 2 (1986): 325; Nanepashemet and James W. Bradley, "Maps and Dreams: Native Americans and European Discovery," in *One Man's Trash Is Another Man's Treasure*, 35; Rebecca K. Shrum, *In the Looking Glass: Mirrors and Identity in Early America* (Baltmore, MD: Johns Hopkins Univ. Press, 2017).

3   On the English merchant community in Málaga, see José Ignacio Martinez Ruiz, "'A Towne Famous for Its Plenty of Raisins and Wines': Málaga en el Comercio Anglo-Español en el Siglo XVII," *Hispania* 71, no. 239 (2011): 665–90. On Spanish slavery during this era, see Robin Blackburn, "The Old World Background to

European Colonial Slavery," *WMQ* 3, no. 1 (1997): 65–102; James H. Sweet, "The Iberian Roots of American Racist Thought," *WMQ* 3, no. 1 (1997): 143–66; Jarbel Rodriguez, *Captives and Their Saviors in the Medieval Crown of Aragon* (Washington, D.C.: Catholic Univ. of America Press, 2007); Andrés Resdéndez, *The Other Slavery: The Uncovered Story of Indian Enslavement in America* (Boston: Houghton Mifflin Harcourt, 2016).

4   On Spanish slave law, see Resdéndez, *Other Slavery*, 46–47. On Slaney, see Nick Bunker, *Making Haste from Babylon: The* Mayflower *Pilgrims and Their World, A New History* (New York: Alfred A. Knopf, 2010), 294; Gillian T. Cell, "The Newfoundland Company: A Study of Subscribers to a Colonizing Venture," *WMQ* 22, no. 4 (1965): 615.

5   Cell, "Newfoundland Company," 622; Peter E. Pope, *Fish into Wine: The Newfoundland Plantation in the Seventeenth Century* (Chapel Hill: Univ. of North Carolina Press for the Omohundro Institute of Early American History and Culture, 2004), 33, 48–52, 55–56.

6   E. M. Rose, "Did Squanto Meet Pocahontas, and What Might They Have Discussed?" *The Junto* (blog), https://earlyamericanists.com/2017/11/21/did-squanto -meet-pocahontas-and-what-might-they-have-discussed/ (accessed 01/18/2019).

7   Camilla Townsend, *Pocahontas and the Powhatan Dilemma* (New York: Hill and Wang, 2004).

8   Vaughan, *Transatlantic Encounters*, 57–76; Salisbury, *Manitou and Providence*, 86–96.

9   James Phinney Baxter, ed., *Sir Ferdinando Gorges and His Province of Maine*, 3 vols. (Boston: Prince Society, 1890), 2:21 ("goodly"); John Smith, *The Generall Historie of Virginia, New-England, and the Summer Isles* (1624), in Philip L. Barbour, ed., *The Complete Works of Captain John Smith (1580–1631), in Three Volumes* (Chapel Hill: Univ. of North Carolina Press for the Institute of Early American History and Culture, 1986), 2:403 ("wit").

10 Nathaniel Morton, *New England's Memorial: Or, A Brief Relation of the Most Remarkable Passages of the Province of God* (1669) (Boston: Congregational Board of Publication, 1855), 37 ("sad").

11 George Parker Winship, *Sailor's Narratives of the Voyages along the Northeast Coast* (Boston: Houghton, Mifflin & Company, 1905), 252.

12 Winship, 254–55 ("savage friends"; "strange manner"); Morton, *New England's Memorial*, 43.

13 Baxter, *Gorges and His Province of Maine*, 2:29.

14 Dermer letter from Bradford, *Of Plymouth Plantation*, 1:206–9 (all quotes); Morton, *New England's Memorial*, 42.

15 Baxter, *Gorges and His Province of Maine*, 1:219; John Smith, *New England's Trials* (1620), in Barbour, *Complete Works of Smith*, 1:428.

16 Phineas Pratt, *A Declaration of the Affairs of the English People That First Inhabited New England*, ed. Richard Frothingham Jr. (Boston: Press of T. R. Marvin & Son, 1858), 8–9; Wood, *New England's Prospect*, 95–96.

17   David B. Quinn, *North America from Earliest Discovery to First Settlements: The Norse Voyages to 1612* (New York: Harper & Row, 1977), 62–64, 114, 513–32; Harold A. Innis, *The Cod Fisheries: The History of an International Economy* (Toronto: Univ. of Toronto Press, 1978); Pope, *Fish into Wine*, 11–44, 73–74; Kathleen L. Ehrhardt, *European Metals in Native Hands: Rethinking Technological Change, 1640–1683* (Tuscaloosa: Univ. of Alabama Press, 2005); Laurier Turgeon, "French Fishers, Fur Traders, and Amerindians during the Sixteenth Century: History and Archaeology," *WMQ* 55, no. 4 (1998): 585–610; James Axtell, "At the Water's Edge: Trading in the Sixteenth Century," in *After Columbus: Essays in the Ethnohistory of Colonial North America* (New York: Oxford Univ. Press, 1988), 144–81; Bruce J. Bourque and Ruth Holmes White-head, "Tarrentines and the Introduction of European Goods in the Gulf of Maine," *Ethnohistory* 32, no. 4 (1985): 327–41; James W. Bradley, "Native Exchange and European Trade," *Man in the Northeast* 33 (1987): 31–46; Calvin Martin, "The Four Lives of a Micmac Copper Pot," *Ethnohistory* 22, no. 2 (1975): 111–33.

18   Lawrence C. Wroth, ed., *The Voyages of Giovanni da Verrazzano, 1524–1528* (New Haven: Yale Univ. Press, 1970), 138–40 (all quotes).

19   On Indian aesthetics as a factor in early trade, see Miller and Hamell, "New Perspective on Indian-White Contact"; William Howard Carter, "Chains of Consumption: The Iroquois and Consumer Goods, 1500–1800" (PhD diss., Princeton University, 2008).

20   Quinn, *North America from Earliest Discoveries*, 160; "Estevão Gomes," *Dictionary of Canadian Biography*, http://www.biographi.ca/en/bio.php?BioId=34383 (accessed 01/18/2019).

21   On colonial precedents, see Karen Ordahl Kupperman, *The Jamestown Project* (Cambridge, MA: Harvard Univ. Press, 2007); Mancall, *Hakluyt's Promise*. On Gilbert, see Nathan Probasco, "Researching North America: Sir Humphrey Gilbert's 1583 Expedition and a Reexamination of Early Modern English Coloni-zation in the North Atlantic World" (PhD diss., University of Nebraska, 2013); Quinn, *North America from Earliest Discovery*, 387–88; Salisbury, *Manitou and Providence*, 86. On the growth of the Newfoundland fishery, see Quinn, *North America from Earliest Discovery*, 348–68; Jeffrey W. Bolster, *The Mortal Sea: Fishing the Atlantic in the Age of Sail* (Cambridge, MA: Belknap Press of Harvard Univ. Press, 2012), 44. On metal remains, see Bradley, "Native Exchange and European Trade," 35; Robert S. Grumet, *Historic Contact: Indian People and Colonists in Today's Northeastern United States in the Sixteenth through Eighteenth Centuries* (Norman: Univ. of Oklahoma Press, 1995), 110–13.

22   "Gabriel Archer's Account of Captain Bartholomew Gosnold's Voyage to 'North Virginia' in 1602," and John Brereton, *A Briefe and True Relation of the Discoverie of the North Part of Virginia* (1602), in David B. Quinn and Alison M. Quinn, eds., *The English New England Voyages, 1602–1608* (London: Hakluyt Society, 1983), 117,

145–46; Matthew R. Bahar, *Storm of the Sea: Indians and Empires in the Atlantic's Age of Sail* (New York: Oxford Univ. Press, 2018).

23 "Archer's Account," 124.

24 Here I'm following Quinn and Quinn's research for the course of Gosnold's voyage in appendix 2 of *English New England Voyages*, contrary to the course set out by Warner F. Gookin and Philip L. Barbour, *Bartholomew Gosnold* (Hamden, CT: Archon Books, 1963). All quotes from "Archer's Account" and Brereton, *Briefe and True Relation*, 125, 149–50, 156.

25 "Archer's Account," 130–31.

26 "Archer's Account," 134.

27 "Archer's Account," 134 ("mustard"); Brereton, *Briefe and True Relation*, 157–58 ("beards"; "saucy"; "huge cries").

28 "Archer's Account," 135 ("fear"), 136 ("lusty"). On Roanoke, see Michael Leroy Oberg, *The Head in Walter Nugent's Hand: Roanoke's Forgotten Indians* (Philadelphia: Univ. of Pennsylvania Press, 2007); Karen Ordahl Kupperman, *Roanoke: The Abandoned Colony* (New York: Rowman & Littlefield Publishers, 2007).

29 Martin Pring, "A voyage set out from the Citie of Bristoll . . . in the yeere 1603," in Quinn and Quinn, *English New England Voyages*, 221 ("let loose"), 222 ("Io, Ia, Io"), 227–28 ("jest"); David B. Quinn, "Martin Pring at Provincetown in 1603?" *NEQ* 40, no. 1 (1967): 79–91.

30 James Rosier, "A True Relation of the most prosperous voyage made in this present yeere 1605, by Captain George Waymouth, in the Discovery of the land of Virginia," in Quinn and Quinn, *English New England Voyages*, 257n2; "Journal of Samuel de Champlain," in Charles Herbert Levermore, ed., *Forerunners and Competitors of the Pilgrims and Puritans*, 2 vols. (Brooklyn: New England Society in the City of Brooklyn, 1912), 121 (all quotes).

31 "Journal of Champlain," 121; W. Sears Nickerson, *Early Encounters: Native Americans and Europeans in New England*, ed. Delores Bird Carpenter (East Lansing: Michigan State Univ. Press, 1994), 54–58; David Hackett Fischer, *Champlain's Dream* (New York: Simon & Schuster, 2008), 189–92.

32 Mark Lescarbot, *Nova Francia: A Description of Acadia, 1606*, ed. H. P. Biggar, trans. P. Erondelle (New York: Harper & Brothers, 1928), 111–12 ("wolves"); "Journal of Champlain," 150–54.

33 Christopher J. Bilodeau, "The Paradox of Sagadahoc: The Popham Colony, 1607–1608," *Early American Studies* 12, no. 1 (2014): 10–11, 16; Vaughan, *Transatlantic Encounters*, 58, 65; Salisbury, *Manitou and Providence*, 92.

34 Smith, *Generall Historie*, 2:399 ("sorely wounded"); Quinn and Quinn, *English New England Voyages*, 480 ("false and malicious"); Vaughan, *Transatlantic Encounters*, 67; Baxter, *Gorges and His Province of Maine*, 1:210 ("slaughter").

35 Bunker, *Making Haste from Babylon*, 48; John Smith, *A Description of New England* (1616), in Barbour, *Complete Works of Smith*, 1:340 (all quotes); Smith, *Generall Historie*, 2:418.

36   Vaughan, *Transatlantic Encounters*, 70 ("worthless"; "silly"); Weaver, *Red Atlantic*, 57–60; Baxter, *Gorges and His Province of Maine*, 1:211 ("war"); *Mourt's Relation*, 52 ("incensed"), 70 ("weeping").

37   Johan De Laet, "New World," in J. Franklin Jameson, ed., *Narratives of New Netherland, 1609–1664* (New York: Charles Scribner's Sons, 1909), 41 ("somewhat shy"), 43 ("enemies"). Block's claim that the "Wapanoos" were enemies of the Pequots probably refers to the Wappingers of the Housatonic River valley rather than the Wampanoags. I am grateful to William Starna for this clarification in email correspondence of October 23, 2017.

38   Smith, *Description of New England*, 1:323–24; Pratt, *Declaration*, 8–9 ("dogs"); Morton, *New England's Memorial*, 44 ("make sport"). See also Dermer's account in Winship, *Sailor's Narratives*, 252.

39   Pratt, *Declaration*, 8–9 ("We think"); John Smith, "Advertisements: Or, the Pathway to Experience to erect a Plantation," in Barbour, *Complete Works of Smith*, 3:275–76; Morton, *New England's Memorial*, 44.

40   Pratt, *Declaration*, 8–9.

CHAPTER 3: GOLGOTHA

1   Jennings, *Invasion of America*, 15; Thomas Morton, *The New English Canaan*, ed. Charles Francis Adams Jr. (Boston: Prince Society, 1883), 133.

2   Raymond D. Fogelson, "The Ethnohistory of Events and Nonevents," *Ethnohistory* 36, no. 2 (1989): 143–44.

3   Smith, *Description of New England*, 1:330.

4   Smith, 1:329 ("language"); Gookin, "Historical Collections," 148 ("amity").

5   Smith, *Generall Historie*, 2:418 ("Bashabes"); Salisbury, *Manitou and Providence*, 60–72, 76–77; Bahar, *Storm of the Sea*, 56–58.

6   Gookin, "Historical Collections," 148.

7   Smith, *Description of New England*, 1:330.

8   Thomas Dermer, 1619, quoted in Winship, *Sailor's Narratives*, 251 ("utterly void"); Morton, *New England's Memorial*, 37–38 ("great mortality"; "twentieth"; "sad spectacles"), 44 ("never heard"); *Mourt's Relation*, 63 ("thousands").

9   Alfred W. Crosby, "Virgin Soil Epidemics as a Factor in the Aboriginal Depopulation in America," *WMQ* 33, no. 2 (1976): 289–99; Crosby, *Ecological Imperialism: The Biological Expansion of Europe, 600–1900* (New York: Cambridge Univ. Press, 1986); William H. McNeil, *Plagues and Peoples* (New York: Anchor Books, 1977), 86–88; Suzanne Austin Alchon, *A Pest in the Land: New World Epidemics in Global Perspective* (Albuquerque: Univ. of New Mexico Press, 2003).

10   Bradford, *Of Plymouth Plantation*, 194.

11   Bruce G. Trigger, *The Children of Aataentsic: A History of the Huron People to 1660* (Kingston, ON: McGill-Queen's Univ Press, 1976), 499–50, 526–28, 588–89. See also Alfred W. Crosby, *The Columbian Exchange: Biological and Cultural Consequences of 1492* (Westport, CT: Praeger, 1972), 42–43, 49; John Smith, *Advertisements for the*

Unexperienced Planters of New England (1631), in Barbour, *Complete Works of Smith*, 3:275 ("three plagues"). In addition to the citations in note 8, see William A. Starna, "The Biological Encounter: Disease and the Ideological Domain," *American Indian Quarterly* 16, no. 4 (1992): 512; Catherine C. Carson, George J. Armelagos, and Ann L. Magennis, "Impact of Disease on the Precontact and Early Historic Populations of New England and the Maritimes," in John W. Verano and Douglas H. Ubelaker, eds., *Disease and Demography in the Americas* (Washington, D.C.: Smithsonian Institution Press, 1992), 144–45.

12   David S. Jones, "Virgin Soils Revisited," *WMQ* 60, no. 4 (2003): 703–42; Paul Kelton, *Epidemics and Enslavement: Biological Catastrophe in the Native Southeast* (Lincoln: Univ. of Nebraska Press, 2009); Catherine M. Cameron, Paul Kelton, and Alan C. Swedlund, eds., *Beyond Germs: Native Depopulation in North America* (Tucson: Univ. of Arizona Press, 2015).

13   Sir Ferdinando Gorges, *A Brief Narration of the Originall Undertakings of the Advancement of Plantations into the Parts of America* (1658), in James Phinney Baxter, ed., *Sir Ferdinando Gorges and His Province of Maine*, 3 vols. (Boston: Prince Society, 1890), 2:19 ("cabins"; "sore"); Dermer, quoted in Winship, *Sailor's Narratives*, 251 ("remnant"); Timothy L. Bratton, "The Identity of the New England Indian Epidemic of 1616–19," *Bulletin of the History of Medicine* 62, no. 3 (1988): 366–70.

14   Edward Johnson, *Johnson's Wonder-Working Providence, 1628–1651*, ed. J. Lawrence Jameson (New York: Charles Scribner's Sons, 1910), 41 ("consumption"); Paul J. Lindholdt, ed., *John Josselyn, Colonial Traveler: A Critical Edition of Two Voyages in New-England* (Hanover, NH: Univ. Press of New England, 1988), 89 ("great mortality"); John Eliot, *The Day-Breaking, If Not The Sun-Rising of the Gospel With the Indians in New-England* (1647), in *Eliot Tracts*, 94 ("plague and pox"); Wood, *New England's Prospect*, 63–64 ("sweeping"); Gookin, "Historical Collections," 148 ("pestilential"); Arthur E. Speiss and Bruce D. Speiss, "New England Pandemic of 1616–1622: Cause and Archaeological Implication," *Man in the Northeast* 34 (1987): 74.

15   Noble David Cook, *Born to Die: Disease and New World Conquest, 1492–1650* (New York: Cambridge Univ. Press, 1998), 172–73 (smallpox and measles). Bratton, "Identity of the New England Indian Epidemic," contains a thorough discussion of the earlier literature and advances the smallpox argument. On the new theory that lice and ticks from humans spread bubonic plague, see Michael Greshko, "Maybe Rats Aren't to Blame for the Black Death," *National Geographic*, January 15, 2018, news.nationalgeographic.com/2018/01/rats-plague-black-death -humans-lice-health-science/ (accessed 01/18/2019).

16   John S. Marr and John T. Cathey, "New Hypothesis for Cause of Epidemic among Native Americans, New England, 1616–1619," *Emerging Infectious Diseases* 16, no. 2 (2010), www.ncbi.nlm.nih.gov/pmc/articles/PMC2957993 (accessed 01/18/2019); Frances Robles, "Puerto Rico's Health Care Is in Dire Condition, Three Weeks after Maria," *New York Times*, October 10, 2017; Elizabeth A. Fenn, *Encounters at*

the Heart of the World: A History of the Mandan People (New York: Hill and Wang, 2014), 290–310.

17   On the cycle of smallpox, see Elizabeth A. Fenn, *Pox Americana: The Great Smallpox Epidemic of 1775–82* (New York: Hill and Wang, 2002), 15–18; Elizabeth A. Fenn, "Biological Warfare in Eighteenth-Century North America: Beyond Jeffery Amherst," *Journal of American History* 86, no. 4 (2000): 1561.

18   Bradford, *Of Plymouth Plantation*, 1:194.

19   Winslow, *Good News*, 103–5 ("undoubted" on 105); Eliot, *Day-Breaking*, 92 ("fall into"), 97 ("two days"); *Conquests and Triumphs*, 17 ("immediate"), 18 ("observing"); Whitfield, *Strength out of Weakness*, 186, 239; Henry Whitfield, *The Light appearing more and more towards the perfect Day or a farther discovery of the present state of the Indians in New England* (1651), in *Eliot Tracts*, 178 ("37"); Williams, *Key into the Language*, 190. This discussion is informed broadly by William S. Simmons, "Southern New England Shamanism: An Ethnographic Reconstruction," in William Cowan, ed., *Papers of the Seventh Algonquian Conference, 1975* (Ottawa: Carleton Univ. Press, 1976), 217–56; and Bragdon, *Native People, 1500–1650*, 203–14.

20   Wood, *New England's Prospect*, 101 ("bear"; "bellowing"); Williams, *Key into the Language*, 192; Winslow, *Good News*, 81.

21   Winslow, *Good News*, 103 ("Kiehtan"; "conceived anger"; "calling"), 105 ("Skooke"); Williams, *Key into the Language*, 108 (in this case, "the sun" appears to represent Kiehtan); *Conquests and Triumphs*, 19–20 ("leather"), 21; John Eliot and Thomas Mayhew Jr., *Tears of Repentance: Or, A Further Narrative of the Progress of the Gospel amongst the Indians in New-England* (1653), in *Eliot Tracts*, 253–54 ("notable").

22   Johnson, *Wonder-Working Providence*, 41.

23   Whitfield, *Light appearing*, 177 ("strange"); Williams, *Key into the Language*, 125 ("bewailing"), 247; David E. Stannard, *The Puritan Way of Death: A Study in Religion, Culture, and Social Change* (New York: Oxford Univ. Press, 1977).

24   Williams, *Key into the Language*, 116 ("affections"), 125 ("profane"), 189 ("lamenting").

25   Winslow, *Good News*, 108–9 ("bury"; "mourn"); Williams, *Key into the Language*, 248 ("dead sachem"); Wood, *New England's Prospect*, 111.

26   Winslow, *Good News*, 79; Williams, *Key into the Language*, 243.

27   *Conquests and Triumphs*, 14–15 ("many families"); Christina Snyder, *Slavery in Indian Country: The Changing Face of Captivity in Early America* (Cambridge, MA: Harvard Univ. Press, 2010), 5–6.

28   The paucity of excavated precolonial southern New England Indian cemeteries, and the subsequent lack of studies about what the remains tell us about human health, means this assertion is open to question, but see the following: Ann L. Magennis, "The Physical Anthropology of the Indian Neck Ossuary," in McMannamon, Bradley, and Magennis, *Indian Neck Ossuary*, 49–143; Carlson, Armelagos, and Magennis, "Impact of Disease"; Marc A. Kelley, T. Gail Barrett, and Sandra D. Saunders, "Diet, Dental Disease, and Transition in Northeastern

Native Americans," *Man in the Northeast* 33 (1987): 113–25; and Marc A. Kelley, Paul S. Sledzik, and Sean P. Murphy, "Health, Demographics, and Physical Constitution in Seventeenth-Century Rhode Island Indians," *Man in the Northeast* 34 (1987): 1–25.

29 *Conquests and Triumphs*, 17–20, 49–50 ("his god"); Eliot, *Day-Breaking*, 92; Whitfield, *Light appearing*, 181 ("power"); Trigger, *Children of Aataentsic*, 537.

30 Morton, *New English Canaan*, 130–34 ("angry"); Benjamin Basset, "Fabulous Traditions and Customs of the Indians of Martha's Vineyard," *MHSC*, 1st ser., vol. 1 (1792): 139–40 ("sprightly").

31 Morton, *New England's Memorial*, 37–38 ("ancient"); Johnson, *Wonder-Working Providence*, 39–40 ("befell a great mortality"); Bunker, *Making Haste from Babylon*, 16–19; Roger Williams to John Winthrop, early June 1638, in *Williams Correspondence*, 160 ("earthquake").

32 Winslow, *Good News*, 106; Paul Alden Robinson, "The Struggle Within: The Indian Debate in Seventeenth-Century Narragansett Country" (PhD diss., State University of New York at Binghamton, 1990), 76–77, 81–82, 88–89.

33 Smith, *New England's Trials*, 1:428 ("God"); Johnson, *Wonder-Working Providence*, 40 ("Christ"); John Winthrop, *Generall Considerations of the Plantation in New England* (1629), in *Winthrop Papers*, vol. 2, ed. Stewart Mitchell (Boston: Massachusetts Historical Society, 1931), 120 ("miraculous"). Generally, see Christobal Silva, *Miraculous Plagues: An Epidemiology of Early New England Narrative* (New York: Oxford Univ. Press, 2011), 24–61.

34 James H. Merrell, "The Indians' New World: The Catawba Experience," *WMQ* 41, no. 4 (1984): 543.

35 Cushman's Discourse (November 1621), quoted in Alexander Young, ed., *Chronicles of the Pilgrim Fathers of the Colony of Plymouth, from 1602 to 1628* (Boston: Charles C. Little and James Brown, 1841), 258 ("courage"); Kai Erikson, *A New Species of Trouble: The Human Experience of Modern Disasters* (New York: W. W. Norton, 1994), 228 ("scan"), 233 ("blow"), 242 ("at its worst"). See also Jack Saul, *Collective Trauma, Collective Healing: Promoting Community Resilience in the Aftermath of Disaster* (New York: Routledge, 2014), esp. 1–29; Daya Somasundaram, "Addressing Collective Trauma: Conceptualisations and Interventions," *Intervention* 12, suppl. 1 (2014): 43–60.

36 Johnson, *Wonder-Working Providence*, 41 ("fear"). The challenges of such adjustments are skillfully treated in Merrell, "Indians' New World," 543–49. See also Heidi Bohaker, "*Nindoodemag*: The Significance of Algonquian Kinship Networks in the Eastern Great Lakes Region, 1600–1701," *WMQ* 63, no. 1 (2006): 23–52.

37 Bradford, *Of Plymouth Plantation*, 1:211 ("strong"); Johnson, *Wonder-Working Providence*, 41; John R. Bartlett, ed., *Records of the Colony of Rhode Island and Providence Plantations in New England*, 10 vols. (Providence, RI: A. C. Greene and Brothers, 1856–65), 1:25–26 ("destitution"); Howard M. Chapin, *Documentary History of*

Rhode Island, 2 vols. (Providence, RI: Preston & Rounds, 1916), 1:54–55 ("subject"; "subdued"). See also testimony of Roger Williams relative to the purchase of lands at Seekonk and Providence, Dec. 13, 1661, *Publications of the Narragansett Club*, 1st ser., vol. 6 (Providence, RI: Providence Press, 1874), 316–17.

38   Smith, *New England's Trials*, 1:428.

39   Bradford, *Of Plymouth Plantation*, 1:228–29 ("Tarrentines"); John Lee Daly, "No Middle Ground: Pennacook–New England Relations in the Seventeenth Century" (MA thesis, Memorial University of Newfoundland, 1997), 25–57; David Stewart-Smith, "The Pennacook Indians and the New England Frontier, circa 1604–1733" (PhD diss., Union Institute, 1998), 61–67, 95, 97–98; Bahar, *Storm of the Sea*, 56–58; *The Journal of John Winthrop, 1630–1649*, ed. Richard S. Dunn, James Savage, and Laetitia Yeandle (Cambridge, MA: Harvard Univ. Press, 1996), 55; Salisbury, *Manitou and Providence*, 176 ("walls"), 184; Morton, *New English Canaan*, 163–65.

40   For instructive cautions against making disease the prime mover of European expansion at Native Americans' expense, see Cameron, Kelton, Swedlund, *Beyond Germs*; Reséndez, *The Other Slavery*.

CHAPTER 4: REACHING OUT TO STRANGERS

1   Among a voluminous literature informing this and the following paragraphs, see Edmund S. Morgan, *Visible Saints: The History of a Puritan Idea* (New York: New York Univ. Press, 1963), 1–63; Stephen Bracklow, *The Communion of Saints: Radical Puritan and Separatist Ecclesiology, 1559–1625* (Oxford: Oxford Univ. Press, 1988).

2   For the best recent studies, see Bunker, *Making Haste from Babylon*; Joke Kardux and Eduard van de Bilt, *Newcomers in an Old City: The American Pilgrims in Leiden, 1609–1620*, 3rd ed. (Leiden: Burgersdijk & Niermans, 2007); Jeremy Dupertuis Bangs, *Strangers and Pilgrims, Travellers and Sojourners: Leiden and the Foundations of Plymouth Plantation* (Plymouth, MA: General Society of Mayflower Descendants, 2009); and Nathaniel Philbrick, *Mayflower: A Story of Courage, Community, and War* (New York: Penguin Books, 2006). The following paragraphs also draw on these works. Bangs makes a compelling case that most of the *Mayflower* passengers were Separatists or their friends, not Church of England men (pp. 178–80, 227–79, 614–16), contrary to the influential argument that Separatists were the minority, as posited by George F. Willison, *Saints and Strangers: Being the Lives of the Pilgrim Fathers and Their Families, with Their Friends and Foes* (New York: Reynal & Hitchcock, 1945). On the business terms of the colony, see Ruth A. McIntyre, *Debts Hopeful and Desperate: Financing the Plymouth Colony* (Plymouth, MA: Plimoth Plantation, 1963).

3   *Mourt's Relation*, 20–21 ("odious"); Bradford, *Of Plymouth Plantation*, 1:191; Christopher Heaney, "A Peru of Their Own: English Grave-Opening and Indian Sovereignty in Early America," *WMQ* 73, no. 4 (2016): 609–46.

4   *Mourt's Relation*, 27–28.

5   *Mourt's Relation*, 27–28 ("remains"); Caleb Johnson, "The True Origin of Stephen Hopkins of the *Mayflower*: With Evidence of His Earlier Presence in Virginia," *American Genealogist* 73, no. 3 (1998): 161–71.

6   Bradford, *Of Plymouth Plantation*, 1:56–57 ("savage"); Quinn, "Martin Pring," 79–91.

7   Bradford, *Of Plymouth Plantation*, 1:165 ("baskets"), 166–67 ("God's good providence"); *Mourt's Relation*, 26, 29 ("bowls"; "best things").

8   *Mourt's Relation*, 32 ("cold"), 35 ("company").

9   *Mourt's Relation*, 35–37 (all quotes); Bradford, *Of Plymouth Plantation*, 1:168–72.

10   *Mourt's Relation*, 31 ("Thievish Harbor"), 39 ("Indian house"), 41 ("land cleared"); Bradford, *Of Plymouth Plantation*, 1:173; Morton, *New England's Memorial*, 37 ("first plantation").

11   Russell G. Handsman, "Landscapes of Memory in Wampanoag Country—and the Monuments upon them," in Patricia E. Rubertone, ed., *Archaeologies of Placemaking: Monuments, Memories, and Engagement in Native North America* (Walnut Creek, CA: Left Coast Press, 2008), 174; Bradford, *Of Plymouth Plantation*, 1:193.

12   Morton, *New England's Memorial*, 44 ("God was angry"); Bradford, *Of Plymouth Plantation*, 1:211–12; William Hubbard, *A General History of New England, from the Discovery to 1680*, MHSC, 2nd ser., vols. 5, 6 (Boston: Massachusetts Historical Society, 1848), 5:54–55.

13   *Mourt's Relation*, 42 ("cry"), 43 ("smokes"), 48 (deer killed), 49 (stalking fowl), 49 (hill; "noise"). See also Bradford, *Of Plymouth Plantation*, 1:198.

14   Bradford, *Of Plymouth Plantation*, 1:211–12 ("swamp"); Bragdon, *Native People, 1500–1650*, 192–93; Kevin A. McBride, "Prehistoric and Historic Patterns of Wetland Use in Eastern Connecticut," *Man in the Northeast* 43 (Spring 1992): 10–24.

15   Salisbury, *Manitou and Providence*, 92, 266n15; Vaughan, *Transatlantic Encounters*, 57–58, 60–65, 75–76; *Mourt's Relation*, 51–52 ("boldly"; "saluted"), 53; Bradford, *Of Plymouth Plantation*, 1:199 ("marveled").

16   *Mourt's Relation*, 51–52.

17   *Mourt's Relation*, 51–52.

18   *Mourt's Relation*, 53–54.

19   *Mourt's Relation*, 53–54. On the symbolism of black, see Bragdon, *Native People, 1500–1650*, 173, 222–24.

20   *Mourt's Relation*, 54.

21   James Phinney Baxter, *Christopher Levett of York: The Pioneer Colonist in Casco Bay* (Portland, ME: printed for the Gorges Society, 1893), 102 ("Somerset"), 103, 108–9, 111, 112.

22   Bradford, *Of Plymouth Plantation*, 1:202–3.

23   Winslow, *Good News*, 106–7 ("courage"; "discreet"); *Mourt's Relation*, 55; Bradford, *Of Plymouth Plantation*, 1:202–20. Neal Salisbury, "Squanto: Last of the Patuxet," in Ian K. Steele and Nancy L. Rhoden, eds., *The Human Tradition in Colonial America*

(Wilmington, DE: Scholarly Resources, 1999), 21–32, raises the possibility that Tisquantum was a pniese. Kupperman, *Indians and English*, 190, calls attention to Tisquantum as one of the Wampanoag names for the god of the dead.

24   *Mourt's Relation*, 58 ("great chain"; "strong"). On color symbolism, see Miller and Hamell, "New Perspective on Indian-White Contact," 325; Hamell, "Wampum."

25   *Mourt's Relation*, 55–56.

26   *Mourt's Relation*, 58. On pipes, see Gibson, *Burr's Hill*, 42–45; Williams, *Key into the Language*, 126–27.

27   The English versions of the treaty appear in Bradford, *Of Plymouth Plantation*, 1:201–2; *Mourt's Relation*, 56–57; and Morton, *New England's Memorial*, 40. On jurisdictional disputes over murder leading to war, see Alfred A. Cave, *The Pequot War* (Amherst: Univ. of Massachusetts Press, 1996); James Drake, *King Philip's War: Civil War in New England, 1675–1676* (Amherst: Univ. of Massachusetts Press, 1999); Evan Haefeli, "Kieft's War and the Systems of Violence in Colonial America," in Michael A. Bellesiles, ed., *Lethal Imagination: Violence and Brutality in American History* (New York: New York Univ. Press, 1999), 17–40; Paul Otto, *The Dutch-Munsee Encounter in America: The Struggle for Sovereignty in the Hudson Valley* (New York: Berghahn Books, 2006), 113–26.

28   *Mourt's Relation*, 56, 58 ("willing"), 60 ("greatest"). On the Powhatans and James-town, see J. Frederick Fausz, "An 'Abundance of Blood Shed on Both Sides': England's First Indian War, 1609–1614," *Virginia Magazine of History and Biog-raphy* 98, no. 1 (1990): 3–56.

29   On English impressions of sachem authority, see Kupperman, *Indians and English*, 77–109.

30   *Mourt's Relation*, 58. On this issue, see also Jeffrey Glover, *Paper Sovereigns: Anglo-Native Treaties and the Law of Nations, 1604–1664* (Philadelphia: Univ. of Pennsyl-vania Press, 2014), 118–57.

31   On the contested meanings of subjecthood between Indians and colonists, see Jenny Hale Pulsipher, *Subjects unto the Same King: Indians, English, and the Contest for Authority in Colonial New England* (Philadelphia: Univ. of Pennsylvania Press, 2005).

32   Bradford, *Of Plymouth Plantation*, 1:219 ("gratuity"); Robert A. Williams Jr., *Linking Arms Together: American Indian Treaty Visions of Law and Peace, 1600–1800* (New York: Oxford Univ. Press, 1999); Russel L. Barsh, "The Nature and Spirit of North American Political Systems," *American Indian Quarterly* 10, no. 3 (1986): 181–98; Colin G. Calloway, *Pen and Ink Witchcraft: Treaties and Treaty Making in American Indian History* (New York: Oxford Univ. Press, 2013).

33   *Mourt's Relation*, 62–64.

34   *Mourt's Relation*, 65 ("pacified"); Williams, *Key into the Language*, 158, 234; Joan M. Vastokas and Roman K. Vastokas, *Sacred Art of the Algonkians* (Petersborough, ON: Mansard Press, 1973), 93–94; Bragdon, *Native People, 1500–1650*, 187–88, 212; Thomas Harriot, *A briefe and true report of the new found land of Virginia* (1588), in

David B. Quinn and Alison M. Quinn, eds., *The First Colonists: Documents on the Planting of the First English Settlements in North America, 1584–1590* (Raleigh: North Carolina Dept. of Cultural Resources, Division of Archives and History, 1982), 72 ("kill and slay").

35   *Mourt's Relation*, 65.

36   *Mourt's Relation*, 66 ("King James"). On these speeches, see Kathleen J. Bragdon, "Emphatical Speech and Great Action: An Analysis of Seventeenth Century Native Speech Events Described in Early Sources," *Man in the Northeast* 33 (1987): 101–11.

37   *Mourt's Relation*, 66.

38   *Mourt's Relation*, 66.

39   *Mourt's Relation*, 69 ("special friend"), 70 ("personable"; "grievous").

40   *Mourt's Relation*, 70–71 (all quotes); Bradford, *Of Plymouth Plantation*, 1:222–24.

41   *Mourt's Relation*, 73 ("spoiled"; "draw"); Bradford, *Of Plymouth Plantation*, 1:225; Pratt, *Declaration*, 14.

42   *Mourt's Relation*, 74 ("lost their tongue"); Bradford, *Of Plymouth Plantation*, 1:225–27.

43   *Mourt's Relation*, 74.

44   *Mourt's Relation*, 75–76 ("revenged"), 77–78 ("threatened"); Bradford, *Of Plymouth Plantation*, 1:228–29.

45   W. Sears Nickerson, "Some Lower Cape Indians" (unpub. ms., 1933), MS 52, Sturgis Library, Barnstable, MA, 10, 12; Salisbury, *Manitou and Providence*, 120–21. On Weetamoo and Wootonekanuske, see Milton A. Travers, *The Wampanoag Indian Federation: Indian Neighbors of the Pilgrims* (New Bedford, MA: Reynolds-De Walt, 1957), 101–6; Gina M. Martino-Trutor, "'As Potent a Prince as any Around about Her': Rethinking Weetamoo of the Pocasset and Native Female Leadership in Early America," *Journal of Women's History* 27, no. 3 (2015): 37–60.

46   Winslow, *Good News*, 517–20 (all quotes); Bradford, *Of Plymouth Plantation*, 1:240–41, 242, 244.

47   *Mourt's Relation*, 82, 84; Bradford, *Of Plymouth Plantation*, 1:230–31; and, generally, Deetz and Deetz, *Times of Their Lives*, 2–9. The next several paragraphs also draw on these sources.

48   Bradford, *Of Plymouth Plantation*, 1:230–31; John Josselyn, *New-Englands Rarities Discovered* (London: printed for G. Widdowes, 1675), 52–53.

49   *Mourt's Relation*, 84; Bunker, *Making Haste from Babylon*, 299. See also the following interviews with Plimoth Plantation's Foodways Culinarian, Kathleen Wall: Erin Blasco, "Five Questions with a Colonial Culinarian," *O Say Can You See?* (blog), National Museum of American History, November 9, 2012, http://americanhistory .si.edu/blog/2012/11/fire-questions-for-a-colonial-culinarian-yum.html (accessed 01/20/2019); Megan Gambino, "What Was on the Menu at the First Thanksgiving?" *Smithsonian Magazine*, November 21, 2011, https://www.smithsonianmag.com/history /what-was-on-the-menu-at-the-first-thanksgiving-511554 (accessed 01/20/2019).

50 *Mourt's Relation*, 82.

51 *Mourt's Relation*, 82; Baker, *Thanksgiving*, 14–30; Deetz and Deetz, *Times of Their Lives*, 1–30; "Wampanoag on Thanksgiving," Many Hoops, http://www.manyhoops .com/wampanoag-on-thanksgiving.html (accessed 01/20/2019).

CHAPTER 5: OUSAMEQUIN'S POWER PLAY

1   McIntyre, *Debts Hopeful and Desperate*, 21–24 (quotes on 22); Michelle Burnam, "Merchants, Money, and the Politics of 'Plain Style' in William Bradford's *Plymouth Plantation*," *American Literature* 72, no. 4 (2000): 695–720; George D. Langdon, *Pilgrim Colony: A History of New Plymouth, 1620–1691* (New Haven, CT: Yale Univ. Press, 1966), 26–37; Salisbury, *Manitou and Providence*, 76–78, Daly, "No Middle Ground," 25–57; Stewart-Smith, "Pennacook Indians."

2   Winslow, *Good News*, 61–62.

3   Winslow, *Good News*, 63–64; Bradford, *Of Plymouth Plantation*, 1:252–53.

4   Winslow, *Good News*, 64. On other cases of rumor and power play in Native southern New England, see Robinson, "Struggle Within"; Michael Oberg, *Uncas: First of the Mohegans* (Ithaca, NY: Cornell Univ. Press, 2003), 34–40; Eric S. Johnson, "Uncas and the Politics of Contact," in Robert S. Grumet, ed., *Northeastern Indian Lives, 1632–1816* (Amherst: Univ. of Massachusetts Press, 1996), 29–47; Julie A. Fisher and David J. Silverman, *Ninigret, Sachem of the Niantics and Narragansetts: Diplomacy, War, and the Balance of Power in Seventeenth-Century New England and Indian Country* (Ithaca, NY: Cornell Univ. Press, 2014).

5   Winslow, *Good News*, 66. For other, similar cases, see Jeffrey Ostler, "'To Extirpate the Indians': An Indigenous Consciousness of Genocide in the Ohio Valley and Lower Great Lakes, 1750s–1810," *WMQ* 72, no. 4 (2015), 387–622; Gregory Evans Dowd, *Groundless: Rumors, Legends, and Hoaxes on the Early American Frontier* (Baltimore: Johns Hopkins Univ. Press, 2015), 38–62.

6   Morton, *New English Canaan*, 255 ("another sachem"); Roger Williams to Henry Vane and John Winthrop, May 1, 1637, in *Williams Correspondence*, 72 ("accused the English"); Winslow, *Good News*, 66 ("God of the English").

7   This line of interpretation is inspired by Anna Brickhouse, *The Unsettlement of America: Translation, Interpretation, and the Story of Don Luis de Velasco* (New York: Oxford Univ. Press, 2014), 44. Willison, *Saints and Strangers*, notes that Tisquantum had traveled more widely than any of the colonists. The most thorough examinations of Tisquantum are Salisbury, "Squanto: Last of the Patuxet," 21–32; and Neal Salisbury, "Squanto: Last of the Patuxets," in David Sweet and Gary B. Nash, eds., *Struggle and Survival in Colonial America* (Berkeley: Univ. of California Press, 1981), 228–46. See also John H. Humins, "Squanto and Massasoit: A Struggle for Power," *NEQ* 60, no. 1 (1987): 54–70; Vaughan, *Transatlantic Encounters*, 70–74; Weaver, *Red Atlantic*, 57–62; Thrush, *Indigenous London*, 33–61; Caleb Johnson, "Tisquantum ('Squanto')," http://mayflowerhistory.com/tisquantum/

(accessed 01/20/2019). I have also profited from Andrew Lipman's early versions of his forthcoming biography of Tisquantum.

8   Winslow, *Good News*, 65. On the pattern among Native New Englanders of severing the heads and hands of enemies, see Andrew Lipman, "'A Meanes to Knitt Them Togeather': The Exchange of Body Parts in the Pequot War," *WMQ* 65, no. 1 (2008): 3–28, esp. 11–13.

9   Winslow, *Good News*, 68.

10 Winslow, *Good News*, 68 ("cast forth"); Bradford, *Of Plymouth Plantation*, 1:255.

11 Bradford, *Of Plymouth Plantation*, 1:286.

12 Pratt, *Declaration*, 11.

13 Pratt, 8 ("great plague"; "half"); Winslow, *Good News*, 72 ("not unlike"), 74; Cook, *Indian Population of New England*, 36; *Records of the Council for New England* (Cambridge, MA: Press of J. Wilson & Son, 1867), 30 ("robbed").

14 Bradford, *Of Plymouth Plantation*, 1:270.

15 J. Frederick Fausz, "The Powhatan Uprising of 1622: A Historical Study of Ethnocentrism and Cultural Conflict" (PhD diss., College of William and Mary, 1977).

16 Winslow, *Good News*, 70–72; Bradford, *Of Plymouth Plantation*, 1:276 ("continual"), 281–83. On Plymouth's response to the news from Jamestown, see Cynthia J. Van Zandt, *Brothers among Nations: The Pursuit of Intercultural Alliances in Early America, 1580–1660* (New York: Oxford Univ. Press, 2008), 86–87. On fears of poisoning among southern New England Indians, see Simmons, *Spirit of the New England Tribes*, 92; Fisher and Silverman, *Ninigret*, 12, 91. Philbrick, *Mayflower*, 138, raises the possibility that Tisquantum was poisoned.

17 Winslow, *Good News*, 73 ("smart").

18 Winslow, 73–74.

19 Winslow, 77–78; Bragdon, "'Emphatical Speech and Great Action,'" 101–11.

20 Winslow, *Good News*, 77–78.

21 Winslow, 79 ("gentleman"), 80 ("loving sachem").

22 Winslow, 79–81.

23 Winslow, 81–82.

24 Winslow, 82–83.

25 Winslow, 83.

26 Winslow, 83. Bunker, *Making Haste from Babylon*, 327, raises the shaman comparison.

27 Winslow, *Good News*, 84.

28 Winslow, 86. On p. 87, Winslow specifies that Hobbamock shared this intelligence when they were west of Nemasket.

29 Winslow, 86.

30 Gookin, "Historical Collections," 154.

31 Winslow, *Good News*, 90, 91 ("traps").

32 Pratt, *Declaration*; Winslow, *Good News*, 91–93 ("encouragement"), 97.

33 Winslow, *Good News*, 93–95.

34 Winslow, 95–96.

35 Emanuel Altham to Sir Edward Altham, September 1623, James, *Three Visitors*, 29 (flag); Cave, *Pequot War*, 46–47 (cutthroats); Winslow, *Good News*, 97–98 ("manifold"; "God").

36 Bradford, *Of Plymouth Plantation*, 1:367–68.

37 *Mourt's Relation*, 83 ("walk"); *Plymouth Records*, 1:7; Morton, *New England's Memorial*, 87; *Journal of John Winthrop*, 51; Wood, *New England's Prospect*, 89–90; Bradford, *Of Plymouth Plantation*, 1:367–99 ("more glorious"); Winslow, *Good News*, 55 ("loose").

38 Matthew Mayhew, *A Brief Narrative of the Success which the Gospel Hath Had, among the Indians, of Martha's-Vineyard (and the Places Adjacent) in New-England* (Boston: printed by Bartholomew Green, 1694), 32–33; Elizabeth A. Little, "Three Kinds of Indian Land Deeds at Nantucket, Massachusetts," in William Cowan, ed., *Papers of the Eleventh Algonquian Conference* (Ottawa: Carleton Univ. Press, 1980), 64–65; *Mourt's Relation*, 83 ("great peace"); Emanuel Altham to Sir Edward Altham, September 1623, in James, *Three Visitors*, 29; Gibson, *Burr's Hill*.

39 *Journal of John Winthrop*, 64–65. Generally on the point that the Wampanoags found the English "preferable to the Narragansetts," see Salisbury, *Manitou and Providence*, 116.

40 Pratt, *Declaration*, 14 ("wonders"); Bradford, *Of Plymouth Plantation*, 1:353; Bunker, *Making Haste from Babylon*, 300, 361.

41 Williams, *Key into the Language*, 97, 99, 104, 106; Wood, *New England's Prospect*, 88; Morton, *New English Canaan*, 137; Gookin, "Historical Collections," 153; *Mourt's Relation*, 92 ("what place").

42 Wood, *New England Prospect*, 88.

CHAPTER 6: A GREAT MAN AND A LITTLE CHILD

1 Franklin B. Hough, ed., *Narrative of the Causes which Led to Philip's Indian War, of 1675 and 1676, by John Easton of Rhode Island* (Albany: J. Munsell, 1858), 12.

2 Winslow, *Good News*, 106; Robinson, "Struggle Within," 76–77, 81–82, 88–89.

3 Williams, *Key into the Language*, 193; Roger Williams to John Winthrop, August 20, 1637, in *Williams Correspondence*, 113.

4 Gibson, *Burr's Hill*, 14, 16, 17–21, 96; Elsie M. Brenner, "Sociopolitical Implications of Mortuary Ritual Remains in Seventeenth-Century Native Southern New England," in Mark P. Leone and Parker B. Potter Jr., eds., *The Recovery of Meaning: Historical Archaeology in the Eastern United States* (Washington, D.C.: Smithsonian Institution Press, 1988), 172; James Axtell, "The First Consumer Revolution: The Seventeenth Century," in his *Beyond 1492: Encounters in Colonial North America* (New York: Oxford Univ. Press, 1992), 125–51.

5   Miller and Hamell, "New Perspective on Indian-White Contact," 311–28 ("trading in metaphors" on 326); Nanepashemet and James W. Bradley, "Maps and Dreams: Native Americans and European Discovery," in van Donegan et al., *One Man's Trash*, 35; Williams, *Key into the Language*, 158, 234; Bragdon, *Native People . . . 1500–1650*, 187–88, 212; David J. Silverman, *Thundersticks: Firearms and the Violent Transformation of Native America* (Cambridge, MA: Belknap Press of Harvard Univ. Press, 2016), 11–12.

6   Salisbury, *Manitou and Providence*, 116–17, 129; Darrett B. Rutman, *Husbandmen of Plymouth: Farms and Villages in the Old Colony, 1620–1692* (Boston: published for Plimoth Plantation by Beacon Press, 1967); Daniel H. Usner Jr., *Indians, Settlers, and Slaves in a Frontier Exchange Economy: The Lower Mississippi Valley before 1783* (Chapel Hill: Univ. of North Carolina Press for the Institute of Early American History and Culture, 1992); *Plymouth Records*, 2:4 ("small things"). Suggestive evidence of these exchanges can also be found in *Plymouth Records*, 2:20, 89, 4:183, 190; *Mourt's Relation*, 62; Winslow, *Good News*, 148–49; Morton, *New English Canaan*, 162; Gookin, "Historical Collections," 434.

7   Kevin A. McBride, "The Source and Mother of the Fur Trade: Native-Dutch Relations in Eastern New Netherland," in Laurie Weinstein, ed., *Enduring Traditions: The Native Peoples of New England* (Westport, CT: Bergin & Garvey, 1994), 31–52; Andrew Lipman, *The Saltwater Frontier: Indians and the Contest for the American Coast* (New Haven, CT: Yale Univ. Press, 2015), 105–12; Francis X. Maloney, *The Fur Trade in New England, 1620–1676* (Hamden, CT: Archon Books, 1967), 41–42.

8   Bradford, *Of Plymouth Plantation*, 1:343–45 ("few beads"); Emmanuel Altham to Sir Edward Altham, March 1623–24, in James, *Three Visitors*, 36; William I. Robert, "The Fur Trade of New England in the Seventeenth Century" (PhD diss., University of Pennsylvania, 1958), 27, 34–35; Carl Bridenbaugh, *Fat Mutton and Liberty of Conscience: Society in Rhode Island, 1636–1690* (Providence, RI: Brown Univ. Press, 1974), 23; Roger H. King, *Cape Cod and Plymouth Colony in the Seventeenth Century* (Lanham, MD: Univ. Press of America, 1993), 30.

9   Robert, "Fur Trade," 32; Salisbury, *Manitou and Providence*, 145.

10   Langdon, *Pilgrim Colony*, 31–32, 36; Eugene Aubrey Stratton, *Plymouth Colony: Its History and People* (Salt Lake City: Ancestry Publishing, 1986), 27–28; James, *Three Visitors*, 74–75 ("house"); Willison, *Saints and Strangers*, 284; King, *Cape Cod and Plymouth Colony*, 34. Percival Hall Lombard, *The Aptucxet Trading Post: The First Trading Post of the Plymouth Colony, with an Account of Its Restoration on the Original Foundations* (Bourne, MA: Bourne Historical Society, 1934), 26, makes a convincing case that this stout post replaced an insubstantial structure at the same site.

11   Cronon, *Changes in the Land*, 95; M. J. Becker, "Wampum Use in Southern New England: The Paradox of Bead Production without the Use of Political Belts," in

Chilton and Rainey, *Nantucket and Other Native Places*, 137–58; Lois Scozzari, "The Significance of Wampum to Seventeenth Century Indians in New England," *Connecticut Review* 17, no. 1 (1995): 59–69; Frank G. Speck, "The Functions of Wampum Among the Eastern Algonkian," *Memoirs of the American Anthropological Association* 6, no. 1 (1919): 3–71; Hamell, "Wampum," 45–46; William Engelbrecht, *Iroquoia: The Development of a Native World* (Syracuse, NY: Syracuse Univ. Press, 2003), 156. On the evolving terminology of these beads, see Paul Otto, "'This is that which . . . they call Wampum': Europeans Coming to Terms with Native Shell Beads," *Early American Studies* 15, no. 1 (2017): 1–36.

12 James W. Bradley, *Before Albany: An Archaeology of Native-Dutch Relations in the Capital Region, 1600–1664* (Albany: Univ. of the State of New York, State Education Dept., 2006), 128; Engelbrecht, *Iroquoia*, 156; Martha M. Sempowski, "Fluctuations through Time in Use of Marine Shell at Seneca Iroquois Sites," in Charles F. Hayes, Lynn Ceci, and Connie Cox Bodner, eds., *Proceedings of the 1986 Shell Bead Conference* (Rochester, NY: Research Division of the Rochester Museum and Science Center, 1986), 83, 86; Paul Otto, "Henry Hudson, the Munsees, and the Wampum Revolution," in Jaap Jacobs and Louis Roper, eds., *The Worlds of the Seventeenth Century Hudson Valley* (Albany: State Univ. of New York Press, 2014), 91–92; Salisbury, *Manitou and Providence*, 151; Cronon, *Changes in the Land*, 95–97; Wood, *New England's Prospect*, 81.

13 McBride, "Source and Mother"; Bradford, *Of Plymouth Plantation*, 42–43; James, *Three Visitors*, 63. On later manifestations of the Dutch-Chesapeake trade, see James R. Perry, *Formation of a Society on Virginia's Eastern Shore, 1615–1655* (Chapel Hill: Univ. of North Carolina Press for the Institute of Early American History and Culture, 1990), 14; April Lee Hatfield, *Atlantic Virginia: Intercolonial Relations in the Seventeenth Century* (Philadelphia: Univ. of Pennsylvania Press, 2004), 77, 103.

14 Bradford, *Of Plymouth Plantation*, 2:190, 226–27, 2:26 ("at our doors"), 43–44 ("scarce"); Langdon, *Pilgrim Colony*, 31–32, 36; Bunker, *Making Haste from Babylon*, 233; William B. Weeden, *Indian Money as a Factor in New England Civilization* (Baltimore: Johns Hopkins University, 1884), esp. 22–25; Alden T. Vaughan, *New England Frontier: Puritans and Indians, 1620–1675*, 3rd ed. (Norman: Univ. of Oklahoma Press, 1995), 220; Lynn Ceci, "Native Wampum as a Peripheral Resource in the Seventeenth-Century World-System," in Laurence M. Hauptman and James D. Wherry, eds., *The Pequots in Southern New England: The Fall and Rise of an American Indian Nation* (Norman: Univ. of Oklahoma Press, 1990), 48–64; Mary W. Herman, "Wampum as Money in Northeastern North America," *Ethnohistory* 3, no. 1 (1956): 21–33.

15 Bradford, *Of Plymouth Plantation*, 2:43–44 ("none or very little"; "drug"); Morton, *New England's Memorial*, 89; Gibson, *Burr's Hill*, 118–19, 158–59, 160. On the assumption of Narragansett and Pequot dominance, see, for example, Drake, *King Philip's War*, 22; Cronon, *Changes in the Land*, 96. A notable exception to this trend is Ceci, "Wampum as a Peripheral Resource," 48–49. On the actual

distribution of the shells, see Clyde L. MacKenzie Jr. et al., "Quahogs in Eastern North America: Part I, Biology, Ecology, and Historical Uses," *Marine Fisheries Review* 64, no. 2 (2002): 3; Bhae-Jin Peemoeller and Bradley G. Stevens, "Age, Size, and Sexual Maturity of Channeled Whelk (*Busycotypus canaliculatus*) in Buzzards Bay, Massachusetts," *Fishery Bulletin* 111, no. 3 (2013): 265–78; Frank G. Speck and Ralph W. Dexter, "The Utilization of Marine Life by the Wampanoag Indians of Massachusetts," *Journal of the Washington Academy of Sciences* 38, no. 8 (August 1948): 257–65.

16 Bradford, *Of Plymouth Plantation*, 2:52–53 ("mad"), 56–57; William Bradford to Sir Ferdinando Gorges, June 15, 1627, and Bradford to Council for New England, June 9, 1628, in *Governor William Bradford's Letter Book* (Bedford, MA: Applewood Books, 2001), 36, 41–44; Morton, *New England's Memorial*, 91–93. Other historians are more skeptical of Plymouth's rationales for the mission. See Michael Zuckerman, "Pilgrims in the Wilderness: Community, Modernity, and the Maypole at Merry Mount," *NEQ* 50, no. 2 (1977): 255–77; Salisbury, *Manitou and Providence*, 157–62.

17 Elizabeth S. Chilton and Dianna L. Doucette, "Archaeological Investigation at the Lucy Vincent Beach Site," 19, MS in the author's possession; personal correspondence with Holly Herbster of Public Archaeological Laboratory; Franklin B. Hough, ed., *Papers Relating to the Island of Nantucket, with Documents Relating to the Original Settlement of the Island, Martha's Vineyard and Other Islands Adjacent, Known as Dukes County, While under the Colony of New York* (Albany: [J. Munsell], 1865), 108; New York Colonial MS, 3:68–71, quoted in Charles E. Banks, ed., *History of Martha's Vineyard, Dukes County, Massachusetts*, 3 vols. (Boston: George H. Deans, 1911), 1:150 ("sewan").

18 On Plymouth's population, Robert Charles Anderson, *The Pilgrim Migration: Immigrants to Plymouth Colony, 1620–1633* (Boston: New England Historical Genealogical Society, 2004), xxxix; Stratton, *Plymouth Colony*, 50. On the Great Migration, Virginia DeJohn Anderson, *New England's Generation: The Great Migration and the Formation of Society and Culture in the Seventeenth Century* (New York: Cambridge Univ. Press, 1991); Robert Charles, "A Note on the Changing Pace of the Great Migration," *NEQ* 59, no. 3 (1986): 406–7. On demographic growth, see John M. Murrin, "Review Essay," *History and Theory* 11 (1972): 226–75; Murrin, "Beneficiaries of Catastrophe: The English Colonies in America," in Eric Foner, ed., *The New American History* (Philadelphia: Temple Univ. Press, 1997), 3–30; Gloria L. Main, *Peoples of Spacious Lands: Families and Cultures in Colonial New England* (Cambridge, MA: Harvard Univ. Press, 2001). On the Indian population, see Fisher and Silverman, *Ninigret*, 108, 170n56.

19 Stratton, *Plymouth Colony*, 70; Samuel Hugh Brockunier, *The Irrepressible Democrat, Roger Williams* (New York: Ronald Press, 1940), 82–100; Sydney V. James, *Colonial Rhode Island: A History* (New York: Charles Scribner's Sons, 1975), 13–32.

20 Salisbury, *Manitou and Providence*, 191; Dean R. Snow and Kim M. Lanphear, "European Contact and Indian Depopulation in the Northeast: The Timing of the First Epidemics," *Ethnohistory* 35, no. 1 (1988): 23; Bradford, *Of Plymouth Plantation*, 1:193–94 ("mortality"); John Winthrop to Nathaniel Rich, May 22, 1634, in Allyn B. Forbes, ed., *Winthrop Papers*, 5 vols. (Boston, 1929–45), 3:167 ("near all dead"); Stratton, *Plymouth Colony*, 46.

21 Whitfield, *Light appearing*, 177 ("strange disease"), 178 ("universal"); *Indian Converts*, 171 ("sore Distemper"; "many of them"); Dane Morrison, *A Praying People: Massachusett Acculturation and the Failure of the Puritan Mission, 1600–1690* (New York: P. Lang, 1995), 6. On the blackface mourning ritual, see Gookin, "Historical Collections," 153; Morton, *New English Canaan*, 170; Williams, *Key into the Language*, 115–16, 247–50; *John Josselyn*, 95.

22 On these developments, see Cave, *Pequot War*, 69–121; Fisher and Silverman, *Ninigret*, 32–38; Andrew Lipman, "Murder on the Saltwater Frontier: The Death of John Oldham," *Early American Studies* 9, no. 2 (2011): 268–94.

23 Cave, *Pequot War*; Oberg, *Uncas*.

24 John Mason, *A Brief History of the Pequot War* (Boston: S. Kneeland and T. Green, 1736), in Charles Orr, ed., *History of the Pequot War: The Contemporary Accounts of Mason, Underhill, Vincent, and Gardener* (Cleveland: Helman-Taylor, 1897), 84 ("Lord judge"); *Mass. Bay Recs.*, 1:200.

25 Michael J. Fickes, "'They Could Not Endure That Yoke': The Captivity of Pequot Women and Children After the War of 1637," *NEQ* 73, no 1. (2000): 58–81; Margaret Ellen Newell, *Brethren by Nature: New England Indians, Colonists, and the Origins of American Slavery* (Ithaca, NY: Cornell Univ. Press, 2015), 17–42; Clinton Alfred Weslager, *The English on the Delaware, 1610–1682* (New Brunswick, NJ: Rutgers Univ. Press, 1967), 96; Daragh Grant, "The Treaty of Hartford (1638): Reconsidering Jurisdiction in Southern New England," *WMQ* 72, no. 3 (2015): 461–98.

26 *Journal of John Winthrop*, 256; *Plymouth Records*, 1:133 ("against all"); Morton, *New England's Memorial*, 141–42. That these were Mohicans is indicated by Ousamequin's identification of their homeland as lying "beyond Connecticut [River] and Pakontuckett." Pakontuckett probably meant Pocumtuck, or modern Deerfield, Massachusetts. Both the Connecticut River and Pocumtuck were west of Mohegan territory. "Beyond," which is to say, west of those places, were the Mohicans of the Housatonic and Hudson Rivers.

27 John Underhill, *Newes from America; Or, A New and Experimentall Discoverie of New England* (1638), in Orr, *History of the Pequot War*, 84 ("machit"); Cave, *Pequot War*; Oberg, *Uncas*.

28 *Papers and Biography of Lion Gardiner, 1599–1663*, ed. Curtiss C. Gardiner (St. Louis, MO: Levison & Blythe, 1883), 29–30; Michael Leroy Oberg, "'We Are all Sachems from East to West': A New Look at Miantonomi's Campaign of Resistance," *New England Quarterly* 77, no. 4 (2004): 478–99.

29 *Journal of John Winthrop*, 399 ("attended"), 406–7 ("terror"); *United Colonies Records*, 1:10 ("labor").

30 William Hubbard, *A General History of New England, from the Discovery to 1680*, 2nd ed., *MHSC*, 2nd ser., vols. 5, 6 (Boston, 1848), 33 ("some have said"); *Journal of John Winthrop*, 494, 497, 498–99.The Wampanoag sachem's relationship to the Nipmucs has confused historians for more than a century because a Nipmuc sachem had a similar name, Woosamequin, and Pokanoket claimed the Nipmuc community of Quabaug as a protectorate. Yet Ousamequin and Woosamequin were undoubtedly two different people because Ousamequin was dead by June 13, 1660, whereas the Nipmuc sachem, Woosamequin, was not. Nine months later, the Nipmuc figure changed his name to Matchippa before helping Quabaug to fend off attacks by Uncas and the Mohegans. On this question, see John Eliot to John Endicott, March 28, 1661, *Proceedings of the Massachusetts Historical Society*, vol. 3 (1855–58): 312–13; Samuel G. Drake, *Biography and History of the Indians of North America, from Its First Discovery*, 11th ed. (Boston: Benjamin B. Mussey & Company, 1851), 105–6; J. H. Temple, *History of North Brookfield, Massachusetts* (North Brookfield, MA: The Town of North Brookfield, 1887), 28, 45–46; Dennis A. Connole, *The Indians of the Nipmuck Country in Southern New England, 1630–1750: An Historical Geography* (Jefferson, NC: McFarland & Co., 2001), 66, 77; and Richard W. Cogley, *John Eliot's Mission to the Indians before King Philip's War* (Cambridge, MA: Harvard Univ. Press, 1999), 275n23.

31 *United Colonies Records*, 1:10–11; *Winthrop Journal*, 471–73; Vaughan, *New England Frontier*, 163–66; Salisbury, *Manitou and Providence*, 234–35; Oberg, *Uncas*, 87–109.

32 John Brown to John Winthrop, June 26, 1644, and William Coddington to John Winthrop, August 5, 1644, in *Winthrop Papers*, 4:465, 491 ("one heart"); Fisher and Silverman, *Ninigret*, 59–65.

33 Howard M. Chapin, ed., *Documentary History of Rhode Island*, 2 vols. (Providence, 1916–19), 1:2 ("spared"), 14, 15.

34 Roger Williams to the Assembly of Commissioners, Nov. 17, 1677, in *Williams Correspondence*, 751–52.

35 Among the first historians to realize that the Wampanoags and Narragansetts were using the English as a buffer was Thomas Williams Bicknell, *Sowams: With Ancient Records of Sowams and Parts Adjacent—Illustrated* (New Haven, CT: Connecticut Associated Publishers of American Records, 1908), 26–27. On other themes, see Chapin, *Documentary History of Rhode Island*, 1:2 ("gratuity"), 52, 2:40; James, *Colonial Rhode Island*, 8; Robinson, "Struggle Within," 123; *Rhode Island Records*, 1:22 ("monies," "peaceable"), 47 ("carriage"); Anne Keary, "Retelling the History of the Settlement of Providence: Speech, Writing, and Cultural Interaction on Narragansett Bay," *NEQ* 69, no. 2 (1996): 250–86.

36 Chapin, *Documentary History of Rhode Island*, 1:240–42. See also *Rhode Island Records*, 1:32, 33–34.

37   Chapin, *Documentary History of Rhode Island*, 1:239–40 ("could not"); *The Early Records of the Town of Portsmouth* (Providence, RI: E. L. Freeman, 1901), 29; *Rhode Island Records*, 1:81; Roger Williams to the Massachusetts General Court, Nov. 1, 1655, in *Williams Correspondence*, 445 ("dangers"). Generally, Allan Greer, *Property and Dispossession: Natives, Empires, and Land in Early Modern North America* (New York: Cambridge Univ. Press, 2018), 81–95.

38   The documents for these sales appear in Jeremy Duperituis Bangs, ed., *Indian Deeds: Land Transactions in Plymouth Colony, 1620–1691* (Boston: New England Historic Genealogical Society, 2002), 260, 263–64 ("annoyed"), 269–70. See also Bicknell, *Sowams*, 27–28.

39   On Brown, see Robert Charles Anderson, *The Great Migration Begins: Immigrants to New England, 1620–1633* (Boston: New England Historic Genealogical Society, 1995), 420–29; *Plymouth Colony Records*, 2:120, 3:21 ("damage"), 3:133–34; Bangs, *Indian Deeds*, 250, 256, 269–70, 387–88; John Frederick, *Profits in the Wilderness: Entrepreneurship and the Founding of New England Towns in the Seventeenth Century* (Chapel Hill: Univ. of North Carolina Press for the Institute of Early American History and Culture, 1991), 81–82; Richard Lebaron Bowen, *Early Rehoboth: Documented Historical Studies of Families and Events in This Plymouth Colony Township*, vol. 1 (Rehoboth, MA: privately printed [by the Rumford Press], 1945), 25–26.

40   On Willet, see Anderson, *Great Migration Begins*, 1997–2002; Martin, *Profits in the Wilderness*, 80–81; Rhode Island/Massachusetts Boundaries, 1:46, Rhode Island State Archives, Providence; Bangs, *Indian Deeds*, 269–70, 297, 301–2, 310, 319, 326, 327 ("loving friend"), 344, 356–57, 371–73, 382, 387, 391–92; *Plymouth Colony Records* 3:167, 180, 192, 4:8, 18, 31, 51, 54, 109–10, 5:24.

41   On gun-related issues, see *Plymouth Colony Records*, 2:8, 99 ("affray"), 135, 3:2. On liquor, see *Plymouth Colony Records*, 3:61, 5:159, 339, 40, 81, 107, 148. Generally, see Peter C. Mancall, *Deadly Medicine: Indians and Alcohol in Early America* (Ithaca, NY: Cornell Univ. Press, 1995), esp. 105.

42   Lion Gardiner, "Relation of the Pequot Warres" (1660), in Charles Orr, ed., *History of the Pequot War: The Contemporary Accounts of Mason, Underhill, Vincent, and Gardener* (Cleveland: Helman-Taylor, 1897), 142–43.

43   Bangs, *Indian Deeds*, 260, 263–64.

44   The sales can be traced in Bangs, *Indian Deeds*, 252–54, 255, 271–72, 277, 277–78, 284, 299–301, 332–24, 346, 362–63, 364, 401, 432–34. On English expansion on the Cape, see *Plymouth Colony Records*, 1:79, 95, 148, 255, 2:5, 9, 11; King, *Cape Cod and Plymouth Colony*. On area resources, Anne E. Yentsch, "Farming, Fishing, Whaling, Trading: Land and Sea as Resource on Eighteenth-Century Cape Cod," in Marcy C. Beaudry, ed., *Documentary Archaeology in the New World* (New York: Cambridge Univ. Press, 1988), 138–60; Susan M. Ouellette, "Divine Providence and Collective Endeavor: Sheep Production in Early Massachusetts," *NEQ* 69, no. 3 (1995): 355–80; Patricia E. Rubertone, "Changes in Coastal Wilderness:

Historical Land Use Patterns on Outer Cape Cod, 17th–19th Centuries," in Francis P. McManamon, ed., *The Historic Period and Historic Period Archeology*, vol. 3 of *Chapters in the Archeology of Cape Cod* (Boston: Division of Cultural Resources, North Atlantic Regional Office, National Park Service, U.S. Dept. of the Interior, 1986), 83–87.

45 Bangs, *Indian Deeds*, 252–54; Jeremy Dupertuis Bangs, ed., *The Town Records of Eastham during the Time of Plymouth Colony, 1620(43)–1692* (Leiden: Leiden American Pilgrim Museum, 2012), 3. See also pp. 43, 47, 53, 89–90. On George, see W. Sears Nickerson, "Some Lower Cape Indians" (1933), MS 52, p. 12, Sturgis Library, Barnstable, MA. On English authorities' insistence on respecting reserved Indian rights, see *Plymouth Court Records*, 3:84 ("not cause"), 85, 123, 175, 181, 4:18.

46 On Nepoyetum, see Bangs, *Indian Deeds*, 257; *Plymouth Colony Records*, 2:22. On Seeknout, see Testimony of James Pease, Sarah Natick, and Thomas Mayhew, Suffolk Files, no. 14047, MA Archives.

47 William Bradford to John Winthrop, Dec. 10, 1646, *Winthrop Papers*, 5:57 ("not to pay"); Roger Williams to John Winthrop Jr., May 23, 1650, in *Williams Correspondence*, 314 ("sturgeon"). On horses: Bangs, *Eastham Town Records*, 3, 110–11; Jeremy Dupertuis Bangs, ed., *The Town Records of Sandwich during the Time of Plymouth Colony* (Leiden: Leiden American Pilgrim Museum, 2014), 80, 82–84, 90, 214–15.

48 Generally, see William Kellaway, *The New England Company, 1649–1776* (New York: Barnes and Noble, 1961); Cogley, *John Eliot's Mission*; Silverman, *Faith and Boundaries*.

49 Silverman, *Faith and Boundaries*; Cogley, *John Eliot's Mission*. Generally, see Edward E. Andrews, *Native Apostles: Black and Indian Missionaries in the British Atlantic World* (Cambridge, MA: Harvard Univ. Press, 2013).

50 Anonymous, *New England's First Fruits* (1643), in *Eliot Tracts*, 61 ("mosquito"); John Eliot, "A Breif [*sic*] History of the Mashepog Indians" (1666), ed. J. Patrick Cesarini, *WMQ* 65, no. 1 (2008): 129 ("angry"), 131 ("deliver"). On disease, see Whitfield, *Light appearing*, 148–50, 177; Whitfield, *Strength out of Weakness*, 221; Edward Winslow, *The Glorious Progress of the Gospel amongst the Indians of New England* (1649), in *Eliot Tracts*, 77–78; James Naeher, "Dialogue in the Wilderness: John Eliot and the Indians' Exploration of Puritanism as a Source of Meaning, Comfort, and Ethnic Survival," *NEQ* 62, no. 3 (1989): 346–68.

51 Thomas Shepard, *The Clear Sun-shine of the Gospel breaking forth upon the Indians in New-England* (1648), in *Eliot Tracts*, 119 ("forefathers," "moosquantum"); Winslow, *Glorious Progress*, 78 ("wise men"); William S. Simmons, "Of Large Things Remembered: Southern New England Indian Legends of Colonial Encounters," in Anne Elizabeth Yentsch and Mary C. Beaudry, eds., *The Art and Mystery of Historical Archaeology: Essays in Honor of James Deetz* (Boca Raton, FL: CRC Press, 1992), 322–23; Thomas Mayhew Jr. to John Winthrop, August 15, 1648, Mayhew Papers, Muger Library Special Collections, Boston University.

52 John Eliot, *A Further Account of the progress of the Gospel Amongst the Indians in New England* (1660), in *Eliot Tracts*, 370, 375 ("might kill"); Roger Williams to Massachusetts General Court, Oct. 5, 1654, in *Williams Correspondence*, 409 ("high sachems"); Henry M. Ward, *The United Colonies of New England, 1643–1690* (New York: Vantage Press, 1961); Kellaway, *New England Company.*

53 Winslow, *Glorious Progress*, 83 ("distribute"); Shepard, *Clear Sun-shine*, 134 ("mattocks"); Lisa Brooks, *Our Beloved Kin: A New History of King Philip's War* (New Haven, CT: Yale Univ. Press, 2018), 72–106.

54 Gookin, "Historical Collections," 196–98; Kathleen J. Bragdon, "Vernacular Literacy and Massachusett Worldview, in Peter Benes, ed., *Algonkians of the Northeast: Past and Present* (Boston: Boston University, 1993), 26–34; E. Jennifer Monaghan, "'She loved to read in good Books': Literacy and the Indians of Martha's Vineyard, 1643–1725," *History of Education Quarterly* 30, no. 4 (1990): 492–521; Kristina Bross and Hillary Wyss, eds., *Early Native Literacies in New England: A Documentary and Critical Anthology* (Amherst: Univ. of Massachusetts Press, 2008); Silverman, *Faith and Boundaries*, 93, 117, 161; Cogley, *John Eliot's Mission*, 121–24, 219–23; Kellaway, *New England Company*, 122–65; Jill Lepore, *The Name of War: King Philip's War and the Origins of American Identity* (New York: Alfred A. Knopf, 1998), 28–41. Gookin's figures were that 142 of 461 Christian Wampanoags (adults and children) from the Cape could read Wampanoag and 72 of 461 could write it.

55 On Massachusetts praying towns, see Cogley, *John Eliot's Mission*, 105–46; Jean M. O'Brien, *Dispossession by Degrees: Indian Land and Identity in Natick, Massachusetts, 1650–1790* (New York: Cambridge Univ. Press, 1997), 31–64. On Mashpee, see *Plymouth Records*, 6:159 ("forever"); MA Archives, 33:149–50; Jack Campisi, *The Mashpee Indians: Tribe on Trial* (Syracuse, NY: Syracuse Univ. Press, 1991), 77–78. On Bourne's land speculation, see *Plymouth Records*, 3:85, 193–94, 201, 208, 216–17, 4:4.

56 Len Travers, ed., "The Missionary Journal of John Cotton, Jr.," *Proceedings of the Massachusetts Historical Society*, 3rd ser., vol. 109 (1997): 77 ("righteous"). On Christiantown, see Ayer MS 589, Newberry Library, Chicago; Suffolk Files nos. 953, 3068, 4974, p. 12, Mass. State Archives. Histories commonly date the formation of this town to 1659 based on a vague statement made in 1699 that it had been founded "about forty years ago." The formal grant was made in 1669–70. See DCD, 1:357, 378, 402, 2:142.

57 Henry W. Bowden and James P. Ronda, eds., *John Eliot's Indian Dialogues: A Study in Cultural Interaction* (Westport, CT: Greenwood Press, 1980), 122; Whitfield, *Light appearing*, 202 ("plainly see"), 203–4; John Eliot to the New England Company, October 10, 1652, *NEHGR* (1882), 294–95 ("professed").

58 William Hubbard, *A Narrative of the Troubles with the Indians in New England* (1677), in Samuel G. Drake, ed., *The History of the Indian Wars in New England, from the First Settlement to the Termination of the War with King Philip, in 1677*, 2 vols.

(Roxbury, MA: printed for W. E. Woodward, 1865), 1:47; *Indian Converts*, 116–17; *Conquests and Triumphs*, 23, 39 ("prince"); Thomas Prince, *Some Account of those English Ministers who have Successfully Presided Over the Work of Gospelizing the Indians on Martha's Vineyard and the Adjacent Islands*, appendix to Experience Mayhew, *Indian Converts: Or, Some Account of the Lives and Dying Speeches of a Considerable Number of the Christianized Indians of Martha's Vineyard* (London: printed for Samuel Gerrish, 1727), 293–94; Eliot and Mayhew, *Tears of Repentance*, 258 ("great enemy").

59 Weeden, *Indian Money as a Factor in New England Civilization*, 19–20, 25–29; William B. Weeden, *Economic and Social History of New England, 1620–1789*, 2 vols. (Boston: Houghton, Mifflin and Company, 1890), 1:40–44.

60 Williams to John Winthrop, Aug. 20, 1637, in *Williams Correspondence*, 113.

61 Samuel D. Drake, *The Old Indian Chronicle: Being a Collection of Exceedingly Rare Tracts, Written and Published in the Time of King Philip's War* (Boston: printed by the author, 1867), 31.

CHAPTER 7: UNGRATEFUL

1 *Plymouth Records*, 3:192. On the practice of subtle threats, see Seth Mallios, *The Deadly Politics of Giving: Exchange and Violence at Ajacan, Roanoke, and Jamestown* (Tuscaloosa: Univ. of Alabama Press, 2006).

2 Fisher and Silverman, *Ninigret*, 107–8, 170n56; Bridenbaugh, *Fat Mutton and Liberty of Conscience*, 27–42; Wendy Warren, *New England Bound: Slavery and Colonization in Early America* (New York: Liverlight, 2016), 49–82; Martin, *Profits in the Wilderness*; Cronon, *Changes in the Land*, 127–57; Pastore, *Between Land and Sea*, 1–49.

3 Bangs, *Indian Deeds*, 286–87 ("I Wamsutta"), 291–93, 298, 301–2 ("plant"); DCD, 3:12–13; MA Archives, 30:102.

4 *Plymouth Records*, 4:8 ("in case").

5 *Plymouth Records*, 4:18; William Read Staples, ed., *Annals of the Town of Providence: From Its First Settlement to the Organization of the City Government* (Providence, RI: printed by Knowles and Vose, 1843), 574–75; Suffolk Deeds, 7:161–63, Mass. State Archives; *Plymouth Records*, 4:8, 16–17, 18; Martino-Trutor, "'As Potent a Prince,'" 43.

6 Increase Mather, *A relation of the troubles which have happened in New-England* (Boston: printed by John Foster, 1677), 70–72; Hubbard, *Narrative of the Troubles*, 1:49–51; John Cotton Jr. to Increase Mather, March 19–20, 1677, in Sheila McIntyre and Len Travers, eds., *The Correspondence of John Cotton Junior* (Boston: Colonial Society of Massachusetts, 2009), 188 ("report").

7 Hubbard, *Narrative of the Troubles*, 1:49–51 ("dead man" on 50); Mather, *Relation of the Troubles*, 70–71; Cotton Mather, *Magnalia Christi Americana: Or, The Ecclesiastical History of New England*, 2 vols. (Hartford, CT: published by Silas Andrus;

Roberts & Burr, printers, 1820), 2:485; Cotton to Mather, March 19–20, 1677, in *Cotton Correspondence*, 188 ("freely"); Hough, *Narrative of the Causes*, 12–13 ("forced"); Brooks, *Our Beloved Kin*, 50–52. Historians accepting the pistol story include Jennings, *Invasion of America*, 289; Russell Bourne, *The Red King's Rebellion: Racial Politics in New England, 1675–1678* (New York: Oxford Univ. Press, 1990); Philbrick, *Mayflower*, 203.

8   Mather, *Relation*, 72 ("Fuller"); Hough, *Narrative of the Causes*, 12–13 ("judged").

9   *Plymouth Records*, 4:25. On Sonkanuhoo, see Ebenezer Pierce Weaver, *Indian History, Biography, and Genealogy: Pertaining to the Good Sachem Massasoit of the Wampanoag Tribe* (North Abington, MA: Z. G. Mitchell, 1878), 211; Bangs, *Indian Deeds*, 388.

10   On the Quabaug dispute, see *United Colonies Records*, 2:269; Temple, *History of North Brookfield*, 45–46. On Namumpum's marriage to Quequegunent, see Brooks, *Our Beloved Kin*, 58–59. On Pumetacom's disagreement with Namumpum, see *Plymouth Records*, 4:24–25; Thomas Prince to Josiah Winslow, October 8, 1663, Winslow Family Papers II, 1638–1760, MHS; Martino-Trutor, "'As Potent a Prince,'" 58.

11   Bangs, *Indian Deeds*, 330–31, 387–88, 392–93. On evidence of public consent, see Bangs, *Indian Deeds*, 330–31, 353–55, 355–56, 382, 387–88, 392–93, 406–7, 444–47.

12   Mattapoisett Indians to Thomas Prince, August 9, 1667, Winslow Family Papers II, MHS ("afraid"); Roger Williams to John Winthrop Jr., May 28, 1664, in *Williams Correspondence*, 528 ("God Land"); Bangs, *Indian Deeds*, 406–7, 444–47. See also Jeremy Dupertuis Bangs, ed., *The Seventeenth-Century Town Records of Scituate Massachusetts*, 3 vols. (Boston: New England Historic Genealogical Society, 1997), 3:70.

13   Bangs, *Indian Deeds*, 308–9, 381, 400 ("neither Tispaquin"), 408–10, 415–16, 436–37, 461–63, 468, 482–84; Curwen Family Mss., box 1, folder 2, AAS. On Buzzards Bay sales, see Bangs, *Indian Deeds*, 302, 316–18, 319, 324–25, 335–36, 340, 350–51, 353, 355–56, 379–80, 425–26. On Narragansett and Nipmuc sales, see Connole, *Indians of Nipmuck Country*, 138–58; James, *Colonial Rhode Island*, 82–87; Fisher and Silverman, *Ninigret*, 89–93.

14   *Plymouth Records*, 4:34–35 ("long practiced"). On timber, *Plymouth Records*, 4:54. On livestock, *Plymouth Records*, 3:21, 89–90, 91, 106, 119–20, 132, 167, 192, 200, 222, 4:17, 53–54, 68, 92–93, 109, 191; Bangs, *Town Records of Eastham*, 109.

15   *Plymouth Records*, 4:66, 5:6, 11–12, 22, 85; *Rhode Island Records*, 2:172–73; *The Early Records of the Town of Portsmouth* (Providence, RI: Freeman & Sons, 1901), 149–50; Winslow, *Good News*, 81. Generally on these points, see Virginia DeJohn Anderson, "King Philip's Herds: Indians, Colonists, and the Problem of Livestock in Early New England," *WMQ* 51, no. 4 (1994): 601–24; Anderson, *Creatures of Empire: How Domestic Animals Transformed Early America* (New York: Oxford Univ. Press, 2004).

16   *Plymouth Records*, 4:168 ("several Indians"); Bangs, *Indian Deeds*, 391 ("a cheat").

17 *Plymouth Records*, 4:185–86; Petition of Josias Wampatuck and Weetama, June 3, 1668, Winslow Family Papers II, MHS ("preserve her interest").

18 Bangs, *Indian Deeds*, 328–29 ("peaceably"), 332–33, 358–59, 361–62, 464–65, 468, 469–70, 473–74; Silverman, *Faith and Boundaries*, 125–26; DCD, 1:6, 12; *Plymouth Records*, 4:115; Barnstable Town Records, 1:85–86, microfilm, MA Archives.

19 *Records of the Court of Trials of the Colony of Providence Plantations, 1647–1670*, 2 vols. (Providence: Rhode-Island Historical Society, 1920–22), 1:57; Newell, *Brethren by Nature*, 108, 125; Langdon, *Pilgrim Colony*, 203. Generally, see Katherine A. Hermes, "'Justice Will Be Done Us': Algonquian Demands for Reciprocity in the Courts of European Settlers," in Christopher L. Tomlins and Bruce H. Mann, eds., *The Many Legalities of Early America* (Chapel Hill: Univ. of North Carolina Press for the Omohundro Institute of Early American History and Culture, 2001), 123–49; Brian P. Owensby and Richard J. Ross, eds., *Justice in a New World: Negotiating Legal Intelligibility in British, Iberian, and Indigenous America* (New York: New York Univ. Press, 2018). On harsh punishments, Lyle Koehler, "Red-White Power Relations and Justice in the Courts of Seventeenth-Century New England," *American Indian Culture and Research Journal* 3, no. 4 (1979): 11–14; *Plymouth Records*, 4:136–37, 167, 5:106.

20 *Plymouth Records*, 3:179; *Rhode Island Records*, 2:295–97; Rhode Island to Plymouth, General Assembly and Court, October 25, 1671, John Davis Papers, MHS; Joshua Micah Marshall, "'A Melancholy People': Anglo-Indian Relations in Early Warwick, Rhode Island, 1642–1675," *NEQ* 68, no. 3 (1995): 421, 427.

21 *Plymouth Records*, 5:156; Harris to Williamson, August 12, 1676, *Collections of the Rhode Island Historical Society*, vol. 10 (1902): 167; *Rhode Island Records*, 2:519–21; *Colonial State Papers Online*, 9:442–43, CO 1/37, No. 47; *Rhode Island General Court of Trials, 1671–1704* (Boxford, MA: Jane Fletcher Fiske, 1998), 37–38; Ann Marie Plane, *Colonial Intimacies: Indian Marriage in Early New England* (Ithaca, NY: Cornell Univ. Press, 2000), 84–85.

22 *Rhode Island Records*, 2:51.

23 Marshall, "Melancholy People"; *Rhode Island Records*, 1:343; Roger Williams to Massachusetts General Court, May 12, 1656, and Williams to Robert Carr, March 1, 1666, in *Williams Correspondence*, 451, 550–51 ("promise"); *Rhode Island Records*, 2:136; Robinson, "Struggle Within," 76–77, 116–19, 182.

24 King Philip to the Chief Officer of the town of Long Island, May 7, 1666, *Colonial State Papers Online*, 1/20, no. 68.

25 *Plymouth Records*, 4:151, 164–66 ("recover" on 164); Emerson Woods Baker II, "New Evidence on the French Involvement in King Philip's War," *Maine Historical Society Quarterly* 28, no. 2 (1988): 85–91; Daniel K. Richter, "Dutch Dominos: The Fall of New Netherland and the Reshaping of Eastern North America," *Trade, Land, Power: The Struggle for Eastern North America* (Philadelphia: Univ. of Pennsylvania Press, 2013), 97–112.

26 *Rhode Island Records*, 2:192–93 ("deportments"; "hazarded"), 194; *Plymouth Records*, 4:164–65 ("first reporter").

27 Charles Banks Papers Relating to Martha's Vineyard, pp. 48, 50, MHS ("his people"); *Plymouth Records*, 4:164–66 ("vile"; "disclaimed"; "tongue").

28 Thomas Stanton to John Mason, July 8, 1669, Yale Indian Papers, 1669.07.08.00; Oberg, *Uncas*; Fisher and Silverman, *Ninigret*; Shawn G. Wiemann, "Lasting Marks: The Legacy of Robin Cassacinamon and the Survival of the Mashantucket Pequot Nation" (PhD diss., University of New Mexico, 2011).

29 *Rhode Island Records*, 2:264–65, 269–74 ("bark").

30 Deposition of John Gallup and John Stanton, July 1669, Yale Indian Papers, 1669.07.00.01 ("must go"); Fisher and Silverman, *Ninigret*, 68, 73–78, 111–12.

31 John Mason to John Allyn, July 4, 1669, Yale Indian Papers, 1669.07.04.00 ("meddle"); Richter, *Ordeal of the Longhouse*, 102–4; Jon Parmenter, *Edge of the Woods: Iroquoia, 1534–1701* (East Lansing: Michigan State Univ. Press, 2010), 122–27; Jeriah Bull, Susquench, and Ninigret to John Winthrop Jr., July 29, 1672, and Tobias Sanders to Fitz John Winthrop, July 3, 1675, *MHSC*, 5th ser., vol. 1 (1871): 426; Thomas Stanton to John Winthrop Jr., September 22, 1675, Winthrop Family Papers, MHS.

32 Daniel Gookin to Thomas Prince, April 12, 1671, and Prince to Gookin, April 26, 1671, *MHSC*, 1st ser., vol. 6 (1799): 199–201; Anderson, *Creatures of Empire*, 222–23, 232; Hugh Cole Deposition, March 8, 1670/71, Misc. Bound Ms., MHS. Also in *MHSC* 1st ser., vol. 6 (1799): 211 ("better armed").

33 Bellingham to Thomas Prince, March 24, 1671, Winslow Family Papers II, MHS ("multitudes"); Thomas Hinckley and Nathaniel Bacon to Thomas Prince, April 6, 1671, Winslow Family Papers II, MHS ("why"); *Rhode Island Records*, 2:370 ("continuous").

34 Josiah Winslow to Thomas Prince, undated, Winslow Family Papers II, MHS ("one wiser"); John Richards to John Winthrop Jr., April 18, 1671, Winthrop Family Transcripts, MHS ("foul weather").

35 *Plymouth Records*, 5:63–64 ("preparation"); Thomas Prince to Richard Bellingham, May 8, 1671, Winslow Family Papers II, MHS ("six score").

36 John Pynchon to John Winthrop Jr., May 10, 1671, in *The Pynchon Papers*, vol. 1, *Letters of John Pynchon, 1654–1700*, ed. Carl Bridenbaugh (Boston: Colonial Society of Massachusetts, 1982), 87 ("industriously"); Hubbard, *Narrative of the Troubles*, 1:44; Grandjean, *American Passage*, 150–52.

37 *Plymouth Records*, 5:63–64 ("compliance"), 69; Thomas Prince to Rhode Island General Assembly, June 16, 1671, Winslow Family Papers II, MHS ("scarce").

38 *Plymouth Records*, 5:73–74, 75 ("help her"; "incendiaries"); Articles of Agreement with Awashunks, July 24, 1671, Boston Athenaeum; Plymouth General Court to John Cotton Jr., in *Cotton Correspondence*, 81–82 and editors' note; Awashonks to Prince, Aug. 11, 1671, Davis Papers, oversize box, MHS; Awashonks pledge of

fidelity, Aug. 31, 1671, Misc. Bound Ms., MHS; Thomas Prince, Submission of Indians at Dartmouth, September 4, 1671, Boston Athenaeum.

39 *Plymouth Records*, 5:76 ("reducement"; "unkind"); James Walker to Thomas Prince, September 1, 1671, MHS Misc. Bound Ms., and *MHSC*, 1st ser., vol. 6 (1799): 197–98; *Rhode Island Records*, 2:408 ("treacherously"), 410; Thomas Prince to Rhode Island, Aug. 23, 1671, Winslow Family Papers II, MHS.

40 Lindholdt, *John Josselyn*, 101 ("coat"); Instructions to William and Anthony from John Eliot on behalf of the church at Natick, Aug. 1, 1671, MHS Misc. Bound Ms., and *MHSC*, 1st ser., vol. 6 (1799): 201–3; Richard Bellingham to Thomas Prince, September 5, 1671, Davis Papers, oversize, MHS; *Plymouth Records*, 5:79–80 ("neighborly"); Pulsipher, *Subjects unto the Same King*, 96–98; Cogley, *John Eliot's Mission*, 200–206.

41 *Plymouth Records* 5:76 ("common enemy"; "professed"), 78–79 ("humble"; "amend"; "smart").

42 *Plymouth Records* 5:76–80; Jon T. Coleman, *Vicious: Wolves and Men in America* (New Haven, CT: Yale Univ. Press, 2004), 62–64; Jonathan Perry, in person conversation with author, Providence, RI, May 2018.

43 On Pumetacom's sales, see *Plymouth Records*, 5:97, 98, 101, 102; Philbrick, *Mayflower*, 219. On Awashonks's sales, see Bangs, *Indian Deeds*, 434; *Rhode Island Land Evidence* (Providence: Rhode Island Historical Society 1921), 1:49, 53. On Mamaneway and his sales, see Bangs, *Indian Deeds*, 460–61, 463, 465–67, 474–75, 477–79; Brooks, *Our Beloved Kin*, 119–21; Ann Marie Plane, "Putting a Face on Colonization: Factionalism and Gender Politics in the Life History of Awashunkes, the 'Squaw Sachem' of Saconet," in Robert Grumet, ed., *Northeastern Indian Lives, 1632–1816* (Amherst: Univ. of Massachusetts Press, 1996), 144–45; John Cotton Jr. to Daniel Gookin, September 14, 1674, *Cotton Correspondence*, 98–99; Gookin, "Historical Collections," 199–200.

44 Bangs, *Indian Deeds*, 474–75; Brooks, *Our Beloved Kin*, 119–21; John Easton to Josiah Winslow, May 26, 1675, NEHGS ("dependence"); Martino-Trutor, "As Potent a Prince," 45–46.

45 1672 Deed, Pilgrim Hall, Plymouth, MA, http://www.pilgrimhallmuseum.org/in_their_own_write.htm#1672_deed (accessed 01/22/2019); *Plymouth Records*, 8:170 ("Tispaquin"); Philbrick, *Mayflower*, 214. On Prince, see Stratton, *Plymouth Colony*, 104, 151.

46 *Plymouth Records*, 8:180, 190–91.

47 *Plymouth Records*, 4:80 ("homage"); Prince, *Some Account of those English Ministers*, 293–94.

48 DCD, 1:211; New York Deeds 1:78, quoted in Charles Banks Papers, vol.: 1600–1699, pp. 80–85, MHS; Prince, *Some Account of those English Ministers*, 293–94; Plane, *Colonial Intimacies*, 41–66; Elizabeth A. Little, "Three Kinds of Indian Land Deeds at Nantucket, Massachusetts," in William Cowan, ed., *Papers of the Eleventh Algonquian Conference* (Ottawa: Carleton Univ. Press, 1980), 63 ("council"); Elizabeth A. Little,

"Sachem Nickanoose of Nantucket and the Grass Contest," *Historic Nantucket* 23 (1976): 19–20; Little, "Indian Politics on Nantucket," in Cowan, ed., *Papers of the Thirteenth Algonquian Conference* (Ottawa: Carleton Univ. Press, 1982), 286, 288–89; NCR, 2:70 verso; Bangs, *Eastham Town Records*, 118; Henry W. and James P. Ronda, eds., *John Eliot's Indian Dialogues: A Study in Cultural Interaction* (Westport, CT: Greenwood Press, 1980), 71 ("English men"). There is a Nantucket oral tradition extending from an unreliable eighteenth-century source that Pumetacom traveled to the island to execute the Wampanoag preacher Assassamough, or John Gibbs, for violating taboo by speaking the name of Ousamequin. See Nathaniel Philbrick, *Abram's Eyes: The Native American Legacy of Nantucket Island* (Nantucket, MA: Mill Hill Press, 1998), 118–22. No contemporary accounts make any such statement.

49 For a sampling of such occasions, see Whitfield, *Strength out of Weakness*, 230–31; Eliot, "A Breif [*sic*] History of the Mashpeog Indians," 110n7, 122; Morton, *New England's Memorial*, 208; John Eliot, "Brief Narrative" (1671), in *Eliot Tracts*, 400–401; Gookin, "Historical Collections," 204.

50 Sheila McIntyre, "John Cotton, Jr.: Wayward Puritan Minister?" in Ian K. Steele and Nancy L. Rhoden, eds., *The Human Tradition in Colonial America* (Wilmington, DE: Scholarly Resources, 1999), 119–40.

51 Whitfield, *Strength out of Weakness*, 152 ("young Ousamequin"); John Eliot to the Commissioners of the United Colonies, Aug. 24, 1664, *NEHGR* 9 (1885): 131–33 (we know the son was John Jr. because he received salary as a missionary from the New England Company during these years); Eliot, *Indian Dialogues*, 121 ("you praying Indians"); Gookin, "Historical Collections," 200 ("chief men"). Historians frequently quote Cotton Mather's claim that Pumetacom once took a button off Eliot's coat and declared "that he cared for his gospel, just as much as he cared for that button." Given that Mather was writing decades after the fact, that no statement of this sort appears in contemporary documents, and that he wished to attribute Pumetacom's loss in King Philip's War to providential judgment, his provocative claim carries less weight than the accounts of Eliot himself and Gookin. See Mather, *Magnalia Christi Americana*, 514.

52 *Plymouth Records*, 5:70; Thomas Mayhew Sr. to Thomas Prince, Aug. 19, 1671, *MHSC*, 1st ser., vol. 6 (1799), 196 ("subject themselves").

53 James Walker to Thomas Prince, September 1, 1671, MHS Misc. Bound Ms., and *MHSC*, 1st ser., vol. 6 (1799): 197–98 ("reporting"); Hough, *Narrative of the Causes*, 4. Several historians have wrongly understood Pumetacom's charge that Sassamon deliberately mistranslated his "will" to mean that Sassamon forged a documentary will, in the sense of a personal list of final instructions. The actual meaning is that Sassamon mischaracterized Pumetacom's wishes, probably in a land deed (of which we have many by him) or a letter (of which we have one) rather than in a will (of which we have none).

54 Lepore, *Name of War*, 21–47; Brooks, *Our Beloved Kin*, 63–64, 122–24; *United Colonies Records*, 2:362 ("endeavoring").

55 *Plymouth Records*, 5:159, 167–68.

56 Jennings, *Invasion of America*, 288–97; Brooks, *Our Beloved Kin*, 50–53, 68–71, 118–21, 131–37.

CHAPTER 8: RUINING THANKSGIVING

1   Hough, *Narrative of the Causes*, 4.

2   Hough, 6.

3   Hough, 7–8.

4   Hough, 8–9.

5   Hough, 9–10. On Andros, see Mary-Lou Lustig, *The Imperial Executive in America: Sir Edmund Andros, 1637–1714* (Madison, NJ: Fairleigh Dickinson Univ. Press, 2002). On Pumetacom's talk as a lament, see Drake, *King Philip's War*, 72.

6   Hough, *Narrative of the Causes*, 12–13.

7   Hough, 14–15.

8   Hough, 11 ("mischievous"; "lying"), 13 ("testified").

9   Hough, 4.

10 Hough, 15.

11 Josiah Winslow and Thomas Hinckley, "Narrative shewing the manor of the beginning of the present Warr with the Indians of Mount hope and Pocasett," *United Colonies Records*, 2:362–64 ("dismissed"); Mather, *Relation of the Troubles*, 74–75 ("twisting"); Yasuhide Kawashima, *Igniting King Philip's War: The John Sassamon Murder Trial* (Lawrence: Univ. Press of Kansas, 2001), 99–100; Robert P. Brittain, "Cruentation in Legal Medicine and Literature," *Medical History* 9, no. 1 (1965): 82–88.

12 Brooks, *Our Beloved Kin*, 102–12; James P. Ronda and Jeanne Ronda, "The Death of John Sassamon: An Exploration in Writing New England Indian History," *American Indian Quarterly* 1, no. 2 (1974): 91–102; Lepore, *Name of War*, 21–47; James Drake, "Symbol of a Failed Strategy: The Sassamon Trial, Political Culture, and King Philip's War," *American Indian Culture and Research Journal* 19, no. 2 (1995): 111–41. On Indian reactions to imprisonment, see Ian Steele, "Shawnee Origins of Their Seven Years' War," *Ethnohistory* 53, no. 4 (2006): 657–87. On legal culture, see John M. Murrin, "Magistrates, Sinners, and a Precarious Liberty: Trial by Jury in Seventeenth-Century New England," in David D. Hall, John M. Murrin, and Thad Tate, eds., *Saints and Revolutionaries: Essays on Early American History* (New York: Norton, 1984), 152–206.

13 Hough, *Narrative of the Causes*, 5 ("confessed they three"); Increase Mather, *A Brief History of the Warr with the Indians in New-England* (1676), in Richard Slotkin and James K. Folsom, eds., *So Dreadful a Judgment: Puritan Responses to King Philip's War, 1676–1677* (Middletown, CT: Wesleyan Univ. Press, 1978), 87 ("that his father"); Hubbard, *Narrative of the Troubles*, 1:63; *Plymouth Records*, 5:167 ("shot").

14 Hough, *Narrative of the Causes*, 4 ("hide"), 10–11 ("lying"; "prosecute").

15   Hough, 4 ("their law"; "please"), 11 ("mischievous"); instructions from the Church at Natick to William and Anthony, August 1, 1671, *MHSC*, 1st ser., vol. 6 (1799): 201–3; Lepore, *Name of War*, 40.

16   Winslow and Hinckley, "Narrative" ("gather strangers"); *United Colonies Records*, 2:363 ("blow over"). See also Roger Williams to John Winthrop Jr., June 13, 1675, and Williams to Winthrop, June 27, 1675, in *Williams Correspondence*, 691, 699; Josiah Winslow to Leverett, July 6, 1675, Davis Papers, MHS.

17   John Brown, Swansea, to Gov. Winslow, June 15, 1675, Winslow Family Papers II, MHS.

18   Benjamin Church, *Entertaining Passages Relating to King Philip's War* (1716), ed. Martyn Dexter (Boston: printed by B. Green, 1865), 6–7 ("custom").

19   Church, *Entertaining Passages*, 8–11.

20   Church, 12–14 ("rifle"); Martino-Trutor, "'As Potent a Prince,'" 45 46; Josiah Winslow to Mr. Freeman, June 28, 1675, Winslow Family Papers II, MHS ("undoubted").

21   Hough, *Narrative of the Causes*, 24 ("priests"); Edward Rawson, *The Present State of New England with Respect to the Indian War* (1675), in Samuel D. Drake, ed., *The Old Indian Chronicle: Being a Collection of Exceedingly Rare Tracts, Written and Published in the Time of King Philip's War* (Boston: printed by the author, 1867), 111 ("God's day"), 126 ("caution"); Douglas Edward Leach, *Flintlock and Tomahawk: New England in King Philip's War* (New York: Macmillan, 1958), 37.

22   Hough, *Narrative of the Causes*, 17.

23   Josiah Winslow to Massachusetts, June 21, 1675, MA Archives, 67:202 ("few days").

24   Leach, *Flintlock and Tomahawk*, 50–54.

25   Leach, 62–67; *Plymouth Records*, 5:201–3; Hough, *Narrative of the Causes*, 17 ("fury"); Church, *Entertaining Passages*, 47; Martino-Trutor, "'As Potent a Prince.'"

26   Church, *Entertaining Passages*, 50 ("many people"); John Freeman to Josiah Winslow, July 3, 1675, Winslow Family Papers II; Leach, *Flintlock and Tomahawk*, 66; Daniel R. Mandell, *King Philip's War: Colonial Expansion, Native Resistance, and the End of Indian Sovereignty* (Baltimore: Johns Hopkins Univ. Press, 2010), 59, 70; Eric B. Schultz and Michael J. Tougias, *King Philip's War: The History and Legacy of America's Forgotten Conflict* (Woodstock, VT: Countryman Press, 1999), 146–47; Thomas Walley to John Cotton Jr., July 25, 1675, and August 2, 1675, in McIntyre and Travers, *Cotton Correspondence*, 111, 112–13.

27   James Cudworth to Josias Winslow, July 20, 1675 ("never"), Cudworth to Josiah Winslow, July 9/10, 1675, and John Freeman to Josiah Winslow, July 18, 1675, Winslow Papers II, MHS; William Bradford, *A Letter from Major William Bradford to the Reverend John Cotton: Written at Mount Hope on July 21, 1675* (Providence: Society of Colonial Wars in the State of Rhode Island, 1914), 15–16.

28   Richard Greenwood et al., "The Battles of Nipsachuck: Research and Documentation," National Park Service, August 2011, 51–53, Ms. in author's possession;

Nathaniel Thomas, "Account of the Fight with the Indians," August 10, 1675, John Davis Papers, MHS.

29 Brian D. Carroll, "From Warrior to Soldier: New England Indians in the Colonial Military, 1675–1763" (PhD diss., University of Connecticut, 2009), 41, 44–45; Oberg, *Uncas*, 174–77; Roger Williams to John Leverett, Oct. 11, 1675, in *Williams Correspondence*, 705 ("long grass"); Thomas, "Account of the Fight with the Indians"; Leach, *Flintlock and Tomahawk*, 75–77; Brooks, *Our Beloved Kin*, 166–68; Greenwood et al., "Battles of Nipsachuck."

30 Wait Winthrop to John Winthrop Jr., July 9, 1675, Colonial War Series, Connecticut State Archives, Hartford ("Bay and Plymouth"); Rawson, *Present State of New England*, 131–32, 152–53 ("Eliot's"); Newell, *Brethren by Nature*, 141–42.

31 Church, *Entertaining Passages*, 45–46 ("terms"); Rawson, *Present State of New England*, 131–32 ("perpetual"); Newell, *Brethren by Nature*, 158, 175–80; Linford D. Fisher, "'Why Shall Wee Have Peace to Bee Made Slaves': Indian Surrenderers during and after King Philip's War," *Ethnohistory* 64, no. 1 (2017): 91–114. On the Eells garrison, see Schultz and Tougias, *King Philip's War*, 118.

32 Church, *Entertaining Passages*, 45–56 ("fairly" on 45–46); Newell, *Brethren by Nature*, 150 ("prolongation").

33 Oberg, *Uncas*, 145–50; Fisher and Silverman, *Ninigret*, 69–70, 80–84; Thomas Walley to John Cotton Jr., November 18, 1675, in *Cotton Correspondence*, 119 ("innocent"); Solomon Stoddard, "An Account of the Reasons Alledged for Demanding the Armes of the Indians of Northampton and Hadley," Yale Indian Papers, 1675.09.15.00; Hubbard, *Narrative of the Troubles*, 1:92 ("discover"), 111, 121–33 ("devil" on 120); Leach, *Flintlock and Tomahawk*, 85–91; Pulsipher, *Subjects unto the Same King*, 114–16; Brooks, *Our Beloved Kin*, 194; Richard Melvoin, *New England Outpost: War and Society in Colonial Deerfield* (New York: Norton, 1989), 99–105.

34 Daniel Gookin, "An Historical Account of the Doings and Sufferings of the Christian Indians in New England in the Years 1675, 1676, 1677," *Transactions and Collections of the American Antiquarian Society* 2 (1836): 450.

35 Gookin, 504; Jenny Hale Pulsipher, "Massacre at Hurtleberry Hill: Christian Indians and English Authority in Metacom's War," *WMQ* 53, no. 3 (1996): 459–86.

36 Gookin, "Historical Account," 474 ("fear"), 476 ("two evils"); Brooks, *Our Beloved Kin*, 228 ("all the praying Indians").

37 "The Examination and Relation of James Quannapaquait," in Neal Salisbury, ed., *The Sovereignty and Goodness of God, Together with the Faithfulness of His Promises Displayed: Being a Narrative of the Captivity and Restoration of Mrs. Mary Rowlandson and Related Documents* (Boston: Bedford/St. Martin's, 1997), 121 ("somewhat").

38 Gookin, "Historical Account," 434 ("jealous").

39 NCR, 2:4 verso ("disown"); Letter of Thomas Macy, May 9, 1676, in Peter R. Christoph and Florence A. Cristoph, eds., *Files of the Provincial Secretary of New York during the Administration of Governor Sir Edmund Andros*, 3 vols. (Syracuse,

NY: Syracuse Univ. Press, 1989), 1:365–67; *Plymouth Records*, 5:177–78 ("strange Indians"); Barnstable Town Records, 1:56–58, microfilm, MA Archives.

40 Simon Athearn to Governor Edmund Andros, 1675, in Charles Edward Banks, *Papers Relating to Martha's Vineyard*, pp. 105–7, MHS; *Conquests and Triumphs*, 34–36 ("mostly"); DCD, 6:369–73 (Wampanoag version); translation in Ives Goddard and Kathleen Bragdon, eds., *Native Writings in Massachusett*, 2 vols. (Philadelphia: American Philosophical Society, 1988), 1:82–89.

41 *Conquests and Triumphs*, 34–36.

42 *Indian Converts*, 141–42 ("preservation"), 370; Thomas Mayhew Sr. to John Winthrop Jr., October 7, 1675, MHSC, ser. 4, vol. 7 (1865): 43 ("temporal").

43 Frederick Freeman, *The History of Cape Cod: The Annals of Barnstable County, Including the District of Mashpee*, 2 vols. (Boston: printed for the author, by Geo. C. Rand & Avery, 1858), 293; *Plymouth Records*, 5:183, 187 ("not to depart"); Thomas Walley to John Cotton Jr., April 17, 1676, in *Cotton Correspondence*, 144–45 ("some hope").

44 William S. Simmons, "Narragansett," in Trigger, *Northeast*, 196.

45 Hough, *Narrative of the Causes*, 23.

46 Brooks, *Our Beloved Kin*, 143 ("threatening"), 156; Roger Williams to John Winthrop Jr., June 27, 1675, in *Williams Correspondence*, 698–99.

47 Fisher and Silverman, *Ninigret*, 122–24; Richard Smith to John Winthrop Jr., September 3, 1675, in Daniel Berkeley Updike, *Richard Smith, First English Settler of the Narragansett Country* (Boston: Merrymount Press, 1937), 110–11 ("take notice"); William Harris to Joseph Williamson, Aug. 12, 1676, in Harris Papers, *Collections of the Rhode Island Historical Society*, vol. 10 (Providence: Rhode Island Historical Society, 1902), 167–68.

48 Brooks, *Our Beloved Kin*, 237; Martino-Trutor, "As Potent a Prince," 47; Patrick M. Malone, *The Skulking Way of War: Technology and Tactics among the New England Indians* (Baltimore: Johns Hopkins Univ. Press, 1991), 99; Hubbard, *Narrative of the Troubles*, 1:58, 136.

49 Leach, *Flintlock and Tomahawk*, 118–44.

50 Malone, *Skulking Way of War*, 67–98; "A Reinterpretation of the Attack on the Clark Garrison/RM Site Plymouth, MA," http://plymoutharch.tripod.com/id16.html (accessed 01/22/2019); Schultz and Tougias, *King Philip's War*, 124–25; Leach, *Flintlock and Tomahawk*, 55–81; Mandell, *King Philip's War*, 134–35, 137.

51 Drake, *King Philip's War*, 4; Langdon Jr., *Pilgrim*, 182.

52 Pulsipher, *Subjects unto the Same King*, 207–37; Evan Haefeli and Kevin Sweeney, "Wattanummon's World: Personal and Tribal Identity in the Algonquian Diaspora, c. 1660–1712," in William Cowan, ed., *Proceedings of the Twenty-Fifth Algonquian Conference* (Ottawa: Carleton Univ. Press, 1993), 212–24.

53 Nathaniel B. Shurtleff, ed., *Records of the Governor and Company of the Massachusetts Bay in New England*, 5 vols. (Boston: W. White, 1853–54), 5:58–63 ("strange"); Mather, *Brief History*, 105; Thomas Walley to John Cotton Jr., July 25, 1675, and

Aug. 2, 1675, *Cotton Correspondence*, 111, 112–13. On colonial New England's crisis of conscience, see Lepore, *Name of War*; Pulsipher, *Subjects unto the Same King*, 179–206. For a critical view of colonists' providential explanation for the war by an official from London, see Michael Leroy Oberg, *Dominion and Civility: English Imperialism and Native America, 1585–1685* (Ithaca, NY: Cornell Univ. Press, 1999), 113–14.

54   Silverman, *Thundersticks*, 112–14.

55   Charles J. Hoadly, ed., *The Public Records of the Colony of Connecticut*, 15 vols. (Hartford, 1850–90), 2:407 ("engage"); John Cotton Jr. to Thomas Walley, February 4, 1676, in *Cotton Correspondence*, 134; Church, *Entertaining Passages*, 51–52 ("Mohawks' country").

56   Oberg, *Dominion and Civility*, 162–63; Jennings, *The Invasion of America*, 314–15.

57   Hubbard, *Narrative of the Troubles*, 1:217–19, 231, 239; I. Mather, *Brief History*, 128–29.

58   Thomas Hinckley to John Leverett, April 16, 1676, Davis Papers, Oversize, MHS ("Wepunuggs"); Noah Newman to John Cotton Jr., Apr. 19, 1676, in *Cotton Correspondence*, 148–50. On the warring Indians' food scarcity, see Salisbury, *Sovereignty and Goodness of God*, 83, 85, 92–93, 105.

59   All quotes in this and the following two paragraphs come from Roger Williams to [Robert Williams?], Apr. 1, 1676, in *Williams Correspondence*, 721.

60   Christopher William Hannan, "'After This Time of Trouble and Warr': Crisis and Continuity in the New England Anglo-Indian Community, 1660–1725" (PhD diss., Boston College, 1999), chaps. 6–7; Jason W. Warren, *Connecticut Unscathed: Victory in the Great Narragansett War, 1675–1676* (Norman: Univ. of Oklahoma Press, 2014); Gookin, "Historical Account," 434, 442; Hubbard, *Narrative of the Troubles*, 1:175–76, 250–51; Church, *Entertaining Passages*, 122–23; *Conquests and Triumphs*, 49 ("forward"); Carroll, "From Warrior to Soldier," 49–52; Francis G. Hutchins, *Mashpee: The Story of Cape Cod's Indian Town* (West Franklin, NH: Amarta Press, 1979), 55.

61   Matther, *Relation of the Troubles*, 133, 143 ("terror"); Silverman, *Thundersticks*, 117–18; Hubbard, *Narrative of the Troubles*, 1:249 ("at other times").

62   On Church as a source, see "Benjamin Church: King of the Wild Frontier," in Slotkin and Folsom, *So Dreadfull a Judgment*, 370–91; Jill Lepore, "Plymouth Rocked: Of Pilgrims, Puritans, and Professors," *New Yorker*, April 24, 2006.

63   Church, *Entertaining Passages*, 73–87 ("convenient" on 80), 91 ("eat clams").

64   Church, 87–91.

65   *Plymouth Records*, 5:201 ("secured"); Church, *Entertaining Passages*, 91–100; Moody to Cotton, April 1, 1677, in *Cotton Correspondence*.

66   Church, *Entertaining Passages*, 99–100; Carroll, "Warrior to Soldier," 53–54.

67   Mandell, *King Philip's War*, 112–13, 116 ("so faithfully"); Hubbard, *Narrative of the Troubles*, 1:83, 173, 175–76 ("continued faithful"); Church, *Entertaining Passages*, 95; Pulsipher, "Massacre at Hurteberry Hill."

68 Hubbard, *Narrative of the Troubles*, 1:271–72 ("seven hundred"; "broke"); Thomas Walley to John Cotton Jr., July 18, 1676, in *Cotton Correspondence*, 158 ("greatest success"); William Harris to Joseph Williamson, Aug. 12, 1676, in *Harris Papers*, 163.

69 This and the following paragraph draw on William Harris to Sir Joseph Williamson, Aug. 12, 1676, in *Harris Papers*, 177; Hubbard, *Narrative of the Troubles*, 1:183–84, 190, 191–92, 205–7, 220; Mather, *Brief History*, 135–36; Mandell, *King Philip's War*, 113; Leach, *Flintlock and Tomahawk*, 199–241, esp. 211, 221–22, 233–36; Carroll, "Warrior to Soldier," 59.

70 *Plymouth Records*, 5:207, 209, 225, 244; *Rhode Island Records*, 2:549–50, 586; Mandell, *King Philip's War*, 128; Newell, *Brethren by Nature*, 158, 170–71, 175–80.

71 *Plymouth Records*, 5:191; Leach, *Flintlock and Tomahawk*, 248; Martin, *Profits in the Wilderness*, 82–83n86, 85–86; Brian D. Carroll, "The Effect of Military Service on Indian Communities in Southern New England, 1740–1763," *Early American Studies* 14, no. 3 (2016): 530; *A Letter from Major William Bradford*, 3.

72 Church, *Entertaining Passages*, 138 ("ready"); Samuel Arnold and John Cotton Jr. to the Commissioners of the United Colonies, September 7, 1676, in *Cotton Correspondence*, 173; Lepore, *Name of War*, 150–54.

73 Hubbard, *Narrative of the Troubles*, 1:264; Mather, *Brief History*, 138 ("horrid").

74 Newell, *Brethren by Nature*, 219–21; Caroll, "From Warrior to Soldier," 157–207; Plane, "Putting a Face on Colonization," 140–65; *Conquests and Triumphs*, 42; MA Archives, 30:227; DCD, 1:3. For the Sakonnets' immediate aftermath of the war, see *Plymouth Records*, 5:209, 215, 224–25, 239, 248; *Rhode Island Land Evidence* (Providence: Rhode Island Historical Society, 1921), 1:175; John Smith to Josiah Winslow, October 23, 1678, Winslow Family Papers II, MHS.

75 Church, *Entertaining Passages*, 151–52; Newell, *Brethren by Nature*, 150–51.

76 Mather, *Brief History*, 189 ("marvelous"); Church, *Entertaining Passages*, 151–52; Mandell, *King Philip's War*, 130; Lepore, *Name of War*, 150–54, Newell, *Brethren by Nature*, 150–51.

77 Hubbard, *Narrative of the Troubles*, 1:268; Mather, *Brief History*, 139.

CHAPTER 9: "DAYS OF MOURNING AND NOT JOY"

1   In *The Name of War: King Philip's War and the Origins of American Identity*, Jill Lepore examines the origins of these themes. Even the classic study by Douglas Edward Leach, *Flintlock and Tomahawk: New England in King Philip's War*, sometimes traffics in them (see p. 24) while raising the possibility that "Philip's eager and hot-blooded young warriors were dragging him, reluctant, into open violence and hostilities" (36).

2   My thinking here has been influenced by Ramona Louise Peters, "Community Development Planning with a Native American Tribe in a Colonized Environment: Mashpee Wampanoag, a Modern Native American Tribe in Southern New

England Seeking to Maintain Traditional Values and Cultural Integrity" (MS thesis, California School of Professional Psychology, 2003).

3   Richard Lebaron Bowen, *Early Rehoboth: Documented Historical Studies of Families and Events in this Plymouth Colony Township*, vol. 1 (Rehoboth, MA: privately printed [by the Rumford Press], 1945), 11, provides the figure for the English based on a census count of families and an estimate of six people per family. In 1685 Plymouth authorities tallied 1,439 Wampanoags over the age of twelve within the colony and judged there to be three times as many children as adults (defined as those over the age of twelve). See Thomas Hinckley to William Stoughton and Joseph Dudley, April 2, 1685, *Hinckley Papers, MHSC*, 4th ser., vol. 5 (1861): 133. On other themes, see Edward Byers, *The Nation of Nantucket: Society and Politics in an Early American Commercial Center, 1660–1820* (Boston: Northeastern Univ. Press, 1987), 60; Silverman, *Faith and Boundaries*, 285–87; Drake, *King Philip's*, 169–70; Baker and Reid, "Amerindian Power in the Early Modern Northeast"; Collin G. Calloway, *The Western Abenakis of Vermont, 1600–1800: War, Migration, and the Survival of an Indian People* (Norman: Univ. of Oklahoma Press, 1990); Evan Haefeli and Kevin Sweeney, *Captors and Captives: The 1704 French and Indian Raid on Deerfield* (Amherst: Univ. of Massachusetts Press, 2003).

4   Linford Fisher, *The Indian Great Awakening: Religion and the Shaping of Native Cultures in Early America* (New York: Oxford Univ. Press, 2012).

5   Grindal Rawson and Samuel Danforth, "Account of an Indian Visitation, A.D. 1698," *MHSC*, 1st ser., vol. 10 (1809): 129–30; *Indian Converts*, 129, 130, 132–33 ("pious"), 142–44 ("faithful"), 177, 232–33 ("worthy"; "merciful"), 243–45; New England Company Ledger, 1680–1719, MHS, p. 60; Increase Mather, *A Brief Relation of the State of New England* (1689), in William H. Whitmore, ed., *The Andros Tracts: Being a Collection of Pamphlets and Official Papers*, 3 vols. (Boston: Prince Society, 1868–74), 2:165–66, 168 ("great").

6   *Conquests and Triumphs*, 52–68; John Cotton Jr. to Increase Mather, March 23, 1693, *Cotton Correspondence*, 429–31; John Cotton Jr. Diary, entry for July 22, 1678, MHS; Rawson and Danforth, "Indian Visitation," 129–34; Thomas Hinckley to William Stoughton and Joseph Dudley, April 2, 1685, Hinckley Papers, *MHSC*, 4th ser., vol. 5 (1861): 133–34; Gideon Hawley to Samuel Cooper, Dec. 31, 1770, Ayer MS 374, Newberry Library, Chicago; Nickerson, *Early Encounters*, 174, 177; Josiah Paine, *A History of Harwich, Barnstable County, Massachusetts, 1620–1800* (Rutland, VT: Tuttle, 1937), 406–7; Increase Mather, *A Letter About the Present State of Christianity among the Christianized Indians of New England* (Boston: T. Green, 1705), 4–5, 5–6; Cotton Mather, *A Brief Account of the Evangelical Work among the Christianized Indians of New England*, appendix to his *Just Commemorations: The Death of Good Men, Considered* (Boston: printed by B. Green, 1715), 49–50 ("thousands"); C. Mather, *Concerning the Essays that are made, for the Propagation of Religion among the Indians*, appendix to his *Bonifacius* (Boston: printed by B. Green,

1710), 195–99; John W. Ford, ed., *Some Correspondence Between the Governors and Treasurers of the New England Company in London and the Commissioners of the United Colonies in America* (London: privately printed, 1896), 84; Experience Mayhew, *A Brief Account of the State of the Indians on Martha's Vineyard*, appendix to his *Discourse Shewing that God Dealeth with Men as with Reasonable Creatures* (Boston: printed by B. Green, 1720), 2–3, 5; Experience Mayhew to Roland Cotton, July 1699, Misc. Bound MSS, MHS; NE Co. Mss. 7956, p. 103, 7955/2, pp. 100, 109–10; CPGNE, box 1, February 25, 1731.

7   An Account of Monument Ponds Indians taken by Josiah Cotton their Minister in the year 1710, Curwen Papers, box 2, folder 1, AAS ("further end"); Gideon Hawley Journal, entry for May 5, 1777, Congregational Library, Boston; "Report of a Committee on the State of the Indians in Mashpee and Parts Adjacent," *MHSC*, 2nd ser., vol. 3 (1815): 12–17 ("celebrate" on 12–13). On Christian Indian belief and practice, see David J. Silverman, "Indians, Missionaries, and Religious Translation: Creating Wampanoag Christianity in Seventeenth-Century Martha's Vineyard," *WMQ* 62, no. 2 (2005): 141–74; Douglas L. Winiarski, "A Question of Plain Dealing: Josiah Cotton, Native Christians, and the Quest for Security in Eighteenth-Century Plymouth County," *NEQ* 77, no. 3 (2004): 368–413; Linford Fisher, "Native Americans, Conversion, and Christian Practice in Colonial New England," *Harvard Theological Review* 102, no. 1 (2009): 101–24; Neal Salisbury, "Embracing Ambiguity: Native Peoples and Christianity in Seventeenth-Century North America," *Ethnohistory* 50, no. 2 (2003): 247–59. On frolics, see Josiah Cotton Memoirs, p. 122, MHS.

8   Increase Mather, *A Letter About the Present State of Christianity*, 5 ("Christianized"), 11 ("foundation"); Rawson and Danforth, "Indian Visitation," 129–34.

9   Rawson and Danforth, "Indian Visitation," 129–34; "An Account of Monument Ponds Indians"; *Conquests and Triumphs*, 37. On farming reforms, see Silverman, "'We Choose to Be Bounded': Native American Animal Husbandry in Colonial New England," *WMQ* 60, no. 3 (2003): 531–32; M. Halsey Thomas, ed., *The Diary of Samuel Sewall, 1674–1729*, 2 vols. (New York: Farrar, Straus and Giroux, 1973), 1:465; E. Mayhew, *Brief Account*, 11–12. On conversion narratives, see C. Mather, *Concerning the Essays*, 51–52; I. Mather, C. Mather, and Nehemiah Walker to William Ashhurst, March 2, 1705, *Some Correspondence*, 86–87.

10   *Conquests and Triumphs*, 33 ("disparagement"); *Indian Converts*, 91 ("hardly be persuaded"; "dishearten"); E. Mayhew, *Mankind by Nature*, 25 ("no worse"). On Indians as royal subjects, see Pulsipher, *Subjects unto the Same King*. On Indians' legal status, Hermes, "'Justice Will Be Done Us'"; Yasuhide Kawashima, *Puritan Justice and the Indian: White Man's Law in Massachusetts, 1630–1763* (Middletown, CT: Wesleyan Univ. Press, 1986). On civilized claims to the land, see Silverman, "'We Choose to Be Bounded'"; Greer, *Property and Dispossession*.

11   Bangs, *Town Records of Eastham*, 205–6; MA Archives, 113:607 ("distressed").

12   Franklin B. Hough, ed., *Papers Relating to the Island of Nantucket . . . While under the Colony of New York* (Albany: [J. Munsell], 1865), 107–8 ("forbear"); Elizabeth A. Little, "Sachem Nickanoose of Nantucket and the Grass Content: Part 2," *Historic Nantucket* 24 (1976): 28 ("forcing"); NCR, 1:3, 113, 2:7; Byers, *Nation of Nantucket*, 73; Alexander Starbuck, *The History of Nantucket, County, Island and Town* (Boston: C. E. Goodspeed & Co., 1924), 139; MA Archives, 31:147.

13   DCD, 6:463–64; DCCR, 1:243, 244, 246, 247, 249; Silverman, *Faith and Boundaries*, 149–54; MA Archives, 31:129 ("flee"); Daniel R. Mandell, *Behind the Frontier: Indians in Eighteenth-Century Eastern Massachusetts* (Lincoln: Univ. of Nebraska Press, 1996), 117–63.

14   *Plymouth Records*, 6:159–60; Hugo A. Dubuque, *Fall River Indian Reservation* (Fall River, MA, 1907), 3–4, 10, 28 ("serviceable"), 61; *Earle Report*, 78–79; Mandell, *Behind the Frontier*, 51; Newell, *Brethren by Nature*, 219–21.

15   NE Co. MSS, 8004; DCD, 1:35, 349, 2:344, 4:128; Goddard and Bragdon, *Native Writings*, 1:96–97; MA Archives, 31:10.

16   MA Archives, 31:17, 32:268–70; *The Acts and Resolves, Public and Private, of the Province of the Massachusetts-Bay*, 21 vols. (Boston: Wright & Potter, 1869–1922), 2:723, 724, 732, 8:118, 9:29.

17   MA Archives, 31:17 ("not true"); Thomas Walcut Papers, 1671–1866, file 4, MHS; NE Co. Mss., 7953, p. 17 ("threatened"); *Some Correspondence*, 94 ("scattered").

18   NE Co. Mss., 7953, pp. 69, 70, 7955/2, pp. 22–23.

19   Nickerson, *Early Encounters*, 184–85; Paine, *Harwich*, 191, 199; Mandell, *Behind the Frontier*, 54 ("use forever").

20   *Acts and Resolves . . . , Public and Private, of the Province of Massachusetts Bay*, 10:ch.88:p.464; Mandell, *Behind the Frontier*, 75; CPGNE, box 2, entry for July 16, 1741; MA Archives, 31:320–22.

21   Banks, Papers Relating to Martha's Vineyard, unbound vol., pp. 65–71 (160 acres), MHS; DCD, 1:123, 4:173, 6:97 ("Legall Town meeting"), 8:196; Suffolk Files, no. 43637, p. 81, no. 69495, Mass. State Archives; Goddard and Bragdon, *Native Writings*, 1:134–35; MA Archives, 31:19, 32:386a ("town people").

22   MA Archives, 33:222; O'Brien, *Dispossession by Degrees*; Mandell, *Behind the Frontier*.

23   Goddard and Bragdon, *Native Writings*, 1:370–73; Jessie Little Doe Baird from the Anne Makepeace documentary, *We Still Live Here: Âs Nutayuneân* (2010).

24   Kawashima, *Puritan Law*, 32–35; Suffolk Files no. 29178 ("devil"); Superior Court of Judicature, Recs., Reel no. 3, p. 105, Mass. State Archives; MA Archives 31:523–24, 550, 551, 643 ("before"), 645, 32:424 ("good as right"), 356; Goddard and Bragdon, *Native Writings*, 1:173–75 ("poorer"); Petition of the Mashpee Indians to the Commissioners of Indian Affairs, Aug. 4, 1757, Hawley Letters, MHS ("more hurt"; "hearken").

25   Vaughan, *Transatlantic Encounters*, 176–77 (all quotes); Mandell, *Behind the Frontier*, 157–58; Campisi, *Mashpee Indians*, 84–85.

26 *Conquests and Triumphs*, 42–43.

27 *Plymouth Records*, 5:270, 6:98, 108, 116; Francis G. Hutchins, *Mashpee: The Story of Cape Cod's Indian Town* (West Franklin, NH: Amarta Press, 1979), 60–61; DCR, 1:59, 61–62.

28 Kawashima, *Puritan Law*, 32; MA Archives, 30:491 ("young men"); Paine, *Harwich*, 404–5; E. Mayhew to Cotton Mather, Aug. 28, 173, Misc. Bound Mss., MHS ("disgusted").

29 David Thomas Konig, ed., *Plymouth Court Records, 1686–1859*, 16 vols. (Wilmington, DE: M. Glazier/Pilgrim Society, 1978), 1:228, 247, 268, 273, 294, 2:26, 31, 41–42, 44, 66, 79, 81, 86, 87, 82, 91, 98–99, 109, 118, 155; DCGSP, 866–67; NCD 3:171; Newell, *Brethren by Nature*, 211–36.

30 Daniel Vickers, *Farmers and Fishermen: Two Centuries of Work in Essex County, Massachusetts, 1630–1830* (Chapel Hill: Univ. of North Carolina Press, for the Institute of Early American History and Culture, 1994); Margaret Ellen Newell, *From Dependency to Independence: Economic Revolution in New England* (Ithaca, NY: Cornell Univ. Press, 1998); James E. Wadsworth, ed., *The World of Credit in Colonial Massachusetts: James Richards and His Daybook, 1692–1711* (Amherst: Univ. of Massachusetts Press, 2017); NCD, 1:110 ("Judges and Jurors").

31 DCCR, 1:100, 143, 144. See also "1723 Indenture, Alice Sachemus, Indian Woman," http://www.pilgrimhallmuseum.org/in_their_own_write.htm#1723 _indenture (accessed 01/24/2019); *Indian Converts*, 282–84, 338–41; Plane, *Colonial Intimacies*, 96–128; Silverman, *Faith and Boundaries*, 215–17.

32 Samuel Moody, *Summary Account of the Life and Death of Joseph Quasson, Indian* (Boston: printed for S. Gerrish, 1726); Covenant of Indenture, April 28, 1728, Misc. Bound Mss., MHS; "Indenture of Robin Meserick," July 6, 1737, Misc. Bound Mss., MHS.

33 Petition of Simon Popmonet, George Wapock, and John Terkins, Mashpee Indians to the Governor of the Province of Massachusetts, May 24, 1700, https:// yipp.yale.edu/annotated-transcription/digcoll1700052400 ("Great Jehovah," accessed 01/24/2019); Hawley to Andrew Oliver, Dec. 9, 1760, Hawley Journal, Congregational Library ("Every Indian"); Mashpee Indians to a Committee Appointed to Hear Indian Grievances, August 13, 1761 ("we can't"), and Hawley to Anon., June 1, 1794, Hawley Letters, MHS; Gideon Hawley to Samuel P. Savage, July 31, 1794, Samuel P. Savage Papers, MHS ("being children"); James Freeman, "A Description of Dukes County, Aug. 13th 1807," *MHSC*, 2nd ser., vol. 3 (1815): 94.

34 Zaccheus Macy, "A Short Journal of the First Settlement of the Island of Nantucket," *MHSC*, 1st ser., vol. 3 (1794): 161; Daniel F. Vickers, "Maritime Labor in Colonial Massachusetts: A Case Study of the Essex Cod Fishery and the Whaling Industry of Nantucket, 1630–1775" (PhD diss., Princeton University, 1981), 150–57; Richard C. Kugler, "The Whale Oil Trade, 1750–1775," in Philip Chadwick Foster Smith, ed., *Seafaring in Colonial Massachusetts* (Boston: Colonial

Society of Massachusetts, 1980), 153–73; Byers, *Nation of Nantucket*, chaps. 4, 7; Alexander Starbuck, *History of the American Whale Fishery: From Its Earliest Inception to the Year 1876*, 2 vols. (1878) (New York: pub. by the author, 1964), 1:1–42; J. Hector St. John de Crèvecour, *Letters from an American Farmer* (New York: E. P. Dutton, 1957), 115; "A Summer in New England: Paper One," *Harper's New Monthly Magazine* 124 (June 1860): 9 ("greater variety"); Daniel Ricketson, *The History of New Bedford, Bristol County, Massachusetts* (New Bedford: published by the author, 1858), 58, 59, 72, 300–302; James Freeman, "Notes on New Bedford," *MHSC*, 2nd ser., vol. 3 (1815): 18.

35 Brian D. Carroll, "'Savages' in the Service of Empire: Native American Soldiers in Gorham's Rangers, 1744–1762," *NEQ* 85, no. 3 (2012): 383–429; Carroll, "Effect of Military Service"; Carroll, "From Warrior to Soldier," i, 68, 260; Richard R. Johnson, "The Search for a Usable Indian: An Aspect of the Defense of Colonial New England," *Journal of American History* 64, no. 3 (1977): 622–51; Colin G. Calloway, "New England Algonkians in the American Revolution," in Peter Benes, ed., *Algonkians of New England: Past and Present* (Boston: Boston Univ., 1993), 51–62.

36 Carroll, "Warrior to Soldier," 95–98, 101.

37 Byers, *Nation of Nantucket*, 99. See also Daniel Vickers, "The First Whalemen of Nantucket," *WMQ* 40, no. 4 (1983): 560–83; Kelly K. Chaves, "Before the First Whalemen: The Emergence and Loss of Indigenous Maritime Autonomy in New England, 1672–1740," *NEQ* 87, no. 1 (2014): 46–71; Mark A. Nicholas, "The Mashpee Wampanoags of Cape Cod, the Whalefishery, and Seafaring's Impact on Community Development," *American Indian Quarterly* 26, no. 2 (2002): 165–97; Starbuck, *History of Nantucket*, 154 ("How").

38 Hawley Journal, entry for Dec. 9, 1760, Congregational Library ("First"); PLP, Acts 1804, chap. 84 ("Our men").

39 *Indian Converts*, 200 ("pressed"); Carroll, "Warrior to Soldier," 95–96, 111–15 ("recruitment" on 113), 232, 259, 286, 310 ("ventured"); MA Archives, 1:576 ("never been").

40 Wait Winthrop, *Some Meditations Concerning our Honourable Gentlemen and Fellow-Soldiers, in Pursuit of Those Barbarous Natives in the Narragansit-Country* (New London, CT: reprinted at N. London [by Timothy Green], 1721) ("swarm"); David J. Silverman, *Red Brethren: The Brothertown and Stockbridge Indians and the Problem of Race in Early America* (Ithaca, NY: Cornell Univ. Press, 2010), 79; Daniel R. Mandell, "'The Indian's Pedigree' (1794): Indians, Folklore, and Race in Southern New England," *WMQ* 61, no. 3 (2004): 521–38.

41 Alden T. Vaughan, *Roots of American Racism: Essays on the Colonial Experience* (New York: Oxford Univ. Press, 1995), 21 ("too apt"); Stephen Badger, "Historical and Characteristic Traits of the American Indians in General, and Those of Natick in Particular," *MHSC*, 1st ser., vol. 5 (1798): 39–40 ("considered"); Richard J. Boles,

"Dividing the Faith: The Rise of Racially Segregated Northern Churches, 1730–1850" (PhD diss., George Washington University, 2013).

42 In a lengthy literature, see Roy Harvey Pearce, *Savagism and Civilization: A Study of the Indian and the American Mind*, rev. ed. (Berkeley: Univ. of California Press, 1988); Robert F. Berkhofer, *The White Man's Indian: Images of the American Indian from Columbus to the Present* (New York: Alfred A. Knopf, 1978); Reginald Horsman, *Race and Manifest Destiny: Origins of American Racial Anglo-Saxonism* (Cambridge, MA: Harvard Univ. Press, 1981); Dippie, *Vanishing Indian*.

43 William Tudor, *Letters on the Eastern States* (New York: Kirk & Mercein, 1820), 236, 244 ("hopeless"); "A Visit to Martha's Vineyard," *Atlantic Monthly* 4 (September 1859): 292–93 ("exchanging"); O'Brien, *Firsting and Lasting*.

44 William Apess, "The Experiences of Five Christian Indians," in Barry O'Connell, ed., *On Our Own Ground: The Complete Writings of William Apess, a Pequot* (Amherst: Univ. of Massachusetts Press, 1992), 118; *Report of the Commissioners*, 14.

45 On population, see *U.S. Bureau of the Census, Historical Statistics of the United States, Colonial Times to 1970* (Washington, D.C.: U.S. Dept. of Commerce, Bureau of the Census, 1970), II, 1168, 1170 (Ser. Z 2-8, Ser. Z 24-132); Mandell, *Behind the Frontier*, 163; James W. Bradley et al., *Historic and Archaeological Resources of Cape Cod and the Islands: A Framework for Preservation Decisions* (Boston: Massachusetts Historical Commission, 1986), 92. On deaths at sea, see "List of Vessels Lost," notebook A, file 18, Macy Family Papers, Nantucket Historical Association; Crèvecour, *Letters from an American Farmer*, 175–76; Starbuck, *History of the American Whaling Fishery*, 1:33, 34, 77, 170, 171. On 1730, see *Boston News-Letter*, no. 1400, November 19, 1730 ("scarce"); Nickerson, "Some Lower Cape Indians" (1933), p. 119, MS 52, Sturgis Library, Barnstable, MA. On smallpox in Yarmouth, see *Boston News-Letter*, no. 1763, Jan. 2, 1738. On Mashpee, see CPGNE, box 1, entry for Nov. 10, 1738, and box 2, entry for Oct. 23, 1738. On yellow fever, see Letter of Jasper Manduit, Jan. 5, 1765, box 1, CPGNA; *Boston News-Letter*, no. 3127, Jan. 26, 1764; *Newport Mercury*, no. 283, February 6, 1764; *Boston Evening Post*, no. 1482, Jan. 30, 1764; Elizabeth A. Little, "The Nantucket Indian Sickness," in William Cowan, ed., *Papers of the Twenty-First Algonquian Conference* (Ottawa: Carleton Univ. Press, 1990), 181–96; Edouard A. Stackpole, "The Fatal Indian Sickness of Nantucket that Decimated the Island Aborigines," *Historic Nantucket* 23 (1975): 8–13; Donald Pelrine, "The Indian Sickness in the Town of Miacomet," *Historic Nantucket* 39 (1991): 67–69; "Account of Those Who Died at Mashpee in 1763," Gideon Hawley Journal, Congregational Library. On the Revolution, see Colin G. Calloway, *The American Revolution in Indian Country: Crisis and Diversity in Native American Communities* (New York: Cambridge Univ. Press, 1995), 34; Campisi, *Mashpee Indians*, 88; Mashpee Births and Deaths for 1778, Hawley Journal, Congregational Library.

46 On 1815, see Report of a Committee on the State of the Indians in Mashpee, *MHSC*, 2nd ser., vol. 3 (1815): 14; Freeman, "Description of Dukes County," 93–94. On these places before the war, see Report of Elisha Tupper, Aug. 7, 1757, Misc.

Bound Mss., MHS; Franklin Bowditch Dexter, ed., *Extracts from the Itineraries and Other Miscellanies of Ezra Stiles, D.D., LL.D., 1755–1794* (New Haven, CT: Yale Univ. Press, 1916), 59, 118; Petition of Indians at Potonumecut, November 24, 1765, Misc. Bound Mss., MHS; and the recollections of Gideon Hawley in his letter to the General Court, Jan. 29, 1794, Hawley Journal, Congregational Library. On hamlets, see Mandell, *Behind the Frontier*, 172–73, 174; Mandell, *Tribe, Race, History: Native Americans in Southern New England* (Baltimore: Johns Hopkins Univ. Press, 2008); Report of the Commissioners to determine the title of certain lands claimed by Indians, Governor's Council Files, box Jan. 1859–Dec. 1860, Mass. State Archives; *Report of the Commissioners*; *Earle Report*. On Mashpee, see Hawley to Rev. Peter Thatcher, Aug. 5, 1800, Society for Propagating the Gospel among the Indians and Others in North America, Records, 1791–1875, Phillips Library, Peabody Essex Museum, Salem, MA (hereafter SPGNA), box 2, folder 16. On Herring Pond, see A. Williams to John Eliot, June 20, 1778, CPGNE, box 3, folder 61. On Aquinnah, see Freeman, "Description of Dukes County," 93–94. For an 1827 census, see D. L. Child, H. Stebbins, and D. Fellows Jr., *Report on Condition of the Native Indians and Descendants of Native Indians, in This Commonwealth*, Massachusetts House Report No. 68 (Boston: printed by True and Greene, 1827). On Indians in urban "colored" neighborhoods, see Daniel R. Mandell, "Shifting Boundaries of Race and Ethnicity: Indian-Black Intermarriage in Southern New England, 1760–1880," *Journal of American History* 85, no. 2 (1998): 466–501; Jason Mancini, "Beyond Reservation: Indian Survivance in Southern New England and Eastern Long Island, 1713–1861" (PhD diss., University of Connecticut, 2009); Russell Lawrence Barsh, "'Colored' Seamen in the New England Whaling Industry: An Afro-Indian Consortium," in James F. Brooks, ed. *Confounding the Color Line: The Indian-Black Experience in North America* (Lincoln: Univ. of Nebraska Press, 2002), 76–107; Petition of Essex Boston, Peter Boston, and Jeffrey Sammons, May 17, 1822, SPGNA, box 1, ("colored").

47 Hawley to Andrew Eliot, July 18, 1787, Hawley Journal, Congregational Library ("asylum"); Hawley to Rev. Peter Thatcher, Aug. 5, 1800, SPGNA, box 2, folder 16. See also Moses Howwoswee, Account of the Indians Resident at Gay Head, March 19, 1792, Misc. Mss., MHS; A List of Children Under Eighteen Years of Age, the 14th Day of May, 1798; PLP, Resolves 1789, chap. 57; *Gay Head Report*, 37, 39; *Report of the Commissioners*, 62.

48 ULRIA, box 2, file 9419-1824; *Report of the Commissioners*, 20–21 ("no heart-burning"; "communists"); Tudor, *Letters on the Eastern States*, 243–44; *Earle Report*, 33, 42; *Mass. Acts and Resolves, 1845*, chap. 22, 522–23; box 4S, env. 25, Martha's Vineyard Museum; "Visit to the Elizabeth Islands," 318; Ebenezer Skiff to Frederick Baylies, May 3, 1823, Misc. Bound Mss., MHS; Leavitt Thaxter to John Milton Earle, February 3, 1860, John Milton Earle Papers, box 2, file 2, AAS.

49 Zachariah Howwoswee Papers, file 1777 My 12-Ag 28, file 1784 Ap. 16-22, John Carter Brown Library, Providence, RI; Petition and Address of the Indians of

Mashpee [n.d.], Hawley Journal, Congregational Library ("Negroes and English"); Moses Howwoswee, Account of the Indians Resident at Gay Head, March 19, 1792, Misc. Mss., MHS; Petition of "the Proprietors, Nation, and Tribe of Gay Head," May 18, 1816, ULRIA, 8029-1816 (4); "Enumeration of Proprietors and Non-Proprietors (Negroes of Mashpee)," Nov. 1832, GIP, folder 13.

50 PLP, Acts 1804, chap. 84; *Report of the Commissioners*, 88 ("not right"); "Zacheus Howwoswee to John Milton Earle, Aug. 25, 1859," Earle Papers, box 2, file 3, AAS; *Earle Report*, 44–45; Petition of Christiantown, Dec. 25, 1823, ULRIA, box 2, folder: House Unpassed 9419-1824; Resolve on the Petition of Hannah Cappen, Resolves-1822, Ch. 22, PLP; Petition of Benjamin Allen, February 11, 1850, ULRIA, box 2, folder SU 13034-1850 (4) ("arose"); Petition of the Indians of Chappaquiddick, May 25, 1826, Acts-1827, Ch. 114, PLP ("difficulties").

51 *Report of the Commissioners*, 26; GIP, box 2, file 13; Howwoswee to John Milton Earle, 27 Jan. 1860," Earle Papers, box 2, file 3, AAS ("we the proprietors"); Bird, Griswold, and Weekes, *Report of the Commissioners*, 16 ("liberty"); *Earle Report*, 20. See also the interview between the Mashpee women Anne Foxx and Joan Tavares Avant, ca. 1950, in Senier, *Dawnland Voices*, 470–72.

52 E. Mayhew, *Brief Account*, 9–10 ("much better"); Samuel Sewall to William Ashhurst, October 6, 1724, NE Co. Recs., 7955/2, p. 10 ("unless"); Goddard and Bragdon, *Native Writings*, 1:179 ("no need"); "At a meeting of the Indians in Mashpee, July 28, 1754," Hawley Letters, MHS ("did not understand"); "Report of a Committee on the State of the Indians in Mashpee," *MHSC*, 1st ser., vol. 10 (1815): 13 ("fond"); *Boston News-Letter*, no. 3351, December 24, 1767.

53 Hawley to R.D.S., August 1802, Savage Papers, MHS ("English language"); Frederick Baylies, Names and Ages of the Indians on Martha's Vineyard, Jan. 1, 1823, Shattuck Collection, Mss. A/S53, NEHGS ("six"); Samuel Davis Papers, uncatalogued, May 1841, MHS ("infancy").

54 Edward S. Burgess, "The Old South Road of Gay Head," *Dukes County Intelligencer* 12 (1970): 22.

55 Patrick Wolfe, "Land, Labor, and Difference: Elementary Structures of Race," *American Historical Review* 106, no. 3 (2001): 866–905.

56 Report of Joseph Thaxter and Federick Baylies, September 22, 1818, GIP, box 3, folder 15 ("pure"); Indians on Martha's Vineyard, Shattuck Collection, Mss. A/S53, folder 1HA, NEHGS ("probable"); *Report of the Commissioners*, 6 ("admixture"); Report of a Committee Appointed to Investigate the Condition of the Indians, March 1, 1827, PLP, Acts 1827, chap. 114 ("full blood"); "A Visit to Martha's Vineyard," *Atlantic Monthly* 4 (1859): 292 ("half-breeds"); Christine Tracey Grabowski, "Coiled Intent: Federal Acknowledgment Policy and the Gay Head Wampanoags" (PhD diss., City University of New York, 1994), 295 ("monig").

57 "Report on the care of Holden Wordell as Guardian of the Troy Indians, May 15, 1845," Governor's Council Files, box May 1845–Jan. 1846, Mass. State Archives ("kindness"); Donald M. Nielsen, "The Mashpee Indian Revolt of 1833," *NEQ* 58,

no. 3 (1985): 500 ("do not believe"); GIP, box 2, folder 1, MA Archives ("free and equal"); Apess, *Indian Nullification of the Unconstitutional Laws of Massachusetts Relative to Mashpee* (1835), in O'Connell, *On Our Own Ground*, 163–274; Philip F. Gura, *The Life of William Apess, Pequot* (Chapel Hill: Univ. of North Carolina Press, 2015), 77–99; Mandell, *Tribe, Race, History*, 96–103.

58   Joanna Brooks, ed., *The Collected Writings of Samson Occum, Mohegan: Leadership and Literature in Eighteenth-Century Native America* (New York: Oxford Univ. Press, 2006).

59   Apess, *Eulogy on King Philip* (1836), in O'Connell, *On Our Own Ground*, 278, 280.

60   Apess, 305–6.

61   Apess, 286.

62   Campisi, *Mashpee*, 105.

63   Morse, *Report to the Secretary of War*, 69; Daniel Wrighte to Adlen Bradford, April 9, 1839, Andrews-Eliot Coll., MHS; Bird, Griswold, and Weekes, *Report of the Commissioners*, 7 ("pictures"), 9–10, 14–16, 18–19, 20–21; B. G. Marchant to J. M. Earle, August 27, 1859, Earle Papers, box 2, file 3, AAS; *Earle Report*, 17, 18, 26–27, 36; Albert C. Koch, *Journey through a Part of the United States*, trans. and ed. Ernst A. Stadler (Carbondale: Southern Illinois Univ. Press, 1972), 16; Glover and McBride, "Old Ways and New Ways," 15; B. G. Marchant to J. M. Earle, September 17, 1859, and Leavitt Thaxter to John Milton Earle, February 3, 1860, Earle Papers, box 2, file 3; *Report of the Select Committee of the Society for the Propagation of the Gospel in North America* (Cambridge, MA, 1861), 21, 24; *Vineyard Gazette*, June 1, 1848, vol. 3, no. 4; Wrighte to Bradford, April 9, 1839, SPGNA, Recs., box 6, MHS ("parents"); Gay Head Town Records, 1858–1866, box 174, env. S1, Martha's Vineyard Museum; Report on Account of the Commissioners . . . for the Herring Pond Indians, March 20, 1839, Governor's Council Files, box June 1838–March 1839, Mass. State Archives; Report of the Guardians of the Herring Pond Indians, March 1840, GIP, box 2, folder 3; Report of the Guardians of the Troy Indians, 1857, GIP, box 3, folder 11; House Report 46 (1849); *Earle Report*.

64   Bird, Griswold, and Weekes, *Report of the Commissioners*, 11 ("feel"); *Earle Report*, 13 ("vague"), 24 ("shrewder").

65   *Gay Head Report*, 28 ("exist"); Petition of Aaron Cooper, Thomas Jeffers, and Isaac D. Rose, Selectmen and Treasurer of the Gay Head Indians . . . February 4, 1869, PLP, Acts 1870, chap. 213 ("incorporated"); Plane and Button, "Massachusetts Indian Enfranchisement Act"; D. Elliotte Draegor, "Losing Ground: Land Loss among the Mashantucket Pequot and the Mashpee Wampanoag Tribes in the Nineteenth Century" (PhD diss., University of Connecticut, 2009), 82–94.

66   Mandell, *Tribe, Race, History*, 218–30; Dubuque, *Fall River Reservation*.

67   *Earle Report*; Grabowski, "Coiled Intent," 320; Hutchins, *Mashpee*, 142; Campisi, *Mashpee*, 119–50; Draegor, "Losing Ground," 129, 138–39, 156, 158.

68   Gabrowski, "Coiled Intent," 278 ("always"). These sentiments cut through Levitas, "No Boundary Is a Boundary"; Campisi, *Mashpee*; Starna, "'We'll All Be

Together Again,'" 3–12; and the narratives accompanying the Gay Head Wampanoag and Mashpee Wampanoag petitions for federal recognition.

69 Campisi, *Mashpee*, 130–38; Ann McMullen, "What's Wrong with This Picture? Context, Conversion, Survival, and the Development of Regional Native Cultures and Pan-Indianism in Southeastern New England," in Weinstein, *Enduring Traditions*, 123–50.

70 Campisi, *Mashpee*; and Grabowski, "Coiled Intent."

71 James Clifford, "Identity in Mashpee," in *The Predicament of Culture: Twentieth-Century Ethnography, Literature, and Art* (Cambridge, MA: Harvard Univ. Press, 1988), 217–48.

72 Clifford, "Identity in Mashpee"; Smith and Warrior, *Like a Hurricane*; Cornell, *Return of the Native*; Nagel, *American Indian Ethnic Renewal*.

73 Administrative Policies and Procedures of the Coalition of Eastern Native Americans, Inc., CENA Records, folder 1973, National Museum of the American Indian Cultural Resources Center, Suitland, MD.

74 Campisi, *Mashpee*; Grabowski, "Coiled Intent"; Starna, "'We'll All be Together Again.'" For local coverage of the Gay Head Wampanoags' federal recognition, see John Robinson, "US Recognizes Wampanoag Indians as Tribe," *Boston Globe*, February 5, 1987; Steven Marantz, "Wampanoags See Better Days Ahead after Ruling," *Boston Globe*, February 6, 1987; Elaine Lembo, "Historic Ruling Grants Gay Head Indians Federal Recognition," *Vineyard Gazette*, February 12, 1987. On Mashpee, see Andrew Ryan, "Mashpee Tribe Wins Federal Recognition," *Boston Globe*, February 16, 2007; Jason Kolnos, "A Nation Reborn: The Mashpee Wampanoag Indian Tribe Gets Federal Recognition after a Years-Long Battle," *Cape Cod Times*, February 15, 2007.

75 Local newspapers, the *Cape Cod Times*, the *Vineyard Gazette*, and the *Vineyard Times*, regularly cover these developments. These issues can also be traced from the perspective of Mashpee tribal authorities in the official newsletter, *Mittark*: https://mashpeewampanoagtribe-nsn.gov/mittark-archives/ (accessed 01/24/2019).

76 The story of Baird and her language work is treated on the Wôpanâak Language Reclamation Project website: http://www.wlrp.org; the MacArthur Foundation website: https://www.macfound.org/fellows/24/ (accessed 01/24/2019); the 2001 MIT *Spectrum* newsletter article by Orna Feldman, "Inspired by a Dream," https://spectrum.mit.edu/spring-2001/inspired-by-a-dream/ (accessed 01/24/2019); the following articles: http://www.wikinow.co/topic/jessie-little-doe-baird; and in the 2010 film *We Still Live Here*, directed by Anne Makepeace. See also Jessie Little Doe Fermino (Baird), "You are a Dead People," *Cultural Survival Quarterly* 25, no. 2 (2001): 16–17.

77 "Wampanoag Massasoit Returns to Grave," *Nashauonk Mittark*, May 2017, https://static1.squarespace.com/static/59ca33c0f09ca4a9c5845529/t/5a4e61bbf9619a322 db89437/1515086272810/mittark-may-2017.pdf (accessed 01/24/2019); Jason Daley,

"Massasoit, Chief Who Signed Treaty with the Pilgrims, to Be Reburied," *Smithsonian Magazine*, April 21, 2017; Chris Lindahl, "Objects Returned to Native American Leader Massasoit's Burial Site in Warren," *Providence Journal*, May 15, 2017.

EPILOGUE: TOWARD A DAY WITH LESS MOURNING

1   "Native Americans Marking Thanksgiving with Day of Mourning," Associated Press, November 23, 2017, https://www.boston.com/news/local-news/2017/11/23 /native-americans-marking-thanksgiving-with-day-of-mourning ("No thanks"; accessed 01/24/2019); *People of the First Light: An Indigenous Perspective on Thanksgiving*, https://archive.org/details/PACTV_Summer_Documentary_2016_People _of_the_First_Light_-_An_Indigenous_Perspective_on_Thanksgiving (accessed 01/24/2019); "Episode 40—Wampanoag Nation: Jonathan Perry—Native American," LightupwithShua, June 12, 2018, https://www.youtube.com/watch?v=83F4X NugSOo (accessed 01/24/2019); Aquinnah's Tobias Vanderhoop in the Thomas Bena documentary, *One Big Home* (2016).

2   Quoted in Meg Anderson, "How to Talk to Kids About Thanksgiving," NPR, November 25, 2015, https://www.npr.org/sections/ed/2015/11/25/457105485/how-to -talk-to-kids-about-thanksgiving (accessed 01/24/2019).

3   "Wampanoag on Thanksgiving," Many Hoops, http://www.manyhoops.com /wampanoag-on-thanksgiving.html ("complicated," "ten"; accessed 01/24/2019).

4   Amanda Morris, "Teaching Thanksgiving in a Socially Responsible Way," Teaching Tolerance, November 10, 2015, https://www.tolerance.org/magazine/teaching-thanks giving-in-a-socially-responsible-way ("indoctrination"; accessed 01/24/2019); Victoria Pasquantonio, "Lesson plan: After helping Pilgrims at Plymouth, today's Wampanoags fight for their ancestral lands," PBS NewsHour Extra, http://www .pbs.org/newshour/extra/lessons_plans/on-thanksgiving-giving-thanks-to -todays-native-americans-lesson-plan/ (accessed 01/24/2019); "Teaching About the First Thanksgiving," Scholastic, https://www.scholastic.com/teachers/collec tions/teaching-content/teaching-about-first-thanksgiving/ (accessed 01/24/2019); Phil Nast, "Thanksgiving Ideas for the Classroom, Grades 6–8," National Education Association, last updated October 19, 2018, http://www.nea.org/tools/lessons /thanksgiving-ideas-for-the-classroom-grades-6-8.html (accessed 01/24/2019); Anderson, "How to Talk to Kids About Thanksgiving," http://www.npr.org/secti ons/ed/2015/11/25/457105485/how-to-talk-to-kids-about-thanksgiving (accessed 01/24/2019); "Differing Views of Pilgrims and Native Americans in Seventeenth-Century New England," History Now, Gilder Lehrman Institute of American History, https://www.gilderlehrman.org/content/differing-views-pilgrims-and-native -americans-seventeenth-century-new-england (accessed 01/24/2019); National Museum of the American Indian Education Office, "American Indian Perspectives on Thanksgiving," teaching poster, https://nmai.si.edu/sites/1/files/pdf /education/thanksgiving_poster.pdf (accessed 01/24/2019); *Investigating "The First*

Thanksgiving": An Educator's Guide to the 1621 Harvest Celebration, Plimoth Planta-tion Educational Materials (Plymouth, MA: Plimoth Plantation, 2003); Cathe-rine O'Neill Grace and Margaret M. Bruchac, *1621: A New Look at Thanksgiving* (Washington, D.C.: National Geographic Society, 2001).

5   Paula Peters, "Cultural Lives Matter," *Dawnland Voices 2.0: Indigenous Writing from New England and the Northeast*, https://dawnlandvoices.org/paula-peters -issue-2/ ("degradation"; accessed 01/24/2019); Ramona Peters, "How Should Thanksgiving Be Taught in Schools?" *Nashauonk Mittark*, November 2016, 12, https://static1.squarespace.com/static/59ca33c0f09ca4a9c5845sa9/t/5a4e622fe 2c4835f86b33c76/1515086385369/mittark-november-2016.pdf ("gratitude"; accessed 01/24/2019).

6   "Tribe Gives Thanks at Seventh Annual Native American Thanks Giving," *Nashauonk Mittark*, December 2016, 7, https://static1.squarespace.com/static /59ca33c0f09ca4a9c5845sa9/t/5a4e5e21c8302529ed90bb2d/1515085348132/mittark -december-2016.pdf (accessed 01/24/2019).

7   Paula Peters, "Wampanoag Reflections," in Senier, *Dawnland Voices*, 479.

8   "October 19, 1998 Settlement," United American Indians of New England, www .uaine.org/settlement.htm (accessed 01/24/2019); "Native American March Becomes a Melee," *Boston Globe*, November 28, 1997; "Confrontation Continues in Courtroom," *Boston Globe*, November 29, 1997; "Plymouth Protest Pact Reached," *Boston Globe*, October 25, 1998; "Two Views of History Converge in Plymouth," *Boston Globe*, November 22, 1998; Tall Oak, phone conversation with author, August 31, 2018.

INDEX

Note: Page numbers in italics refer to figures.

Abbomocho. *See* Cheepi
Abenakis, 53, 89, 104, 105, 106, 144, 145, 148, 275, 336, 359
Acadia, 84
Acoaxet, 361, 391
Acushnet, 218, 287, 361, 391
Adena, 36
Adventurers, 133, 177
Agawam, 123, 349
Ahhunnut, Hannah, 360
AIM. *See* American Indian Movement
Albany, NY, 56, 278, 336
Alderman, 315, 348, 352
Alexander. *See* Wamsutta
Algonquian language, 52
Allen, John, 288
American Indian Congress, 415
American Indian Movement, 11, 15, 415
Amos, Blind Jo, 401
Amos, Rachel, 360
Andros, Edmund, 219, 302, 337
Apess, William, 12, 290, 402–5, *404*
Apponagansett, 218, 233, 236, 321, 361, 391
Aptucxet, 213–14, *214*, 217
Aquidneck Island, 74, 221, 232, 299
Aquinnah (sachemship, reservation, and town; also Gay Head), 2, 31, 53, 367–71
    division of common lands in, 410
    federal reservation of, 416
    incorporation of as a town, 410
    population of, 410–11
Aquinnah Wampanoags, 2, 21, 248, 383, 389
    Christianity of, 249, 359–63
    citizenship of, 405–10
    federal recognition of, 414–16
    governance of, 395–96, 406
    guardians and, 375

    intermarriages of, 394–98, 406
    King Philip's War and, 328–29
    land management of, 394
    land sales and, 257
    language change among, 397–99, 400
    missions among, 249, 257
    New England Company and, 367–71
    oral traditions of, 31, 117
    population of, 392
    protests of, 368–69, 375
    reservation status of, 370–71
    sachem removal by, 372
    town as tribe among, 411–13
    values of, 411–12
    women's authority among, 396
Archer, Gabriel, 81
Ascook, 281–82
Aspinet, 161, 163, 186–87, 199
Assamough (John Gibbs), 241, 480n48
Assaweta (Betty Sassamon), 294
Assawompset, 349, 360, 361, 362, 369, 391
Assawompset Pond, 265, 294, 306–8, 350
Assonet Neck, 318, 349
Awashonks, 258, 282–83, 286–87, 292, 310–11, 319, 342–46, 350
Awashonks, Peter, 315, 344–45

Baird, Jessie Little Doe, 374, 417
Baptists, 234, 401
Barnstable (Ply. and MA), 237, 239, 327, 329, 391
Barnstable Harbor, 86, 162
Bass River, 371
Baylies, Frederick, 398, 400
Bellingham, Richard, 280
Bernard, Francis, 375
Betty's Neck, 294, 391

Bible, Wampanoag language, 244–46, *247*, 324, 399, 417
Billington, John, 161–64, 172, 187
Blackstone River, 213, 231, 232, 338
Block, Adrian, 92
Block Island, 211, 223, 273
Boston, MA, 222, 228, 234, 240, 246, 284, 308, 317, 321, 324, 325, 334, 336, 347, 348, 372, 381, 388
Bourne, Joseph, 397
Bourne, Lt. Richard, 386
Bourne, Rev. Richard, 240, 246, 290
bow and arrow, 36
Bradford, Gov. William, 7, 23, 24, 102–3, 108–9, 122, 137, 148, 167, 168–71, 178, 181, 182, 183, 199, 213, 288, 350
Bradford, Maj. William, 313, 344–45, 346
Briant, Solomon, 397
Bridgewater (Ply. and MA), 233, 236, 347, 372
Bristol (Ply., MA, and RI), 350
Brown, James, 283
Brown, John, 229, 233–35, 252, 283, 310
Bureau of Indian Affairs, 12, 416
Buzzards Bay, 78, 80, 211, 213, 218, 233, 265, 268, 361, 391

Cabot, John, 73
Cádiz, 322
Cagenhew, 244
Canacum, 161, 187, 199
Canonchet, 332
Canonicus (I), 54, 122, 166–67, 179, 230, 251, 272, 330
Canonicus (II), 347
Cape Breton, 78
Cape Cod, 7, 184, 200, 213, 217, 260
    European exploration of, 67, 68, 71, 75, 76, 83, 84, 86, 89, 129
    geography of, 33–34
    King Philip's War and, 305, 325, 329–30
    land sales on, 207, 237–40
    Mayflower landing on, 23, 134
    missions of, 207, 220, 240–50, 289–94
    Pilgrim exploration of, 135–39
    population of, 359
    Wampanoags of, 23, 78, 89, 158, 185–87, 194, 198–99, 207, 218, 219, 237–50, 289–94, 305, 325–30, 341, 346, 359, 361–65, 378, 397
Captain Amos, 341
captivity, 62–66, 68–69, 115, 334
Caribbean. *See* West Indies
Carlisle Indian School, 412

Carver, John, 150, 151, 288
Cassacinamon, Robin, 276
Cautantowwit. *See* Kiehtan
Champlain, Samuel de, 84–88
Chappaquiddick, 239, 248, 366–67, 372, 375, 376, 391, 392, 395, 407, 410
Charles I, 220
Charles II, 327, 340
Charles River, 123, 212
Chawum, 99
Cheepi, 110, 111, 117, 148, 164, 243
Cheesebrough, William, 234–35
Cheeshahteaumuck, Caleb, 244, *245*, 416–17
Chowahunna, David, 345
Christianity
    Indian survival and, 359–63
    Mohegans and, 360
    Narragansetts and, 360
    Pequots and, 360
    role of in Thanksgiving myth, 5, 9
    Wampanoags and, 240–50, 291–92, 330, 359–65, 398
Christian missions. *See* missions
Christiantown, 247–49, 367, 386, 390, 395, 410
Church, Benjamin, 287, 310–12, 315, 322, 337, 342–46, 348, 350, 351, 352, 383
Church of England, 130–31
citizenship, 405–10
Civil War (American), 408
Civil War (English), 220
Clafflin, William, 209
Clark's Garrison, 334
Clark's Island, 329, 341
Coalition of Eastern Native Americans, 415
Coddington, William, 229, 231
Cogenhew, Reuben, 375–76
Cole, Hugh, 279, 288
Cole's Hill, 12, 15, 425
colonialism, 20, 356, 358
Connecticut
    enslavement of Indians by, 225, 251
    founding of, 132, 221
    King Philip's War and, 330, 340–41
    Pequot War and, 14, 223–24
    United Colonies of New England and, 228
    war scares and, 278, 284–85, 302
Connecticut River, 99, 102–3, 175, 211, 213, 221, 222, 323–24, 327, 328, 334, 348
Constitution, United States, 7
Coombs, Darius, 420
Coombs, Linda, 421, 424

Corbitant, 55, 164, 165–66, 175, 180, 189, 193, 194–95, 263
Cosens, John, 361
Coshaug, Tom, 361
Cotton, John, Jr., 240, 248, 259–60, 287, 292, 361
Cotton, Josiah, 361, 363
Coweset, 57, 100, 310, 338
Cromwell, Cedric, 421, 424
Cudworth, James, 317
Cummaquid, 91, 162
Cushman, Robert, 26
Cutshamekin, 228

Danforth, Samuel, 363
Dartmouth (Ply. and MA), 317, 321, 350, 360, 391
debt peonage, 378–82, *384*
Deer Island, 324–25, 326, 341, *343*, 346, 360
Department of the Interior, 416, 417
Dermer, Thomas, 61, 66, 68–71, 90, 100–101, 104, 140, 145, 146, 148
Dohoday, 99
Dongan, Thomas, 368–70
Duke of York (James Stuart). *See* James II
Dutch, 276
    arms trade of, 278
    explorations of 91–92
    Indian trade of, 91–92, 189, 210, 211–12, 215
    King Philip's War and, 321
    war scares and, 251, 275
Dutch Island, 211
Dutch Reformed Church, 132
Dutch Republic. *See* Netherlands

Eastham (Ply. and MA), 62, 139, 237, 365–66, 391
Easton, John, 299
Eells, Samuel, 321
Eliot, John, 105, 240, 243, 244, 246, 267, 283, 292–93, 321, 322
Eliot, John, Jr., 292
Elizabeth Islands, 80, 83, 351, 361, 369
enslavement, 63, 66, 76, 90–91, 128, 162, 225, 251, 253, 319–22, 329–30, 340–41, 348–49, 351, 352, 376
Epenow, 67, 70, 89–90, 128, 130, 145, 166, 170
epidemic disease, 39, 101–2
    of 1616–1619, 67–68, 93, 95–98, 101, 104–8, 112, 114–21, 146, 175, 179, 180, 184, 193, 210, 222, 253, 272
    of 1622, 105, 184, 186, 199, 222

    of 1633–1634, 103, 105, 107, 108–9, 222
    of 1643, 223
    of 1645, 223
    of 1730, 391
    of 1736, 391
    of 1738, 391
    of 1763–64, 391
    colonialism and, 104, 124–25
    English explanations for, 119
    Indian explanations for, 116–21, 157–58, 175, 179
    trauma from, 120–21
    virgin soil, 102–3
Eulogy on King Philip (1836), 12, 402
explorers, 59, 61
    in New England, 66, 68–71, 83–94
    trade of, with Indians, 62
    violence of, with Indians, 62–63, 66–67, 70, 76, 82–94
    See also Block, Adrian; Cabot, John; Champlain, Samuel de; Dermer, Thomas; Gilbert, Humphrey; Gomez, Estevão; Gosnold, Bartholomew; Harlow, Edward; Hobson, Nicholas; Hudson, Henry; Hunt, Thomas; Mons, Pierre de Gaust; Poutrincourt, Jean de Biencourt; Pring, Martin; Smith, John; Waymouth, George; Verrazzano, Giovanni da

Fall River, MA, 257, 367, 410
Federated Eastern Indian League, 3, 415
Fifteenth Amendment, 409
firearms, 157–58, 210, 218–19, 229, 234, 277, 279, 282, 336
First Thanksgiving, 4, 128, 168–71, 419
The First Thanksgiving (Brownscombe), *6*
Fish, Phineas, 401, 405
Five Nations Iroquois. *See* Iroquois League
Folger, Peter, 240
Forefathers' Day, 5
Fort Orange, 212
Fourteenth Amendment, 409
Freetown, MA, 350
French, 276
    colonization by, 92
    explorations of, 73–75, 84–88, 92, 93
    Indian trade of, 176
    war scares and, 275
fur trade, 62, 70, 73, 80, 88, 92, 99, 103, 147, 158, 176, 177, 183, 189, 201, 210–20, 230, 234, 336

Gardiner's Neck. *See* Mattapoisett Neck
Gay Head. *See* Aquinnah
George (Nauset sachem), 238
Gibbs, John (Assamough), 241
Gilbert, Humphrey, 76
Gomez, Estevão, 75
Gookin, Daniel, 58, 99, 105, 293, 325, 346
Gorges, Ferdinando, 66, 67, 70, 88, 89, 90, 91,
    104, 144
Gosnold, Bartholomew, 76, 78–82
Governor Drummer's War, 383
Grand Banks, 63, 73, 76
Great Migration, 202, 220–22, 229, 250, 255
Great Swamp Fort Massacre, 333–34, 388
Gulf of Maine, 78, 100

Hale, Sarah Josepha, 4
Hamden, John, 189, 195
Hannit, Japheth, 328, 360
Harlow, Edward, 67, 89
Harris, William, 332
Harvard College, 244–45, 273, 291, 292, 294
Haskins, Amos, *384*
Hassanamesit, 324, 325
Haudenosaunee. *See* Iroquois League
Hawley, Gideon, 381–82, 392, 397
Hazzleton, Charles, 310–11
Hedge, Jacob, 361
Herring Pond Wampanoags, 361, 392, 410
Hiacoomes, 241
Hiacoomes, Joel, 244, 290, 417
Hiacoomes, John, 360
Hobbomock (deity). *See* Cheepi
Hobbomock (Wampanoag), 164, 165–66, 177,
    180, 182, 189, 194, 197–98, 200–201
Hobson, Nicholas, 70
Hog Island, 266
Honorable, Dorcas, *393*
Hoosic River, 336–37, 341
Hopkins, Stephen, 101, 137, 143, 155–61, 172,
    179
horticulture, 36–45, 51, 56
Hossueit, Zachariah, *368*
Housatonic Indians, 336
Howwoswee, Zachariah, 399
Howwoswee, Zacheus, 396
Hubbard, William, 228, 254, 308, 346
Hudson, Henry, 91
Hudson River, 7, 133, 134, 212, 213, 225, 227,
    278, 336–37
Hunt, Thomas, 61–63, 66, 67, 90–91, 92, 162
Hurons (Wendats), 42, 103, 116
Hutchinson, Thomas, 388

indentured servitude. *See* Indian servitude
Indian Converts (1727), *364*, 365
Indian-English relations. *See* debt;
    enslavement; fur trade; interpreters;
    jurisdictional disputes; King Philip's
    War; land sales; liquor trade; livestock;
    missions; murder; trade; wage work; war
    scares.
Indian Removal, 402
Indian Reorganization Act (1934), 416
Indians
    ancient civilizations of, 9, 28–29
    authenticity and, 29
    bow and arrow technology of, 36
    colonialism and, 9
    history and, 18–20
    military service of, 17, 384
    modernity and, 9, 29
    myth of disappearance and, 10, 29,
        398
    race and, 9, 16, 29
    role of in Thanksgiving myth, 5, 7, 8
    trade of, 36, 38–39
    See also Abenakis; Cayugas; Hurons;
        Iroquois; Iroquois League; Long
        Island Indians; Maliseet-
        Passamaquoddies; Massachusetts
        Indians; Mohawks; Mohegans
        Mohicans; Montauketts; Munsees;
        Narragansetts; New England
        Indians; Nipmucs; Oneidas;
        Onondagas; Pequots;
        Pocumtucks; River Indians;
        Senecas; Wabanakis;
        Wampanoags; Wappingers
Indian servitude, 378–82, 384–87, 396–97
Indian Town, 371, 391
interpreters, 99, 162, 164, 176, 177, 182, 187, 230,
    233–35, 274, 294–97, 310–11, 339. *See also*
    Brown, John; Dohoday; Hazzleton,
    John; Hobbomock; Samoset; Sassamon,
    John; Sassamon, Rowland; Stanton,
    Thomas; Tatum; Tisquantum;
    Tokamahamon; Whitman, Valentine;
    Willet, Thomas; Williams, Roger
Iroquois (language group), 40
Iroquois League (Haudenosaunee), 40–44,
    122, 175, 215, 216, 336, *339*
Iyanough, 162, 186, 199

Jackson, Andrew, 402, 405
James I, 133, 155, 158
James II, 302

James, Frank (Wamsutta), 2–3, 9, 10, 12, 13, 14, 419
James, Roland, 419
James, Samuel, 387
Jamestown, 65–66, 76, 133, 137, 154, 199
Jennings, Francis, 96
Johnson, Edward, 105, 121
Johnson, Simon, 407, 408
Jones, Ralph, 361
Josselyn, John, 105, 169
jurisdictional disputes, 269–72, 296, 299–300, 303, 308, 326, 376–78

Keencomsett, 327
Kennebec River, 66, 88, 213, 217
Kickamuit, 255
Kieft's War, 297
Kiehtan (Cautantowwit), 31, 47, 48, 59, 110, 111, 117, 118, 208
King George's War, 383
King Philip. See Pumetacom
King Philip's War, 287, 320
    on Cape Cod, 305, 325–29
    causes of, 299–309
    colonial histories of, 19, 259
    in Connecticut River Valley, 322–24, 327, 328, 334, 348
    English captivity in, 334
    English interpretations of, 335–36
    English losses in, 334
    English spoils of, 348–50
    English victories in, 349–50
    enslavement of Indians by English during, 319–22, 329–30, 340–41, 348–49, 351, 352, 355
    histories of, 355
    Indian allies of English during, 305, 330, 333, 340–41, 343, 346–47, 351–52
    Indian interpretations of, 336, 360
    Indian losses in, 336–50, 348, 349, 355
    Indian victories in, 334
    last phase of, in southern New England, 347–53
    Maine and, 335, 347, 348
    Martha's Vineyard and, 219, 305, 325–29
    Mohawks' involvement in, 336–38, 341
    Mount Hope Neck and, 314–15, 316
    Nantucket and, 219, 305, 325–29
    Narragansetts' involvement in, 330–34
    Nipmuc country and, 324–25
    opening phase of, 309–19
    Pocasset and Sakonnet and, 314–19, 342–46

praying Indians and, 323–30, 341, 346, 349
River Indians and, 322–23
spread of, 322–24
start of, 153, 254
Thanksgiving myth and, 254, 353
Wampanoag country and, 314–19, 342–53
King William's War, 383

Landing of the Pilgrims (Cusici), 8
land sales, 206
    fines and, 283, 296, 300, 302
    fraud and, 255, 267–68, 286–87, 296, 303
    joint-use agreements and, 230–33, 236, 238–39, 250, 266, 365–76
    King Philip's War and, 296
    Narragnasetts and, 265
    New England Indians and, 52–53
    Nipmucs and, 265
    Ousamequin and, 226, 230–37
    payments to Indians in, 236
    planting rights and, 268–69
    praying town protection against, 246
    sachem rights and, 268–69
    speculation and, 256
    straw sellers and, 255, 287, 303
    Wampanoags and, 52–53, 125, 230–33, 240–50, 256–58, 263–66
    Wampanoag resistance to, 268–69, 368–70
Laud, William, 220
Leiden, 132, 133, 199
leptospirosis, 106–7
Leveridge, William, 240
Levett, Christopher, 148
liquor trade, 73, 212, 218, 234–36, 304
Little Compton (Ply., MA, and RI), 350, 360
livestock, 202, 211, 250, 255, 256, 266, 279, 303, 366–67
London, 63, 64, 180, 184
Long Island, 56, 211, 220
Long Island Indians, 56, 175, 220, 225, 226, 273, 277
Long Island Sound, 74, 215, 216, 227
Long Pond (Yarmouth), 371
Lovelace, Francis, 219

Mahicans. See Mohicans
Maine, 73, 75, 76, 78, 79, 84, 88, 92, 104, 105, 144, 148, 177, 212, 216, 234, 335, 347, 348, 351, 359, 383
Málaga, 63, 180

Maliseet-Passamaquoddies, 84
Maliseets, 415
Mamaneway, 286–87
Manifest Destiny, 9, 389, *393*
Manisses, 223, 273
Manomet, 161, 187, 246, 363
Manomet River (Monument River), 213, *214*
Marshfield (Ply. and MA), 260
Martha's Vineyard, 2, 71, 80
    court system of, 377
    epidemics of, 223, 391
    European explorers and, 67, 70, 71, 78,
        79, 89
    King Philip's War and, 305, 325–30
    land sales on, 207, 237–40, 268–69
    missions of, 207, 220, 240–50,
        289–94
    population of, 359
    Wampanoags of, 54, 67, 70, 79–80, 89,
        112, 194, 200, 207, 218, 219, 223,
        237–50, 257, 268–69, 276, 289–94,
        305, 325–30, 359, 360, 361, 366–67,
        369, 377, 378, 382, 391
    war scare of 1671 and, 293–94
Mashpee Pond, 246
Mashpee reservation, district, and town, 2,
    367, 405
    division of common lands in, 410
    incorporation of as a town, 410
    federal reservation of, 416
    federal revocation of reservation, 416
    population of, 410–11
Mashpee Wampanoags, 12, 390
    Christianity among, 242, 246, 249, 290,
        360–65
    courts of, 290
    debt peonage of, 376–77, 380
    epidemics among, 391
    federal recognition of, 414–16
    governance of, 395
    guardians and, 375–76, 401–2
    intermarriages of, 392–94
    land management of, 394
    language change among, 397–99, 400
    meeting house of, *362*
    military service of, 282, 386
    population of, 392
    protests of, 373–75, 381, 382, 397, 401–2
    town as tribe among, 411
    values of, 411–12
    war scare of 1671 and, 293–94
Mason, John (of Connecticut), 224, 278–79
Massachusetts (colony and state), 13

annexation of Plymouth and the islands
    by, 238, 374, 377
confiscation of Indian land by, 349–50
enslavement of Indians by, 225, 251,
    319–22, 326, 340–41, 348–49, 378
founding of, 132, 202, 220
governors of. *See* Bellingham, Richard;
    Bernard, Francis; Clafflin,
    William; Hutchinson, Thomas;
    Winthrop, John, Sr.
Great Migration of, 220–22, 250, 255
Indian allies of during King Philip's
    War, *343*, 346
Indian citizenship in, 405–10
Indian guardian system of, 377, 401
King Philip's War and, 313, 316, 319, 335
Miantonomo's plot and, 228
Pequot War and, 14, 223–24, 225
population of, 221–22
praying towns of, 246
Rhode Island and, 230
United Colonies of New England and,
    228
Wampanoag federal recognition and,
    415
war scare of 1671 and, 284–85, 302
Massachusett Indians
    epidemic disease among, 106, 222
    European sailors and, 76, 90, 92–94
    French captives of, 69, 92–93, 117
    geography of, 54
    Indian attacks on after King Philip's
        War, 359
    Indian population of, 390
    King Philip's War and, 305, 321, 323–25
    Miantonomo's plot and, 228
    missions among, 105, 240, 246–47
    Narragansetts and, 123, 177, 188
    political organization of, 54
    population of, 49, 390
    Plymouth and, 166, 194–98
    praying Indians and, 324–25, 326
    praying towns of, 246
    trade of, 100
    Wampanoags and, 99, 123–24, 175, 188,
        195, 452n41
    wampum and, 218
    Wessagusset and, 183–85, 194–98
Massachusetts Bay, 68, 69, 90, 92–94, 166,
    183, 212, 213, 216, 240
Massasoit. *See* Ousamequin
Mather, Cotton, 363
Mather, Increase, 259, 308, 338, 350, 360, 361

Matoonas, 282, 317, 318, 347
Mattakeeset (Pembroke), 362, 391
Mattakeeset (Yarmouth), 186, 239, 293, 371
Mattapoisett Neck (Gardiner's Neck), 263, 314, 317
Mattaquason, 238, 361
Mattashunannamo, 306–8, 316
Mayflower, 23, 69, 71, 91, 93, 96, 97, 121, 127, 128, 129, 130, 132–34, 139–42, 162, 198
Mayflower Compact, 7
Mayhew, Experience, 328, *364*, 365, 377, 387, 397
Mayhew, John, 240
Mayhew, Matthew, 110, 115, 240, 249, 327, 364, 368
Mayhew, Thomas, Jr., 46, 116, 240, 243
Mayhew, Thomas, Sr., 219, 237, 240, 248, 249, 290, 294, 327, 329
Means, Russell, 15
Meeshawin, 241
Melville, Herman, 383
Mendon, MA, 317, 318
Merrell, James, 120
Merrimac River, 123, 177
Merrymount, 219
Metacom. *See* Pumetacom
Mexican-American War, 389
Miantonomo, 54, 122, 227–29, 231, 236, 237, 254, 272, 330, 331
Middleboro (Ply. and MA), 316, 372
Mi'kmaq, *72*, 73, 78, 99, 100, 123
missionaries, 240–41
        See also Assamough (John Gibbs); Bourne, Richard; Cotton, John, Jr.; Eliot, John; Folger, Peter; Hiacoomes; Mayhew, Matthew; Mayhew, Thomas, Jr.; Mayhew, Thomas, Sr.; Meeshawin; Mummeecheeg; Nohnoso, John; Sakantucket; Tackanash, John; Tupper, Thomas; Wuttananmatuk
missions, 251
        to Cape and island Wampanoags, 240–50, 290–92, 400
        to Massachusett Indians, 240, 246–47
        to Nipmucs, 240, 246–47
        sachem opposition to, 240, 248–50, 304
        tribute and, 248–49
        to Wampanoags, 172, 200, 220, 240–50
Mississippians, 38–39
Mittark, 249, 327–28, 369, 452n41
Mittark, Joseph, 368–69, 372

Mixano, 274
Moby-Dick (1851), 383
Mohawks
        anticolonial resistance and, 278–79
        horticulture of, 44
        Iroquois League and, 41
        King Philip's War and, 323, 330–31, 336–38, *339*, 341
        Narragansetts and, 251
        territory of, 222
        wampum trade and raids of, 56–57
        warfare of, 44, 105, 281
Mohegans, 392
        Christianity of, 360
        English alliance of, 263
        geography of, 54
        King Philip's War and, 305, 318, 323, 330, 334, 336, 337, 340–51
        missions and, 249
        Narragansetts and, 220, 224, 226, 228, 229, 277
        Nipmucs and, 252
        Pequots and, 220, 224, 225, 226
        Pequot War and, 223–27
        political organization of, 54
Mohicans, 53, 216, 225, 336, 470n26
Momonaquem, John, 360
Monhegan Island, 67, 68, 89, 144, 146, 198
Monomoyick, 69, 86–88, 129, 134, 186, 293, 361, 371, 372, 380, 391
Monponsett Pond, 259, *261*
Mons, Pierre de Gaust, 84–86
Montauketts, 273
Montaup, 217, 233, 255, 261, 263, 264, 279, 281, 283, 295, 299, 300, 309, 312–15, 331, 350
Monument Pond. *See* Manomet
Monument (Manomet) River, 213, *214*
Mooanum. *See* Wamsutta
Morton, Nathaniel, 68, 93, 101
Morton, Thomas, 96, 219
Mosely, Samuel, 321, 324, 325
Moshassuck River, 230
Moshup, 31–32, *32*
Mount Hope (Wampanoag village). *See* Montaup
Mount Hope Bay, 301, 315
Mount Hope Neck, 55, 217, 218, 279, 299, *300*, 312, 316
Mummeecheeg, Joshua, 241
murder, 223, 233, 270–71, 281–82, 290–91, 296–97, 299–300, 303, 306–9
Mystic Fort massacre, 14, 224, 333

Nahuaton, William, 306, 309
Namumpum. *See* Weetamoo
Nanapashemet, 54
Nantucket
    epidemics on, 391
    European explorers and, 89
    King Philip's War on, 219, 305, 325–30
    land sales on, 207, 237–40
    missions of, 207, 210, 240–50, 289–94
    New Guinea neighborhood of, 392
    population of, 359
    Wampanoags of, 31, 54, 89, 194, 200,
        207, 218, 290–91, 325–30, 359, 361,
        366–67, 369, 372, 378, 382, 385–86,
        391, 480n48
    whaling of, 382, 385, 390
Nashobah, 246
Narragansett Bay, 55, 56, 68, 73–75, 76, 92, 122,
    158, 211, 221, 230, 232, 258, 334
Narragansetts, 392
    archaeology of, 37
    Christianity of, 360
    of Coweset, 100, 310, 338
    ceremonies of, 118, 208–9
    deities of, 31
    epidemics among, 107, 222
    enslavement of, 348–49
    European sailors and, 73–74, 76, 92
    geography, 54
    Great Swamp Fort Massacre of, 333–34
    Iroquois and, 122, 215, 251
    King Philip's War and, 310, 318, 325,
        330–34, 348
    land sales of, 265, 272
    language of, 52–53
    Massachusett Indians and, 123, 177
    missions and, 243, 249
    Mohawks and, 251
    Mohegans and, 220, 224, 277, 331
    mourning ways of, 112–13
    Nipmucs and, 273–75
    Pequots and, 220, 224
    Pequot War and, 223–21
    Plymouth and, 166–67, 185
    Pocumtucks and, 251
    political organization of, 52, 54
    population of, 49, 222
    Rhode Island courts and, 270–71
    of Shawomet, 100, 272–73, 310
    subjugation of, after King Philip's War,
        355–56
    trade of, 57, 122, 158, 176, 215, 217
    tribute politics of, 224, 226–27, 272–73

United Colonies of New England and,
        232, 242, 251, 331, 332–33
    Wampanoags and, 54, 55, 56–58, 100,
        122–23, 128, 153, 154, 158, 164,
        166–67, 175, 193, 201, 229, 272–80,
        331, 334
    wampum and, 215, 217
Nashuakemuck, 372
Natick, 246, 283, 293, 295, 325, 388
National Day of Mourning, 2, 13, 14, 15–16,
    419–20, 424, 425–26
Nauset, 62, 83–84, 99, 129, 146, 161–64,
    186–87, 238, 239, 293, 365, 372
Nemasket, 68, 71, 156, 165, 165–66, 172, 175,
    178, 184, 209, 265, 282, 292, 329, 362
Nepoeof, 165
Nepoyetum, 239
Netherlands, 132, 137, 176, 200, 234
New Amsterdam, 211
New Bedford, 80, 317, 383, 384
New England Company, 243, 244, 370–71, 397
New England Indians
    ancient geology of, 32–35
    archaeology of, 35–36
    citizenship of, 405–10
    copper of, 57, 78–79
    diaspora of, after King Philip's War, 355
    epidemic diseases among, 67–68
    enslavement of, 61–62, 66, 348–49, 355
    European sailors and, 61–63, 66, 72,
        73–94
    gender roles of, 44–45
    geography of, 54
    horticultural development among,
        37–38, 42, 44
    justice ways of, 270–71
    King Philip's War and, 336, 348
    land sales and, 236–37
    military service of, 383–87
    political organization of, 43–44, 53–54
    population of, 49, 221, 256
    sachems of, 51–52
    social structure of, 43–44
    subjugation of, after King Philip's War,
        355
    trade of, 36, 42, 72, 73, 74, 75, 79, 100, 107
    warfare of, 44
    wealth ways of, 207–10
    women's roles among, 37–38
    See also Abenakis; Mohegans;
        Narragansetts; Niantics (Eastern);
        Nipmucs; Norwottucks;
        Pawtucket Indians; Penobscots;

Pennacooks; Pequots;
Pocumtucks; Sokokis; Wabanakis;
Wampanoags
New England
economy of, 256
population of, 256
Newfoundland, 63, 65, 67, 73, 76, 78, 92, 180
Newfoundland Company, 63, 67
New France, 92, 275, 278, 335
New Guinea, 392
New Haven (colony), 132, 221, 225, 228
New Netherland, 133, 211, 212, 216, 217, 250,
251, 260, 278
Newport, RI, 74, 221, 229, 257, 269, 280, 286,
297, 299, 348
New World, myth of, 24–25, 28–29
New York (colony and state), 41, 219, 238, 275,
278, 336–37, 368
Niantics (Eastern), 305
Nickanoose, 291
Ninigret, 249, 263, 272, 273–79, 305, 331, 332
Nipmucs, 54, 281
King Philip's War, 316–17, 318, 324, 325,
338, 348
land sales of, 265
missions among, 246–47
Mohegans and, 252, 262
of Pakachoog, 282
of Quabaug, 121, 252, 262
of Quantisset, 273–75
subjugation of, after King Philip's War,
355–56
Wamapanoags and, 121, 228, 252, 262, 318
Nipsachuck, 318–19
Nobscusset, 293, 361
Nohnoso, John, 241
Nohtouaussuet (Notooksact), 249
Norwottucks, 322–23
Nova Scotia, 36, 73, 76, 79
Nunnepog, 372
Nunnuit, Peter. See Petonowowet

Obbatinewat, 166
Obtakiest, 196
Okommakamesit, 246
Old Colony Club, 5
Ompohhunnut, 327
Ousamequin (Massasoit), 2, 54
authority of, 28, 30, 55, 58–59, 154, 200
brother of, 148
death of, 252, 253
dissent against, 161–62, 163–66, 175–76,
192–93, 200, 202, 219–20, 237

Eulogy on King Philip (1836) and, 402–3
father of, 55, 122
First Thanksgiving and, 171
land sales of, 226, 230–37
mark of, 235
marriage alliances of, 55, 193
Miantonomo's plot and, 227–28
missions and, 240, 248–50, 292
Narragansetts and, 122–23, 153, 227–28
Pequot War and, 225
Plymouth and, 26, 129, 143–61, 164–66,
167, 185, 187, 193, 200, 205, 226,
250–52, 303, 308, 313, 350, 352, 356
Pumetacom's memory of, 303
reburial of, 418
Rhode Island and, 230–33
Roger Williams and, 221, 230–31, 349
role of, in Thanksgiving myth, 7, 9,
171–72
Samoset's service to, 144–48
sickness of, 189–94
sons of, 55
Tisquantum and, 71, 128, 155–61, 178–82,
193

Pakachoog, 282
Pamantaquash, 265, 288
Paomet, 99, 129, 188, 293, 371, 372
Papmunnuck, 249, 290, 361
Papmunnuck, Simon, 361
Passamaquoddies, 414
Patuckson, 206, 306, 309
Patuxet (Wampanoag), 61–62, 68, 84, 85, 90,
140, 141, 146, 161, 176, 180, 194, 195, 222,
250
Pawtucket Indians, 123, 177
Pawtucket River, 258
Pawtuxet (Narragansett), 57
pawwaws, 46–47, 110–12, 116, 143, 189
peag. *See* wampum
Pecksuot, 93–94, 183–84, 196–98
Pemaquid, 84
Pennacooks, 177
Penobscot Indians, 99, 100
Penobscot River, 99, 123, 213, 217
Pequots, 392
Christianity of, 360
geography of, 54
King Philip's War and, 305, 332, 333, 341
and Pequot War, 14, 223–27, 251, 254
political organization of, 54
Narragansetts and, 201, 220
wampum and, 215, 217–28

Pequot War, 153, 223–27, 251, 330, 332
Perry, Hannah, 401
Perry, Jonathan, 420
Perry, Leroy C., 413
Pessacus, 272, 332
Peters, Paula, 423, 425
Peters, Ramona, 423
Petonowowet (Peter Nunnuit), 315
Philip. *See* Pumetacom
Pilgrim Progress March, 12
Pilgrims
    contact with Wampanoags of, 25
    grave-robbing by, 136–37
    exile of, in Netherlands, 132–33
    explorations of, 23–28
    first winter of, 141–42
    plundering by, 136–37, 138–39, 161, 162,
        163
    profile of, 130
    settlement of at Plymouth, 140
    Thanksgiving myth and, 3, 5, 7, *8*
    voyage of, to America, 132–34
    Wampanoags and, 135–40, 142–61, 303
    See also English; Plymouth colony;
        Separatists
Piscataqua River, 347
Pleasant Bay (Orleans, Chatham, Harwich),
    371
Plimoth Plantation, 15, 421
Plymouth (colony)
    alliance of, with Wampanoags, 152–55,
        167–68, 172, 200, 313
    anniversaries of, 10
    confiscation of Indian land by, 349–50
    corn trade of, 158, 184, 185–86, 211
    courts of, and Indians, 269–70
    Dutch relations of, 216–20
    enslavement of Wampanoags by, 319–22,
        329–30, 340–41, 348–49, 351, 352,
        376–77, 378
    expansion of, 202
    exploitation of Wampanoags by, 206
    financiers of, 133
    fishing economy of, 211
    founding of, 140
    fur trade of, 177, 201, 210–11, 234
    General Court of, 211, 225, 258, 283, 322
    governors of, 150. *See also* Bradford,
        William; Carver, John; Prince,
        Thomas; Winslow, Josiah
    Indian allies of during King Philip's
        War, 341, 346–47
    Indian land purchases of, 232–37, 237–40

Indian trade of, 177, 201, 210–20
jurisdictional disputes with
        Wampanoags of, 299–300, 303,
        306–9, 326, 376–77
King Philip's War and, 309–22, 329–30,
        334, 335, 340–41, 344–47
livestock of, 202, 211, 250, 255, 256, 279
Maine and, 335
Massachusett Indians and, 177, 194–98
migrants to, 166
population of, 201, 202, 220
Narragansetts and, 153, 185
Rhode Island and, 230, 258, 259, 267, 350
subjugation of Wampanoags to, 285–86,
        288–89, 296, 301
treaties of, with Wampanoags, (1621)
        152–55, 156, 181; (1671) 280–86
Wamsutta and, 258–62
war scare of 1671 and, 280–86
Wessagusset and, 183, 185, 193, 194–98
Plymouth (town), 2, 5, 16, 140, 234, 347, 348,
    425
Plymouth Harbor, 15, 68, *85*, 141, 211, 212, 329
Plymouth Rock, 5, 12
pniesok, 149, 187, 197
Pocahontas, 65–66, 185
Pocasset, 55, 164, 209, 218, 257–58, 263, 267,
    277, 292, 310, 311, 314–19, 331, 334, 347,
    348
Pochet Island, 238
Pocumtucks, 251, 322–23, 337, 348, 470n26
Pokanoket, 26, 54, 57, 68, 70, 99, 101, 178, 179,
    194, 201, 207, 209, 218, 219, 233, 237, 275,
    276, 291, 310, 340
Pomham, 272, 347
Pompano, Peter, 341
Popmonet, Simon, 381
population
    of Aquinnah, 410–11
    of Cape Cod, 359, 390
    of colonial New England, 221, 256, 359
    of Martha's Vineyard, 359
    of Mashpee, 410–11
    of Massachusett Indians, 49
    of Massachusetts, 220, 390
    of Nantucket, 359
    of Narragansetts, 49, 222
    of Plymouth colony, 201, 202, 221–22,
        359
    of Southern New England Indians, 49,
        221, 256
    of Wampanoags, 49, 98–99, 146, 359,
        390, 391–92

Portsmouth, RI, 221, 231, 266, 267, 297, 299, 301

Potonumecut, 291, 361, 371, 391

Poutrincourt, Jean de Biencourt, 69, 86–88

Powhatan Indians, 65–66, 90, 137, 154, 185

Pratt, Phineas, 72, 93, 184

praying Indians, 323–30, 341, 346, 349

praying towns, 246–49, 282. *See also* Christiantown; Mashpee; Nashobah; Natick; Okommakamesit; Punkapoag; Wamesit

Prince, Thomas, 260, 281, 282

Pring, Martin, 83–84, 137, 138

Printer, James, 244, 324

Providence, RI, 55, 221, 230, 231, 258, 269, 278, 297, 338–40

Provincetown Harbor, 135

Pumetacom

    arbitration of, 268, 290–91

    criticism of English by, 129, 205–26, 260–61, 266–67, 299–310

    death of, 348

    dismemberment of, 352, 355

    dissent against, 263–66

    dress of, 284

    Eulogy on King Philip (1836) and, 403

    escape of, from Mount Hope, 315

    escape of, from Pocasset, 317–18

    flight of, to Nipmuc country, 319, 326

    hog-raising of, 266–67

    intertribal diplomacy of, 206

    King Philip's War and, 308–14, 319, 326, 347–53

    land sales of, 256–57, 263–65, 286

    mark of, *264*

    missions and, 290–91, 292–93, 295, 480n51

    Mohawks and, 336–38

    name change of, 254–55

    Narragansetts and, 263, 272–75

    Plymouth and, 155, 205–6, 254–55, 256–57, 260–61, 263–65, 266–67, 275–76, 277–79, 279–86

    Sassamon, John, and, 295–96, 480n53

    sister of, 347

    son of, 350–51

    subjugation of, to Plymouth, 285–86, 288–89, 296, 301

    resistance movement of, 206, 207, 252, 253–54, 262–64, 272–80, 286, 298, 302

    uncle of, 347

    war scare of 1667 and, 275–76

    war scare of 1669 and, 277–79

    war scare of 1671 and, 279–86

    wife of, 55, 166, 350, 353

Punkapoag, 240, 246, 306, 325

puritans, 2, 4, 132

Quabaug, 121, 262

Quadaquina, 148, 151, 154, 155

Quaiapen, 263, 274–75, 318, 331, 347

Quakers, 234

Quannapaquait, James, 325, 337

Quantisset, 273–75

Quatchatisset, 246, 268

Québec, 84, 92

Queehequassit, 361

Queen Anne's War, 383

Queppish, Eben, 412

Quequegunent, 263

race

    Christianity and, 364–65, 388–89

    Indian notions of, 399, 408

    King Philip's War and, 355

    Manifest Destiny and, 400

    myth of Indian disappearance and, 356, 398, 400–401, 415–16

    prehistory and, 29

    Thanksgiving myth and, 5, 6, 9, 16, 29

    white nationalism, 427

    white notions of, 400–401, 408

    white stereotypes of Indians and, 387–90

racism, 364–65

Rasieres, Isaack de, 216

Rawson, Grindal, 363

Reconstruction, 408

Red Power, 11, 415

Rehoboth (town, Ply. and MA), 232, 234, 255, 266, 297, 301, 338

Revolution (American), 382, 384, 391, 393

reservations

    elimination of, by Massachusetts, 2. *See also* Aquinnah; Christiantown; Indian Town; Mashpee; Potonumecut; praying towns; Titicut; Watuppa

Rhode Island (colony)

    courts of, and Indians, 269–71

    enslavement of Indians by, 348–49

    founding of, 132, 221, 230

    Indian land purchases of, 226, 230–33, 258, 263, 286

    Indian trade of, 218

reservations (*continued*)
  King Philip's War and, 314, 330
  Narragansetts and, 227, 230–31
  Plymouth and, 258, 259, 267, 350
  United Colonies of New England
    and, 228
  Wampanoags and, 230–33
  war scares and, 276, 277–79, 280
River Indians, 322–24, 337, 338. *See also*
  Norwottucks; Pocumtucks; Sokokis
Roanoke, 76, 82, 157
Robinson, John, 199–200

sachems, 51–52, *150*, 196, 208–10, 248–49, 270
  See also Abel, Ben; Aspinet; Awashonks;
    Canacum; Canonchet; Canonicus;
    Cassacinamon, Robin; Corbitant;
    Cutshamekin; George;
    Iyananough; Keencomsett;
    Matoonas Mattaquason;
    Miantonomo; Mittark; Mittark,
    Joseph; Mixano; Nanapashemet;
    Nepoeof; Nepoyetum;
    Nickanoose; Ninigret;
    Nohtouassuet; Obbatinewat;
    Obtakiest; Ompohhunnut;
    Ousamequin; Pamantaquash;
    Papmunnuck; Pessacus; Pomham;
    Pooskin, Zachariah; Pumetacom;
    Quaiapen; Quachatasett;
    Seeknout; Seeknout, Jacob;
    Tatobem; Tawanquatuck;
    Tispaquin; Tookenchosin; Uncas;
    Wampatuck, Josias; Wamsutta;
    Wassapinewat; Weetamoo;
    Wepquish; Weunquesh
sachemships, 53–54, 58
  See also Aquinnah; Chappaquiddick;
    Coweset; Cummaquid; Manomet;
    Mattakeesett; Monomoyick;
    Nauset; Nemasket; Nunnepog;
    Paomet; Patuxet; Pawtuxet;
    Pocasset; Pokanoket; Sakonnet;
    Satucket; Sengekontacket;
    Shawomet; Takemmy; Titicut;
    Wequaquet
Saco River, 104, 213
Sagadahoc, 66, 88–89
Sakantuket (Peter), 241
Sakaweston, 89
Sakedan, 372
Sakonnet
  Christianity of, 360, 361
  King Philip's War and, 314–19, 338,
    342–46, 347, 349
  land sales and, 258, 286–87
  military service of, 383
  post-war settlement of, 350, 351
  wampum and, 218
  war scare of 1671 and, 282–83
Samoset, 7, 127, 144–48, 151–52
Samponock, 286
Sanders, John, 183
Sandwich (town, Ply. and MA), 237, 322,
    329, 361
Sanford, John, 267
Santuit River, 246
Sassacomit, 144
Sassamon, Betty (Assaweta), 294
Sassamon, John, 273, *274*, 292, 294–97,
    299–300, 306–9, 329, 480n53
Sassamon, Rowland, 310–11
Satucket, 69, 293, 372
Seeknout, 239, 376
Seeknout, Jacob, 366
Seekonk (Ply. and MA), 275, 281
Seekonk River, 55, 230, 234, 258
Sengekontacket, 248, 372, 387, 391
Separatists, 130–32, 460n2
servitude. *See* Indian servitude
Seven Mile River, 257
Seven Years' War, 383, 388
sewan. *See* wampum
Shawomet, 57, 100, 310
Shinnecocks, 273
Simons, Nelson Drew, 412
Sippican, 361, 391
Sippican River, 345, 349
Sissetom, Thomas, 360
Slaney, John, 63, 65, 148
smallpox, 102–3, 105, 107–9, 222
Smith, John, 65, 66, 90, 91, 93, 98–99,
    100, 103
Smith, Richard, 267
Society of Friends. *See* Quakers
Society or Company for the Propagation of
    the Gospel in New England and the
    parts adjacent. *See* New England
    Company
Sokokis, 322–23
Southworth, Constant, 283, 287
Sowams, 26, 27, 55, 156–60, 189–94, 233
Speedwell, 133
Squant, 31
Squanto. *See* Tisquantum
Squantum. *See* Cheepi

Standish, Miles, 137, 143, 177, 183, 186–88,
    197–98, 201, 213
Stanton, Thomas, 277
St. Lawrence River, 73, 212, 222, 275
Stone, John, 223
Stuart, James (Duke of York). See James II
Sudbury, MA, 334
Swansea (Ply. and MA), 233, 234, 265, 279, 281,
    297, 300–301, 310, 314, 317
sunksquaws, 51–52. See also Awashonks;
    Quaiapen; Weetamoo

Tackanash, John, 241
Takemmy, 248, 372, 452n41
Tall Oak, 426–27
Talman, Peter, 257–58, 288
Tangier, 322
Tarrentines. See Mi'kmaq
Tashtego, 383
Tatobem, 54
Tatum, 99
Taunton (Ply. and MA), 232, 234, 265, 266,
    280–91, 286, 297, 301, 313, 317, 322, 416, 417
Taunton River, 27, 35, 49, 54, 55, 68, 101, 156,
    209, 233, 244, 259, 265, 282, 287, 292, 293,
    316, 318, 347, 350, 371
Tawanquatuck, 243, 249
Thanksgiving holiday, 2, 3–4, 16, 224
Thanksgiving myth, 3–12, 16, 124, 127–29,
    144, 148, 205, 419
    King Philip's War and, 254, 353
    race and, 5, 6, 9, 17, 29, 427
    school curricula and, 17–18, 422
    See also First Thanksgiving
Thanksgiving pageants, 8, 422
Thaxter, Joseph, 400
Three Mile River, 265
Tispaquin, 265, 282, 287–88, 292, 294, 295, 307,
    316, 319, 347
Tispaquin, William, 282, 287–88, 307
Tisquantum, 130
    assault against, 165, 175
    captivity of, 61–66
    death of, 186, 199
    English captivity of, 63–66, 145, 201
    linguistic skills of, 151–52, 164, 176
    name of, 148–49
    Newfoundland voyages of, 63–64
    Ousamequin and, 128, 155–61, 178–82,
        186, 201
    Patuxet and, 61–62, 68, 85, 140
    Plymouth and, 147–52, 155–61, 162, 167,
        168

political ambitions of, 148, 157–58, 176,
    178–82, 183
return of, 61, 67–71
role of in Thanksgiving myth, 7, 127
Spanish captivity of, 63
Titicut, 240, 265, 269, 349, 361, 367, 371–72,
    387
Tiverton (MA and RI), 350
Tobias, 306–8, 316
Tokamahamon, 162, 164, 167
Tom, the interpreter (Saunkussecit/
    Sansawest/Sansuett/Sancsuick/Tom of
    Wackemocket), 295
Tookenchosin, 246
Totoson, 316–17
trade
    Indian-European, 62, 71, 72, 73, 74, 75,
        78, 79–80, 88, 92, 99, 103, 147, 158,
        176, 177, 183, 189, 201, 206, 207,
        209, 210–20, 234–36, 239, 250
    intertribal, 36, 38–39, 48, 57, 78, 79, 107,
        208
Treat, Samuel, 361
treaties
    of 1621 (I), 152–55, 161, 181
    of 1621 (II), 166
    of Hartford (1638), 225
    of Taunton (1671), 281–91
tribute, 28, 57, 58, 175, 176, 193, 195, 215,
    219–20, 226–27, 228, 237, 272–74, 290,
    296, 304
Tupper, Thomas, 240, 361

Uncas, 224, 225, 226–27, 228, 249, 251, 252,
    276–77, 318, 331
Uncompoen, 347
United Colonies of New England, 228, 229,
    232, 242, 243, 251, 278, 331, 332–34
United Indians of New England, 425

Verrazzano, Giovanni da, 56, 57, 73–76, 80
Vines, Richard, 104
Virginia, 65, 70, 71, 90, 184, 185, 217

Wabanakis, 73, 78, 107, 177, 213, 217, 335, 351,
    383
Wamesit, 246
Wampanoags
    of Acoaxet, 361, 391
    of Acushnet, 218, 361, 391
    aftermath of King Philip's War among,
        356–65
    ancient history of, 30–38

Wampanoags (*continued*)
  animal husbandry of, 266–67, 363, 398
  of Apponagansett, 218, 361, 391
  of Aquinnah, 2, 21, 31, 117, 248, 249,
      257–58, 328–29, 367–71, 372, 375,
      392, 394–98, 410–18
  archaeology of, 30, 31–38
  of Assawompset, 240, 282, 287, 310, 349,
      360, 361, 362, 369, 391
  Bible of, 244–46, 247, 324, 399, 417
  boats of, 34
  burial ways of, 47–48, 113
  of Buzzards Bay, 78, 80, 92, 211, 218, 265,
      268, 361, 391
  of Cape Cod, 48, 78, 99, 121, 136, 158,
      162–63, 194, 195, 198–99, 218, 219,
      237–50, 289–94, 305, 325, 329–30,
      338, 341, 346, 351, 359, 361–65, 378,
      397
  captivity among, 92–93, 115
  ceremonies of, 45, 345–46
  of Chappaquiddick, 239, 248, 366–67,
      372, 375, 376, 391, 392, 395, 407, 410
  children of, 378–80, 386
  Christianity of, 240–50, 291–92, 330,
      359–65, 398
  of Christiantown, 248, 367, 386, 390,
      395, 410
  citizenship of, 405–10
  civilization of, 98–99
  color symbolism of, 62, 75, 110, 147,
      149–50, 210
  courts of, 377
  of Cummaquid, 91, 162
  deer drives of, 26, 27
  deities of, 31, 110
  economy of, 26
  of Elizabeth Islands, 80, 361, 369
  enslavement of, 13, 63, 67, 70–71, 90–91,
      162, 319–22, 348–49, 351, 352, 377, 378
  epidemics among, 67–68, 95–125, 146,
      184, 391
  European sailors and, 30, 59, 61–63,
      66–67, 68–94, 128
  First Thanksgiving and, 170–71
  food ways of, 48, 169
  geography of, 33–34, 54
  guardians of, 374–74
  of Herring Pond, 240, 361, 392, 410
  historical source and, 19
  history ways of, 26
  horiticulture of, 27, 30, 48
  houses of, 23–24, 24

  of Indian Town, 371
  intermarriages of, 356, 392–98, 406
  jurisdictional disputes of, with English,
      269–71, 296, 299–300, 303, 306–9,
      326, 376–77
  King Philip's War and. *See* King Philip's
      War
  kinship among, 53–54
  landholding of, 268–69
  land loss of, 229–40, 256–58, 263–66,
      356, 365–76
  land sales of, 229–40, 256–58, 263–66
  language of, 52–53, 125, 230, 241, 244–47,
      328, 356, 369, 374, 396–99, 400, 417
  literacy of, 18, 244–46, 360, 363, 380,
      399, 474n54
  of Manomet, 161, 187–88, 197, 240, 246,
      363
  of Martha's Vineyard, 31, 46, 48, 49, 52,
      54, 67, 78, 79–80, 89–90, 112, 194,
      200, 218, 219, 240–50, 257, 268–69,
      276, 289–94, 305, 325–30, 351, 359,
      361, 366–67, 369, 378, 382, 397
  of Mashpee, 2, 12, 242, 246, 249, 290,
      292, 294, 361, 367, 375–76, 380, 381,
      382, 390, 391, 392–95, 401–2, 410–18
  Massachusett Indians and, 52, 54, 58,
      99–100, 188, 452n41
  matawaûog of, 26
  material culture of, 209–10
  material resources of, 33–35
  of Mattakeeset (Pembroke), 362, 391
  of Mattakeeset (Yarmouth), 186, 239,
      293, 371, 391
  of Mattapoisett, 361
  medical ways of, 109–112
  military service of, 3, 383–87, 390
  missions among, 172, 200, 220, 240–50,
      304, 360–61, 400
  Mohawks and, 56
  Mohegans and, 252, 262
  of Monomoyick, 69, 86–88, 129, 186,
      293, 361, 371, 372, 380, 391
  of Montaup, 283, 309, 314–19
  mourning ways of, 12, 14–15, 16, 112,
      350–51, 358, 405
  of Nantucket, 31, 48, 49, 54, 89, 194,
      200, 218, 219, 240–50, 290–91, 305,
      325–30, 359, 361, 369, 372, 378, 382,
      385–86
  of Narragansett Bay, 73–75, 92, 121, 211
  Narragansetts and, 54, 55, 56–58, 100,
      122–23, 128, 153, 154, 158, 164,

166–67, 171, 175, 188, 193, 195, 201, 227–28, 229, 262–63, 272–80, 331, 334
of Nashuakemuck, 372
of Nauset, 62, 83–84, 129, 146, 161–64, 186–87, 238, 239, 293, 365–66, 372
of Nemasket, 68, 156, 165–66, 175, 184, 209, 265, 282, 292, 329, 362
Nipmucs and, 221, 228, 252, 262, 273–75, 318
of Nobscusset, 361
of Nunnepog, 372
nutrition of, 48, 49
of Paomet, 99, 129, 188, 293, 371, 372
of Patuxet, 49, 176, 180
pawwaws of, 110–12, 116, 143, 189
Pequot War and, 225–26, 241–42
perseverance of, 2, 9, 349, 355–56, 359
Pilgrims and, 135–40
Plymouth and, 128, 142–61, 167–68, 171–72, 200, 203, 250–52
pniesok of, 149, 197
of Pocasset, 209, 218, 257–58, 263, 267, 277, 292, 310, 311–12, 314–19, 334, 347, 348
of Pokanoket, 57, 189–94, 209, 218, 282, 340
political disputes among, 58 161–62, 164, 172, 175–76, 192–93, 202, 206–7, 219–20, 248–49, 289–94, 304
political organization of, 26, 28, 42, 52, 53–55, 58, 99
population of, 49, 98–99, 146, 390, 391–92
of Potonumecut, 291, 361, 371, 391
poverty among, 372–73
preachers of, 361. See also Apess, William; Assamough; Cosens, John; Coshaug, Tom; Hedge, Jacob; Hiacoomes; Hiacoomes, John; Hossueit, Zachariah; Howwoswee, Zachariah; Howwoswee, Zacheus; Jones, Ralph; Papmunnuck, Simon; Sissetom, Thomas; Tackanash, John; Wuttananmatuk
protocols of, 27, 189
of Queehequassit, 361
religious life of, 45–48, 62
religious specialists among, 42, 46–47
reservations of, 246–48, 367–71. See also Aquinnah; Christiantown; Indian Town; Mashpee; Potonumecut; Titicut; Watuppa

revivals of, 412, 416
roadways of, 23, 26
sachems of, 42, 372
of Sakonnet, 218, 258, 282–83, 286–87, 314–19, 338, 342–46, 347, 349, 350, 351, 360, 361, 383
of Satucket, 69, 293, 372
schools of, 244–45, 399
of Sengekontacket, 248, 372, 387, 391
servitude of, 378–82, 384–87, 396–97
of Sippican, 361, 391
subjugation of, after King Philip's War, 355–56
of Takemmy, 248, 372
of Taunton River, 49, 54, 194, 209
Thanksgiving and, 419–27
of Titicut, 240, 361, 367, 371–72, 387
trade of, 48, 57, 79, 99, 100, 107, 201, 208, 209–10, 215–20
treaties of, with English, (1621, I) 152–55, 161, 181; (1621, II), 166
wage work of, 211, 250, 382–83
wampum and, 26, 215–20
war scares and, 275–86
of Watuppa, 367, 371, 392, 401, 410
of Waweantick, 361
wealth ways of, 207–10
weaponry of, 210
whaling by, 382–83, 384–86, 390
witchcraft among, 110–12, 116, 208
women's authority among, 396
Wampapaquan, 306–8, 316
Wampatuck, Josias, 265, 268
wampum, 26, 42, 56–57, 163, 175, 206, 214–20, 228, 231, 232, 250, 258
wampumpeag. See wampum
Wamsley, Jane, 407
Wamsutta (Mooanum, Alexander), 2
death of, 259–62, 303, 312
intertribal diplomacy of, 206
land sales of, 256–58
missions and, 292
Mohegans and, 262
name change of, 251–52, 254–55
Narragansetts and, 262
Nipmucs and, 262
Plymouth and, 155, 225
resistance movement of, 206, 207, 252, 253–54, 257, 259, 262, 298
as sachem, 255–61
Sassamon, John, and, 294
wife of, 55, 166
Waopam, 242

Wapock, George, 381
Wappingers, 336
Waquoit Bay, 246
War of 1812, 383
wars. See Civil War (American); Governor
    Drummer's War; Kieft's War; King
    George's War; King Philip's War;
    Mexican-American War; Pequot War;
    Queen Anne's War; Revolution
    (American); Seven Years' War; War of
    1812; World War II
war scares, 206, 251
    of 1622, 185–89, 194–203
    of 1662, 262, 303
    of 1667, 275–76
    of 1669, 277–79
    of 1671, 279–86, 290, 293–94, 301, 309
Warwick, RI, 221, 272, 278, 332
Washington, Bethia, 420
Wassapinewat, 196
Watuppa, 367, 371, 392, 401, 410
Wawaus. See Printer, James
Waweantick, 361
Wawweeyowit, 286
Waymouth, George, 66, 84, 88, 144
Weetama, 267–68
Weetamoo (Namumpum), 55
    King Philip's War and, 311–12, 315–18,
        332, 347, 352
    land sales and, 257–58, 267–68, 287, 312
    marriages of, 166, 259, 262–63
    Narragansetts and, 262–63, 319
    resistance movement of, 262–63, 298
    war scare of 1671 and, 280
Wepquish, 246

Wessagusset, 183–85, 187, 193, 194–98, 200,
    202, 219, 240
West Indies, 225, 256, 349, 352
Weston, Thomas, 133, 177
Wequaquet, 293
Weunquesh, 277
whaling, 382–83, 384–86, 390
whiteness, 5, 17
Whitman, Valentine, 339
Willet, Thomas, 233–35, 258, 260
Williams, Roger, 112, 113, 114, 118, 122, 180,
    208, 221, 225, 230–31, 232, 233, 243, 251,
    265, 276, 332, 339, 340, 349
Winslow, Edward, 26, 53, 101, 111, 114, 115, 118,
    119, 150, 151, 153, 155–61, 163, 169, 170, 172,
    179, 182, 187, 189–95, 200, 213
Winslow, Job, 312
Winslow, Josiah, 259–61, 275, 281, 282, 283,
    288, 289, 295, 300, 311, 312, 313, 344
Winthrop, John, Jr., 329
Winthrop, John, Sr., 119, 208, 222, 225
Winthrop, Wait, 319, 388
Wituwamat, 187–88, 197
Wood, William, 72, 105, 111, 203
Woonasquetucket River, 230, 318
Woosamequin, 471n30
Wootonekanuske, 55, 166, 312, 350, 352
Wôpanâak Language Revitalization Project,
    418
World War II, 413
Wuttananmatuk, 241, 242

Yarmouth (Ply. and MA), 237, 239, 327, 371,
    380, 391
Young, Alexander, 4

A NOTE ON THE AUTHOR

David J. Silverman is a professor at George Washington University, where he specializes in Native American, Colonial American, and American racial history. He is the author of *Thundersticks*, *Red Brethren*, *Ninigret*, and *Faith and Boundaries*. His essays have won major awards from the Omohundro Institute of Early American History and Culture and the New York Academy of History. Silverman lives in Philadelphia.